A GLOBAL LAW OF JURISDICTION AND JUDGMENTS: LESSONS FROM THE HAGUE

A GLOBAL LAW OF JURISDICTION AND JUDGMENTS: LESSONS FROM THE HAGUE

Edited by

JOHN J. BARCELÓ III

and

KEVIN M. CLERMONT

KLUWER LAW INTERNATIONAL
THE HAGUE / LONDON / NEW YORK

Published by:
Kluwer Law International
P.O. Box 85889, 2508 CN The Hague, The Netherlands
sales@kli.wkap.nl
http://www.kluwerlaw.com

Sold and Distributed in North, Central and South America by:
Kluwer Law International
101 Philip Drive, Norwell, MA 02061, USA
kluwerlaw@wkap.com

Sold and Distributed in all other countries by:
Kluwer Law International
Distribution Centre, P.O. Box 322, 3300 AH Dordrecht, The Netherlands

Library of Congress Cataloging-in-Publication Data

A global law of jurisdiction and judgments: lessons from The Hague / edited by John J. Barceló and Kevin M. Clermont.
p. cm.
ISBN 9041118861 (hb : alk. paper)
1. Jurisdiction (International law) 2. Judgments. I. Barceló, John J. II. Clermont, Kevin M.

2002029698

Printed on acid-free paper.

ISBN 90-411-1886-1

Kluwer Law International incorporates the imprint Martinus Nijhoff Publishers.

Printed and bound in Great Britain by MPG Books Limited, Bodmin, Cornwall.

Table of Contents

PART II: JUDGMENTS PROVISIONS AND THE CONVENTION'S FUTURE

APPENDICES

John J. Barceló III[†] *and Kevin M. Clermont*[‡]

General Introduction

In 1992, the Hague Conference on Private International Law launched a project to draft a worldwide convention on territorial jurisdiction and recognition and enforcement of judgments in civil and commercial matters. By 1999, the project had achieved a Draft Convention (included in the appendix) intended for adoption at a final conference, originally scheduled for the fall of 2000.

The 1999 Draft Convention, however, proved too controversial. The United States, in particular, refused to go forward on the basis of the 1999 text. Instead, the countries most interested in achieving a successful convention agreed to continue more informal discussions and to seek changes in the 1999 text at a special drafting session held in June 2001. (The changes proposed at that 2001 Hague session are also reproduced in the appendix.)

The papers included in this volume address the provisions of the 1999 Draft Convention and the state of the negotiations as of the summer of 2000. They were presented at a symposium held July 7–8, 2000, at the Centre Panthéon (University of Paris I Law Faculty) as a part of the Cornell-Paris I Summer Institute of International and Comparative Law.

The symposium was entitled: A Global Law of Jurisdiction and Judgments–Lessons from The Hague. The papers prepared for the symposium and this volume were originally intended to be a contemporary scholarly exegesis of the 1999 Draft Convention, the text many expected and at least some hoped would become – at least in its core provisions – a new global law of jurisdiction and judgments. When the 1999 Draft Convention ran into difficulty, however, the nature of some of our papers shifted to more of a focus on the future, and so we added that subtitle to the symposium's name and to the title of this volume.

The papers in Part I of this volume focus, as originally intended, on the jurisdiction provisions of the 1999 Draft Convention. They analyze those provisions and shed light on many of the basic difficulties that must be resolved if a global law of jurisdiction is to be achieved. Indeed, all of the stumbling blocks impeding a successful convention concern the 1999 Draft's jurisdiction provisions.

[†] William Nelson Cromwell Professor of International and Comparative Law and Reich Director of the Berger International Legal Studies Program, Cornell University.

[‡] Flanagan Professor of Law, Cornell University.

J.J. Barceló and K.M. Clermont (eds.), A Global Law of Jurisdiction and Judgments: Lessons from The Hague, vii–viii

The papers in Part II deal only briefly with the judgments provisions of the 1999 Draft, which, as just mentioned, are not so controversial. For the most part, the papers in the second half of the volume look to the future. One paper takes up changes in European Union law that will significantly affect future negotiations concerning the Draft Convention. The other two offer analyses of the major hurdles blocking the way to a successful convention and proposals for vaulting those hurdles.

As joint organizers of the symposium and editors of this volume, we have included at the beginning of each of the two parts brief commentary on the papers presented in each part.

The symposium was sponsored by Cornell Law School and the University of Paris I Law Faculty and enjoyed generous support from the Berger International Legal Studies Program.

As work on the Hague Jurisdiction and Judgments Convention continues, the papers in this volume will serve, we believe, as a major reference point. They will form a part of the historical background and commentary on what may become before long a global law of jurisdiction and judgments. And should that achievement be delayed, we hope this volume will help to spur it along to completion.

Part I
Jurisdiction

Kevin M. Clermont[†]

An Introduction to the Hague Convention

Back in July 1789, Louis XVI went to bed after writing in his diary: "*14 juillet, rien.*" So Duc de La Rochefoucauld-Liancourt[1] had to wake him in the night with news of the taking of the Bastille. The King queried:

"*Mais, c'est une révolte?*"
"*Non, Sire, c'est une révolution!*"

In July 2000, a humbler but more aware group of delegates, practitioners, and academics gathered in Paris to discuss the Convention on Jurisdiction and Foreign Judgments in Civil and Commercial Matters, which is currently under negotiation through the Hague Conference on Private International Law.[2] Already apparent was that the Convention's envisaged changes for the legal world, although in large part desirable rather than "revolting," would indeed be revolutionary.

The Hague Convention's Background

Brussels Convention

The principal European countries appear ahead of the United States on the treatment of foreign judgments. The European Union has an enlightened, albeit far from perfect, treaty dating from 1968. That treaty is the Brussels Convention on Jurisdiction and the Enforcement of Judgments in Civil and Commercial Matters, which morphed into a European Union Regulation on March 1, 2002.[3]

By the Brussels Convention, the member states agree to provide virtually automatic recognition and enforcement of the judgments of the other member states. This provision is like the Full Faith and Credit Clause of the U.S. Constitution. In order to make this agreement acceptable, the Brussels Convention is a "double convention" that also defines the bases of territorial jurisdiction – the doctrine that must, in a

† Flanagan Professor of Law, Cornell University.

1 Grand Master of the King's Wardrobe, as well as deputy for the nobility of Clermont-en-Beauvaisis in the Estates-General.

2 *See infra* Appendix 1 (draft of October 1999). The more recent, refined version appears as Appendix 2 (draft of June 2001).

3 *See infra* Appendix 3.

J.J. Barceló and K.M. Clermont (eds.), A Global Law of Jurisdiction and Judgments: Lessons from The Hague, 3–13

judgment-respecting regime, serve almost alone in ensuring adjudicative restraint. The European member states can give respect to the others' judgments because they know that the Brussels Convention restricts the others to appropriate jurisdictional reach. This latter restriction works as the Due Process Clause does in the United States. The current time is indeed exciting in Europe as the supranational European Court of Justice, overseeing the national courts, actively works out the details, much as the Marshall Court united the U.S. judicial systems two centuries ago.

Of course, the Brussels Convention's jurisdictional bases follow the civil-law approach. The defendant's domicile is the usual place for suit, although there is additionally long-arm-like jurisdiction for tort and contract actions. Certain disadvantaged plaintiffs, such as consumers, can often sue at home. Moreover, there is authorization for forum selection agreements. There is exclusive local jurisdiction in actions concerning real property and the like. Further on the prohibited side, each member state gave up its exorbitant jurisdiction, so that for example France gave up its personal jurisdiction based on the plaintiff's French nationality.

England too is now a signatory. It gave up transient jurisdiction and attachment jurisdiction. Additionally, the Brussels Convention not only prohibits exorbitant jurisdiction, but also makes mandatory the permissible bases of jurisdiction. So, England abandoned its judicial practice of sometimes declining jurisdiction on expressly discretionary grounds.

Europe does not always appear superior in terms of approach to jurisdiction and judgments, however. Note that the Brussels Convention applies only to defendants domiciled in a member state. Indeed, the Brussels Convention openly discriminates against outsiders. Accordingly, although France cannot use its exorbitant jurisdiction in a suit by a French person against an English person, it can still use it when the defendant is an American instead. Moreover, the resulting French judgment gets recognition and enforcement in England, Germany, and elsewhere in the European Union against the American or the American's assets there.

Similarly, the virtually automatic recognition and enforcement under the Brussels Convention does not extend to judgments rendered by countries that are not member states. The European countries, in fact, have traditionally been and continue to be rather stingy in extending respect to foreign judgments not covered by treaty, such as American judgments.

A hypothetical example is necessary to drive home this astounding reality. Assume that Linda Silberman, a New York law professor with property in London, had a car collision in New York City with Bernard Audit, a law professor visiting from France. Imagine that Professor Audit sues Professor Silberman in Paris. This jurisdiction is okay under the French Civil Code's Article 14, being personal jurisdiction based on the plaintiff's French nationality. Moreover, a judgment for Audit will be entitled under the Brussels Convention to recognition and enforcement against Silberman's property in England. Now assume conversely that the collision was in Paris. Imagine that Silberman sues Audit in New York. This jurisdiction is impermissible under U.S. law. If a default judgment were rendered, neither France nor England would enforce it, because the lack of personal jurisdiction made the judgment invalid. Even a litigated judgment would enjoy far less than automatic recognition and enforcement abroad.

This cxamplc is an cxtrcmc onc, without much importance in actual practice. But it works to illustrate the legal context. And it works to suggest the U.S. motivation for seeking a treaty. In short, Americans are being whipsawed. Not only are they still subject in theory to the far-reaching jurisdiction of European courts and the wide recognition and enforceability of the resulting European judgments, but also U.S. judgments tend in practice to receive short shrift in European courts.

Hague Negotiations

This international situation, exacerbated by the Brussels Convention, is untenable in the long run for the United States. Therefore, in 1992 the United States initiated a push to conclude a worldwide convention on jurisdiction and judgments, having naturally chosen to work through the Hague Conference on Private International Law. A convention would resolve the whipsawing predicament in which Americans today find themselves regarding jurisdiction as well as recognition and enforcement of judgments.

Will such a convention come into existence? As negotiations now enter their final phase, the possibility still persists that a multilateral convention will emerge for signature, ratification, and implementation in the near future. But the United States has little bargaining power. It needs a convention, while the Europeans have little to gain over their presently favorable situation. The expectation therefore is that any eventual convention will be similar to the Brussels Convention. That is, the Hague Convention will agree on certain bases of territorial jurisdiction, but chiefly those palatable to the Europeans – and judgments based thereon will receive virtually automatic recognition and enforcement in other signatory countries, except perhaps those judgments that the Europeans consider too generous or punitive. Such a prospect is not to the United States' liking. Reaching agreement on a Hague Convention is therefore far from a certainty. What is certain is that the final segment of the path to international agreement will not be smooth.

In the end, perhaps the United States would have to pay too great a price for securing agreement to a Hague Convention. The Europeans have exhibited some fixed positions and bloc voting. Or perhaps the document emerging from the intermittent and contentious drafting sessions would be too imperfect. Some of its current provisions remain maddeningly awkward or vague. Until recently, generalist drafters had not treated very well technical matters, such as intellectual property. Also, their lack of foresight has thus far prevented the crafting of handles on future developments, such as e-commerce.

Yet drafting and agreeing on a multilateral Hague Convention could yield great returns for the United States on both jurisdictional law and judgments law. A Hague Convention would rationalize the law on an international level. In the specific matter of treatment of foreign judgments, a Hague Convention appears quite desirable. It would mean that the United States could get returns for the respect it is already according other nations' judgments. As to the jurisdictional side, a Hague Convention would cause other countries to renounce their own exorbitant jurisdiction. It also could improve U.S. jurisdictional law in international cases.

Regardless of ultimate outcome, the fruits of negotiation have definitely been worth the effort so far. Merely negotiating a Hague Convention has taught a lot about jurisdiction and judgments as well. Indeed, it has given the United States the opportunity to untangle its law in domestic cases.

The Hague Convention's Provisions on Jurisdiction

Basic Provisions

The key to understanding the jurisdictional half of the Hague Convention is the notion of a "mixed convention," as distinguished from a double convention. The United States has pushed a mixed convention from the beginning as a way to bridge the negotiators' wide differences on jurisdictional approaches. This mixed convention includes not only a so-called whitelist of required jurisdictional bases and a so-called blacklist of prohibited bases, but also a catchall gray zone of permitted bases. In the gray zone, a signatory country could exercise jurisdiction on any basis under its own law not prohibited by the convention, but other countries would not have to recognize or enforce the resulting judgment. Although such a mixed convention does not go as far in providing global uniformity as a double convention, a more limited ambition greatly facilitates international agreement. It also provides a means to handle jurisdiction in areas where diversity of practice is beneficial at present or where significant changes are foreseeable in the near future.

1. Whitelist

Each signatory country must exercise the whitelist's bases of jurisdiction in international cases. That is, the Hague Convention makes these bases part of the national law.

General jurisdiction exists as the foundational basis of jurisdiction at the defendant's home, so that normally the plaintiff can there bring suit on any personal claim whatsoever against the defendant. More precisely, under the Hague Convention the foundational basis is the defendant's habitual residence or, for a corporation, its place of incorporation or its principal place of business (Art. 3).

Specific jurisdiction supplements general jurisdiction by allowing suit on a personal claim related to the defendant's consent or to the defendant's acts directed at the forum country. Under the Hague Convention, the consent basis extends to forum selection agreements (Art. 4) and to the defendant's appearance (Art. 5). Long-arm-like jurisdiction exists for contract actions (Art. 6) and tort actions (Art. 10). Certain disadvantaged persons – consumers (Art. 7) and employees (Art. 8) – enjoy special treatment allowing them often to litigate at home.

Exclusive jurisdiction provisions override this scheme to fix one proper forum in a few instances. These provisions cover trusts (Art. 11) and real estate and the like (Art. 12).

2. Blacklist

Each signatory country must renounce the blacklist's bases of jurisdiction, which have been deemed exorbitant.

In its generalized terms, the Hague Convention prohibits a signatory country from exercising jurisdiction, with respect to a defendant habitually resident in any other signatory country, if there is no "substantial connection" between the forum country and the dispute (Art. 18(1)).

In its precise terms, the Hague Convention expansively, but not exhaustively, lists prohibited bases (Art. 18(2)). The blacklist includes the traditional U.S. bases of transient or tag jurisdiction, "doing business" as a basis for general jurisdiction, and attachment jurisdiction. Of course, the blacklist also includes other countries' exorbitant bases. For instance, France would renounce jurisdiction based on the French nationality of the plaintiff.

3. Gray Zone

Even with respect to a defendant habitually resident in another signatory country, a signatory country can continue to utilize additional bases under its national law of jurisdiction, as long as those bases do not fall on the blacklist and do not contravene a forum selection agreement or the exclusive jurisdiction provisions (Art. 17). The Hague Convention, however, does not require the other signatory countries to recognize or enforce the resulting judgment; they can treat the judgment as they would absent a treaty.

Under the current Hague Convention draft, this gray zone is not big, because of the expansiveness of the general and specific blacklist. But the gray zone would reach international human rights cases (Art. 18(3)). And it offers a neat way to overcome the Hague Convention's shortcomings in not providing all the needed jurisdiction (e.g., the useful parts of U.S. in rem and quasi in rem jurisdiction) and in not foreseeing all future developments (e.g., Internet jurisdiction).

Special Provisions

Any convention comprehensively treating territorial jurisdiction must contain a number of articles handling special matters. Accordingly, the Hague Convention goes on to authorize jurisdiction for provisional and protective measures (Art. 13), to manage redundant litigation by creating a vigorous role for lis pendens (Art. 21), and to reduce the role of judicial discretion by restricting forum non conveniens

(Art. 22). However, it does not cover all the special matters that perhaps it should, such as antisuit injunctions.

These special provisions can raise serious and devilishly difficult problems, on which big differences of view exist. The Brussels Convention, for instance, provides for so-called derivative jurisdiction, an idea coming from French law. This provision yields personal jurisdiction over codefendants if normal personal jurisdiction based on domicile exists over one defendant, as well as personal jurisdiction over any third-party defendants. U.S. lawyers, used to testing personal jurisdiction separately and independently for each defendant, find this doctrine so foreign that they have trouble even comprehending it. So, how should the negotiators compromise on this point? Does the European laxness rest primarily on administrative convenience? Does the U.S. fetish derive primarily from its power heritage? What does fairness dictate? The Hague Convention might provide for derivative jurisdiction (arts. 14–16), but this remains up in the air. Because of this point and many more significant points, reaching agreement on a Hague Convention remains tricky to predict.

U.S. Implications

On the level of international cases, the Hague Convention will fundamentally alter U.S. jurisdictional law. It will federalize the law. But it will also change the content of the law. It will both contract and expand current bases of jurisdiction. Both these changes of direction raise perplexing concerns.

On the one hand, the eventuality of a Hague Convention means that the United States might soon abandon – on the international level, but not necessarily with respect to its courts' actions against its own habitual residents (Art. 2) – transient jurisdiction, "doing business" as a basis for general jurisdiction, attachment jurisdiction, and much of forum non conveniens. The Europeans' objection is to the U.S. proclivity to base general jurisdiction on rather thin contacts, namely, allowing any and all causes of action to be brought on the basis of the defendant's physical presence, doing business in the forum, or property ownership. They do not object to specific jurisdiction, as long as a rules-based approach controls its mandatory application. Thus, jurisdiction under the Hague Convention would exist at the unconsenting defendant's habitual residence or where a specific part of the events in suit occurred, but would not extend to the broader bases of jurisdiction now authorized by U.S. law.

On the other hand, the Hague Convention by mandating new bases of jurisdiction, such as the favorable treatment in allowing a consumer to bring suit at home regardless of the defendant's contacts with that forum, might stretch U.S. ideas of the permissible outer limits on jurisdictional reach, namely, the power and unreasonableness tests imposed by the Due Process Clauses. Such stretching, however, likely falls within the U.S. treatymakers' constitutional mandate. Although a treaty cannot trump the Constitution, this Hague Convention could supplant the moribund power test in its function of allocating territorial authority on the international level.

Presumably, the negotiated and agreed Hague Convention's terms would satisfy any unreasonableness test, especially given that the Supreme Court's jurisdiction cases have accorded considerable weight to legislative views on reasonableness.

On the level of domestic cases, the Hague Convention ironically promises even greater benefits than on the international level. The negotiations hand lawmakers a hidden benefit in providing the opportunity to straighten out the jurisdiction law applied at home. Rethinking jurisdiction would permit the United States to improve its interstate law. The negotiators' efforts might inspire Congress some day to enact the Hague Convention's jurisdictional provisions as national law, just as Italy has recently done with the Brussels Convention. That is, Congress could legislate in effect that federal and state courts, not only in all international cases but also even in interstate cases, possess jurisdiction only if the case's circumstances satisfy the Hague Convention's analogous jurisdictional provision. Alternatively, state legislatures could enact reform of their own jurisdiction law.

Even if the Hague negotiations were ultimately to fail, Congress could work such a domestic reform by enacting as national law the gist of the jurisdictional provisions in the United States' final proposal at The Hague. (In fact, the American Law Institute by its International Jurisdiction and Judgments Project is already building on the Hague Conference's work by drafting a federal statute to govern the recognition and enforcement of foreign judgments in the United States.) Thus, from an unexpected direction for domestic reform, the United States might arrive at the optimal law on territorial authority to adjudicate: a law under which the constitutional limits fade into the background, and legislative rules move to the fore by providing certainty and restraint.

In brief, then, the Hague negotiations represent a major legal development in U.S. jurisdictional law, even though so far they are proceeding without much professional awareness. Regardless of the negotiations' outcome, the United States – as well as the rest of the world – could learn much from the Hague experience. Accordingly, Cornell Law School and the University of Paris I convened a Symposium in July 2000 on Lessons from The Hague.

The Paris Symposium's Papers and Comments on Jurisdiction

Basic Provisions

The Symposium's first group of three major papers sequentially cover the above-described three aspects of the Hague Convention's jurisdictional provisions: basic provisions, special provisions, and U.S. implications.

Georges A.L. Droz starts us off, in Chapter Two, with a more detailed overview of the jurisdictional provisions. He is a true expert in this area. As the former Secretary General of the Hague Conference, he played an active role in the elaboration of some thirty international conventions. As an academic, he has authored numerous publications on international private law, the unification of law, and the law of treaties. His paper for the Symposium goes provision by provision through the jurisdictional half of the Hague Convention, giving the sources and content of each provision, along with a discussion of some of the persisting problems. This paper oriented the whole discussion of jurisdiction. It also triggered a flurry of published comments.

First, Olivier Tell elaborates the basic choice for the negotiators between a double convention and a mixed convention. His appointments and employments locate him critically to discuss the choice. He is an official French delegate to the Hague Conference for a jurisdiction and judgments convention. Also, he was at the time of the Symposium a judge in the Central Administration of the Ministry of Justice of France, Bureau of European and International Affairs, but he has since moved on to work at the European Commission. So, should the treaty specify each signatory country's international jurisdictional reach, exhaustively imposing a whitelist and a blacklist, or should it merely regulate the extremes, mandating minimum jurisdiction and outlawing the most exorbitant jurisdiction while leaving a gray zone? His comment makes a powerful statement of the European point of view in favor of a double convention. He contends that a mixed convention is inherently destructive of the Hague aims of predictability and certainty, and also that plaintiffs would heavily utilize the gray-zone bases to subvert the agreement. More specifically, he argues against the authorization, in the gray zone or elsewhere, of any jurisdiction based on the defendant's commercial activity or any substantial doctrine of forum non conveniens.

Second, Joaquim-J. Forner Delaygua, a Professor of Law at the University of Barcelona, focuses in on the provisions covering jurisdiction in contract cases. His focus narrows to business-to-business contracts formed and performed on the Internet. Within that illustrative context, he demonstrates the considerable expertise required of the drafters in their treatment of each of the myriad of specialized areas covered by the Hague Convention's jurisdictional provisions. Although his broad-gauged survey of the emerging problems of such B2B contracts calmly reveals them to be ultimately solvable, he nevertheless concludes that the drafters would better leave this representative area to the gray zone for now. Here, then, is a European opinion that the drafters should utilize the strengths of the mixed-convention approach.

Third, Professor Ronald A. Brand, Director of the Center for International Legal Education at the University of Pittsburgh School of Law, and also an official U.S. delegate to the Hague Conference for a jurisdiction and judgments convention, shifts the narrow focus to the provisions covering jurisdiction in tort cases. In fact, he starts off with the Hague Convention's subsection on tort jurisdiction at the place of injury, but shows how such narrow consideration can lead back to broad and profound reconsideration of the whole treatymaking process. His comment centers on three themes. First, he argues that the Hague draft's tort subsection, as well as the rest of the draft, is far too ambitious in its pursuit of perfection. It should instead aim at the acceptable, by sticking to the common ground of first principles. Second, he argues that some of the jurisdiction provisions improperly focus on the relation between court and claim, instead of keeping the focus on the relation between court and defendant. The draft's tort subsection, which inappropriately generalizes a European defamation decision by codifying a broad limit on tort recovery to locally incurred damages when the forum is merely the place of injury, suffers also from this fault. Third, he argues that the draft retains too much allegiance to the Brussels Convention. The draft's structure should instead be expressive of its essence as a mixed convention. Finally, the comment closes with a masterful integration and implementation of these themes: it presents a whole alternative treaty, minimalist but feasible, that would indeed make the world a better place for transnational litigation.

Special Provisions

Stephen B. Burbank, in Chapter Six, undertakes the challenge of dissecting and integrating the Hague Convention's provisions on lis pendens and forum non conveniens, as well as considering its missing coverage of antisuit injunctions. He is the David Berger Professor for the Administration of Justice at the University of Pennsylvania Law School. As in his other research, he wrestles the problem of these three special provisions to the ground, and then takes them even deeper.

Professor Burbank's paper begins by surveying U.S. and European approaches to these special devices by which courts protect or decline jurisdiction. Against this background survey, the Hague Convention's provisions appear to promise great advance. On the one hand, the author is remarkably positive on the draft's treatment of lis pendens and forum non conveniens, although he does offer some valuable suggestions for minor improvement. On the other hand, he leans toward altering the draft to provide courts with a limited power to issue antisuit injunctions. Nevertheless, despite the Hague Convention's promise, he remains calmly accepting of its slowing progress and uncertain prospects. The reason is that he believes in the negotiations' educational benefits. He accordingly closes with his own proposals: first, a U.S. congressional statute treating lis pendens and antisuit injunctions for domestic cases in federal and state courts, with separate and somewhat different treatment of these matters for international cases; and perhaps, second, another such statute regulating forum non conveniens for international cases in federal and state courts.

U.S. Implications

Linda Silberman, in Chapter Seven, provides another perspective from the United States. She too is critically positioned for this discussion. Twice a delegate to the Hague Conference for earlier conventions, and now Martin Lipton Professor of Law at New York University, she is sufficiently recognized an expert in private international law to have become Co-Reporter for the American Law Institute's aforementioned International Jurisdiction and Judgments Project. This nascent ALI Project is drafting a federal statute to govern the recognition and enforcement of foreign judgments in the United States, but it will not rework the direct jurisdiction of U.S. courts.

Professor Silberman's paper describes her ALI Project. Primarily, however, the paper performs a careful and cautious, but ultimately positive, evaluation of the various provisions of the current Hague draft. Her realistic assessment of its chances for adoption stresses the need for European concessions to certain U.S. concerns. Her prime example is the draft's proposed abolition of "doing business" as a basis for general jurisdiction, a basis existing under U.S. law. She suggests shifting a carefully worded core of that basis from the draft's blacklist to its gray zone. This change would allow U.S. courts to continue to exercise such jurisdiction when the defendant has a substantial presence in the U.S. and the plaintiff is habitually resident there, but would not obligate other countries to recognize or enforce the resulting judgment. This clever solution to a "deal-breaker" problem demonstrates that compromise of very different national visions is indeed feasible under a mixed convention.

Last in this part of the book, but not in my humble opinion least, comes the comment by Kuo-Chang Huang and me. It suggests a way of converting the Hague Convention negotiations into national jurisdictional law. As already suggested, those negotiations have given the United States the opportunity to rethink jurisdiction and make improvements on the interstate level. A federal statute could extend the substance of the negotiated provisions to state courts not only in international cases but also in all interstate cases. Earlier work foresaw such jurisdictional salvation and argued for its desirability and constitutionality, but just sketched its content. Calls for reform are relatively easy to utter. Actually drafting the reform – fully formulating the law of territorial jurisdiction – is a much harder task. This comment presents a draft of a proposed statute, so adding feasibility to the arguments made to the legislators. In general, the proposed statute aims to pare general jurisdiction down to its proper scope and codify specific jurisdiction into restrained and clear mandatory rules, while pushing constitutional limits into the background where they belong.

The closing comment's effort to draft a federal statute to govern the states' interstate and international territorial jurisdiction, whether or not there is a treaty, is thus complementary to Professor Silberman's ALI Project, which will treat only the judgments half of the Hague Convention.

A Preliminary Glance at the Hague Convention's Provisions on Judgments

The Hague Convention, in its basic treatment of foreign judgments, [i] requires recognition and enforcement of another signatory country's judgment that has the effect of res judicata in the rendering country, as long as that country was exercising whitelist jurisdiction (Art. 25), and [ii] prohibits recognition and enforcement of another signatory country's judgment rendered on blacklist jurisdiction or in contravention of a forum selection agreement or of the exclusive jurisdiction provisions (Art. 26). The second court could verify the jurisdiction of the rendering court, although a nondefault judgment's findings of jurisdictional fact would bind that second court (Art. 27).

An obvious concern with a multilateral treaty is that the United States might be forced to give respect to distasteful foreign judgments. Americans are confident about sister-state and federal judgments, but there the substantive and procedural aspects of the Due Process Clauses apply, with the U.S. Supreme Court in place to review their application. Perhaps Americans could muster confidence in the judgments of a small number of like-minded legal systems, even in the absence of a supranational oversight authority. But a worldwide treaty is altogether another matter. Americans could not be sure of the fundamental fairness of all foreign judgments. Accordingly, any treaty would probably have to contain a provision giving each signatory country some control over which countries can sign on vis-à-vis that country, as well as a narrowly drawn public-policy exception for procedural due process violations and other repugnancies (Art 28).

Georges A.L. Droz[†]

Preliminary Draft of the Convention on Jurisdiction and Foreign Judgments in Civil and Commercial Matters: Provisions of Jurisdiction

Preliminary Comments

Before commenting on the articles pertaining to bases of jurisdiction, it is appropriate to make two tentative comments regarding the structure of the Convention and the character of the bases of jurisdiction.

Structure of the Convention

The structure of the Convention is very different from the Brussels and Lugano Conventions, which provide a list that allocates the authority to adjudicate. Courts must (in the case of exclusive jurisdiction) or may exercise this authority when the defendant is domiciled in a contracting state. The use of any other factor to grant jurisdiction is forbidden (the list of prohibited bases for jurisdiction, provided as an example in Article 3, is not exhaustive). Outside of the exclusive jurisdiction rule, when a defendant is not domiciled in a contracting state, courts may use national rules of jurisdiction, including those granting exceptional jurisdiction that may exist in contracting states. In both cases, the conventional device applies to the recognition and execution of court decisions rendered in a contracting state.

The Hague Preliminary Draft first establishes a list of bases of jurisdiction, which courts may always use (the "whitelist"), except in cases stated in Articles 21 and 22. By contrast, the Draft also establishes a list of bases of jurisdiction that are forbidden when the defendant's place of habitual residence is in a contracting state (non-exhaustive "blacklist" also found in the Brussels/Lugano Conventions).

Finally, the Convention recognizes a "gray zone" by allowing the use of national bases of jurisdiction for contracting states that would differ from those included in the whitelist and yet that would not fall under the scope of the blacklist. This structure will be reflected at the recognition level since whitelist judgments will have to be recognized and executed. Moreover, blacklist-based judgments will not receive recognition, and the general law of the relevant state will determine whether or not gray zone-judgments will receive recognition.

[†] Former Secretary General of The Hague Conference on Private International Law.

J.J. Barceló and K.M. Clermont (eds.), A Global Law of Jurisdiction and Judgments: Lessons from The Hague, 15–36

Nature of the Bases of Jurisdiction

The Brussels/Lugano Conventions, like the present Preliminary Draft, recognize general as well as special jurisdiction rules. General jurisdiction occurs when subject-matter jurisdiction is granted to the courts of a contracting state while leaving the choice of proper venue to this same state's adjective law. Special jurisdiction occurs when the Convention itself determines the proper venue such as the court of the place of execution of a contract, over any court of the state in which the parties executed the contract.

In the Brussels and Lugano Conventions, the only general jurisdictions are those based either on the defendant's domicile or on exclusive jurisdiction. All other bases for jurisdiction are special jurisdiction bases. On the contrary, in the present Preliminary Draft, all jurisdiction bases are general, except those derived and already linked to a chosen court. Such a difference may be explained by observing the Brussels/Lugano recognition system: the relevant court does not have to confirm the correctness of the special jurisdiction of the foreign court. If the latter wrongly found itself competent, and if its judgment has become final, this does not matter in either this judge's state or in the state of enforcement. However, as set forth by the Preliminary Draft, the judge, on recognition, must verify the competence of the foreign court. If special competencies had been provided for, several matters of dispute would have arisen, for instance, whether the defendant maintained habitual residence in Sydney and not in Melbourne, whether the damage was incurred in Hamburg and not in Berlin, or whether the contract was executed in Shanghai and not in Canton. Thanks to general jurisdictions, the mere observance that the habitual residence, the offense, or the execution of a contract were located in the country of first instance, without further investigation, is sufficient.

Bases for Jurisdiction Under the Conventions

The Whitelist – Bases for Jurisdiction Plaintiff May Always Assert

General Jurisdiction

Article 3: The Defendant's Forum

Article 3 provides for the competence of the courts of the state where the defendant as a physical person maintains habitual residence. The Preliminary Draft uses the adage "actor sequitur forum rei," which is applied in many civil-law systems. Though difficult to apply at first sight in common-law countries, the implementation of this rule is actually easy. It is the primary forum provided for in the Brussels/Lugano Conventions; the British and Irish systems have conformed to it without difficulty. The retained connecting factor is habitual residence, a question of fact, and not a matter of domicile, a question of law that is interpreted in several different ways in comparative law, as it is in the Brussels/Lugano Conventions. In practice, the notion of habitual residence used in several Hague conventions to found jurisdiction or to determine applicable law has not resulted in any difficulties.

Article 3 paragraph (2) pertains to entities or persons other than physical persons. The provision mainly concerns corporations, associations, and foundations, as well as entities that are not moral persons yet who possess standing.

Four bases of jurisdiction are listed: (a) the courts of the state in which the registered seat is located, an existing corporate-law notion for some legal systems; (b) the courts of the state under whose law the entity was created, that is, the place of incorporation for countries that use this system; (c) the courts of the state where the entity has its administrative core; and (d) the courts of the state where the entity has its principal place of business. In practice, these bases of jurisdiction will often overlap (even though the development of electronic commerce will allow the small-size administrative core to exist in a country other than the one of the principal place of business).

The spectrum offered to the plaintiff is thus large and, even if a company incorporated in one country has its central administration in a second and maintains its principal place of business in a third, one must not limit the plaintiff's freedom of choice because it is the defendant who provides several angles of attack.

Article 4: Forum Selection

In sanctioning forum selection choice, worldwide and by an international substantive rule, the Preliminary Draft reinforces the predictability and security of private international relations. The first sentence of Article 4 paragraph (1) sets down the principle of exclusivity of the chosen court's jurisdiction when the parties have not decided otherwise. In some states, exclusivity is in practice not the rule; under the Preliminary Draft the chosen court cannot refuse jurisdiction on the grounds that, for instance, it has no contact with the dispute. The parties may have chosen this forum because of its neutrality, precisely because it had no contact with the dispute. Such a choice must be respected. The second sentence of the last paragraph confirms the validity on its face of the agreed choice of court while specifying that the exclusive jurisdiction attributed by the parties to the court or courts of a non-contracting state must be respected, except in cases where the elected court – unbound by the Convention – declined jurisdiction. The parties may choose a court of determined venue – making it a special jurisdiction case – or the courts of a contracting state, which will be a general jurisdiction case.

The combined operation of Article 2, paragraph (1)(a) and Article 4 allows two parties with habitual residence in a contracting state to choose the courts of another contracting state in order to settle their dispute. The Convention is silent on whether the dispute must be international. In the context of the Brussels/Lugano Conventions, the doctrine widely admits that the Convention is inapplicable when the agreement on choice of court involves a mere domestic dispute.

The formal requirements set forth in Article 4, paragraph (2) are traditional and have adapted to the needs of international trade. They are directly inspired by the text of Article 17 of the Brussels/Lugano Conventions. The parties must have concluded or confirmed their agreement in writing, a way they commonly use, or in a way that parties to similar contracts in the same industry employ. More modern and inspired by developments in electronic commerce, paragraph (2)(b) validates the form of the agreement concluded or confirmed "by any other means of communication which makes information accessible so as to be subsequently consulted." The retained criterion is thus conservation of information, just as for electronic signatures, the value of which is increasingly and largely recognized in comparative law.

Article 4, paragraph (3), which is a very traditional provision, declares void agreements that confer jurisdiction contrary to protective or exclusive rules jurisdiction. Noticeably, this provision assimilates agreements that confer jurisdiction and stipulations of instruments creating a trust. One should wonder whether Article 11 on trusts would not be a more suitable location for such a provision.

Article 5: Appearance by the Defendant

These provisions are directly inspired by the Brussels/Lugano Conventions and by several procedural systems that make no distinction between voluntary appearance and forum's selection. Voluntary appearance of the defendant makes a court competent where it otherwise would not be. If the plaintiff brings an action before an incompetent court, voluntarily or not, and is unhappy with the conflict-of-forum rule – the plaintiff would not be able to withdraw if the defendant appeared for the purpose of obtaining an application of the said conflicting rule from the now competent court.

From a procedural point of view, Article 5, paragraph (1) has the great advantage of eliminating all disputes regarding the verification of the jurisdiction of the foreign court's jurisdiction: as soon as the defendant appears before the court and the proceedings become adversarial, the court acquires jurisdiction and all defenses are barred. The defendant, however, must have voluntarily appeared with the intention of consolidating the jurisdiction of the court at stake. It is possible that the defendant would have to present a defense based on the merits, for example, to overturn a seizure of goods. In such a case, appearance is no longer voluntary. To prove this, however, the defendant must have contested the court's jurisdiction before filing the first defense on the merits. Article 5, paragraph (2) provides for just this. Finally, paragraph (1) traditionally preserves Article 12 concerning exclusive jurisdiction since neither the plaintiff nor the defendant may depart from it.

Article 6: Contracts

A Preliminary Draft of an international convention on jurisdiction in civil and commercial matters could not "politically" abstain from formulating rules applicable to contracts. Yet, the disappointing experience of the Brussels Convention, as interpreted by the Court of Justice of the European Communities, could have frozen enthusiasm. We know that Article 5 of the Brussels Convention resulted in substantial disputes, whereas a good convention should aim at reducing the number of lawsuits. Problems arose because of the Brussels/Lugano allocation of jurisdiction to the courts of the place of execution of the different obligations set forth in the contract.

This "spin off" of obligations could trigger contradictory judgments in several countries regarding the same contract. Moreover, the Court of Justice decided that under the forum rules governing choice of law, the determination of the place of execution of an obligation must be made according to the law applicable to the contract. True, today, the Convention of Rome governs conflict of laws in contractual matters within the European Union, but differences remain among domestic laws. Concerning the obligation of payment, some systems (the Netherlands, Germany, and the Vienna Convention on Sales) consider payment to be payable at the creditor's residence, whereas others, France and Belgium for example, consider it to be requestable at the debtor's domicile. In the first case regarding payment, jurisdiction is attributed to the plaintiff's court – forum actoris being an exception – and, in the second case, to that of the defendant's domicile, which is the standard rule. In such a system, the forum of the contract has no autonomy per se, which accounts for revision of the Brussels/Lugano Conventions in the areas of sales and performance of services, the most common types of contracts. It suppresses the splitting of obligations, pushes away the jurisdiction of the place of payment, and grants jurisdiction to the court where goods were or were to be delivered or where services were or were to be provided by virtue of the contract.

The solution presently adopted in the Preliminary Draft is a minimalist one. Article 6 eliminates the splitting of obligations and therefore, makes the problem related to the place of execution of payment disappear. Inspired by the revision of the Brussels/Lugano Conventions, the Preliminary Draft allows a plaintiff to bring an action in contract before the courts, in cases relating to the supply of corporeal movables, where these goods were provided in full or in part, or in cases relating to the provision of services, where the services were rendered in whole or in part. In cases of hybrid contracts, where the agreement deals with the provision of corporeal movables and performance of services, the place where the main obligation was executed, in whole or in part, governs.

Therefore, the court of the state in which merchandise or services were to be provided or rendered, but were actually not, lacks jurisdiction. Such a court, which would be competent under the preliminary revision of the Brussels/Lugano Conventions, is not so under the Hague Draft because it lacks minimum contact with the contract. Thus, it will be necessary, under the current text, to use the basis for jurisdiction provided for in Article 3 regarding the defendant's habitual residence or, alternatively, the basis for jurisdiction set forth in brackets in Article 9 based on the defendant's habitual commercial activity.

The same solution will govern for contracts that do not fall into the categories targeted by Article 6. For example, this involves contracts of carriage and insurance, contracts between professionals, contracts governing stock transactions, bonds, or claims, that are not corporeal movables in the language of Article 6.

Moreover, the Convention does not exclude, thus necessarily includes, contracts linked to electronic commerce. If such a contract results in an actual delivery of goods, Article 6 would be easy to apply. If, on the other hand, the delivery or service is provided on-line (downloading a film, book, or software, for example), determining the place of execution is problematic. A working group of the Hague Conference met in Ottawa to deal with these problems. The result of these sessions might be submitted for consideration to the delegations, and it is possible that ad hoc solutions might be sought. In any case, there is clear unanimity that disputes arising from electronic commerce should fall under the scope of the Convention.

Article 7: Contracts Concluded by Consumers

The provision of Article 7 is drawn directly from the consumer-protection rules widely used in Europe and established in the Brussels/Lugano Conventions. Consumers, individuals who have concluded a contract for motives other than professional or commercial activities, may bring suit in the state of habitual residence when the other contracting party is a professional who conducted promotional activity (Article (7)(a)) in this state and when that professional completed the proceedings required for the conclusion of the contract in this state (Article (7)(b)). A consumer may benefit from Article 7 if when making a purchase from a catalogue abroad, from a door-to-door salesperson, or by completing a form provided in a publication. However, Article 7 does not apply when a person travels abroad to sample a special menu in a renowned restaurant on the basis of an advertisement published in local press.

While the consumer may exceptionally use the forum actoris, the professional may only bring an action against the consumer before the courts of the consumer's state of habitual residence (Article 7, paragraph (2)).

As stated above, Article 4, paragraph (3) renders forum-shopping agreements void when concluded by consumers. This is a preventive measure. But, when the consumer has had enough time to consider the consequences of the contract entered into, and accepts, in case of dispute, the jurisdiction of another court, the forum-shopping agreement becomes valid. An agreement that allows the consumer to bring suit in a court other than that of habitual residence or that of the defendant's habitual residence is valid as well.

Article 7 is thus drafted on the same scheme as the Brussels/Lugano Conventions. But, since these conventions were drafted, consumer contracts related to electronic commerce have developed lightening speed. Whether the agreed-upon text could be applied to electronic commerce as it is or whether it would be more appropriate to adopt specific e-commerce friendly provisions is an issue requiring further contemplation.

Is there not a factual difference between a consumer who is solicited at home by catalogue, by an ad, or by a door-to-door salesperson and a consumer who, from a desk and with the help of a search engine, takes the initiative to compare prices of desired goods in several different countries and orders them from the supplier whose products and prices are best? Even if the consumer did not take such an initiative, how could it be determined whether a commercial activity was executed or managed in the consumer's home state when the messages involved are not geographically localized? Further, does the mere act of "clicking" constitute a necessary step towards concluding a contract? Finally, the trickiest question remains how to deal with forum-shopping agreements in the electronic commerce context. Here, the trend in the European market seems to lean towards the protection, thus prohibition, of forum-shopping agreements; whereas, in North America, the trend looks more towards the protection of e-commerce companies against lawsuits brought by consumers from far-off lands. The working group that met in Ottawa also discussed these issues; concrete solutions must be sought. At the very least, the state should be permitted to authorize consumers residing in their territory to conclude forum-shopping agreements in e-commerce.

Article 8: Individual Employment Contracts

The solution set forth concerning employment contracts comes directly from the Brussels/Lugano Convention rules. In international relations, employment contracts often create disputes. In Europe, this is one of the areas that entails the greatest amount of case law. Nevertheless, one may ask what fate awaits these provisions when they reach the diplomatic conference, since enormous social and economic gaps exist among countries worldwide. Over the course of the debate, the fact emerged that, in Latin America, employment contracts, like every labor law issues, are administrative matters that fall outside of the reach of the Convention.

According to paragraph (1), an employee bringing an action may do so before the courts of the state in which the employee's work is usually performed. When the employee does not usually work in any one state, however, an action can be brought in the courts of the state where the hiring company is located. The employer can bring an action against an employee in the court of the state of the employee's habitual residence or before the courts of the state in which the employee's work is usually performed.

Article 4 prohibits forum-shopping agreements. However, paragraph (2) allows consumers to enter in such an agreement after the dispute has arisen or to the extent that it allows the employee to bring an action before courts different from those ordinarily available.

Article 9: Branch [and Regular Commercial Activity]

The forum of a branch agency or firm is a traditional one and was established by Article 5(5) of the Brussels/Lugano Conventions. A defendant, when acting abroad through the expedient of a branch office, agency, or firm, can expect to be subject to suit in the country where the branch is located for disputes related to the activities of the same. By virtue of Article 3, however, the plaintiff may also bring suit in the defendant's country of habitual residence or where the statutory headquarters are located. It would also be possible for the plaintiff to bring an action against the defendant in the place where merchandise at stake was delivered or where services were rendered. Indeed, the place where the branch runs its activity is not necessarily identical to the place where the branch was established. This was clearly demonstrated in the Court of Justice of the European Communities decision *Lloyd's Register of Shipping v. Société Campenon Bernard* (6 April 1995). In this case, an English firm was cited in France at the registered office of its branch that entered a contract for the inspection of public works materials. The contract was executed in Spain. The plaintiff could also have brought action in England, where the company was incorporated, or in Spain, where the obligation was executed.

A new element found in Article 9 that should become essential through the negotiations of the diplomatic conference is provided in brackets. The courts of the state "where the defendant has carried on regular commercial activity by other means ... provided that the disputes relate ... to that regular commercial activity" are competent. This drafting results from a proposition of the United States Delegation and is very important for the United States of America.

Let us recall that the provision will only operate against a defendant when neither a branch nor an agency nor an establishment in the implicated country exists, when the sales or service contract is not executed in this country, and finally, when the defendant is neither a consumer who maintains a habitual residence in the country of the court dealing with the case nor an employee who usually works in the same country. Indeed, in all listed cases, Articles 6 through 9 already confer jurisdiction. The activity must also be *habituelle (regular* in English, which does not seem to be identical in meaning). This implies some permanence in the exercise of the activity in question. The condition does not seem to be satisfied when the defendant comes to the country to negotiate a contract executed in a third country. Moreover, the dispute must be directly linked to this regular commercial activity, which excludes the doing business jurisdiction (an exception to the general law).

Given what was discussed, it is somewhat difficult to find real examples where the proposed aggregation would be at play. It is not rare for a cosmetic surgeon to travel abroad on a regular basis to examine potential patients, in a hotel room or ad hoc location, and to discuss the details of surgery that would occur in the physician's private clinic. If the contract were concluded in the patient's country, Article 7 would apply. The provisions of Article 9 would only apply when the patient does not sign the contract until arriving in the country where the physician's practice is located and where the surgeon's performance does not conform to its industry-standard practice. Another example would be where, a tourist information office or chamber of commerce of a ski resort area opens information desks abroad and, using free gifts, sale prices, or particular advantages, attracts potential clients to the resort. If contracts are executed on site, Article 7 applies. Otherwise, to the extent that the benefits, as stated by the tourist information office, make the defendant resort appear attractive and the actual services are inconsistent with what was represented, Article 9 applies. Another common example in Europe is that of part-time vacation real estate companies established in one state, which would attract clients from another state, by organizing parties and product exhibitions. On-site drawings for vacations are usually organized. When clients arrive, they are harassed until they sign a contract, the terms of which clients cannot truly ascertain. As this situation is neither a sale of non-movable goods nor a lease of non-movable goods, Article 12 does not apply, but the provisions of Article 9 could. Nevertheless, in the majority of cases, the client, who has been taken advantage of and signed the contract, accepts a choice-of-forum clause. As the conditions of Article 7 are not satisfied, the agreement is valid unless one can plead defect in consent.

Article 10: Torts
The provision on civil liability jurisdiction is of great importance because the amount of international litigation is substantial. Indeed, insurance companies are very often subrogated to the rights of perpetrators or victims of injury, and such practice fuels international litigation.

Paragraph (1) asserts the principle of alternative jurisdiction, created in Europe by the European Court of Justice in the *Potasses d'Alsace* case. The plaintiff may bring action in either the state where the occurrence (whether it be an act or omission) that resulted in injury took place or where the injury originated. This opens the door to a forum-shopping that is not blameworthy because it tends to protect the victim by allowing suit to be brought in the court that will favor the plaintiff's interests most. Beyond divergences in conflict of jurisdiction rules, it is necessary to consider the fundamental differences that exist between domestic laws that do, and those that do not, allow recovery for pain and suffering in cases of bodily injury.

However, the defendant, who will often be an insurance company, is corrected when it establishes that the person allegedly at fault could not have reasonably foreseen that the act or omission was susceptible to produce an injury of such nature in the state at stake. An example would be the case of an injury caused by a defective product made in one country that brings an injury in another country, even though its exportation to the second country was not contemplated or was even prohibited, due to, for instance, the fact that it did not conform to domestic regulations (commercial norms, pharmaceutical norms, and so on). This exception will scarcely apply, however, in instances of damage to the environment of another state because, in the majority of cases, the injury is foreseeable. For example, let us imagine a case where, due to a river's course or to dominant winds, pollution that occurs in one country will result in damage to the territory of country downwind or downstream.

Article 10, paragraph (2) restricts the scope of application of paragraph (1)(b). This exception does not apply to injuries resulting from unfair competition practices or conspiracies aiming to create economic losses. International business actors, especially European companies, fear conviction by judgments rendered in states where plaintiffs could contend that they suffer from the effects of antitrust violations. Under the current letter of the text, only the courts of the state where the antitrust violations or prohibited conspiracies originate are competent. The underlying political problem demonstrates a reservation concerning a desire on the part of certain states to see widespread application of their antitrust laws before their courts to facts that occurred outside of their territory but which are asserted to have caused injury in the territory of the forum.

Article10, paragraph (4) also restricts the scope of application of paragraph (1)(b). If a plaintiff brings suit before the courts of a state whose jurisdiction is acquired solely because of the place where damages originated, these courts' jurisdiction is limited to the damages that might arise in this state. The purpose of this provision is to avoid a plaintiff from bringing suit in a state where fewer damages occurred compared to another state, simply because the laws and social and legal environment of the former offer the best prospects in terms of recovery. For instance, some countries, like France, severely punish invasions of privacy under French civil law. On the contrary, in other countries, invasions of privacy are of less importance in the eyes of the judges and of public opinion, which justifies lighter sentences. Consider the case of an invasive publication, displaying pictures of an individual shot by "paparazzi" that is largely distributed in "softly regulated" countries but with a very low circulation in France. The victim is entitled to seek remedy in France for the global damages sustained. Rather, remedy is rewarded in relation to the circulation and notoriety of the publication in the French territory.

Article 10, paragraph (4) contains an exception to the exception described above. It is possible to request an aggregate compensation for all injuries in the country where part of the injury originated, provided the victim maintains habitual residence in this country. In this case, consolidation is allowed. To use the preceding example, if an Italian or English periodical were to interfere with an actor's private life (or that of a princess), an aggregate compensation could be requested in France, notwithstanding the periodical's low circulation there, as long as the victim maintained habitual residence there. It is not unheard of in comparative international private law to take into account a number of facts pointing in the same direction.

Article 10, paragraph (3) (whose place in the article could be reconsidered) states that one can bring an action in conformity with the provisions set forth in Article 10, paragraph (1), when the offensive act or omission, or the injury is "susceptible to reoccur." This is done to permit preventive measures that, for example, would prohibit the construction of a factory whose waste could potentially pollute a river crossing a neighboring country. This is not a simple temporary or precautionary measure, but indeed, a substantive measure that seeks to obligate the defendant to act before damage occurs.

Just as was indicated regarding to contracts and consumer protection, the development of international relations through electronic networks complicates the situation somewhat. Injuries may be caused through the intermediary of these networks; these injuries may include slanderous acts, counterfeiting, or even plagiarism, to name a few. It is often difficult to pinpoint the location of the wrongful activity. The defendant should not be too readily able to avoid jurisdiction in the place where the injury occurred by invoking the exception set forth in Article 10, paragraph (1)(b) on the pretext that it could not have been reasonably anticipated that the defendant's action could produce injury here or there. These questions remain on the table.

Article 11: Trusts

The need for a provision on trust jurisdiction arose after the first revision of the Brussels Convention in 1978, the United Kingdom and Ireland having joined the European Community since its original drafting. In Article 5(6), the Brussels/Lugano Conventions deal with normal jurisdiction in trust matters. Article 17, paragraph (3) enumerates provisions on jurisdiction resulting from choice-of-forum agreements. Article 11 combines these situations by including measures that apply when an instrument creating a trust contains a choice-of-forum clause. This is a rather common practice in international relations. Exclusive jurisdiction is attributed to the court designated by the instrument creating the trust for suits that deal with the validity, interpretation, effects, administration, or modification of the voluntary trust whose proof of existence is provided in writing. Therefore, the provision essentially targets the relationship among trustor, trustee, and beneficiary. On the other hand, relations between the trustee and third parties are governed by the general rules of jurisdiction provided by the Convention. When the court designated by the document is located in a non-contracting state, the same mechanism found in the second sentence of Article 4, paragraph (1) applies: The courts of contracting states respect this choice unless the chosen tribunal declines jurisdiction.

According to paragraph (2)(a), if there is no choice-of-forum clause, a suit can be brought in the courts of the state where the trust is principally administered. The Hague Draft avoids the notion of "trust domicile" as employed in the Brussels/Lugano Conventions; this concept is, in fact, unknown to the English and Irish substantive laws and, obviously, to countries where trusts do not exist. Article 45 of the Civil Jurisdiction and Judgment Act of 1982, regarding the domicile of trusts, indicates that a trust is situated in a part of the United Kingdom if, and only if, the legal system of this region is that to which the trust has the closest and most tangible relationship. This logically leads to Article 11, paragraph (2), which provides for the possible jurisdiction of a state (b) whose law is applicable to the trust, and (c) with which the trust has the closest connection for the purpose of the proceedings.

This provision will facilitate the regulation of lawsuits related to the internal dealings of the trust, just as the Brussels/Lugano Conventions previously did. However, paragraph (2), part (c) might well cause some uncertainty to the extent that it allows a court to decline jurisdiction if it believes that it is not the forum with which the trust has the closest connection for the purpose of the proceedings. Nonetheless, part (c) is inoperative if parts (a) or (b) could apply.

In addition to the options available under Article 11, paragraph (2), the general jurisdiction of the court of the defendant's habitual residence, namely that of the trustee (which is most often the same as the principal place of administration of the trust), trustor, or beneficiary, must be added.

A particular difficulty arises when jurisdiction is based on the habitual residence of the trust actors and the suit is, therefore, brought before the courts of a state whose laws do not recognize the existence of the institution at all. It would be a rather difficult undertaking to supervise the internal workings of an American or

English trust, subject to norms such as the English cy-près doctrine, which applies to charitable trusts or spendthrift clauses constructed under American jurisprudence in France, Italy, or Spain. The ratification of the Hague Convention on Recognition and Laws Applicable to Trusts would facilitate a better knowledge of the institution of trust.

To conclude, it is important to note that Article 11 does not apply to implicit or judicial trusts, whereas the Brussels/Lugano Conventions targeted judicial trusts. Pertaining to the internal workings of judicial trusts, the governing rule will be that of the prevailing defendant's habitual residence or that of Article 10, if there is question of civil liability. These cases are rather rare, however, because the majority of judicial trusts covers matters such as the protection of minors, inheritance, or bankruptcy, which fall outside of the scope of the Convention.

Article 12: Exclusive Jurisdiction

Compared to the Brussels/Lugano Conventions, Article 12 provisions appear classical in style. However, a range of options put into brackets complicates such provisions.

Article 12, paragraph (1) contemplates a basis of exclusive jurisdiction that is accepted in comparative real estate law. The courts of the contracting state in which the property is situated have exclusive jurisdiction. As in the Brussels/Lugano Conventions, the Preliminary Draft extends this exclusivity to leases of buildings. Domestic legislation, in a great number of legal systems, are very complex in matters related to leases of buildings or agricultural tenancy. Restricting systems regarding the amount of rent, the right to maintain the property, the duration of a lease contract, and the preferential award of a tenant's right to a lease, are progressively created all over the world. Therefore, jurisdiction is attributed to the local judge because of the subject matter. In fact, in some countries, there are specialized jurisdictions presided over by lease judges or agricultural-tenancy judges. However, when changing the Brussels/Lugano Conventions, some pointed out that, in cases of short term or vacation rentals, the exclusivity of jurisdiction did not necessarily apply. This was particularly true when the lessor and the lessee were ready to submit their dispute to the courts in the place of one's residence or the other. Complex rules have been introduced into these conventions. The Preliminary Draft takes these difficulties into account by creating a simpler solution: in real estate lease matters, the exclusive jurisdiction attributed to the place where the real property is located no longer governs when the lessee maintains habitual residence outside this state. In most instances, this will be a case of a vacation rental, and thus, suit will be brought in the lessor's or lessee's place of residence with Article 3. As the prohibition found in Article 4, paragraph (2) no longer applies, the lessor and lessee, in such a case, could also conclude an agreement by choosing the jurisdiction.

Paragraph (2) states the action on the validity, nullity, or dissolution of a moral person, or the validity or nullity of the decisions of its organs. The Brussels/Lugano Conventions give exclusive jurisdiction to the courts of the state of the legal person's headquarters. Both the revisions of these conventions as well as the Preliminary Draft, prefer to give exclusive jurisdiction to the courts of the contracting state whose law governs the moral person. True, the determination of this law could be based upon the notions of a registered or factual place of incorporation. Nonetheless, it seems that when a company is clearly subject to the law of a given state, due to its incorporation, and when it operates business abroad, there is no reason why jurisdiction should be given to the courts of that foreign country to determine the validity or the nullity of the incorporation under the law of the state of incorporation. On the contrary, the validity or nullity of the decisions of its organs may be reasonably determined under another national law: one must hesitate and ask whether it is possible to exclude the jurisdiction of the courts of the state where the company operates, i.e., where the decisions of the outcome take effect and become public.

It is of note that subparagraph (2) uses the notion of "moral person" that Article 3 avoids. The author believes that "moral person" also means, as in Article 3, a juridical person without moral personality.

For proceedings that have as their object the validity or nullity of entries in public registers, paragraph (3) gives exclusive jurisdiction to the courts of the contracting state in which the registers are kept. This is a traditional provision insofar as a foreign authority could not order a correction to entries or an addition in public registers of another state without affecting its sovereignty.

Paragraphs (4) and (5) on registered intellectual property rights, patents, trademarks, and designs are much more complex, due to the diversity of options that appear in the text.

Without taking into account the brackets that appear in paragraph (4), the first sentence is similar to Article 16(4) of the Brussels/Lugano Conventions. The courts of the contracting state in which the deposit or registration has been applied for, has taken place, or is deemed to have taken place under the terms of an international convention, have exclusive jurisdiction (these last words particularly target the case of a European patent whose registration is deemed to have taken place in the member states of the European Patent Organization). While the Brussels Convention only targets registration and validity issues, the present Preliminary Draft also aims at the nullity of a patent. What was implicit in the Brussels/Lugano Conventions (an action of nullity is a dispute of validity) fortunately becomes explicit in the Preliminary Draft. Indeed, there are more proceedings related to the nullity of a patent than for declarations of validity. Moreover, a nullity action is generally part of the main proceedings whereas a question related to validity is often incidental to an infringement of a registered intellectual property right. In effect, if one disregards the brackets, like in the Brussels/Lugano Conventions, as interpreted by their authors, the exclusive jurisdiction only extends to issues in the main proceedings; the courts of other contracting states can still examine the incidental question of the patent's validity when raised by a defendant accused of patent infringement. While omitted in the Brussels Convention, the Preliminary Draft explicitly states, in paragraph (6) in brackets, that the previous paragraphs do not apply when such matters referred to the court arise as incidental questions. Such a rule can apply, for instance, in cases of nullity of corporations, but the situation will more commonly arise, in practice, in matters related to registered intellectual property rights.

The brackets that appear in the first sentence of Article 4 target the termination or violation of rights resulting from patents, trademarks, and the like. Certain delegations would indeed like to concentrate the entirety of the proceedings relating to patents and trademarks, including those regarding their termination, in the place where the registration is made. In such a case, as all suits related to patents and trademarks must be brought before the courts of the state of registration, paragraph (6) will lose its utility in matters that concern them. However, other delegations oppose the view that exclusive jurisdiction regarding the termination or the infringement of registered intellectual property rights is necessary. Therefore, paragraph (5) provides another option by stating that, in relation to proceedings of infringement of patents, paragraph (4) does not exclude the jurisdiction of any other court that would be competent under the Convention or under the national law of a contracting state. Therefore, the suit will be brought in the country of the defendant's domicile or registered domain (there is no need to consider the place of infringement here as it will always be identical to the place of registration. In a given country, one can only infringe upon patents and trademarks, which are registered, or said to be registered, there. If a patent is not registered there, its use does not constitute an infringement).

Paragraph (5), in brackets, only targets proceedings relating to the infringement of patents. This seems to exclude violations related to trademark, model, or design, and it is unclear whether the authors of the text intended such exclusion. As this situation remains somewhat confused, a working group made up of experts from the Hague Conference and the World Intellectual Property Organization is to gather to discuss such issues and maybe to propose solutions to be discussed within the diplomatic conference.

Be that as it may, the rule of exclusivity does not apply to copyright or any neighboring rights, even though registration or deposit of such rights is possible according to the second sentence of paragraph (4). It is known that a significant difference exists between the European systems (in which these rights are not registered) and the American copyright practice. In this last instance, the general rules of the Convention would govern jurisdiction, which would not be exclusive.

Article 13: Temporary and Protective Measures

This area created the greatest difficulty under the Brussels/Lugano Conventions. Article 24 of these conventions, being too simplistic, gave rise to a number of questions. Article 13 of the Preliminary Draft clearly sets forth a range of solutions that gained general approval.

Paragraph (1) provides that the court, which is competent to examine the merits of the dispute under Articles 3 through 12, is also competent to order any temporary or protective measures, even if these orders are to be executed in another contracting state.

Article (23)(b) expressly confirms this rule and states that the Convention understands that "a decision ordering temporary or protective measures in accordance with Article 13, paragraph (1)" is a judgment susceptible to recognition and execution under the Convention. Thus, an order to repatriate goods or a preventive attachment pronounced by the court competent to adjudicate the merits would take effect in all the contracting states. Frequently, the courts of several contracting states will be competent to judge the dispute on the merits. For example, both the court located where the injurious facts or damage took place and the court of the defendant's habitual residence would be competent. Yet, the text does not state that, in order to issue a provisional or protective measure, the court competent to examine the suit on the merits must have the case already before it. The issuance of the provisional or protective measure often occurs prior to the adjudication on the merits. Thus it is possible that the plaintiff would go before the courts of several states potentially competent to hear the merits, and the judgments of these courts would be executable under the Convention. The risk of incompatibility between the judgments is rather improbable since the plaintiff is the beneficiary of the various judgments and will therefore seek the execution of the most beneficial judgment. But, once one of the courts competent to examine the merits of the dispute actually has the case under consideration, the other potentially competent courts should no longer benefit from paragraph (1); priority should be given, as in lis alibi pendens cases, to the court first-seized to adjudicate the merits. These courts will, however, be able to act under paragraphs (2) and (3).

Paragraph (2) provides that the courts of a state in which property is located have jurisdiction to order any provisional or protective measures with respect to that property. In this case, comparative law generally admits the jurisdiction of the forum of the situs.

Paragraph (3) is of particular interest. It deals with the case where a court of a state does not have jurisdiction on the merits and that would order measures limited to goods situated in the forum of the situs. Such a court may, nevertheless, order in personam provisional or protective measures that apply to the defendant; for example, an order to act (such as the obligation to disclose the purchase of stock or agreements signed with a local company) or not to act (not to use a logo or not to create a play whose copyright is being considered before the courts of another contracting state). A first restriction is found in part (a) and conditions the preventive measure on its enforcement being limited to the territory of the state of the forum. A state cannot issue an injunction that requires a person to retransfer property located abroad, to disclose agreements entered abroad with foreign corporations, to refrain from the use of a logo, or not to put on a play in another state.

But, this was not enough. Indeed, the application of the Brussels/Lugano Conventions has revealed the danger of some procedural devices known in certain European countries as the Dutch "*kort geding*", the French "*référé provision*", or the

German "*Mahnbescheid*". In these countries, it is frequent practice, notably in cases where monetary damages are sought, to provisionally award the plaintiff a substantial advance (often up to 80 per cent of the amount sought) without requiring the plaintiff to litigate the case on the merits before the competent court. In a number of cases, the plaintiff that received a substantial advance does not pursue the action any further. In the hypothetical situation where a court in one state holds jurisdiction to decide on the merits while the request for an advance is made in a state where the courts lack jurisdiction, such habits completely divert from the conventional system. That is why the European Court of Justice issued its decision in *Van Ulden Maritime v. Deco-Line* (November 17, 1998, Recueil 1998.I, p. 7091), which called for the defendant's guaranteed reimbursement of the advance, in cases where the plaintiff loses the case on the merits after the defendant enters an appeal. This is the reason why paragraph (3), part (b), adds the cumulative condition that the purpose of the provisional or protective measures must be to protect, on an interim basis, a claim on the merits that is pending or that must be brought by the petitioner. If the action is already pending, the court will wait until the end of the trial before affirming or reversing the order. If the petitioner must make the motion, and does not do so within a reasonable amount of time, the court should cancel its order and have the advance refunded.

Special Jurisdiction

The Preliminary Draft establishes special bases of jurisdiction in case of multiple defendants, counterclaims (*demandes conventionnelles*), and third party claims (*appel en garantie et intervention*). These are necessarily bases for special jurisdiction because of their direct link to a court whose general jurisdiction was granted by the Convention and before whom the plaintiff has or will bring suit. This is an instance of derived jurisdiction admitted by reason of the specific nexus existing among several suits. This consolidation of proceedings was thought to be a useful means to avoid contradictory judgments.

Article 14: Multiple Defendants

Jurisdiction based on multiple defendants, which was admitted by Article 6.1 of the Brussels/Lugano Convention in a rather lax manner, is reluctantly considered by certain legal systems. Indeed, this basis for jurisdiction creates the risk that a defendant would be forced to appear in a proceeding before a court with which the said defendant has no significant or reasonable link. The European Court of Justice has improved upon the text by requiring that there be some specific nexus (*lien de connexité*) between the suits brought against the defendants. The present Article 14 is even more protective in this regard. It confirms that a plaintiff who brings suit before the courts in the defendant's state of habitual residence may also do so against defendants who do not maintain habitual residence in this state. However, part (a) mandates that claims against the defendant who habitually resides in that state and the other defendants must be so closely connected that they should be adjudicated together to avoid a serious risk of inconsistent judgments. Even when this is true, there must also be, under part (b), concerning each defendant not habitual resident in that state, a substantial connection between that state and the dispute involving the defendant. Maybe this goes too far; a specific nexus between the claims ought to be sufficient. The insistence on a substantial connection between the state and the dispute runs the risk of creating further litigation and bogging down the proceedings. One may ask whether it would not have been preferable to leave this question to the domestic law of each of the contracting states.

Article 14, paragraph (2), specifies that the forum provided for in multiple-defendant cases does not apply to a co-defendant invoking an exclusive choice-of-forum clause stipulated by the plaintiff and conforming with Article 4. The European Court of Justice recognized this principle in the context of the Brussels/Lugano Conventions.

Although it seems obvious that a choice-of-forum clause should be the primary reference, it is useful to state it expressly here.

Article 15: Counterclaims

This rule is somewhat traditional and presents fewer dangers than the preceding rule. In fact, in this case, the defendant initiates a counterclaim "arising out of the transaction or occurrence on which the original claim is based." In commercial matters, an action seeking termination or indemnification is frequently asserted as a counterclaim to a request for payment if the defendant is sued in the country of the defendant's habitual residence. In cases where an opponent maintains habitual residence abroad and a sales or service contract was also executed abroad, the ordinary rules of the Convention would not permit an individual to seek termination of the contract or to have it nullified in the individual's country of habitual residence. This Article allows the defendant to bring counterclaims before the defendants own courts. Of course, nothing prohibits the said defendant from bringing suit as a separate action, before a court that would normally be competent, running the risk of contradictory judgments.

Article 16: Third-Party Claims

Comparative law does not generally recognize an action to enforce a guarantee. However, such jurisdiction is very useful and, indeed, common, in actions involving insurance companies. A court that has jurisdiction to hear a case becomes competent to hear a defendant's claim against a third party for indemnity or contribution regarding the claim against that defendant. If one brings suit for breach of contract against a defendant in the defendant's forum of habitual residence, for breach of contract, the defendant can call the indemnitor before this court, even if the indemnitor maintains a registered office or habitual residence in another contracting state. Certain restrictions, however, demonstrate the hesitations that exist regarding an action against a third-party guarantor. On one hand, such an action must be permitted under national law (that is, the law of the forum). On the other hand, there must be a substantial connection between that state and the dispute involving that third party. This last rule is rather vague and could result, did was the case with multiple defendants, in frivolous litigation. Additionally, as with multiple defendants, choice-of-forum clauses stipulated between the defendant and a third party must be respected.

The Blacklist – Prohibited Grounds of Jurisdiction

Even though a plaintiff may always use the grounds for jurisdiction found in the whitelist, a plaintiff may never use the grounds for jurisdiction that appear in the blacklist against a defendant whose habitual residence is in a contracting state, the exception to this rule being when the defendant makes a voluntary appearance and therefore validates the grounds for jurisdiction.

The forbidden grounds for jurisdiction are listed in Article 18, paragraph (18). Nonetheless, the experience of the Brussels/Lugano Conventions shows that it was impossible to establish an exhaustive list of exceptional grounds for jurisdiction. Over the course of the ratification process, grounds for jurisdiction that new member states used and that no one had previously considered, appeared. Thus, the Draft Article 18, paragraph (1) forbids the application of a ground for jurisdiction rooted in the domestic law of a contracting state when there is no substantial connection between this state and the dispute. This idea of substantial connection was previously seen in the articles on multiparty defendants and third-party guarantee claims. The vagueness of the rule, which could create litigation when it is invoked as an exception to trump a general rule, is subject to less criticism with current Article 18. Indeed, this is meant to be a basis on which to interpret a ground for jurisdiction that is rooted in domestic law but does not appear in the Preliminary Draft.

The list that appears in paragraph (2) is directly inspired from the Supplemental Protocol to the Hague Convention on the Recognition and Execution of Foreign Judgments in Civil and Commercial Matters of February 1, 1971. The Protocol was concluded in order to prevent, among contracting states, the recognition and execution of judgments among contracting states rendered in the context of exceptional rules of jurisdiction. As almost everything was said on this point during the 1966 debates, the establishment of this list was not very difficult.

Courts cannot exercise jurisdiction on the sole basis of one or more of the following criteria.

Part (a) states that the presence or the seizure of property belonging to the defendant, except where the dispute is directly related to that property, is not grounds for jurisdiction. The forum of sequestration, of patrimony, or the forum arresti are recognized by a great number of comparative law states. During the 1966 works, the Danish Delegate caricatured that it was sufficient to seize the defendant's umbrella during a stopover in Denmark in order to give Danish courts jurisdiction over a contract whose entire existence took place in Latin America. This base of jurisdiction is, thus, prohibited "except where the dispute is directly related to that property."

This exception is important. The whitelist does not include rules that give jurisdiction, in actions to establish title over movable property, to the courts where the property is located. Yet, it is not abnormal to demand the restitution of movable property, in cases where the ownership of the property is contested, before the courts of the place where it is located. This is frequently the case with stolen or diverted works of art; in fact, the UNIDROIT Convention of June 24, 1995 contains a rule of express jurisdiction in this situation, in order to facilitate the restitution of stolen cultural works.

Parts (b), (c), and (d) forbid jurisdiction based on the parties' nationality, domicile, habitual or temporary residence, or the presence of the plaintiff in a given state. Thus, Article 14 and 15 of the French Civil Code, as well as the principle of forum actoris that exists in the Nordic, Dutch, and other legal systems, are declared inapplicable.

Part (e) targets doing business jurisdiction. The Hague Protocol condemned the existence of jurisdiction based on the fact that the defendant "had conducted business in the state of first instance." The Preliminary Draft speaks of "the carrying on of commercial or other activities by the defendant within the territory of the state at issue." The substance and form are the same as those in the sentence that appears in brackets in Article 9. Jurisdiction that is based solely on the conduct of commercial activity is prohibited except "where the dispute is directly related to those activities." In the latter case, and in the context of the provisions listed in brackets in Article 9, the forbidden basis of jurisdiction becomes permissible and is offered to the plaintiff by the Convention.

Part (f) prohibits the common-law practice of giving jurisdiction to the courts of a state solely because the service of summons occurred there.

Part (g) condemns the unilateral designation of a forum by the plaintiff because of misuses of the "forum of invoice" when the designation of forum is found in the bill of sale.

Part (i) is somewhat linked to part (f). It actually envisions the case where a summons to appear in a local court is served on an individual who is only temporarily present in the territory; for example, this would apply to someone in an airport.

Finally, part (j) renders irrelevant the place where the contract from which the dispute arises was signed. The place where a contract is signed can be totally fortuitous. Many airports provide businessmen with facilities and secretarial staff in order to permit individuals to meet in a neutral location and to conduct business there. Moreover, it is well-known that many international contracts are settled at a distance, by mail, fax, or electronic network. It was good to nip all attempts at using this ground for jurisdiction in the bud.

The bases for jurisdiction found in the blacklist are only prohibited when the defendant maintains habitual residence in a contracting state. If habitual residence is maintained in another state, the prohibition has no effect. In fact, the Brussels/Lugano Conventions fortunately specify, in Article 4, paragraph (2), that all persons domiciled in the territory of a contracting state may, just as nationals of this state, bring suit against a defendant domiciled outside of the contracting states, under the rules of competence of the state of this domicile including those provided for in Article 3, paragraph (2) (exceptional jurisdiction). The Preliminary Draft does not dare to be as straightforward; the result is the same, however, and those who criticized the provisions of the Brussels/Lugano Conventions in the past admit today that the solution is not that bad.

It is perfectly natural that contracting states reserve the right to exercise exceptional jurisdiction over a defendant domiciled in a non-contracting state. This is done to defend the plaintiff's right by permitting the plaintiff to bring suit before courts that are close to the said plaintiff's residence or place of activity, without first obligating the plaintiff to seek remedy in far-off courts, whose judgments may or may not be enforced in the countries where the defendant's property is located. Those prohibited grounds for jurisdiction included in the blacklist will give rise, regarding defendants domiciled in non-contracting states, to the gray zone, which will be addressed later.

However, it is important to first speak about Article 18, paragraph (3), which attempts to establish an allowance for the use of exceptional jurisdiction in cases where a remedy to a human rights violation is sought.

The creation of the International Criminal Court and the Hague International Criminal Tribunal bears witness to the fact that the modern world is very sensitive to human rights violations. The nongovernmental human rights defense organizations that hold observer status in the Conference's proceedings wanted victims who could not obtain reparations through the normal rules of competence of the Convention to be able to do so by pleading grounds for exceptional jurisdiction based, for example, on nationality, domicile, or the location of the adversary's property. Assuming everyone agreed on this, in principle, the plan is carried out in several variants, which appear in brackets. Although this is a rather sensitive issue, it is worth tempering. If a party allegedly guilty of a heinous crime under international law is physically located in a country that is not party to the Convention, which is often the case, all of the grounds for jurisdiction that appear in paragraph (2) can, as explained, usually be asserted. Thus, it is necessary to go back to the case where an alleged criminal actor is located in the territory of a contracting state and to assert that, in this particular case, the judges of this state can hardly be expected to sanction the conduct of the alleged criminal through a civil judgment. This will take shape when the state in which the extortion took place eventually becomes party to the Convention and then assures, through a legislative or regulatory mechanism, the impunity of past crimes. In this context, it is the basis for actions that caused the greatest difficulty. A first analytical variant describes reprehensible conduct like genocide, crimes against humanity, war crimes, and serious crimes against natural persons under international law, including substantial violations of inalienable, fundamental rights, torture, slavery, and forced labor. A second variant deals simply with the case of a serious crime under international law, when the state whose courts' competence is put forward, has established its criminal jurisdiction over that crime in accordance with an international treaty to which it is a party and the claim is for civil compensatory damages for death or serious bodily injury. This link-up from the civil trial to the criminal trial limits the effectiveness of the provision considerably.

The above-stated problem should be discussed anew within the diplomatic conference.

The Gray Zone – Jurisdiction based on National Law

Article 17 provides that the Convention does not prevent contracting states from applying rules of jurisdiction under their national law.

The primary rule is subject to two restrictions. First, these national rules of jurisdiction cannot go against the Convention's provisions regarding choice of forum and voluntary appearance (Articles 4 and 5), jurisdiction designed to protect consumers and workers (Articles 7 and 8), rules of exclusive jurisdiction (Article 12), and temporary and protective measures (Article 13). Moreover, the national rules must not be prohibited under Article 18.

The bases of jurisdiction that arise under national law consist, above all, of those that are neither included in the whitelist nor prohibited under the blacklist. For example, the jurisdiction of the courts where a piece of movable property is located, when the dispute is directly related to the ownership of this object, would fall into this category. One could also imagine the jurisdiction of the courts of the state where the obligation to pay is to be executed; this is similar to provisions in the Brussels/Lugano Conventions. Above all, however, it is important to note that the gray zone will be mostly fed by the exceptional grounds for jurisdiction mentioned in the Article 18 blacklist, concerning those who do not maintain habitual residence in a contracting state.

A judgment founded on national rules of jurisdiction, exceptional or not, can only be executed in other contracting states on the basis of the general law. In order not to encroach upon the official reports that will come later, the author will restrict himself by noting that, in comparative law, a court will generally refuse to execute judgments (exequatur) founded on exceptional bases of jurisdiction, even if the country in which the court is located itself recognizes such jurisdiction.

Verifications Made by Relevant Court

Verification of Jurisdiction

Where the defendant does not enter an appearance, Article 20, paragraph (1), of the Brussels/Lugano Conventions requires the judge in the first instance to systematically verify whether jurisdiction may be exercised. It was difficult to generalize this process worldwide because of the differences that exist among procedural rules. In the judicial practice of some states, when the defendant does not enter an appearance, the plaintiff's motion is granted; sometimes, even the court clerk, rather than a judge, issues a default or ex parte judgment. It was necessary, nonetheless, to provide for a minimum level of verification in order to determine that such claim was not prohibited under the provisions of Article 18.

Article 19 attempts to resolve this problem by proposing several options. In cases where the defendant does not make an appearance, the court shall verify whether it is prevented from exercising its Article 18 jurisdiction if (a) international law requires it to do so – which corresponds to the expectations of the countries bound by the Brussels/Lugano Conventions – or (b) the plaintiff so requests in order to benefit from a sort of "seal of approval" that will allow execution of the judgment elsewhere to be obtained more easily execution of the judgment elsewhere. A variant provides, in brackets, that the court should also verify its jurisdiction (c) at the request of the defendant, even after judgment is entered; in this case, the goal is to cause refusal of such registration. Finally, two variations on part (d) deal with the automatic triggering of the verification function when the document that instituted the proceedings was served on the defendant in another contracting state, or if it appears from the documents filed by the plaintiff that the defendant's address is in another contracting state; for legal purposes, both situations bring about the same result. The advantage of both variations in part (d) is that they render the preceding provisions useless.

Verification of the Rights of the Defense

In line with the traditional path taken by the Brussels/Lugano Conventions, Article 20, paragraph (1), provides that a judge must interrupt the proceedings so long as it is not established that the document that instituted the proceedings, or an equivalent document including the essential elements of the claim, was transmitted to the defendant in sufficient time and in such a way as to enable the defendant to arrange for a defense. This is also the case, so long as all necessary steps have been taken to that effect. This rule clearly targets the case of a defendant that fails to appear, because a defendant who enters an appearance is obviously aware that the proceedings are to take place. The provision requires that the transmitted document contain the essential elements of the claim. This is a useful stipulation inspired by the Hague Convention on the Service Abroad of Judicial and Extra-Judicial Documents in Civil or Commercial Matters of November 15, 1965.

Paragraph (2), in brackets, deals with the use of national instruments on the service and notice abroad of court processes. This paragraph clearly refers to the previously cited Hague Convention, which was the first, in its Article 15, to provide for a stay in proceedings, as well as to applicable inter-American conventions.

Paragraph (3) provides that the interruption of proceedings does not apply, in case of urgency, to any provisional or protective measures. All of this is rather difficult to contest, and it is hoped that the brackets will be removed.

Olivier Tell[†]

Tentative Draft on the Jurisdiction and the Enforcement of Foreign Judgments: Can a Mixed Convention Work?

After several years of preliminary work, the Hague Conference envisions the drafting of a convention whose structures would be more flexible than that of the Brussels Convention of September 27, 1968, and of its twin sister, the 1988 Lugano Convention. This convention would be based on three pillars by providing for: (1) authorized bases of direct jurisdiction (the "whitelist"), some of which would confer exclusive jurisdiction, (2) forbidden bases of jurisdiction, those lacking sufficient nexus with a nonexhaustive list of forbidden instances (the "blacklist" as established in Article 18), and (3) bases of jurisdiction found in domestic law (the "graylist" as established in Article 17).

It is, however, necessary to recall that until this Preliminary Draft in 1999, the negotiators believed that the recognition of a "gray zone" within the conventional framework would obviously be limited in scope when granting direct jurisdiction.

The negotiators have aimed to establish a convention that would help users of the justice system, lawyers, and judges, by increasing both the predictability and certainty of solutions to international issues. The author is thus convinced that only a convention capable of reducing the current fragmentation of international law in this area would have a reasonable chance of being successful and somewhat useful. The 1997 Special Commission laid out initial goals of the Preliminary Draft relating to this attempt of harmonization. First, the draft had to propose pragmatic solutions, as efficient and simple as possible, so that everybody would understand them and lawyers and judges would be able to apply them very easily.[1] Second, the draft had to increase the predictability and certainty of the jurisdictional solutions at the international level.[2] Third, the draft had to balance the interest of both plaintiffs and defendants.[3]

Allowing the states to continue using jurisdictional rules on the basis of their

† The opinions developed by the author in this article are not binding on and do not represent the position of the French government.

1 *See* Report of the President of the Special Commission, session of March 3, 1998 to March 13, 1998.

2 *Id.*

3 *Id.*

J.J. Barceló and K.M. Clermont (eds.), A Global Law of Jurisdiction and Judgments: Lessons from The Hague, 37–46

domestic rules might seem to oppose the aim of an international convention governing direct jurisdiction. International law inherently implies a partial abandonment of sovereignty in instances relating to the international realm.

Providing Legal and Jurisdictional Certainty

The obvious goal of an international instrument in this area is to allow some international unification of the rules conferring jurisdiction, thus avoiding the conflicts of jurisdiction that naturally mushroom when no international instrument exists and when national jurisdictional systems are in direct confrontation. Private international law instruments that deal with specific subject matter and that provide rules granting direct jurisdiction have achieved such a goal (e.g., the Warsaw Convention of October 12, 1929, on the unification of certain rules regulating international air transportation, and the Berne International Convention of October 25, 1952, on railroad passengers and baggage).[4]

The actual aim is to curb over-litigation and dilatory schemes within international proceedings. We are dealing with litigation that involves a foreign element, that is to say, international lawsuits. International jurisdiction vis-à-vis foreign parties cannot be treated like its domestic counterpart.

Taking into account the economic globalization and the successive removal of burdens to international trade (e.g., suppression of tariffs and investment barriers) that progressively integrate industrialized countries on both sides of the Atlantic, a convention more flexible than the Brussels/Lugano framework is not the answer. The relative unification of the conflicts of jurisdiction rules within the European territory, which curb competition among the legal systems and make the conditions resulting from this competition fair to companies, is rooted in the original idea of a European interior market (*marché interieur*). The aim was to avoid providing advantages to any one particular company and to prevent companies from using their domestic jurisdiction rules as an economic weapon against competitors, clients, or providers of goods and services. Smoothing the business decision process was also a priority. The Brussels/Lugano framework worked well for countries that had reached a similar economic development level. Moreover, this system is open to other states, be they European or not. The author thinks a broader Brussels/Lugano-kind of system would be perfectly viable among countries achieving similar business and economic development.

The existence of a large gray zone, especially if the whitelist is shortened as a consequence of applying the principle of the communicating vessels, would pervert the conventional framework of the Hague Conference. Indeed, the problem lies in the arbitrage that parties would make between the use of domestic jurisdiction rules (gray zone) and the basis of direct jurisdiction provided for in the whitelist. This

4 There is a list of these conventions in the Jénard Report on the Brussels Convention, JOCE, March 5, 1997. C59/59.

arbitrage would be to the detriment of the worldwide convention. The bases of direct jurisdiction found in the whitelist would become purely facultative, which would make this convention not so different from a convention simple. If the doing business basis of jurisdiction were to be transferred from the blacklist (forbidden bases) to the graylist, this risk would be greatly increased.[5] A mixed and very flexible convention could legitimize the general jurisdiction based upon the "doing business" factor, which is not compatible with the Brussels/Lugano framework and which is limited to a national system. The basis that vests French courts with jurisdiction vis-à-vis foreign defendants is found in Article 14 of the French Civil Code. Jurisdiction based upon citizenship of the plaintiff provides such an illustration: Currently, the decision issued by French courts that took jurisdiction on this ground is not recognized internationally. In some respects, the basis of jurisdiction labeled as "transacting business" and originating from the American "long-arm statutes," which this article will deal with later, is not so different in its consequences from the French Article 14 jurisdiction and would not be better received in the international framework.

The only limited interest – and yet some oppose even its scope – of a mixed convention is found in the definition of a nonexhaustive list that includes some bases of jurisdiction (blacklist). Actually, regarding the recognition and enforcement of foreign judgments, the Convention could be less favorable than some of the bilateral conventions of which France is a part, and even than the ordinary exequatur law as quite liberally defined in case law originating in from the French Cour de cassation.[6] Such a convention, if the list of authorized bases of jurisdiction were limited (whitelist), would not be of practical interest for European business sectors, since the conventional framework for the recognition and enforcement of foreign judgments is inherently limited to the bases of jurisdiction found in the whitelist, and it could not be otherwise.

The Issue of Jurisdiction Based on Commercial Activity

Among the forbidden bases of jurisdiction listed in the draft of the Hague Convention, one can find the doing business basis well-known in American law (Article 18(2)(e)). However, transacting business, as a specific basis of jurisdiction, is found in brackets in Article 9 of the draft relating to branches, because there was no agreement on its insertion in the whitelist. Thus, the transacting business basis of jurisdiction would remain in the gray zone.

While negotiating, it clearly appeared that the majority of the participating states opposed the insertion of any basis of jurisdiction relating to the specific commercial activity (transacting business as set forth in Article 9) that is supposed to differ from

---

5 For a premonitory analysis, *see generally* Friedrich K. Juenger, *A Hague Judgments Convention?*, 24 Brook. J. Int'l L.39 (1998).

6 *See* Muntzer, Cass. le civ., Jan. 7, 1964, RC 1964.244; *see also* Bachir, Cass. le civ., Oct. 4, 1967; and *see* Simitch, Cass. le civ., Feb. 6, 1985, RC 85.369.

the doing business general basis of jurisdiction. The author thinks that the inclusion of such a basis of jurisdiction in the draft would be potentially dangerous, for the following reasons.

First, unlike a branch or establishment, the exercise of commercial activity is not a physical notion. It is a very vague notion and could characterize any business conduct: pre-arrangement talks between companies by way of business representative in the U.S., existence of a bank account, existence of a subsidiary[7] or even of a Website, phone calls, etc. The mere fact of purchasing or selling products in the state where the court is located would be sufficient to vest jurisdiction. The notion even encompasses strictly noncommercial activities.

Second, the transacting business basis of jurisdiction inherently carries serious possibilities of being a slippery slope. The courts that will use the transacting business notion might move towards the doing business notion by relaxing, or even by omitting, the requirement of a direct connection between the activity and the dispute. This connection is extremely difficult to define. After *Helicopteros*,[8] the American doctrine showed how difficult it is to draw a distinction between general jurisdiction and specific jurisdiction as a practical matter.[9] Above all, it seems that the transacting business notion derived from the long-arm statutes is used more and more in the U.S. as a basis of general jurisdiction and no longer as a basis of specific jurisdiction. This trend is due to an extensive case law interpretation that led to the implementation of catch-all provisions,[10] which supposed less contact between the defendant and state where the court dealing with the case is located, than the doing business basis of jurisdiction. From a European perspective, the profusion of American cases on this matter, sometimes contradictory and imprecise, leaves the naïve user of the justice system with a feeling of great uncertainty and total lack of predictability for the vesting of jurisdiction on these grounds. Europeans also know that the American doctrine itself denounces this uncertainty.[11] Therefore, it is easy to conclude that, in the framework of an international convention, the transacting business notion would carry with itself too great a jurisdictional uncertainty.

Third, if judges were to adopt a wide concept of transacting business, it would render inoperative the other traditional bases of jurisdiction relating to the contract

[7] This would pertain to the issue of piercing the corporate veil.

[8] *See* Helicopteros de Columbia, S.A. v. Hall, 466 U.S. 408 (1984).

[9] *See* Agnès Mirandès, La Compétence inter-étatique et internationale des Tribunaux en Droit des Etats-Unis [The Interstate and International Jurisdiction in the American Legal System] (March 20, 1999) (unpublished Ph.D. dissertations, Univeristé Paris II, France) (on the broadening of the special jurisdiction as favored by the American doctrine and applied by some courts and some statutes).

[10] *See* Agnès Mirandès, *supra* note 9 (citing numerous cases, articles, statutes and stating that "although the defendant may not have been negligent or have committed any of the acts enumerated in the test (of the long-arm statute), a court might nonetheless take jurisdiction solely on the basis of the defendant's contracts with the state where the court is located.").

[11] *See* R. Casad, *Jurisdiction in Civil Actions* (1998), Lexis Publishing.

or tort at issue, as set forth in the draft and applied in Europe on a regular basis.[12] It would render inoperative the basis of jurisdiction found in the place of execution because the mere carrying on of contractual relations would sufficiently to vest the courts of the state of the lawful habitual residence with jurisdiction. This would be the case even when a dispute arose before the breach of the contract at stake. In other words, the adoption of the transacting business approach could possibly disturb, in a radical way, the balance of the Convention.

Finally, it is unclear as to what instances that do not already fall under the Convention's bases of jurisdiction (consumer contracts or torts), the specific basis of jurisdiction relating to the commercial activity would apply. The author finds that Article 10 (basis of jurisdiction found in the locus delictus) and, even better, Article 7 of the Preliminary Draft of the Convention largely deprive Article 9's bracketed provisions effect, particularly in disputes concerning consumers who entered into a contract in their home state. In other instances, and in the case of a tort action for damages, vesting jurisdiction in the courts of the plaintiff's state would be neither equitable nor desirable when the transaction in question is not affected, or when the damages are not suffered, in this state.

No one in the negotiation process seriously challenged the presence of the doing business basis of general jurisdiction in the blacklist. International law has traditionally considered doing business as a basis of jurisdiction constituting an exception to the general law, such as the basis of jurisdiction found in the defendant's domicile or nationality, which already placed it in the blacklist of the Hague Protocol of February 1, 1971.[13] The author already stressed that as long as there was no relation between the litigation and the defendant's presence or activity within the territory where the court dealing with a case is situated, there would be no difference from the French Civil Code Article 14 that relates to the plaintiff's nationality.[14] This actual similarity is found in both the implementation and the consequences of the doing business notion, as from now on any person who is domiciled in the French territory can use it just as French nationals can against a defendant domiciled outside of the Brussels Convention contracting states.[15] Article 4(2) of the Brussels

[12] European judges, unfamiliar with the transacting business notion, would more easily apply the place where the contract was executed or where the damage occurred and would strictly construe the conventional terms relating to the place where the commercial activity is carried on. There would not be any balance.

[13] *See* Additional Protocol to the Hague Convention on the Recognition and Execution of Foreign Judgments in Civil and Commercial Matters, Art. 4 (asserting "the fact that the defendant operated the transactions in the original state whereas the dispute was not relating to these operations").

[14] "The foreigner, even though he does not reside in France, can be brought to French courts, for matters relating to the execution of obligations he has entered into with a French party; he can be brought (to the same courts), for obligations he has entered into with a French party in a foreign country.".

[15] In 1999, during the negotiations on the revision of the Warsaw Convention on air transportation, the U.S. delegation issued a paper that came to the same conclusion by drawing an analogy between the basis for jurisdiction said to be the "Fifth jurisdiction" and French Civil Code Article 14 jurisdiction (forum actoris and basis of jurisdiction found in the activity).

Convention makes it clear that the ban on the use of Article 3 bases of jurisdiction, which constitutes an exception to the general law, is only applicable vis-à-vis residents of contracting states. Therefore, anybody residing in France, including an American, can take advantage of the doing business basis of jurisdiction, which applies against French citizens domiciled in a state not party to the Convention. Thus, the nationality of the plaintiff's basis of jurisdiction applies as a general forum actoris. Moreover, the application of forum non conveniens theory, which is sometimes used before U.S. courts, especially as applied to victims of damages relating to U.S. companies, strengthens the analogy described above.

United States courts tend to deny their jurisdiction when the defendant is an American and the plaintiff does not reside in the territory where the court is located, referring to case law that allows for a distinction based on the plaintiff's domicile or citizenship.[16] As a consequence, in the case of an action to establish liability in tort, American citizens would always benefit from U.S. forum when they oppose European companies, virtually all of which have, either directly or not, a commercial presence in the U.S. through subsidiaries (or even through an accessible Website). Those American citizens' disputes might have originated in any remote part of the world and have no relation with the commercial activity of these companies. For instance, an American citizen living in Europe and having a residence or beneficiaries in the U.S. would be entitled to bring a French restaurateur, who owns a restaurant in New York, to U.S. courts for a dispute relating to indigestion that occurred in one of the French restaurateur's establishments in Bombay! However, this rule does not systematically apply when a foreign plaintiff who seeks recovery for damages wants to bring a U.S. global company before U.S. courts.[17] The doing business theory has been devised as a tool to bring foreign defendants, which include unincorporated companies,[18] to the forum courts when they do business in the territory where the forum courts are located, in order to protect the interests of the citizens of this forum.[19] This is the evidence of a "territorialist" and "sovereignist" conception of

---

16 *See* Nolan v. Boeing Co., 919 F.2d 1058 (5th Cir. 1990); *see also* Piper Aircraft v. Reyno, 454 U.S. 235 (1981). A document issued by the U.S. delegation at the international conference on air law held in Montreal (May 1–28, 1999) mentioned these decisions as significant ones, *see* OACI, DCW Doc. n° 27 (May 12, 1999). In a recent case following the TWA flight 800 accident, Boeing and TWA counsels made a motion to remove the case to French courts in reference to the doctrine and to these two cases.

17 *See* G. Droz, *Les droit de la demande dans les relations privées internationales* [Plaintiff's rights in the framework of international private relations] (May 6, 1994) statement before the Comité français de droit international privé, Travaux du Comité, years 1993–94, Pedone, at 104 (the author mentioned a talk by Ch. Bernarsconi and A. Gerber before the Swiss Institute of Comparative Law, entitled *La théorie du forum non conveniens*, issued in IPRax (1994) at 3).

18 *See* Agnès Mirandès, *supra* note 9, at 260, 267.

19 *See* Linda J. Silberman, *Can the Hague Judgments Project Be Saved? A Perspective from the United States* (July 8, 2000), Paris-I Cornell Symposium (explaining how the doing business basis of jurisdiction is used against foreign multinationals when they possess assets in the U.S., which renders useless the enforcement of the decision abroad, notably for infringements of corporal property, and even though the act that caused the damages occurred outside of U.S. territory).

the exercise of sovereign international jurisdiction and is not really compatible with the enactment of international norms. An international convention that would establish, as a basis of jurisdiction, an exception to the general rules could harm international trade and the development of investments,[20] notably the development of electronic commerce. Companies, in particular small and medium-sized ones, might well be discouraged from operating business if potentially obliged to be part of a costly litigation in a remote forum only because of their commercial activities. The thorniest issue is the completely unpredictable nature of this doing business basis of jurisdiction. This kind of jurisdiction is practically the equivalent of the jurisdiction based on citizenship that European law recognizes, subject to the restrictions of the Brussels Convention.

Thus, if the doing business basis of jurisdiction were transferred to the graylist, the other European bases of jurisdiction found in Article 18 of the Preliminary Draft should be subject to the same treatment as a matter of reciprocity. These European bases of jurisdiction notably include the plaintiff's domicile, the defendant's or the plaintiff's citizenship, or the location of the defendant's property in the forum court territory. Such a measure could cause the implosion of the conventional framework as it is today. Europeans have relinquished their bases of jurisdiction, creating exceptions to the general law within their intra-European relations and in the Preliminary Draft of the Hague Convention, for two reasons. First, they rely on the judges of all the states that are members of the Brussels and Lugano Conventions. Second, all of the contracting states have mutually relinquished their bases of exorbitant jurisdiction.

For these reasons, it is doubtful that the civil law countries will accept the defendant's activity as a basis of jurisdiction at the international level, whatever look it may have.

The Issue of Forum Non Conveniens

The recognition of the existence of a gray zone favors the development of forum non conveniens, which depends on the will of the court dealing with the case and on whether or not a substantial connection exists between the dispute and the forum. Actually, the Convention provides authorized bases for the vesting of jurisdiction that are assumed to have a connection with the dispute and that would not be possible to decline. Forum non conveniens is in opposition to the objective of predictability to which the Hague Convention gives priority. For these reasons, the framework of the Brussels Convention does not really allow the use of forum non conveniens, even for states that use this notion as part of their general law. Furthermore, forum non conveniens entails a significant increase in the length and

[20] *See* Helicopteros de Columbia, *supra* note 8 (*Amicus Curiae* memorandum introduced by the U.S. government before the U.S. Supreme Court).

cost of judicial procedures. Québec, a civil law country, tried out forum non conveniens and it led to serious abuses.[21] In order not to affect the predictability and the legal certainty of the parties, the introduction of a forum non conveniens mechanism of the Convention's Preliminary Draft has been strictly limited.

However, the above-discussed disadvantages of a mixed convention referred to previously by the author are even greater in the Preliminary Draft because of the introduction of flexible rules on lis alibi pendens and, more importantly, because of the incorporation of forum non conveniens at the location of the defendant's residence. The author considers the application of forum non conveniens doctrine to the defendant's forum to be in opposition to a predictable conventional system. This doctrine stands for the maximal perversion of a system based on predictable rules, which are available and provide for in advance, to vest jurisdiction. These rules hinge on jurisdiction based on the defendant's domicile or residence. Actually, in the Brussels and Lugano frameworks, the use of the defendant's domicile as a basis of jurisdiction is the keystone,[22] and the system that develops jurisdiction is mainly based on this keystone insofar as: (1) it determines the scope of the Convention (its burden in relation to other systems); (2) it determines the acceptable exceptions (special bases of jurisdiction still acceptable if the defendant is domiciled in a member state, save under some exceptions, and the exclusive bases of jurisdiction). This aims at avoiding jurisdictional "territorialism" and the extraterritorial nature of jurisdictional rules that would provide for the jurisdiction of courts of the European Community regarding disputes without an object nexus with the forum (for instance, based only upon the citizenship or the domicile of the plaintiff or even on the localization of some of the defendant's property or the exercise of his activities in the forum territory, when the dispute did not directly originate from this property or these activities).[23]

Other Concerns

In order to preserve the plaintiff's rights in the enforcement of a decision issued in a state that is not a member to the Hague Convention, more security devises must be provided (attachment of the defendant's property, for instance). This mechanism, when at play, should never be facultative, left to the states' discretion and to national laws. Such a solution would considerably affect the significance of the bases of jurisdiction that vest direct jurisdiction (whitelist), and in particular, the significance of the forum of the defendant's domicile or residence.

In sum, such a mixed convention may not fit the scheme implemented under the

[21] *See* S. Guillemard, A. Prujiner and F. Sabourin, *Les difficultés du forum non conveniens et droits québecois* (1995), Les Cahiers du Droit, vol. 36, at 913–51.

[22] Case 412/98, Group Josi (2000), point 34, 47 (holding that "it is only in very exceptional instances when Title II of the Convention provides for a determinative influence, in order to vest jurisdiction, to the localization of the defendant's domicile in a contracting state.").

[23] *See* Brussels Convention, Article 3.

Brussels and Lugano Conventions. Such a system could be jeopardized by the implementation of this harmful convention, even if a suitable deconnection clause were stipulated.

Conclusion

As unpopular as it may be, the author still favors a single straightforward system that is efficient in practice and based on a double convention with specific bases of jurisdiction that would turn on a pivotal forum without any way to avoid it on the ground of forum non conveniens.[24] The pivotal forum would be the defendant's domicile, rather than residence, which is still a vague notion in some countries. In addition, the Convention would provide a sufficiently attractive list of special and exclusive bases of jurisdiction, of which the forum of the activity would not be part, as its general character would disturb the application of the other special forum. This list would provide for a genuine forum for contracts and would not be limited to the execution of the contract,[25] a forum for torts, fora to protect weak parties[26] (particularly useful in an electronic environment), and exclusive fora for disputes relating to rights in rem, including leases of buildings and patents. This system would clarify the principle of recognition and enforcement of judgments. It is useless in such a system, which is simpler than those combined under Article 17 and Article 24 of the Preliminary Draft, to deal with a gray zone of jurisdiction bases that inherently fall outside of the conventional system[27] since decisions reached upon

[24] During the next to last Special Commission, the French delegation proposed a double geographical criterion that would impose that both the defendant's domicile and the court dealing with the case be in the same contracting state. As in Article 4 of the Brussels Convention, the proposal avoids protecting a defendant who is in a non-contracting state. Therefore, the Convention would apply if the court is located in a contracting state *and* the defendant is domiciled in a contracting state. Actually, if the defendant is domiciled in a non-contracting state, there is no reason to deprive this defendant from the exceptional basis for jurisdiction that could exist in relations to this non-contracting state under the Convention while this non-contracting sate will keep using its own exceptional basis of jurisdiction against a defendant domiciled in a contracting state. The current text seems to reach the same result but by using a mechanism that is unnecessarily complicated. Furthermore, the French proposal can make the play of the Hague Convention easier in relation with the other European tools.

[25] Note that Article 6 of the Preliminary Draft of the worldwide convention on contracts has been limited to a forum executionnis in order to meet the U.S. Delegation's demands. The U.S. Delegation put forward the incompatibility of a contractual forum like the one found in Article 5–1 of the Brussels Convention with Due Process.

[26] What would be the interest of a worldwide convention that would not deal with disputes involving consumers in the era of e-business?

[27] The Convention states that, besides some dispositions that are more mandatory than others, it "does not infringe bases of jurisdiction settled in national law." However, what does it mean 'not to infringe' in the gray basis of jurisdiction? The Nygh-Pocar report on the Preliminary Draft of the Convention only states a patently obvious thing when it stresses that the contracting states have some leeway regarding the issue of jurisdiction as long as they respect the provisions of the Convention. The actual contribution of the text is principally found in the bans on the basis of jurisdiction that are set forth in the blacklist.

these bases are not respected on the basis of the Convention. A possible compromise would be to recognize some decisions rendered by courts that are connected to the dispute, as long as these decisions do not contradict the whitelist. However, in return, an easier recognition should be instituted for judgments rendered on an authorized jurisdictional basis.

Joaquim-J. Forner Delaygua[†]

International Jurisdiction in "Business to Business" On-line Performed Contracts: Lessons From The Hague?

Introduction

Codification of International Jurisdiction Rules and E-Commerce

The Hague

In 1992, the Hague Conference on Private International Law began the task of codifying rules of recognition and enforcement of foreign judgments, in what I shall refer to here as the Judgments Convention or the Hague works.[1] Since then, the number and economic importance of contracts made, and even performed, through distant computers has rapidly increased.[2] This increase is clearly noticeable even if we look back only to 1997 and 1998, when discussion of concrete terms of jurisdictional rules on contracts began.[3]

---

† *Profesor titular* of private international law, Facultat de dret, Universitat de Barcelona (Spain).

1 May 5, 1992 is only the date of the American proposal, contained in a letter addressed by Edwin D. Williamson, Legal Adviser for Private International Law of the Department of State, to the Permanent Bureau of the Hague Conference of Private International Law. The decision to include the subject in the agenda of the works of the 19th Session (2000) of the Conference was made four years later in 1996, during the 18th Session (1996) of the Conference (I *Proceedings of the Eighteenth Session. Miscellaneous matters*, p. 29). From 1992 until the 18th Session (1996), a 1992 Working Group session, followed by two meetings of a Special Commission in 1994 and 1996, took place. See Catherine Kessedjian, *International Jurisdiction and Foreign Judgments in Civil and Commercial Matters*, Preliminary Document No. 7 of April 1997 for the attention of the Special Commission of June 1997 on the question of jurisdiction, and recognition and enforcement of foreign judgments in civil and commercial matters. For this and other (not all) documents of the Hague Conference mentioned henceforth, see *http://www.hcch.net*.

2 Presentation by Mr. Pearl on behalf of the World Information Technology and Services Alliance (WITSA) February 28, 2000, Ottawa. See *http://www.witsa.org*.

3 Catherine Kessedjian, *Synthesis of the Work of the Special Commission of June 1997 on International Jurisdiction and the Effect of Foreign Judgments in Civil and Commercial Matters* [hereinafter *1997 Synthesis*] *and Synthesis of the Work of the Special Commission of November 1998 on International Jurisdiction and the Effects of Foreign Judgments in Civil and Commercial Matters* [herinafter *1998 Synthesis*]. Catherine Kessedjian, Deputy Secretary General of the Bureau Permanent of the Conference, has drawn the attention of the delegates to the incidence of modern electronic communications, especially in certain torts (Preliminary document 7 *International Jurisdiction and Foreign Judgments in Civil and Commercial Matters*, April 1997, for the attention of the Special Commission on Jurisdiction and Judgments – meeting on June 1997), and has also recorded some ideas advanced during the meetings of the Special Commission (Preliminary document 8 *1997 Synthesis*, November

J.J. Barceló and K.M. Clermont (eds.), A Global Law of Jurisdiction and Judgments: Lessons from The Hague, 47–73

The Hague Conference produced a Preliminary Draft in October 1999, during the fifth and final meeting of the Special Commission on Jurisdiction and Judgments. Only then, in Ottawa from February 28 to March 1, 2000, was a special meeting of the Conference[4] devoted to the study of the questions raised by jurisdiction and e-commerce.[5] During this meeting, experts examined the language of the Preliminary Draft articles within an e-commerce scenario. The Ottawa meeting was preceded by, among other events,[6] a round table symposium held in Geneva in September 1999, co-organized by the Hague Conference and the Université de Genève. The Geneva Round Table was not limited to the study of international jurisdiction issues, but dealt with most private international law aspects of e-commerce.[7]

Jurisdictional aspects of e-commerce, and especially in business-to-consumer contracts, along with several other problems confronting the Special Commission on General Affairs and Policy of the Conference, could have contributed to the delay in concluding the Judgments Convention until the end of 2001, and probably even later.[8]

1997, for the attention of the Special Commission on Jurisdiction and Judgments – meeting on March 1998). In particular, electronic commerce concerns were made explicit both in relation to jurisdictional based on activities (Preliminary document 9 *1998 Synthesis*, for the attention of the Special Commission on Jurisdiction and Judgments and in matters related to contract). No further Synthesis documents seem to have been produced since July 1998, i.e., after the meetings of the Special Commission on Jurisdiction and Judgments in November 1998 (3rd), June 1999 (4th), and October 1999 (5th).

4 The Ottawa Meeting of Experts on Jurisdiction and E-Commerce was a Hague Conference of Private International Law event that, for the first time in the history of the Conference, did not take place in The Hague. The Report of the Special Commission, drawn up by Peter NYGH and Fausto POCAR (Preliminary Document No. 11 for the attention of the 19th Session (2000)) has been circulated by e-mail on August 9, 2000 to the participants of the Hague works; although a interim version of the Report has been circulating from April 2000, the current version stills refers to the Ottawa meeting as a forthcoming event and thus does not deal with the work carried on in the meeting.

5 The opportunity was also taken to deliver a translation of the Preliminary Draft into Spanish, prepared by Professor Alegria Borràs of the Universitat de Barcelona and Spanish delegate at the Hague Conference. Spain was the only Spanish speaking country present at the meeting.

6 Mention has also to made to the Colloquium organized in 1997 by the Hague Conference and the Molengraaff Institute of the Utrecht Faculty of Law in honor of Michel Pelichet, published under Katharina Boele-Woelki Catherine Kessedjian (eds.), Internet. Which Court Decides? Which Law Applies, the Hague, 1998; see, on the subject, Gabrielle Kauffmann-Kokler's contribution, "Internet: mondialisation de la comunication – mondialisation de la résolution des litiges?"

7 The information concerning the Geneva Round Table comes from Preliminary Document 7 *Electronic Data Interchange, Internet and Electronic Commerce* for the attention of the Special Commission on General Affairs and Policy of the Conference of May 2000 (April 2000) and from the substantially identical – for the present purposes – document Information note *Electronic Commerce and International Jurisdiction* for the attention of the experts Meeting at Ottawa from February 28 to March 1, 2000. The work in Geneva was organized in several Commissions: Commission I dealt with contracts whereas Commission III dealt with forum selection clauses.

8 Information concerning the Special Commission on General Affairs and Policy of the Conference (May 2000) provided by Professor Alegria Borràs of the Universitat de Barcelona and Spanish delegate at the Hague Conference. See in this volume the contributions by Arthur T. von Mehren and Peter D. Trooboff.

Brussels

In the meantime, at the European Community (EC) level, jurisdictional aspects of business-to-consumer e-commerce may also be among the factors preventing the Brussels Convention of September 27, 1968,[9] from being replaced by a "Brussels I Regulation," at least at the same speed as the recently published EC Regulations on matrimonial causes,[10] insolvency,[11] and service abroad[12] were accepted.[13] There is a so-called Brussels I Regulation proposal[14] (BIRP) intended to become the Brussels I Regulation.[15] Of course, the Brussels Convention does not specifically contemplate

---

9 Brussels Convention "codified" version is published in *OJ* C 27 January 26, 1998. Although it is an unofficial version, it is a practical single text containing all the amendments deriving from successive adhesions to the original Convention, including the most recent ones on Austria, Finland and Sweden's adhesion by Treaty of November 29, 1996.

10 Council Regulation (EC) No. 1347/2000 of 29 May 2000 on jurisdiction and the recognition and enforcement of judgments in matrimonial matters and in matters of parental responsibility for children of both spouses, *OJ* L 160, June 30, 2000.

11 Council Regulation (EC) No. 1346/2000 of May 29, 2000 on insolvency proceedings, *OJ* L 160, June 30, 2000.

12 Council Regulation (EC) No. 1348/2000 of May 29, 2000 on the service in the Member States of judicial and extrajudicial documents in civil or commercial matters, *OJ* L 160, June 30, 2000.

13 *See id.*

14 Proposal for a Council Regulation on jurisdiction and the recognition and enforcement of judgments in civil and commercial matters of September 7, 1999, *OJ* C 376, December 28, 1999. The opinion of the European Parliament is now expected for September 2000. The proposal is currently under examination by the Civil Law Committee of the Council whose last meeting on the issue took place on June 21, 2000. No other meeting is expected until the Parliament delivers its opinion. I shall use the last version used in the mentioned works, *Justciv* 64 dated May 29, 2000, distributed to the participants of the Seminar on "*La reconnaissance mutuelle des décisions civiles*" held at the French Senate on July 3–4, 2000 (organized by *ARPEJE, Association pour le Renouveau et la Promotion des Échanges Juridiques Internationaux* – the French *Ministère de la Justice* and the European Commission).

15 Before the entry into force of the Amsterdam Treaty on May 1, 1999, an ad hoc group prepared an amended version of the Brussels and Lugano Conventions. See Mariano Aguilar Benitez de Lugo and Andrés Rodríguez Benot, "La revisión de los Convenios de Bruselas de 1968 y de Lugano de 1988 sobre competencia judicial y ejecución de resoluciones judiciales en materia civil y mercantil. Una primera lectura", 50 *Revista española de Derecho Internacional* 1998-2. Assuming that BIRP will eventually follow the course of the works of revision of the old 1968 Brussels Convention, just finished on April 30, 1999, it is not surprising to find in the BIRP the e-commerce provisions for business-to-commerce contracts already incorporated into the revised text. Art. 15 of BIRP reads: "*In matters relating to a contract concluded by a person, the consumer, for a purpose which can be regarded as being outside his trade or profession, jurisdiction shall be determined by this Section, without prejudice to Article 4 and point 5 of Article 5, if: ... or (3) in all other cases, the contract has been concluded with a person who pursues commercial or professional activities in the Member State of the consumer's domicile or*, by any means, directs such activities to that Member State or to several countries including that Member State, and the contract falls within the scope of such activities." (emphasis added); Art. 16(1) and (2) provides for these cases: "*1. A consumer may bring proceedings against the other party to a contract either in the courts of the Member State in which that party is domiciled or in the courts for the place where the consumer is domiciled. 2. Proceedings may be brought against a consumer by the other party to the contract only in the courts of the Member State in which the consumer is domiciled.*"

electronic contracts, but for the same reason, it does not exclude them from its scope.[16] Moreover, as time goes by, the alignment of the Lugano Convention with the Brussels Convention, not yet initiated but scheduled to begin upon the conclusion of the Brussels revision, could prove increasingly troublesome because the outcome of the BIRP will merge into EC law.[17] While the European Community's E-Commerce Directive[18] could have added new jurisdictional rules to the picture, it did not.

Granted, the BIRP suffers mainly from its own unclear future relationship with the in pectore Judgments Convention. It also suffers from the internal debate within the EC concerning the relative powers of the member states and the EC,[19] and, maybe too, from its own old underpinnings (as evidenced by the Seminar on "*La reconnaissance mutuelle des décisions civiles*," held at the French Senate July 3–4, 2000,[20] to be placed within the current trend towards an enlargement of the recognition principle following the conclusions of the European Council at Tampere[21]). So, while not the gravest of problems, e-commerce causes considerable concern in the drafting of any new jurisdictional instrument.[22] At the same time, codification in one context is influenced by parallel works within a different context:[23] a view of how

---

16 Same with the "parallel" Lugano Convention of September 16, 1988.

17 Moreover, due to its special status after Arts. 1 and 2 of the Protocol on the position of Denmark annexed to the Treaty on European Union (EU) and the Treaty establishing the European Community (EU), Denmark will not be bound by the outcome of the BIRP. Therefore, the Brussels Convention will continue to apply between Denmark and other members states (Art. 60(2(1)) BIRP).

18 Directive 2000/31/EC of the European Parliament and of the Council of June 8, 2000, *OJ* L 178, July 17, 2000 [hereinafter E-Commerce Directive].

19 *See* Horatia Muir Watt in this volume; *see also* Alegria Borràs, *Derecho internacional privado y Tratado de Amsterdam*, 51 Revista española de Derecho internacional 1999-2 (forthcoming).

20 *See supra* note 14.

21 October 15/16, 1999. See ¶¶ 33, 34 and 37 in <http://ue.eu.int/en/info/eurocouncil>.

22 The Commission of the European Community organized a public hearing on jurisdiction and law applicable on November 4/5, 1999.

23 The fact that the Brussels Convention provisions I refer to are normally applicable to defendants domiciled in member states (see Articles 2, 3 and 5) shall be deliberately omitted. The BIRP shows the same feature. On the well-known discriminatory aspect of this feature of the Brussels Convention, see Juenger, Friedrich K., *La Convention de Bruxelles du 27 septembre 1968 et la courtoisie internationale. Reflexions d'un Américain*, 72 Revue critique de Droit international privé 38 (1983). Georges A.L. Droz points out in his intervention in this volume that states currently participating in the Hague works could accept a similar regime resulting from Article 18(1) of the Preliminary Draft

> "*Where the defendant is habitually resident in a Contracting State, the application of a rule of jurisdiction provided for under the national law of a Contracting State is prohibited if there is no substantial connection between that State and the dispute*",

but the resulting judgment, although Articles 24 to 26 do not explicitly provide for this case, falls under Article 17 typology and therefore, unlike under the Brussels Convention, does not qualify for the conventionally privileged regime of Article 25. *See* Georges A.L. Droz, "Tentative Draft of the Convention on Jurisdiction and Foreign Judgments in Civil and Commercial Matters," 72 Revue Critique de Droit International Privé (1983).

some EC regulations are implemented in Spain will illustrate the importance of sensible jurisdictional rules.

Choice of Business-to-Business Contracts

Computers progressively interact among themselves through human or automatic orders and comprehensively integrate and combine former technological achievements (computers and multimedia, computers and telecommunications).[24] Thanks to computers' interface with the operator, they create, in some fields, a vivid sensation of reality or virtual reality. This leads to talk of a cyberspace, parallel to but separate from real space. The most salient characteristic of computer networks is that they provide operators with a wide range of communications with people far away and access to other information provided from distant and rapidly-varying sources. Therefore, an alternative image, such as the information superhighway, seems more appropriate than cyberspace. The law concerns only itself with the regulation of consequences within the real world;[25] it is here that various state laws or international organizations operate, each within the territorial or personal scope that public international law distributes.[26] Thus, cyberspace is an expression that can only be used within certain limits of significance.

For several reasons, the simplest legal scenario regarding electronic contracts seems to be business-to-business contracts; specifically on-line performed contracts. In business-to-business contracts, there are no additional considerations to the judicial jurisdiction problem. Unlike in consumer contracts, there are no systematic problems related to weak parties; unlike in the tort realm, there are no untreatable multi-localization problems. Moreover, business-to-business contracts cover a highly relevant field, should we be in agreement with the reasons advanced for the codification of international jurisdiction rules.[27] Compared to torts, the need for uniform foreseeable rules for contractual matters is much greater. Compared to consumer contracts, the need for foreseeable business-to-business rules is perhaps greater, simply because significant conventional international litigation is unlikely to arise in

---

24 See Paloma Llaneza González, *Internet y comunicaciones digitales. Régimen legal de las tecnologías de la información y la comunicación*, Barcelona, Bosch, p. 17 (2000).

25 By which I mean common sense three-dimensional space. Law is also concerned with other spaces and models of spaces, at least from the point of view of copyright law.

26 See Pierre-Yves Gautier "Rapport de synthèse", *Le droit et l'immatériel*, 43 *Archives de philosophie du droit* 233 (1999). *See also* Neil Weinstock Netanel, *Cyberspace Self-Governance: A Skeptical View from Liberal Democratic Theory*, 88 California L. Rev. 2000, Henry H. Perritt, Jr., *The Internet as a Threat to Sovereignty? Thoughts on the Internet's Role in Strengthening National and Global Governance*, 5 Ind. J. Global Legal Stud. 423 (1998), Joel P. Trachtman, *Cyberspace, Sovereignty, Jurisdiction, and Modernism*, 5 Ind. J. Global Leg. Stud. 475; Jack L. Goldsmith, *The Internet and the Abiding Significance of Territorial Sovereignty*, 5 Ind. J. Global Leg. Stud. 561 (1998).

27 Already in the context of the Hague works, see Arthur T. von Mehren, *Recognition and Enforcement of Foreign Judgments: A New Approach for the Hague Conference?*, 57 Law and Contemporary Problems 271 (1994).

a field so dramatically in need of new, alternative vehicles to satisfy relevant juridical interests.

The last reason given above for discriminating a priori between business-to-business and business-to-consumer contracts is in itself avowedly weak. There is another reason for discriminating a posteriori: the solution approach suggested for the codification of a rule of judicial jurisdiction for business-to-business on-line performed contracts only applies to business-to-business contracts and does not seek to affect on the business-to-consumer realm.[28]

Problems and Solution Approach

Some Problems

Electronic contracts can raise problems related to the location of the parties to the transaction and to the time and place of formation and performance. Moreover, there are problems related to the record of one, several, or all of these circumstances of fact.

If taken into consideration by an international jurisdiction rule, the location of the parties to a business-to-business electronic contract is not likely to raise many problems. The international character of the situation, as a condition for the application of the international jurisdiction rule or as a condition for the validity of the choice-of-forum agreement, is one aspect to be considered. Here, the only relevant issue seems to be possible false statements concerning the physical situation of the parties. The other aspect is their location, taken either as a direct circumstance by the jurisdiction rule – actor sequitur forum rei – or as an indirect circumstance by the jurisdiction rule, provided such circumstance depends on the location of the parties (place of conclusion or place of performance). While, as a direct circumstance, the issue is the merits of the rule itself; as an indirect circumstance, the issue is better viewed within the examination of the merits of the respective rules in Parts III on *Place of Conclusion* and IV on *Place of Performance*.

More precisely, international business-to-business electronic contracts raise problems regarding place of formation for international jurisdictional purposes if the circumstances relating to the formation are taken into consideration by international jurisdiction rules. In the case of rules now under consideration in the Hague Judgments Convention and in Brussels (BIRP), this circumstance is of no relevance because the conclusion of the contract is not an issue.[29] In Spain, however, one of

---

[28] Concerning business-to-business contracts, in the Ottawa Meeting a near consensus arose on the convenience of keeping e-commerce within the future convention and on the need for a special rule for on-line performed contracts. *See infra* Part IV (A).

[29] Article 58(1) of the BIRP refers to its applicability *ratione temporis*, taking into consideration the date of the institution of proceedings, not of the transaction underlying. The Hague Preliminary Draft seems not yet to have achieved this level of detail because it lacks a provision on the matter of *ratione temporis* applicability.

the two special jurisdiction rules for any business-to-business contract[30] gives international competence to Spanish courts, provided the contractual obligation has arisen ("has been given birth") in Spain and therefore the place of conclusion of the contract must be determined. Since this rule is one of the two ordinary rules to be applied when the Brussels or Lugano Conventions do not apply, I shall consider it and illustrate its possible functioning coupled with a far-reaching choice-of-law rule[31] (*infra* Part III).

Finally, if international jurisdiction rules consider circumstances related to performance, international business-to-business electronic contracts performed on-line also raise problems of place of performance for international jurisdictional purposes. As we shall see in Part IV, this is the case of rules now under consideration in The Hague and in Brussels and is also the case of a second special jurisdiction rule for any business-to-business contract in Spain.[32] As this kind of rule is the candidate most likely to succeed in giving content to a special jurisdiction rule in business-to-business electronic contracts, it is useful to clearly identify the relevant questions: (a) does the place of performance have a meaning in business-to-business on-line performed contracts? if so, (b) is this meaning of any significance for international jurisdiction rules? and if so, (c) does place of performance deserve a uniform juridical content?

Solution Approach

If there are more general and immediate legal issues deserving primary attention, they are not litigation issues. Instead, daily issues such as records of facts that help to prevent litigation, deserve primary attention. Law must provide the world with an equivalent to paper documents where electronic transactions are concerned. The features of a proper equivalent[33] are authenticity,[34] reliability of the fidelity of the record to the recorded data, integrity, and durability of the record. In other words, a record on the mentioned points has to make past events accessible in the present when a fact or a statement must be verified or merely consulted ex post. Rules of the applicable law could then provide answers to the questions that arise in the following two particularly important situations of particular importance in electronic transactions: (a) what facts prevail when a record of the facts depends solely on the parties' statements and the parties have made false statements? and, (b) what facts are presumed or what are the default rules for facts if there is no proper record of

30 *Ley Orgánica* 6/1985 Article 22(3) (July 1, 1985).

31 *Real Decreto* 1906/1999 Article 1(4) (December 17, 1999). *See infra* Part III(B).

32 *Ley Orgáncia* 6/1985 Article 22(3), (July 1, 1985).

33 *See* Guide to Enactment of the UNCITRAL Model Law on Electronic Commerce and Article 6 of the Model Law [hereinafter *Guide to Enactment*], ¶ 47; and UNCITEAL Model Law on Electronic Commerce [1996] I.Y.B. Int'l. Law Comm'n. 237 U.N. Doc. A/CN.9/SER.A/1996 [hereinafter *the UNCITRAL Model Law*] Article 6 available in <http://www.uncitral.org/en-index.htm>.

34 *See* Guide to enactment ¶ 53, the UNCITRAL Model Law Article 7.

the facts? The international jurisdiction rules regarding the location of parties or the location of one or another aspect of the transaction require three things as a foundation: (a) reliable, adapted records of the facts, (b) adapted rules to settle contradictions between recorded facts and real facts, and (c) adapted default rules when the record does not disclose the relevant facts.

If there exist proper material (as opposed to conflict of laws) rules on how to deal with such eventualities, then the jurisdiction rule can contribute to certainty of transactions. That is, of course, assuming it establishes the jurisdictional consequence of the facts recorded. For example, this is what happens when, as we shall see below, rules adapt formal aspects of choice-of-court to electronic contracts. In other words, international jurisdiction must first assume the degree of development of material law in the field related to the record of facts, and then establish jurisdictional consequences. I point to two aspects of the relationship between background material law and international jurisdiction rules.

First, there is a primary level at which material rules clearly depend on choice-of-law rules. Roughly speaking, choice-of-law rules became useful instruments of private law when conflict of laws, due to different national laws, became a reality. Choice-of-law rules still remain an acceptable tool, as long as conflicts are modest in quantity and in scope. Precisely the opposite is true in a field where the relevant characteristics can be seen as the converse: many electronic contracts are international contracts and the private law aspects of international trade constitute a field that traditionally resisted being based on conflicts theory.[35] There is a shift from "exceptional-internationality" to "immaterial-internationality." Therefore, the very same reasons that have traditionally prompted a relatively separate set of material rules for international trade are present in business-to-business electronic contracts. If background material aspects of international jurisdiction rules are made dependent on choice-of-law rules, in one way or another, judicial resolution of business-to-business disputes could prove very unpredictable. This is not a desirable situation; a trend towards globalization naturally calls for more globally reliable solutions. In this sense, material rules that are prepared at a global level by the United Nations Commission on International Trade Law (UNCITRAL) or at a regional level, but that intended to be harmonious with the former in the EC,[36] should be used to their full capacity. Once rules like the UNCITRAL Model Law on Electronic Commerce have obtained wide endorsement, judges, lacking powerful reasons to do otherwise, should find inspiration in their material solutions. There is little sense in applying choice-of-law rules when conflicts are already avoided or can be avoided through the application of a body of ad hoc material rules to which parties to the transaction would rarely have a bona fide objection. The possible objection, based on the lack of mandatory character of some of these rules, can be resisted on the same basis frequently used

[35] See Ole Lando, *The Eternal Crisis, Festschrift für Ulrich Drobnig*, Tübingen, Mohr 32, 375 (1998).

[36] *See, e.g.*, the E-Commerce Directive *supra* note 18, recital 58.

to advocate, for instance, the application of the UNIDROIT Principles of International Commercial Contracts.[37]

Second, there is also a second level where material rules are raised to the category of principles, whose applicability is not dependent on conflict-of-laws rules and are systematically applied qua lex fori. One way or another, these principles or general clauses make it possible to escape from the general, well-known private international law formulae: that material law is a function of forum-conflict-of-laws rules and forum-conflict-of-laws rules are a function of international jurisdiction rules.[38] Moreover, they are so strong that they normally prevail over any other rule of the primary level. They need not necessarily be labeled as "*lois de police*" or "*lois d'application immédiate*" because they embody principles and categories commanding other rules, including international jurisdiction rules.[39] At most, only small parts of these concepts that provide a basic, albeit flexible, judicial frame deserve a place in the codification of the law of international transactions, including jurisdictional rules. They can be left within judges' hands, even in situations like the present one in which a trend towards global or pervasive concepts is perceived. This second level of material rules and principles will provide the proper solutions to cope with such problems as false statements and the reliability of statements. For example, a probable principle is one that prevents a party to the contract from taking jurisdictional advantage of a behavior contrary to the good faith or to common practice in the trade.

Choice of Court and Actor Sequitur

Choice of Court

Both the Hague Preliminary Draft and the BIRP admit choice-of-court clauses and establish the corresponding rule and its jurisdictional effects.[40] Concerning substance

---

37 For a recent appraisal of the context and further references, see Filip de Ly, *Emerging New Perspectives Regarding Lex Mercatoria in an Era of Increasing Globalization*, Festschrift für Otto Sandrock, 183 (2000). *See* UNIDROIT Principles of International Commercial Contracts in <http://www.unidroit.org>.

38 Forum necessitatis makes an abstract application of this exceptional device: There is a rule to apply, and the necessity of applying it creates the forum. Rules advancing strong policies tend to create a similar effect. *See infra* Part III(B).

39 This idea, which is almost reciprocal to the idea of the preceding footnote, has been used in Spanish legal doctrine to find a feasible functional equivalent to forum non conveniens. See Francisco-José Garcimartin Alférez, *¿Caben reducciones teleológicas o 'abuso de derecho' en las normas sobre competencia judicial internacional? (Nota a R. CARO, REDI, 1995-1)*, 47 Revista española Derecho Internacional 2, 121 (1995).

40 Preliminary Draft, Article 4(1):

> If the parties have agreed that a court or courts of a Contracting State shall have jurisdiction to settle any dispute which has arisen or may arise in connection with a particular legal relationship, that court or those courts shall have jurisdiction, and that jurisdiction shall be exclusive unless the parties have agreed otherwise. Where an agreement having exclusive effect designates a court or courts of a non-Contracting State, courts in Contracting States shall decline jurisdiction or suspend

(as opposed to procedure), they only regulate formal requirements.[41] Therefore, the corresponding rules look like a guide directed to grasp their variable shape around a generally simple and straightforward content. In business-to-business contracts, the main concern of rules seems to be reaching the limits of informal agreement to avoid invalidating a choice-of-court unless such choice appears to be completely unilateral.[42] In this sense, formal requirements tend to invade material (as opposed to form and procedure) aspects and, thus, achieve a greater level of uniformity. Consequently, the Preliminary Draft and the BIRP make express reference to agreements entered into or confirmed

(a) in writing;
(b) by any other means of communication which renders information accessible so as to be usable for subsequent reference; ...[43]

or specify that agreements shall be

(a) in writing or evidenced in writing ... Any communication by electronic means which provides a durable record of the agreement shall be equivalent to 'writing'.[44]

---

proceedings unless the court or courts chosen have themselves declined jurisdiction.

BIRP, Article 23(1) and (3):

(1) If the parties, one or more of whom is domiciled in a Member State, have agreed that a court or the courts of a Member State are to have jurisdiction to settle any disputes which have arisen or which may arise in connection with a particular legal relationship, that court or those courts shall have jurisdiction. Such jurisdiction shall be exclusive unless the parties have agreed otherwise ...

(3) Where such an agreement is concluded by parties, none of whom is domiciled in a Member State, the courts of other Member States shall have no jurisdiction over their disputes unless the court or courts chosen have declined jurisdiction.

41 Moreover, the Rome Convention on the law applicable to contractual obligations of June 19, 1980, excludes from its material scope the choice-of-court clause (Article 1(2)(d) and 10(1)(b)). For the "Codified" version of the Rome Convention, *see* 1998 O.J. (C 27). As with the Brussels Convention, although it is an unofficial version, it is a practical single text containing all the amendments deriving from successive adhesions to the original convention, including the most recent ones on Austria, Finland and Sweden's adhesion by treaty of November 29, 1996.

42 *See* Case C-159/97, Trasporti castelletti Spedizioni Internazionali SpA v. Hugo Trumpy SpA, 1999 ECJ CELEX LEXIS 2436 (1999).

43 Article 4(2) of the Preliminary Draft read:

(c) in accordance with a usage which is regularly observed by the parties; (d) in accordance with a usage of which the parties were or ought to have been aware and which is regularly observed by parties to contracts of the same nature in the particular trade or commerce concerned.

44 Article 23(1) and 23(2) of BIRP, whose relevant part reads:

(1) Such an agreement conferring jurisdiction shall be either: (a) in writing or evidenced in writing; or (b) in a form which accords with practices which the parties have established between themselves; or (c) in international trade or commerce, in a form which accords with a usage of which the parties are or ought to have been aware and which in such trade or commerce is widely known to, and

While the Preliminary Draft is consistent with the UNCITRAL Model Law on Electronic Commerce,[45] the BIRP is also consistent with the E-Commerce Directive.[46]

Nevertheless, a potentially rigid and parochial application of national rules that could strongly limit the efficacy of choice-of-court clauses[47] is not prevented by the E-Commerce Directive, precisely in international cases where forum contractus or forum of performance could apply and challenge a choice-of-court clause. These are the cases in which rules governing the form of choice-of-court clauses like the ones in the Preliminary Draft or in the BIRP do not apply to overcome national standard terms statutes.[48]

Actor Sequitur Forum Rei

Under both the Preliminary Draft and the BIRP, further reference to business-to-business electronic contracts regarding the actor sequitur rule is unnecessary. The reason seems obvious and stems from its nature as a general jurisdictional rule: the rule refers directly to the situation of persons, regardless of the location of their activities or their property.[49] The E-Commerce Directive purports to identify the service provider: the service provider will have to provide, inter alia, its name and physical address.[50] At a de facto level, the other party to the contract will have to provide the equivalent information required by the service provider, who controls the process of formation of the contract.[51]

---

regularly observed by, parties to contracts of the type involved in the particular trade or commerce concerned.

(2) Any communication by electronic means which provides a durable record of the agreement shall be equivalent to 'writing'.

45 Commission III of the Geneva Round Table, considered that Article 4(2) of the text (then Working Document 144, *Proposal by the Drafting Committee*, (November 1998)) met the requirements of e-commerce, especially if its provisions are read according to the "functional-equivalent" principle advanced by the UNCITRAL Model Law. *See* Guide to Enactment Articles 5, 15. During the Ottawa Meeting, regulation of choice-of-court clauses in the Preliminary Draft was welcomed and was not the object of significant debate.

46 Article 9 of the E-Commerce Directive, *supra* note 18, refers in general to the validity of electronic contracts from the point of view of formation: Members States may not object to the validity of electronic contracts on the basis that they are formed by electronic means.

47 See *infra* Part III(B), where I refer to Spanish *Real Decreto* 1906/1999, (December 17, 1999).

48 See Dirk Langer, *Initiation and Conclusion of Contracts in the Internet*, International Legal Forum n. 1, 10 (1999).

49 Commission I of the Geneva Round Table took notice of the problem of identification and localization of the parties to the contract. Commission I was of the opinion that the parties to the contract must disclose and provide information about the place of their residence or establishment, and disclose their identity where necessary.

50 Article (1)(a) and (b).

51 The E-Commerce Directive refers to several aspects of the formation of contracts in Articles 10 and 11. In business-to-business contracts these rules are default rules except for the right of access to the standard contractual terms (Article 10(3)). Standard contractual terms usually contain choice-of-court clauses. Moreover, in business-to-business contracts these articles do not apply, with the exception of

It is worthwhile to note that a forum actoris rule proposed as variant four of Article 6 of a treaty draft outline published by the Bureau Permanent in September, 1998[52] was discarded before the Preliminary Draft.[53] The rule read:

> For contracts made and performed entirely by electronic means, the plaintiff may bring a claim in respect of all his losses in the court of his ... habitual residence.[54]

Another aspect of actor sequitur is that, in spite of the different modality of the basic rule used by the Preliminary Draft and the BIRP,[55] entities and persons other than natural persons are, in both texts, subject to general jurisdiction, among other places, in the state of their principal place of business.[56] Therefore, although computers are not the place where a business operates per se, certain business could be carried on through computers making possible to consider the actual location of a computer to be the defendant's principal place of business. This consequence may be greatly facilitated by the fact that the principal place of business can be only one of several places retained by the text.[57] A fortiori, although computers are not

---

the rules in Articles 10(3) and 11(1) second part, if communication is made by e-mail or the like (Articles 10(4) and 11(3)).

52 Information document 2: *Preliminary Draft Outline To Assist in the Preparation of a Convention on International Jurisdiction and the Effects of Foreign Judgments in Civil and Commercial Matters* (September 1998).

53 Working document 144: *Proposal by the Drafting Committee* (November 1998).

54 Variant four of Article 6 was in tune with the end of ¶ 72 of *Preliminary Document 9*. It soon received critics: see Kevin M. Clermont, *Jurisdictional Salvation and the Hague Treaty*, 85 Cornell Law Review 117 (1999).

55 Preliminary Draft, Article 3(1) provides:

> "Subject to the provisions of the Convention, a defendant may be sued in the courts of the State where that defendant is habitually resident." BIRP, Article 2(1): "Subject to the provisions of this Regulation, persons domiciled in a Member State shall, whatever their nationality, be sued in the courts of that Member State."

56 Preliminary Draft, Article 3(2)(d); BIRP, Article 60.

57 Preliminary Draft, Article 3(2) provides:

> "For the purposes of the Convention, an entity or person other than a natural person shall be considered to be habitually resident in the State – (a) where it has its statutory seat, (b) under whose law it was incorporated or formed, (c) where it has its central administration, or (d) where it has its principal place of business."

BIRP, Article 60 provides:

> (1) For the purposes of this Regulation, a company or other legal person or association of natural or legal persons is domiciled at the place where it has its: (a) statutory seat; (b) central administration; (c) principal place of business.
>
> (2) For the purposes of the United Kingdom and Ireland 'statutory seat' means the registered office or, where there is no such office anywhere, the place of incorporation or, where there is no such place anywhere, the place under the law of which the formation took place.
>
> (3) In order to determine whether a trust is domiciled in the Member State whose courts are seised of the matter, the court shall apply its rules of private international law."

This result will be easier to reach in Europe once the EC Court of Justice has ruled that

> It is contrary to Articles 52 and 58 of the EC Treaty for a Member State to refuse to register a branch of a company formed in accordance with the law of another Member State in which it has

establishments per se, the semi-personification of secondary establishments made by private international law in the fields of international jurisdiction[58] and choice-of-law[59] may well lead to consider a computer, in certain circumstances, as a secondary establishment for the purposes of Article 9 of the Preliminary Draft and Article 5(5) of the BIRP.

Place of Conclusion

Jurisdiction

Neither the Preliminary Draft nor the BIRP declare that the place of conclusion of the contract confers judicial jurisdiction in business-to-business contracts (forum contractus). However, in Spanish law, formation of the contract gives jurisdiction to Spanish courts, provided a treaty does not prevent this result.[60] This being the case, a few words are appropriate to underline two different, related aspects. First, forum contractus can be viewed as mainly providing a forum actoris in order to obtain a judgment against a foreign defendant deciding either (a) that there is a valid contract to be performed by the defendant, or (b) that there is not a valid contract and that, as a consequence, the plaintiff need not perform.[61] Therefore, the winning plaintiff can try to enforce in either the judgment forum or abroad, the judgment against the

its registered office but in which it conducts no business where the branch is intended to enable the company in question to carry on its entire business in the State in which that branch is to be created, while avoiding the need to form a company there, thus evading application of the rules governing the formation of companies which, in that State, are more restrictive as regards the paying up of a minimum share capital.

See Case C-212/97, Centros Ltd. v. Erhvervs-og Selskabsstyrelsen, 1999 E.C.R. I-1495 [1992] 2 C.M.L.R. 55.

58 Because they are amenable in their own forum for any activity related to the branch or agency, but not for those not related even if the activity is related to the company they belong to: Preliminary Draft Article 9 and BIRP Article 5(5).

59 Article 4.2 in fine of the Rome Convention on the law applicable to contractual obligations.

60 *Ley Orgáncia* 6.1985 Article 22(3) (July 1, 1985).

61 This is the "natural defendant" hypothesis. See in general but also at the origin of the current solution of the Preliminary Draft, Arthur T. von Mehren, *The Transmogrification of Defendants into Plaintiffs: Herein of Declaratory Judgments, Forum Shopping, and Lis Pendens*, Festschrift für Ulrich Drobnig 419 (1998). In a non-conventional situation, lis pendens devices would depend on national law and Spanish procedural law statutes do not contemplate international lis pendens. If the hypothesis were instead that the Judgments Convention is in force with the current version of the Preliminary Draft, situation (b) described in the text would be covered by Article 21, in particular by its paragraph 6:

> If in the action before the court first seised the plaintiff seeks a determination that it has no obligation to the defendant, and if an action seeking substantive relief is brought in the court second seised – (a) the provisions of paragraphs 1 to 5 above shall not apply to the court second seised, and (b) the court first seised shall suspend the proceedings at the request of a party if the court second seised is expected to render a decision capable of being recognised under the Convention

provided the second court is competent on a "whitelist" basis (Article 21.1 subjects the lis pendens effect to the condition that the court "seised has jurisdiction and is expected to render a judgment capable of being recognised under the Convention," i.e., after Article 25 a whitelist judgment) and judgment debtor or, to avoid in its own forum, the enforcement of an inconsistent foreign judgment based on a place-of-performance forum. This very parochial picture of forum contractus can be reinforced in business-to-business electronic contracts by material and conflict rules that try to ensure the in forum control of standard contractual terms and by indetermination concerning the place of facts related to the conclusion of the contract.[62] Article 1262 of the Spanish Civil Code presumes that the contract has been entered into in the place where the offer was made. This is a nineteenth century rule that can easily be manipulated in on-line concluded contracts to achieve the desired jurisdictional result, albeit not to challenge a choice-of-court clause included in standard terms of the offer.[63]

Second, a forum contractus rule for a discrete contractual occurrence is undoubtedly placed behind the outer limits of a very large, hypothetical, activity-based international jurisdiction rule. Nevertheless, in the absence of uniform interpretation of the future Hague convention,[64] such a forum contractus rule designated for a single contractual relationship could survive and, again, even be reinforced under an international jurisdiction rule referring to "regular commercial activity" to which the dispute "relates directly," like the one under the bracketed part of Article 9 of the Preliminary Draft.[65]

Choice of Law (and Recognition and Enforcement) Issues

The general framework in EC law for consumer contracts is to provide a consumer forum under certain circumstances;[66] then the consumer can rely on its forum-of-residence law[67] because such law's more protective rules prevail, even in the case of a valid choice of another law.[68] No similar device exists at the EC law level for

irrespective of the basis used by the first court (*ex.* Article 21.4). *See* Stephen B. Burbank, "Jurisdictional Equilibrium, the Proposed Hague Convention and Progress in National Law," in this volume.

62 See *infra* Part III(B).

63 Article 1.262 of the Spanish Civil Code has been construed by one author as a rule designed to establish the place of entering into of *inter ausentes* international contracts, *see* Miguel Virgós Soriano, Lugar de celebración y de cumplimiento en la contratación internacional (1989). He is probably right, but problems of electronic transactions aside, (a) Article 1262 creates a presumption, see Pedro A. de Miguel Asensio, Derecho privado de Internet 404 (2000); (b) case law has not settled the issue in one sense or another; and (c) some authors endorse a wider interpretation of the jurisdictional rule precisely in order to give it a wider scope than that to be gathered *ex.* Article 1262 of the Civil Code, see José-Carlos Fernández Rozas and Sixto-Alfonso Sanchez Lorenzo, Derecho internacional privado 514 (1999).

64 But *see* Articles 38 of the Preliminary Draft.

65 See *infra* Part IV(A).

66 Article 13 of the Brussels Convention. BIRP follows the same pattern and tends to enlarge the situations where the consumer is forum protected, see *supra* note 15.

67 Article 5 of the Rome Convention on the law applicable to contractual obligations.

68 Article 5(2) of the Rome Convention on the law applicable to contractual obligations. *See also* Council Directive 93/13/EEC on Unfair Terms in Consumer Contracts, 1993 O.J. (L 95) 29 [hereinafter *the Unfair Contractual Terms Directive*] Article 6(2) and Council Directive 97/7 of the European Parliament and the Council of February 17, 1997 on the Protectuion of Consumers in Respect of Distant Contracts, 1997 O.J. (L 144) 19 [hereinafter *the Distant Contracts Directive*].

business-to-business contracts, and therefore, the party claiming not to be bound by a contract[69] or by one or several of its clauses may have to litigate in a foreign forum for his claim to prevail. I should stop here as only jurisdictional issues are concerned. Nevertheless, I shall enter for a moment into the related field of choice-of-law to illustrate that the "de-localization" of activities through e-commerce can find its counterpart in a certain "de-localization of applicable law." By de-localization of applicable law, I simply refer to a situation in which the law applied has a weak connection to the issue to which it is applied. The chosen example refers to Spanish law and involves some critical aspects that I will not fully develop here.[70]

The starting points are two consumer protection directives. The first is the Unfair Contractual Terms Directive 93/13 of April 5, 1993,[71] implemented in Spain by the *Ley* 7/1998, of April 13, 1998.[72] This law has two parts. Its second part implements the Unfair Contractual Terms Directive and, in order to do so, it amends a previous consumer-law statute (*Ley* 26/1984, July 19, 1984). The first part introduces a new general regulation of standard contractual terms. This first part is neither limited to consumer contracts nor is it a directive-implementing device. *Ley* 7/1998 declares[73] itself applicable (a) when Spanish law applies to the contract, and also,[74] (b) when foreign law applies, provided the party adhering to the standard terms is both habitually resident in Spain and has adhered in Spain. The article dealing precisely with the conditions for incorporation of the standard terms into the contract[75] refers to a further statutory development for cases in which the contract is concluded *by telephone or by electronic means.*

Here, we see the second directive, the Distance Contracts Directive 97/7 of May 20, 1997,[76] come onto the scene. Article 12(2) of this Directive, much in the same way as Article 6(2) of the Unfair Contract Terms Directive, instructs member states to implement the directive to ensure that the consumer protection provided by the implementing rules cannot be circumvented by choosing a non-member state law, when the contract is closely related to the territory of one or more member states.

---

69 For instance, Article 8(2) of the Rome Convention on the law applicable to contractual obligations.

70 See Pedro A. de Miguel Asensio Derecho Privado de Internet 318, n. 62, 461 (2000). I shall also disregard the many exclusions from their material scope contained in directives mentioned in the forthcoming text and their Spanish implementing legislation.

71 The Unfair Contractual Terms Directive, 1993, O.J. (L 95) 29.

72 *Boletín Oficial del Estado* (April 14, 1998).

73 Ley 7/1998 Article 3. See Blanca Vilà Costa *Artículo 3. Ámbito territorial. Disposiciones imperativas,* Comentario a la Ley sobre condiciones generales de la contratación. Ley 7/1998, de 13 de abril, sobre Condiciones Generales de la Contratación, Modificaciones de la Ley 26/1984, de 19 de julio, General para la Defensa de los Consumidores y Usuarios, y de la Ley Hipotecaria 37 (Ignacio Arroyo Martínez and Jorge Miquel Rodríguez coordinarores (1999)).

74 "Without prejudice of international treaties," the article says in a redundant reference made mainly to the Rome Convention on the law applicable to contractual obligations. It is of course also redundant to declare the Spanish *Ley* applicable when Spanish law applies.

75 *Ley* 7/1998 Article 5.

76 1997 O.J. (L 144) 19.

We have just seen that *Ley* 7/1998 (standard terms) has taken this step; it is applicable when the party adhering to the standard terms is resident in Spain *and* has adhered in Spain. The statutory rule that develops this *Ley* for contracts concluded by telephone or by electronic means and, at the same time, implements the Distance Contracts Directive, is *Real Decreto* 1906/1999, December 30, 1999.[77] The *Real Decreto* declares[78] itself applicable every time adhesion to the contract with standard terms takes place in Spain, regardless of the law applicable to the contract and it does *not require the adhering party to be resident in Spain.*

What is relevant to our purposes now is that, in spite of the fact that both directives are consumer-protection directives, both *Ley* 7/1998 and *Real Decreto* 1906/1999 apply to business-to-consumer and to business-to-business contracts.[79] The subject matter of these statutory regulations is the incorporation, the validity, and the interpretation of standard contractual terms and, in the case of contracts concluded by telephone or by electronic means, pre-contractual information duties.[80] The application of these substantial rules depends, of course, on the forum. They would apply if the forum is Spain and their conditions for application are met. We have already seen that, for one side, the forum can easily be Spain following a forum contractus international jurisdiction rule.[81] The resulting judgment would be recognized and enforced under the Brussels[82] and Lugano Conventions.

---

77 *Boletín Oficial del Estado* (Dec. 30, 1999).

78 *Real Decreto* 1906/1999 Article 1(4).

79 As a consumer protection rule, national legislation implementing the Distant Contracts Directive could provide more protection than the directive itself, see the Distant Contracts Directive, *supra* note 67, Article 14. Nevertheless, *Real Decreto* 1906/1999 Article 1(4) is not covered by Article 14 of the Distant Contracts Directive because it is submitted that Article 14 refers to material law rules, not to conflict rules like Article 1(4). Therefore, *Real Decreto* 1906/1999 Article 1(4) is not covered by Article 12(2) of the Distant Contracts Directive because (a) if the law of a third state has been chosen as applicable law, adhesion in Spain does not in itself reveal a close relationship of the contract with the member states territory as required by Article 12(2); (b) if the law of a member state has been chosen as applicable law, Article 12(2) is not applicable. While regarding business-to-business contracts, consumer protection directives do not count, we shall see in the text that there is room for a rule like Article 1(4) under the Rome Convention on the law applicable to contractual obligations. *Real Decreto* 1906/1999 Article 1(4) must nevertheless be considered illegal because it is contrary to Article 3(2) of the Ley 7/1998 provision, already examined in the text. *See* Pedro A. de Miguel Asensio, Direcho Privado de Internet 461, n. 62 (2000).

80 *Real Decreto* 1906/1999 Article 2 makes no exception to the duty to send to the party adhering to the contract the standard terms and other terms of the contract at least three days before the conclusion of the contract. This rule does not exist in the text of Distant Contracts Directive.

81 *Supra* Part III(A).

82 It is worth mentioning here that the relevant part of the rule of Article 22(3) of *Ley Orgánica* 6/1985, of July 1, 1985 has not been blacklisted in Article 3 of the Brussels and Lugano Conventions. Article 28(3) of both Conventions reads:

> the jurisdiction of the court of the State of origin may not be reviewed; the test of public policy referred to in point 1 of Article 27 may not be applied to the rules relating to jurisdiction."

The EC Court of Justice has reinforced Article 28.3 in its ruling of March 28, 2000, C-98, Krombach v. Bamberski.

On the other hand, such "de-localized" rules that make themselves applicable only because adhesion takes place in Spain also have a chance to "circulate" to another European forum within the EC on the law applicable to contractual obligations under the regime of Article 7(1) of the Rome Convention of June 19, 1980.[83] Eventually, a non-Spanish court could, therefore, eventually apply such rules. Article 7(1) of the Rome Convention allows a court to apply mandatory rules (lois de police or lois d'application immédiate) other than the forum and the lex contractus mandatory rules under certain circumstances. This is the possible, although not certain,[84] result of a statute that declares itself to be in accordance with forthcoming or already existing EC e-commerce legislation.[85]

The EC legislation referred to here is the aforementioned E-Commerce Directive. The text is framed around the "origin" and "freedom of services"[86] principles, together with, but not conditioned to, certain harmonization, such as the admissibility and conclusion of electronic contracts.[87] Even if certain features of EC law distort the normal operations of the ordinary classic choice-of-law methods, the E-Commerce Directive will not affect jurisdictional rules (as stated in recital 23 and in Article 1(4)[88]). When directives do not introduce jurisdictional rules, they do not ordinarily declare that they are not introducing them. The purpose of the recital and of Article 1(4) is to avoid further confusion in an already complicated text, and to highlight the point for further careful consideration, for instance, within the BIRP.[89]

---

83 *See supra* note 41.

84 Article 7(1) is a very open and flexible rule. Moreover, Germany, Ireland, Luxembourg, Portugal and the United Kingdom have made the reservation of Article 22 of the Rome Convention and therefore their courts are not bound by Article 7(1).

85 *Real Decreto* 1906/1999 specifically mentions legislation on electronic signature. *See* Council Directive 99/93 2000 O.J. (L 13) 12, implemented in Spain *avant la lettre* by *Real Decreto-Ley* 14/1999 of September 17, 1999.

86 *See* E-Commerce Directive, *supra* note 18, Article 3 and recital 19.

87 *See* E-Commerce Directive, *supra* note 18, Article 1(2).

88 The E-Commerce Directive, *supra* note 18, recital 23 and Article 1(4) make the same statement as to conflict-of-laws rules. Article 1(4) provides: "*This Directive does not establish* additional *rules on the private international law nor does it deal with the jurisdiction of Courts*" (emphasis added). But recital 23 also says that the law applicable as a result of conflict-of-laws rules "must not restrict the freedom to provide information society services as established in this Directive".

89 Text of recital 23 and of Article 1(4) of the E-Commerce Directive has its origin in a document issued in the afternoon meeting of the Committee on Civil Law of November 18, 1999 sent to the Coreper for its meeting the following day. Since the Committee on Civil Law is at the same time working with BIRP and with its relationship with the Hague works, it is quite understandable that it wanted to ensure that the jurisdictional question remained open. *Supra* note 18.

Place of Performance

Hague Works

The Geneva Round Table[90] took place without variant 4 of Article 6[91] and without further reference to e-commerce in the Preliminary Draft. Commission I distinguished between contracts concluded on-line (but not wholly performed on-line) and contracts concluded and performed or to be performed on-line. Whereas traditional rules based on off-line activities such as contractual performance would remain appropriate, contracts fully performed on-line would face a situation where neither place of conclusion nor place of performance are, after Commission I, workable as to jurisdictional effects. However, Commission I did not advance any alternative rule.

The proper jurisdictional solution for on-line performed contracts in the framework of the text is logically influenced by the opinion of Article 6. Article 6 was the text examined by the experts at the Ottawa meeting.[92] Article 6 (contracts) reads as follows:

> A plaintiff may bring an action in contract in the courts of a State in which – (a) in matters relating to the supply of goods, the goods were supplied in whole or in part; (b) in matters relating to the provision of services, the services were provided in whole or in part; (c) in matters relating both to the supply of goods and the provision of services, performance of the principal obligation took place in whole or in part.

One possible solution was to exclude on-line performed contracts from Article 6 rather than from the Convention. Therefore, an action derived from such a contract should find its place anywhere in the Convention,[93] normally in Article 4 (choice of court) or in Article 3 (actor sequitur forum rei). Another sensible course of action was to try to adapt Article 6 to business-to-business on-line performed contracts, looking for a "functional equivalent" of the general solution embodied in it. This course of action could lead either to a proper rule or to a reinforcement of the reasons that militate against a rule following the line of off-line performed transactions.

A very active United Kingdom delegation proposed a paragraph (d) to be added in Article 6 of the Preliminary Draft. The proposal[94] was designed to provide a "place of delivery" language, specific for on-line performed contracts that "*shall be deemed to be the geographical address given by the receiver for delivery of that*

---

90 See *supra* Introduction A.

91 See *supra* p. 58.

92 *Id.*

93 I refer later in this Part IV (A) to Article 9 of the Preliminary Draft.

94 *See* Paul Beaumont, *UK Position on the Hague Preliminary Draft Convention on Jurisdiction and Foreign Judgments in Civil and Commercial Matters adopted by the Special Commission* on October 30, 1999 (on file with author).

information." The practical problems concerning how to make this solution workable are among the reasons put forward by those wanting to keep on-line performed contracts out of Article 6. Other reasons invoked in favor of the exclusion include those focusing on the rank that Article 6 is conceded within the Preliminary Draft. Tacit submission apart,[95] since (a) Article 4(1) allows the parties a choice of court that would normally[96] make Article 6 inapplicable, and (b) in absence of a valid choice, Article 3 (actor sequitur) would also be applicable, there is no need to offer on-line performed contracts a product similar to the one that suits their off-line counterparts. This was the opinion vehemently expressed by the New Zealand delegate,[97] thus reproducing a very well-known controversy in Europe.[98]

The experts at the Ottawa meeting also focused on the role of Article 9 of the Preliminary Draft:

> Branches [and regular commercial activity] a plaintiff may bring an action in the courts of a State in which a branch, agency or any other establishment of the defendant is situated, [or where the defendant has carried on regular commercial activity by other means,] provided that the dispute relates directly to the activity of that branch, agency or establishment [or to that regular activity].[99]

In Ottawa, there was certain agreement on the "branches part" of Article 9 in the sense that computers and parts of computers are not branches, agencies or establishments per se. Nevertheless, problems could arise regarding the quality and amount of electronic activity, the "regular commercial activity" required by bracketed part of Article 9. Here, e-commerce could be precisely one of the weapons against Article 9 activity used by its opponents, because it dramatically highlights that the article is far from concrete.[100]

---

95 The E-Commerce Directive, *supra* note 18, Article 5.

96 See *supra* pp. 55–57.

97 Also in a document distributed during the meeting, on file with the author.

98 *See infra* note 112.

99 Article 9 on "branches" and "activities" has a double origin corresponding respectively to the part outside and to the part inside the brackets: the "branches" provision comes from Article 9 of the Treaty Draft outline of September 1998 and remains since then in Article 9, and the "activities" provision comes from Article 11 of the Treaty Draft outline: "Specific jurisdiction based on business activity: A defendant, whether acting directly or through a third party, shall be subject to the jurisdiction of a State for a claim arising out of activities regularly carried on within or directed to that State." After the Treaty Draft outline, the origin of this language is to be found in Working Documents 89 (produced by the U.S. Delegation) and 91 (produced by the representative of the Commonwealth Secretariat), but in reality the text assumes literally one point of Working Document 89. Then Article 11 of the *Proposal by the Drafting Committee* (of November 1998) was left without content, but the provision, although amended, has regained a conditional life within Article 9 during the 5th meeting of Special Commission in October 1999, after which Article 9 reads as quoted in the text.

100 See *supra* pp. 58–59.

Brussels Works

Under the Brussels Convention, tacit submission aside, in the absence of a valid choice of court, the plaintiff has the choice between the domicile of the defendant and the place of performance of the obligation forming the basis of the action.[101] I look now to this second possibility, however, no cases dealing with business-to-business contracts performed by electronic means have been the object of a preliminary ruling by the European Court of Justice, so the question of how to decide these cases remains open.

Article 5(1) of the BIRP reads:

> "A person domiciled in a Member State may, in another Member State, be sued: 1) (a) in matters relating to a contract, in the courts for the place[102] of performance of the obligation in question; (b) for the purpose of this provision and unless otherwise agreed, the place of performance of the obligation in question shall be: – in the case of the sale of goods, the place in a Member State where, under the contract, the goods were delivered or should have been delivered; – in the case of the provision of services, the place in a Member State where, under the contract, the services were provided or should have been provided; (c) if paragraph (b) does not apply then paragraph (a) applies.

This article follows in paragraph (a) the current Brussels Convention rule. However, in paragraph (b), the article tries to alleviate the main difficulties experienced in its application,[103] by bypassing choice-of-law issues by allowing the parties to establish the place of performance by agreement,[104] which, if not otherwise provided, will be

---

[101] *See, e.g.*, Harry Duintjer Tebbens, *Possible Revision of the Brussels and Lugano Conventions in the Light of the Case Law of the Court of Justice of the European Communities*, in La revisión de los Convenios de Bruselas de 1968 y Lugano de 1988 sobre competencia judicial y ejecución de resoluciones judiciales: una reflexión preliminar española (Seminario celebrado en Tarragona, 30–31 de mayo de 1997) 42 (Alegria Borràs ed., 1998). In business-to-business contracts, the EC Court of Justice has consistently said that it is the obligation corresponding to the claim and not the characteristic obligation of the contract that counts for jurisdictional purposes in Article 5(1). *See* Case 45/75, De Bloss v. Soc. Bouyer, 1977 E.C.R. 2359; Case C-420/97, Leathertex v. Bodetex, 1999 ECJ CELEX LEXIS 2645. Since the entry into force of the treaty of October 9, 1978 of adhesion of Denmark, Ireland and the United Kingdom the Brussels Convention reads "in the courts for the place of performance of the obligation in question" and that the place of execution is determined by the law applicable to the contractual obligation according to the choice-of-law rules of the national court, *See* Case 12/76, Tessili v. Dunlop, 1976 E.C.R.; Case C-288/92, Custom Made Commercial v. Stawa Metallbau, E.C.R. I-2913; Case C-440/97, GIE Groupe Concorde v. Captain of the "Suhadiwarno Panjan", 1999 E.C.R.

[102] Document *Justciv* 64, *supra* note 14, warns: "This text will be revised by the Legal/linguistic experts in due course."

[103] As illustrated by the cases decided by the EC Court of Justice, Case 12/76, Tessili v. Dunlop, 1976 E.C.R.; Case C-288/12, Custom Made Commercial v. Stawa Metallbau, 1994 E.C.R. I-2913; Case C-440/97, GIE Groupe Concorde v. Captain of the "Suhadiwarno Panjan", 1990 E.C.R.

[104] The solution is not present in the text of the Convention but has been accepted by the EC Court of Justice since Case 56/79, Zelger v. Salitrini, 1980 E.C.R. 89. For the characterization of such agreements under the Brussels Convention, and the scope of EC Court of Justice doctrine after *Zelger v. Salitrini*

the place where, according to the contract, merchandise is to be delivered or where services are to be provided. Whereas the Preliminary Draft concentrates litigation in the forum of performance of the "characteristic obligation," the BIRP keeps alive the Brussels Convention approach of "obligation in question."[105]

In the absence of a specific solution for on-line performed contracts, the places to which Article 5(1)(b) of the BIRP refers could provide a more direct link between "facts" and their "jurisdictional consequence" than the current Article 5(1) of the Brussels Convention allows. There are no formal requirements in Article 5(1)(b) and, hence, the agreement need not satisfy the formal requirements of the BIRP Article 2 because Article 5(1)(b) and Article 23 agreements necessarily differ according to the instrument structure: Article 23 envisions a choice-of-court clause and Article 5(1)(b) envisions a "material law" clause,[106] whose wording would normally be clear enough to avoid confusion. Nevertheless, due to the fact that the formal requirements in Article 23 are quite loose,[107] it could theoretically be difficult to distinguish between Article 5(1)(b) and Article 23 in a given case.[108] In other words, because the particular contents of an Article 5(1)(b) clause cannot be known in advance, and because it is indeed difficult to envisage an agreement the only purpose of which is to say that the place of performance is not the place of delivery of the merchandise or the performance of the services, it may be difficult to avoid the confusion with Article 23. Although hypothetically the competent court will be situated in Europe, in an Article 23 situation, a member state domiciled would be bound on equal grounds to a non-member state domiciled.[109] By contrast, in an Article 5(1)(b) situation a member state domiciled may use Article 5(1)(b) place of performance as

especially in cases such as *Custom Made Commercial v. Stawa Metallbau*, and Case C-106/95, *MSG v. Les Gravières Rhénanes*, 1997 E.C.R. I-911, see Andrés Rodríguez Benot, "Acuerdos para la determinación del lugar de ejecución de las obligaciones contractuales y acuerdos atributivos de competencia en los Convenios de Bruselas y Lugano" in *La Revisíon de los Convenios de Bruselas de 1968 y Lugano de 1988 Sobre Compentencia Judicial y Ejecución de Resoluciones Judiciales: Una Feflexión Preliminar Española (Seminario celebrado en Tarragona, 30–31 de mayo de 1997)* 42 (Alegria Borràs ed., 1998).

105 I shall pass now sub silentio two important differences between Article 6 of the Preliminary Draft and Article 5(1) of the BIRP. While it is assumed that Article 5(1) covers both issues, the text of Article 6 is unclear concerning (a) whether it deals with contractual actions concerning the formation of the contract and (b) whether it is applicable when no performance at all has occurred. For some of these issues, in the context of a critical appraisal of forum of performance in general and in e-commerce contracts, see Andreas Bucher, Vers une convention mondiale sur la compétence et sur les jugements étrangers, La Semaine juridique 85 (2000).

106 The first is regulated by the BIRP (Article 23), while the second is a matter of the applicable law in general determined through the Rome Convention, which in turn, as already said, *supra* note 41, excludes from its material scope the choice-of-court clause (Article 1(2)(d) and 10(1)(b)).

107 *See supra* note 44.

108 See Andrés Rodríguez Benot, *supra* note 104, at 186.

109 Choice of court regulated by Article 17 of the Brussels Convention (and by Article 23 of the BIRP) is the one giving international competence to a court of one state party (or member state) provided at least one of the parties to the agreement is domiciled in a state party (member state).

a defendant with the same practical effect as Article 23 if the place is his or her domicile while its non-member state domiciled counterpart would not be covered by the BIRP in this case.[110]

Discussion

We have seen above that, compared to Article 5(1) of the Brussels Convention, the corresponding provisions of the Preliminary Draft, and the BIRP, to a different extent, have been largely freed of their conflicts of laws component. As we have also seen, in Article 5(1) the place-of-performance rule somehow winks at the choice-of-forum rule.

Critics of the place-of-performance rule argue that, in practice, the rule turns out to be redundant either because (a) performance occurs within the defendant's premises and coincides with the defendant's forum rule, or (b) it embodies a forum actoris rule because performance, alternatively, occurs within the plaintiff's premises. Other issues raised by the place of performance rule–like plurality of obligations or places, where to perform, and place of payment of money or equivalent–do not contribute to the prestige of the rule. In the first case, the rule in fact multiplies the number of potentially available fora, and in the second case, the place of performance lacks any real material significance as it is difficult to localize and is frequently deprived of practical effect. Both the Preliminary Draft and the BIRP limit the applicability of the place-of-performance rule to the cases where performance has a factual significance like the supply of goods and the provision of services. In business-to-business contracts performed by electronic means, the extreme rule resulting from the current Article 5(1) of the Brussels Convention as interpreted by the Court of Justice[111] is unacceptable, because rules needed to deal with international jurisdiction must be straightforward and provide certain predictability.[112] In Spain, the aforementioned

[110] BIRP Article 4(1). This article amends the omission in Convention Article 4(1): if there is a choice of court under Article 23, the choice prevails over national law and international jurisdiction rules otherwise applicable should the defendant not be domiciled in a member state.

[111] *See supra* note 103.

[112] See Harry Duintjer Tebbens, *Possible Revision of the Brussels and Lugano Conventions in Light of the Case Law of the Court of Justice and of the European Communities*, in *La Revisíon de los Convenios de Bruselas de 1968 y Lugano de 1988 Sobre Compentencia Judicial y Ejecución de Resoluciones Judiciales: Una Feflexión Preliminar Española (Seminario celebrado en Tarragona, 30–31 de mayo de 1997)* 47 (Alegria Borràs ed., 1998) referring to the various positions authors have adopted concerning Article 5(1). Add the very strong defense of the current Brussels Convention solution made by Miguel Virgós Soriano and Francisco J. Garecimartín Alférez, *El Convenio de Bruselas y las propuestas para su reforma: una crítica radical. Arts. 5.1.I, 21, 24 y 27–2*, in *La Revisíon de los Convenios de Bruselas de 1968 y Lugano de 1988 Sobre Compentencia Judicial y Ejecución de Resoluciones Judiciales: Una Feflexión Preliminar Española (Seminario celebrado en Tarragona, 30–31 de mayo de 1997)* 93 (Alegria Borràs ed., 1998).

second rule of specific jurisdiction (place of performance) for business-to-business contracts[113] is affected by uncertainty similar to that of the first rule (place of conclusion or forum contractus).[114] Therefore, except where a uniform material rule cannot provide an adapted, precise meaning to the place of performance of business to-business contracts performed by electronic means, this place of performance should not be made dependent on a choice-of-law rule.

However, a unique, uniform, material place-of-performance rule does not exist yet. Only a two-step device that gives preference to the parties' agreement can achieve this goal.

First, the definition of both initial and final points of an electronic performance, as opposed to a non-electronic performance, must be established.[115] Once again, following the "functional-equivalent" principle, the UNCITRAL Model Law on E-Commerce defines the place of dispatch and place of reception of data messages in Article 15(4):

> Unless otherwise agreed between the originator and the addressee, a data message is deemed to be dispatched at the place where the originator has its place of business, and is deemed to be received at the place where the addressee has its place of business. For the purposes of this paragraph: (a) if the originator or the addressee has more than one place of business, the place of business is that which has the closest relationship to the underlying transaction or, where there is no underlying transaction, the principal place of business; (b) if the originator or the addressee does not have a place of business, reference is to be made to its habitual residence.[116]

Second, the choice of one of these two places, or another place in between, as the place of performance, must be established. This should be done with the help of the most specific legal text. This text would again normally give precedence to the parties' agreement on the issue. The most specific, uniform text would be a text dealing specifically with electronic performance prepared by the UNCITRAL or the International Chamber of Commerce (ICC).[117] Less specific, but still adequate

---

113 Article 22(3), in the relevant part, of *Ley Orgánica* 6/1985, of July 1, 1985.

114 *See supra* note 63. While the courts have not settled the issue, Miguel Virgós Soriano advocates a conflict-of-laws solution, see Lugar de Celebración y de Culplimento en la Contratación Internacional (1989); but José-Carlos Fernández Rozas and Sixto-Alfonso Sánchez Lorenzo endorse a more free-floating approach, see José-Carlos Fernández and Sixto-Alfonso Sánchez Lorenzo *Derecho Internacional Privado* (1999).

115 *See* Pedro A. de Miguel Asensio, Derecho Privado de Internet 400, n. 62 (2000).

116 Article 11(1), second part of the E-Commerce Directive, *supra* note 18, only refers to the time of the acts of communication among the parties.

117 Information concerning law of e-commerce transactions of the International Chamber of Commerce *available in* <http://www.iccwbo.org>.

according to the context,[118] could be to refer either to the UNIDROIT Principles of International Commercial Contracts[119] or the Principles of European Contract Law.[120]

In the absence of a uniform material rule, it is submitted that the rule in Article 5(1) of the BIRP is preferable to the rule in Article 6 of the Preliminary Draft when taking into account the current needs of business-to-business contracts performed by electronic means. Article 5(1) of the BIRP clearly allows the parties to agree on the place of performance, which could prove to be a useful tool of certainty when data transfers are at stake, since they occur among computers whose constantly evolving features may both recommend and tolerate less dependence on rigid rules. This open solution is consistent with the current development of EC law: (a) contracts performed by electronic means can be characterized as contracts of services according to the E-Commerce Directive characterization of "services of the information society"[121] but (b) at the private-law level, the E-Commerce Directive avoids introducing rules of private international law and of place of performance. For our purposes, more important than this is the fact that the BIRP will be, in contrast to the Brussels Convention, an EC regulation, therefore more open to EC law influence than the latter. Other regulations as well as national legislation implementing directives could, in the future, contain jurisdictional rules.[122] Moreover, some substantive rules, such as those defining places where things are situated or happen, can impact the conceptual framework of the BIRP.

By contrast, Article 6 of the Preliminary Draft does not clearly allow parties to manipulate the place of performance in order to adapt it to electronic performance, nor is there a safety net of an evolutionary, undisputed material law framework. An ad hoc material rule in the text of the Convention would theoretically solve the problem, but supposing this result could be achieved, the price would also be high. The risk is that the ad hoc material rule would freeze in the Convention until it was amended, and without a court having authority in the meantime to deem it obsolete.[123]

---

118 *See, e.g.*, Katharina Boele-Woelki, *The Unidroit Principles of International Commercial Contracts and the Principles of European Contract Law: How to Apply them to International Contracts?* 1 Uniform L. Rev. 1996; Michel Joachim Bonell, *The Unidroit Principles of International Commercial Contracts and the Principles of European Contract Law: Similar Rules for the Same Purpose*, 1 Uniform L. Rev. (1996).

119 Article 6(1)(6), *available in* <http://www.unidroit.org>.

120 Article 7-101. *See* Parts I and II of Ole Lando and Hugh Beale, *Principles of European Contract Law* 329 (comb. and rev. ed., 2000).

121 The E-commerce Directive, *supra* note 18, Article 1(1).

122 This seemed natural to the point that the provision of the Brussels Convention in this sense (Article 57(3)) is not found in the BIRP.

123 It is obvious that this reasoning hardly conceals a more general dislike for international treaties in matters of private law, an argument that I partially develop elsewhere (*Hacia un convenio mundial de* exequatur*: Algunos aspectos del Derecho estadounidense de interés para España*, Barcelona, Bosch (1999)).

Article 6 clearly shows the dilemma: either Article 6 deals with business-to-business contracts containing no special rule for them, or it tries to offer them a specific rule of international jurisdiction, seizing the time of codification for an agreement that does not yet exist. The second possibility could ruin Article 6. The first one condemns business-to-business contracts performed by electronic means to a significant uncertainty until the law is clarified. And since the law could be clarified in nationally divergent ways, the first possibility would frustrate both those wanting a clear "whitelist" of jurisdictional bases and those wanting a frankly recognized gray zone open to evolution.

Questions formulated at page 53 are then answered here. Does the place of performance have meaning in business-to-business on-line performed contracts? It has, because despite the character of the subject matter, there is a place of performance. The importance of this place of performance is highlighted in law (a) because of the real distance taken into account by international jurisdiction rules and private international law in general, and (b) because the medium through which performance is carried out is normally not within the control of the parties to the contract. While the vendor has an interest in a rule declaring that the performance has taken place in its own establishment, the purchaser does not want this result attained until he obtains effective control of the object of the performance. Therefore, we encounter a similar situation to the one law has already encountered when merchandise has to travel from the vendor's to the purchaser's establishment. This situation has already been solved by means of international commercial terms concerning delivery and transfer of risks.[124]

Since there *is* a place of performance, this place is of significance for international jurisdiction rule purposes, as long as the place of performance is used to build a rule specific for contracts. If one of the rationales of the rule is that it provides easy access to evidence, business-to-business contracts performed by electronic means may require discovery in very similar terms to off-line performed contracts. There are also other rationales for the rule,[125] and they point to a jurisdiction rule not dependent on the real place of performance, as opposed to the contractual one, and one even independent of actual facts of performance. However, this only makes the jurisdiction rule more dependent on the material law in evolution.

This leads to the answer of the third question, although it has already been given. The place of performance deserves to have uniform juridical content. Lacking uniform contents at the particular time of elaboration of the jurisdiction rule, the jurisdiction rule should invite parties to the contract to agree on the place as to jurisdictional

[124] *See, e.g.*, International Commercial Terms (INCOTERMS), International Chamber of Commerce Publication N1 460.

[125] See Miguel Virgós Soriano and Francisco J. Garecimartín Alférez, *El Convenio de Bruselas y las propuestas para su reforma: una crítica radical. Arts. 5.1.I, 21, 24 y 27-2*, in *La Revisíon de los Convenios de Bruselas de 1968 y Lugano de 1988 Sobre Compentencia Judicial y Ejecución de Resoluciones Judiciales: Una Feflexión Preliminar Española (Seminario celebrado en Tarragona, 30–31 de mayo de 1997)* 97(Alegria Borràs ed., 1998).

effects and to promote this agreement without a premature crystallization of a specific solution.

Concluding Remarks

There is no need for super high-speed jurisdictional rules designed for business-to-business on-line performed contracts. To a similar extent, as with a wide range of national laws,[126] EC law is currently showing that business-to-business contracts can be left free floating among other contracts waiting for a specific rule or for a European Court of Justice decision. The law will stabilize with specific solutions, if needed, when material rules for business-to-business on-line performed contracts, if needed, begin to crystallize.

The present situation is characterized by potential rather than actual difficulties on the jurisdiction-localization of business-to-business on-line performed contracts, the current state of evolution of international jurisdiction law including EC law, and the current language of Article 6 of the Preliminary Draft. In The Hague, this leads to a choice between two possible solutions when two premises are met. The premises are (a) that no specific solution for business-to-business on-line performed contracts either could be achieved or is now desirable, and (b) that these contracts cannot be excluded from the future convention. The two possible solutions are of course the non-exclusion of business-to-business on-liner performed contracts from Article 6 – without any further special provision for them – or their exclusion from Article 6, while at the same time not excluding them from the Convention in Article 1(2) of the Preliminary Draft.

The first possibility entails a theoretical complete assimilation of business-to-business on-line and off-line performed contracts, from the point of view of the recognition and enforcement of judgments given in the state of origin, as well as other conventional devices such as lis pendens. However, since the determination of the place of performance jurisdictional basis and the findings of the court of origin are not shielded by Article 27(2) of the Preliminary Draft, different national approaches to the place of performance issue could reveal an unexpected gray zone inside the white Article 6 excluding volens nolens some contracts from the Article 25 regime.

The Preliminary Draft contains a gray zone in Article 18 mainly to the effect of the Article 24 regime. The gray zone was designed to allow evolution of national laws otherwise frozen by a rigid system of conventional black and whitelists.[127] In order to avoid a scenario which undermines the prestige of the treaty, (and also in

[126] *See, e.g.*, Martin H. Redish, *Of New Wine and Old Bottles: Personal Jurisdiction, The Internet and the Nature of Constitutional Evolution*, 38 Jurimetrics (1998), and Allan R. Stein, *The Unexceptional Problem of Jurisdiction in Cyberspace*, 32 International Lawyer (1998).

[127] See Arthur T. von Mehren, *Enforcing Judgments Abroad: Reflections on the Design of Recognition Conventions*, 24 Brooklyn J. Int'l. L. (1998).

order to use the mixed-convention structure or approach openly for one of the cases it was designed for), exclusion of business-to-business on-line performed contracts from Article 6 and automatic transfer to the gray "non-list" of Article 18 seems the proper solution in the current situation.[128]

[128] This seems to be the solution advanced by Kevin M. Clermont and Kuo-Chang Huang in paragraph 203(b) of their proposal of a U.S. Federal Statute implementing the Hague Convention. *See* Kevin M. Clermont and Kuo-Chang Huang, *Converting the Draft Hague Treaty into Domestic Jurisdictional Law, infra* p. 191.

Ronald A. Brand[†]

Current Problems, Common Ground, and First Principles: Restructuring the Preliminary Draft Convention Text

Introduction

On October 30, 1999, a Special Commission of the Hague Conference on Private International Law adopted a Preliminary Draft Convention on Jurisdiction and Foreign Judgments in Civil and Commercial Matters (Preliminary Draft Convention or "PDC").[1] Originally scheduled for a diplomatic conference in the fall of 2000, the negotiating process has now been delayed by serious questions concerning the language of the PDC text. Those questions arise from three basic problems inherent in the Preliminary Draft Convention text: (1) a structure that fails to take into account the global goals of a Hague convention, (2) too many provisions based on a desire to carry the Convention too far, and (3) jurisdictional rules built on a court's relationship to the claim rather than a court's relationship to the defendant.

In this article, I begin by elaborating on these problems, and use Article 10(4) of the PDC text to demonstrate, in particular, the latter two problems. I then offer a restructured convention text that I believe responds to the three problems and builds on common ground among parties to the Hague negotiations. I offer restructured text not as a final product, but rather as an alternative designed both to take into account a first principles approach to the Convention and to use the work that has been done to date in important provisions. My hope is that discussions such as this

---

† Professor of Law and Director, Center for International Legal Education, University of Pittsburgh. David Goddard provided helpful comments on a prior draft and Monica A. Stubanas provided valuable research and editorial assistance in the preparation of this paper. The author is a member of the United States delegation to the Special Commission on negotiating the Convention on Jurisdiction and Foreign Judgments in Civil and Commercial Matters. The opinions expressed in this comment are those of thc author and should not be taken to represent the position of the United States government or any other member of the United States delegation.

Author's Note: This paper suggests an approach to revising the Preliminary Draft Convention text in order to help reach a convention that has some chance of acceptance on more than a regional scale. It addresses concerns in the general approach taken toward reaching a final convention text and does not purport to provide "perfect" solutions to any single problem or final language for any single provision. It is offered to further the dialogue necessary to making progress, and not to suggest final positions on the part of any delegation.

1 The text of the Preliminary Draft Convention is available in <http://www.hcch.net/e/conventions/draft36e.html>.

J.J. Barceló and K.M. Clermont (eds.), A Global Law of Jurisdiction and Judgments: Lessons from The Hague, 75–116

might contribute to movement from the stalled PDC text to a successful Hague convention.

The Problems with the PDC Text

The first problem with the PDC text is its structure. The construction of the PDC text is primarily a result of the existing models found in the Brussels and Lugano Conventions.[2] The fact that 17 of the delegations began the negotiations as parties to these conventions, combined with the fact that these two conventions represent the principal existing models for a jurisdiction and judgments convention, resulted in a natural tendency to make the PDC text look much like the Brussels and Lugano models.

The Brussels Convention structure has worked well in European Union member states for more than 30 years, but that regional experience does not necessarily translate well to a global convention. The delegations at the Hague negotiations made a very deliberate decision to have a mixed convention (with three categories of bases of jurisdiction), and not a double convention (with only two jurisdictional categories), and yet kept the structure of a double convention.[3] Under the mixed-convention approach, there would exist a list of required bases of jurisdiction and a list of prohibited bases of jurisdiction. All contracting states would have to offer jurisdiction founded on required bases, and other contracting states would have to recognize and enforce any resulting judgment. Since courts would not take jurisdiction on bases found in the "prohibited" list, only limited exceptions to recognition

---

2 European Convention on Jurisdiction and Enforcement of Judgments in Civil and Commercial Matters, done at Brussels, Sept. 27, 1968, 41 O.J. Eur. Comm. (C 27/1) (Jan. 26, 1998) (consolidated and updated version of the 1968 Convention and the Protocol of 1971, following the 1996 accession of the Republic of Austria, the Republic of Finland and the Kingdom of Sweden) ("Brussels Convention"); European Communities-European Free Trade Association: Convention on Jurisdiction and Enforcement of Judgments in Civil and Commercial Matters, done at Lugano, Sept. 16, 1988, O.J. Eur. Comm. (L 319/9) (Nov. 25, 1988), *reprinted in* 28 I.L.M. 620 (1989) ("Lugano Convention").

3 For a complete description of, and discussion of the rationale for, a mixed convention, *see* Arthur T. von Mehren, *Enforcing Judgments Abroad: Reflections on the Design of Recognition Conventions*, 24 Brook. J. Int'l L. 17 (1998).

A mixed convention is a hybrid form of the traditional "single" and "double" conventions. Single conventions, like the earlier Hague Conventions, deal only with indirect jurisdiction and apply only to the decision of the court asked to enforce a foreign judgment – thus, jurisdiction of the court issuing a judgment is considered "indirectly" by the second court in deciding whether to recognize the judgment of the issuing court. Convention on the Recognition and Enforcement of Foreign Judgments in Civil and Commercial Matters and Supplementary Protocol, done Feb. 1, 1971, *reprinted in* 15 Am. J. Comp. L. 362 (1967); Convention on the Recognition of Divorces and Legal Separations, opened for signature fall 1969, *printed in* 8 Int'l Legal Materials 31 (1969). Double conventions, like Brussels and Lugano, provide direct jurisdiction rules applicable in the court in which the case is first brought – thus addressing the matter from the outset and preempting the need for indirect consideration of the issuing court's jurisdiction by the court asked to recognize the resulting judgment.

would apply. Any jurisdictional basis not included in one of the two lists would be permitted, but subject to review by the recognizing court in the manner applicable absent a treaty. The retention of a double-convention structure is likely to frustrate the goal of uniform interpretation in courts of different states. Courts in Brussels Convention states will naturally look at the structure of the PDC text and see something very similar to the Brussels Convention, and thus be tempted to read the jurisprudence of the Brussels Convention into interpretations of the PDC text. On the other hand, courts not from Brussels Convention states may have trouble with the structure and language of the PDC text, which do not make clear the three categories of jurisdiction or the manner in which those categories are of principal importance to issues of recognition and enforcement. Thus, by following the Brussels Convention format and failing to provide clarity in terms of mixed-convention structure, the PDC text poses a real risk of improper interpretation in both Brussels and non-Brussels contracting states. This undercuts an important purpose of addressing jurisdiction in the first place: the desire to move toward harmonization of international practice.

The second problem with the PDC text is that it represents an attempt to do too much. It thus goes too far by including rules that will make constituencies in a significant number of states likely to find strong arguments against its ratification. In other words, the problem with the PDC text is that it is the product of an effort to reach perfection, where no single concept of perfection exists and the multiple ideas of perfection are irreconcilable. The goal should simply be to go as far as possible in making the world a better place for transnational litigation, realizing that perfection (by anyone's definition) is not an attainable goal. The world will be much better off with a convention of limited ambition, providing a foundation for future developments, than with a convention that will leave out important states and never result in true global adherence. Thus, it is worth the effort to back up a bit and focus on first principles, building a convention through a focus on those provisions for which there is a consensus. This will result in a shorter list of required bases of jurisdiction and a shorter list of prohibited bases of jurisdiction, with more left in the permitted category. If it means success in reaching a truly global convention, it will be worth the effort.

The third problem with the PDC text is that many of its jurisdictional provisions do not focus on the relationship that (1) is the relationship on which the jurisdictional rules supported by greatest consensus are built, (2) is the relationship on which jurisdictional rules of differing legal systems seem to converge, and (3) is arguably the relationship most important to a convention that combines jurisdiction with recognition and enforcement of judgments: the relationship between the court and the party (the defendant). Article 2 of the Brussels Convention gives priority to this relationship by providing for jurisdiction at the defendant's domicile. Likewise, U.S. constitutional jurisprudence in jurisdictional issues provides a focus on the contacts of the defendant with the state in which the court exercising authority is located.[4] Ultimately, when a court is faced with recognition and enforcement of a foreign judgment, the question is whether the originating court had legitimate authority over the *party* against whom enforcement of the judgment is sought. This means that consensus (and ultimate success of the Convention) is more likely to result from inclusion of jurisdictional provisions built on the relationship between the court and the party. Since this is the preferred relationship in the systems most often discussed in the negotiations, it should be possible to move in this direction.

Article 10(4) of the PDC Text as Illustrative of the Problems

The Purpose and Effect of Article 10(4)

Article 10(4) deals with jurisdiction in tort cases. It is one of the provisions of the PDC text that illustrates the second problem noted above: it goes beyond first principles and consensus development and thus impedes the conclusion of a successful convention. At the same time, it also illustrates the third problem, providing insight into the general question of the appropriate nexus by which jurisdiction is to be judged. It is useful to first consider the entirety of Article 10, which reads as follows:

> Article 10 – Torts or delicts
> (1) A plaintiff may bring an action in tort or delict in the courts of the State –
> (a) in which the act or omission that caused injury occurred, or
> (b) in which the injury arose, unless the defendant establishes that the person claimed to be responsible could not reasonably have foreseen that the act or omission could result in an injury of the same nature in that State.
> (2) Paragraph (1)(b) shall not apply to injury caused by anti-trust violations, in particular price-fixing or monopolisation, or conspiracy to inflict economic loss.
> (3) A plaintiff may also bring an action in accordance with paragraph 1 when the act or omission, or the injury may occur.
> (4) If an action is brought in the courts of a State only on the basis that the injury arose or may occur there, those courts shall have jurisdiction only in respect of the injury that occurred or may occur in that State, unless the injured person has his or her habitual residence in that State.

Paragraph (1) of this Article provides the basic rule that, in a tort case, a defendant may be sued (in addition to suit at the defendant's habitual residence under Article 3), either in the state where the event causing the injury occurs or in the state where the injury is felt. This is a codification of the European Court of Justice interpretation

[4] *See, e.g.*, Ronald A. Brand, *Due Process, Jurisdiction and a Hague Judgments Convention*, 60 U. Pitt. L. Rev. 661 (1999). Canada takes a similar approach, sometimes combining the state/defendant nexus with a state/claim nexus. *See, e.g.*, Morguard Investments Ltd. v. De Savoye, 76 D.L.R.4th 256 (1990); United States v. Ivey, 27 B.L.R.2d 221, 130 D.L.R.4th 674, 26 O.R.3d 533 (Ont. Gen. Div. 1995).

of Article 5(3) of the Brussels Convention in *Bier v. Mines de Potasse d'Alsace*.[5] The remaining three paragraphs of Article 10 modify this first paragraph in specific instances. Paragraph (2) prevents the use of paragraph (1)(b) in antitrust cases;[6] paragraph (3) authorizes paragraph (1) jurisdiction even where the injury has not yet occurred (allowing injunctive relief); and paragraph (4) purports to limit the jurisdiction of courts to the "injury that occurred or may occur in [the] State" in which jurisdiction exists under paragraph (1)(b).

My approach here is first to examine the problem Article 10(4) is designed to address (or at least the problem from which it originates). Next, I will discuss the solution the European Court of Justice chose in addressing this problem under Article 5(3) of the Brussels Convention. I will then consider how Article 10(4) serves to generalize that solution beyond existing jurisprudence in the European Union or elsewhere, as well as the effects of such generalization. Ultimately, it is my hope that this analysis will illustrate the fundamental distinction in approaches to jurisdiction that must be addressed in a successful global convention.

The Problem of English Libel Judgments

Article 10(4) is a child of the judgment of the European Court of Justice in *Shevill v. Presse Alliance S.A.*[7] *Shevill* began in the English courts when an English plaintiff brought suit against a French defendant. The plaintiff alleged defamation in the publication of a newspaper whose circulation was mainly in France and involved events occurring while the plaintiff was employed in France. When the case reached the House of Lords, it was referred to the European Court of Justice for a preliminary ruling concerning the interpretation of Article 5(3) of the Brussels Convention. The reasons for bringing the action in the United Kingdom were clear, even though only 230 out of more than 253,500 copies of the newspaper were sold in England and Wales.[8] Those reasons are captured in the following statement of two Scottish legal academics:

> London is known as "the libel capital of the world." Under the law of England, the tort of libel is committed where the libelous statement is "published" (communicated to third parties). Thus, any report in the European media that reaches England can be the subject of an English libel suit. English defamation law is singularly favorable to plaintiffs seeking civil remedies for harm to reputation. Plaintiffs benefit from a combination of substantive and procedural advantages largely unavailable elsewhere in the European Union, the most important of which is the determination of damage awards by juries rather than by judges.

5 Case 21/76, 1976 E.C.R. 1735.

6 This provision obviously has U.S. antitrust judgments as its target, and indicates another "deal-breaker" effort to go too far in this convention.

7 Case C-68/93, 1995 E.C.R. I-415.

8 *Id.* at ¶ 9.

> Jury awards can be quite substantial, particularly in London, where the cost of living is high and there is popular distrust of newspapers animated by Britain's infamous tabloid press.[9]

It is not only the presence of juries that creates concern with the law of defamation in England. Two additional aspects of English libel law create substantial incentive for plaintiffs. First, consistent with the doctrine that "whenever a man publishes he publishes at his peril,"[10] English law of defamation is based on the strict liability rule similar to what existed in the United States prior to the U.S. Supreme Court's 1964 decision in *New York Times v. Sullivan.*[11] A defendant in an English libel case has available to him three defenses: truth, fair comment and criticism, and the privilege of providing a fair report.[12] These are limited defenses, however, and the plaintiff has the benefit of allocating of the burden of proof. Thus, the mere filing of a libel action results in a presumption of falsity of the defendant's statements, placing the burden on the defendant to prove the truth of the statement alleged to be defamatory.[13] In addition, under English law, there is also a presumption of damages in libel cases, and plaintiffs do not have to produce evidence of actual damages

---

9 Douglas W. Vick and Linda Macpherson, *Anglicizing Defamation Law in the European Union*, 36 Va. J. Int'l L. 933, 934–35 (1996) *quoting* Geoffrey Robertson and Andrew Nicol, Media Law 38 (3d ed. 1992).

10 Lord Mansfield in The King v. Woodfall, [1774] Lofft 776, 781, 98 Eng. Rep. 914, 916, *quoted in* Peck v. Tribune Co., 214 U.S. 185, 189 (1909), *as* "whatever a man publishes he publishes at his peril.".

11 376 U.S. 254 (1964). For a comparison of U.S. and English law on these matters, *see* Kyu Ho Youm, *The Interaction Between American and Foreign Libel Law: US Courts Refuse to Enforce English Libel Judgments*, 49 Int'l & Comp. L. Q. 131 (2000).

12 *See* Youm, *supra* note 11, at 135–37.

13 Morgan v. Odhams Press Ltd., [1971] All E.R. 1156, 1170 (opinion of Lord Morris of Borth-Y-Guest) (jury could find for the plaintiff in defamation action if "some readers (knowing certain circumstances) would reasonably understand that the article referred to the plaintiff"); Hough v. London Express Newspaper, [1940] 3 All E.R. 31, 35 (Goddard, L.J.) (C.A.) ("In the case of words defamatory in their ordinary sense, the plaintiff has to prove no more than that they were published. He cannot call witnesses to prove what they understood by the words. Nor will it avail the defendant to call any number of witnesses to say that they did not believe the imputation. The only question is whether reasonable people might understand them in a defamatory sense."); Youssoupoff v. Metro-Goldwyn-Mayer Pictures, Ltd., 50 T.L.R. 581, 583 (Scrutton, L.J.) (C.A. 1934) ("we follow the law that though the person who writes and publishes the libel may not intend to libel a particular person and, indeed, has never heard of that particular person, the plaintiff, yet, if evidence is produced that reasonable people knowing some of the circumstances, not necessarily all, would take the libel complained of to relate to the plaintiff, an action for libel will lie."); Affidavit of Geoffrey Robertson in Opposition to Plaintiff's Motion to Enforce a Foreign Judgment, at 4, Bachchan v. India Abroad Publications, Inc., 585 N.Y.S.2d 661 (N.Y. Sup. Ct. 1992) ("The burden of proof on the media defendant in libel actions is a good example of how English law makes no presumption in favour of freedom of expression; on the contrary, it presumes that a tort has been committed from the very fact that a criticism has been published, and leaves the publishers to exculpate themselves as best they can."). A defendant who pleads truth but fails to prove it, runs the additional risk of punitive damages. *See, e.g.*, Cassell & Co. Ltd. v. Broome, [1972] A.C. 1027, [1972] 1 All E.R. 801, [1972] 2 W.L.R. 645 (H.L.).

caused by the publication of the questioned article.[14] These rather significant advantages to the plaintiff create obvious incentive to forum-shop for an English court in a libel action.

While some have predicted that developments regarding the European Convention for the Protection of Human Rights and Fundamental Freedoms would result in a change in English libel law,[15] as recently as October, 1999, in *Reynolds v. Times Newspapers Ltd.*,[16] the House of Lords rejected the argument that "political information" should be treated under the "actual malice" rule of the U.S. Supreme Court in *New York Times v. Sullivan.* Thus, at least for the foreseeable future, the problem English libel law creates for transnational litigation is likely to continue.

In the United States, courts have addressed this problem by refusing to recognize English libel judgments. Despite the fact that U.S. courts are perhaps the most liberal in the world in recognizing and enforcing foreign judgments, recent English libel judgments have not fared well on U.S. soil. Two cases provide special perspective on this development. In *Bachchan v. India Abroad Publications Inc.*,[17] an Indian plaintiff sued a New York defendant in the High Court of Justice in London, alleging defamation as a result of a story written in London and wired by the defendant to a news service in India. The resulting publication in Indian and New York newspapers received some distribution in the United Kingdom. After an English jury awarded GBP40,000 in damages, plus attorney fees, the plaintiff sought to enforce the judgment in New York. The New York court noted its concern with the English allocation of the burden of proving truth of the defendant's statement, and concluded that this was inconsistent with U.S. Supreme Court decisions holding such an allocation unconstitutional under the First Amendment of the U.S. Constitution.[18] The court stated:

> The "chilling" effect is no different where liability results from enforcement in the United States of a foreign judgment obtained where the burden of proving truth is upon media defendants. Accordingly, the failure of [the plaintiff] to prove falsity in the High Court of Justice in England makes his judgment unenforceable here.[19]

Relying on the public policy ground for denial of recognition as stated in the New

---

[14] *See* Opinion of Advocate General Darmon, in Shevill v. Press Alliance, Case C-68/93 1995 E.C.R. I-419, ¶ 11 ("[U]nder English law the tort (known as 'libel') is committed where the writing is regarded as defamatory by the jury, without there being any requirement for the person harmed to show actual damage and without any consideration of the question of good faith.").

[15] *See, e.g.*, Youm, *supra* note 11, at 141–43; Bruce W. Sanford, *Libel and Privacy* § 2.3.4, at 48.9 (2d ed. 1999).

[16] [1999] 4 All E.R. 609, 3 W.L.R. 1010 (H.L.).

[17] 585 N.Y.S.2d 661 (N.Y. Sup. Ct. 1992).

[18] *Id.* at 664, *citing* Philadelphia Newspapers v. Hepps, 475 U.S. 767, 777 (1986).

[19] *Id.* at 664.

York version of the Uniform Foreign Money-Judgments Recognition Act (Uniform Act),[20] the court thus refused recognition and enforcement of the English judgment.

The case of *Telnikoff v. Matusevitch*[21] is perhaps even more telling in that the American court (the D.C. Circuit Court of Appeals applying Maryland law) refused recognition and enforcement of an English libel judgment against a defendant who was, at the time of the alleged libel, living in England.[22] Looking to federal and state constitutional principles to determine Maryland public policy, the Maryland Court of Appeals answered the certified question by finding "[t]he principles governing defamation actions under English law ... are so contrary to Maryland defamation law, and to the policy of freedom of the press underlying Maryland law, that Telnikoff's judgment should be denied recognition under principles of comity."[23] It further determined that, under Maryland's version of the Uniform Act, "Telnikoff's English 'cause of action on which the judgment is based is repugnant to the public policy of the State.'"[24] Thus, there is a clear modern position in U.S. courts against the recognition and enforcement of English libel judgments.

The European Court's Solution to the Problem of English Libel Judgments

While the *Shevill* case provides the direct genesis of Article 10(4) of the PDC text, the development of the law regarding tort jurisdiction under the Brussels Convention leading up to this decision is worth explaining. Article 5(3) of the Brussels Convention reads as follows:

> A person domiciled in a Contracting State may, in another Contracting State, be sued:
>
> ...
>
> (3) in matters relating to tort, delict or quasi-delict, in the courts for the place where the harmful event occurred.

In *Bier v. Mines de Potasse d'Alsace* SA,[25] the European Court of Justice interpreted the words "place where the harmful event occurred" to include both the place where the damage occurred and the place of the event that gave rise to the damage, allowing the plaintiff the choice of locations in bringing suit. Thus, where the defendant discharged saline into the Rhine River in France, resulting in injury to

[20] *Id.* at 662.

[21] 347 Md. 561, 702 A.2d 230 (Md. Ct. App. 1997).

[22] The D.C. Circuit Court of Appeals, in Matusevitch v. Telnikoff, 1998 U.S. App. LEXIS 10628 (unpublished opinion of May 5, 1998), refused recognition and enforcement, relying on the answer of the Maryland Court of Appeals to the question of whether recognition would violate Maryland public policy. The principal decision is that of the Maryland Court of Appeals. Telnikoff v. Matusevitch, *supra* note 21.

[23] 702 A.2d at 249.

[24] *Id.*

[25] Case 21/76, 1976 E.C.R. 1735.

the plaintiff's horticultural interests in The Netherlands, the plaintiff could bring suit in either France or The Netherlands under Article 5(3).

The *Bier* case was followed by *Dumez France v. Hessische Landesbank*,[26] in which the European Court faced the question of whether the two-pronged jurisdictional rule of *Bier* applied where the plaintiff bringing suit suffered only indirect injury as a result of the defendant's wrongful conduct. Two French companies set up subsidiaries in Germany to develop certain property, and the German bank providing financing for the project terminated the loan contracts, causing the German subsidiaries to go into receivership. The Court ruled that the French parent corporations could not bring suit against the bank in France as the state where the damage occurred. The *Bier* rule on jurisdiction under Article 5(3) of the Brussels Convention

> cannot be interpreted as permitting a plaintiff pleading damage, which he claims to be the consequence of the harm suffered by other persons who were direct victims of the harmful act to bring proceedings against the perpetrator of that act in the courts of the place in which he himself ascertained the damage to his assets.[27]

Only direct damage to the immediate victim triggers the jurisdictional benefits of the second prong of the *Bier* rule, otherwise allowing suit in the courts of the state in which the damage was suffered.

Such was the status of the jurisprudence on Article 5(3) when the Court of Justice was called upon to decide *Shevill v. Press Alliance*.[28] Fiona Shevill, domiciled in England, was temporarily employed during the summer in Paris. When she and her temporary employer became the subjects of a story published in *France Soir*, which allegedly defamed them, suit was brought in the High Court of England and Wales, based on local distribution of 230 out of some 253,500 copies of the newspaper.[29] Determining that jurisdiction hinged on an interpretation of Article 5(3) of the Brussels Convention, the House of Lords submitted the matter to the European Court of Justice for a preliminary ruling.

> The *Shevill* court began by describing the *Bier/Dumez* rule as a rule of special jurisdiction, the choice of which is a matter for the plaintiff, ... based on the existence of a particularly close connecting factor between the dispute and the courts other than those of the state of the defendant's domicile which justifies the attribution of jurisdiction to those courts for reasons relating to the sound administration of justice and the efficacious conduct of proceedings.[30]

As to the first prong of the *Bier* rule, the Court stated that "the place of the event giving rise to the damage ... can only be the place where the publisher of the

---

[26] Case C-220/88, 1990 E.C.R. I-49.

[27] *Id.* at I-81.

[28] Case C-68/93, 1995 E.C.R. I-415.

[29] *Id.* at I-455, ¶ 9.

[30] *Id.* at I-459, ¶ 19.

newspaper in question is established, since that is the place where the harmful event originated."[31] As to the second prong, the Court stated that, in a defamation case, "the injury ... occurs in the places where the publication is distributed, when the victim is known in those places,"[32] and that "the courts of [those states] are territorially the best placed to assess the libel committed in that State and to determine the extent of the corresponding damage."[33]

The Court then turned to concerns about English libel law, noting that "the object of the [Brussels] Convention is not to unify the rules of substantive law and of procedure of the different Contracting States."[34] It went on to discuss English law, stating:

> The fact that under the national law applicable to the main proceedings damage is presumed in libel actions, so that the plaintiff does not have to adduce evidence of the existence and extent of that damage, does not therefore preclude the application of article 5(3) of the Convention in determining which courts have territorial jurisdiction to hear the action for damages for harm caused by an international libel through the press.[35]

The result of this analysis was a gloss on the two-pronged jurisdictional rule of *Bier*, holding that, under Article 5(3):

> the victim of a libel by a newspaper article distributed in several Contracting States may bring an action for damages against the publisher either before the courts of the Contracting State of the place where the publisher of the defamatory publication is established, which have jurisdiction to award damages for all the harm caused by the defamation, or before the courts of each Contracting State in which the publication was distributed and where the victim claims to have suffered injury to his reputation, which have jurisdiction to rule solely in respect of the harm caused in the State of the court seised.[36]

Perhaps the most interesting aspect of the *Shevill* decision is that the European Court, admitting its own concern about the substantive and procedural law of England in defamation cases, although acknowledging that it could not affect that law, the European Court chose to use the law it could "interpret" (the Brussels Convention), first to acknowledge that under its own decisions in *Bier* and *Dumez* the English courts had jurisdiction, but then to place limitations on the damages those courts could award by limiting that "jurisdiction" to consideration of "the harm caused in the state of the court seised." The case thus addressed a problem of the English law of burden of proof (on both liability and damages), saving the other

---

31 *Id.* at I-460–61, ¶ 24.
32 *Id.* at I-461, ¶ 29.
33 *Id.* at I-462, ¶ 31.
34 *Id.* at I-463, ¶ 35.
35 *Id.* at I-464, ¶ 40.
36 *Id.* at I-462, ¶ 33.

states of the European Union from the acknowledged problems of the English rule by the legal fiction of an indirect limitation on jurisdiction. In other words, the English court did have jurisdiction, it just did not have jurisdiction to deal with damages beyond the territory of the United Kingdom. A problem of burden of proof was addressed through a limitation on damages, under the rubric of a limitation on jurisdiction.

The Generalization of the Shevill *Rule in Article 10(4) of the Preliminary Draft Convention Text*

Article 10(4) of the PDC text generalizes the holding in *Shevill* beyond defamation actions (and thus modifies the *Shevill* rule), allowing a court to have jurisdiction under Article 10(1)(b), but limiting that jurisdiction to consideration of the damages caused in the state in which the court sits. To an American observer of the Brussels Convention process, this extension of *Shevill* in a global setting presents at least four concerns:

(1) It addresses a problem in the allocation of the burden of proof and questions of damages through jurisdictional limitations not directly related to the problem,
(2) it generalizes a solution for defamation cases to all tort cases,
(3) it globalizes a rule that no single state or regional legal arrangement has adopted either by statute, code, or treaty (or, for that matter by judicial decision if one considers the general application of the rule beyond defamation cases), and
(4) it adopts this generalized rule without any clear understanding of how it will affect substantive areas of the law other than defamation.

This seems simply too much (with results that are too uncertain) in a global convention intended to move the world forward in the process of transnational litigation. It may be that the only way to deal with the English rule on the relationship between defamation law and freedom of press and speech is to limit the impact of the resulting cases to damages suffered in the United Kingdom. If this is the case, and if it is appropriate to address this concern in a global convention, then it should be done in a provision honestly limiting damages, not in a rule on jurisdiction.

The results of the *Bier-Dumez-Shevill* cases themselves provide reasons against addressing a damages or burden of proof problem with a rule of limited jurisdiction. While the discussion by the Advocates General and the Court in all three of these cases expresses concern over the plaintiff's opportunity to forum shop in a tort case, under the *Shevill* result, forum shopping remains likely. By tying jurisdiction to damages, the local courts will separately determine the *amount* of the damages suffered in each jurisdiction, but the question of how other courts treat the first court's basic decision on liability is left confused. It is not entirely clear whether this part of the original judgment is subject to convention rules on recognition and enforcement. The irony is that, if the first court's liability decision is subject to recognition and enforcement, then the burden of proof problem really has not been cured, since courts in every other contracting state must then simply accept the liability determination and only compute local damages. If, however, other contracting states need not recognize the liability portion of the judgment, but must recognize and enforce the damages portion (which seems to be the result of *Shevill*), then this promotes both the proliferation of litigation, by carving the case into territorial damages components, and the incongruity of deciding the original court had jurisdiction to bind the recognizing court on the issue of damages, but did not have jurisdiction to bind the recognizing court on the issue of liability. It is difficult to find in any legal system, a situation comparable to this, in which a rule provides for the acknowledgment of an obligation to pay damages without recognition of liability. Even if such a rule makes sense, it facilitates the proliferation of inconsistent judgments, allowing courts in each state to provide a different result on the question of liability, but nonetheless requiring them to recognize and enforce judgments on damages from other states based on contrary liability determinations.[37] It certainly does not further the goals of predictability and efficiency.

The PDC text already has a provision designed to deal with the limitation of damages. Article 33 authorizes less than full recognition of damages when they include either non-compensatory damages (punitive and multiple damages), or "grossly excessive" compensatory damages.[38] The real issue in *Shevill* was damages,

---

[37] Advocate General Darmon wrestled valiantly with this problem in his opinion in *Shevill*, but failed to reach a coherent conclusion, despite his apparent syllogistic support of a backdoor limitation on damages through a frontdoor limitation on jurisdiction. Case C-68/93, 1995 E.C.R. I-436 (Opinion of Advocate General Darmon at ¶ 98, *et seq.*). He indicates the difficulty with this effort when he ends this discussion with the rather curious statement that "[t]he jurisdiction of any of the courts seised by reason of the damage suffered is not affected by the risk of conflicting decisions which may result from the multiplicity of courts having jurisdiction." *Id.* at I-439, ¶ 111. Advocate General Léger similarly twists through this problem, again with unconvincing result:

> It is true that the judgments of courts seised in different Contracting States may conflict with one another, since they are governed by different substantive laws. They will not be *irreconcilable*, because they will each relate to *compensation for a distinct head of damage* (that arising in the territory of the Contracting State concerned).

Id. at I-443 (Opinion of Advocate General Léger at ¶ 23) (emphasis in original).

[38] Article 33 of the PDC text reads as follows:

Article 33 – Damages

(1) In so far as a judgment awards non-compensatory, including exemplary or punitive, damages, it shall be recognised at least to the extent that similar or comparable damages could have been awarded in the State addressed.

(2) (a) Where the debtor, after proceedings in which the creditor has the opportunity to be heard, satisfies the court addressed that in the circumstances, including those existing in the State of origin, grossly excessive damages have been awarded, recognition may be limited to a lesser amount.

(b) In no event shall the court addressed recognise the judgment in an amount less than that which could have been awarded in the State addressed in the same circumstances, including not jurisdiction. If the Hague Convention is to deal with that concern, it should do so directly and not through a troublesome rule on jurisdiction. Further, the concern in *Shevill* was with *damages in defamation cases*, and no convincing argument has been made for the extension of any limitation (on damages or on jurisdiction) to other causes of action. Problems in the United States generated by the single publication rule and cases such as *Keeton v. Hustler Magazine, Inc.*,[39] may well lead one to conclude that, in defamation cases, there are circumstances under which it is appropriate to limit damages to those occurring within the state in which the court sits. If that is an appropriate conclusion, and if it is a globally desirable result, then the provisions of a Hague convention should address the matter directly by providing a limitation on such damages.

If the Article 10(4) jurisdictional rule is important to a global convention as a result of the illumination brought to the subject by the *Shevill* case in the European Union context, it would also seem to be important within the European Union to make that rule clear, especially if the intent is to generalize the rule beyond the holding in *Shevill*, which is by its terms limited to a defamation action. Recent detailed discussions concerning the amendment of the Brussels Convention, which now have taken the form of proposed internal European Community legislation,[40] have not resulted in any language that would do this. It is odd that a rule not appropriate for clear statement within the regional organization from which it arose would be considered appropriate for clear statement *and broad generalization* in a global convention.

It seems unwise to adopt in a global convention on jurisdiction and recognition of judgments a general rule that (1) does not deal with jurisdiction so much as with damages, (2) does not exist in the written law of any state or regional organization, and (3) is generalized in a manner that goes beyond the existence of any clear rule of law resulting from judicial opinion anywhere. The uncertainties are simply too great. To the extent that predictability is important to both courts and private parties subject to the Convention's rules, such a provision defeats an important goal of the process.

While Article 10(4) has limited application when one considers the entire Preliminary Draft Convention, its impact can be significant. Moreover, that impact cannot be fully understood in light of its generalization in areas never covered by a similar rule in any existing legal system to date. Thus, whether on a simple first

---

those existing in the State of origin.

(3) In applying paragraph 1 or 2, the court addressed shall take into account whether and to what extent the damages awarded by the court of origin serve to cover costs and expenses relating to the proceedings.

39 465 U.S. 770 (1984).

40 *See, e.g.*, Council of the European Union, Draft Council Regulation (EC) on jurisdiction and the recognition and enforcement of judgments in civil and commercial matters, Doc. No. 5733/00, Justiciv 10 (February 8, 2000).

principles approach or on the basis of the quality of the rule, it is best left out of the Hague Convention.[41]

General Lessons from Article 10(4): The Appropriate Jurisdictional Nexus

A review of Article 10(4) is useful beyond its own terms, as it furnishes insight into a more general concern: the relationship with a court that justifies a jurisdictional rule. Two fundamental approaches to this issue exist, with a combination of those approaches present in the PDC text, as well as in the Brussels Convention. The first approach requires a *connection between the court and the party* over whom jurisdiction is being exercised (the defendant).[42] The second approach requires a *connection between the court and the claim.*[43]

Like the Brussels Convention, the PDC text incorporates both of these approaches to jurisdiction. Articles 3 (the defendant's habitual residence) and 9 (branch, agency or establishment of the defendant) require a relationship between the court and the defendant. Articles 4 (choice of court) and 5 (appearance by the defendant) are also arguably related to the nexus between the court and the defendant, representing the defendant's voluntary acceptance of the jurisdictional authority of the court. Articles 6 (contracts), 7 (consumer contracts), 8 (employment contracts), 10 (torts or delicts), 11 (trusts), and 12 (exclusive jurisdiction) follow the second approach, requiring a nexus between the court and the claim.

---

[41] An additional problem may exist with Article 10(4) as a result of the mixed convention nature of the PDC text. The effect of 10(4) is to provide a required basis of jurisdiction (Article 10(2)) in order to assess damages suffered within the territory of the state, but to leave in the permitted category the ability of the court to exercise "jurisdiction" in order to assess damages suffered elsewhere (Article 10 does not provide rules of prohibition on jurisdiction). This is a concern with a mixed convention structure that does not arise in the exclusive, double convention structure of the Brussels Convention. What then happens to a defendant who appears to contest the case based on the required basis of jurisdiction (with limited damages), but is also faced with the possibility of a permitted jurisdictional basis for damages suffered elsewhere? It appears that there would then be jurisdiction under the permitted basis found in Article 5 of the PDC text (dealing with appearance). This only leads to further problems supporting the deletion of 10(4).

[42] This is the approach found in the general jurisdictional rule of Article 3 of the Brussels Convention (jurisdiction founded on the presence of the defendant, who is domiciled in the forum state). It is also the approach followed in U.S. courts, with the ultimate question governed by the Due Process clauses of the Fifth and Fourteenth Amendments of the U.S. Constitution. *See, e.g.*, Ronald A. Brand, *Due Process, Jurisdiction and a Hague Judgments Convention*, 60 U. Pitt. L. Rev. 661 (1999). Analysis of "in personam" jurisdiction in U.S. courts generally involves a two-step process. The first step is the application of the state long-arm statute, to determine if the necessary statutory jurisdiction exists. The second step is the constitutional analysis by which it is determined whether the exercise of statutory jurisdiction is within the limits of the Due Process Clause. While some state long-arm statutes may have language similar to that of some of the special jurisdiction provisions of the Brussels Convention (providing reference to the cause of action), it ultimately is the due process analysis that is determinative. *See id.* at 669–71.

[43] This is the approach followed in most of the special jurisdictional rules of the Brussels Convention found in Articles 5–16.

The connection between the court and the defendant is the preferred nexus in both the PDC text and the Brussels Convention, as well as the focus of U.S. jurisdictional jurisprudence. Article 3 of the PDC text provides for jurisdiction in the courts of the state in which the defendant is habitually resident. Likewise, Article 2 of the Brussels Convention provides for jurisdiction in the courts of the state of the defendant's domicile. In the Brussels context, Article 2 jurisdiction is referred to as the general rule of jurisdiction, with other rules (including the tort provision of Article 5(3)) referred to as special rules of jurisdiction.

> Pursuant to Article 2 of the Convention, persons domiciled in a Contracting State are, subject to the provisions of the Convention, 'whatever their nationality, to be sued in the courts of that State'. Section 2 of Title II of the Convention, however, provides for 'special jurisdictions', by virtue of which a defendant domiciled in a Contracting State may be sued in another Contracting State. ...[44]
>
> The principle laid down in the Convention is that jurisdiction is vested in the courts of the State of the defendant's domicile and that the jurisdiction provided for in [the "special jurisdiction" articles are] exception[s] to that principle.[45]
>
> [T]he 'special jurisdictions' enumerated in Articles 5 and 6 of the Convention constitute derogations from the principle that jurisdiction is vested in the courts of the State where the defendant is domiciled and as such must be interpreted restrictively.[46]

Thus, in *Kalfelis v. Schröder*,[47] the European Court held that, in an action in both tort (Article 5(3)), and contract (Article 5(1)) cases, "a court which has jurisdiction under Article 5(3) over an action in so far as it is based on tort or delict does not have jurisdiction over that action in so far as it is not so based."[48] The existence of tort jurisdiction in the German courts over a Luxembourg defendant did not bring with it the existence of contract jurisdiction over the same defendant resulting from the same set of facts.

The restrictive interpretation of the Brussels Convention special jurisdiction provisions was also a part of the decision in the *Shevill* case, when the Court stated that the Article 5(3) tort rule of jurisdiction, as interpreted in *Bier*, to provide the plaintiff with a two-pronged choice.

> is based on the existence of a particularly close connecting factor between the dispute and the courts other than those of the State of the defendant's domicile, which justifies the attribution of jurisdiction to those courts for reasons relating

44 Case 189/87, Kalfelis v. Schröder, 1988 E.C.R. 5565, 5583, ¶ 7.

45 *Id.* at 5583, ¶ 8.

46 *Id.* at 5585, ¶ 19.

47 *Id.*

48 *Id.*

> to the sound administration of justice and the efficacious conduct of the proceedings.[49]

Thus, the Court emphasized the court/claim nexus that is the foundation of the special jurisdiction rules of the Brussels Convention.

The Brussels Convention clearly establish three rules of interpretation:

(a) Article 2 jurisdiction is more general than the rules of special jurisdiction;
(b) the special jurisdiction rules (Articles 5–16) are to be narrowly interpreted; and
(c) the rules of special jurisdiction are based on a "close connecting factor between the dispute and the courts."

These rules generate several observations about a convention that mixes jurisdictional rules based on different relationships to the court. First, it is instructive that the general rule of jurisdiction focuses on the court/defendant nexus. However, the fact that so many problems have arisen from the court/claim nexus explains why there underlies the subsidiary special rules of jurisdiction. The *Bier-Dumez-Shevill* line of cases indicates the difficulties the European Court has had with the interpretation of the Article 5(3) rule providing jurisdiction in the "place where the harmful event occurred." Even more difficult problems have resulted from the court/claim nexus found in the Article 5(1) Brussels Convention rule, which states that jurisdiction in a contract case lies in the courts of the "place of performance of the obligation in question."[50] The result of the expressed preference for jurisdictional rules that focus on the court/defendant nexus, and the myriad of problems encountered in applying rules focused on a court/claim nexus, would seem to lead to an even stronger preference for a Hague convention focused on the court/defendant nexus approach to jurisdiction.

Two other results of the European Court's jurisprudence under Article 5(3) add to the problems created by a focus on a court/claim connection. The first is "the hostility of the Convention towards the attribution of jurisdiction to the courts of

---

49 Shevill, 1995 E.C.R. at I-459, ¶ 19.

50 *See, e.g.*, Case C-420/97, Leathertex Divisione Sintetici SpA v. Bodetex BVBA, 1999 E.C.R. I-6747, at ¶ 40 ("the same court does not ... have jurisdiction to hear the whole of an action founded on two obligations of equal rank arising from the same contract when, according to the conflict rules of the State where that court is situated, one of those obligations is to be performed in that State and the other in another Contracting State"); Case 266/85, Shenavai v. Kreischer, 1987 E.C.R. 239 ("the obligation to be taken into consideration in a dispute concerning proceedings for the recovery of fees commenced by an architect commissioned to draw up plans for the building of houses is the contractual obligation which forms the actual basis of legal proceedings"); Case 133/81, Ivenel v. Schwab, 1982 E.C.R. 1891 (in an employment contract, the obligation to be taken into consideration is that which characterized the contract and was normally the obligation to carry out work); Case 13/76, De Bloos v. Bouyer, 1976 E.C.R. 1497 (the important obligation was the obligation on which the plaintiff's action was based); and Case 12/76, Tessili v. Dunlop, 1976 E.C.R. 1473 (the location of the place of performance of a contract is to be determined pursuant to the law governing the obligation at issue).

the plaintiff's domicile."[51] The second is the assumption that the "scheme and objectives of the Convention"[52] (including both the structure of Article 2 jurisdiction in the courts of the state of the defendant's domicile and the special jurisdiction rules based on a court/claim nexus) result in a presumption against a proliferation of forums.[53]

In the *Dumez* case, the European Court acknowledged concerns with rules that lead to jurisdiction in the plaintiff's home state:

> [T]he hostility of the Convention towards the attribution of jurisdiction to the courts of the plaintiff's domicile was demonstrated by the fact that the second paragraph of article 3 precluded the application of national provisions attributing jurisdiction to such courts for proceedings against defendants domiciled in the territory of a Contracting State.[54]

This hostility to the forum actoris often goes so far as to omit any discussion of real fairness to the defendant, or predictability in allowing parties to plan for potential judicial proceedings. Of course, jurisdiction based *only* on the plaintiff's domicile (or habitual residence), is undesirable. Under *Bier*, however, if the place where the harm occurs (the place where the damage arises) happens to be the plaintiff's home jurisdiction, that does not mean jurisdiction there is bad, any more than it is bad (or good) if it is also the defendant's home jurisdiction. The real question is what makes it bad or good. If the jurisdiction in the courts of the state where the damage arises is good when that state is not the plaintiff's domicile (or habitual residence), it should be no less good when that state *is* the plaintiff's domicile. Otherwise, the connection has no legitimacy of its own. Thus, for an outsider, it seems that either Article 5(3) of the Brussels Convention is a good rule, or it is a bad rule. The fact that it may lead to the forum actoris should not of itself affect this determination. Certainly, in an action brought by multiple plaintiffs at the defendant's domicile under Article 2 of the Brussels Convention, jurisdiction is no less good if the defendant's domicile is also the domicile of one or more of the plaintiffs. Neither should it be a negative factor if one of the rules of special jurisdiction leads to jurisdiction in the plaintiff's domicile or habitual residence, *if the special jurisdiction rule has underlying integrity of its own.* This seems to demonstrate once again the European Court's own recognition of the undesirability of court/claim connectors that have little to do with whether a court can fairly exercise authority *over a specific person.*

---

51 *Dumez*, 1990 E.C.R. at I-79, ¶ 16.

52 Kalfelis v. Schröder, 1988 E.C.R. at 5585, ¶ 16.

53 "[T]he Convention provides a collection of rules which are designed *inter alia* to avoid the occurrence, in civil and commercial matters, of concurrent litigation in two or more Member States and which, in the interests of legal certainty and for the benefit of the parties, confer jurisdiction upon the national court territorially best qualified to determine a dispute." Case 38/81, Effer SpA v. Kantner, 1982 E.C.R. 825, 834, ¶ 6.

54 *Dumez*, 1990 E.C.R. I-79, ¶ 16.

In *Dumez*, the Court also stated "it is necessary to avoid the multiplication of courts of competent jurisdiction which would heighten the risk of irreconcilable decisions."[55] While a convention concerned with recognition of judgments should help avoid irreconcilable decisions, expressions of concern over a proliferation of fora ignore the fact that avoiding concurrent litigation does not require avoiding concurrent jurisdiction. The basic premise should be that any proliferation of available fora is a direct result of the conduct of the defendant, not the result of arbitrary factors by which courts may manipulate the connection between the claim and the court. If convention rules are built on this premise, then parties involved in global commercial relationships will be able to predict the likelihood of being sued in the courts of various states as a result of their own decisions to participate in commerce in a given state. The rules of both the Brussels Convention and the PDC text that allow such predictability are those that create jurisdiction based on a connection between the defendant and the court.

For a U.S. observer, cases under the Brussels Convention provide strong support for a principal focus on jurisdictional rules based on the nexus between the court and the defendant. In *Marinari v. Lloyds Bank*,[56] the European Court dealt with the tension between Article 2 of the Brussels Convention and the special jurisdiction rules (specifically Article 5(3)) when it stated

> The choice thus available to the plaintiff cannot however be extended beyond the particular circumstances which justify it. Such extension would negate the general principle laid down in the first paragraph of Article 2 of the Convention that the courts of the Contracting State where the defendant is domiciled are to have jurisdiction.[57]

This type of statement begs application of the "so what?" test. Why is Article 2 so important while other special jurisdiction articles are less important? I would submit this is primarily because Article 2 is based on the court/defendant nexus that is, and should be, the principal focus of the jurisdictional inquiry. If we are determining when a court should have authority to dictate the conduct of a person, then we must ask, what it is that justifies the exercise of *that authority* over *that person.* Rules that answer this question by reification of the place of performance of a contract (by which party?) or the place of injury in tort (notably to the plaintiff – the party to whom the European Court wants to avoid giving too much choice), work to remove the analysis from a focus on the person over whom authority is being exercised. The Court of Justice thus seems correct in moving its jurisprudence in a direction that reduces the importance of the Brussels Convention's special jurisdiction rules. We should learn from this experience and should avoid providing a foundation for similar jurisprudential roller coasters in a global convention that will not have

---

55 *Dumez*, 1990 E.C.R. at I-80, ¶ 18.

56 Case C-364/93, 1995 E.C.R. 2719.

57 *Id.* at I-2739, ¶ 13.

a single source of authoritative interpretation, and would thus provide even less predictability if it contained such troublesome heads of jurisdiction.

It may be that the fundamental jurisdictional rules of every state except the United States are based on a court/claim nexus, and, thus, that the analysis set forth above can be characterized as too parochial to be of real value. I hope this is not the case. It does seem, however, that rules tying jurisdiction to the place where some "event" or element of "performance" occurs rather than to the presence or conduct of the party over whom jurisdiction is asserted, are destined to produce rather arbitrary debates.[58] In a convention designed to deal with the future (including electronic commerce), and not just the past, tying jurisdictional rules to the "place" where something "happens" seems an unwise choice. The reification of electronic and other commercial events as "things" that "occur" in physical space creates a system in which we rely on combinations of legal fictions that may no longer have conceptual significance.[59] The result seems too often to avoid any discussion of *the question of whether it is reasonable for a court to exercise authority over a specific person.*[60] It seems that a global convention should address this question directly, and that the only way to do so is to deal with the only nexus existing in the question: the relationship between the court and the person over whom judicial authority is to be exercised.

Conclusions Regarding Article 10(4)

If we are to learn from this tension between the general and special jurisdiction rules of the Brussels Convention, it seems important to draft the Hague Convention with a focus on the preferred rules of the Brussels Convention, and at the same time to avoid the troublesome special jurisdiction rules that are both less favored and more restricted in their application. In other words, we should focus on rules based on the connection between the court and the defendant, and avoid wherever possible rules based *only* on the connection between the court and the claim.

In sum, Article 10(4) of the Preliminary Draft text of the Hague Convention provides both an example of a specific provision that goes farther than is wise in a

---

58 For a thorough discussion of this element, in the context of indirect harm under Article 5(3) of the Brussels Convention, *see* the comparison of member state approaches catalogued in the Opinion of Advocate General Darmon in *Dumez*, 1990 E.C.R. I-65 through I-71, ¶¶ 19–46.

59 This is demonstrated in the U.S. by the cases under the Foreign Sovereign Immunities Act dealing with the "location" of a debt. *See, e.g.*, Republic of Argentina v. Weltover, Inc., 504 U.S. 607, 619 (1992) ("because New York was ... the place of performance for Argentina's ultimate contractual obligations, the rescheduling of those obligations necessarily had a 'direct effect' in the United States," removing the immunity of Argentina from jurisdiction in U.S. courts).

60 *See, e.g.*, the distinction in *Dumez* between Advocate General Darmon's opinion that indirect damage is included under the two-prong test of *Bier*, but is suffered where the direct damage occurs, and the Courts opinion that the location of indirect damage (assumed to be at the domicile of the plaintiff) is not encompassed in the *Bier* second prong. Case C-220/88, 1990 E.C.R. I-49 (opinion of Advocate General Darmon at I-63, *et seq.* and Judgment at I-78 *et seq.*).

global convention and a demonstration of the general problem with jurisdictional rules that focus on the relationship between the court and the claim. The global preference (including that of the Brussels and Lugano Conventions) for jurisdiction based on a connection between the court and the defendant, as well as the myriad of problems the European Court of Justice has experienced with jurisdiction based on a court/claim nexus, supports a Hague convention with jurisdictional rules grounded in the court/defendant nexus. The following section of this article provides a restructuring of the convention text designed to take account of these problems.

Responding to the Problems: A Revised Convention Text

Problems and Goals

The problems of the PDC text noted above can be summarized as follows:

(1) The structure of the PDC text does not allow for a clear understanding of the categories of jurisdiction and how they affect the rules regarding recognition and enforcement, thus creating significant risk of inconsistent interpretation.
(2) The PDC text goes too far by providing rules that many states will likely find untenable and an impediment to ratification.
(3) Many jurisdictional provisions of the PDC text focus on the relationship between the court and the claim rather than on the relationship between the court and the party over whom the court's authority is being exercised.[61]

While the PDC text cannot be adopted as a global treaty, or even easily "tweaked" into a globally acceptable text, the time and effort spent on its creation should not be wasted. Many of the provisions of the PDC text can be used to construct a convention that is acceptable to a significant number and variety of states. The problems with the current text generate corresponding guidelines for accomplishing this goal:

(1) The structure of the Convention must make clear its purpose, organization, and application, even to the uninitiated reader, as well as its differences from the Brussels Convention.
(2) The Convention provisions must go far enough to provide a substantial improvement over the status quo, but not so far as to include provisions that provide substantial reason for significant states to oppose ratification in significant states; it must focus on first principles.

[61] It may be that this problem is better stated as too many heads of jurisdiction that are without common support in the member state legal systems. If we then look to the core that commands widespread acceptance, however, we are left with a limited class of defendant-related bases of jurisdiction. Thus, either way, the result seems to be the same.

(3) The provisions on jurisdiction must focus on whether a court in a given state may properly exercise authority over *parties* to the dispute before it.

Chapter I – Scope

The Convention should, of course, begin with provisions defining its scope. Articles 1 and 2 of the current draft provide the relevant focus for these provisions, though they have been the targets of significant criticism. Most of the criticism here concerns the definition of the exclusions from scope contained in Article 1. It is not this paper's purpose to deal with all criticisms of Article 1. Indeed, some of them may be resolved through future uniform global interpretation and application of the Convention. Terms such as "maritime," "maintenance," "succession," and "insolvency," may well have different scope in different legal systems. Any attempt to provide detailed definitions of each such term in the Convention itself may lead only to frustration. Some risk of non-uniform interpretation may be necessary here. Similar general categories of exclusion from scope exist in the Brussels and Lugano Conventions. Whether their use in a global convention will create problems not encountered in a regional convention is uncertain.

Article 2 is generally acceptable for a global convention in defining when the Convention is to be applied in terms of the parties. As currently drafted, however, and as the following discussion will demonstrate, Article 2(1) contains unnecessary provisions, since they apply to other articles not necessary to a first principles approach to the Convention. As indicated below, deletion of articles on exclusive jurisdiction, lis pendens, and forum non conveniens will remove the need for subparagraphs (1)(b) and (c) of Article 2. The other change to Article 2 is a simple reversal of paragraphs (1) and (2) to reflect the restructuring of the Convention suggested below. Thus, the following demonstrates the restructured Article 2:

Article 2 – Territorial Scope

(1) The provisions of Chapter II (recognition) apply to the recognition and enforcement in a Contracting State of a judgment rendered in another Contracting State.

(2) The provisions of Chapter III (jurisdiction) shall apply in the courts of a Contracting State unless all the parties are habitually resident in that State. However, even if all the parties are habitually resident in that State, Article [jurisdiction based on choice of court] shall apply if they have agreed that a court or courts of another Contracting State have jurisdiction to determine the dispute.

Chapter II – Recognition and Enforcement of Judgments

Having established the above-stated guidelines, a revised text can next include rules on recognition and enforcement of foreign judgments. While this runs counter to the structure of the Brussels Convention and the PDC text, it is logical to begin the Convention with the provisions on recognition and enforcement. As noted above, part of this logic lies in constructing a convention that will both be understood by the uninitiated reader and not be inappropriately confused with the Brussels Convention.

A basic assumption of the PDC text, which is that recognition and enforcement will depend largely on the jurisdictional basis exercised by the originating court, is appropriate, and should be retained in a restructured convention. The further assumption that it is appropriate to consider all bases of jurisdiction falling into three categories as both appropriate and useful. Thus, the recognition and enforcement provisions should (1) provide that judgments based on jurisdictional bases acceptable to all contracting states ("required bases") receive a presumption of recognition, (2) provide that judgments based on jurisdictional bases considered to be inappropriate by all contracting states ("prohibited bases") should receive a presumption of non-recognition, and (3) provide that judgments based on jurisdictional bases for which there is no consensus on their acceptability ("permitted bases") should be subject to neither a presumption of recognition nor a presumption of non-recognition. The existence of three categories of jurisdictional bases is the source of coordination with the jurisdictional provisions of the Convention, and should be made clear in the final text. Thus, reference to "required," "prohibited," and "permitted" bases of jurisdiction should be explicit in the convention text. This arguably is implied in the PDC text in Articles 24 through 26, but without language that helps the uninitiated reader understand the relationships involved. The following is a reconstruction of Articles 24–26 that both moves these provisions to the beginning of the convention text and provides clear categorization in order to make the text more readable:

Article 3 – Judgments based on required bases of jurisdiction to be recognised and enforced

(1) A judgment based on a ground of jurisdiction provided for in Articles 16 to 23, or which is consistent with any such ground, shall be recognised and enforced under this Chapter.

(2) In order to be recognised, a judgment referred to in paragraph 1 must have the effect of res judicata in the State of origin.

(3) In order to be enforceable, a judgment referred to in paragraph 1 must be enforceable in the State of origin.

(4) Recognition or enforcement may be postponed if the judgment is the subject of review in the State of origin or if the time limit for seeking a review has not expired.

Article 4 – Judgments based on prohibited bases of jurisdiction not to be recognised or enforced

A judgment based on a ground of jurisdiction which is prohibited by this Convention shall not be recognised or enforced.

Article 5 – Judgments based on permitted bases of jurisdiction to be subject to national law rules on recognition and enforcement

A judgment based on a ground of jurisdiction which is neither required nor prohibited by this Convention shall be subject to the rules of recognition and enforcement provided under the national law of the Contracting State in which it is presented for recognition and enforcement, without regard to the rules of this Convention.

Once the basic recognition provisions are set, the next question is what further provisions are necessary to support these articles. Again, the PDC text is helpful in providing Articles 23, 27–32, and 34–36. These provisions can be incorporated with little change to the PDC text, thus providing guidance on the definition of a "judgment;" a rule on the extent to which a recognizing court may "verify" the basis of jurisdiction in the originating court; grounds for refusal of recognition; a list of the documents to be produced by the party seeking recognition; basic rules on procedure, costs, and legal aid; and rules on severability, authentic instruments, and settlements. This would complete the Convention's basic chapter on recognition and enforcement of foreign judgments. It would also set up the Chapter III provisions on jurisdiction by making clear that the rules on jurisdiction are determined, in large part (if not entirely), by the extent to which there is agreement on the adequacy of the basis of jurisdiction to support a judgment.

As thus structured, Chapter II of the Convention would satisfy the first and second goals set forth above. It would begin with three articles that illuminate the basic structure and purpose of the Convention, thus facilitating a better understanding of the Convention by its readers, and ultimately making it more likely that the Convention would be properly interpreted and applied. It would also focus on first principles, emphasizing the basic purpose of the Convention (facilitation of the free movement of judgments) and the manner in which that purpose is to be realized, without adding extraneous detail.

Chapter III – Jurisdiction

Once the basic provisions on recognition and enforcement are provided in Chapter II, the provisions on jurisdiction may be provided in Chapter III. This is the part of the Convention in which the most opportunity exists for consideration of alternative approaches. The jurisdiction chapter of the PDC text begins with what has been referred to as the general jurisdiction rule, which states that a defendant may be sued in the courts of a contracting state in which the defendant has habitual residence. This article guarantees that every defendant may be sued in at least one state (assuming all problems with the interpretation of habitual residence are resolved). Experience with the Brussels Convention, however, demonstrates an alternative organizational scheme that provides better guidance to convention users. The general "suit at the defendant's domicile" rule of the Brussels Convention is sometimes misleading in that other jurisdictional rules actually preempt jurisdiction at the defendant's domicile. Provisions on exclusive jurisdiction, protective jurisdiction for certain types of parties (consumers and insureds), and preference to choice-of-court clauses, all prevail over the general rule of suit at the defendant's domicile in the Brussels system. Thus, a structure based on priority of application of jurisdictional rules presents itself as a logical alternative that provides additional guidance to the Convention user.

Assuming such a structure has value, it makes sense to begin Chapter III with the choice of court provision found in Article 4 of the PDC text. By placing this article at the beginning of Chapter III, the reader will have a clearer sense of the priority of provisions within the chapter on jurisdictional rules. This assumes that, unlike the Brussels and Lugano Conventions, there will be no provisions on exclusive or protective jurisdiction, matters addressed in further detail below.

The second priority rule in a restructured convention would be that a court has jurisdiction over a defendant who appears without contesting jurisdiction. Thus, the current Article 5 of the PDC text would become Article 17 of the restructured text. In addition, as noted above and discussed below, since no provisions on exclusive jurisdiction will be necessary, reference to such provisions may be eliminated from this article. Otherwise, the language of PDC text Article 5 may be retained.

In a restructured convention, choice-of-court and defendant's appearance without contesting jurisdiction would be the only rules having priority over the general rule of jurisdiction at the defendant's habitual residence. Thus, the general rule of suit at the habitual residence (found in Article 3 of the PDC text) would logically follow as Article 18 of the restructured text. This article has been criticized as providing a term "habitual residence" that is fundamental to the application of the Convention, but at the same time is nowhere defined in the Convention. This is a legitimate criticism, and should be addressed before a final text is reached. Habitual residence is a preferable focus over the Brussels Convention use of the defendant's domicile for two reasons: first, it is the term traditionally used in Hague Conference texts; moreover, it is a fact-based concept, whereas domicile is a law-based concept. Thus, it is less likely that national legislation could be used to redefine the term for domestic courts and thereby frustrate the hope of uniform interpretation.

While it may not be possible to provide a fail-safe definition of habitual residence in the Convention, it is possible to provide greater guidance than that of the current language of Article 3 of the PDC text. Thus, a second paragraph may be added to provide guidance in the application of the term to natural persons. This can be done by providing a presumption that any person present in a state for three months (or other appropriate period of time) who cannot clearly demonstrate the intent that such stay be temporary, is habitually resident in that state. The burden to disprove habitual residency would then be on a natural person present in a state for the stated time, thus creating a guiding presumption, with a clear allocation of the burden of proof on the issue. A perfect rule would make clear that each person always has a habitual residence, and would also deal with the possibility of multiple habitual residences, but that may not be possible in the Convention at this time, and is not necessary to a first principles approach. The following is suggested language for the restructured habitual residence rule, to be placed in Article 18 of the restructured text:

Article 18 – Jurisdiction based on defendant's habitual residence

(1) Subject to the provisions of the Convention, a defendant may be sued in the courts of the State where that defendant is habitually resident.

(2) For purposes of this Convention, a natural person shall be presumed to be habitually resident in a State in which he has been physically and continuously present for at least three months, unless he shall demonstrate the existence of another habitual residence and the intention not to remain.

(3) For the purposes of the Convention, an entity or person other than a natural person shall be considered to be habitually resident in the State –

(a) where it has its statutory seat,

(b) under whose law it was incorporated or formed,

(c) where it has its central administration, or

(d) where it has its principal place of business.

The next article of the PDC text is Article 6, providing rules for jurisdiction in contract cases. Given the guidelines set forth above for a restructured text, this article is not necessary for a number of reasons. First, its absence does no harm to the status quo and detracts little from the proposed treaty. Unlike tort cases, contract cases begin with a pre-existing relationship. Parties to international contracts have the opportunity, and often exercise it, to include either a choice-of-court or other dispute resolution forum in the contract. If they choose a court, then jurisdiction has been established under Article 16 in a manner that takes priority over any other contract jurisdiction rule. If the parties choose arbitration as the forum for dispute settlement, then under Article 1, they have already placed themselves outside the scope of the Convention. Further, Article 6 of the PDC text does not deal with all contract disputes and is limited to cases of partial or full performance, providing no rule for non-performance cases. Even then, the rule is arbitrarily based on place of performance concepts that have proved problematic in both the application of the Brussels Convention and in similar application in conflict of laws problems. Other provisions for jurisdiction in contract cases exist in most national laws, and those rules remain available if necessary. Since the restructured convention makes clear in Article 5 that the Convention does not "taint" such permitted jurisdictional bases, no harm is done in omitting a contract jurisdiction provision when no satisfactory language exists to improve on the status quo. The absence of such a provision is also consistent with the guideline requiring a jurisdictional focus on the relationship between the state in which the court is located and the person over whom judicial authority is being exercised. Article 6 of the PDC text fails entirely to focus on this relationship.

The next two articles of the PDC text, Articles 7 and 8, provide "protective" jurisdictional rules designed to give certain benefits to categories of parties considered to be in need of special protection. Thus, Article 7 allows consumers to sue merchants in contract disputes in the courts of the state of the consumer's habitual residence, and Article 8 allows the same benefits to an employee suing an employer "in matters relating to individual contracts of employment." These rules have created significant problems for specific types of cases. Thus, under a first principles approach, as well as a "do no harm" approach to drafting, they are better left out of a global convention. Given the ability of employers and merchants to frustrate these provisions through the use of arbitration clauses (placing the dispute outside the scope of the Convention entirely), the extent of their protective function is limited at best. Even in the Brussels system, on which these provisions are modeled, recent discussions have demonstrated significant objection to the "no predetermined choice-of-court" rule for consumer contracts, especially that applied to electronic commerce.

The one concept that ties jurisdictional provisions together, and upon which there seems to be near complete agreement, is that it is appropriate to sue a defendant in the courts of the state where the defendant *is*. This is the underlying principle behind the general rule that a defendant may be sued in the courts of the state of the defendant's habitual residence. Article 18 of the restructured convention should retain this rule, as noted above. Closely related to this article is Article 9 of the PDC text, which provides jurisdiction over a party in the courts of a state in which that party has "a branch, agency or any other establishment ... provided that the dispute relates directly to the activity of that branch, agency or establishment."[62] This is a logical extension of the general rule, and acknowledges the importance of a relevant relationship between the state exercising jurisdiction and the party over whom jurisdiction is exercised. Thus, this is an appropriate basic jurisdictional rule for the Hague Convention, and it is logical to place it as Article 19, immediately following the Article 18 habitual residence jurisdiction rule.

Three matters regarding Article 19 are worth mention. First, the concept of "branch, agency or establishment," implies some type of physical presence in a particular place. Comparisons may be made to the "permanent establishment" concept in the Organisation for Economic and Co-operative Development (OECD) and U.S. model bilateral income tax treaties.[63] Thus, for this provision to apply, logically

---

62 The full text of Article 9 of the PDC text reads as follows:

> **Article 9 – Branches [and regular commercial activity]**
>
> A plaintiff may bring an action in the courts of a State in which a branch, agency or any other establishment of the defendant is situated, [or where the defendant has carried on regular commercial activity by other means,] provided that the dispute relates directly to the activity of that branch, agency or establishment [or to that regular commercial activity].

The bracketed language indicates text that is under consideration, but which has not been approved by a majority of the delegations voting.

63 The 1995 OECD Model Double Taxation Convention can be found at <http://www.oecd.org/daf/fa/treaties/articles.pdf> (visited June 12, 2000). The U.S. Model Income Tax Treaty of September 20, 1996 can be found at <http://www.ustreas.gov/taxpolicy/t0txmod1.html> (visited June 12, 2000). Article 5 of both treaties defines "permanent establishment" as "a fixed place of business through which the business of an enterprise is wholly or partly carried on."

there must be some type of office, warehouse, or similar physical facility. Second, the language logically applies to legal persons (corporations) adopting the accepted legal fiction that a corporation *is someplace*, and that such a place can be clearly identified. While Article 18 places a corporation at its place of incorporation, principal place of business, seat, or central place of administration, Article 19 extends the location of the corporation for jurisdictional purposes to additional states in which it has a physical presence.[64] To the extent this article results in a proliferation of available fora, it does so only as a result of specific conduct of the defendant related to each forum state. The defendant has chosen to be in each of these states, and jurisdiction over conduct there is imminently reasonable. Finally, by requiring that "the dispute relates directly to the activity of that branch, agency or establishment," this article not only requires a court/defendant nexus, it combines that requirement with a court/claim nexus, thus adopting both tests and providing consistency with multiple jurisdictional systems.

The bracketed language in Article 9 of the PDC text is the source of significant discussion and dispute.[65] The concept of activity-based jurisdiction is quite common to U.S. lawyers familiar with the "minimum contacts" analysis developed by the Supreme Court under the due process clauses of the Fifth and Fourteenth Amendments.[66] While to the uninitiated this concept seems at times vague, it provides a logical extension of the habitual residence concept in Article 18 and the branch, agency, and establishment concepts in Article 19. Thus, each of these concepts serves to determine where a corporation *is* for purposes of jurisdiction. It is eminently fair to subject to jurisdiction a corporation active in a state and deriving significant profits and other benefits from that activity, especially when the claim relates to that activity. It should not matter whether the activity is local incorporation, operation of a local physical facility, or business regularly conducted by employees or officers present there. The development of transportation, communication, and electronic interchange of data and services requires that concepts of presence for legal persons include more than just place of formal incorporation or permanent physical establishment. As with the "branches" article, the extent to which this article results in jurisdiction in the courts of additional states is a result only of the conscious conduct of the defendant.

The legal fiction of a corporation *being there* is the same, regardless of the form the conduct takes. Thus, it is logical to follow Articles 18 and 19 with an article on commercial presence jurisdiction that acknowledges the range of activities that can subject a legal person to jurisdiction, requiring also that the claim be related to the activity involved. Given the debate over inclusion of such language in the "branches"

---

64 This does not, however, change the concept of legal status, and a subsidiary should continue to be treated as a separate legal entity, except to the extent that its conduct justifies a piercing of the corporate veil or it acts as an agent of the parent corporation such that it effectively is an "agency or establishment" of the parent.

65 *See supra* note 62.

66 *See, e.g.*, Brand, *supra* note 42, at 667–87.

article, it is also logical to place this rule in a separate article, but immediately following the habitual residence rule of Article 18, and the branch, agency and establishment rule of Article 19. The following is suggested as language for this new Article 20:

Article 20 – Jurisdiction based on defendant's regular commercial activity

A plaintiff may bring an action in the courts of a State in which the defendant has conducted regular commercial activity, provided the action is based on a claim that relates to such activity.

Unlike Article 19, this article would not require the defendant to have a permanent or fixed establishment in the forum state. It is important to note, however, that though this new article adds an activity-based form of jurisdiction to the category of required bases, such jurisdiction is limited to cases in which the claim relates to the defendant's activity within the forum state. Thus, it would require both a court/defendant nexus and a court/claim nexus. In the United States, this is consistent with specific jurisdiction concepts applied by the courts,[67] and in no way reaches as far as the more criticized general doing business jurisdiction that becomes an issue in the prohibited bases article.[68] It is extremely important for other states to understand that a Hague convention that both prohibits general doing business jurisdiction *and* fails to have an activity-based jurisdictional basis in the required category of jurisdictional bases will be dead on arrival in the United States. Such a complete absence of compromise on the part of other states would experience no chance of approval in the U.S. Senate.

Given the three guidelines established above, it would be possible to construct the jurisdictional chapter of a convention on Articles 18, 19, and 20 alone. This would authorize jurisdiction over defendants who are present in some form, so long as that presence is sufficient to make the exercise of jurisdiction both reasonable and fair, requiring the addition of a court/claim nexus in every instance except where the defendant is habitually resident in the forum state. It also is possible, however, to include some of the "heads of jurisdiction" provisions of the PDC text without being unfaithful to the stated guidelines. A pared-down PDC Article 10 providing jurisdiction in tort cases may fit a first principles approach without going so far as to harm the status quo. As noted in the earlier discussion, paragraph (1) of this article restates the *Bier* analysis of the Brussels Convention's Article 5(3), allowing jurisdiction either in the state where the act causing the injury occurs or in the state where the injury is felt. The second prong of the *Bier* test is modified in the PDC text by adding a foreseeability requirement. This is not the foreseeability requirement applied

[67] The distinction between general and specific jurisdiction was first suggested in Arthur T. von Mehren and Donald T. Trautman, *Jurisdiction to Adjudicate: A Suggested Analysis*, 79 Harv. L. Rev. 1121, 1144–1164 (1966). It was adopted by the U.S. Supreme Court in *Helicopteros Nacionales de Colombia, S.A. v. Hall*, 466 U.S. 408 (1984).

[68] *See infra* note 70 and accompanying text.

by the U.S. Supreme Court in *World-Wide Volkswagen*[69] and similar cases, but may be capable of modification to fit with that analysis (such a modification is not attempted here).

The more troublesome provisions of Article 10 are paragraphs (2) through (4). Paragraph (2), which denies the application of paragraph (1)(b) to antitrust cases, is simply inappropriate. It extends the text into areas beyond the status quo in a manner aimed at a specific state, and thus creates the kind of roadblock to acceptance of the Convention that should not be included in the basic text. Paragraph (3), which provides for injunctive relief in tort cases, raises concerns beyond a first principles approach that justify its exclusion. The reasons for omitting paragraph (4) are provided in detail in earlier parts of this article, and need not be restated here. The result of this analysis is an Article 21, based on the PDC text Article 10, that could read as follows:

Article 21 – Jurisdiction for torts or delicts

A plaintiff may bring an action in tort or delict in the courts of the State –

(a) in which the act or omission that caused injury occurred, or

(b) in which the injury arose, unless the defendant establishes that the person claimed to be responsible could not reasonably have foreseen that the act or omission could result in an injury of the same nature in that State.

Unlike the contracts provision of Article 6 of the PDC text, there exists some rationale for including a torts provision that can fit with the general guidelines discussed above. Parties to a tort case often have no prior relationship that allows the kind of planning for jurisdiction found in the contract setting. Thus, there is greater benefit to providing a rule of jurisdiction; it is less likely that the parties would choose a forum for dispute resolution on a consensual basis.

Article 11 of the PDC text, which provides a rule for jurisdiction in trust cases, could also be retained with minor modification. Only two words need be changed. First, in paragraph (1) the word "exclusive" should be removed. As with Article 12, below, there exists no need to change the status quo by providing exclusive bases of jurisdiction. Doing so only creates problems, and provides no significant advantages over the transnational status quo sufficient to counterbalance those problems. Further, the concerns behind both the Article 11 trust provision and Article 12 can be met with provisions on recognition and enforcement that will make it generally unwise for any plaintiff to bring suit on the types of claims dealt with in any jurisdiction other than that provided for in these provisions. There is no good reason to provide this additional level of priority within the Convention; the problems it creates detract from any value of an exclusive jurisdiction approach.

The second change to PDC Article 11 would be to insert the word "or" after subparagraph (2)(b), making clear that any of the three alternatives to this paragraph

[69] 444 U.S. 286, 297 (1980).

is available, and preventing any indication of priority among the alternatives. The most appropriate alternative would differ from case-to-case, and thus, all should be equally available. For example, in a case where the trustee has absconded with the trust res to a jurisdiction totally unrelated to the trust purposes (but now the "principal place of administration of the trust"), a frustrated beneficiary should be able to bring the case against the trustee in the state in which "the trust has the closest connection for the purpose of the proceedings." This is the third alternative of Article 10(2), but the one most appropriate to a trust designed to benefit specific individuals all located in that state. Thus modified, PDC text Article 11 can be included as Article 22 of the restructured text.

Likewise, Article 12 of the PDC text can be modified to be Article 23 of the restructured text. The basic modification would be the deletion of the word "exclusive" throughout its provisions (with corresponding elimination of language that is necessary only if the rules create exclusive jurisdiction). There is no clearly demonstrated need to provide exclusive jurisdiction provisions such as these, and discussion in the area of intellectual property rights indicates a myriad of problems with such exclusive jurisdiction. If necessary, a provision can be added in Article 8 authorizing non-recognition of judgments brought on such claims in states other than the Article 24 state (*e.g.*, recognition in state A would not be required of a state B judgment determining title to Blackacre, which is located in state A). In the alternative, it may be that the general public policy ground for non-recognition fulfills this purpose. This is primarily a recognition problem, not a jurisdiction problem, and as such, it would be a waste of time and money for a plaintiff to bring such an action in a state that does not have the authority definitively to determine *and enforce* the type of title being considered in each provision of this article.

Given that the Convention is a mixed convention, with significant permitted-area jurisdiction, the provisions of Article 13 of the PDC text that deal with provisional and protective measures, add little and are not necessary to a first principles approach. Thus, they may be omitted from the restructured text.

Articles 14–16, which deal with multiple-party cases, are inconsistent with the basic guideline calling for a focus on the relationship between the state exercising jurisdiction and the party in question. In addition, they incorporate what generally constitute rules of procedure rather than rules of jurisdiction. Jurisdiction over each party is an important consideration, and is separate from the procedural ability to join multiple parties or claims in a single action. Finally, these articles arguably pull too much out of the permitted category and insert it in the required bases category, all without careful consideration of the results. Thus, again on a first principles rationale, these articles may be omitted from a restructured convention.[70]

---

[70] If these articles were to be retained, they would better be combined into a single article, providing the additional requirement of a connection between the forum state and the defendant. For example:

Article X – Jurisdiction over multiple defendants, third party claims and counterclaims

(1) A plaintiff bringing an action against a defendant in a court of the State in which that defendant is habitually resident may also proceed in that court against other defendants not habitually resident in that State if – (a) the claims against the defendant habitually resident in that State and the other

This brings us to the articles dealing with permitted and prohibited jurisdictional bases. Here, it makes sense to place the prohibited bases provision ahead of the permitted bases provision, to be consistent with the structure of the recognition provisions already established above. Thus, Article 18 of the PDC text (prohibited bases) would become Article 24 of the reconstructed text. This article, however, requires some important adjustments. Paragraph (1) adds nothing to the list of objectionable bases of jurisdiction found in paragraph (2). Despite repeated requests in the negotiations at The Hague, not one delegation has offered an example of a jurisdictional rule that would be covered by paragraph (1) that is not already listed in paragraph (2). Further, the primary result of inclusion of paragraph (1) will be to guarantee lack of uniform interpretation of the Convention. Thus, an originating state is likely to find that the asserted basis of jurisdiction is not within paragraph (2), but rather within the permitted category falling outside the Convention. Upon presentation for recognition, a second state's court could then determine that the originating state's jurisdictional basis falls not within the permitted category, but rather within the rule of paragraph (1) of this article. As such, paragraph (1) would have little purpose other than to facilitate (guarantee?) such non-uniform interpretation. It is simply poor drafting to include such a provision in any convention intended for global acceptance.

Likewise, no delegation in The Hague has identified, in any state, an existing jurisdictional rule falling within subparagraphs 2(i) or (j) of Article 18 of the PDC text. Thus, without such support for their inclusion, they too should be deleted.

Finally, subparagraph (2)(e), aimed at the concept of general doing business jurisdiction in the United States, should be excluded from this article. Having such jurisdictional bases within the permitted category, and thus not subject to the recognition rules of the Convention, simply maintains the status quo of current international jurisdiction rules. It may be that some form of acceptable compromise on language regarding general jurisdiction exists. Professor Linda J. Silberman has suggested a compromise approach:

---

defendants are so closely connected that they should be adjudicated together to avoid a serious risk of inconsistent judgments, and (b) as to each defendant not habitually resident in that State, there is a substantial connection between that State and the dispute involving that defendant and a substantial connection between that State and that defendant.

(2) A court that has jurisdiction to determine a claim under the provisions of the Convention shall also have jurisdiction to determine a claim by a defendant against a third party for indemnity or contribution in respect of the claim against that defendant to the extent that such an action is permitted by national law, provided there is a substantial connection between that State and the dispute involving that third party, and a substantial connection between that State and the third party defendant.

(3) A court that has jurisdiction to determine a claim under the provisions of the Convention shall also have jurisdiction to determine a counterclaim arising out of the transaction or occurrence on which the original claim is based.

(4) Paragraphs 1 and 2 shall not apply to a co-defendant or third party invoking an exclusive choice of court clause agreed with the applicable party and in conformity with Article [choice of court].

> One possible modification of Article 18 that might appeal to both sides in the debate over general jurisdiction would be to thus narrow the area of general doing business jurisdiction on the prohibited list and permit general jurisdiction in those situations where the argument for such jurisdiction is the strongest. Article 18 could be modified to prohibit jurisdiction on the basis of the "carrying on of commercial activity by the defendant when the activity did not give rise to the claim *except where the defendant's activity in the forum is evidence of a substantial presence there, and the plaintiff is habitually resident in the forum state.*"[71]

Any restructured text should retain the paragraph (3) provision of the prohibited bases article, which allows human rights claims brought on otherwise prohibited bases but makes clear that such bases fall in the permitted category.

After inclusion of the prohibited bases list as Article 24 of the restructured text, the PDC text Article 17 may be included to provide the permitted bases jurisdictional rule. With the elimination of former Articles 7 and 8, and the alteration of former Articles 12 and 13 to avoid exclusive jurisdiction, however, the reference to those articles is now unnecessary. Only the choice-of-court priority of Article 16 (PDC text Article 4) requires reference. Thus, the restructured permitted jurisdiction article will be more easily understood by the uninitiated reader of the text and may read as follows:

Article 25 – Permitted grounds of jurisdiction based on national law

> Subject to a valid choice of court clause under Article 16, nothing in this Convention shall prevent the application by Contracting States of rules of jurisdiction under national law that are neither required nor prohibited by this Convention.

Articles 19 (authority of the court seised) and 20 (stay of proceedings in the event of proper notification) may be retained as Articles 26 and 27 of a restructured text, so long as the latter of these articles is clear in both the English and French text that "notification" refers to actual notification (in the English sense) and not to any one state's interpretation of the formalities of service.

The provisions on lis pendens and forum non conveniens in the PDC text (Articles 21 and 22) are provisions unnecessary to a first principles approach to drafting a convention. It may be that they can be molded into an acceptable form, but at this point, their inclusion in a restructured text is not required, and their potential for creating objections weighs in favor of their exclusion. However, it is important to provide in their place, a provision that makes clear the retention of the status quo. The following is suggested as such a provision, to be designated Article 28 in the restructured convention:

---

[71] Linda J. Silberman, *Can the Hague Judgments Project Be Saved?: A Perspective from the United States*, *infra* p. 159.

Article 28 – Declining jurisdiction

(1) Nothing in this Convention shall preclude the operation of any national law under which the courts of a Contracting State decline jurisdiction in favor of another forum that has jurisdiction under its national law and is deemed to be the proper forum for the trial of the action. Neither shall this Convention require the adoption of any such national law by any Contracting State.

(2) Nothing in this Convention shall preclude the operation of any national law under which the courts of a Contracting State may stay or dismiss an action, despite the presence of jurisdiction under this Convention, where a court in another Contracting State also having jurisdiction was first seised of a case involving the same parties and the same cause of action. Neither shall this Convention require the adoption of any such national law by any Contracting State.

Chapter IV – General Provisions

This completes the restructured convention, except for the Chapter IV general provisions that need further work even in the PDC text. Article 33 of the PDC text, which allows a recognizing court to restructure the damages awarded in the originating court, would be excluded from a first principles restructured text. Omitting Article 23, however, would cause obvious objection from non-U.S. delegations, and may make this a necessary provision in arriving at an acceptable text (leaving aside for the moment the problems with U.S. ratification).

CONCLUSION

The full restructured text is provided as an appendix to this paper. Such a text should be consistent with the guidelines requiring that (1) the Convention be structured in a manner that makes clear its purpose, organization, and application, as well as its difference from the Brussels Convention; (2) the Convention provisions go far enough to provide a significant improvement over the status quo, but not so far as to include provisions that provide substantial reason for opposition to ratification; and (3) the provisions on jurisdiction be founded on the preferred jurisdictional nexus between the court and the defendant. Thus, it would represent a legitimate attempt to make the world a better place for transnational litigation through greater likelihood of free movement of judgments, while at the same time clearly channeling jurisdictional practice toward the required bases upon which all contracting states could agree, and away from the prohibited bases all contracting states would agree are exorbitant. It would allow, but not promote, use of jurisdictional bases falling within the permitted category. At the same time, it would leave enough in this third category to make clear that the Convention does not taint these bases simply as a result of their omission from the required bases category.

Appendix

Restructured Convention Text

Chapter I – The Scope of The Convention

Article 1 – Substantive scope

(1) The Convention applies to civil and commercial matters. It shall not extend in particular to revenue, customs or administrative matters.

(2) The Convention does not apply to –

(a) the status and legal capacity of natural persons;

(b) maintenance obligations;

(c) matrimonial property regimes and other rights and obligations arising out of marriage or similar relationships;

(d) wills and succession;

(e) insolvency, composition, or analogous proceedings;

(f) social security;

(g) arbitration and proceedings related thereto;

(h) admiralty or maritime matters.

(3) A dispute is not excluded from the scope of the Convention by the mere fact that a government, a governmental agency, or any other person acting for the State is a party thereto.

(4) Nothing in this Convention affects the privileges and immunities of sovereign States or of entities of sovereign States, or of international organisations.

Article 2 – Territorial scope

(1) The provisions of Chapter II (recognition) apply to the recognition and enforcement in a Contracting State of a judgment rendered in another Contracting State.

(2) The provisions of Chapter III (jurisdiction) shall apply in the courts of a Contracting State unless all the parties are habitually resident in that State. However, even if all the parties are habitually resident in that State, Article 16 shall apply if they have agreed that a court or courts of another Contracting State have jurisdiction to determine the dispute.

Chapter II – Recognition of Foreign Judgments

Article 3 – Judgments based on required bases of jurisdiction to be recognised and enforced

(1) A judgment based on a ground of jurisdiction provided for in Articles 16 to 23, or which is consistent with any such ground, shall be recognised or enforced under this Chapter.

(2) In order to be recognised, a judgment referred to in paragraph 1 must have the effect of res judicata in the State of origin.

(3) In order to be enforceable, a judgment referred to in paragraph 1 must be enforceable in the State of origin.

(4) However, recognition or enforcement may be postponed if the judgment is the

subject of review in the State of origin or if the time limit for seeking a review has not expired.

Article 4 – Judgments based on prohibited bases of jurisdiction not to be recognised or enforced

A judgment based on a ground of jurisdiction which is prohibited by this Convention under Article 26 shall not be recognised or enforced.

Article 5 – Judgments based on permitted bases of jurisdiction to be subject to national law rules on recognition and enforcement

A judgment based on a ground of jurisdiction which is neither required nor prohibited by this Convention shall be subject to the rules of recognition and enforcement provided under the national law of the Contracting State in which it is presented for recognition and enforcement, without regard to the rules of this Convention.

Article 6 – Definition of "judgment"

For the purposes of this Chapter, "judgment" means –

(a) any decision given by a court, whatever it may be called, including a decree or order, as well as the determination of costs or expenses by an officer of the court, provided that it relates to a decision which may be recognised or enforced under the Convention;

(b) decisions ordering provisional or protective measures in accordance with Article 14, paragraph 1.

Article 7 – Verification of jurisdiction

(1) The court addressed shall verify the jurisdiction of the court of origin.

(2) In verifying the jurisdiction of the court of origin, the court addressed shall be bound by the findings of fact on which the court of origin based its jurisdiction, unless the judgment was given by default.

(3) Recognition or enforcement of a judgment may not be refused on the ground that the court addressed considers that the court of origin should have declined jurisdiction in accordance with Article 24.

Article 8 – Grounds for refusal of recognition or enforcement

(1) Recognition or enforcement of a judgment may be refused if –

   (a) proceedings between the same parties and having the same subject matter are pending before a court of the State addressed, if first seised in accordance with Article 21;

   (b) the judgment is inconsistent with a judgment rendered, either in the State addressed or in another State, provided that in the latter case the judgment is capable of being recognised or enforced in the State addressed;

   (c) the judgment results from proceedings incompatible with fundamental principles of procedure of the State addressed, including the right of each party to be heard by an impartial and independent court;

(d) the document which instituted the proceedings or an equivalent document, including the essential elements of the claim, was not notified to the defendant in sufficient time and in such a way as to enable him to arrange for his defence;
(e) the judgment was obtained by fraud in connection with a matter of procedure;
(f) recognition or enforcement would be manifestly incompatible with the public policy of the State addressed.

(2) Without prejudice to such review as is necessary for the purpose of application of the provisions of this Chapter, there shall be no review of the merits of the judgment rendered by the court of origin.

Article 9 – Documents to be produced

(1) The party seeking recognition or applying for enforcement shall produce –
(a) complete and certified copy of the judgment;
(b) if the judgment was rendered by default, the original or a certified copy of a document establishing that the document which instituted the proceedings or an equivalent document was notified to the defaulting party;
(c) all documents required to establish that the judgment is res judicata in the State of origin or, as the case may be, is enforceable in that State;
(d) if the court addressed so requires, a translation of the documents referred to above, made by a person qualified to do so.

(2) No legalisation or similar formality may be required.

(3) If the terms of the judgment do not permit the court addressed to verify whether the conditions of this Chapter have been complied with, that court may require the production of any other necessary documents.

Article 10 – Procedure

The procedure for recognition, declaration of enforceability or registration for enforcement, and the enforcement of the judgment, are governed by the law of the State addressed so far as the Convention does not provide otherwise. The court addressed shall act expeditiously.

Article 11 – Costs of proceedings

No security, bond, or deposit, however described, to guarantee the payment of costs or expenses shall be required by reason only that the applicant is a national of, or has its habitual residence in, another Contracting State.

Article 12 – Legal aid

Natural persons habitually resident in a Contracting State shall be entitled, in proceedings for recognition or enforcement, to legal aid under the same conditions that apply to persons habitually resident in the requested State.

Article 13 – Severability

If the judgment contains elements which are severable, one or more of them may be separately recognised, declared enforceable, registered for enforcement, or enforced.

Article 14 – Authentic instruments

(1) Each Contracting State may declare that it will enforce, subject to reciprocity, authentic instruments formally drawn up or registered and enforceable in another Contracting State.

(2) The authentic instrument must have been authenticated by a public authority or a delegate of a public authority and the authentication must relate to both the signature and the content of the document.

[(3) The provisions concerning recognition and enforcement provided for in this Chapter shall apply as appropriate.]

Article 15 – Settlements

Settlements to which a court has given its authority shall be recognised, declared enforceable, or registered for enforcement in the State addressed under the same conditions as judgments falling within the Convention, so far as those conditions apply to settlements.

Chapter III – Jurisdiction

Article 16 – Jurisdiction based on choice of court

(1) If the parties to an action have agreed that a court or courts of a Contracting State shall have jurisdiction to settle any dispute which has arisen or may arise in connection with a particular legal relationship, that court or those courts shall have jurisdiction, and that jurisdiction shall be exclusive unless the parties have agreed otherwise. Where an agreement having exclusive effect designates a court or courts of a non-Contracting State, courts in Contracting States shall decline jurisdiction or suspend proceedings unless the court or courts chosen have themselves declined jurisdiction.

(2) An agreement within the meaning of paragraph 1 shall be valid as to form, if it was entered into or confirmed –

- (a) in writing;
- (b) by any other means of communication which renders information accessible so as to be usable for subsequent reference;
- (c) in accordance with a usage that is regularly observed by the parties;
- (d) in accordance with a usage of which the parties were or ought to have been aware and that is regularly observed by parties to contracts of the same nature in the particular trade or commerce concerned.

Article 17 – Jurisdiction based on appearance by the defendant

(1) A court has jurisdiction if the defendant proceeds on the merits without contesting jurisdiction.

(2) The defendant has the right to contest jurisdiction at least until the time of the first defence on the merits.

Article 18 – Jurisdiction based on defendant's habitual residence

(1) Subject to the provisions of the Convention, a defendant may be sued in the courts of the State where that defendant is habitually resident.

(2) For purposes of this Convention, a natural person shall be presumed to be habitually resident in a State in which he has been physically and continuously present for at least three months, unless he shall demonstrate the existence of another habitual residence and the intention not to remain.

(3) For the purposes of the Convention, an entity or person other than a natural person shall be considered to be habitually resident in the State –
   (a) where it has its statutory seat,
   (b) under whose law it was incorporated or formed,
   (c) where it has its central administration, or
   (d) where it has its principal place of business.

Article 19 – Jurisdiction based on defendant's branch, agency or establishment

A plaintiff may bring an action in the courts of a State in which a branch, agency or any other establishment of the defendant is situated, provided that the dispute relates directly to the activity of that branch, agency or establishment.

Article 20 – Jurisdiction based on defendant's regular commercial activity

A plaintiff may bring an action in the courts of a State in which the defendant has conducted regular commercial activity, provided the action is based on a claim that relates to such activity.

Article 21 – Jurisdiction for torts or delicts

A plaintiff may bring an action in tort or delict in the courts of the State –
   (a) in which the act or omission that caused injury occurred, or
   (b) in which the injury arose, unless the defendant establishes that the person claimed to be responsible could not reasonably have foreseen that the act or omission could result in an injury of the same nature in that State.

Article 22 – Jurisdiction for trusts

(1) In proceedings concerning the validity, construction, effects, administration or variation of a trust created voluntarily and evidenced in writing, the courts of a Contracting State designated in the trust instrument for this purpose shall have jurisdiction. Where the trust instrument designates a court or courts of a non-Contracting State, courts in Contracting States shall decline jurisdiction or suspend proceedings unless the court or courts chosen have themselves declined jurisdiction.

(2) In the absence of such designation, proceedings may be brought before the courts of a State –
   (a) in which is situated the principal place of administration of the trust;
   (b) whose law is applicable to the trust; or

(c) with which the trust has the closest connection for the purpose of the proceedings.

Article 23 – Special categories of jurisdiction based on national authority over property rights and legal persons

(1) In proceedings that have as their object rights in rem in immovable property or tenancies of immovable property, the courts of the Contracting State in which the property is situated have jurisdiction.

(2) In proceedings that have as their object the validity, nullity, or dissolution of a legal person, or the validity or nullity of the decisions of its organs, the courts of a Contracting State whose law governs the legal person have jurisdiction.

(3) In proceedings that have as their object the validity or nullity of entries in public registers, the courts of the Contracting State in which the register is kept have jurisdiction.

(4) In proceedings that have as their object the registration, validity, [or] nullity[, or revocation or infringement,] of patents, trade marks, designs or other similar rights required to be deposited or registered, the courts of the Contracting State in which the deposit or registration has been applied for, has taken place or, under the terms of an international convention, is deemed to have taken place, have jurisdiction.

Article 24 – Prohibited grounds of jurisdiction

(1) Jurisdiction shall not be exercised by the courts of a Contracting State on the basis solely of one or more of the following –
   (a) the presence or the seizure in that State of property belonging to the defendant, except where the dispute is directly related to that property;
   (b) the nationality of the plaintiff;
   (c) the nationality of the defendant;
   (d) the domicile, habitual or temporary residence, or presence of the plaintiff in that State;
   (e) the service of a writ upon the defendant in that State;
   (f) the unilateral designation of the forum by the plaintiff;
   (g) proceedings in that State for declaration of enforceability or registration or for the enforcement of a judgment, except where the dispute is directly related to such proceedings.

(2) Nothing in this Article shall prevent a court in a Contracting State from exercising jurisdiction under national law in an action [seeking relief] [claiming damages] in respect of conduct which constitutes –

[Variant One:

(a) genocide, a crime against humanity or a war crime[, as defined in the Statute of the International Criminal Court]; or
(b) a serious crime against a natural person under international law; or

(c) a grave violation against a natural person of non-derogable fundamental rights established under international law, such as torture, slavery, forced labour and disappeared persons.

Subparagraphs [(b) and] (c) above apply only if the party seeking relief is exposed to a risk of a denial of justice because proceedings in another State are not possible or cannot reasonably be required.]

[Variant Two:

a serious crime under international law, provided that this State has established its criminal jurisdiction over that crime in accordance with an international treaty to which it is a party and that the claim is for civil compensatory damages for death or serious bodily injury arising from that crime.]

Article 25 – Permitted grounds of jurisdiction based on national law

Subject to a valid choice-of-court clause under Article 16, nothing in this Convention shall prevent the application by Contracting States of rules of jurisdiction under national law that are neither required nor prohibited by this Convention.

Article 26 – Authority of the court seised

Where the defendant does not enter an appearance, the court shall verify whether Article 26 prohibits it from exercising jurisdiction if –

(a) national law so requires; or
(b) the plaintiff so requests; or
[(c) the defendant so requests, even after judgment is entered in accordance with procedures established under national law; or]
[(d) the document which instituted the proceedings or an equivalent document was served on the defendant in another Contracting State.]

or

[(d) it appears from the documents filed by the plaintiff that the defendant's address is in another Contracting State.]

Article 27 – Stay of proceedings in the absence of proper notification

(1) The court shall stay the proceedings so long as it is not established that the document which instituted the proceedings or an equivalent document, including the essential elements of the claim, was notified to the defendant in sufficient time and in such a way as to enable him to arrange for his defence, or that all necessary steps have been taken to that effect.
[(2) Paragraph 1 shall not affect the use of international instruments concerning the service abroad of judicial and extrajudicial documents in civil or commercial matters, in accordance with the law of the forum.]
[(3) Paragraph 1 shall not apply, in case of urgency, to any provisional or protective measures.]

Article 28 – Declining jurisdiction

(1) Nothing in this Convention shall preclude the operation of any national law under which the courts of a Contracting State decline jurisdiction in favor of another forum that has jurisdiction under its national law and is deemed to be the proper forum for the trial of the action. Neither shall this Convention require the adoption of any such national law by any Contracting State.

(2) Nothing in this Convention shall preclude the operation of any national law under which the courts of a Contracting State may stay or dismiss an action, despite the presence of jurisdiction under this Convention, where a court in another Contracting State also having jurisdiction was first seised of a case involving the same parties and the same cause of action. Neither shall this Convention require the adoption of any such national law by any Contracting State.

Chapter IV – General Provisions

Article 29 – Relationship with other conventions

[See annex to PDC text]

Article 30 – Uniform interpretation

(1) In the interpretation of the Convention, regard is to be had to its international character and to the need to promote uniformity in its application.

(2) The courts of each Contracting State shall, when applying and interpreting the Convention, take due account of the case law of other Contracting States.

[Article 31

(1) Each Contracting State shall, at the request of the Secretary General of the Hague Conference on Private International Law, send to the Permanent Bureau at regular intervals copies of any significant decisions taken in applying the Convention and, as appropriate, other relevant information.

(2) The Secretary General of the Hague Conference on Private International Law shall, at regular intervals, convene a Special Commission to review the operation of the Convention.

(3) The Commission may make recommendations on the application or interpretation of the Convention and may propose modifications or revisions of the Convention or the addition of protocols.]

[Article 32

(1) Upon a joint request of the parties to a dispute in which the interpretation of the Convention is at issue, or of a court of a Contracting State, the Permanent Bureau of the Hague Conference on Private International Law shall assist in the establishment of a committee of experts to make recommendations to such parties or such court.

[(2) The Secretary General of the Hague Conference on Private International Law shall, as soon as possible, convene a Special Commission to draw up an optional protocol setting out rules governing the composition and procedures of the committee of experts.]]

Article 33 – Federal clause

Stephen B. Burbank[†]

Jurisdictional Equilibration, the Proposed Hague Convention, and Progress in National Law

INTRODUCTION

Time will tell whether resolution can be achieved regarding the problems that caused the United States to seek to put the proposed Hague Convention on Jurisdiction and Foreign Judgments in Civil and Commercial Matters on a slower track.[1] The fact that the process has been put on a slower track should not be cause for regret in any country desiring a workable international agreement. Like reform of judicial administration in the United States, international law reform is "no sport for the short-winded."[2] When speed is a goal, the result will probably be disappointing. To see the wages of inadequate opportunities for mutual education and understanding, we need only look at the Hague Evidence Convention. It is fitting that, having led the rush on that occasion,[3] the United States has called for the application of brakes on this one.

It may be that, given the incentives of the major players to participate in the negotiations, a resolution satisfactory to the United States is critical to the success of the project as treatymaking. Such a resolution should not be necessary, however, to its success in enhancing knowledge about, and understanding of, current approaches to jurisdiction and the recognition of judgments in other countries, and the needs of the international legal order in the future. Symposia like this one provide opportunities for scholars from countries with different traditions to educate each other and, through their writing, to educate domestic and foreign audiences, including courts, about those approaches and needs.

---

† © Stephen B. Burbank 2000, David Berger Professor for the Administration of Justice, University of Pennsylvania. I have profited immensely in this work from the teaching, scholarship, and generous colleagueship of Professor Arthur T. von Mehren. In addition, I have received helpful comments from Samuel Baumgartner, George Bermann, Paul Carrington, Kevin Clermont, Trevor Hartley, Charles Mooney, Arnaud Nuys, Martin Redish, Linda Silberman, Allan Stein, and participants in a University of Pennsylvania Law School faculty retreat.

1 *See* letter from Jeffrey D. Kovar, Assistant Legal Advisor for Private International Law, United States Department of State, to J.H.A. van Loon, Secretary General, Hague Conference on Private International Law (Feb. 22, 2000) (on file with author) [hereinafter *State Department letter*].

2 Arthur T. Vanderbilt, *Minimum Standards of Judicial Administration* xix (Arthur T. Vanderbilt ed., 1949).

3 *See* Stephen B. Burbank, *The Reluctant Partner: Making Procedural Law for International Civil Litigation*, 57 Law & Contemp. Probs. (No. 3) 103, 131–35 (1994).

J.J. Barceló and K.M. Clermont (eds.), A Global Law of Jurisdiction and Judgments: Lessons from The Hague, 117–157

Those who framed the Brussels Convention[4] realized, as did the framers of the Full Faith and Credit Clause of the United States Constitution,[5] that civil courts can be instruments of economic warfare and, conversely, that shared judgment recognition standards can be powerful facilitators of economic cooperation and integration. From this perspective, the proposed Hague Convention represents an attempt to translate lessons of regional enlightenment to a global audience and, hence, to add to the forces for economic cooperation the contributions of a public private international law. That is a very ambitious task, requiring statesmanship of a high order. Its success will also require a healthy measure of realism.

The proposed Hague Convention proceeds from a platform of recognition practice, set both in the United States and under the Brussels Convention, that does not permit general reexamination of either the choice of law or the adjudication on the merits in the rendering court and that, therefore, invests with great importance the jurisdiction of that court.[6] In such a recognition system, jurisdiction becomes, as Professor Arthur T. von Mehren has termed it, the "hallmark" of the fairness and impartiality of the adjudicative process in the rendering court.[7]

Moreover, to the extent that it follows the Brussels model of a double convention, directly constraining the freedom of contracting state to apply domestic jurisdictional law, the proposed Hague Convention seeks a measure of jurisdictional orthodoxy with effects beyond the international recognition and enforcement of judgments.[8] It is thus no surprise that, the decision having been made to fashion a mixed convention,[9] two of the most difficult and contentious problems remaining in the negoti-

---

4 European Communities, Brussels Convention on Jurisdiction and the Enforcement of Judgments in Civil and Commercial Matters, 1972 O.J. (L 299) 32, *reprinted as amended in* 29 I.L.M. 1413 (1990) [hereinafter *Brussels Convention*]. Unless otherwise noted, references to the Brussels Convention include the related Lugano Convention, 1988 O.J. (L 319) 40.

5 "Full Faith and Credit shall be given in each State to the public Acts, Records, and Judicial Proceedings of every other State. And the Congress may by general Laws prescribe the Manner in which such Acts, Records and Proceedings shall be proved and the Effect thereof." U.S. Const. art. IV, § 1.

6 *See* Hilton v. Guyot, 159 U.S. 113 (1895); Unif. For. Money-Judg. Recognition Acts, §§ 3–4, 13 U.L.A. 265, 268 (1986); Brussels Convention, *supra* note 4, art. 29. *But see id.*, art. 27(4) (limited choice-of-law test for preliminary questions concerning "the status or legal capacity of natural persons, rights in property arising out of a matrimonial relationship, wills or succession"). Of course, both regimes permit a limited public policy defense to recognition. In addition to such a defense, any treaty emerging from the negotiations at The Hague might contain a provision permitting a contracting state to decline to assume the Convention's obligations with respect to other states (i.e., who have not participated in the negotiations) seeking to become parties. *See* Louise Lussier, *A Canadian Perspective*, 24 Brook. J. Int'l L. 31, 64–65 (1998).

7 *See* Arthur T. von Mehren and Donald T. Trautman, *Recognition of Foreign Adjudications: A Survey and a Suggested Approach*, 81 Harv. L. Rev. 1601, 1610 (1968).

8 That is because prohibited grounds of jurisdiction cannot be used by a contracting state, in cases within the draft Convention's territorial scope, even if the judgment could be enforced in that state. *See* Hague Conference on Private Int'l Law, *Preliminary Draft Convention on Jurisdiction and Foreign Judgments in Civil and Commercial Matters*, art. 2, 18 (Oct. 30, 1999) [hereinafter *Hague Draft*].

9 The U.S. proposal to the Hague Conference is for a *convention mixte*. Like a *convention double*, a *convention mixte* contains a "whitelist" specifying approved grounds of jurisdiction. Judgments

ations concern (1) the appropriateness of various grounds of jurisdiction acceptable in the United States or under the Brussels Convention,[10] and (2) the extent of the so-called gray zone, the area under a mixed convention in which national jurisdictional law, neither required nor forbidden under the proposed convention, can be applied to cases within its scope but without triggering any treaty obligation to recognize the resulting judgment.[11]

Compared to problems like these, which test notions of jurisdictional exorbitance and ultimate negotiating ambitions, the matters that I will address – lis pendens, antisuit injunctions, and forum non conveniens – seem like details. Yet these matters, which I have gathered under the rubric of jurisdictional equilibration,[12] are nonetheless difficult, and their satisfactory resolution is, I believe, critically important to the success of any treaty that may be concluded. For here are located devices easing the agony of foresight by which jurisdiction is protected or declined and its potential to yield an enforceable judgment fructified or frustrated.[13]

---

rendered in a contracting state and resting on an approved jurisdictional basis are entitled to recognition and enforcement under the Convention. However, unlike a true *convention double*, the U.S. proposal allows contracting states to assume jurisdiction on other jurisdictional bases not listed in the Convention. Judgments resulting from the exercise of jurisdiction on such bases are not assured of recognition under the Convention, but a state may – unless the Convention expressly provides otherwise – grant recognition and enforcement under its general law. The U.S. mixed convention proposal also contemplates a "blacklist" of exorbitant jurisdictional bases. With respect to matters covered by the Convention, contracting states would be required to forgo exercise of jurisdiction on these bases. Arthur T. von Mehren, *Recognition and Enforcement of Foreign Judgments: A New Approach for the Hague Conference?*, 57 Law & Contemp. Probs. (No. 3) 271, 283 (1994).

10 *See Hague Draft*, *supra* note 8, art. 18.

11 *See id.*, art. 17. The scope of the authority there conferred to apply rules of jurisdiction under national law is expressly limited by the proposed Convention's provisions on choice-of-court agreements, appearance by the defendant, contracts concluded by consumers, individual contracts of employment, exclusive jurisdiction, and provisional and protective measures. It is also expressly limited by the prohibited grounds of jurisdiction in draft Article 18. As the latter list expands, the size of the gray zone contracts, and a putatively mixed convention looks more like a double convention. *See* State Department letter, *supra* note 2, at 4–5, 8–9; Arthur T. von Mehren, *Drafting a Convention on International Jurisdiction and the Effects of Foreign Judgments Acceptable Worldwide: Can the Hague Conference Project Succeed?*, *infra* p. 281, at 289 ("the Commission's product remains, in spirit and approach, much more a close-knit double convention than a loose-jointed mixed convention").

12 The English word "equilibration" denotes a state of equilibrium or balance, and achieving balance is the essential function I associate with the matters to be discussed. Our French colleagues may imagine a tightrope walker, *un équilibriste*, a helpful image whether one thinks only of problems of jurisdiction under the proposed Convention or of the current state of the negotiations.

13 On this view of jurisdictional equilibration, one should perhaps also consider provisional and protective measures. I do not do so here for a number of reasons. First, I do not wish unduly to lengthen this contribution. Second, although regulating these matters to some extent, the Brussels Convention leaves most questions to national law, *see* Brussels Convention, *supra* note 4, art. 24, and that is the model adopted in draft Article 13 of the proposed Hague Convention. Finally, domestic United States law on the subject is unsettled. For a discussion of the last point and an argument that federal legislation is needed, see Stephen B. Burbank, *The Bitter with the Sweet: Tradition, History and Limitations on Federal Judicial Power – A Case Study*, 75 Notre Dame L. Rev. 1291 (2000). The form that such legislation should take remains to be worked out, but it would sensibly combine the treatment

The prospect of an enforceable judgment concentrates the attention of litigants and their attorneys, shaping plaintiffs' choice of forum and sometimes leading defendants to take evasive action, whether by seeking to have the lawsuit dismissed or by filing a preemptive or competing lawsuit.[14] The prospect also concentrates the attention of courts and sometimes leads them to take evasive action, by dismissing or staying actions pending before them or enjoining litigants from pursuing actions pending or impending elsewhere. Such moves can be threats not only to a smoothly functioning system of judgment recognition but also to the system of jurisdictional allocation on which it is based. Fashioning rules of jurisdictional equilibration that attend to the reasons for these phenomena in a world without treaties, and to the fact that no treaty can eliminate the impulses behind them, will also require very considerable statesmanship and realism, not just about human behavior but about jurisprudential assumptions. The negotiations at The Hague present an opportunity for enlightened comparative procedural lawmaking, the results of which could prove to be a model for law reform in or among states from both of the dominant traditions represented there.

My plan for this contribution to the symposium is first to describe how the matters that concern me are treated in litigation in the United States and, more briefly, how they are treated under the Brussels Convention, with attention to some of the jurisprudential assumptions underlying such treatment. Second, in the light of that background, I propose to examine the treatment of these matters in the current draft of the proposed Hague Convention, with attention to possible improvements. The improvements I have in mind include not just revisions to the Draft Convention. For this American scholar of international civil litigation, the prospects for changes in and the development of national law, under the influence, if not the command, of a private international law treaty, are among the most exciting aspects of the current project.[15]

Jurisdictional Equilibration in United States Practice

An understanding of domestic recognition practice in the United States is helpful to an understanding of what I have called "United States practice," by which I mean the practice obtaining in international cases. An understanding of the former is

---

of provisional and protective measures with the provisions on lis pendens, antisuit injunctions, and forum non conveniens that I recommend below. *See infra* text accompanying notes 113–53, 183–201. I also leave out of account the use by potential litigants and treatment by courts of forum selection agreements.

[14] Evasive action by defendants may also include dissipating assets or removing them from the jurisdiction. *See supra* note 13.

[15] Others see the same potential. *See* Kevin M. Clermont, *Jurisdictional Salvation and the Hague Treaty*, 85 Cornell L. Rev. 89 (1999). For this purpose, "national law" includes both the law in the United States for domestic and international interjurisdictional cases, and the interjurisdictional law of other states participating in the negotiations at The Hague, including (for member states) the interjurisdictional law contained in the Brussels Convention.

helpful in understanding the latter. And so it is for the subject of my inquiry, "devices by which jurisdiction is protected or declined and its potential to yield an enforceable judgment fructified or frustrated."[16] Of course, here as elsewhere in the American legal landscape, there is ambiguity in the use of the term "domestic,"[17] and here as elsewhere, there is a need to paint with a broad brush both that part of the domestic landscape that is relevant, which for these purposes is the territory of interjurisdictional cases, and United States practice.

The precise nature of the community to which the people of the United States aspired when they ratified the United States Constitution remains in dispute,[18] although it is not disputed that the framers of the Constitution perceived and sought to avoid corroding the new nation by disregarding judgments of sister states.[19] Yet, inspirational as it may be and has been, the text of the Constitution's Full Faith and Credit Clause is not very nourishing for one who seeks guidance on interstate recognition practice in the United States;[20] neither it nor the statute that since 1790 has implemented, by giving content to, its command[21] speaks directly to the question of jurisdiction.

For almost half of the country's history, jurisdictional orthodoxy bred of a shared legal heritage, coupled with the power to police indirectly jurisdiction by denying recognition, sufficed.[22] Thereafter, a federal constitutional law of substantive due process, whose content was initially borrowed from state-law arrangements and justified in the territorial terms of public international law, ensured a measure of direct control. It also had the effect of rationalizing the power of states to deny recognition.[23] With federal checks over jurisdiction and recognition in place, and given the potential of the system to police state choice of law directly,[24] the American

---

16 *Supra* text accompanying note 13.

17 *See* Stephen B. Burbank, *Interjurisdictional Preclusion, Full Faith and Credit and Federal Common Law: A General Approach*, 71 Cornell L. Rev. 733, 744 (1986). *Cf. supra* note 15 ("national law").

18 *See*, e.g., United States v. Morrison, 120 S. Ct. 1740 (2000); Kimel v. Florida Bd. of Regents, 120 S. Ct. 631 (2000); Alden v. Maine, 119 S. Ct. 2240 (1999); City of Boerne v. Flores, 521 U.S. 507 (1997).

19 The framers sought "not merely to demand respect from one state for another, but rather to give us the benefits of a unified nation by altering the status of otherwise 'independent, sovereign states.'" Willis L.M. Reese and Vincent A. Johnson, *The Scope of the Full Faith and Credit to Judgments*, 49 Colum. L. Rev. 153, 161 (1949) (*quoting* Sherrer v. Sherrer, 334 U.S. 343, 355 (1948)).

20 *See* U.S. Const. art. IV, § 1, *quoted supra* note 5.

21 Act of May 26, 1790, ch. 11, 1 Stat. 122 (codified as amended at 28 U.S.C. § 1738 (1994)). In pertinent part the statute currently provides that state "judicial proceedings ... shall have the same full faith and credit in every court within the United States ... as they have by law or usage in the courts ... from which they are taken." Note that, although the constitutional obligation is imposed only on states, the statutory obligation extends to "every court within the United States" and thus to federal courts. *See* Burbank, *supra* note 17, at 740. A similar obligation exists to respect federal court judicial proceedings, and it can most plausibly be founded in federal common law. *See id.* at 740–47.

22 *See* James Weinstein, *The Early American Origins of Territoriality in Judicial Jurisdiction*, 37 St. Louis U.L.J. 1 (1992).

23 *See* Pennoyer v. Neff, 95 U.S. 714 (1878).

24 For many years, the Supreme Court of the United States appeared of two minds, one that the Constitution required the application of territorial choice-of-law rules, *see, e.g.*, New York Life Ins.

law of full faith and credit could, with relative equanimity, forbid non-recognition because of disagreement about the rendering court's adjudication on the merits.[25]

The influence of American interjurisdictional practice in shaping United States practice is undoubtedly due to a complex of structural, historical, and cultural factors that defy brief summary. As brevity is demanded on this occasion, I offer as a cause the fact that, at the founding, the states of the United States were regarded as distinct sovereignties and that the history of both interjurisdictional recognition and jurisdictional equilibration since their founding has been a history of accommodating the perceived needs of sovereignty under constitutional language long on aspiration but short on details. It was, I suggest, easier for such a country and its constituent states to treat other countries like other constituent states than it was or would be for countries without a history of and experience in accommodating internal sovereign claims.

This disposition to assimilate international to domestic interjurisdictional cases has been reinforced by the very powerful impulse of modern American procedural law, including choice of law for these purposes, to apply the same rules to all cases. American courts have pursued domestic doctrinal uniformity, even when doing so resulted in international disuniformity, as in the interpretation of treaties.[26]

The effects of this process of assimilation can be seen throughout the landscape of international litigation. The process itself helps to explain both the generous treatment accorded internationally foreign judgments in United States practice, which requires no elaboration, and the schizophrenic attitudes of American courts towards existing or potential litigation abroad, to which I now turn.

The capacious language of the Full Faith and Credit Clause of the Constitution could have been used to fashion a federal law of lis pendens, as perhaps could the less capacious language of its implementing statute, at least in the service of wholly domestic lis pendens or "other action pending" doctrine in the state to which the federal obligation was owed. Notwithstanding some early movement in that direction, however, the obligation came to be tied to the existence of a judgment,[27] with the courts of other states and the federal courts free to entertain parallel litigation even if such litigation would be barred in the courts of the state in which the first lawsuit

---

Co. v. Dodge, 246 U.S. 357 (1918), and the other that it had nothing to do with choice of law. *See* Kryger v. Wilson, 242 U.S. 171,176 (1916). The modern Court's approach reposes great latitude in the states to choose the governing law. *See, e.g.*, Allstate Ins. Co. v Hague, 449 U.S. 302 (1981).

25 *See* Fauntleroy v. Lum, 210 U.S. 230 (1908).

26 *See* Burbank, *supra* note 3, at 135–39.

27 *See* Stephen B. Burbank, *Where's the Beef? The Interjurisdictional Effects of New Jersey's Entire Controversy Doctrine*, 28 Rutgers L.J. 87, 110–12 (1996). "But Congress had no problem barring duplicative simultaneous litigation in the child custody area, and its action in that regard may be further support for the proposition that at least the 'judicial proceedings' referred to in the Constitution need not have culminated in a judgment." *Id.* at 112 (footnote omitted). American readers will have noted that "lis pendens" for these purposes has to do with doctrine governing a court's response to "parallel litigation" rather than the effect of litigation on the marketability of property. *See, e.g.*, 28 U.S.C. § 1964 (1994) ("Constructive Notice of Pending Actions").

was filed.[28] In hindsight, the resulting system was calculated to promote forum-shopping and a race to judgment. But hindsight should in this case acknowledge the impediments to forum-shopping imposed for much of United States history by jurisdictional law and the nature of the society whose needs it served.

On this view, the absence of a federal lis pendens obligation and the incentives created by a system of full faith and credit to domestic interjurisdictional judgments did not become seriously inconvenient until the needs of the society prompted changes in the federal law constraining state jurisdictional freedom. And on this view, the greater latitude to assert jurisdiction afforded the states by *International Shoe*[29] and its progeny dramatically enhanced the opportunities for interstate forum-shopping and, coupled with loose federal control of state choice of law,[30] the incentives for both litigants and state courts to run a race to judgment. This created a market for litigation in which the voluntary extension of wholly domestic lis pendens doctrine to interjurisdictional litigation would constitute surprising self-restraint.[31]

Under this model of litigation, one would expect to encounter frequent attempts to preempt the recognition problem through the use of antisuit injunctions. The fact that such injunctions apparently do not plague modern interstate litigation may suggest limitations in the model, in particular the failure to capture behavior that is not self-regarding; that is surely part of the explanation. But it may also reflect the bitter lessons of experience in a system that does not require recognition of antisuit injunctions and, therefore, in which they can proliferate.[32] Moreover, the self-regarding behavior of courts may affect the stay or dismissal rather than the jealous maintenance of litigation.

---

28 The reference to "parallel litigation" is intended to include both duplicative and related litigation and thus to reflect the fact that American courts today do not draw a sharp distinction between the two for purposes of jurisdictional equilibration devices. As Samuel Baumgartner has suggested, this elision of matters that are treated separately in the Brussels Convention, *see infra* text accompanying notes 70–72, is due to differences in doctrine and in jurisprudential assumptions, including with respect to the proper role of judicial discretion, the breadth and aggressiveness of preclusion law, and the importance accorded to comprehensive dispute resolution within one proceeding. *See* Samuel P. Baumgartner, *Related Actions*, ZZPInt 3 at 203 (1998).

For a thoughtful discussion of different ways to give content to the concept of parallel litigation for the purpose of implementing a "zero tolerance solution" to the problem of redundancy between the federal and state courts in the United States, see Martin H. Redish, *Intersystemic Redundancy and Federal Court Power: Proposing a Zero Tolerance Solution to the Duplicative Litigation Problem*, 75 Notre Dame L. Rev. 1347, 1362–67 (2000).

29 International Shoe Co. v. Washington, 325 U.S. 310 (1945).

30 *See, e.g.*, Allstate Insurance Co. v. Hague, 449 U.S. 302 (1981); *supra* note 24.

31 For an unusual example, see 735 Ill. Comp. Stat. 5/2–619(a)(3) (West 1992); Burbank, *supra* note 27, at 120 n. 165; Redish, *supra* note 28, at 1352 n. 30.

32 *See, e.g.*, James v. Grand Trunk Western R.R., 14 Ill.2d 356, 152 N.E.2d 858, *cert. denied*, 358 U.S. 915 (1958); Restatement (Second) of Conflict of Laws § 103, comment b (1988 rev.). The Supreme Court has not ruled on the question, but a recent decision strongly suggests that it will not require states to recognize antisuit injunctions issued by the courts of other states as a matter of full faith and credit. *See* Baker v. General Motors Corp., 522 U.S. 222, 236 n. 9 (1998).

Courts, through judges, serve interests in addition to these animating domestic substantive law and the interests of litigants or their lawyers, including their own institutional interests.[33] When state legislatures directed state courts to take full advantage of the constitutional freedom accorded by *International Shoe* and its progeny or the courts seised that advantage themselves,[34] they were opening the courthouse door to additional litigation with which the state had very little connection and in which it might have no regulatory interest.[35] Means of self-protection, of achieving balance in a system where federal constitutional and statutory law had proved inadequate, were needed. Although not required by federal law, interstate lis pendens remained available at the option of the individual states, but that doctrine operates only when another lawsuit is pending. Jurisdictional imposition is not so confined. Thus the doctrine of forum non conveniens was given a scope of operation more wide-ranging than its previous employment would have suggested.[36]

Those who are conversant with the history of forum non conveniens in the United States know that it became a real litigation force in that country as a result of the U.S. Supreme Court decisions in the 1940s,[37] decisions that involved federal courts but that were contemporaneous with the loosening of federal constitutional restraints on state court jurisdiction. They also know that, with the advent of a statutory transfer mechanism in 1948, the doctrine became irrelevant in federal litigation that could be properly lodged in another federal court.[38] Finally, they know that, although

---

Although Professor Bermann notes that "over the years a large number of antisuit injunctions have been directed against proceedings in sister-state courts," George A. Bermann, *The Use of Anti-Suit Injunctions in International Litigation*, 28 Colum. J. Transnat'l. L. 589, 594–95 (1990), in all of the interstate cases he cites, it is difficult to find one decided less than sixty years ago. *See id.* at 594–604. In comments on a draft of this article, Professor Bermann suggested that the most baffling interpretation of the full faith and credit obligation is that which has permitted state courts to issue sister-state antisuit injunctions in the first place.

33 *See* Richard A. Posner, *Overcoming Law* ch. 3 (1995).

34 For a discussion of the costs of linking or eliding state and federal constitutional law concerning jurisdiction to adjudicate, see Stephen B. Burbank, *Jurisdiction to Adjudicate: End of the Century or Beginning of the Millennium?*, 7 Tulane J. Int'l. & Comp. L. 111 (1999).

35 The courts were already open to some such litigation because of the traditional grounds of general jurisdiction on the basis of the presence within the state of the person ("tag jurisdiction") or of property ("attachment jurisdiction") at the time of service, and the development of general "doing business" jurisdiction for corporate and other business entities added to the burden. For these purposes, the importance of *International Shoe* and its progeny is the proliferation of choice resulting from their expansion of the opportunities for specific jurisdiction. For criticism of the Supreme Court's failure to inform due process analysis with a comparative and dynamic consideration of jurisdictional possibilities, see Burbank, *supra* note 34, at 117–19.

36 *See* Allan R. Stein, *Forum Non Conveniens and the Redundancy of Court Access Doctrine*, 133 U. Pa. Law Rev. 781, 795–812 (1985); Gulf Oil Corp. v. Gilbert, 330 U.S. 501, 512 (1947) (Black, J., dissenting).

37 *See* Gulf Oil Corp. v. Gilbert, 330 U.S. 501 (1947); Koster v. (American) Lumbermens Mutual Casualty Co., 330 U.S. 518 (1947).

38 *See* Act of June 25, 1948, ch. 646, 62 Stat. 869, 937 (codified at 28 U.S.C. § 1404(a) (1994)) ("For the convenience of parties and witnesses, in the interests of justice, a district court may transfer any civil action to any other district or division where it might have been brought."); Ravelo Monegro v. Rosa,

the doctrine has not been embraced in all states, federal decisional law has proved to be a substantial continuing influence on the tenor of many states' law whose reach includes cases that could, as well as those that could not, be lodged in another American court.[39]

Therefore, to the extent that it is possible to speak of a modern American law of forum non conveniens, it has both a federal inspiration and a strong continuing federal influence. Moreover, although initially invigorated to deal with problems created by domestic litigation, the vagaries of its development have led to law for domestic cases being shaped, in those states that follow the federal lead, by the responses of federal courts to international civil litigation.

Ostensibly a tool to implement litigation convenience for litigants and courts, as formulated by the Supreme Court in the 1940s, forum non conveniens doctrine invited attention to regulatory concerns, and hence to choice of law, through consideration of what the Court called "public interest factors."[40] Ironically, such attention became essentially irrelevant in the context in which the doctrine was (re)born, because a change in the governing substantive law was held to be impermissible in diversity of citizenship cases that could be transferred under the mechanism enacted in 1948.[41] Yet, the presence or absence of a perceived domestic regulatory interest often seems critical to the result of a forum non conveniens motion in international cases.[42] Moreover, although the justification for treating foreign plaintiffs differently from domestic plaintiffs is framed in terms of inferences concerning litigation convenience,[43] judgments about regulatory interest are not very far beneath the surface, if beneath the surface at all.[44] As a result, the consequence of even dramatic changes in the substantive law may not defeat a forum non conveniens motion,[45] but choice-of-law concerns are hardly irrelevant.

The dynamic of doctrine applicable in domestic cases changing shape because of international litigation is not unique to forum non conveniens law. International civil litigation in the United States has involved doctrinal cross-fertilization between domestic and international cases.[46] Unfortunately, state courts' continuing use of

---

211 F.3d 509, 513 (9th Cir. 2000) ("The doctrine of forum non conveniens survives in federal court only when the alternative forum is in a foreign country.").

39 *See* Gary B. Born, *International Civil Litigation in United States Courts* 298 (3d ed. 1996).

40 *See* Gulf Oil Co. v. Gilbert, 330 U.S. 501, 508–09 (1947).

41 *See* Van Dusen v. Barrack, 376 U.S. 612 (1964) (defendant's motion); Ferens v. John Deere & Co., 494 U.S. 516 (1990) (plaintiff's motion); Ravelo Monegro v. Rosa, 211 F.3d 509, 513 n. 3 (9th Cir. 2000).

42 *See* Stein, *supra* note 36, at 784, 831–40; David R. Robertson, *Forum Non Conveniens in America and England: "A Rather Fantastic Fiction,"* 103 L.Q. Rev. 398, 406–07 (1987); Lonny Sheinkopf Hoffman and Keith A. Rowley, *Judicial Discretion and Legislative Intent: Forum Non Conveniens in Federal Statutory Cases* (forthcoming in 49 Emory L.J. 1137 (2000)).

43 *See* Piper Aircraft Co. v. Reyno, 454 U.S. 235, 261 (1980).

44 *See id.* at 251–52, 260–61.

45 *See id.* at 247 ("The possibility of a change in substantive law should ordinarily not be given conclusive or even substantial weight in the forum non conveniens inquiry.").

46 *See* Stephen B. Burbank, *The World in Our Courts*, 89 Mich. L. Rev. 1456 (1991) (book review); Burbank, *supra* note 3, at 125–27.

contemporary federal foreign non conveniens doctrine may suggest that the models borrowed are not always appropriate, either in their original or in their transplanted contexts.

We have seen that, among American state courts, there is no federally imposed obligation of lis pendens and that there are reasons for state courts to be sparing in the use of antisuit injunctions against litigation in other states. When the question is whether a federal court will dismiss or stay litigation before it because of, or enter an injunction against, parallel litigation pending elsewhere in the United States, different answers are likely depending on whether the other litigation is pending in a federal or state court. Although the differences can be explained, the answers are not immune to criticism. Moreover, it is indefensible that *both* approaches have been borrowed for, and coexist in case law treating, the same problems in international cases.

When parallel litigation is pending in two federal courts, something very close to a system of lis pendens operates, with a strong preference for the first-filed case. For these purposes, federal courts consider themselves part of the same system of courts, even when different states' substantive laws would govern in the respective cases. They are not shy about implementing the first-filed preference through antisuit injunctions as well as dismissals or stays.[47]

When parallel litigation is pending in state and federal courts, on the other hand, the federal courts follow different rules.[48] The ability of a federal court to dismiss a case in favor of state court litigation is constrained by that branch of the Supreme Court's abstention doctrine associated with the *Colorado River* case,[49] while its ability to enjoin the continued prosecution of such litigation is constrained by the Court's interpretation of the federal Anti-Injunction Act.[50] The former imputes a "virtually unflagging obligation"[51] to federal courts to exercise the subject-matter jurisdiction conferred by statute, tolerating a dismissal only in "exceptional circumstances."[52] The latter confines their ability to protect their jurisdiction against

---

47 *See* Landis v. North American Co., 299 U.S. 248 (1936) (stay); National Equipment Rental, Ltd. v. Fowler, 287 F.2d 43 (2d Cir. 1961) (injunction). True lis pendens or "other action pending" doctrine may be available when the cases are pending before the same federal court. *See* Chinn v. Giant Food, Inc., 100 F. Supp.2d 331 (D. Md. 2000); Sutcliffe Storage & Warehouse Co. v. United States, 162 F.2d 849 (1st Cir. 1947).

48 *See* Stephen B. Burbank, *The United States' Approach to International Civil Litigation: Recent Developments in Forum Selection*, 19 U. Pa. J. Int'l Econ. L. 1, 15–16 (1998); Redish, *supra* note 28, at 1356–60.

49 Colorado River Water Conservation Dist. v. United States, 424 U.S. 800 (1976).

50 "A court of the United States may not grant an injunction to stay proceedings in a State court except as expressly authorized by Act of Congress, or where necessary in aid of its jurisdiction, or to protect or effectuate its judgments." 28 U.S.C. § 2283 (1994). *See* Vendo Co. v. Lektro-Vend Corp., 433 U.S. 623 (1977).

51 *Colorado River*, 424 U.S. at 817. *See also* Moses H. Cone Memorial Hospital v. Mercury Constr. Corp., 460 U.S. 1 (1983).

52 *Colorado River*, 424 U.S. at 813.

pending state litigation by injunction to situations involving or analogous to those involving tangible property.[53] The perceived jurisdictional constraint dissolves, and a federal court has broad discretion to dismiss (or stay) parallel litigation, in a case seeking a declaratory judgment.[54]

When parallel litigation is pending in a federal court and in the court of another country, the rules governing a motion to dismiss or stay and a motion for an antisuit injunction may depend on the federal circuit in which that federal court sits. It appears that a reason for such differences in circuit law on lis pendens and antisuit injunctions in international cases has been the choice of "domestic" models, the model of litigation entirely within the federal court system (federal-federal) or the interjurisdictional (federal-state) model.[55] A court that follows the former model perceives that it has broad discretion to dismiss or stay parallel litigation in favor of litigation filed abroad,[56] and also to enjoin litigation abroad in favor of the case before it.[57] A court that follows the latter model will dismiss or stay parallel litigation before it, and similarly, will enjoin parallel litigation abroad, only in exceptional circumstances.[58]

For different reasons, both Professor Martin H. Redish and I have argued that the treatment of parallel federal-state litigation is incoherent.[59] The perceived requirements of separation of powers appear to have been a source of difficulty, coupled with the Supreme Court's failure to distinguish adequately among the circumstances

---

53 *See Vendo Co.*, 433 U.S. at 641–42; In re Baldwin-United Corp., 770 F.2d 328, 337 (2d Cir. 1985); Redish, *supra* note 28, at 1359. The text concerns the "in aid of jurisdiction" exception. Note, however, the two other exceptions to the Anti-Injunction Act's bar. *See supra* note 50. For other limitations on the ability of a federal court to enjoin pending state litigation, see Redish, *supra* note 28, at 1372–73.

54 *See* Wilton v. Seven Falls Co., 515 U.S. 277 (1995).

55 *See* Born, *supra* note 39, at 461–65, 475–78; Burbank, *supra* note 48, at 15–17. I do not mean to suggest that this is the only explanation for the differences among the circuits. Mr. Baumgartner has helpfully analyzed the cases from the perspective of "exclusive adjudication of a case in the forum in which the entire transaction or occurrence can be resolved." Baumgartner, *supra* note 28, at 214. He continues:

> [I]t is interesting that those federal decisions that favor a more restrained approach to antisuit injunctions in the United States happen to involve simple reverse-action situations with identical parties and causes of action. Perhaps, the prospect that the judgment in one litigation cannot be used as *res judicata* by or against all parties in the other significantly weakens the rule in favor of parallel proceedings.

Id. at 215–16 (footnote omitted). Note that the federal-federal model would best enable "having all aspects of a dispute adjudicated in a single forum," which he recognizes is "a general policy of common-law procedure, particularly of federal procedure in the United States." *Id.* at 216 (footnote omitted). It may not be an appropriate model in the international context, however. *See infra* text accompanying note 62.

56 *See, e.g.*, Continental Time Corp. v. Swiss Credit Bank, 543 F. Supp. 408 (S.D.N.Y. 1982).

57 *See,* e.g., Cargill, Inc. v. Hartford Accident & Indemnity Co., 531 F. Supp. 710 (D. Minn. 1982).

58 *See, e.g.*, Neuchatel Swiss General Ins. Co. v. Lufthansa Airlines, 925 F.2d 1193 (9th Cir. 1991) (dismissal/stay); Laker Airways, Ltd. v. Sabena, Belgian World Airlines, 731 F.2d 909 (D.C. Cir. 1984) (injunction).

59 *See* Redish, *supra* note 28, at 1355–60; Burbank, *supra* note 48, at 16–17.

in which a federal court may be asked to decline to exercise, or to postpone the exercise of, subject-matter jurisdiction. The Court *has* recently distinguished the refusal to grant declaratory relief from abstention[60] and distinguished the power of a federal court to stay, an action from dismissal.[61] These decisions suggest both that additional changes are necessary in the doctrine for federal-state cases and that, at least until such changes are made, it is not an appropriate model for international litigation. The federal-federal model is coherent, but in the absence of a treaty, it is not obviously more appropriate for international cases.[62]

Jurisdictional Equilibration Under the Brussels Convention

The extraordinary achievement of the Brussels Convention is apparent when considering the tenor and variety of the national recognition law for international cases that it replaced in signatory states. Indeed, as Professor Walter and Mr. Baumgartner have recently made clear, although the Brussels Convention has "cross-fertilized" the recognition doctrine that some states apply in cases outside its scope, even today there is a stark contrast between its regime and the law that some other states apply to foreign judgments.[63]

In one sense, the contrast is not surprising, insofar as the traditional recognition laws of many countries "developed during a time of pronounced nationalism,"[64] yielding a "strict territorialist approach."[65] As a result, some states refused to recognize foreign judgments in the absence of a treaty, while others implemented sovereign prerogatives through practices and/or requirements that had the effect of one hand taking back what the other conferred. For nations desiring more favorable treatment, the answer lay in treaties. Thus, the Brussels Convention can be seen as the most ambitious of a "staggering number of treaties that the continental European states have concluded over the last 150 years."[66]

---

60 *See* Wilton v. Seven Falls Co., 515 U.S. 277 (1995).

61 *See* Quackenbush v. Allstate Ins. Co., 517 U.S. 706 (1996). "Because it is not clear that dismissal and stay are functionally distinguishable for these purposes ... the case may represent a knowing wink in the direction of, rather than an effort to honor, separation of powers." Burbank, *supra* note 13, at 1295 n. 18 (citation omitted). *See infra* text accompanying note 112.

For a thoughtful critique of separation of powers arguments in connection with decisions by federal courts to decline jurisdiction, see David L. Shapiro, *Jurisdiction and Discretion*, 60 N.Y.U. L. Rev. 543 (1985).

62 *See* Burbank, *supra* note 48, at 17.

63 *See* Gerhard Walter and Samuel P. Baumgartner, The Recognition and Enforcement of Judgments Outside of the Brussels and Lugano Conventions (Sept. 1998), forthcoming in 3 *Civil Procedure in Europe, The Recognition and Enforcement of Judgments Outside the Scope of the Brussels and Lugano Conventions* (Gerhard Walter and Samuel P. Baumgartner eds.) (on file with author). For examples of cross-fertilization from the Brussels Convention to national jurisdictional law, see J.J. Fawcett, *General Report*, in *Declining Jurisdiction in Private International Law* 10 (J.J. Fawcett ed. 1995).

64 *Id.* at 2.

65 *Id.* at 5.

66 *Id.*

What is more striking than the ambition of using a multilateral treaty to achieve the purposes of the European Community, by liberalizing judgment recognition practice, is the legal and political ambition to pursue and successfully conclude a double convention. The signatory states thus secured agreement to displace national law with uniform rules concerning the grounds of adjudicatory jurisdiction required to be afforded, as well as those prohibited, in cases within the Convention's scope. It seems likely that the dominance of a shared tradition among the original signatory states eased the task, in both the form and content of the jurisdictional rules prescribed.[67] That legal tradition puts a very high premium on certainty and predictability in general, and particularly as to adjudicatory jurisdiction. Moreover, it only grudgingly admits a role for judicial discretion, if it admits any such role at all. Both are reasons to withhold from a court vested with jurisdiction the discretionary power to decline to exercise that jurisdiction, and they help to explain why the forum non conveniens doctrine is rejected in most of the civil-law world and in the Brussels Convention.[68]

Yet, even when states aspire to more than community, and have the confidence and collective political will to agree upon a closed list of jurisdictional bases, the choice of forum remains important to litigants; even a double convention cannot prevent the filing of lawsuits in inappropriate fora or in multiple fora. A regime seeking to avoid judgments that are denied recognition because they are irreconcilable with domestic judgments or rendered in conflict with a grant of exclusive jurisdiction[69] also needs either a requirement or authority for a contracting state to stay or dismiss litigation in favor of potential or existing litigation elsewhere. It requires jurisdictional equilibration devices.

And so, Article 19 of the Brussels Convention requires a contracting state's court to "declare of its own motion that it has no jurisdiction" of a claim concerning "a matter over which the courts of another contracting state have exclusive jurisdiction by virtue of Article 16." Where actions are brought in different contracting states, Article 21 gives strict precedence to the court first seised, to the extent that the actions involve the same cause of action and are between the same parties,[70] while

---

67 *See* Arthur von Mehren, *supra* note 11, at 284.

68 *See* Joachim Zekoll, *The Role and Status of American Law in the Hague Judgments Convention Project*, 61 Albany L. Rev. 1283, 1297–1300 (1998); Burbank, *supra* note 37, at 119–20; Fawcett, *supra* note 63, at 21–24.

69 *See* Brussels Convention, *supra* note 4, Articles 27(3) and (5) (recognition denied in the event of certain irreconcilable judgments); *id.*, Article 28 (recognition denied if judgment conflicts with, *inter alia*, exclusive jurisdiction provisions).

70 Article 21 of the Brussels Conventions provides:

> Where proceedings involving the same cause of action and between the same parties are brought in the courts of different Contracting State, any court other than the court first seised shall of its own motion stay its proceedings until such time as the jurisdiction of the court first seised is established.
>
> Where the jurisdiction of the court first seised is established, any court other than the court first seised shall decline jurisdiction in favour of that court.

Article 23 does the same "[w]here actions come within the exclusive jurisdiction of several courts."[71] For related actions, Article 22 permits any court other than the court first seised to stay its proceedings ("while the actions are pending at first instance"), and, upon application of a party, to decline jurisdiction if the court first seised has jurisdiction over both and consolidation is permitted.[72]

An appreciation of experience under Articles 21 and 22 of the Brussels Convention can perhaps best be gained, and it can be gained most economically, by considering the differences between those provisions and the comparable provisions of the proposed Hague Convention, which were drafted in the light of that experience.[73] A few observations may, however, usefully precede, by framing that discussion.

Experience with interjurisdictional lis pendens in Europe, both prior to and independent of the Brussels Convention, reveals a close link between that doctrine and recognition practice,[74] a link that is obscured by Article 21's requirement that the court second seised decline jurisdiction as soon as "the jurisdiction of the court first seised is established." The same experience indicates awareness, which is not apparent from the Brussels Convention text, that the doctrine fosters a race to the courthouse, which may be part of a litigation strategy wholly unconcerned with, and perhaps fearful of, adjudication on the merits and that it should therefore be relaxed in circumstances of undue delay.[75]

If Article 21 of the Brussels Convention may, for such reasons, be considered insufficiently progressive even within Europe, Article 22 was venturesome indeed. Although the laws of many countries on the continent address the problem of related litigation that is wholly domestic, as Baumgartner reports, "these code provisions

---

[71] Article 23 of the Brussels Convention provides: "Where actions come within the exclusive jurisdiction of several courts, any court other than the court first seised shall decline jurisdiction in favour of that court."

[72] Article 22 of the Brussels Convention provides:

> Where related actions are brought in the courts of different Contracting States, any court other than the court first seised may, while the actions are pending at first instance, stay its proceedings. A court other than the court first seised may also, on application of one of the parties, decline jurisdiction if the law of that court permits the consolidation of related actions and the court first seised has jurisdiction over both actions.
>
> For the purposes of this Article, actions are deemed to be related where they are so closely connected that it is expedient to hear and determine them together to avoid the risk of irreconcilable judgments resulting from separate proceedings.

[73] *See infra* text accompanying notes 85–112. To the extent reported decisions are a guide, there appears to be little experience under Article 23.

[74] *See* Baumgartner, *supra* note 28, at 205–06; Fawcett, *supra* note 63, at 28.

[75] *See* Baumgartner, *supra* note 28, at 205–06. Note, however, that both the Lugano and San Sebastian Conventions *did* address the problem of the court first seised deciding that it did not have jurisdiction after the court second seised had declined jurisdiction, with the possible running of the applicable limitations period, by distinguishing between a stay and declining jurisdiction. *See* Wendy Kennett, *Lis Alibi Pendens: A View from the UK*, in *The European Judicial Area in Civil and Commercial Matters*, 104 (R. Fentiman, A. Nuyts, H. Tagaras, and N. Watté eds., 1999). This change is now reflected in the text of the Brussels Convention, quoted *supra* note 70.

have not found their way into transnational practice the way the doctrine of lis pendens has."[76] In considering possible reasons for this, he suggests the traditional civil-law concerns about courts surrendering jurisdiction and exercising discretion.[77] More interesting, I believe, is his empirical observation that "the stay in favor of related actions does not seem to be used very often in purely domestic proceedings,"[78] and his jurisprudential speculation that "[a] further reason for the reluctant use of related-action stays may lie in a procedural philosophy that views a civil proceeding more as an efficient adjudication of the plaintiff's claim than as an equitable resolution of a dispute or, as in the United States, of an entire 'transaction or occurrence'."[79] This philosophy, he suggests, may help explain why there are so few published opinions involving Article 22 of the Brussels Convention from the European Court of Justice or "the courts of the Convention's civil-law member states."[80] There are limits to a treaty's power to cross-fertilize domestic law and to alter jurisprudential assumptions.

Even expert drafters' most painstaking efforts cannot prevent interpretative dissonance. When the effort involves languages that are to serve as authoritative prescriptions in countries to which they are foreign, the risk is great. It is greater still when those prescriptions are silent on questions necessarily and obviously included within their scope. The risk becomes a virtual certainty when the languages are brought into service in countries from different legal traditions. Thus, it is no surprise that a need to enable the European Court of Justice to reduce the interpretative noise by making binding interpretations of the Brussels Convention was soon acknowledged.[81]

Finally, although the lis pendens provision in Article 21 of the Brussels Convention may appear "rigid, mechanical and crude"[82] to common-law eyes, in recent years the costs of discretionary justice within a highly entrepreneurial adversarial system have become apparent.[83] The negotiations at The Hague are taking place at a time when signals from both domestic law and other international initiatives point toward a rapprochement between the jurisprudential assumptions of the common-law and

---

76 Baumgartner, *supra* note 28, at 207.

77 *See id.* at 207–10.

78 *Id.* at 209.

79 *Id.* at 210 (footnotes omitted).

80 *Id.*

81 As originally adopted, the Brussels Convention "did not give the European Court jurisdiction to interpret its provisions; consequently, a protocol was signed in Luxembourg on June 3, 1971 to make provision for preliminary references." Trevor C. Hartley, *Introduction to the Brussels Jurisdiction and Judgments Convention*, in V *Collected Courses of the Academy of European Law*, Book 1, at 229 (1996) (footnote omitted). For the protocol, see 1978 O.J. (L304) 50. On the preliminary reference procedure, see Koen Lenaerts and Dirk Arts, *Procedural Law and the European Union* ch. 6 (Robert Bray ed., 1999).

82 Neste Chemicals S.A. v. DK Line S.A., [1994] 3 All E.R. 180 (Eng. C.A. 1994).

83 *See, e.g.*, Stephen B. Burbank, *Implementing Procedural Change: Who, How, Why, and When?*, 49 Ala. L. Rev. 221 (1997).

civil-law traditions with regard to the proper roles of rules and discretion, and of judges and lawyers, in seeking procedural justice.[84]

The Proposed Hague Convention, the Road Ahead at The Hague, and Progress in National Law

Lis Pendens and Antisuit Injunctions

The proposed Hague Convention's lis pendens provisions, contained in draft Article 21,[85] are an excellent example of the fruits of "enlightened comparative procedural lawmaking, ... which could prove a model for law reform in or among countries from both of the dominant traditions represented [at The Hague]."[86] The draft provisions sensitively reflect experience under the Brussels Convention, greatly improving the treatment of the subject in that treaty. They also reflect experience under common-law systems, appropriating a common-law device in order to impart greater flexibility.

---

84 *See, e.g., American Law Institute, Transnational Rules of Civil Procedure* (Preliminary Draft No. 2, March 17, 2000).

85 Draft Article 21 provides:

1. When the same parties are engaged in proceedings in courts of different Contracting States and when such proceedings are based on the same causes of action, irrespective of the relief sought, the court second seised shall suspend the proceedings if the court first seised has jurisdiction and is expected to render a judgment capable of being recognised under the Convention in the State of the court second seised, unless the latter has exclusive jurisdiction under Article 4 or 12.

2. The court second seised shall decline jurisdiction as soon as it is presented with a judgment rendered by the court first seised that complies with the requirements for recognition or enforcement under the Convention.

3. Upon application of a party, the court second seised may proceed with the case if the plaintiff in the court first seised has failed to take the necessary steps to bring the proceedings to a decision on the merits or if that court has not rendered such a decision within a reasonable time.

4. The provisions of the preceding paragraphs apply to the court second seised even in a case where the jurisdiction of that court is based on the national law of that State in accordance with Article 17.

5. For the purpose of this Article, a court shall be deemed to be seised – (a) when the document instituting the proceedings or an equivalent document is lodged with the court, or (b) if such document has to be served before being lodged with the court, when it is received by the authority responsible for service or served on the defendant.

[As appropriate, universal time is applicable.]

6. If in the action before the court first seised the plaintiff seeks a determination that it has no obligation to the defendant, and if an action seeking substantive relief is brought in the court second seised – (a) the provisions of paragraphs 1 to 5 above shall not apply to the court second seised, and (b) the court first seised shall suspend the proceedings at the request of a party if the court second seised is expected to render a decision capable of being recognised under the Convention.

7. This Article shall not apply if the court first seised, on application by a party, determines that the court second seised is clearly more appropriate to resolve the dispute, under the conditions specified in Article 22.

86 *See supra* text accompanying notes 14–15.

As previously described, the Brussels Convention treats the subject of lis pendens briefly and, from a common-law perspective, rigidly. As a result, both the European Court of Justice and national courts have been given a load of interpretative work that has tested jurisprudential assumptions of the civil-law tradition. The proposed Hague Convention has profited from the evidence furnished by those cases and, although following the basic preference for the court first seised, has sensibly resolved many of the problems they reveal. In taking this approach, the drafters have not only advanced the goals of certainty and predictability, they have provided greater hope of uniformity for a regime that lacks a mechanism to ensure it.

Thus, for instance, the drafters at The Hague have acknowledged the difficulties arising from the Brussels Convention's failure to define the critical determinant of precedence, when a court is seised, a gap that the European Court declined to fill when it held that the matter was to be determined by national law.[87] Also, recognizing from experience under the Brussels Convention that the condition requiring the proceedings to be based "on the same causes of action" could greatly limit the scope of the provision's application,[88] The Hague drafters included the qualifier "irrespective of the relief sought." Indeed, they went much farther, drawing on experience in common-law jurisdictions, suggesting that, in some circumstances, precedence should not be given to cases in which the plaintiff seeks only declaratory relief, and crafting a provision that reverses the normal rule where (1) such relief is sought in the court first seised, (2) "an action seeking substantive relief is brought in the court second seised," and (3) "the court second seised is expected to render a decision capable of being recognized under the Convention."[89]

The last-quoted qualification from draft Article 21(6)(b) implements a broader rule that itself constitutes an advance in the proposed Hague Convention, again reflecting experience under the comparable provision in the Brussels Convention. For, under draft Article 21(1), the obligation of the court second seised to suspend proceedings arises only "if the court first seised has jurisdiction and is expected to render a judgment capable of being recognised under the Convention in the State of the court second seised, unless the latter has exclusive jurisdiction under Article 4 or 12."

This provision, which responds to the authority to apply national jurisdictional law under a mixed convention, also answers a question apparently still open under the Brussels Convention, to wit, whether lis pendens applies when the court second

---

87 *See* Case C-129/83, Zelger v. Salinitri, 1984 E.C.R. 2397, [1985] 3 C.M.L.R. 366 (1984).

88 *See, e.g.*, Case C-144/86, Gubisch Maschinenfabrik KG v. Palumbo, 1987 E.C.R. 4861, [1989] E.C.C. 420 (1987).

89 *See, e.g.*, Capitol Indemnity Corp. v. Haverfield, 218 F.3d 872 (8th Cir. 2000); Wilton v. Seven Falls Co., 515 U.S. 277 (1995); Brillhart v. Excess Ins. Co. of America, 316 U.S. 491 (1942); *supra* text accompanying note 54. *But see* Case C-406/92, The Maciej Rataj, Tatry v. Maciej Rataj, [1995] All E.R. (EC) 229 (1994). This categorical treatment of declaratory relief cases may be too broad. *See infra* notes 131, 145.

seised has exclusive jurisdiction.[90] Indeed, it appears to be partially redundant in that regard, since judgments based on grounds of jurisdiction that conflict with Articles 4 and 12 are among those denied recognition and enforcement under draft Article 26.[91] Moreover, by permitting the court second seised to consider whether a judgment of the court first seised is "capable of being recognized under the Convention," this provision appears to affirm the power of the court second seised independently to determine the jurisdiction of the court first seised. If so, it answers a question suggested by the condition, "if the court first seized has jurisdiction," and does so, except perhaps in instances of exclusive jurisdiction, contrary to the solution worked out under the Brussels Convention.[92]

A strict lis pendens regime is most palatable where, as in the Brussels Convention, participating states have confidence in an existing closed jurisdictional system. The required confidence concerns not only the likelihood that the jurisdictional standards will ensure an appropriate relationship between the forum and the defendant(s), but, where neither a choice of law test nor reexamination of the merits (*révision au fond*) is permitted, also an appropriate relationship between the forum and the matter in controversy. To the extent that required jurisdictional bases do not inspire such shared confidence and/or that other jurisdictional bases are permitted, a safety valve is needed that permits the equilibration of competing jurisdictional claims by means other than a strict first-filed (or first-seised) rule.

The proposed Hague Convention draft Article 21(7) contains such a safety valve, borrowed from the common-law, rendering the Convention's lis pendens rule inapplicable "if the court first seised, on application by a party, determines that the court second seised is clearly more appropriate to resolve the dispute under the conditions specified in Article 22."[93]

---

90 *See* Case C-351/89, Overseas Union Insurance Ltd v. New Hampshire Ins. Co., [1991] E.C.R. I-3317 (1991); Continental Bank NA v. Aeakos Compania Naviera S.A., [1994] 1 Lloyd's Rep. 505, [1994] 1 W.L.R. 588 (Eng. C.A. 1993); Glencore International AG v. Metro Trading International, Inc., [1999] 2 Lloyd's Rep. 632 (Q.B. 1999); Paul R. Beaumont, *A United Kingdom Perspective on the Proposed Hague Judgments Convention*, 24 Brook. J. Int'l L. 75, 100 (1998); Kennett, *supra* note 75, at 118–20. *Cf.* Toepfer International GmbH v. Société Cargill France, [1998] 1 Lloyd's Rep. 379 (Eng. C.A. 1997) (referring to European Court questions concerning applicability of Brussels Convention, including Article 21, to litigation arising out of relationship governed by arbitration agreement). For an interesting argument distinguishing Articles 16 and 17 of the Brussels Convention for these purposes, see Richard Fentiman, *Exclusive Jurisdiction and Article 17*, in *The European Judicial Area*, *supra* note 75, at 127.

91 Draft Article 26 provides: "A judgment based on a ground of jurisdiction which conflicts with Articles 4, 5, 7, 8 or 12, or whose application is prohibited by virtue of Article 18, shall not be recognised or enforced."

92 *See* Case 351/89, Overseas Union Insurance Ltd. v. New Hampshire Insurance Co., [1991] E.C.R. I-3317 (1991). Note, however, that in connection with recognition, although draft Article 27(1) provides that "[t]he court addressed shall verify the jurisdiction of the court of origin," in doing so it is "bound by the findings of fact on which the court of origin based its jurisdiction, unless the judgment was given by default" under draft Article 27(2).

93 Draft Article 22 is set forth *infra* at note 163. Note, however, that draft Article 21 as a whole, and hence this provision, does not operate where *the court first seised* is exercising jurisdiction under national law pursuant to draft Article 17.

Two other, conceptually linked advances over the comparable provisions in the Brussels Convention should be noted. Whereas under Article 21 of the Brussels Convention, the court second seised is required to decline jurisdiction "[w]here the jurisdiction of the court first seised is established,"[94] under draft Article 21 of the proposed Hague Convention, suspension and declining jurisdiction are treated separately, with the latter required only when the court second seised "is presented with a judgment rendered by the court first seized that complies with the requirements for recognition or enforcement under the Convention." In addition, draft Article 21(3) permits the court second seised, upon application of a party, to "proceed with the case if the plaintiff in the court first seized has failed to take the necessary steps to bring the proceedings to a decision on the merits or if that court has not rendered such a decision within a reasonable time." These aspects of the proposed Hague Convention constitute an important hedge against the risks of strategic behavior that are inevitable in any system of jurisdictional equilibration and an important protection of a court's ability to do justice against the demands of efficiency and consistency.[95]

This is an impressive record of progress that should inspire diffidence in anyone suggesting additional refinements. One matter should not be controversial, although it may resist solution because of technical difficulties and differences in national law. Unless the addition of the condition, "irrespective of the relief sought" and its French counterpart in draft Article 21[96] are thought to cover the matter, the proposed Hague Convention imports from the Brussels Convention the ambiguity raised by the use of different conditions in the English and French versions ("same causes of action" in English and "*la même cause et le même objet*" in French), ambiguity that has engaged the attention of the European Court on more than one occasion and to which that tribunal assigns some importance.[97]

---

94 *See supra* note 75 and accompanying text.

95 *See* Re Proceedings in Two Fora (II ZR 3/85), [1987] E.C.C. 273 (BGHZ 1985). For forerunners of such provisions in Swiss (as of 1987) and Italian (as of 1995) law, see Baumgartner, *supra* note 28, at 205–06.

96 The French language version of draft Article 21(1) provides:

> Lorsque les même parties sont engagées dans des procédures devant des tribunaux d'Etats contractants différents et que ces procedures ont la même cause et le même objet, quelles que soient les prétentions des parties, le tribunal saisi en second lieu suspend la procédure si le tribunal premier saisi est compétent et s'il est à prévoir que ce tribunal rendra un jugement susceptible d'être reconnu en vertu de la Convention dans l'Etat du tribunal saisi en second lieu, sauf si ce dernier est exclusivement compétent en vertu des articles 4 ou 12.

97 *See* Case C-144/86, Gubisch Maschinenfabrik v. Palumbo, 1987 E.C.R. 4861, [1989] E.C.C. 420 (1987); Case C-406/92, The Maciej Rataj, Tatry v. Maciej Rataj, [1995] All ER (EC) 229 (1994). *See also* Haji-Ioannou v. Frangos, [1999] 2 Lloyd's Rep. 337 (Eng. C.A. 1999); Kennett, *supra* note 75, at 105–08. The notion that the addition of the words "irrespective of the relief sought" ("*quelles que soient les prétentions des parties*" in the French version) was intended to bridge the gap finds support in the official report explaining the provisions of the preliminary draft of October 30, 1999. *See* Peter Nygh and Fausto Pocar, *Report of the Special Commission* 85 (2000). Samuel Baumgartner informs me that "'*la même cause*' has no technical meaning in French" and that the wording chosen was deemed "better (because known from Brussels as interpreted in *Gubisch*) than inserting some explanat-

More controversially, one might question the decision to exclude from the operation of draft Article 21 situations in which the court first seised is exercising jurisdiction under national law as permitted by draft Article 17. The recognition check in draft Article 21(1) (deleting "under the Convention") might be thought to provide adequate protection to the court second seised.

Moreover, acknowledging that an interjurisdictional lis pendens provision can only reach so far without ignoring or affecting domestic law, including procedural and res judicata law,[98] it is worth asking whether draft Article 21 goes as far as it properly can and should go in other respects to advance shared interests in efficiency and consistency. Thus, experience under the Brussels Convention might at least counsel elaboration of the concept of "same parties."[99] And should concern for the integrity of national procedural law prevent this provision from reaching claims that are in fact compulsory counterclaims in the court first seised?[100]

One answer to the last question might be that draft Article 21 is less concerned with efficiency than with the prevention of irreconcilable judgments (consistency). Even if that is a plausible account of the Brussels regime,[101] however, both the departures from that regime described above and the fact that the proposed Hague Convention does not, while the Brussels Conventions does, contain a separate article on related actions,[102] deprive it of persuasive force.

---

ory phrase into the French text." Letter from Samuel P. Baumgartner to Stephen B. Burbank 3 (Sept. 30, 2000). *See also* International Law Association, Committee on International Civil and Commercial Litigation, Third Interim Report: Declining and Referring Jurisdiction in International Litigation 32 (2000) (Principle 4.1 of the Leuven/London Principles on Declining and Referring Jurisdiction in Civil and Commercial Matters) ("proceedings involving the same parties and the same subject-matter"); *id.* at 37 ("des demandes ayant le même objet et la même cause ... entre les mêmes parties").

98 For example, an American might be tempted to formulate a lis pendens provision so as to comprehend claims that the defendant in the court first seised has against the plaintiff that arise out of the same transaction or occurrence, taking inspiration from Fed. R. Civ. P. 13(a)'s definition of a compulsory counterclaim. One problem with such a broad formulation is that other states may not countenance counterclaims, or require that they be asserted, and any such provision would therefore operate so as to upset the policy judgments implicit in their normal rules of procedure in the cases to which it applies. A second problem is that even a legal system that is aggressive in requiring the assertion of counterclaims, like the American federal system, recognizes that there must be limits to the compelled loss of choice of forum, and the perceived need for such limits is likely to be more insistent in the international context.

99 *See* Case C-351/96, Druot Assurances SA v. Consolidated Metallurgical Industries, [1999] Q.B. 497 (1998); K.R. Handley, *Res Judicata in the European Court*, 116 L.Q.R. 191 (2000); Kennett, *supra* note 75, at 108–11.

100 *See* Turner v. Grovit, [1999] 3 All E.R. 616, [1999] 1 W.L.R. 794 (Eng. C.A. 1999); *supra* note 98. If in these respects the Special Commission may be thought to have kept its ambition too well under control, that cannot be said about draft Article 2(1)(c), pursuant to which "even if all the parties are habitually resident in [a Contracting] State" "Articles 21 and 22 shall apply where the court is required to determine whether to decline jurisdiction or suspend its proceedings on the grounds that the dispute ought to be determined in the courts of another Contracting State."

101 *See* Case C-144/86, Gubisch Maschinenfabrik KG v. Palumbo, 1987 E.C.R. 4861, [1989] E.C.C. 420 (1987); Case C-406/92, The Maciej Rataj, Tatry v. Maciej Rataj, [1995] All E.R. (EC) 229 (1994).

102 *See supra* text accompanying notes 70–72; *infra* text accompanying notes 103–06.

Of course, this line of reasoning raises perhaps the most difficult question for one who admires this aspect of the work at The Hague but who desires to make a constructive contribution to the process as it goes forward. Why is it that the current draft does not contain a provision on related actions comparable to Article 22 of the Brussels Convention? Granted that the co-existence of Articles 21 and 22 has posed some serious interpretative problems for the European Court[103] and for national courts,[104] and acknowledging again the progress that draft Article 21 represents, it is still a provision of quite limited scope, hardly adequate to meet the strategic ingenuity of modern litigants or otherwise to eliminate the inefficient consumption of scarce judicial resources. It does not appear that draft Article 22 of the proposed Hague Convention could, even if it was intended to, serve the purpose.[105] Moreover, particularly in light of extensive discussion of mechanisms for judicial cooperation during the deliberations of the Special Commission,[106] it seems a shame that what is perhaps the best vehicle for the development of experience along those lines is absent from the proposed convention.

As experience under the Brussels Convention demonstrates, it is not easy wholly to banish antisuit injunctions from a legal culture accustomed to them.[107] Moreover,

---

[103] *See* Case C-406/92, The Maciej Rataj, Tatry v. Maciej Rataj, [1995] All E.R. (EC) 229 (1994).

[104] *See, e.g.*, Glencore International AG v. Metro Trading International Inc., [1999] 2 Lloyd's Rep. 632 (Q.B. 1999); Kennett, *supra* note 75, at 115–17, 124–26.

[105] Draft Article 22, which is set forth in full *infra* note 163, permits suspension/dismissal only "[i]n exceptional circumstances," only if "it is clearly inappropriate for [the court seised] to exercise jurisdiction," and only "if a court of another State has jurisdiction and is clearly more appropriate to resolve the dispute." These conditions are cumulative and to be taken seriously. *See* Nygh and Pocar, *supra* note 97, at 99. The second of them in particular deprives the provision of utility for the consolidation of related actions. Compare the proposal for a "combination of a narrowly defined *lis pendens* rule and a widely defined related actions rule modelled on *forum non conveniens*," Beaumont, *supra* note 90, at 101, which the author suggested "might prove a negotiable compromise in the Hague even if it cannot be achieved in the Brussels and Lugano revision." *Id.* See in that regard Leuven/London Principle 4.2, *supra* note 97 (where related actions are pending, "either court may suspend or terminate its proceedings and refer the matter to the alternative court ... provided that the actions can be consolidated in the alternative court").

[106] *See* Hague Conference on Private Int'l Law, Special Commission on International Jurisdiction and the Effects of Foreign Judgments in Civil and Commercial Matters, Working Document No. 144 E, 8–10 (Nov. 20, 1998) [hereinafter *Working Document No. 144 E*]; Catherine Kessedjian, *Synthesis of the Work of the Special of March 1998 on International Jurisdiction and the Effects of Foreign Judgments in Civil and Commercial Matters*, 1998 Synthesis, at 40–44 (1998) [hereinafter *1998 Synthesis*]. Note also Leuven/London Principle 5.2, *supra* note 97, providing for direct communication between courts, when permitted by the respective states, and encouraging states to "permit their courts to make, and respond to, such communication."

[107] *See* Turner v. Grovit, [1999] 3 All E.R. 616, [1999] 1 W.L.R. 794 (Eng. C.A. 1999); Trevor C. Hartley, *Antisuit Injunctions and the Brussels Jurisdiction and Judgments Convention*, 49 Int'l. & Comp. L. Q. 166 (2000). Note, however, substantial German authority for the proposition that Articles 21 and 22 of the Brussels Convention occupy the field, excluding antisuit injunctions. *See* Letter from Samuel P. Baumgartner to Stephen B. Burbank, *supra* note 97, at 4 (*citing* Rolf Stürner, Anmerkung, 109 ZZP 224, 228 (1996)).

even in a closed jurisdictional system that relies primarily on a strict lis pendens regime, and even where binding interpretation of governing jurisdictional and lis pendens law is possible, antisuit injunctions may have a (very) limited role to play. Duplicative litigation may reflect more than a litigant's attempt to secure a more favorable forum in a world of choice. It may represent an attempt to evade a grant of, or an agreement to submit to, exclusive jurisdiction in another tribunal. It may also represent an attempt to wear down the opponent, to prevail without prevailing on the merits.[108] In both situations, the potential for ultimate correction pursuant to the binding interpretation of a central tribunal may not suffice to deter, as under the Brussels Convention, and neither may the ability of the court that possesses exclusive jurisdiction to continue to judgment, as under the proposed Hague Convention.[109]

Therefore, there is an argument in both situations to be made in favor of limited power in a court properly vested with jurisdiction to enjoin the abuse. Some countries participating in the Hague negotiations may regard antisuit injunctions issued unilaterally by the courts of another country as an infringement of territorial sovereignty. However, this should not deter the effort since agreement in the treaty would solve the problem. Moreover, the absence of a tribunal empowered either to resolve differences among signatory states or to issue interpretations binding on them suggests that the need is greater than it is under the Brussels Convention. Perhaps, however, the subject of antisuit injunctions is too controversial to broach in negotiations, leaving their availability open to national interpretation, which will be influenced by national legal culture, tradition, and rules.[110]

When one looks to see what lessons those who have been considering changes in the Brussels regime have drawn from the experience under that convention to date, and what, if anything, they have drawn from the deliberations at The Hague, one finds only that "the date on which an action is 'pending' for the purposes of [Article 21] is defined autonomously, and a mistake in the framing of the related actions

---

[108] *See id.*; Toepfer International GmbH v. Société Cargill France, [1998] 1 Lloyd's Rep. 379 (Eng. C.A. 1997).

[109] *See Hague Draft*, *supra* note 8, art. 21(1); *supra* text accompanying notes 90–91. For some of the means to facilitate uniform interpretation of the proposed Hague Convention considered to date, see Preliminary Doc. No., *supra* note 106, at 45–46; Zekoll, *supra* note 68, at 1286 n. 16.

[110] As Mr. Baumgartner has pointed out, this could lead to serious mischief if common-law countries interpreted the Convention as simply not dealing with antisuit injunctions and civil law countries took the view that they were preempted. *See* Letter from Samuel P. Baumgartner to Stephen B. Burbank, *supra* note 97, at 3–4.

Except in the case of an exclusive jurisdiction clause that "has been manifestly breached according to the law applicable in the courts of both states," the Leuven/London Principles do not permit antisuit injunctions where the respective states are parties to a convention providing common jurisdictional rules or where the court from which an injunction is sought "is satisfied that these Principles will be applied by the court in which proceedings have been instituted." Leuven/London Principle 7, *supra* note 97.

rule in the Brussels Convention has been corrected."[111] If nothing else were changed, in this respect at least it would be hard to avoid the conclusion that an opportunity had been missed.[112] Let us hope that more will be done to bring the Brussels Convention's provisions on lis pendens in line with experience, and to inform them with comparative insight. Let us hope, moreover, that the United States can profit from both sources, as well as from recent scholarship on domestic law.

The Supreme Court's recent decisions distinguishing a federal court's power to refuse declaratory relief from its power to abstain and, within the domain of abstention, distinguishing a stay from dismissal, suggest that the "exceptional circumstances" requirement of *Colorado River* abstention may have been responsive to the separation of powers concerns to which those distinctions speak.[113] They also suggest that, so long as a federal court desiring to give precedence to parallel litigation pending in a state court stays, rather than dismisses, the case before it, such concerns are satisfied. They also suggest that, as a result, exceptional circumstances should not be required for that reason.[114]

In a recognition system that mandates application of the preclusion (res judicata) law of the rendering court and subjects that law to very modest federal checks, as does the Full Faith and Credit statute,[115] a stay may appear, ex post, functionally indistinguishable from dismissal.[116] The ex ante difficulties of predicting the extent of duplication and the likelihood and extent of potential preclusion may provide some functional support for the stay alternative, as may potential limitations bars

---

[111] Commission of the European Communities, Proposal for a Council Regulations (EC) on Jurisdictional and the Recognition and Enforcement of Judgments in Civila and Commercial Matters 19 (1999) (on file with author). For a discussion of this not uncontroversial effort, see Beaumont, *supra* note 90; Horatia Muir Watt, *New Perspectives for Jurisdiction and Judgments Within Europe: A Critical View*, *infra* p. 245.

[112] *Cf.* Fentiman, *supra* note 90, at 159 (remarking failure of Commission proposals to clarify the problem of exclusivity within Article 17).

[113] *See supra* text accompanying notes 47–62. In Wilton v. Seven Falls Co., 515 U.S. 277 (1995), the Court emphasized its oft-repeated characterization of the Declaratory Judgment Act as "an enabling act, which confers a discretion on the courts rather than an absolute right on the litigant." *Id.* at 287 (*quoting* Public Service Comm'n of Utah v. Wycoff Co., 344 U.S. 237, 241 (1952)). On that view neither a stay nor a dismissal of a declaratory judgment action presents separation of powers concerns.

[114] *See* Burbank, *supra* note 48, at 16–17. In Moses H. Cone Memorial Hospital v. Mercury Const. Corp., 460 U.S. 1 (1983), the Court applied *Colorado River's* "exceptional circumstances" test in concluding that the district court's stay (not dismissal) of the federal action was inappropriate. That decision long antedated the rationalization of precedent in Quackenbush v. Allstate Ins. Co., 517 U.S. 706 (1996), and as an action to compel arbitration, it would not have been subject to the prohibition on dismissal that *Quackenbush* discerned for common-law damages cases. In any event, there were reasons other than concern about separation of powers that supported the result, if not the test. *See* further *infra* note 118 and accompanying text.

[115] *See* Burbank, *supra* note 17, at 797–829.

[116] *See* Wilton v. Seven Falls Co., 515 U.S. 277, 283 (1995); Lewis Yelin, Note, *Burford Abstention in Actions for Damages*, 99 Colum. L. Rev. 1871 (1999); *supra* note 61.

in the absence of a tolling rule.[117] Moreover, even for separation of powers purposes, one should perhaps distinguish between situations in which a federal court yields, or yields provisionally, to a state court seised of parallel litigation and a situation in which a federal court refuses for other reasons to adjudicate a case, no other litigation has yet been filed and the federal plaintiff is therefore forced to file a lawsuit in state court.[118]

Professor Redish has called for a "zero tolerance solution to the duplicative litigation problem."[119] His effort is concerned with federal courts law and is avowedly preliminary. He is agnostic about the scope of application of the regime he favors,[120] the standards for determining forum preference,[121] and about whether the regime should be implemented by decisional or statutory law.[122] Although he does not discuss the federal-federal context,[123] the changes he proposes in federal law governing both dismissal and antisuit injunctions for parallel litigation between the federal and state courts could substantially assimilate the two contexts. This would then remove both supposed separation of powers and federalism roadblocks and leave the development of lis pendens and antisuit injunction jurisprudence free to focus on litigant convenience and institutional needs.

Although I share Professor Redish's view that current federal law in this area is incoherent,[124] I suspect that his proposed "zero tolerance solution" goes both too far and not far enough. Thus, it is not clear to me that the circumstances in which a federal court should decline to dismiss or stay duplicative litigation in favor of state court litigation are *always* circumstances in which an antisuit injunction would

---

[117] *See Wilton*, 515 U.S. at 288 n. 2; Preliminary Doc. No. 9, *supra* note 106, at 41. *Cf.* Kevin M. Clermont and Kuo-Chang Huang, *Converting the Draft Hague Treaty into Domestic Jurisdictional Law*, *infra* p. 191, at 225 (proposed statutory tolling provision in connection with dismissal for lack of territorial jurisdiction).

[118] Congress' extension of the constitutional obligation of full faith and credit to the federal courts and its use of state preclusion law as the referent necessarily mean that federal litigation can be cut short by a state court judgment. At least in cases governed by substantive state law, it is difficult to see why a federal court's unwillingness to run the race to judgment with parallel state court litigation should be thought any different. It is more difficult to reconcile with the larger statutory context the action of a federal court which, rather than responding to a motion stimulated by state court litigation, creates the need for such litigation by refusing to adjudicate a case within its statutory subject-matter jurisdiction, and, where that is true, the functional similarities of a stay and a dismissal may dwarf any theoretical distinctions. *See* Note, *supra* note 116. *Cf.* Federal Reserve Bank of Atlanta v. Thomas, 2000 U.S. App. LEXIS 18288, at *38 (11th Cir. July 31, 2000) ("It is an abuse of discretion ... to dismiss a declaratory judgment action in favor of a state court proceeding that does not exist."). *But see* Aetna Casualty & Surety Co. v. Ind-Com Electric Co., 139 F.3d 419 (4th Cir. 1998).

[119] Redish, *supra* note 28.

[120] *See id.* at 1362–67.

[121] *See id.* at 1374–75.

[122] *See id.* at 1375–76.

[123] *See supra* text accompanying note 47.

[124] *See* Burbank, *supra* note 48, at 14–17.

be appropriate.[125] In other words, zero tolerance may be too little tolerance of parallel litigation, even within the United States. In addition, recognizing that state courts represent half of the problem of federal-state parallel litigation, and much more than that when the problem is defined to account for all of the litigation in the United States, I do not see the wisdom in baking less than half a loaf, particularly if preheating the oven will require overcoming legislative inertia. Agreeing that the Supreme Court's interpretation of the "in aid of jurisdiction" exception in the Anti-Injunction Act has been unfortunate,[126] I nonetheless doubt that a system that relied on injunctions rather than reciprocal forbearance pursuant to uniform federal law would best serve federal, state, or interjurisdictional interests.

In other words, I am inclined to believe that, having inspired those who negotiated the Brussels Convention to emulate our full faith and credit approach to the recognition of judgments, we can benefit by seeking to emulate, if not precisely to replicate, that convention's approach to the problem of equilibration when there is parallel litigation, as refined and improved in the proposed Hague Convention. It is time to implement the Full Faith and Credit Clause, the grants of judicial power in Article III, and federal statutes conferring subject-matter jurisdiction, with legislation that provides federal lis pendens standards, binding in state and federal courts alike, whose decisions interpreting and applying those standards can be reviewed by the Supreme Court.[127] The standards should not usually permit parallel litigation,[128] and they should make it impossible to suggest that normative thinking about American law generally supports such litigation.[129] At the same time, pace Professor Redish, the standards should not implement any general preference for federal or state courts, or usher in a multifactored "case-by-case form of systemic and/or litigant

[125] *Cf.* SNI Aerospatiale v. Lee Kui Jak, [1987] 3 All E.R. 510 (P.C. 1987); Workers' Compensation Board v. Amchem Products, Inc., 1 Can.S.C.R. 897 (1993). The tribunals deciding both of these cases were at pains to distinguish the standards governing a forum non conveniens dismissal or stay from those governing issuance of an antisuit injunction. *See* Paul Beaumont, *Great Britain*, in *Declining Jurisdiction*, *supra* note 63, at 230–31.

[126] *See supra* text accompanying notes 50, 53; Redish, *supra* note 28, at 1371. *See also* Lonny S. Hoffman, *Removal Jurisdiction and the All Writs Act*, 148 U. Pa. L. Rev. 401, 459–69 (1999).

[127] Changes in current law regarding the timing of appellate review may be necessary. *Cf.* Redish, *supra* note 28, at 1367–69.

For a suggestion that the Full Faith and Credit Clause might ground both a rule prohibiting interstate antisuit injunctions and a rule of lis pendens, see Bermann, *supra* note 32, at 602–03 n. 58. As he points out, "[i]f a lis pendens rule risks provoking races to the courthouse, it should at least avoid a more treacherous race to judgment." *Id.* at 603 n. 58.

[128] Note that the definition of "parallel litigation" is likely to differ for the domestic, as opposed to the international, interjurisdictional context. *See supra* note 28. Even domestically, however, acknowledgment of differences in procedural and preclusion rules should probably result in a definition that does not seek to impose on the country as a whole the broadest conceptions of litigation efficiency and consistency. *See* Burbank, *supra* note 27, at 98–102; *supra* note 98; *infra* text accompanying note 144.

[129] *See* Redish, *supra* note 28, at 1350–55. This is not the only example of the phenomenon of something that under current conceptions must be tolerated because of the perceived requirements of federalism being transmogrified into a normative good. *See* Burbank, *supra* note 34, at 113.

'interest analysis,'"[130] as opposed to a defeasible preference for the court in which litigation seeking a coercive (that is, not declaratory) remedy was first filed.

Because federal constitutional law places minimal restraints on both jurisdiction and choice of law in the United States, while federal constitutional and statutory law strictly constrain the freedom to deny recognition, a "safety valve ... that permits the equilibration of competing jurisdictional claims by means other than a strict first-filed (or first-seised) rule"[131] should be part of the suggested federal lis pendens statute. Such a provision would constitute a limited but mandatory federal doctrine of forum non conveniens, to be considered apart from any broader proposal to federalize forum non conveniens law.[132] It would be limited, as under the proposed Hague Convention,[133] because such a provision would be applicable only where parallel litigation was pending interjurisdictionally. Unlike the proposed Hague Convention provision, it would be mandatory, and federal appellate review would be available to ensure that a federal or state court did not ignore or seriously misapply the governing standards.[134]

If even a closed jurisdictional system backed by strict lis pendens doctrine cannot deter evasive action that inflicts substantial costs on litigants and courts,[135] the

---

130 Redish, *supra* note 28, at 1374. Of course, neither a preference for federal court nor a preference for state court would serve to resolve problems of interstate parallel litigation, with which the proposed statute would also deal. *See* also *infra* note 132.

131 *Supra* text accompanying notes 92–93. If the categorical lis pendens treatment of declaratory relief cases under the proposed Hague Convention is deemed too broad, *see supra* note 89, *infra* note 145, the overbreadth can be cured through the application of this limited forum non conveniens safety valve.

132 *See infra* text accompanying notes 178–201. Just because we may be stuck with multi-factored case-by-case analysis as the basis of decision in one corner of the law, *but see infra* note 200, does not mean that we should sweep it into others, even if they are adjacent. Moreover, there is probably a greater need for flexibility, and hence discretion, in international than in domestic cases. I am here advocating, for wholly domestic cases, a rule that presumptively favors the court in which the first coercive suit is filed, with statutory specification of the considerations that might lead to another choice. Realism about what really motivates most forum non conveniens motions – and it is not litigation convenience – should prompt Congress not simply to ape the doctrine that formally governs the resolution of such motions when specifying exceptions to the statutory lis pendens rule. If so, it would be "a limited ... federal doctrine of forum non conveniens" in more than one sense.

133 *See Hague Draft*, *supra* note 8, art. 21(7); *supra* text accompanying note 93.

134 Other problems of appellate review aside, *see supra* note 127 and accompanying text, any forum non conveniens provision is likely to present serious obstacles to effective review. *See* American Dredging Co. v. Miller, 510 U.S. 443 (1994). Those problems could be reduced if there were, as I advocate, statutory specification of the considerations that could lead to defeasance of the first-filed rule and if those specifications did not simply repeat current forum non conveniens doctrine. As Allan Stein has helpfully observed:

> Particularly where the forum choice turns on regulatory choices, there is absolutely no reason for appellate deference under an abuse of discretion standard. Moreover, effective appellate review of forum choices must be interlocutory. The final judgment rule here is as undermining of coherent policy as the standard of review.

Letter from Allan Stein to Stephen Burbank 1 (Sept. 22, 2000).

135 *See supra* text accompanying notes 107–09.

proposed federal lis pendens statute should permit, but strictly control the grant of antisuit injunctions. It is worth considering whether, as an aspect of the statutory controls, must the litigant seeking the injunction in the (few) situations permitted first seek a stay from the other court. Any such requirement might also have to negate the possibility of preclusion arising from the first court's decision on the statutory requirements.[136] Moreover, careful attention would be required to the alternatives of asymmetric treatment of federal and state courts, on one hand, and reversal of current law barring in almost all cases state court injunctions against federal litigation, on the other.[137]

How then should American courts respond to parallel international litigation *in the absence of a treaty or in cases that are not within the scope of any treaty concluded*? I have sketched a model for a federal solution to parallel interjurisdictional litigation within the United States, one that is based in a federal statute binding on federal and state courts alike. Federal legislative power to dictate a national solution for international cases is as clear as it is for domestic interjurisdictional cases. Whichever serves as the lead in the effort to move Congress to action, the argument from legislative inertia extends to all litigation contexts where there is a plausible national need.

The federal courts have used inappropriate domestic models to deal with parallel international litigation in the past, inconsistently treating litigation in Italy as if it were litigation in another federal court or in a state court. The models used have been inappropriate either because their extension to international cases lacked normative justification, or because the model itself was incoherent in the context in which it was initially used, or for both reasons.[138] Having suggested the unitary treatment of parallel interjurisdictional litigation that is wholly domestic, I turn to the question whether it would be an appropriate model for international litigation.

The generous recognition treatment of international foreign judgments characteristic of American law for more than a century has represented a remarkable act of faith, one that has been tested, if only because put in relief by the discriminatory provisions of the Brussels Convention,[139] and that would be tested again if proposed changes were implemented to eliminate the mechanism by which the United States could escape such discriminatory treatment.[140] A due-process check on jurisdictional

---

[136] *Cf.* Parsons Steel, Inc. v. First Alabama Bank, 474 U.S. 518 (1986) (state court ruling on preclusive effect of prior federal litigation itself entitled to full faith and credit in proceeding seeking injunction from federal court otherwise permitted under the relitigation exception to the Anti-Injunction Act).

[137] *See* Donovan v. City of Dallas, 377 U.S. 408 (1964).

[138] *See supra* text accompanying notes 59–62, 119–26.

[139] *See* Brussels Convention, *supra* note 4, art. 4; von Mehren, *supra* note 9, at 278–79; Hartley, *supra* note 81, at 231–33. The scope of potential discrimination was, of course, increased with the Lugano Convention.

[140] Article 59 of the Brussels Convention "allows a Contracting State ... to enter into a convention ... with a non-Contracting State ... in which it undertakes not to recognize judgments given in other Contracting States against a defendant domiciled or habitually resident in the other party to the convention ... in those cases in which the judgment-granting court only had jurisdiction on one of the grounds expressly outlawed by Article 3 of the Convention." Hartley, *supra* note 81, at 233

exorbitance can provide no greater assurance internationally than it does in domestic interjurisdictional litigation. Moreover, as an anterior matter, it is not clear whether standards of adjudicatory jurisdiction can be properly taken as the hallmark of fairness and impartiality of the rendering court in a judgment recognition world that comprehends vastly different cultures and legal traditions. Due process also does not provide much protection against procedural unfairness; a truly limited public policy defense is hardly a replacement for choice-of-law control.

Whatever the force of these concerns regarding recognition practice, they do suggest that, in the absence of a treaty, international cases should not be assimilated to domestic cases for purposes of lis pendens and antisuit injunctions, whether in case law as it develops in the federal and state courts, or under the proposed federal lis pendens statute.

So long as the inquiry concerns the content of a proposed federal statute, an important concern that may attend unilateral judicial lawmaking for international cases need not detain us.[141] Congress and the President are competent to decide whether and when dismissing or staying litigation in the United States in response to, or enjoining, parallel litigation abroad, would well serve the nation's interests. Indeed, the fact that federal and state courts are currently making such decisions, and doing so inconsistently, is one argument for legislation as the vehicle of change.

An argument can be made that, at least in the absence of reciprocity, American courts should not generally defer to parallel litigation abroad. The argument would probably acknowledge that it is too late in the day to reverse the historic generosity of American courts in recognizing international foreign judgments. Indeed, it might well rely on that proposition, as well as the realities of modern international forum-shopping,[142] for the normative stance that the United States should not further handicap itself and its people by refusing to enter the race to judgment.

This argument is not without force. Yet, some of the costs of parallel international litigation are visited on domestic parties and domestic courts. Moreover, the general faith in other legal systems evidenced by the United States' generous judgment recognition practice surely has a firmer basis today than it did 100 years ago. Both considerations suggest that an attempt to rely on a normative principle of dual jurisdiction would ring hollow. Unless the goal were to take back part of the territory surrendered by international recognition practice, such a crude rule would not be necessary to protect the interests that, according to that practice, are relevant. And

---

(footnote omitted); *see also* Zekoll, *supra* note 68, at 1289 n. 33. The proposed Council Regulation of the Commission of the European Communities would eliminate that authority prospectively. *See* Proposed Council Regulation, *supra* note 108, at 26, 51. This would be a result far different from that urged by the United Kingdom's representatives, namely, abolition of the underlying discrimination. *See* Beaumont, *supra* note 90, at 102–04. Discussion at the Symposium suggested that this proposal is highly controversial and may not be part of any final regulation.

141 *See* Burbank, *supra* note 3, at 138–39.

142 *See* Andreas F. Lowenfeld, *Forum Shopping, Antisuit Injunctions, Negative Declarations and Related Tools of International Litigation*, 91 Am. J. Int'l L. 314 (1997).

such a goal would be hard to defend at a time when "[t]he need for courts to rely on each other in order to serve justice has been recognized in an increasing number of international civil litigation cases."[143]

Assuming then that some rule of deference is appropriate, the existence of litigation in different countries that may follow different procedural rules and reflect different legal traditions counsels caution or modesty in giving content to the concept of parallel litigation. This is one justification for the very narrow scope of Article 21 of the Brussels Convention and the narrow scope of Article 21 of the proposed Hague Convention.

For these purposes, the focal point of difference is likely to be the content of domestic preclusion law, including, in particular, the scope of the operation of claim preclusion, the treatment of counterclaims, and the existence and scope of issue preclusion. These matters, in turn, may reflect, although for these purposes they do not exhaust, the relevance of domestic procedural rules on such matters as joinder of claims and parties. Although for domestic interjurisdictional cases, consideration of changes in the law on lis pendens can reasonably assume substantial homogeneity as to such matters, that is not true internationally. And United States lis pendens practice should no more impose upon foreign institutions than should United States judgment recognition practice.[144]

At the very least, a lis pendens provision for international cases, inspired by the proposed Hague Convention, should require the second-seised American court to assure itself that a recognizable judgment was in prospect.[145] This element, which is not necessary for domestic interjurisdictional litigation, would enable the American court to satisfy itself that the expense and delay of parallel litigation could be avoided, and that it would be fair to do so, by inquiring whether the basis of jurisdiction in the foreign court met minimum standards and by determining, ex ante, that there was no systemic or insuperable situational barrier to the fair conduct of proceedings abroad and no likelihood of a judgment manifestly incompatible with American public policy. It would also involve engagement with the law of preclusion applicable to the foreign litigation. Finally, since ex ante predictions about recognition and delay are more difficult in the international context, the provision should

---

[143] Lussier, *supra* note 6, *at* 60.

[144] *See supra* note 128; Stephen B. Burbank, *Federal Judgments Law: Sources of Authority and Sources of Rules*, 70 Texas L. Rev. 1551, 1582–87 (1992).

[145] The inspiration derived should extend to other matters not mentioned in the text. Thus, an international lis pendens provision should qualify the obligation to defer to the first-filed case by including a limited forum non conveniens check, but one that conferred greater discretion than that for lis pendens in wholly domestic cases. *See supra* note 132. Whether it should follow the proposed Hague Convention in carving out actions for declaratory relief depends on the view taken of the potential of such actions "to level the forum shopping playing field." Letter from Allan Stein to Stephen Burbank, *supra* note 134, at 2. For a more nuanced treatment, *see* Leuven/London Principles 4.1 and 4.3, *supra* note 97.

require a stay, with dismissal to follow, if appropriate, upon presentation of a judgment eligible for recognition.[146]

American courts and scholars are prone to ignore or dismiss the interests of sovereignty with which some other countries invest procedural mechanisms that operate extraterritorially.[147] As a result, perceived American imperialism may have an intellectual dimension. In any event, one of the many matters in which such a difference of view is likely concerns injunctions entered against litigation abroad. Some Americans may comfort themselves with the notion that the order is directed to a litigant within the court's jurisdiction, resuscitating a distinction akin to the distinction between in personam and in rem actions that has been thoroughly discredited in other contexts.[148] Others take the view that an antisuit injunction has inescapable extraterritorial implications, which is the view taken in the interpretation and application of the federal Anti-Injunction Act.[149]

Precisely because antisuit injunctions in international litigation are reasonably perceived to operate extraterritorially and to constrain courts as well as litigants, their issuance should be governed by a federal statute binding on federal and state courts alike. Moreover, respect for other nations counsels care in specifying the circumstances in which an international antisuit injunction can be issued, as do the risks and costs of error when courts dabble in comparative law.[150] Here, existing law governing parallel federal-state litigation, however incoherent in the context for which it was developed, may in fact be an appropriate model, at least insofar as it would permit an injunction to protect the American court's jurisdiction (the so-called anti-antisuit injunction).[151] American courts should also have the power to prevent a manifest attempt to evade important national policy,[152] but perhaps only in those situations where the policy in question would not be adequately protected through the denial of recognition. Finally, the federal-state model also suggests as appropriate internationally, in the absence of a treaty governing recognition, power in the

---

146 *See supra* text accompanying notes 59–62, 94, 117. Regulation by statute would moot any separation of powers concerns that attended dismissal of litigation involving legal (as opposed to equitable) claims from federal court in deference to litigation abroad. In Posner v. Essex Ins. Co., Ltd., 178 F.3d 1209, 1222–23 (11th Cir. 1999), the Court of Appeals held that the restrictions on abstention announced in Quackenbush v. Allstate Ins. Co., 517 U.S. 706 (1996), did not apply to "international abstention." With respect, the court's reasoning confuses the grounds of the putatively applicable abstention doctrine with the basic separation of powers limitations that, rightly or wrongly, the Quackenbush Court set out to rationalize and enforce.

147 *See* Burbank, *supra* note 3, at 112–23 (service of process and waiver of service).

148 *Cf.* Burbank, *supra* note 13, at 1338–39 (asset freeze orders).

149 *See* Laker Airways v. Sabena, 731 F.2d 909, 927 (D.C.Cir. 1984); 28 U.S.C. § 2283 (1994); County of Imperial v. Munoz, 449 U.S. 54, 58–59 (1980).

150 *See* Bermann, *supra* note 32, at 627–32; Kent Andersen, *What Can the United States Learn from English Anti-Suit Injunctions? An American Perspective on* Airbus Industrie GIE v. Patel, 25 Yale J. Int'l L. 195 (2000).

151 *See Laker*, 731 F.2d 909. For the influence of the federal-state model, see *id.* at 926.

152 *See Laker*, 731 F.2d at 931; China Trade & Development Corp. v. MV Choong Yong, 837 F.2d 33 (2d Cir. 1987).

American court to enjoin the continuation of litigation abroad when that is necessary to protect or effectuate a judgment that it has rendered.[153]

Forum Non Conveniens

It is commonplace to link the forum non conveniens doctrine to the need to discipline jurisdictional law that reaches too far (including, in the United States, federal venue law). As the above summary of American developments suggests,[154] there is force in the observation. Those who make it should admit the possibility, however, that American jurisdictional law does not have a monopoly on overreaching and that the limitations of foresight can call forth a similar need in other systems. Even such a hallowed jurisdictional ground as domicile may benefit from the equilibration that forum non conveniens or some similar device can provide,[155] and functionally similar jurisdictional equilibration may already occur without invocation of that dreaded Latin phrase.[156] Just as by substituting "inquiring" for "inquisitorial," "the bad becomes the good,"[157] so it may be that changing forum non conveniens to "circumstances for declining jurisdiction" lowers a red flag and allows those from different legal traditions to be candid about what courts really do – the discretion that dares not speak its name – and the appropriate measure of equilibration flexibility in a jurisdictional system that is hybrid both because it combines standards from different traditions and because it is neither closed nor open.

Of course, judgments about both jurisdictional overreaching and the acceptable limits of foresight are culturally contingent. Recalling the persistence of attention to regulatory interests in American forum non conveniens cases, one can perhaps identify a normative basis for judgments about overreaching from the American perspective that is broader and more faithful to actual practice than litigation convenience simpliciter. According to this view, the failure of American law to

---

[153] *See Laker*, 731 F.2d at 926–27. Note, however, that the same concerns that caution modesty in the definition of parallel international litigation, *see supra* text accompanying notes 143–44, should restrain the use of antisuit injunctions to export peculiarly American notions of claim or issue preclusion.

Consideration of experience under the Brussels Convention may also suggest scope for a carefully defined power to enjoin litigation abroad that is, and is intended to be, oppressive. *See supra* text accompanying notes 107–10.

[154] *See supra* text accompanying notes 16–46.

[155]
> A civilian mind assumes that the need to have discretion to decline to exercise jurisdiction must be because the country has over broad, or exorbitant, rules of jurisdiction. However, it may simply be the case that it is impossible to devise rules of jurisdiction which will always lead to an appropriate court hearing the case. Even the archetypically fair jurisdiction rule, the domicile of the defendant ... can lead to an inappropriate forum.

Beaumont, *supra* note 90, at 76 (footnotes omitted).

[156] *See* Wendy Kennett, *Forum Non Conveniens in Europe*, 54 Cambridge L.J. 552 (1995); Fawcett, *supra* note 63, at 24–27 ("forum non conveniens substitutes").

[157] *Hearings Before the Commission on Revision of the Federal Court Appellate System*, second phase, vol. I, at 205 (1974) (statement of Friendly, J.).

integrate jurisdictional and choice-of-law doctrine, together with a recognition practice that permits neither a choice-of-law test nor reexamination of the merits, renders it important to consider domestic regulatory interests before jurisdiction is surrendered. Jurisdictional standards that more broadly implement domestic regulatory interests should diminish the need for this equilibration device.[158]

It would be surprising if the jurisdictional standards in the current draft of the proposed Hague Convention, some of which seem more responsive to what Americans would regard as choice of law than to jurisdictional concerns,[159] did not "more broadly implement domestic regulatory interests" than American state jurisdictional law based on the federal constitutional floor of due process.[160] From the American perspective there is still a need for an escape device, however, even if only because the proposed convention preserves some freedom to apply national jurisdictional law that is neither required nor prohibited (the gray zone again). It will also be useful in some cases if the final product contains, as does the current draft, jurisdictional bases that not only overreach but may be exorbitant as a matter of due process.[161] Thus, whether or not forum non conveniens is redundant in domestic cases,[162] a provision for declining jurisdiction under the proposed convention may be important to the United States' ability faithfully to comply both with the treaty and with domestic constitutional law.

In this light, Article 22 of the current draft[163] is an important provision from the

[158] *See* Clermont and Huang, *supra* note 117, at 226.

[159] *See Hague Draft*, *supra* note 8, Article 6 (contracts), Article 11 (trusts).

[160] *See* Burbank, *supra* note 34, at 112–19.

[161] *See Hague Draft*, *supra* note 8, Article 10(1)(b) (torts or delicts), Article 14 (multiple defendants), Article 16 (third-party claims).

[162] *See* Stein, *supra* note 36.

[163] Draft Article 22 provides:

> 1. In exceptional circumstances, when the jurisdiction of the court seised is not founded on an exclusive choice of court agreement valid under Article 4, or on Article 7, 8 or 12, the court may, on application by a party, suspend its proceedings if in that case it is clearly inappropriate for that court to exercise jurisdiction and if a court of another State has jurisdiction and is clearly more appropriate to resolve the dispute. Such application must be made no later than at the time of the first defence on the merits.
>
> 2. The court shall take into account, in particular – (a) any inconvenience to the parties in view of their habitual residence; (b) the nature and location of the evidence, including documents and witnesses, and the procedures for obtaining such evidence; (c) applicable limitation or prescription periods; (d) the possibility of obtaining recognition and enforcement of any decision on the merits.
>
> 3. In deciding whether to suspend the proceedings, a court shall not discriminate on the basis of the nationality or habitual residence of the parties.
>
> 4. If the court decides to suspend its proceedings under paragraph 1, it may order the defendant to provide security sufficient to satisfy any decision of the other court on the merits. However, it shall make such an order if the other court has jurisdiction only under Article 17, unless the defendant establishes that sufficient assets exist in the State of that other court or in another State where the court's decision could be enforced.
>
> 5. When the court has suspended its proceedings under paragraph 1 – (a) it shall decline to exercise jurisdiction if the court of the other State exercises jurisdiction, or if the plaintiff does not bring

American perspective, and it could have a salutary effect on domestic law in other signatory states, since it would authorize courts to exercise openly a measure of jurisdictional equilibration that they may approximate today through other means.[164]

Draft Article 22 permits a court that has jurisdiction under the Convention, other than exclusive jurisdiction or jurisdiction under provisions protective of consumers and employees, to suspend its proceedings "[i]n exceptional circumstances" if the exercise of jurisdiction would be "clearly inappropriate" and "if another State has jurisdiction and is clearly more appropriate to resolve the dispute." The draft article requires the court to consider certain factors, forbids discrimination on the basis of nationality or habitual residence, and prescribes circumstances in which security may or must be required from the defendant seeking suspension. Finally, the draft article provides for a court that has suspended its proceedings (1) to decline jurisdiction if the court of the other state exercises jurisdiction or if the plaintiff does not bring proceedings in that state in the time specified, or (2) to proceed with the case "if the court of the other State decides not to exercise jurisdiction."

By permitting a court seised of jurisdiction under the Convention to suspend its proceedings, and ultimately to decline to exercise jurisdiction, in favor of "a court of another State," rather than only "a court of another Contracting State," draft Article 22 appears to give broad scope to this jurisdictional equilibration device. The drafting history confirms that such was the intent.[165] For one who previously assumed that compromise between the civil-law and common-law traditions would limit the operation of the common-law device to cases in which "an alternative forum [was] available in another signatory state,"[166] this is surprising. Indeed, without the aid of the drafting history and the Special Commission's report, one might have been tempted to conclude that the failure to specify "contracting state" was inadvertent.[167]

---

the proceedings in that State within the time specified by the court, or (b) it shall proceed with the case if the court of the other State decides not to exercise jurisdiction.

164 *See supra* text accompanying note 156. Might the example of Québec have helped to persuade skeptics to accept a limited form of forum non conveniens in the proposed Hague Convention? *See* Lussier, *supra* note 6, at 46, 50; Fawcett, *supra* note 63, at 16–17.

165 *See* Working Document No. 144 E, *supra* note 103, Article 24; Hague Conference on Private Int'l Law, Special Commission on International Jurisdiction and the Effects of Foreign Judgments in Civil and Commercial Matters, Working Document 241 E, Article 24 (June 1999) ("if a court of another [Contracting] State has jurisdiction and is clearly more appropriate to resolve the dispute"). *See also* Nygh and Pocar, *supra* note 97, at 89.

166 Burbank, *supra* note 34, at 122. Wendy Kennett had suggested foreclosing the operation of forum non conveniens "in cases where the plaintiff was domiciled in a Contracting State." Kennett, *supra* note 156, at 568–69.

167 Draft Article 2(1)(c) provides that Article 22, like Article 21, displaces domestic law in situations where all parties to the litigation are habitually resident in the state but the court there "is required to determine whether to decline jurisdiction or suspend its proceedings on the grounds that the dispute ought to be determined in the courts of another Contracting State." Draft Article 22(4) contains a special provision for security in situations where "the other court has jurisdiction only under Article 17." Draft Article 21(7) permits escape from the requirements of lis pendens, requirements that are applicable only when there are proceedings in different contracting states, "under the conditions specified in Article 22." None of these provisions would be dispositive on the question of scope, but

Not wishing to criticize the basic compromise reached, I note only that the provision for security in draft Article 22(4) apparently does not reach cases in which the other court sits in a non-contracting state.[168]

It is difficult to fault the conditions set forth in draft Article 22(1), to wit, the requirement of exceptional circumstances, the carving out of certain bases of exclusive and protective jurisdiction, and the limitations requiring that the exercise of jurisdiction in the court seised be clearly inappropriate and that there be some other clearly more appropriate state whose courts have jurisdiction.[169] Moreover, although draft Article 22(2) requires the court entertaining a motion to suspend to take account of certain factors, it does not exclude the consideration of other factors that might signal "exceptional circumstances" and that might inform judgments about the appropriateness of the respective fora.[170]

However, it is not clear why, and it is a source of considerable controversy in the United States that, draft Article 22 appears to govern dismissals by the courts of contracting state, even when exercising jurisdiction under national law as permitted by draft Article 17.[171] Fortunately, the Special Commission Report flags the issue, notes arguments for and against that interpretation, and wisely concludes that "[t]his point will require clarification at the Diplomatic Conference."[172]

One of the factors that a court is required to consider under draft Article 22(2), "applicable limitation or prescription periods," is often the subject of conditional forum non conveniens stays or dismissals in the United States and other countries, the party seeking to escape the jurisdiction being required to waive any time bar in the alternative forum.[173] The draft article does not explicitly authorize the imposition

all might be thought to suggest what I previously assumed would be the rule if compromise were possible, namely that the proposed Convention would permit a court in a contracting state to decline jurisdiction only in favor of the courts of another contracting state.

168 That provision requires the suspending court to "order the defendant to provide sufficient security to satisfy any decision of the other court on the merits" in situations where "the other court has jurisdiction only under Article 17" and "unless the defendant establishes that sufficient assets exist in the State of that other court or in another State where the court's decision could be enforced." Draft Article 17, in turn, applies only to contracting states.

169 Recall, however, that these conditions make it difficult to credit the notion that this article could effectively serve the purposes of Article 22 of the Brussels Convention on related actions. *See supra* text accompanying note 105. Compare Leuven/London Principle 4.3, *supra* note 97, which requires a court to "decline jurisdiction and refer the matter to an alternative court where it is satisfied that the alternative court is the manifestly more appropriate forum for the determination of the merits of the matter."

170 "The list is not exhaustive, as indicated by the words 'in particular'. Other factors, such as: the substantive law to be applied in resolving the dispute, the availability of legal aid or the extent of the relief which may be granted in each forum, may also be relevant." Nygh and Pocar, *supra* note 97, at 91.

171 At the Symposium a member of the United States delegation went so far as to term the application of Article 22 in cases governed by national jurisdictional law "unacceptable."

172 Nygh and Pocar, *supra* note 97, at 89.

173 *See* John Bies, Comment, *Conditioning Forum Non Conveniens*, 67 Chi. L. Rev. 489, 501–02 (2000). Compare Leuven/London Principle 5.3, *supra* note 97, encouraging the parties and the court to consider "appropriate terms of referral," including submission to jurisdiction and "the terms on which the applicant may assert a defense of limitation or prescription of action in the alternative court."

of such a condition, and the fact that another consideration, "the possibility of obtaining recognition and enforcement of any decision on the merits," is the subject of a separate provision, draft Article 22(4), which authorizes or requires the taking of security from the defendant, might be the basis for a negative inference in that regard.[174] The article should explicitly authorize the imposition of conditions, in addition to the provision of security. Experience in common-law countries indicates that it may be necessary and appropriate to wise jurisdictional equilibration practice.[175]

Divining the motive force behind draft Article 22(3), which forbids discrimination on the basis of the nationality or habitual residence of the parties in deciding whether to suspend proceedings, does not require great imagination. The possibility of invidious discrimination under the Brussels Convention, after all, was an important reason why the United States initiated this process at The Hague.[176] Those on the receiving end of such implied criticism may take the view that discrimination is discrimination,[177] even if, as a result, the poor moth is blocked from the light.[178] But we are all, I hope, discriminating, and thus, if this provision remains in Article 22, capable of distinguishing differences in treatment that are prompted by the consistent application of factors that are nationality-neutral from differences that are causally tied to the consideration of nationality (or habitual residence).

The critical question here, I believe, is the extent to which consideration of what the Supreme Court of the United States has called "public interest factors," which includes, even if not acknowledged as such, the regulatory interests of the forum, is

---

174 The Special Commission's report suggests, although not with great clarity, that such a conditional dismissal is permitted. It states: "In most common law countries it is possible for a defendant to waive the benefit of a limitation period by agreeing not to plead it. Such an agreement may counteract consideration (*sic*) set out in sub-paragraph (c)." Nygh and Pocar, *supra* note 97, at 91.

175 This could be done by enumerating permissible conditions or stating general criteria. If the latter approach were taken, a normative framework would be necessary, and it does not presently emerge from the American cases. *See* Comment, *supra* note 173. The enterprise should also take account of the perverse incentives that a regime of conditional dismissals may create. *See id.* at 517. *Cf.* Robert Braucher, *The Inconvenient Federal Forum*, 60 Harv. L. Rev. 908, 938 (1947) (recommending that proposed federal transfer statute include a provision "that the court may order or deny transfer on condition that any party to the action comply with such terms ... as the court in its discretion considers just"). I agree with Allan Stein, however, that "[u]nless narrowly constrained, ... conditions can totally undermine the point of forum non [conveniens]." Letter from Allan Stein to Stephen Burbank, *supra* note 134, at 2.

176 *See* von Mehren, *supra* note 9, at 278–82.

177 *See* Zekoll, *supra* note 68, at 1299. They may also point out that one's reaction to perceived discrimination may depend upon whether one is a potential victim or beneficiary, using the proposed Hague Convention as Exhibit 1. *See* Georges A.L. Droz, *Preliminary Draft of the Convention on Jurisdiction and Foreign Judgments in Civil and Commercial Matters: Provisions on Jurisdiction*, *supra* p. 15, at 34. Unlike the Brussels Convention, however, the proposed Hague Convention does not *require* contracting state to recognize judgments entered by the courts of other contracting state, pursuant to jurisdictional bases declared to be exorbitant, in cases not within the scope of the Convention.

178 "As a moth is drawn to the light, so is a litigant drawn to the United States." Smith Kline & French Laboratories Ltd. v. Bloch, [1983] 1 W.L.R. 730, 733 (Eng. C.A. 1982).

permissible in declining jurisdiction under draft Article 22.[179] It may be that, at least in most cases where the proposed convention provides the jurisdictional standards, a measure of regulatory interest is assured. But that will not be true in some cases, including, particularly, cases in which jurisdiction is asserted within the gray zone as authorized in draft Article 17.[180]

If further negotiations do not lead to the restriction of Article 22 to cases in which jurisdiction is asserted under the Convention, perhaps draft Article 22(3) should be revised to exempt from the non-discrimination provision cases in which jurisdiction is founded on Article 17. That may not be necessary, however, and it may not be desirable from the perspective of domestic United States law reform "under the influence, if not the command, of a private international law treaty."[181] It would not be necessary if perceived lack of regulatory interest were a permitted factor in making judgments about "exceptional circumstances" and about appropriateness of the forum under Article 22, and if United States courts applying Article 22 were candid about the influence of regulatory considerations on decisions to decline jurisdiction.[182]

This discussion suggests that, apart from the proposed Hague Convention, but in part because of the perception of invidious discrimination in United States forum non conveniens law that it reflects, domestic law should be purged of differential presumptions based on nationality that supposedly implement considerations of litigation convenience but that often mask crude judgments about regulatory interest. At the same time, the doctrine should be explicitly reshaped to comprehend attention to regulatory interest,[183] an important check on jurisdictional equilibration that has nothing to do with convenience and that, indeed, cannot be properly confined to the policies underlying the substantive law. The realities of international forum selection revealed by decisions in the United States and abroad demonstrate that the American legal system is distinctive as much for the rules by which it ensures and fructifies access to court as by its rules of substantive law.[184]

---

179 *See supra* text accompanying notes 40–45. The Special Commission's report suggests that consideration of such matters is appropriate. *See* Nygh and Pocar, *supra* note 97, at 91, *quoted supra* note 170. Note, however, the English view that "public interest considerations not related to the private interests of the parties and the ends of justice have no bearing on the decision which the court has to make." Lubbe v. Cape plc, [2000] W.L.R. 1545 (H.L. 2000). *See* Fawcett, *supra* note 63, at 15–16.

180 The relevance of this point depends, of course, on the answer to the question whether draft Article 22 governs in cases where jurisdiction is asserted under national law pursuant to draft Article 17. *See supra* text accompanying notes 171–72.

181 *Supra* text accompanying note 15.

182 This reorientation would not necessarily eliminate discrimination, however, since the definition of regulatory interest can itself be discriminatory. *See* John Hart Ely, *Choice of Law and the State's Interest in Protecting its Own*, 23 W. & Mary L. Rev. 173 (1981).

183 *See* Hoffman and Rowley, *supra* note 42.

184 *See, e.g.*, Piper Aircraft Co. v. Piper, 454 U.S. 235, 252 n. 18 (1981). In argument before the Appellate Committee of the House of Lords seeking to have an injunction against personal injury litigation in Texas set aside, "the defendants undertook (1) to waive their claim to punitive damages, and (2) to waive reliance on the principle of strict liability." Airbus Industrie GIE v. Patel, [1999] 1 A.C. 119,

If I am correct that regulatory interest is reflected in arrangements, including procedural arrangements, that are consequential to the implementation of substantive law norms, explicit attention to that matter should force American lawmakers finally to confront the relevance, if any, that the loss, not only of more favorable substantive law, but also of the ability to finance a lawsuit, should have on the decision to decline jurisdiction. Although American decisions occasionally discuss that matter, no coherent approach emerges from these decisions.[185] English cases, applying doctrine that explicitly accounts for the loss of litigation advantage, are more informative. There too, however, coherence has been lacking, at least until recently, probably because of differences in views of what is a "legitimate" litigation advantage (which are culturally contingent).[186]

American forum non conveniens law seems generally to contemplate dismissal rather than a stay or suspension of proceedings,[187] although a conditional dismissal may be the functional equivalent of a stay. In this as well, it is different from similar doctrine in some other Anglo-American jurisdictions.[188] It also differs from draft Article 22, which authorizes a suspension of proceedings ripening into action declining jurisdiction if "the court of the other State exercises jurisdiction, or if the plaintiff

---

[1998] 2 All E.R. 257 (H.L. 1998). The American legal system is also distinctive for, and forum non conveniens practice is strongly influenced by, the institution of the jury. *See* Russell J. Weintraub, *Admiralty Choice-of-Law Rules for Damages*, 28 J. Mar. L. & Com. 237, 237, 253 (1992); Hoffman and Rowley, *supra* note 42. "[M]ost often, party selection is dictated by the procedural characteristics of the forum concerned (costs rules, jury trial, provision for discovery etc) or simply by the relative advantage of playing at home rather than abroad." Third Interim Report, *supra* note 97, at 5. *See* Fawcett, *supra* note 63, at 20–21.

185 *Compare* In re Union Carbide Corp. Gas Plant Disaster at Bhopal, India in December, 1984, 634 F. Supp. 842 (S.D.N.Y. 1986), *aff'd*, 809 F.2d 195 (2d Cir.), *cert. denied*, 484 U.S. 871 (1987), *with* Fiorenza v. United States Steel Int'l, 311 F. Supp. 117, 120–21 (S.D.N.Y. 1969) and Waterways Ltd. v. Barclays Bank plc, 571 N.Y.S.2d 208 (App. Div. 1991). *Cf.* Mercier v. Sheraton International, Inc., 981 F.2d 1345 (1st Cir. 1992) (rejecting condition that defendant waive cost-bond requirement under Turkish law).

186 *See* Lubbe v. Cape plc, [2000] 1 Lloyd's Rep. 139 (Eng. C.A. 1999); *see also* Airbus Industrie GIE v. Patel, [1999] 1 A.C. 119, [1998] 2 All E.R. 257 (H.L. 1998). On July 20, 2000, the House of Lords removed the stay upheld in the Court of Appeal in the *Lubbe* case. Critical to that decision were the findings that legal aid would not be available to the plaintiffs in South Africa and that they would have no other means of obtaining the professional representation or expert evidence that would be essential to the just adjudication of their claims. *See* Lubbe v. Cape plc, [2000] W.L.R. 1545 (H.L. 2000).

It appears that the issue can properly be considered in decisions under draft Article 22 of the proposed Hague Convention. *See* Nygh and Pocar, *supra* note 97, at 91, *quoted supra* note 170. Otherwise, if a plaintiff whose case has been suspended thereunder does not bring proceedings in a court of "the other State" within the time specified, the suspending court is required to decline to exercise jurisdiction.

187 *See* David W. Robertson, *The Federal Doctrine of Forum Non Conveniens: "An Object Lesson in Uncontrolled Discretion,"* 29 Texas Int'l L. J. 353, 370 n. 139 (1994) ("In the federal system, dismissal is the unvarying rule.").

188 *See, e.g.*, Kennett, *supra* note 156, at 555.

does not bring the proceedings in that State within the time specified by the court," but which directs the suspending court to "proceed with the case if the court of the other State decides not to exercise jurisdiction."

Apart from the proposed Hague Convention, but again under its influence, American forum non conveniens law should be changed to make a stay, rather than dismissal, the norm.[189] Even if the recommended attention to comparative litigation finance did not yield a change in doctrine, for instance preventing a forum non conveniens dismissal where there was a domestic regulatory interest and the plaintiff lacked the ability to finance litigation elsewhere, conditional dismissals may not always guarantee that there would be a competent court in the more appropriate state.[190] Moreover, whatever the psychological and bureaucratic benefits of getting rid of a case, preserving the opportunity to take a look at developments abroad ex post would ease the agony, or discipline the sincerity, of prediction, thus enabling American courts to respond more sensitively, and on the basis of actual information, to situations in which any relief, let alone justice, proved only theoretically possible in another forum.[191]

It might be argued that another reason for federal forum non conveniens law to change from a norm of dismissal to one of stay or suspension arises from two things: (1) the Supreme Court's bright line approach to that distinction for separation of powers purposes in the cognate area of abstention, and (2) from the Court's failure to date to rationalize the forum non conveniens doctrine for that purpose.[192] Whatever the force of separation of powers concerns in connection with jurisdictional equilibration in general, and whatever functional differences there may be between dismissal and stay, however, it would be difficult to rest on the distinction when suspending or declining jurisdiction did not require the existence of actual litigation in another forum and was not concerned with the potential for a recognizable judgment.

---

189 *See* Alexander M. Bickel, *The Doctrine of Forum Non Conveniens as Applied in the Federal Courts in Matters of Admiralty: An Object Lesson in Uncontrolled Discretion*, 35 Cornell L.Q. 12, 28 n. 69 (1949).

190 *See* 1998 Synthesis, *supra* note 106, at 43.

191 *See* Robertson, *supra* note 187, at 364; *id.* at 371 ("in the real world, everyone knows that international plaintiffs who suffer forum non conveniens dismissals in the United States are typically unable to go forward in the hypothesized foreign forum").

> The Principles address a concern expressed in many quarters about the process of declining jurisdiction, namely the prospect that it could lead to a denial of justice in which a plaintiff is left without an effective forum in which to secure relief. They do so by coupling the process of declining jurisdiction with that of *referral*. This process ensures that, in cases where a court is permitted to decline jurisdiction by these Principles, it shall always refer the matter to an alternative court, and provides a mechanism to ensure that such referral is effective.

Third Interim Report, *supra* note 97, at 18.

192 *See supra* text accompanying notes 47–62, 112. "The Court [in *Quackenbush*] was less successful in bringing within the analytical fold post-1948 cases dismissing damages actions on the ground of *forum non conveniens*, to which it understandably imputed a separate history." Burbank, *supra* note 48, at 17 (footnote omitted).

Having suggested a number of changes in American forum non conveniens law for international cases, some of which are inspired by the proposed Hague Convention, I conclude this discussion by considering how such changes should be implemented and whether there is sufficient need for uniformity that federal law should provide the governing rules, or some of them, for both federal and state courts. The two questions are analytically related.

Under current conceptions of the requirements of federalism, it appears to be difficult, if not impossible, to carry an argument for a federal judge-made law of forum non conveniens that is binding on state courts.[193] Moreover, as I have suggested, it is equally difficult to sustain the continued use of federal forum non conveniens law, the scope of application of which is essentially confined to international cases – here, cases in which no other domestic court is available – as a model for state forum non conveniens law, whose scope is broader.[194] If uniformity is deemed sufficiently important, both considerations support federal statutory treatment of the subject, at least in international cases.

Arguments for legislation as the vehicle of change, although not for uniformity, are that it would put to rest any remaining questions about current federal judge-made doctrine as a matter of separation of powers, and that it could put to rest remaining questions prompted by special venue provisions in federal statutes.[195] More broadly, and a matter that does implicate uniformity where there is concurrent subject-matter jurisdiction in the federal and state courts, legislation could dispose of doubts about the legitimacy of forum non conveniens dismissals under certain federal regulatory statutes.[196] Congress could do so simply by enumerating the federal statutory claims, if there are any, to which the doctrine could not be applied. Alternatively and probably preferably, Congress could articulate the relevance of regulatory interest, broadly defined, to the analysis, and thus perhaps influence the development of doctrine in areas not formally reached by its commands.[197]

---

193 *See* American Dredging Co. v. Miller, 510 U.S. 443 (1994); Burbank, *supra* note 144, at 1571–82.

194 *See supra* text accompanying notes 39, 46.

195 *Compare* United States v. National City Lines, Inc., 334 U.S. 573 (1948), *with* United States v. National City Lines, Inc., 337 U.S. 78 (1949). *See* Hoffman and Rowley, *supra* note 42.

196 *Compare, e.g.*, Industrial Inv. Dev. Corp. v. Mitsui & Co., 671 F.2d 876, 890–91 (5th Cir. 1982), *vacated on other grounds*, 460 U.S. 1007 (1983) (forum non conveniens not available in federal antitrust cases), *with* Capital Currency Exchange, N.V. v. National Westminster Bank plc, 155 F.3d 603, 606–09 (2d Cir. 1998), *cert. denied*, 119 S. Ct. 1459 (1999) (forum non conveniens available in federal antitrust cases). *See* Born, *supra* note 39, at 354–56; Hoffman and Rowley, *supra* note 42. Recall that because of the federal transfer statute, 28 U.S.C. § 1404 (1994), a forum non conveniens dismissal from federal court will usually occur only when the alternative court is located abroad. *See* Robertson, *supra* note 42, at 402.

197 I am inclined to believe that, in cases under federal regulatory statutes like the antitrust laws, a finding of legislative or prescriptive jurisdiction should usually prevent dismissal under the forum non conveniens doctrine. The choice-of-law process usually does not operate so as to permit the courts of another country to apply such a law, and even if inquiry as to functional equivalence is permissible when determining whether to honor a forum-selection clause, *see* Roby v. Corporation of Lloyd's, 996 F.2d 1353 (2d Cir. 1993), I am not persuaded that the two questions need be resolved in the same way,

Another argument in favor of both uniformity and legislation for international cases involves the foreign-relations implications of the doctrine. Although such an argument can be nothing more than theoretical justification for the exercise of federal legislative power, the proposed Hague Convention furnishes concrete evidence that existing American law is perceived to be invidiously discriminatory. Judgments about aspects of doctrine that potentially elicit that response from foreign governments should be made by those charged with the conduct of United States foreign relations, the Congress, and the President.[198]

Without suggesting that this discussion exhausts the arguments in favor of either uniformity or legislation, its ambit suggests, without even reaching contrary arguments, that any federal legislation should be of limited scope, interstitially setting certain ground rules for the application of this jurisdictional equilibration device in cases where no other domestic court is available. Even one who stresses the strategic value of discretion rather than rules to enhance judicial power[199] must acknowledge the need for some flexibility in making comparative assessments in the pursuit of justice in civil litigation, a need that is greater in international than in wholly domestic cases.[200] Moreover, in the absence of a claim under federal law, of evidence that the content of the doctrine can affect foreign relations, or of far more ambitious legislation prescribing federal jurisdictional standards,[201] the case probably cannot be made for legislation that constrains the freedom of state courts to adjust, or to refuse to adjust, their jurisdictional doctrine through the use of forum non conveniens.

---

although they should be considered together. *See also* Mitsubishi Motors Corp. v. Soler Chrysler-Plymouth Inc., 473 U.S. 614 (1985) (arbitration clause); Vimar Seguros y Reaseguros, S.A. v. M/V Sky Reefer, 515 U.S. 528 (1995) (arbitration clause). *But see* Capital Currency Exchange, N.V. v. National Westminster Bank plc, 155 F.3d 603 (2d Cir. 1998), *cert. denied*, 119 S. Ct. 1459 (1999) (antitrust claims subject to forum non conveniens dismissal, court terming "roughly analogous" redress available under Articles 85 and 86 of the Treaty of Rome); Hoffman & Rowley, *supra* note 42.

With respect to U.S. antitrust laws, note Article 137(1) of the Swiss Private International Law Act, which "takes up the suggestions made by scholars under the choice-of-law statutes of a number of continental European countries for years by stating that '[c]lams arising from anti-competitive behavior are controlled by the law of the country on whose market the claimant has immediately been affected by that behavior.'" Letter from Samuel P. Baumgartner to Stephen B. Burbank, *supra* note 97, at 5.

198 *See* Burbank, *supra* note 13, at 1337–40.

199 *See, e.g.*, Burbank, *supra* note 83, at 223–29.

200 Were it thought appropriate to codify the entire doctrine for international cases, I would favor "a narrowly tailored forum non conveniens doctrine" of the sort advocated by Professor Robertson. *See* Robertson, *supra* note 187, at 378–80. *See also* Ravelo Monegro v. Rosa, 211 F.3d 509, 514 (9th Cir. 2000) ("rather than treating forum non conveniens as an exceptional tool to be employed sparingly, the district court perceived it as a doctrine that compels plaintiffs to choose the optimal forum for their claim"); Fawcett, *supra* note 63, at 12–13 (comparing the English and Australian doctrines of forum non conveniens).

201 *See* Clermont and Huang, *supra* note 117.

Conclusion

Although there is room for improvement in the treatment of jurisdictional equilibration in the proposed Hague Convention, the current draft provisions directed to that end represent an impressive achievement, one that marks substantial progress over comparable doctrine in the United States and under the Brussels Convention.

Treaties are not the only, although in private international law they are the best, means to bridge gaps and to resolve conflicts among national laws.[202] If a treaty proves impossible at this time, it is perhaps not too much to hope that what we have learned about other legal systems and about means to mediate between them will promote greater understanding and cooperation among the lawmakers of those systems and thus contribute to wise unilateral lawmaking for international civil litigation.

---

[202] *See* Burbank, *supra* note 3.

Linda J. Silberman[†]

Can the Hague Judgments Project Be Saved?: A Perspective from the United States

INTRODUCTION

The Hague Judgments Project was at a crossroads as the delegates to a first session of a Diplomatic Conference met in June, 2001 at The Hague. As has been reported, the Preliminary Draft Hague Convention on Jurisdiction and Foreign Judgments encountered formal resistance from the United States delegation[1] and substantial informal criticism in other U.S. circles.[2] This paper explains some of the difficulties that the Draft Convention presents for the United States[3] and proposes some possible

† Martin Lipton Professor of Law, New York University School of Law © 2000. The Filomen D'Agostino and Max E. Greenberg Research fund has provided financial support for this and other related research on the proposed Hague Judgment Convention.

This article reflects the collaborations and co-authorships of related papers with my colleague, Professor Andreas F. Lowenfeld. Many of the ideas and much of the research found in this paper are the product of our joint efforts, particularly with respect to the American Law Institute International Jurisdiction and Judgments Project, for which we are Co-Reporters. Were it not for his other commitments, this paper too would have been jointly authored. For those portions of the paper with which he agrees, I am in his debt; as to those, if any, on which we disagree, I take full responsibility.

In addition to the suggestions of Professor Lowenfeld, I have had the benefit of a continuing dialogue with U.S. delegates to the Special Commission, Jeffrey Kovar, Peter Trooboff, Professor Arthur von Mehren and Professor Ronald Brand. Two members of other delegations, Professor Andreas Bucher (Switzerland) and Mr. David Goddard (New Zealand), offered specific and helpful comments on an earlier draft, as did Professors Stephen Burbank, Kevin Clermont, Rochelle Dreyfuss, and Joseph Lookofsky. My thanks also to Professor Rick Cupp and the faculty at Pepperdine Law School and to Megan Richardson and the faculty at the University of Melbourne, Australia, where I presented earlier versions of the paper and received valuable advice.

1 *See* Letter from Jeffrey D. Kovar, Assistant Legal Adviser for Private Int'l Law, U.S. Dep't of State, to J.H.A. van Loon, Secretary General, Hague Conf. on Private Int'l Law (Feb. 22, 2000) (on file with the author) [hereinafter Kovar letter].

2 *See* The Hague Convention on Jurisdiction and Judgments, Records of a Conference held at New York University School of Law, April 30–May 1, 1999 (Andreas F. Lowenfeld and Linda J. Silberman eds.), Juris Publishing, Inc. (forthcoming 2001), for an extensive discussion among world experts on the subject. The formal papers presented at the Conference are included as an Appendix [hereinafter NYU Conference]; *see also* Friedrich K. Juenger, *A Hague Judgments Convention?*, 24 Brook. J. Int'l L. 111 (1998); Russell J. Weintraub, *How Substantial Is Our Need for a Judgments-Recognition Convention and What Should We Bargain Away to Get It?*, 24 Brook. J. Int'l L. 167 (1998).

3 *See* Linda J. Silberman and Andreas F. Lowenfeld, *A Different Challenge for the ALI: Herein of Foreign Country Judgments, an International Treaty, and an American Statute*, 75 Ind. L. J. 635, 640–42 (2000),

J.J. Barceló and K.M. Clermont (eds.), A Global Law of Jurisdiction and Judgments: Lessons from The Hague, 159–189

compromises for the negotiators at The Hague. It also offers details of an ongoing project undertaken by the American Law Institute (ALI) to address issues of jurisdiction and recognition as a matter of U.S. domestic law and to take account of the numerous federalism issues with respect to any implementation of a convention.[4]

Background

Although the initiative for the recent effort by the Hague Conference on Private International Law to negotiate a worldwide treaty on international jurisdiction and judgments came from the United States,[5] the United States has expressed unhappiness with the Preliminary Draft Convention in its present form.[6] There are a number of reasons for this shift in attitude.

Initial U.S. interest in a treaty was the result of a confluence of factors. The U.S. has no treaties – multilateral or bilateral – with respect to the enforcement of foreign country judgments. While the United States is one of the most liberal countries in enforcing the judgments of other countries, enforcement of U.S. judgments abroad has faced substantial resistance.[7] Efforts at a bilateral judgments treaty with the United Kingdom fell apart in the late 1970s, in part because of concern over what the U.K. regarded as excessive damage awards in the United States tort system.[8] Indeed, the U.S. attempt to achieve a convention with the United Kingdom was motivated in part by the consequences and incentives created by the Brussels and Lugano Conventions. Under the Brussels/Lugano Conventions, Member States are obligated to enforce judgments of other Member States rendered against domiciliaries of non-member countries even when a judgment rests on an exorbitant basis of jurisdiction – such as Article 23 of the German Procedure Code or Article 14 of the French Civil Code.[9] However, Article 59 of Brussels/Lugano offers some protection:

---

for prior observations on the same subject; *see also* ALI, International Jurisdiction and Judgments Project, Report (April 14, 2000) [hereinafter ALI Report].

4 *See* ALI Report, *supra* note 3, at xi-xiii.

5 See generally Peter H. Pfund, *The Project of the Hague Conference on Private International Law to Prepare a Convention on Jurisdiction and the Recognition and Enforcement of Judgments in Civil and Commercial Matters*, 24 Brook. J. Int'l L. 7 (1998); Arthur T. von Mehren, *Recognition and Enforcement of Foreign Judgments: A New Approach for the Hague Conference?*, 57 Law & Contemp. Probs. 271 (1994).

6 *See* Kovar letter, *supra* note 1.

7 *See* Volker Behr, *Enforcement of United States Money Judgments in Germany*, 13 J.L. & Com. 211 (1994); Andreas F. Lowenfeld, "*Recognition and Enforcement of Judgments*," in *International Litigation and the Quest for Reasonableness* 109, 129–36 (1996).

8 *See* P.M. North, *The Draft U.K./U.S. Judgments Convention: A British Viewpoint*, 1 Nw. J. Int'l L. & Bus. 219 (1979).

9 *See generally* Convention on Jurisdiction and the Enforcement of Judgments in Civil and Commercial Matters, Sept. 27, 1968, 1990 O.J. C 189/2 (consolidated) [hereinafter Brussels Convention] (where Article 3 identifies exorbitant bases of jurisdiction; where Article 4 provides that exorbitant bases can be used against defendants not domiciled in the European Union; and where Article 28 requires recognition of judgments by other Member States).

if a Member State concludes a treaty or recognition and enforcement of judgments with a non-Member State, the Member State can agree not to enforce convention judgments based on an exorbitant basis of jurisdiction.[10] Thus, the desire to avoid the excesses of jurisdiction and enforcement against U.S. domiciliaries under Brussels and to gain more effective recognition of its own judgments abroad brought the U.S. to the negotiating table.[11]

Still, there have been a chorus of nay-sayers to the Convention all along. Some questioned whether there was any empirical evidence to indicate a serious problem with enforcement abroad.[12] Even if the perception of a problem were accurate, many believed that the price the United States would have to pay too high a price to achieve enforcement of its judgments,[13] and that in any event, certain types of U.S. judgments, such as high damage tort judgments, would never be enforced with or without a convention. Because the Hague Convention was envisioned as a "double convention," dealing with the regulation of judicial jurisdiction as well as enforcement of judgments, there was concern in the U.S. that the price for enforcement of U.S. judgments would be an excessive restriction of U.S. judicial jurisdiction. Because more and more foreign defendants are likely to have assets in the United States, the need for foreign enforcement may be less than one might expect. Accordingly, the U.S. should be reluctant to surrender jurisdictional authority that it now exercises over foreign defendants since many of those judgments may be enforceable against the defendants' assets located in the United States.[14] Concern was also expressed that changes in the rules of jurisdiction as against foreign defendants would create an uneven playing field for American defendants. And as for protection for U.S. domiciliaries against the jurisdictional excesses of Brussels/Lugano, because the dangers seem not to have materialized, the original fears evaporated.[15]

Given the changes in attitude, can a case still be made in the United States to support a worldwide Judgments Convention? I believe the answer to that question

---

10 *See id.* art. 59. However, the new Council Regulation of the Commission of the European Communities appears to have eliminated this option, although agreements previously concluded are preserved. *See* Article 72, Council Regulation on Jurisdiction and the Recognition and Enforcement of Judgments in Civil and Commercial Matters (EC) No. 44/2001, 2001 O.J. L 12/1 (Jan. 16, 2001, effective March 1, 2002). The use of a "regulation" rather than a revision of the Brussels Convention by a new treaty was intended to avoid the need of individual Member States to go through the ratification process with submission of the revised text to their respective parliaments.

11 *See* Weintraub, *supra* note 2, at 168.

12 *See, e.g.*, Matthew H. Adler, *If We Build It, Will They Come? – The Need for a Multilateral Convention on the Recognition and Enforcement of Civil Monetary Judgments*, 26 Law & Pol'y Int'l Bus. 79, 82 (1994) ("[t]here is no catalogue of the actual experiences of U.S. litigants seeking enforcement abroad").

13 *See* Weintraub, *supra* note 2, at 171–73.

14 *See* NYU Conference, *supra* note 2.

15 Indeed, no instance has been reported where a judgment rendered on an exorbitant jurisdiction basis in one Brussels/Lugano state has been enforced against a domiciliary of a non-Member State in another Convention state.

is yes, but I think there will have to be some movement, by the Europeans and other participants in the Convention effort, away from the present Convention draft. A judgments convention would be beneficial both for the United States and for most other countries because it would symbolize closer cooperation and harmonization in the area of dispute settlement. It would also build on the principle expressed in Article 220 of the Treaty of Rome that unification of markets goes together with mutual enforcement of judgments. The ability to arrive at consensus about the allocation of judicial authority in transnational litigation would also represent an important step in the development and growth of private international law, and failure would be understood as a step backwards.

From a purely American perspective, a jurisdiction and judgments convention presents the opportunity to create a national standard with respect to the enforcement of foreign country judgments. Under existing U.S. law,[16] enforcement of foreign judgments is a matter of state rather than federal law – regardless of whether enforcement is sought in state or federal court.[17] Thus, a judgment rendered in France might be enforced in New York, but not in Texas. A uniform state law in the United States – the Uniform Foreign Money-Judgments Recognition Act (Uniform Act)[18] – adopted in over half the states, has mitigated the problem of disuniformity in American recognition practice. A number of substantive differences still remain, however, and even in states that have adopted the Uniform Act, there are deviations. For example, whether there should be a requirement of reciprocity – i.e., a requirement that conditions enforcement of a judgment of Country X upon a showing that the courts of Country X would enforce the judgment of an American court if the facts were reversed – as a condition for enforcement of a foreign judgment is resolved differently under the laws of the various states.[19] Most states reject any requirement of reciprocity to enforce a judgment, but a number of states – including some that have adopted the Uniform Act most recently – make lack of reciprocity a defense to enforcement of a foreign judgment.[20] An international treaty would

16 For a comprehensive overview of that law, *see* Linda Silberman, *Enforcement and Recognition of Foreign Country Judgments in the United States*, International Business Litigation & Arbitration (Practising Law Institute 2001) 257–91.

17 *See, e.g.*, Restatement (Third) of the Foreign Relations of Law of the United States § 481 cmt. a (1987). The rule is not absolute; if an issue of recognition of a foreign country judgment is asserted as a defense to a federal claim, federal rather than state law applies. In addition, a claim in admiralty or under a federal statute or treaty would look to a federal standard.

18 13 U.L.A. 263 (1986 and 2000 Supp.).

19 As a result, in those countries such as Germany whose law requires a finding of reciprocity for the recognition of foreign country judgments, it is often unclear whether the judgment of an American court satisfies the requirement.

20 In some states, the defense is stated as a "mandatory" basis to refuse enforcement. *See* Mass. Gen. Laws Ann. ch. 5, § 23A (2000); Ga. Code Ann. § 9-12-114 (1993). In other states, reciprocity is identified as a "discretionary" basis for non-enforcement. *See* Fla. Stat. Ann. § 55.605(2) (West Supp. 2000); Idaho Code § 10-1404 (1998); Me. Stat. Ann. Title 14 Rev. Code § 8505(2) (2000 Supp.); Ohio Rev. Code Ann. § 2329.92(B) (1996); Tex. Civ. Prac. & Rev. Code Ann. § 36.005 (1997) (where reciprocity is identified as a "discretionary" basis for non-enforcement). Even where the standard is "discretion-

change this aspect of recognition practice and create a uniform national standard for recognition and enforcement.[21]

Quite apart from concerns about non-uniformity, treatment of foreign country judgments in the United States should be seen as an aspect of the relationship between the United States and other countries, and thus as appropriately falling within the ambit of federal law.[22] Both the Uniform Act and common-law principles provide an exception for recognition and enforcement if it is found that the foreign judgment was rendered under a "system which does not provide impartial tribunals or procedures compatible with the requirements of due process of law."[23] In several recent cases, courts in the United States have refused enforcement of judgments of countries and have passed judgment on the fairness and adequacy of the legal systems of other countries.[24] That courts are required to make such assessments is additional support that a national federal standard on recognition and enforcement for the United States is desirable.[25] The creation of a multinational treaty would be an important step in the direction of national law.[26]

A number of commentators also see the establishment of defined jurisdictional rules in an international convention as a means of salvation for an irrational and

---

ary," courts appear to refuse recognition and enforcement where a failure of reciprocity is found. *See, e.g.*, Banque Libanaise Pour Le Commerce v. Khreich, 915 F.2d 1000 (5th Cir. 1990) (refusing to recognize an Abu Dhabi judgment in favor of a French bank against a U.S. defendant, on ground that there was no reciprocity for U.S. judgments; recognition was denied even though the U.S. party had been the plaintiff in the Abu Dhabi action); *see also* Me. Stat. Ann. Title 14 Rev. Code § 8505(2) (2000 Supp.) (illustrating that recent adoptions of the Uniform Act impose a reciprocity requirement of one kind or another).

21 A federal statute, in the absence of a treaty, would have the same effect. However, without the impetus from an international treaty, federal legislation could encounter greater resistance. Nonetheless, the ALI Project (for which the author and her colleague Andreas Lowenfeld are Reporters) will propose such a federal statute as an alternative if no treaty is concluded.

22 *Cf.* Crosby v. National Foreign Trade Council, 530 U.S. 363 (2000) (Massachusetts statute restricting ability of state agencies from buying goods or services from companies doing business with Burma held unconstitutional as interfering with foreign affairs and foreign commerce power of the United States).

23 *See* Uniform Foreign Money-Judgments Recognition Act § 4(a)(1), *supra* note 18, at 268.

24 *See, e.g.*, Bridgeway Corp. v. Citibank, 201 F.3d 134 (2d Cir. 2000) (stating that an action to enforce Liberian judgment rendered against U.S. defendant was refused under New York law because the courts in Liberia were not impartial tribunals); Bank Melli Iran v. Pahlavi, 58 F.3d 1406 (9th Cir.), cert. denied, 516 U.S. 989 (1995) (stating that default judgments obtained in Iran by Iranian banks against the Shah's sister would not be enforced in California for failure of due process in Iranian courts).

25 Among other sources, courts have relied upon State Department Country Reports and human rights reports in assessing the operations and fairness of foreign court systems. *See* Bridgeway Corp. v Citibank, 201 F.3d 134 (2nd Cir. 2000); Bank Melli Iran v. Pahlavi, 58 F.3d 1406 (9th Cir.), cert. denied, 516 U.S. 989 (1995).

26 Legislation to implement an international convention might also address the standards for recognition and enforcement of judgments of non-Convention states. Thus, the Convention proposal is a catalyst for the creation of national U.S. law with respect to the recognition and enforcement of foreign judgments.

confusing jurisdiction jurisprudence that has developed in the United States.[27] Whether or not the Hague Convention on Jurisdiction and Foreign Judgments would create more or less chaos is not clear, but a convention on the order of the proposed Hague draft would encourage litigants to use those jurisdictional bases that have gained the international imprimatur as a way to ensure foreign enforcement. Moreover, other issues of transnational litigation, such as provisional remedies, forum non conveniens, and lis pendens – if embraced in a treaty – would be appropriate subjects for national legislation.[28] At present, treatment of these issues is an odd patchwork of state and federal law, without much coherence.[29] Adding these subjects to a national agenda dealing with recognition and enforcement would help develop an American jurisprudence for transnational litigation. The issues do present complex issues of federalism in the United States, and the details will have to be worked through in implementing legislation – a task that the American Law Institute Project has begun to undertake.

The Specifics of the Hague Preliminary Draft Convention

As observed earlier, the proposed Hague Convention[30] – like the Brussels Convention on Jurisdiction and Enforcement of Judgments in Civil and Commercial Matters

---

27 *See* Kevin M. Clermont, *Jurisdictional Salvation and the Hague Treaty*, 85 Cornell L. Rev. 89, 89 n. 1 (1999) ("[T]he American house of jurisdiction to adjudicate is not a place where any sensible person other than a lawyer (if that is not redundant) wants to live.") (quoting Stephen B. Burbank, *Jurisdiction to Adjudicate: End of the Century or Beginning of the Millennium?*, 7 Tul. J. Int'l & Comp. L. 111, 123 (1999)); Friedrich K. Juenger, *A Shoe Unfit for Globetrotting*, 28 U.C. Davis L. Rev. 1027, 1027 (1995)("American jurisdictional law is a mess").

28 *See generally* Stephen B. Burbank, "*Jurisdictional Equilibration, the Proposed Hague Convention, and Progress in Domestic Law*," in *A Global Law of Jurisdiction and Judgments: Lessons from The Hague* 117 (John J. Barceló III and Kevin M. Clermont eds., 2002) (discussing the current state of U.S. law on forum non conveniens and lis pendens) [hereinafter *Jurisdictional Equilibration*].

29 There is no formal lis pendens provision in U.S. law, and the propriety of staying an action in the face of parallel litigation in another country is unclear under existing law. *See, e.g.*, Posner v. Essex Insurance Company, Ltd., 178 F.3d 1209 (11th Cir. 1999) (describing the issue of "abstention" with respect to parallel foreign litigation as "one of first impression in this, as well as any other, circuit"). Heretofore, forum non conveniens has been regarded as an aspect of "procedural" law, permitting a forum to apply the doctrine as adopted by state statute or developed by common law. *See* American Dredging Co. v. Miller, 510 U.S. 443 (1994). Provisional remedies in the state courts are the product of state statute and procedural rules; the federal courts are often authorized to "borrow" state remedies. *See* Fed. R. Civ. P. 64. In other circumstances the power to grant provisional relief is derived from federal statutes and rules. *See* George A. Bermann, *Provisional Relief in Transnational Litigation*, Colum. J. Transnat'l L. 553 (1997), for the various kinds of provisional relief available in international litigation. *See also* Stephen B. Burbank, *The Bitter with the Sweet: Tradition, History, and Limitations on Federal Judicial Power – A Case Study*, 75 Notre Dame L. Rev. 1291 (2000); Charles E. Dorkey, *Grupo Mexicano and Mareva Injunctions: U.S. as Debtor's Haven*, N.Y.L.J., June 8, 2000, at 5, for more recent developments.

30 *See* Hague Conference on Private International Law, Preliminary Draft Convention on Jurisdiction and Foreign Judgments in Civil and Commercial Matters, (Oct. 30, 1999) [hereinafter Preliminary Draft Convention].

(1968) – addresses both the regulation of judicial jurisdiction and the recognition and enforcement of judgments. The point of departure for both conventions is that a civil judgment rendered in one convention state against a person habitually resident in another convention state will be recognized in all other convention states, subject to a narrow list of defenses, and provided the court that rendered the judgment had jurisdiction over the defendant according to an agreed standard. In addition, the Draft Convention makes elaborate provision for jurisdiction of courts.[31] There are three categories of jurisdiction: (1) prohibited jurisdiction, which may not be used as a basis of jurisdiction by convention countries against defendants from other contracting states, whether or not enforcement will later be sought, (2) required bases of jurisdiction, obligating convention states to provide for such bases of jurisdiction for cases falling within the Convention and requiring recognition and enforcement of judgments predicated on such jurisdiction, and (3) other bases of jurisdiction, which may – but need not be – exercised when authorized by national law; recognition and enforcement of judgment predicated on jurisdiction in this category is left to the national law of the enforcing country.

Thus, the proposed Hague Convention departs from Brussels in creating an area of jurisdiction that may be exercised by states that are party to the Convention, but that other convention states are not required to recognize. The Brussels Convention is a pure double convention in that direct jurisdiction is either mandated or prohibited, and the rules of recognition and enforcement follow accordingly. The additional category or graylist of jurisdiction, which did not appear in earlier drafts of the proposed Hague Convention, was necessary because the participation of a large number of states with different legal systems and cultures made it difficult to reach consensus on what belonged in the respective areas of prohibited and required jurisdiction.[32]

Another difference between the proposed Hague Convention and the Brussels Convention is the absence of a final authority, such as the European Court of Justice, to oversee its operation.[33] Because Brussels has a supranational tribunal to ensure

---

31 The direct regulation of jurisdiction is one major difference between the Draft Hague Convention and an earlier Hague Convention that proved to be unsuccessful. *See* Hague Convention on the Recognition and Enforcement of Foreign Judgments in Civil and Commercial Matters, Feb. 1, 1971, 1144 U.N.T.S. 249 (having only a few signatories and no practical effect).

32 For a discussion of the general framework and nature of the proposed Convention, *see* Peter Nygh and Fausto Pocar, Report of the Special Commission on International Jurisdiction and Foreign Judgments in Civil and Commercial Matters (2000) [hereinafter Report of the Special Commission].

33 When the Brussels Convention was signed in 1968, the European Court of Justice did not have the power to review jurisdictional issues. At that time, a Joint Declaration was adopted committing the contracting states to study the question of conferring jurisdiction on the European Court of Justice to interpret the Brussels Convention. In 1971, a Protocol was adopted that conferred upon the European Court of Justice jurisdiction to give rulings on the interpretations of the Convention. *See* Brussels Convention, *supra* note 9, Protocol, art. 1. The Protocol does not extend to decisions under the Lugano Convention. For the role of the European Court in this area, see C.G.J. Morse, *International Shoe v. Brussels and Lugano: Principles and Pitfalls in the Law of Personal Jurisdiction*, 28 U.C. Davis L. Rev. 999, 1009–10, 1020–25 (1995).

uniformity of interpretation, it can more readily entrust the determination on jurisdiction to the original forum without the need for a jurisdictional check by the enforcing forum. In the absence of any such supranational authority, it was necessary that the proposed Hague Convention find some checking mechanism on the assertion of jurisdiction by the court asserting jurisdiction. Article 27 of the proposed Hague draft provides that the "court addressed shall verify the jurisdiction of the court of origin." This "verification" at least allows the enforcing court to determine for itself whether jurisdiction was properly exercised under the provisions of the Convention; that second court will be bound by the findings of fact on which the court of origin based its jurisdiction (except in default judgments), but not the conclusions of law.[34]

From the perspective of the United States, the overall structure of the Convention – the concept of a mixed convention with a gray zone of jurisdiction and a jurisdictional checking mechanism in the enforcement court – is appealing. The Hague draft proposal rejects the closed-system rigidity of Brussels and attempts to compensate for the lack of a supranational tribunal. However, to use an American colloquialism, the devil is in the details.

The Required Bases of Jurisdiction

If one first looks at the category of required jurisdiction – that is, jurisdictional bases that are to be afforded by every convention state and judgments that are to be enforced if rendered on those grounds – there is not much that is controversial from a U.S. perspective. The grounds for general jurisdiction – habitual residence for an individual and place of incorporation, statutory seat, principal place of business, and central administration for juridical entities – seem appropriate and consistent with U.S. law[35] even if the particular terms are not always completely familiar. It might be useful to provide for a convention definition of habitual residence, particularly for the aid of U.S. courts, which have only recently encountered the term in connection with the application of other international conventions.[36] Both choice-of-forum clauses conferring exclusive jurisdiction[37] and appearance by the defendant other

---

34 Preliminary Draft Convention, art. 27(2).

35 Preliminary Draft Convention, art. 3.

36 "Habitual residence" is an important focus of the 1980 Hague Abduction Convention. *See* Convention on the Civil Aspects of International Child Abduction, Oct. 25, 1980, multilateral, 19 I.L.M. 1501. For a discussion of the use of the concept in multilateral conventions, see E.M. Clive, *The Concept of Habitual Residence*, 1997 Jurid. Rev. Part 3.

The tradition of the Hague Conference has been to resist any formal definition of habitual residence. Although a definition would be preferable from the U.S. point of view, lack of definition would not seem to be a huge stumbling block. *See* Peter Nygh and Fausto Pocar, Report of the Special Commission, *supra* note 32, at 39.

37 Preliminary Draft Convention, art. 4. A forum-selection clause is generally understood by U.S. courts as non-exclusive, but there are good reasons to treat the forum choice as exclusive and such a rule should be compatible with United States' interests. *See* Kevin M. Clermont and Kuo-Chang Huang, "*Converting the Draft Hague Treaty into Domestic Jurisdiction Law*," in *A Global Law of Jurisdiction and Judgments: Lessons from The Hague*, *supra* note 28, at 191, 220.

than for the purpose of challenging jurisdiction[38] are also generally compatible with U.S. law.

There are more questions with respect to the articulated bases for the special rules of jurisdiction – that is, particular provisions for specific kinds of claims. It is agreed that special jurisdictional provisions, such as those for torts, contracts, and intellectual property, should be included in the Convention, but both the substance and particular phrasing of the provisions raise questions. There has also been extensive discussion as to whether jurisdiction should be identified by traditional substantive categories, such as torts and contracts, or left to a more general activity-based formulation.[39]

Several of the provisions of the required jurisdiction are, from a United States perspective, somewhat odd. Article 6 of the Preliminary Draft Convention categorizes two distinct kinds of contracts – contracts for the supply of goods and contracts for the supply of services. The Draft then prescribes jurisdictional criteria for each, and adds an additional provision for contracts that cover both goods and services. There are also specialized provisions for consumer contracts (Article 7) and for employment contracts (Article 8), but no provision for other kinds of contracts, such as licenses or sales of securities.

The required forum for contract actions in Article 6 is geared to the place in which the contract is performed, and the jurisdictional rule identifies the place of performance of the particular obligation.[40] The action may be brought in the state in which the "goods were supplied in whole or in part"[41] or where the "services were supplied in whole or in part."[42] As for contracts involving both goods and services, the required forum is where the "performance of the principal obligation took place in whole or in part."[43] From the U.S. viewpoint, the contract provision of Article 6 is both narrow and formalistic.[44] Many kinds of contracts do not neatly fit the "contracts for goods or services" parameters of Article 6, and requiring courts to ascertain whether the principal obligation concerns goods or services – where contracts involve both – seems an unnecessarily grudging approach.

---

38 Preliminary Draft Convention, art. 5.

39 *See* Peter Nygh, *The Criteria for Judicial Jurisdiction*, NYU Conference, *supra* note 2; *see also* Peter Nygh and Fausto Pocar, Report of the Special Commission, *supra* note 32, at 48–49; Catherine Kessedjian, Synthesis of the Work of the Special Commission of March 1998 on International Jurisdiction and the Effects of Foreign Judgments in Civil and Commercial Matters, Preliminary Document No. 9, at 31–32 (1998) [hereinafter Kessedjian Synthesis].

40 *See* Peter Nygh and Fausto Pocar, Report of the Special Commission, *supra* note 32, at 49. The Brussels Convention, art. 5 (1) adopts the more general "place of performance of the obligation in question" language for matters relating to contract. For some of the difficulties presented by the Brussels approach, *see* Patrick J. Borchers, *Comparing Personal Jurisdiction in the United States and the European Community: Lessons for American Reform*, 40 Am. J. Comp. L. 121, 140–41 (1992).

41 Preliminary Draft Convention, art. 6(a).

42 *Id.* art. 6(b).

43 *Id.* art. 6(3).

44 *See* Kovar letter, *supra* note 1.

The provisions in most U.S. state specific-act statutes offer a more flexible alternative for jurisdictional rules involving contracts. A standard formula for contract actions is to authorize suit in the courts of a state where the defendant "transacts business in the state" when the claim "arises from" that activity.[45] The Preliminary Draft Convention does offer, as a bracketed provision in Article 9, the possibility of a forum in the state where the defendant "has carried on regular commercial activity ... provided that the dispute relates directly to that regular commercial activity."[46] Restricting jurisdiction to situations of "regular commercial activity" has the advantage of limiting the range of possible fora, but certain basic transactions might fall outside such a provision. For example, such language might not encompass a situation where the parties negotiate and execute a transaction in a particular state on a one-time basis even when all contractual activity is centered there. Still, along with the fallback of a choice-of-forum clause, adoption of the bracketed language of Article 9 would help to satisfy U.S. interests.

The specially designed rule for contracts involving consumers allows a consumer to sue in the forum of its habitual residence if the conclusion of the contract on which the claim is based is related to trade or professional activities that the defendant has engaged in or directed to that state and the consumer has taken steps necessary for the conclusion of the contract in that state.[47] Interestingly, the revised Brussels Regulation has expanded jurisdiction over consumer contracts even further[48] and may affect how this provision is ultimately drafted. As to employment contracts, an employee can bring an action against the employer "in the courts of the State in which the employee habitually carries out his work or in the courts of the last State in which he did so."[49] With respect to claims brought by merchants against consumers and employers against employees, only limited fora are available; as to suits against consumers, only the state of the habitual residence of the consumer is an accepted forum;[50] as to actions against employees, suit can be brought only in the state where the employee is habitually resident or in which the employee carries out his work.[51]

---

45 *See* I Robert C. Casad and William B. Richman, *Jurisdiction in Civil Actions* 397–98 (3d ed. 1998); *see also* Clermont and Huang, *supra* note 37, at 207 (discussing the benefits of such a provision).

46 *See* Preliminary Draft Convention, *supra* note 30, at art. 9. The provision without brackets identifies as a required basis of jurisdiction the place where the defendant has a "branch, agency or any other establishment," and the dispute "relates directly to the activity of that branch, agency, or establishment."

47 *See* Preliminary Draft Convention, *supra* note 30, at art. 7(1).

48 Article 15(1)(c) and 16 of Council Regulation (EC) No. 44/2001, 2001 O.J. L 12/1 (Jan. 16, 2001) provide for jurisdiction over a defendant in consumer contract cases whenever the defendant directs, by any means, commercial or professional activities to a state, and the contract falls within the scope of such activities.

49 Preliminary Draft Convention, *supra* note 30, at art. 8(1)(a)(i). If the employee did not habitually carry out his work in one state, suit can be brought in the state in which the business that engaged the employee is situated. *See id.* art. 8(1)(a)(ii).

50 *See id.* art. 7(2).

51 *See id.* art. 8(1)(b).

The specialized provisions of Articles 7 and 8 also prohibit the use of forum selection clauses prior to suit in cases involving consumers and employees.[52]

The jurisdictional balance struck between consumers and merchants and employees and employers is probably about right,[53] but the restriction on the use of forum-selection clauses may be too absolute. Forum-selection causes, and in particular arbitration clauses,[54] are common in international transactions; the U.S. Supreme Court has upheld such clauses in consumer cases if "reasonable",[55] although the European practice is different.

The tort provisions of the Preliminary Draft require jurisdiction to be exercised by the state where either the tortious act or injury occurs. Because the injury may often occur in a place where the defendant did not conduct activity, the Draft Convention eliminates the place of injury as a forum in some circumstances: when "the person alleged to be responsible could not reasonably have foreseen that the act or omission could result in an injury of the same nature in that State."[56] The qualification not only reflects principles of fairness but also attempts to accommodate the constitutional restrictions on assertions of territorial jurisdiction that exist under U.S. law.[57] The provision as drafted may still not satisfy the required nexus between the defendant and the forum currently demanded by U.S. jurisprudence, which has found "mere foreseeability" on the party of the defendant to be constitutionally inadequate.[58] An alternative to redrafting the provision would be to permit the United States (and any other contracting state) to take a reservation if a required ground of jurisdiction would violate its own constitutional norms. It is also possible that the provisions of an international treaty could affect the United States Supreme Court's analysis of the constitutional limits of due process and permit the exercise

52 Both provisions permit a forum-selection clause only if the agreement is entered into after the dispute has arisen and only if the option to bring proceedings in another court is that of the consumer or the employee. *See id.* art. 7(3) (re consumers) and art. 8(2) (re employees).

53 For a fuller discussion of the treatment of these issues by the proposed convention as compared with U.S. law, *see* Clermont and Huang, *supra* note 37, at 207–09. Some Hague delegates have found the scope of Art. 7(1) of the Preliminary Draft Convention too restrictive in requiring the consumer to take steps necessary for the conclusion of the contract in the consumer's state.

54 *See, e.g.*, Preliminary Draft Convention, *supra* note 30, at art. 2(g) (stating that arbitration is outside of the substantive scope of the Convention). This means that arbitration clauses, if not prohibited by the applicable law, can be used by the parties, but choice-of-court clauses cannot. This seems an odd result.

55 *See, e.g.*, Carnival Cruise Lines v. Shute, 499 U.S. 585 (1991) (where the U.S. Supreme Court upheld forum-selection clauses even in "consumer"-type cases, but subject to a "reasonableness" test). The European practice is different, and the Hague Draft adopts the limitations on forum-selection clauses in consumer cases found in Article 15 of the Brussels/Lugano Conventions.

56 Preliminary Draft Convention, *supra* note 30, at art. 10(b).

57 *See* Asahi Metal Indus. Co. v. Superior Court, 480 U.S. 102 (1987); World-Wide Volkswagen Corp. v. Woodson, 444 U.S. 286 (1980); *see generally* Ronald A. Brand, *Tort Jurisdiction in a Multilateral Convention: The Lessons of the Due Process Clause and the Brussels Convention*, 24 Brook. J. Int'l L. 125, 154–55 (1998).

58 *See* World-Wide Volkswagen Corp. v. Woodson, 444 U.S. 286, 295–97 (1980).

of jurisdiction in these circumstances, at least for cases falling within the Convention.[59]

Other aspects of the Draft Convention's jurisdictional tort provisions present more significant obstacles. When the injury in the state is economic and the action is based on an allegation of a violation of antitrust or competition law, the place of injury no longer operates as a required basis of jurisdiction.[60] Jurisdiction in such cases is not prohibited,[61] but plaintiffs in such actions do not gain the enforcement benefits of the Convention. Moreover, plaintiffs in such actions are precluded from obtaining jurisdiction on any of the bases found on the prohibited list. If there is no movement at The Hague to change the provision excluding place of injury from the list of required jurisdiction and mandatory recognition in competition-type cases, the more prudent course might be to eliminate such actions from the Convention altogether. In that case, at least the Convention prohibitions on jurisdiction would also be inapplicable. The result, of course, would be to narrow the operation of the Convention and, to some degree, that might be considered a set-back. However, if the proposed convention is conceived as a stepping stone for continually evolving arrangements, a draft that can marshal consensus even about limited rules of prohibited and required jurisdiction would offer a first step in arriving at international standards of jurisdiction and enforcement. Over time, perhaps additional jurisdictional grounds could be added to the respective lists so that a more limited convention will be regarded as just the beginning of a process.

An additional difficulty arising from the tort provisions of the Draft Convention relates to Article 10(4), which provides that if the action is brought only on the basis that the injury arose in the state, the court has jurisdiction only in respect of the injury that occurred there, unless that state is the habitual residence of the injured party. The effect is to provide a strong incentive for the plaintiff to sue in the place where the tortious act occurred or where the defendant is located if the plaintiff is not habitually resident in the state where the injury arose. Such a rule has some value in defamation-type cases to discourage the plaintiff from forum-shopping in situations where the injury can occur in several states.[62] The Draft Convention departs from the approach adopted by the European Court of Justice in interpreting the Brussels Convention. The Brussels Convention provides for jurisdiction in matters

---

59 The point is not that the treaty would in any way "trump" the constitutional limitation imposed on the exercise of jurisdiction. Rather, the fact that an international treaty and/or federal statute expressly asserted jurisdiction on particular grounds has a bearing on the evaluation of constitutionality. *See* Linda J. Silberman, *"Two Cheers" for International Shoe (And None for Asahi): An Essay on the Fiftieth Anniversary of International Shoe*, 28 U.C. Davis L. Rev. 755, 762–67 (1995); *see also* Walter W. Heiser, *A "Minimum Interest" Approach to Personal Jurisdiction*, 35 Wake Forest L. Rev. 915 (2000) (for a recent critique of the existing constitutional standard and a proposal that would bring the United States into closer alignment with the jurisdictional rule in Europe).

60 *See* Preliminary Draft Convention, *supra* note 30, at art. 10(2).

61 Antitrust and unfair competition actions brought in the state where the injury occurred would be within the graylist; convention states would be free to decide whether or not to enforce the judgment.

62 *Cf.* Keeton v. Hustler Magazine, Inc., 465 U.S. 770 (1984).

relating to tort, "in the courts for the place where the harmful event occurred;" that language has been interpreted to give the plaintiff the option to sue in either the place where the damage occurred or the place of the event giving rise to the damage.[63] However, in *Shevill v. Press Alliance*,[64] the European Court of Justice held that a plaintiff libeled by a newspaper article distributed in several contracting states could bring an action against the publisher in the place where the publisher was located and recover for all the damage suffered; but if the plaintiff sued in any of the contracting states where the publication was distributed and the plaintiff suffered reputational injury, jurisdiction would be limited to recovery of the harm suffered in that state. The *Shevill* approach seems unnecessarily restrictive; the victim of a libel is likely to suffer most of the reputational harm at the habitual residence. Accordingly, the Hague Preliminary Draft Convention offers the plaintiff the ability to sue for the entire damage in the place where the tortious act occurs as well as the place of injury when the plaintiff is an habitual resident of the state where the injury occurred. As appropriate as the rule may be for defamation actions, however, the creation of multiple fora for the recovery of partial damages is likely to be inefficient in other types of cases.[65]

The proposed Draft Convention does not specifically address the complexities around electronic commerce, but delegates have focused on e-commerce issues at informal meetings, and it is clear that e-commerce concerns are significantly affecting the negotiations.[66] How best to incorporate provisions with respect to e-commerce into the Hague Convention remains unclear. Indeed, the new Brussels Regulation in Articles 15(1)(c) and 16(1) did nothing more than to authorize the consumer to sue in his home state when a defendant directs commercial or professional activities to the domicile of the consumer and the contract falls within the scope of such activities. That is somewhat surprising since the European Union has considered e-commerce issues more specifically in other directives.[67]

---

63 *See* Bier v. Mines de Potasses d'Alsace, [1976] E.C.R. 1735; *see generally* Dicey and Morris, *The Conflict of Laws* 353 (13th ed. Collins 2000).

64 [1995] E.C.R. I-415.

65 It should be noted, of course, that a gray zone of permissive jurisdiction does still exist under the Convention, and a plaintiff can sue for the entire damage in the place of injury if permitted to do so under national law. Enforcement of such a judgment, however, is not required by other convention states. The complexities arising from this situation are discussed in Ronald A. Brand, "*Current Problems, Common Ground, and First Principles: Restructuring the Preliminary Draft Convention Test*," in *A Global Law of Jurisdiction and Judgments: Lessons from The Hague*, *supra* note 28, at 75.

66 *See, e.g.*, Hague Conference, *Electronic Date Interchange, Internet and Electronic Commerce* (April 2000) <ftp://hcch.net/doc/gen_pd7e.doc> (summarizing meetings organized by the Hague Conference in Geneva in September 1999); *see generally* David Goddard, *Does the Internet Require New Norms?*, International Law FORUM du droit international 2: 183–195 (2000).

67 *See* Directive 2000/31/EC of the European Parliament and of the Council of 8 June 2000 on certain legal aspects of information society services, in particular electronic commerce, in the Internal Market, 2000 O.J. L/178 (June 17, 2000). *See generally* Francois Dessemontet, *The European Approach to ECommerce and Licensing*, 26 Brook. J. Int'l L. 59 (2000).

The Provisions for Jurisdiction over Counterclaims, Third-Parties, and Multiple Defendants

The Preliminary Draft Convention includes jurisdictional provisions for cases involving multiple defendants,[68] counterclaims,[69] and third-party claims,[70] all of which are included in the Brussels and Lugano Conventions. The Nygh-Pocar Report makes clear that these bases of jurisdiction are to be recognized and enforced by other Member States, even though Article 25 – the recognition and enforcement provision – refers only to judgments based on Articles 3 to 13.[71] The counterclaim rule, which authorizes jurisdiction over plaintiff on the basis of a defendant's counterclaim "arising out of the transaction or occurrence on which the original claim is based" is consistent with U.S. law[72] and presents no difficulty as a required jurisdictional basis. However, the Draft Convention provisions with respect to both multiple and third-party defendants could pose constitutional problems in the U.S. if they are conceived as jurisdictional grounds contracting states are required to exercise. The constitutional due-process standard in the United States stresses the relationship between the individual defendant and the forum – rather than just the relationship between the dispute and the forum. Article 14 of the Preliminary Draft authorizes jurisdiction over multiple defendants when one defendant is habitually resident in the forum state when claims against other nonresident defendants are so closely connected that they should be adjudicated together to avoid a risk of inconsistent judgments, and when a substantial connection exists between the forum state and the dispute involving the nonresident defendant.[73] Article 16 authorizes jurisdiction over a third-party defendant for indemnity or contribution when that court has jurisdiction over the original defendant, provided that the third-party action is permitted by the national law of the forum state and there is a substantial connection between the state and the dispute involving the third-party defendant.[74] However, neither of the multiple defendant provisions can be invoked if the co-defendant or third party has recourse to an exclusive choice-of-court clause.[75]

By demanding a "substantial connection" between the forum state and the dispute

---

[68] *See* Preliminary Draft Convention, *supra* note 30, at art. 14.

[69] *See id.* art. 15.

[70] *See id.* art. 16.

[71] *See* Peter Nygh and Fausto Pocar, Report of the Special Commission, *supra* note 32, at 95: "... there is only one type of jurisdiction which is entitled to recognition or enforcement under the Convention. This is the required jurisdiction ... provided for under Articles 3 to 13 and the associated jurisdictions provided for in Articles 14, 15, and 16."

[72] Indeed, U.S. law, at least domestically, is more expansive in that it treats a plaintiff as consenting to a personal jurisdiction in the state in which suit is brought and does not limit the consent to related claims. *See* Adam v. Saenger, 303 U.S. 59 (1938); *see generally* Casad and Richman, *supra* note 45, at 132–33.

[73] *See* Preliminary Draft Convention, *supra* note 30, at art. 14(1).

[74] *See id.* art. 16(1).

[75] *See id.* art. 14(2) and 16(2).

involving the additional defendant, the Preliminary Draft Convention has created a narrower multiple-defendant jurisdiction than that which exists under Brussels/ Lugano[76] and under the law of many other countries.[77] The multiple defendant provisions in Brussels and other national laws – which are not mirrored in United States practice[78] – contribute to the efficiency of litigation and reduce parallel and inconsistent litigation. However, they can also lead to abusive forum-shopping and a choice of forum that has little relationship to the underlying dispute. A recent case in the House of Lords (although the decision of the Lords addressed only a more technical point under Article 6(1) of the Brussels/Lugano Conventions) is illustrative.[79] In *Canada Trust Co. v. Stolzenberg*,[80] Canadian plaintiffs sought recovery of funds misappropriated through allegedly fraudulent conduct in Canada by numerous defendants from various countries. Suit was brought in England against a German defendant, Mr. Stolzenberg, who was allegedly domiciled in England. The remaining defendants – domiciled or incorporated in Italy, Switzerland, and various other countries – were served under Article 6(2)[81] of Brussels/Lugano and under Order 11 (1)(1)(c) of the English rules. The judge of first instance upheld jurisdiction over all the defendants, and the ruling was affirmed in a 2–1 decision by the Court of Appeal. The dissenting judge, in arguing for a restrictive interpretation of Article 6(2), pointed out that the result reached by the majority gave an English court jurisdiction over litigation brought by non-English plaintiffs against non-English defendants on a cause of action having no connection to England. The House of Lords dismissed the appeal, finding it sufficient that the main defendant was domiciled in England at the time the writ was issued.[82]

---

76 Article 6(1) of Brussels/Lugano provides that jurisdiction over a person domiciled in a contracting state may be sued, when there are multiple defendants "in the courts for the place where any one of them is domiciled." The new Brussels Regulation (art. 6(1)) limits jurisdiction to situation where the claims are so closely connected that they should be heard together to avoid the risk of irreconcilable judgments. Article 6(2) of Brussels/Lugano provides that jurisdiction in a third party action can be brought in the court "seised of the original proceedings, unless these were instituted solely with the object of removing him from the jurisdiction of the court which would be competent in his case."

77 *See, e.g.*, in England, CPR 6.20(3) (2000) (service out of the jurisdiction, with leave of court, is authorized when a claim form has been or will be served against a defendant and there is a real issue to be tried, and where the claimant wishes to serve the claim form on another who is a necessary or proper party to the claim) [formerly Sup. Ct. Prac. Order 11, r. 1(1)(c)].

78 For a more elaborate discussion of U.S. law on jurisdiction in multi-party litigation, see Clermont and Huang, *supra* note 37, at 214–17.

79 The issue before the House of Lords was (1) whether the relevant time for determining when the anchor defendant has been "sued" within the meaning of Article 6(1) is the date that proceedings issued or on the date that service was made and (2) whether the anchor defendant must be served before the other defendants in order to establish jurisdiction.

80 [1998] 1 W.L.R. 547, appeal dismissed 4 A.E.R. 481 (2000).

81 The issue which divided the majority and the dissent was the relevant date for determining the domicile of the principal defendant: whether domicile should be determined on the date of issuance of the writ or on the date of service.

82 4 A.E.R. 481 (2000).

The multiple defendant provision in Article 14 of the proposed Hague Convention would probably not confer jurisdiction in the circumstances of the *Stolzenberg* case because the requisite connection between the defendants and England would be lacking. The Preliminary Draft Convention achieves a better balance in resolving the competing interests of consolidation litigation and allocating cases to the most appropriate forum. Nonetheless, because the provision fails to require a nexus between each individual defendant and the forum, it does not meet the constitutional standard presently imposed by U.S. law.[83] However, if such jurisdiction were left to the graylist[84] rather than "required"[85] – or if a reservation could be made to required grounds of jurisdiction on the basis of constitutional limitations under national law – the U.S. could accept a multiple-defendant provision.

The Prohibited Bases of Jurisdiction

The general concept of a category of exorbitant or prohibited jurisdiction meshes comfortably with U.S. law, which in its national law has elevated an excess of jurisdictional authority to a violation of the U.S. Constitution.[86] Indeed, many of the jurisdictional excesses identified in the Preliminary Draft Convention[87] – jurisdiction based solely on the presence of the defendant's property in the forum state; nationality, domicile, habitual or temporary residence or presence of the plaintiff; nationality, temporary residence or presence of the defendant as well as service of the writ upon the defendant; unilateral designation of the forum by the plaintiff; and the signing of a contract from which the dispute arises – would fall within (or come close to) the unconstitutional zone.[88]

---

83 *See* Clermont and Huang, *supra* note 37, at 217, for the suggestion that U.S. law should be modified in this respect.

84 "Graylist" jurisdiction refers to the category of jurisdiction which may be exercised by convention states, but enforcement of judgments resting on such grounds is not mandated but left to national law in the enforcing state.

85 This possibility has already been noted during the negotiations. *See* Kessedjian Synthesis, *supra* note 39, at 38–39.

86 As early as 1878, the Supreme Court held that the assertion of judicial jurisdiction – whether exercised by state or federal courts – is subject to constitutional scrutiny under the Due Process Clause of the Fourteenth Amendment. *See* Pennoyer v. Neff, 95 U.S. 714 (1878); *see also* Friedrich K. Juenger, *American Jurisdiction: A Story of Comparative Neglect*, 65 U. Colo. L. Rev. 1 (1993) (condemning the constitutionalization of judicial jurisdiction).

87 Article 18(1) of the proposed Hague Convention states: "Where the defendant is habitually resident in a Contracting State, the application of a rule of jurisdiction provided for under the national law of a Contracting State is prohibited if there is no substantial connection between the State and the dispute." Preliminary Draft Convention, *supra* note 30, at art. 18(1). Paragraph (2) identifies particular examples of such exorbitant jurisdiction. Paragraph (3) provides for an exception for some subset of human rights cases. *See id.* art. 18.

88 Note that service of a summons on the defendant due to temporary presence in the state – so-called tag jurisdiction – was upheld by the Supreme Court of the United States in Burnham v. Superior Court. 495 U.S. 604 (1990). However, *Burnham* was a domestic U.S. case and did not involve jurisdiction over a foreign defendant. The Restatement (Third) of the Foreign Relations Law of the United

The aspect of prohibited jurisdiction that is most troubling from a U.S. perspective is the Draft Convention's inclusion of general "doing business" jurisdiction in the exorbitant category. Article 18 identifies as one of the prohibited grounds of jurisdiction "the carrying on of commercial or other activities by the defendant in that State, except where the dispute is directly related to those activities."[89] Courts in the United States have exercised jurisdiction when a defendant conducts systematic and continuous activities within the forum state, even when the claim is unrelated to the activity.[90] Thus, when multinational enterprises have a permanent establishment in the United States, jurisdiction is obtainable in the U.S. under existing law even with respect to a claim that arises outside the United States.[91] In order to join the Convention as it presently stands, however, the United States would have to agree to abandon this type of general jurisdiction against foreign defendants from convention states, whether or not enforcement abroad was necessary. And it should be noted that in many situations these multinational enterprises will have assets in the United States, and foreign enforcement would not be necessary.

It is true, as the Nygh-Pocar Report explains, that "there is a significant margin of uncertainty" as to when a general jurisdiction basis such as doing business applies "because of the difficulty of determining the quality and quantity of activity needed to found jurisdiction."[92] That problem also exists as a matter of domestic U.S. law because if defendants' activities in the forum state are too attenuated, general doing business jurisdiction will be found unconstitutional.[93]

Compromise of some sort appears in order. From the U.S. point of view, many major multinational enterprises – such as Siemens, Phillips, Daimler-Chrysler, and Novartis – have permanent establishments in the United States. Notwithstanding that such companies have their formal incorporation, principal place of business, and legal headquarters outside of the United States, they do have an established presence in the United States. Particularly when U.S. citizens or habitual residents are injured – even with respect to a claim originating outside the United States – there does not seem to be great unfairness in allowing the resident plaintiff to sue such a defendant in plaintiff's home state. In the Report of the American Law Institute on International Jurisdiction and Judgments the following example is used.[94]

States (published prior to *Burnham*) suggests that such transitory presence is not an appropriate basis for jurisdiction under international law. *See* Restatement (Third) of Foreign Relations Law § 421 cmt. e (1987).

89 *See* Preliminary Draft Convention, *supra* note 30, at art. 18(2)(e).

90 *See, e.g.*, Perkins v. Benguet Consol. Mining Co., 342 U.S. 437 (1952); *see generally* Philip B. Kurland, *The Supreme Court, the Due Process Clause and the In Personam Jurisdiction of State Courts – From Pennoyer to Denckla: A Review*, 25 U. Chi. L. Rev. 569, 577–86 (1958).

91 *See* Frummer v. Hilton Hotel Int'l, Inc., 227 N.E.2d 851 (N.Y. 1967).

92 *See* Peter Nygh and Fausto Pocar, Report of the Special Commission, *supra* note 32, at 77.

93 *See* Helicopteros Nacionales de Colombia, S.A. v. Hall, 466 U.S. 498 (1984); Andreas F. Lowenfeld, "*National Jurisdiction and the Multi-National Enterprise*," in *International Litigation and the Quest for Reasonableness*, *supra* note 7, at 81–108.

94 *See* ALI Report, *supra* note 3, at 14.

A U.S. habitual resident, traveling in Europe, ingests a pharmaceutical manufactured by Novartis and has an adverse reaction. She returns home to the United States and wishes to bring suit against the manufacturer. Under U.S. law, she would have no difficulty maintaining the action because the defendant has extensive business activities in the United States; enforcement of a resulting judgment would be relatively easy in the United States because the defendant would have substantial assets in the United States.

Thus, the law of the United States treats foreign defendants who carry on extensive business activities in the United States as if they were a U.S.-based company. Such equivalence is not peculiar to U.S. jurisprudence.[95] An overseas company that carries on business within England is subject to jurisdiction there under English law even if the claim has no connection with the English activity.[96] For example, in *South India Shipping Corp. Ltd. v. Export-Import Bank of Korea*,[97] a foreign bank was held subject to suit in England where it was found to have an "established place of business" from which it conducted external relations with other banks and carried out preliminary work. The Court of Appeal explained that to exercise jurisdiction in such a case was to put such a foreign company on the same footing as an English company in making it subject to suit.

Japan has a similar rule. In *Goto v. Malaysian Airline System*,[98] suit was brought in Japan against Malaysian Airlines by the widow of a Japanese resident traveling between points in Malaysia when the plane crashed in Malaysia. The Japanese Supreme Court sustained jurisdiction on the basis of the defendant's branch office in Japan. *Goto* involved an airline accident between points in Malaysia, and thus was outside the scope of the Warsaw Convention, the international convention covering suits arising out of accidents in international air carriage. Thus, the case was decided on the basis of Japanese domestic law. However, it is interesting to note in this context that the recent amendment to the Warsaw Convention would extend jurisdiction to the state in which the passenger is a "principal and permanent resident" – the so-called "fifth forum"[99] – if the "carrier operates services for the carriage of passengers by air" in that state.[100]

---

95 *See* Linda J. Silberman, *Judicial Jurisdiction in the Conflict of Laws Course: Adding a Comparative Dimension*, 28 Vand. J. Transnatn'l L. 404 (1995).

96 *See* Dicey and Morris, *supra* note 63, at 296–300.

97 [1985] 1 W.L.R. 585 (C.A.); *see also* Saab v. Saudi American Bank, [1998] 1 W.L.R. 937.

98 *See, e.g.*, Andreas F. Lowenfeld, "*Jurisdiction of Courts*," in *International Litigation and the Quest for Reasonableness, supra* note 7, at 48–49 (discussing the *Goto* case); *see also* Kenichiro Hayashida, *Jurisdictional and Applicable Law in Aviation Cases in Japan* (on file with author). The case is reprinted in 26 Jap. Ann. Int'l L. 122 (1983).

99 Other possible fora under the Warsaw Convention are the territory of a contracting state that is the domicile or principal place of business of the carrier, a place of business of the carrier through which the contract has been made, or the place of destination. *See* Convention of the Unification of Certain Rules Relating to International Transportation by Air opened for signature Oct. 12, 1929, 137 L.N.T.S. 11, Art. 28 [hereinafter Warsaw Convention].

100 *See* Convention of the Unification of Certain Rules for International Carriage by Air, Art. 33(2) (1999) (on file with the author).

Although England, the United States, and Japan would all permit general jurisdiction over the foreign airline defendant on the facts in *Goto*, the Brussels/Lugano Convention rejects jurisdiction based on, for example, the establishment of a branch office, unless the dispute arose out of the operations of the branch.[101] The argument against jurisdiction rests on both a desire to achieve certainty and to avoid forum-shopping. In addition, given the availability of other types of special or specific jurisdiction under Brussels/Lugano, the assertion is that another state has a more legitimate interest in the dispute and is the more appropriate forum.[102]

Nonetheless, the position that an injured plaintiff should be able to sue at plaintiff's own habitual residence when the defendant carries on substantial activity in the forum state hardly seems extreme.[103] If such a basis of jurisdiction were relegated to the gray area, states that continue to find such jurisdiction objectionable would still not have to enforce judgments that rest on general jurisdiction of that kind. At the same time, U.S. (or other) courts that are able to enforce judgments against foreign defendants on the basis of forum assets will not have their own domestic rules for jurisdiction curtailed.

One possible modification of Article 18 that might appeal to both sides in the debate over general jurisdiction would be to narrow the area of general doing business jurisdiction on the prohibited list and thus permit general jurisdiction in those situations where the argument for such jurisdiction is the strongest. Article 18 could be modified to prohibit jurisdiction on the basis of the carrying on of the commercial activity by the defendant when the activity did not give rise to the claim "*except where the defendant has a branch office or where the defendant's activity in the forum is evidence of a substantial presence there, and the plaintiff is habitually resident in the forum state.*"[104]

---

[101] *See* Brussels Convention, *supra* note 9, at art. 5(5).

[102] General jurisdiction in the United States was developed when specific jurisdiction was not yet fully available. It has thus been suggested that with the availability of specific jurisdiction only a few cases in which the United States has a legitimate interest in providing a forum will be blocked. *See* Weintraub, *supra* note 2, at 188–89; Clermont and Huang, *supra* note 37, at 204–05.

[103] For example, the recent revision of the Warsaw Convention (though not yet in force) provides for jurisdiction in the state of the principal and permanent residence of the plaintiff if the defendant air carrier operates services there. *See* note 100, *supra*. Also, although perhaps somewhat more tightly drawn, the provision in the proposed Hague Convention for jurisdiction over contract actions concluded by consumers allows suit in the habitual residence of the consumer when the conclusion of the contract is "related to trade or professional activities that the defendant has engaged in or directed to that State." *See* Preliminary Draft Convention, *supra* note 30, at art. 7(1).

It has been suggested to me that the *Goto* case and the Warsaw Convention situation are "one-sided" examples because defendants engage in the same business in the plaintiff's home state as they do in the home state and the place where the even occurred. If that turns out to be the basic objection to my proposal, it might be possible to limit the doing business jurisdiction to those situation where the defendant's business in the forum state bears some relationship to the defendant's business or activity that gives rise to the claim. However, the claim should not have to "arise from" the defendant's activity in the forum state.

[104] My proposal does not contain an express reference to subsidiary corporations, but the activities of subsidiaries should be included here when the relationship of the subsidiary is so closely linked to the

Cases in which foreign defendants have extensive and substantial activities in the forum state represent the strongest claims for general jurisdiction. The exception could follow the English rule, which appears to require an established place of business; alternatively, as I suggest, it could embrace a more flexible standard that would still demand that the activity in the forum state be "substantial and continuous." Where the foreign defendant's relationship with the forum is more attenuated, there is a less compelling claim for jurisdiction, and jurisdiction in such cases would remain on the prohibited list.

From the European or "Brussels" perspective, this narrower area of prohibited general jurisdiction should be acceptable. To the extent that a broader category of general jurisdiction continues to be disfavored, enforcement of judgments based on such jurisdiction would remain within the prerogative of the enforcing forum. As a result, even if the line between the black and gray zones of jurisdiction were less than crystal clear, the interest of other countries would be preserved to a limited degree at the enforcement stage.

The interests of the United States would also be protected by the proposed modification to Article 18. Under the proposal, general doing business jurisdiction would be permitted where the U.S. interests are the strongest – cases brought by habitually resident plaintiffs in a forum where the defendants have an extensive presence. However, general jurisdiction would be prohibited in two categories of cases where it now exists. One category involved plaintiffs not habitually resident in the U.S.; the other relates to a possible increase in the level of commercial activity that would not be required. As to the first, although it is true that formal jurisdiction does turn on the residency or domicile of the plaintiff, most cases with a pattern of foreign plaintiff, foreign defendant and unrelated cause of action would be likely to force dismissal on grounds of forum non conveniens even if technical jurisdiction were sustained.[105] Thus, any change to existing U.S. law would be minimal. With respect to the second category – the level of activity necessary for general jurisdiction – the proposed modification may in fact accurately capture the developing American jurisprudence in this area. The Supreme Court itself, in *Helicopteros Nacionales de Colombia, S.A. v. Hall*,[106] has imposed limits on the level of activity that will support general jurisdiction.[107] And in *Asahi Metal Industry Co. v. Superior Court*,[108] the

---

multinational enterprise by common ownership and control so as to be fairly regarded as a mere department or alter ego of the multinational enterprise. *See Obligations of a company belonging to an international group and their effect on other companies of that group*, 65-I Annuaire de l'Instutut de Droit International 191–326 (1993); *Obligations of Multinational Enterprises and their Member Companies*, 66-II Annuaire de l'Institut de Droit International 463–73 (1996).

[105] The federal courts and most states in the United States recognize the doctrine of forum non conveniens. *See generally* Gary B. Born, *International Civil Litigation in United States Courts* 298 (3rd ed. 1996).

[106] 466 U.S. 408 (1984).

[107] *See* Access Telecom, Inc. v. MCI Telecommunications Corp., 197 F.3d 694 (5th Cir. 1999) (rejecting general jurisdiction over Mexican company on the ground that activities of the foreign defendant fell short of due-process requirements, but finding specific jurisdiction over the defendant on the basis of claims that arose from defendant's Texas activity).

[108] 480 U.S. 102 (1987).

Supreme Court superimposed a "reasonableness" standard on the exercise of judicial jurisdiction with particular regard to foreign defendants.[109] In thinking about the constitutional limitations on general jurisdiction,[110] particularly with respect to foreign defendants, the residency of the plaintiff is an important factor. The modification I propose in Articlc 18 is consistent with the kinds of limits on jurisdiction implicit in *Asahi*, but the proposed rule has the advantage of offering a clearer and more definitive standard.

I have referred to the issue of doing business jurisdiction as a potential "deal-breaker," and thus if modification along the lines I have suggested is acceptable, there is a good chance that the negotiations could move ahead. A compromise along similar lines with respect to a different issue of prohibited jurisdiction in an earlier Special Commission session resolved a different impasse. That compromise is now reflected in Article 18(3) of the Preliminary Draft Convention, which creates an exception to prohibited jurisdiction based on the transient presence of the defendant in the forum state for human rights cases.[111] Two basic alternatives are offered,[112] but the general thrust is to permit a party to bring an action under national law based on conduct that constitutes a crime against humanity or other serious human rights violations under international law. Jurisdiction for these cases would fall within the gray zone of jurisdiction – permitted under national law but not required to be recognized or enforced in other convention states.

Other Convention Provisions

This paper has focused primarily on disagreements over the jurisdictional provisions in the proposed Hague Convention Draft, which, I believe, must be resolved if a

109 The "reasonableness" prong of the *Asahi* test has not been limited to foreign defendants. *See* Linda J. Silberman, "*Two Cheers" for International Shoe, supra* note 59, at 760; Stephen B. Burbank, *Practice and Procedure: The World in Our Courts*, 89 Mich. L. Rev. 1456, 1468–71 (1991) (book review).

110 *See*, for example, Metropolitan Life Ins. Co. v. Roberston-Ceco Corp., 84 F.3d 560 (2d Cir. 1996), where the Second Circuit Court of Appeals applied the *Asahi* "reasonableness standard" – developed in the context of a specific jurisdiction case – to a case of general jurisdiction. One judge on the three-judge panel dissented, urging that the reasonableness inquiry be confined to the specific jurisdiction context until instructed otherwise by the Supreme Court. But the panel majority in *Metropolitan* used the "reasonableness" test to protect a U.S. defendant from suit in a sister state; the claim for imposing a reasonableness standard is considerably stronger in international litigation that involves a foreign country defendant.

111 *See* Kadic v. Karadzic, 70 F.3d 232 (2d Cir. 1995), cert. denied, 518 U.S. 1005 (1996).

112 *See* Preliminary Draft Convention, *supra* note 30, at art. 18(3). Variant one lists in detail particular violations, such as crimes against humanity and war crimes, as defined for purposes of the International Court, as well as crimes against natural persons under international law or violations of fundamental human rights, such as torture and slavery, recognized under international law. Tag jurisdiction can only be used for the latter group of cases if it is impossible to bring proceedings elsewhere. Variant two is more restrictive and jurisdiction on the basis of the defendant's presence is only appropriate when a serious crime has been committed under international law and the State has established criminal jurisdiction over that crime in accordance with an international treaty. *See generally* Peter Nygh and Fausto Pocar, Report of the Special Commission, *supra* note 32, at 80–81.

successful convention is to be concluded. There are, however, other aspects of the Convention that may still prove controversial. The proposed Preliminary Draft addresses lis pendens,[113] that is, the possibility of staying an action in deference to another previously commenced action, and declinations of jurisdiction (akin to forum non conveniens).[114] The provision for lis pendens applies to "proceedings based on the same causes of action" and adopts in general a "first-seised rule" (first-to-file).[115] The first-seised rule does not apply to actions requesting determinations of nonliability,[116] and a court second-seised may proceed if the plaintiff has failed to pursue the action or if the court has not rendered a decision within a reasonable time.[117] The court first-seised may itself decline to proceed if there is a more convenient forum elsewhere.[118] A more general provision for declining jurisdiction – in the forum non conveniens sense – appears in a separate article for application in "exceptional circumstances."[119] A thorough discussion of these provisions has been taken up elsewhere in this symposium.[120]

Nor should the provisions on recognition and enforcement be regarded as settled. The structural aspects of enforcement and recognition appear to be agreed – that is, convention states would be required to recognize and enforce judgments that rest on jurisdiction on the mandated list; those predicated on a prohibited basis of jurisdiction would be denied enforcement; and judgments rendered on a basis of jurisdiction in the gray zone would not have to be recognized by other states, but states would be free to recognize (or not) judgments in this category.[121] The Preliminary Draft also includes a set of discretionary defenses to recognition and enforcement, and Article 28 tracks many of the conventional defenses to recognition and enforcement.[122] More controversial may be the Preliminary Draft provisions that permit recognition in certain cases to be limited to a lesser amount of damages than were awarded by the original judgment.[123]

---

113 *See id.* art. 21.

114 *See id.* art. 22. This article is entitled "Exceptional circumstances for declining jurisdiction.".

115 *See id.* art 21(1).

116 *See id.* art. 21(6).

117 *See id.* art. 21(3).

118 *See id.* art. 21(7).

119 *See id.* art. 22; *see generally* Hague Conference on Private International Law, Note on the Question of Forum Non Conveniens in the Perspective of a Double Convention on Judicial Jurisdiction and the Enforcement of Decisions, Hague Conf. Prelim. Doc. No. 3 (Apr. 1996).

120 *See* Stephen B. Burbank, *Jurisdictional Equilibration, supra* note 28, at 32–56.

121 *See* text accompanying notes 31–32, *supra.*

122 *See* Preliminary Draft Convention, *supra* note 30, at art. 28(1). Among the defenses is that of "public policy" or "*order publique*" – that a judgment need not be recognize or enforced if "recognition or enforcement would be manifestly incompatible with the public policy of the State addressed." *See id.* art. 28(1)(f).

123 *See* Preliminary Draft Convention, *supra* note 30, at art. 33. As regards non-compensatory damages, such as exemplary or punitive damages, recognition is mandatory only to the extent that similar or comparable damages could have been awarded in the state addressed. *See id.* art 33(1). A debtor may also show that the damages awarded were "grossly excessive," and recognition may be limited to a lesser amount; however, in such a case, the court addressed must recognize the judgment in an amount

A Revised Vision for the Convention

My critique of the Hague Preliminary Draft, including the changes I have proposed with respect to the doing business jurisdiction, have a common theme: that the range of countries and cultural and legal traditions make consensus on a multitude of required and prohibited bases of jurisdiction unfeasible. To that end, a slight retreat to a less ambitious convention is in order. There is a limited band of jurisdictional rules where an allocation to either the required or prohibited list has engendered little or no controversy. To the extent that consensus of that kind emerges, placement on the required or prohibited list is appropriate. However, as to those grounds on which there has been substantial opposition to a particular categorization, that basis of jurisdiction should move to the graylist. This would mean that a judgment rendered on that ground would not obligate enforcement in a contracting state nor would it prevent enforcement by such state. It would also allow greater freedom by states to assert jurisdiction under their own domestic law regimes. Both the "human rights" compromise and the modifications with respect to the general doing business jurisdiction that I propose in this paper would enlarge the area of permitted jurisdiction under national law. Indeed, a successful conclusion for the Convention is most likely if convention states are accorded broad flexibility to develop their own jurisdictional regimes. Such an approach could also allow jurisdictional rules with respect to e-commerce and intellectual property[124] to develop over time, and would have the advantage of not restricting jurisdictional developments in these areas by creating an overly expansive list of prohibited jurisdiction.

It helps, I believe, to view the proposed Hague Convention as reflecting a transitional stage for the development of jurisdictional rules for transnational cases and international enforcement of judgments. The treaty would establish a summary and expeditious international enforcement mechanism for cases grounded on "favored" jurisdictional grounds – by this, I refer to the "required list." If foreign enforcement appeared to be necessary, lawyers would gravitate toward using one of the required bases of jurisdiction. Lawyers could still bring suit using other bases of jurisdiction (as long as they were outside the prohibited list), but if they did so they would take their chances on having that judgment enforced elsewhere. It would also be useful if the Convention were to authorize states to declare which bases of gray zone jurisdiction would support judgments that their courts would regard as entitled to recognition. Such a provision would offer flexibility for maximizing recognition and enforcement among particular countries that share similar legal cultures and traditions with respect to jurisdictional regimes, and such declarations would create greater certainty with respect to enforcement and recognition.

---

no less than what could have been awarded in the state addressed in those circumstances. *See id.* art. 33(2).

[124] *See* Rochelle Cooper Dreyfuss, *An Alert to the Intellectual Property Bar: The Hague Judgments Convention*, 2001 U. Ill. L. Rev. 421. With respect to e-commerce, see Allan R. Stein, *The Unexceptional Problem of Jurisdiction in Cyberspace*, 32 Int'l Lawyer 1167 (1998).

A Look at the Federalism Issues: The American Law Institute Project

Because the negotiations at The Hague have focused on the national interests of states, the particular federalism issues that the Convention presents for the United States may have gone undetected by the other delegations at The Hague. However, many aspects of the proposed convention raise controversial issues of federalism in the United States, and they could present political issues for the United States at the ratification stage. To that end, the American Law Institute has undertaken a project to adopt implementing legislation for a successfully concluded treaty. My colleague, Professor Andreas F. Lowenfeld, and I are Co-Reporters for that project. The ALI Project actually has two components: one would implement the proposed Hague Convention's provisions for international jurisdiction and the enforcement of judgments and the other would deal with the treatment of foreign country judgments in the absence of any Convention.[125] The second might also be part of the implementing legislation to deal with judgments issued in states that had not become parties to the Convention. However, the discussion here will be limited to the issues presented by implementation of the Convention in the United States.

The Need for and Scope of Implementing Legislation

Adoption by the United States of any proposed Hague Convention would probably be accompanied by federal authorizing and implementing legislation.[126] Constitutionally, there is little doubt about the existence of federal power to enact legislation to regulate jurisdiction in international cases and the enforcement and recognition of foreign country judgments.[127] And while the establishment of a national standard for recognition and enforcement foreign country judgment has

---

[125] *See generally* ALI Report, *supra* note 3.

[126] The combination of treaty and implementing legislation has been used with respect to both arbitration and international child abduction. *See, e.g.*, Federal Arbitration Act, 9 U.S.C. §§ 201 et seq. (1995) (implementing the UN Convention on the Recognition and Enforcement of Foreign Arbitral Awards); Public Health and Welfare Code 121, 42 U.S.C. §§ 11601 et seq. (1995) (implementing the 1980 Hague Convention on the Civil Aspects of International Child Abduction).

[127] The existence of an international convention clearly places the subject within the powers of the federal government. *See* Missouri v. Holland, 252 U.S. 416 (1920). Even in the absence of a treaty, authority for such legislation can be found in the foreign commerce power and the power to regulate foreign relations. *See, e.g.*, Board of Trustees v. United States, 289 U.S. 48, 59 (1933) ("In international relations and with respect to foreign intercourse and trade the people of the United States act through a single government with unified and adequate national power."); *see also* Japan Line, Ltd. v. County of Los Angeles, 441 U.S. 434 (1979) (striking down California property tax on foreign-owned cargo containers used in international commerce because federal government must "speak with one voice in regulating foreign commerce").

strong support,[128] there have been some detractors.[129] The theme of deference to state regulation is a recurring one in American jurisprudence, and the concerns over federalism must be taken seriously.[130]

As noted earlier, recognition and enforcement of country judgments has been treated as a matter of state law in the United States. A proposed Hague Convention and legislation implementing the Convention would replace that regime with a national standard defined by the Convention. That national Convention standard would be binding on every state in the United States, subject to discretionary Supreme Court review, which offers the vehicle for uniformity of interpretation.

The uniform national standard would clearly apply to a number of issues: the direct regulation of jurisdiction with respect to required and prohibited bases of jurisdiction, the standards of jurisdiction that support a judgment rendered on that basis and require recognition and enforcement of that judgment, the available defenses to recognition and enforcement, and the procedures for enforcement. But the role of the state courts and of state law will continue to be significant. For example, Article 28 of the Preliminary Draft Convention provides that recognition or enforcement may be refused if it "would be manifestly incompatible with the public policy of the State addressed."[131] In the United States, as in other federal states, it is often not clear whether public policy is derived from the nation, or the subdivision in which the forum is located. A uniform national approach to foreign country judgments, as reflected in the context of implementation of an international convention, would suggest that the relevant public policy should be that of the United States.[132] However, in those areas where regulations are primarily a function of state law, U.S. policy will be that of the relevant state. But it should not matter in which court – state or federal – the public policy argument is raised because the substantive rule on enforcement should be the same in every court.[133]

---

128 *See* Andreas F. Lowenfeld, *Nationalizing International Law: Essay in Honor of Louis Henkin*, 36 Colum. J. Transnat'l L. 121, 127–31 (1997).

129 For example, a spokesperson for the National Commissioners on Uniform State Law (NCUSL) speculated as to whether the proposed convention could better be implemented through revision of the Uniform Act.

130 *See* United States v. Morrison, 529 U.S. 598 (2000); Alden v. Maine, 527 U.S. 706 (1999), for the Supreme Court's recent attention to federalism concerns in a different context.

131 *See* Preliminary Draft Convention, *supra* note 30, at art. 28.

132 *Cf.* Jaffe v. Snow, 610 So.2d 482 (Fla. App. 1992), review denied, 621 So.2d 432 (Fla. 1993) (which might have been decided differently if national rather than state policy were controlling). In *Jaffe*, the Florida court refused to enforce an Ontario judgment for loss of consortium resulting from the tortious abduction of plaintiff's husband by U.S. bail bondsmen because plaintiff's husband was a fugitive from justice. The court invoked Florida public policy and refused to enforce the judgment, notwithstanding the urging of the U.S. Secretary of State that the judgment be recognized.

133 For more on public policy exception, see Joachim Zekoll, *The Role and Status of American Law in the Hague Judgments Convention Project*, 61 Alb. L. Rev. 1283, 1300–07 (1998); Linda J. Silberman and Andreas F. Lowenfeld, *A Different Challenge*, *supra* note 3, at 643–45. For recent discussion of the public policy exception in the context of the Brussels Convention by the European Court of Justice, see Regle Nationale des Usines Renault SA v. Maxicar SpA (Case C-38/98), Judgment of 11 May 2000.

Implementing the Convention Provisions on Judicial Jurisdiction

The Required Bases of Jurisdiction

The question of how to implement the provisions on judicial jurisdiction is somewhat complicated. In the United States, the outer limits of judicial jurisdiction are prescribed by federal constitutional standards, but assertion of jurisdiction in diversity and federal question cases (in the absence of an applicable federal statute providing for nationwide jurisdiction)[134] is, in the first instance, a matter of state law.[135]

The underlying claims in many cases falling within the Convention are likely to be state law claims; if there were diversity of citizenship between the parties, the plaintiff would be permitted to bring the case in state or federal court. If two aliens were involved, state court would be the only possible forum. In order to ensure that a court hearing a case falling within the Convention has authority to exercise the Convention's required bases of jurisdiction, federal legislation could authorize the exercise of such jurisdiction in whatever court (state or federal) a convention case is brought.[136] However, such an approach might be thought of as interfering with a state's own regulation of jurisdiction and an inappropriate commandeering of state judicial authority.

As an alternative, federal implementing legislation might be directed to the territorial reach of the federal courts alone, with state courts free to exercise jurisdiction according to their own standards, subject only to the prohibitions set forth in the Convention. Under this alternative, the subject matter jurisdiction capacity of the federal courts might have to be expanded in order to ensure that some court in the United States would be available to exercise a required basis of jurisdiction in a case falling under the Convention.

The Prohibited Bases of Jurisdiction

The Convention's prohibitions on particular exercises of jurisdiction, "the blacklist," would be imposed by federal legislation on both state and federal courts. The prohibitions would be a matter of federal law, to be interpreted by the relevant state or federal court, and subject – other conditions being met – to discretionary Supreme Court review. It would be possible to allow a defendant to remove a case from state

---

[134] Nationwide service provisions are authorized by many federal statutes, including antitrust and securities laws.

[135] An exception is FRCP Rule 4(k)(2), authorizing jurisdiction based on the defendant's contacts with the United States as a whole in cases arising under federal law when there is no single state with which the defendant has the requisite jurisdictional contacts. *See* Fed. R. Civ. P. 4(k)(2).

[136] Such authorization might be necessary because as presently drafted, the Convention includes certain required bases of jurisdiction that are not currently accepted as appropriate grounds for jurisdiction in the U.S. In some situations, the general doing business jurisdiction, which is an appropriate basis of jurisdiction under U.S. domestic law (although not the Convention), could provide the basis for asserting jurisdiction over foreign defendants. This would seem an appropriate substitute – and not considered prohibited – because on the particular facts jurisdiction would be within specific articles of required jurisdiction under the Convention.

to federal court when a jurisdictional defense under the Convention is asserted – that is, when the basis of jurisdiction being asserted in a particular case is a violation of the Convention. Greater confidence in the federal courts to interpret the Convention correctly merits such a removal provision, but such a provision does skew the allocation of cases between state and federal courts and increases the federal court caseload.

Contacts with a Particular State or with the United States

The jurisdictional provisions of the Convention are designed with reference to a defendant's connections with the nation-state. With respect to the United States, a foreign defendant's contacts might be centered in one state or in various states. Two different kinds of implementation questions arise as a result. Although the present convention draft does not so require,[137] when the defendant's relevant connection is with one particular state of the United States, that state of the United States would appear to be the appropriate forum within the United States; legislation implementing the Convention could address this venue question. In some cases, however, the foreign defendant's contacts are spread throughout the United States. In such cases, a national or "aggregate contacts" approach might be called for. Under existing United States practice, an aggregate contacts standard is adopted for the federal courts in cases arising under federal law when no single state is able to exercise jurisdiction over the defendant.[138] Many federal statutes also adopt a standard of nationwide contacts.[139] For international cases, such an aggregate contacts approach could be expanded to cover diversity as well as federal question cases, and the standard might also be the basis for the exercise of jurisdiction by state courts if authorized by Congress.[140] Indeed, when foreign defendants are involved, an "aggregate contacts" standard is appropriate without regard to the defendant's amenability to suit in any particular state.[141] Internal domestic venue rules can then be used to allocate a case to the appropriate forum within the United States.[142]

Implementing the Convention Provisions on Recognition and Enforcement

As noted above, under existing U.S. jurisprudence, a suit to enforce a foreign country judgment is a matter of state and not federal law. Accordingly, a suit to enforce a

137 A particular type of Federal-State Clause could impose such a requirement.

138 Fed. R. Civ. P. 4(k)(2) provides:

> If the exercise of jurisdiction is consistent with the Constitution and laws of the United States, serving a summons or filing a waiver of service is also effective, with respect to claims arising under federal law, to establish personal jurisdiction over the person of any defendant who is not subject to jurisdiction of the courts of general jurisdiction of any state.

139 *See* 15 U.S.C. § 22 (Clayton Act); 15 U.S.C. § 77v (Securities Act of 1933); 15 U.S.C. § 78aa (Securities Exchange Act of 1934).

140 *Cf.* Asahi Metal Indus. Co. v. Superior Court, 480 U.S. 102, 113 (1987).

141 *Cf.* 28 U.S.C. § 1605 (Foreign Sovereign Immunities Act).

142 For example, the defendant could be subject to suit in the state within the United States in which the claim arose, in which the defendant had the most significant contacts, or in which related claims against other defendants were being heard.

foreign country judgment can be brought in (or removed to) a federal court in the United States only if the requisite diversity of citizenship requirements are met. Otherwise, a state court is the appropriate forum.[143]

But if the Preliminary Draft Convention were in effect, a suit to enforce a judgment falling under the Convention would be an action "arising under a treaty" within the meaning of Article III of the U.S. Constitution, and Congress could confer federal jurisdiction over such a suit without regard to the citizenship of the parties. Federal jurisdiction is desirable in ensuring compliance with an international treaty obligation, and Congress has provided for federal jurisdiction in implementing other international conventions.[144]

In implementing the proposed Hague Judgments Convention, Congress could consider making the jurisdiction of the federal courts exclusive of the state courts, but there are reasons to give the state courts concurrent jurisdiction. Committing the subject solely to the federal courts might be taken as a lack of confidence in state courts and is inconsistent with the general philosophy of a shared allocation of cases governed by federal law. Moreover, even an erroneous interpretation of the Convention by the state courts would still be subject to review, albeit discretionary, in the Supreme Court.

Therefore, the Reporters tentatively suggest that legislation implementing the Hague Judgments Convention authorize an action to enforce a foreign judgment to be brought initially in either state or federal court; in addition, as is done with the general scheme of original and removal jurisdiction for actions that "arise under federal law or federal treaties,"[145] the federal legislation should also permit an action for enforcement brought in state court to be removed by the defendant to federal court.[146] Such a jurisdictional regime would thus permit both plaintiff and defendant to have access to a federal court, but would authorize the state courts to hear the case in the absence of such a federal choice by either party.

Whether an action involving recognition (as contrasted with enforcement) of a foreign judgment is heard in federal or state court presents a slightly different problem because the issue of recognition usually arises as a defense to a plenary action. Whether the plenary action is brought in the state or federal court is a function of the nature of the plaintiff's independent claim. Nonetheless, express provision could be made in the implementing legislation for removal of a case to federal court based on the existence of the federal defense invoking recognition of a judgment falling

---

143 Federal courts in the United States have jurisdiction over claims based on state law when the suit is between parties of diverse citizenship. *See* 28 U.S.C. § 1332 (2000).

144 *See* 9 U.S.C. §§ 203, 205 (1995) (providing for original and removal jurisdiction in suits to enforce arbitral agreements and awards under the UN Convention on the Recognition and Enforcement of Foreign Arbitral Awards); 42 U.S.C. § 11603(a) (1995) (providing for concurrent jurisdiction for an action for return of a child under the 1980 Hague Convention on the Civil Aspects of International Child Abduction).

145 *See* 28 U.S.C. § 1331 (2000) and 28 U.S.C. § 1441 (2000).

146 *See* 9 U.S.C. § 205 (1995).

under the Convention,[147] as was done in the legislation implementing the UN Convention on Recognition and Enforcement of Foreign Arbitral Awards in respect to both agreements to arbitrate and arbitral awards.[148]

Other Issues Regarding Implementing Legislation

A host of other issues remain possible targets of implementing legislation. I list several of them briefly.

Definition of Terms

The Preliminary Draft Convention adopts a number of terms often unfamiliar to American lawyers and courts. For example, the principal basis of jurisdiction over a defendant in the U.S. has been domicile, not habitual residence. While the term is used extensively in European conventions, it has been employed less frequently in the United States and rarely in the commercial context.[149] Despite the reluctance of the delegates, and the Hague Conference more generally, to define the term in the Convention itself, a definition in the U.S. implementing legislation might prove beneficial.

Lis Pendens and Forum Non Conveniens

There is no formal lis pendens provision in U.S. law, and the propriety of staying an action in the face of parallel litigation in another country is unclear under existing U.S. law.[150] The Preliminary Draft Convention imposes a lis pendens requirement and makes failure to comply with that provision a defense to a judgment.[151]

Forum non conveniens remains a discretionary defense in the proposed convention to be used only in "exceptional circumstances."[152] Whether or not to adopt a national

---

[147] A specific provision for removal based on the existence of a federal defense is necessary because under the general scheme of original and removal jurisdiction removal is not authorized unless the plaintiff's claim "arises under" federal law. *See* 28 U.S.C. § 1331 as interpreted in Louisville & N.R. Co. v. Mottley, 211 U.S. 149 (1908).

[148] *See* 9 U.S.C. § 205 (1995). The arbitration legislation limits the option of removal to the defendant who is relying on the arbitration agreement or award. The right to remove an action raising the defense of a judgment falling under the proposed Hague Convention could also be limited to the defendant, who is relying on the foreign judgment entitled to recognition. Alternatively, once such a defense is raised, the right of removal could be extended to the plaintiff on the theory that either party should be permitted to seek federal-court interpretation of whether a judgment is entitled to recognition under the standards of the Convention.

[149] The term is used in the 1980 Convention on the Civil Aspects of Child Abduction to which the U.S. is a party, and courts interpreting that convention have applied the concept.

[150] *See* Stephen B. Burbank, *Jurisdictional Equilibration, supra* note 28, at 127.

[151] *See* Preliminary Draft, *supra* note 30, at art. 28(1)(a).

[152] *See* Preliminary Draft Convention, *supra* note 30, at art. 22. Excluded from the scope of forum non conveniens are cases where jurisdiction is based on an exclusive choice-of-court agreement or rests on an exclusive basis of jurisdiction under Article 12. Nor does forum non conveniens displace jurisdiction premised on the protective provisions for consumer and employees in Articles 7 and 8 respectively.

Note that forum non conveniens is not found in the Brussels Convention, but that there has been forum non conveniens standard[153] or merely to require all courts in the United States to take account of the convention standards in exercising their own forum non conveniens rules is an open question.

Provisional Remedies

The Preliminary Draft Convention authorizes the use of provisional remedies,[154] but the propriety of provisional and protective relief is left to national law. The approach to provisional remedies under national law has important convention implications because Article 23(b) of the Draft Convention includes within the definition of a judgment a "decision ordering provisional or protective measures in accordance with Article 13, paragraph 1." Thus, provisional and protective measures, granted by a court exercising a required basis of jurisdiction, are entitled to recognition in other contracting states.

It is tempting to take advantage of U.S. implementing legislation to create via a federal statute a systematic regime of provisional relief for the federal courts.[155] That is particularly true in light of two recent decisions in the U.S., one by the Supreme Court of the United States[156] and the other by the New York Court of Appeals,[157] that rejected the authority of courts in the United States to restrain the transfer of assets abroad in order to ensure future satisfaction of a judgment.

The approach of the U.S. courts provides a stark contrast to the use of Mareva injunctions in England and the Commonwealth countries. If the U.S. position is extreme in denying such provisional relief as an absolute matter, the expanding reach of the English Mareva may have gone too far in the other direction. We have now seen a number of cases where Mareva injunctions have been issued in cases bearing little relationship to the forum other than the fact that the defendant is subject to jurisdiction there.[158] When combined with the more expansive bases of jurisdiction, such as jurisdiction over multiple defendants, the Mareva can be a potentially powerful and abusive weapon.[159] Once mandatory enforcement is added, the Convention may have inadvertently created the elements for a nuclear attack.

---

growing acceptance among civil-law countries of approaches for declining and referring jurisdiction in international and commercial litigation. *See* ILA, Committee on International Civil and Commercial Litigations, Third Interim Report: Declining and Referring Jurisdiction in International Litigation 17 (2000).

153 *See, e.g.*, Stephen B. Burbank, *Jurisdictional Equilibration, supra* note 28, at 155–56 (discussing this point as well as what the substance of such a provision might look like).

154 *See* Preliminary Draft Convention, *supra* note 30, at art. 13.

155 Federalism sensibilities suggest that the legislation be directed to remedies for the federal courts only, and that the states be left to develop provisional relief for their own courts. *See generally* George A. Bermann, *Provisional Relief in Transnational Litigation, supra* note 29.

156 *See* Grupo Mexicano de Desarrollo SA v. Alliance Bond Fund, Inc., 527 U.S. 308 (1999).

157 *See* Credit Agricole Indosuez v. Rossiyskiy Kredit Bank, 94 N.Y.2d 541 (2000).

158 *See* Dicey and Morris, *supra* note 63, at 182–190.

159 *See* Canada Trust Co. v. Stolzenberg, [1998] 1 W.L.R. 547 (Ct. App.), appeal dismissed, 4 A.E.R. 481 (2000).

Procedures for Enforcement

The Preliminary Draft Convention leaves the procedure for recognition and enforcement to the law of the recognizing state and instructs that courts "act expeditiously."[160] Implementing legislation for the United States will need to make provision for summary enforcement in cases falling under the Convention. Again, federalism considerations argue for setting forth specific procedures for the federal courts alone. The legislation could, however, include minimum guidelines to be adopted by the states in enforcing foreign country judgments under the Convention – for instance, the requirement that a summary procedure be made available – but allow the states to control the details in accordance with their prevailing practices.

Conclusion

The differences among the states over the proposed jurisdictional provisions in the Preliminary Draft Convention are attributable to several factors. The Europeans have been wedded in varying degrees to the Brussels/Lugano model while the Americans have found the Preliminary Draft Convention in tension with a constitutionally-rooted jurisdictional tradition and in collision with views deeply-held by certain segments of the American bar about choice of fora for litigation. Nonetheless, the efforts at The Hague have shown that a worldwide convention on jurisdiction and recognition practice is possible. It may be that the Preliminary Draft is in some way too ambitious – that is, finding common ground on all jurisdictional rules may be premature. A revision that offers a much narrower band of required and prohibited jurisdictions could very well be acceptable to the United States, and the possibility of allowing states to elect to recognize judgments resting on particular types of jurisdiction in the gray zone as part of the Convention regime would provide for broader recognition of judgments while preserving flexibility and respecting different legal traditions.

The proposals set forth in this paper for changes in the jurisdictional provisions, most particularly the modification of the prohibition on the doing business jurisdiction, would go a long way in helping to refocus the Convention in this way. They are worth serious consideration.

---

[160] *See* Preliminary Draft Convention, *supra* note 30, at art. 30.

Kevin M. Clermont[†] *and Kuo-Chang Huang*[‡]

Converting the Draft Hague Treaty into Domestic Jurisdictional Law

INTRODUCTION

"Jurisdictional salvation," one of us has pronounced,[1] lies latent in the treaty currently under negotiation through the Hague Conference on Private International Law.[2] The envisaged treaty is a multilateral convention on jurisdiction and foreign judgments in civil and commercial matters that might be approved for signature, ratification, and implementation in the near future.[3] It would ensure mutual respect of judgments among contracting countries, but it would also require agreement on a sensible scheme of territorial jurisdiction.

Any feasible treaty would probably end up at least resembling the European Union's Brussels Convention on Jurisdiction and the Enforcement of Judgments in Civil and Commercial Matters.[4] That is, the United States would probably abandon – on the international level – transient jurisdiction, attachment jurisdiction, and "doing business" as bases for general jurisdiction.[5] The Europeans' principal objection to U.S. jurisdictional law is its proclivity to base general jurisdiction on rather thin

---

† Flanagan Professor of Law, Cornell University. The authors would like to thank Robert Casad, Robert Kent, Emily Sherwin, and Barry Vasios for their very helpful comments.

‡ Rudolf B. Schlesinger Fellow, J.S.D. Candidate, Cornell Law School; LL.B. 1995 National Taiwan University; LL.M. 1999 Cornell Law School. The author would like to take this opportunity to sincerely thank Cornell Law School for financial support while pursuing his J.S.D. degree.

1 Kevin M. Clermont, *Jurisdictional Salvation and the Hague Treaty*, 85 Cornell L. Rev. 89 (1999).

2 For the background of the Hague negotiations, see Peter H. Pfund, *The Project of the Hague Conference on Private International Law to Prepare a Convention on Jurisdiction and the Recognition/Enforcement of Judgments in Civil and Commercial Matters*, 24 Brook. J. Int'l L. 7 (1998).

3 For the best, albeit tentative, suggestion of the content of the eventual treaty, see Hague Conference on Private Int'l Law, *Preliminary Draft Convention on Jurisdiction and Foreign Judgments in Civil and Commercial Matters* (Oct. 30, 1999) [hereinafter *Treaty Draft*], *available in* <http://www.hcch.net/e/conventions/draft36e.html>, *explained in* Peter Nygh and Fausto Pocar, *Report of the Special Commission*, Hague Conf. Prelim. Doc. No. 11 (2000).

4 Sept. 27, 1968, 1972 O.J. (L 299) 32 [hereinafter Brussels Convention], *reprinted as amended in* 29 I.L.M. 1413 (1990). On this Convention, and the related Lugano Convention, see generally Alan Dashwood et al., *A Guide to the Civil Jurisdiction and Judgments Convention* 35–46 (1987); Peter Stone, *Civil Jurisdiction and Judgments in Europe* (1998); or Robert C. Reuland, *The Recognition of Judgments in the European Community: The Twenty-fifth Anniversary of the Brussels Convention*, 14 Mich. J. Int'l L. 559 (1993).

5 On general jurisdiction, see *infra* Proposed Statute § 201.

J.J. Barceló and K.M. Clermont (eds.), A Global Law of Jurisdiction and Judgments: Lessons from The Hague, 191–234

contacts, that is, to allow any and all causes of action to be brought not only on the basis of domicile but also on the basis of the defendant's physical presence, property ownership, or doing business in the forum. They do not object to specific jurisdiction,[6] as long as a rules-based approach controls its mandatory application. Accordingly, jurisdiction under such a treaty would exist at the unconsenting defendant's habitual residence or where a specific part of the events in suit occurred, but would not extend to the broader bases of jurisdiction now authorized by U.S. law. In exchange, the United States would get other countries to respect its judgments and also to renounce their own exorbitant jurisdiction.

Impartially viewed, reaching agreement on a multilateral treaty could yield great benefits.[7] A treaty would rationalize the U.S. law of jurisdiction and judgments on the international level, while moving the world toward justice without regard to international boundaries. Moreover, a treaty would give the United States the opportunity to untangle its jurisdictional law applied at home. That is, rethinking jurisdiction in the course of the treatymaking process could result in improvements on the interstate level.

However, reaching agreement on a treaty is very far from a sure thing.[8] Big differences of view exist, and entrenched interests seem not to be embracing the spirit of compromise and consensus. The efforts already sunk in treatymaking, nevertheless, need not go for naught. Reformers, such as the American Law Institute (ALI),[9] could utilize the best U.S. proposal at The Hague to create a model statute that would rework the U.S. law on jurisdiction and judgments. In particular, reformers might incline toward federalizing the law of recognition and enforcement of foreign judgments. But we would urge them also to reformulate the law of territorial jurisdiction applied in interstate and international cases in the United States.

On this domestic level, then, the treatymaking effort could inspire legislatures to enact the treaty's or the U.S. proposal's jurisdictional provisions as domestic law.

---

6 On specific jurisdiction, see *infra id.* § 202.

7 *See* Linda J. Silberman, *Can the Hague Judgments Project Be Saved?: A Perspective from the United States, supra* p. 159, at 161–64.

8 The United States, although the original proposer of a treaty, has developed serious reservations about going forward in the face of the Europeans' fixed positions and bloc voting. *See* Arthur T. von Mehren, *Drafting a Convention on International Jurisdiction and the Effects of Foreign Judgments Acceptable Worldwide: Can the Hague Conference Project Succeed?, infra* p. 281; Letter from Jeffrey D. Kovar, Assistant Legal Advisor for Private Int'l Law, U.S. Dep't of State, to J.H.A. van Loon, Secretary General, Hague Conf. on Private Int'l Law (Feb. 22, 2000) (on file with authors) [hereinafter Kovar Letter].

9 *See* ALI International Jurisdiction and Judgments Project (Report 2000). The nascent ALI Project intended to pursue two draft federal statutes, one to implement a Hague treaty and one, in the absence of a treaty, to govern the recognition and enforcement of foreign judgments in the United States, but not the territorial jurisdiction of U.S. courts. *See* Linda J. Silberman and Andreas F. Lowenfeld, *A Different Challenge for the ALI: Herein of Foreign Country Judgments, an International Treaty, and an American Statute*, 75 Ind. L.J. 635, 643 n. 57 (2000). The instant article's effort to draft a federal statute to govern the states' interstate and international territorial jurisdiction, whether or not there is a treaty, is thus complementary to the ALI Project.

That is, the states or Congress could legislate that state or federal courts, not only in all international cases but also in interstate cases, possess jurisdiction only if the case's circumstances satisfy the treaty's or the proposal's analogous jurisdictional provision. Thus, with salvation coming from an unexpected direction, the United States might achieve the optimal law on territorial authority to adjudicate: a law under which constitutional limits fade into the background and legislative rules move to the fore.

Legislative action is the preferred route to domestic reform. Legislatures should undertake a much more serious effort to site cases in convenient, efficient, and otherwise desirable courts than they have hitherto. Preferably after wiping the jurisdiction slate clean, their statutes should set out general rules – usually siting cases at the defendant's habitual residence or where a specific part of the events in suit occurred. Such statutes should embrace a rules-based approach to jurisdiction, resisting the allure of delegating to the courts individualized analysis via a standard or a list of factors. The statutes should nudge the law along the spectrum toward certainty, giving outsiders clearer guidance on what activities will and will not subject them to local suit. Furthermore, the new legislation should move toward greater restraint as well as greater certainty. Because the choice of forum can affect a case's just outcome and because the plaintiff currently has a wide choice, lawmakers should take a progressively more restrictive approach to territorial jurisdiction in both state and federal law.

Of course, the courts must subsequently cooperate, by treating the statutes' words as if they mean something. Courts must avoid destroying rules by ad-hoc and result-oriented stretching that would undo the legislative moves toward certainty and restraint. In short, courts must approach the new statutes more as New York courts have respected their long-arm statute than Illinois courts have reworked theirs.[10]

Unfortunately, the states' record on restraining and clarifying their own jurisdiction demonstrates that state reform remains a utopian pipe dream.[11] If the state legislatures do in fact prove reluctant to restrain their own courts, then Congress could legislate that state courts have jurisdiction according to the treaty's or proposal's criteria, regardless of whether the defendant is domiciled in the United States or abroad. Of course, such congressional intervention, highly desirable as it might be, may be even less likely as a political matter than state reform.[12]

---

10 *Compare* Longines-Wittnauer Watch Co. v. Barnes & Reinecke, Inc., 209 N.E.2d 68 (N.Y. 1965), *with* Gray v. American Radiator & Standard Sanitary Corp., 176 N.E.2d 761 (Ill. 1961). *See generally* Richard H. Field et al., *Materials for a Basic Course in Civil Procedure* 982–95 (7th ed. 1997) (comparing states' differing approaches). To encourage a restrained construction, the proposed statute includes a tolling provision that should make courts less reluctant to dismiss. *See infra* Proposed Statute § 301.

11 *See* Martin B. Louis, *The Grasp of Long Arm Jurisdiction Finally Exceeds Its Reach: A Comment on* World-Wide Volkswagen Corp. v. Woodson *and* Rush v. Savchuk, 58 N.C. L. Rev. 407, 431–32 (1980) (noting pressures on states to expand their reach).

12 *See* Kevin M. Clermont, *Restating Territorial Jurisdiction and Venue for State and Federal Courts*, 66 Cornell L. Rev. 411, 442 n. 139 (1981).

The earlier article foreseeing jurisdictional salvation argued for the desirability and constitutionality of such domestic reform by Congress, while just sketching its content.[13] But calls for reform are relatively easy to utter. Actually drafting the reform – fully formulating the law of territorial jurisdiction – is a much harder task. Nevertheless, drafting a proposed statute is worth doing. It would add feasibility to the arguments made to the legislators.

Accordingly, this article offers, with slim hope, the following proposed statute. In brief, this proposal for federal enactment aims to pare general jurisdiction down to its proper scope and codify specific jurisdiction into restrained and clear mandatory rules, while pushing constitutional limits into the background where they belong.

Proposed Statute

Title 1 – General Provisions

§ 101. Scope
§ 102. Preemption of State Law
§ 103. Definitions

Title 2 – Jurisdictional Bases

§ 201. General Jurisdiction
§ 202. Specific Jurisdiction
§ 203. Permitted Jurisdiction
§ 204. Multiple Claims and Parties
§ 205. Choice of Forum
§ 206. Appearance by Defendant
§ 207. Exclusive Jurisdiction

Title 3 – Ancillary Provisions

§ 301. Limitations Tolling
§ 302. Forum Non Conveniens
§ 303. Lis Pendens
§ 304. Antisuit Injunctions
§ 305. Provisional and Final Remedies

Title 1 – General Provisions

§ 101. Scope

This statute applies to all civil actions in the courts of a State, territory, or possession

[13] *See* Clermont, *supra* note 1.

of the United States, the District of Columbia, or the Commonwealth of Puerto Rico, except as otherwise provided in this statute.

Comment: The preferred route to domestic jurisdictional reform would be to extend the congressional implementation of the treaty, if there were a treaty. More precisely, the suggestion is that a federal statute should extend the substance of the treaty's provisions to state courts not only in all international cases but also in interstate cases. The starting point in formulating such a statute would be the treaty. Would the nation really want to tie domestic law to the terms of a treaty? This may seem a concern, but it is not really a problem. Blindly carrying the treaty's terms over into domestic law for non-international cases is neither necessary nor even appropriate. Congress should legislate with attention to domestic needs, and it should take the opportunity in its extensions of the treaty to rewrite any distasteful compromises made to secure international agreement. Nevertheless, *the legislators should treat the treaty as a presumptively appropriate first draft for statutory reform.* After all, international norms deserve some respect. Moreover, the practical benefits of simplicity and consistency would result from the statute's avoiding unnecessary discrepancies with international norms.

A federal statute extending the treaty is politically a long shot. But if the chances for reaching international agreement on a treaty were to go up in smoke, a federal statute based on the draft treaty becomes an even longer shot. The failure of the current treaty negotiations would make reality just too powerful for academic idealism to ignore any longer. The federal government would be very reluctant to impose on the nation a set of jurisdictional reforms that it rejected during treaty negotiations. Still, a federal statute based on the draft treaty, as proposed in this article, deserves some consideration. It does not give away all U.S. interests to foreign interests. By imposing uniform and defensible jurisdictional rules on the nation, the statute would facilitate the recognition and enforcement of U.S. judgments abroad. Also, a fresh and progressive approach to jurisdictional law at home might increase the chances for successful resumption of negotiations for a jurisdiction and judgments convention that would be acceptable in the United States and abroad. Therefore, although the federal statute by no means should follow it slavishly, *the draft treaty remains a presumptively appropriate first draft for statutory reform.*

If the proposed statute were adopted, and later the treaty were ratified, any implementing legislation would of course override the proposed statute in cases that came within the treaty's reach. The proposed statute would then need amendment to mesh the two sets of legislation and thereby avoid any unintended discontinuities between interstate and international cases. In sum, regardless of if or when there is a treaty, a federal statute based on the current draft treaty's treatment of jurisdiction is the essence of this article's proposal.

An approach alternative to a *federal statute* on jurisdiction would be a model *state statute* for adoption by the states. State legislatures could enact uniform jurisdictional provisions as their own law or achieve the same result through an interstate compact.[14] The aim would be to bring interstate and international cases within the sweep of a clear and restrained jurisdictional law. Such a model statute would look much like this article's proposed statute, but for simplicity's sake this article will restrict its drafting effort to the congressional setting.

Neither a federal nor a state statutory route to reform of *state territorial jurisdiction* would directly rework *federal territorial jurisdiction.* Of course, any treaty would reform the federal law for most international cases in the federal courts. And because state jurisdictional law routinely applies in federal court,[15] any state-law reform would automatically reform the federal law for most interstate cases. Nevertheless, an eventual rethinking of federal law on jurisdiction and venue would be in order. Again for simplicity's sake, this article will restrict its drafting effort to the state-court setting.

An entirely different approach to reform would be to expand federal *subject-matter jurisdiction* to open the federal courts whenever a state declines to exercise *territorial jurisdiction* in an international case that meets certain criteria.[16] On the one hand, few cases would follow this route into federal court because the states have little interest in declining their maximum jurisdiction. On the other hand, a new head of federal subject-matter jurisdiction would cause many problems and spawn wasteful litigation. Moreover, it would do nothing to curb the currently excessive reach of state jurisdiction, or to clarify that murky body of law. Accordingly, this article sticks to the direct route of federal reform of the state law on territorial jurisdiction.

§ 102. Preemption of State Law

A state may not exercise territorial jurisdiction on bases other than those specified in this statute or in another federal statute of the United States. Except as otherwise provided in this statute, a state must exercise any properly invoked territorial jurisdiction on one of the bases specified in this statute.

Comment: The recommendation that Congress enact some version of the draft treaty's jurisdictional provisions, for all international and interstate cases in state courts, raises a number of constitutional and prudential concerns. Those concerns intensify when one realizes that the congressional provisions would not supplement but supplant the states' jurisdictional laws. States could thenceforth exercise only the statutorily approved bases of territorial jurisdiction. Moreover, the exercise of those jurisdictional bases would in the main be mandatory.

First, is there power so to federalize jurisdictional law? Congress could intercede to legislate general limits on the states' interstate and international reach by using its powers under the Due Process Clause, Full Faith and Credit Clause, and

---

14 *See* Leonard J. Feldman, *The Interstate Compact: A Cooperative Solution to Complex Litigation in State Courts*, 12 Rev. Litig. 137, 138–41 (1992).

15 *See* Fed. R. Civ. P. 4(k)(1)(A), 4(n)(2).

16 *See* ALI International Jurisdiction and Judgments Project, *supra* note 9, at 25.

Commerce Clause,[17] not to mention its powers with respect to foreign relations.[18] In extending the states' reach, however, Congress must generally stay within the bounds that the Due Process Clause imposes on the states.[19]

Second, does the nation want to federalize jurisdictional law? Recommending congressional intervention, on first impression, seems such a big step. But the actual change from current practice would be both slight and wholly appropriate. The Supreme Court in large part has already federalized the law of state-court territorial jurisdiction, deriving the operative law from the Due Process Clause. Congressional regulation in this particular realm would be preferable to constitutional interpretation by the judiciary. Moreover, the law of interstate and international jurisdiction is inherently a matter of federal interest and within federal powers to regulate. Finally, the states have thus far made poor use of their current powers to restrain their reach and clarify their jurisdictional law.

Third, does Congress have the power to force the states to accept jurisdiction? The congressional authority to legislate on territorial jurisdiction encompasses the power to make the jurisdiction mandatory, and Congress can exercise this authority without violating the Tenth Amendment.[20]

Fourth, does the nation want to force state courts to accept jurisdiction? This concern expresses a more general fear of trying to go too far in the name of reform. Even if the revolution of a jurisdictional statute came to pass, why make its rules mandatory, so that a court with jurisdiction must exercise it? The reason is that the natural corollary of provisions prohibiting jurisdiction to all but a few courts is the requirement that those proper courts exercise their jurisdiction. Because the statute would eliminate exorbitant jurisdiction, forum non conveniens would no longer be justified.[21] Further, the need for fraud-and-force and immunity doctrines would largely disappear with the end of transient jurisdiction. In general, procedural laws that permit courts to decline territorial jurisdiction should suffer repeal.[22]

---

17 *See* Patrick J. Borchers, *Comparing Personal Jurisdiction in the United States and the European Community: Lessons for American Reform*, 40 Am. J. Comp. L. 121, 154–55 (1992); Patrick J. Borchers, *The Death of the Constitutional Law of Personal Jurisdiction: From* Pennoyer *to* Burnham *and Back Again*, 24 U.C. Davis L. Rev. 19, 104–05 (1990); Clermont, *supra* note 12, at 442 n. 139; Israel Packel, *Congressional Power to Reduce Personal Jurisdiction Litigation*, 59 Temp. L.Q. 919 (1986) (Commerce Clause); Ralph U. Whitten, *The Constitutional Limitations on State-Court Jurisdiction: A Historical-Interpretative Reexamination of the Full Faith and Credit and Due Process Clauses* (pts. 1 and 2), 14 Creighton L. Rev. 499, 735 (1981).

18 *See* Patrick J. Borchers, *Judgments Conventions and Minimum Contacts*, 61 Alb. L. Rev. 1161, 1164–73 (1998).

19 *See* Clermont, *supra* note 1, at 124–27.

20 *See id.* at 127–29.

21 *See infra* Proposed Statute § 302. The statute could contain a transfer mechanism in the interest of justice, similar to that under 28 U.S.C. § 1404(a) (1994). *See* Clermont, *supra* note 12, at 450 and n. 186; *cf. infra* Proposed Statute § 301 (opting instead for a tolling provision). The statute should contain a lis pendens provision. *See infra id.* § 303.

22 Presumably, however, a state could apply a more substantive door-closing statute. For example, a statute might close the courthouse doors to any action brought by a foreign corporation that had

Fifth, should the proposed statute follow the draft treaty's lead in including a "graylist" of permitted state jurisdictional bases? The draft treaty includes not only a so-called blacklist of prohibited jurisdictional bases and a so-called whitelist of required bases, but also a catchall gray zone of permitted bases.[23] In the gray zone, a country could exercise jurisdiction on any basis under its own law not prohibited by the blacklist, but other countries would not have to recognize or enforce that judgment. Although such a mixed convention does not go as far in providing global uniformity as a double convention, a more limited ambition greatly facilitates international agreement.

The arguments for a gray zone in the proposed statute are that it would reduce the federal compulsion of states, simplify the drafting task, and provide a handle on future developments in hot areas like Internet jurisdiction. The arguments against a gray zone are that less need exists for one on the national level than on the international level, because less disuniformity exists among one nation's jurisdictional laws; the effect of a gray zone on the national level necessarily differs, because the Full Faith and Credit Clause will obligate other states to respect the judgment of a state exercising a permitted basis; and most importantly, a gray zone will allow state law to remain unrestrainedly broad and confoundingly unclear.

The solution is compromise, changing the catchall gray zone into a list of specified bases (and hence changing the blacklist into a black zone). The proposed statute should specifically list those bases that are left to state law.[24] This approach of including a specific graylist is the partial equivalent of limiting the scope of the proposed statute by listing certain exemptions in the opening section, as the draft treaty does.[25] A specific graylist retains the benefits of a gray zone's flexibility but limits the deleterious effects of unrestrained state reach extending to uncertain bounds. To increase acceptability of the proposed statute, Congress could expand the graylist. With time and emerging consensus, Congress could codify graylist bases by shifting them onto the whitelist. In the meantime, the whitelist serves the purpose of ensuring that the states exercise all the jurisdiction that a treaty would require, and it provides a model of jurisdictional law around which the remaining state law could coalesce.

---

failed to comply with a requirement to register before transacting business in the state. This restriction on the plaintiff's qualifications is sufficiently remote from traditional notions of territorial jurisdiction to avoid violating the treaty or federal statute. Moreover, the policy here is more substantive than the desirable distribution among courts of judicial business. Accordingly, a state door-closing statute of this type would apply in federal court under the *Erie* doctrine. *See* Woods v. Interstate Realty Co., 337 U.S. 535, 538 (1949); *cf. infra* note 166 and accompanying text (nonpersonal jurisdiction).

23 *See Treaty Draft, supra* note 3, art. 17. *See generally* Arthur T. von Mehren, *Enforcing Judgments Abroad: Reflections on the Design of Recognition Conventions*, 24 Brook. J. Int'l L. 17, 19 (1998) (championing the mixed-convention approach).

24 *See infra* Proposed Statute § 203.

25 *See Treaty Draft, supra* note 3, art. 1.

§ 103. Definitions

In this statute:

(a) A "state" means a State, territory, or possession of the United States, the District of Columbia, the Commonwealth of Puerto Rico, or a foreign state.

(b) "Habitual residence" means the place where a natural person dwells in the ordinary course of his or her life or a new place to which the person moves with the intention to dwell for an indefinite period.

(c) "Consumer" means a person or an entity that is not a merchant. For a claim on an insurance contract, "consumer" can include the insured, the policyholder, and the beneficiary if not a merchant.

(d) "Merchant" means a person or an entity that engages in the course of its occupation in the particular transaction on which the claim is based, or that otherwise by its occupation holds itself out as having knowledge or skill peculiar to that transaction.

(e) "Person needed for just adjudication" means a person:

(1) in whose absence complete relief cannot be accorded among those already parties; or

(2) who claims an interest relating to the subject of the action and is so situated that the disposition of the action in the person's absence may (i) as a practical matter impair or impede the person's ability to protect that interest or (ii) leave any of the persons already parties subject to a substantial risk of incurring double, multiple, or otherwise inconsistent obligations by reason of the claimed interest.

Comment: For the purpose of promoting consistent interpretation of legal concepts under the proposed statute, this section provides some uniform definitions.

Because the proposed statute applies to both interstate and international cases, the meaning of state includes the fifty states of the United States and foreign countries with the status of state under international law. The proposed statute follows the ordinary definition in federal statutes of a U.S. state as including other subdivisions of the United States.[26] Obviously, as § 101 recognized, the proposed statute does not apply to foreign countries. But including them here within the meaning of state facilitates the drafting of the later sections on forum selection clauses and exclusive jurisdiction[27] and also facilitates any eventual broadening of the later sections on lis pendens and antisuit injunctions.[28]

The concept of habitual residence is new to U.S. law. In accordance with the purpose of using this concept to provide general jurisdiction,[29] habitual residence is defined in a way to point to the center of the defendant's ordinary life. The phrase "dwells in the ordinary course" focuses on a considerable passage of time and a life's

---

26 *See, e.g.*, 28 U.S.C. §§1332(d), 1367(e) (1994).

27 *See infra* Proposed Statute §§ 205, 207.

28 *See id.* §§ 303–304; *infra* note 197.

29 *See infra* Proposed Statute § 201; text accompanying note 41.

center of gravity[30] but, unlike domicile,[31] does not require the element of intention. The phrase "moves with the intention to dwell for an indefinite period" handles change of habitual residence by providing for immediate acquisition of a new one.[32]

The definition of consumer is a non-merchant. Because this proposed statute will treat a consumer insurance policy as a type of consumer contract,[33] this definition explicitly includes the insured, the policyholder, and the beneficiary.

The definition of merchant basically adopts the definition of merchant provided in the Uniform Commercial Code.[34] An advantage of that definition is the abundant case law already extant. The coverage of this definition is somewhat broader than that provided in the draft treaty.[35]

The definition of a person needed for just adjudication comes right out of Federal Rule of Civil Procedure 19(a), which treats compulsory joinder of parties. The proposed statute uses the term in § 204(c).

Title 2 – Jurisdictional Bases

§ 201. General Jurisdiction

(a) A state has personal jurisdiction, as to any claim, over a natural person whose habitual residence is in that state.

(b) A state has personal jurisdiction, as to any claim, over an incorporated organization organized under the law of or having its principal place of business activity in that state.

(c) A state has personal jurisdiction, as to any claim, over an unincorporated association or other legal person having its principal place of business activity, or for a non-business entity the principal place of administration, in that state.

Comment: This section provides for a court's general jurisdiction. General jurisdiction, which rests on supposedly strong contacts between the defendant and the forum state, gives the state power to adjudicate any personal claim whatsoever against the defendant, whether or not the claim is related to those contacts. The bases of general jurisdiction channel litigation in a workable manner to a predictably certain, and usually fair, forum.

The court's general jurisdiction is supplemented and limited by the subsequent

30 *See generally* Restatement (Second) of Conflict of Laws § 12 (1971) (defining home); E.M. Clive, *The Concept of Habitual Residence*, 1997 Jurid. Rev. 137; J.D. McClean, *The Meaning of Residence*, 11 Int'l & Comp. L.Q. 1153 (1962).

31 *See* Restatement (Second) of Conflict of Laws § 18 (1971) ("To acquire a domicil of choice in a place, a person must intend to make that place his home for the time at least.").

32 *See* Clive, *supra* note 30, at 142–43.

33 *See infra* note 74 and accompanying text.

34 *See* U.C.C. § 2–104 (1990).

35 *See Treaty Draft, supra* note 3, art. 7 ("a person who entered into the contract in the course of its trade or profession").

sections regarding specific jurisdiction[36] and exclusive jurisdiction.[37] Specific jurisdiction denotes personal jurisdiction for related claims only. State-directed acts or consent, resting on lesser contacts between the defendant and the forum state than does general jurisdiction, gives the state additional power to adjudicate, but only with respect to those personal claims related to the contacts. These bases of specific jurisdiction provide needed and useful jurisdiction, although they can give rise to some very difficult problems of line-drawing. Exclusive jurisdiction restricts the court's general jurisdiction in the sense that when another state has exclusive jurisdiction with respect to the action, the court cannot exercise its general jurisdiction over the defendant in that action.

Because general jurisdiction confers broad power to adjudicate any claim against the defendant, without taking into consideration the relation between the particular case and the forum, the basis for this jurisdiction requires a strong nexus between the defendant and the forum. In the draft treaty, as to natural persons, the basis of general jurisdiction looks to the defendant's habitual residence; as to other legal entities, general jurisdiction exists at the statutory seat, the place of incorporation, the place of central administration, and the principal place of business.[38] The draft treaty deviates from the domicile basis adopted in the Brussels Convention.[39] The reason for this deviation is that, as to natural persons, habitual residence is a factual concept preferable to the technical concept of domicile; as to other legal entities, listing four specific criteria is better than using the vague generic term domicile to encompass such criteria.[40]

The proposed statute also uses habitual residence for natural persons, after specifically defining it in § 103(b). Although domicile has long been recognized in the United States as a sufficient basis for the court to exercise general jurisdiction over a natural person,[41] its technical nature might occasionally render the exercise of general jurisdiction unreasonable.[42] For example, even if a person has definitely left his previous domicile with the intention of starting a new life elsewhere, he remains domiciled in the same place until he satisfies all elements for establishing a new domicile.[43] Whether or not the exercise of general jurisdiction by the court in his

---

[36] *See infra* Proposed Statute § 202; *cf. id.* §§ 205–206 (consent).

[37] *See infra id.* § 207.

[38] *See Treaty Draft, supra* note 3, art. 3.

[39] *See* Brussels Convention, *supra* note 4, art. 2.

[40] *See* Catherine Kessedjian, *Synthesis of the Work of the Special Commission of June 1997 on International Jurisdiction and the Effects of Foreign Judgments in Civil and Commercial Matters*, Hague Conf. Prelim. Doc. No. 8, at 17–19 (Nov. 1997) [hereinafter *1997 Synthesis*].

[41] *See* Milliken v. Meyer, 311 U.S. 457 (1940); Unif. Interstate and International Procedure Act § 1.02, 13 U.L.A. 359 (1986) [hereinafter UI&IPA].

[42] *See* Restatement (Second) of Conflict of Laws § 29 reporter's note (1971) (amended 1988); 1 Robert C. Casad and William B. Richman, *Jurisdiction in Civil Actions* 128–29 (3d ed. 1998).

[43] *See* Restatement (Second) of Conflict of Laws § 15 (1971).

technical domicile would be unconstitutional,[44] it is inappropriate as a matter of policy to assume that he still has sufficiently strong ties with his domicile to justify general jurisdiction over him. Given that a court with general jurisdiction can adjudicate any claim against the defendant without regard to the claim's connection with the forum, the most appropriate forum to exercise such jurisdiction is the center of the defendant's ordinary life. Habitual residence, the determination of which focuses on pertinent facts, is a better candidate than legalistic domicile to capture the real center of gravity of the defendant's life.

Habitual residence is also a more appropriate basis for general jurisdiction than is residence, which has sometimes been recognized as a sufficient basis for general jurisdiction.[45] Habitual residence stands for a stronger connection between the forum and the defendant. Moreover, "habitual" can ameliorate the ambiguity of "residence," which can have many, very different meanings.[46] The additional word clarifies that although the defendant need not reside in the forum continuously without absence, the residence must extend for a considerable period of time.

The proposed statute would eliminate transient, or tag, jurisdiction as a basis of general jurisdiction. Under current U.S. law, the ancient basis of presence gives the forum state power to adjudicate any personal claim if the defendant is served with process within the state's territorial limits. Thus, even momentary physical presence of the defendant at the time of service creates power to adjudicate a claim totally unrelated to that transient presence. This basis has long enjoyed judicial approval in the United States and thus is constitutional, as long as its application is not so outlandish that it is unreasonable in the particular circumstances.[47] However, it has also long been the recipient of criticism, from academics and foreigners alike.[48]

---

44 The exercise of general jurisdiction in this situation was upheld in olden days. *See, e.g.*, McDonald v. Mabee, 243 U.S. 90 (1917). But some commentators have argued that, in light of *Shaffer v. Heitner*, 433 U.S. 186 (1977), the exercise of jurisdiction would now be unconstitutional. *See, e.g.*, 1 Casad and Richman, *supra* note 42, at 129.

45 *See* Restatement (Second) of Conflict of Laws § 30 (1971).

46 *See id.* § 11 cmt. k (amended 1988); Willis L.M. Reese and Robert S. Green, *That Elusive Word, "Residence,"* 6 Vand. L. Rev. 561 (1953).

47 *See* Lawrence W. Newman and Michael Burrows, *The Practice of International Litigation* I-120 to -121 (2d ed. 1998); Sarieddine v. Moussa, 820 S.W.2d 837, 840 (Tex. Ct. App. 1991) (implicitly rejecting the minority opinion of Justice Scalia in *Burnham v. Superior Court*, 495 U.S. 604, 607 (1990), which had suggested that transient jurisdiction merely by its historical pedigree always satisfies the unreasonableness test).

48 *See* Gary B. Born, *International Civil Litigation in United States Courts* 121–23 (3d ed. 1996); Mathias Reimann, *Conflict of Laws in Western Europe* 78 (1995) (explaining that most Western European countries do not recognize transient jurisdiction); Stephen B. Burbank, *The United States' Approach to International Civil Litigation: Recent Developments in Forum Selection*, 19 U. Pa. J. Int'l Econ. L. 1, 13–14, 18 (1998); Peter Hay, *Transient Jurisdiction, Especially over International Defendants: Critical Comments on* Burnham v. Superior Court of California, 1990 U. Ill. L. Rev. 593, 599–601; Russell J. Weintraub, *An Objective Basis for Rejecting Transient Jurisdiction*, 22 Rutgers L.J. 611, 613–16 (1991); Joachim Zekoll, *The Role and Status of American Law in the Hague Judgments Convention Project*, 61 Alb. L. Rev. 1283, 1296–97 (1998) (explaining that transient jurisdiction conflicts with international standards).

Formerly the most important basis of U.S. jurisdiction but today far from essential, transient jurisdiction is needed by courts, albeit inappropriately, only when all appropriate bases of jurisdiction are unavailing. Given transient jurisdiction's dubious propriety and general unnecessariness, the United States should adopt the draft treaty's prohibition.[49] Possibly, however, there should be a new provision for jurisdiction against terrorists and other human rights violators, for whom the human rights community has relied on tag jurisdiction.[50] The proposed statute provides for jurisdiction over such wrongdoers by preserving state law.[51]

With regard to corporations, we follow the draft treaty to allow general jurisdiction at the place of incorporation and the principal place of business, but we drop as bases of general jurisdiction the corporation's statutory seat and place of central administration. We use the phrase "principal place of business activity" to help focus the appropriate inquiry for territorial jurisdiction and to avoid the baggage of case law on diversity jurisdiction. The close relation of an incorporated organization with both its place of incorporation and its principal place of business activity leaves no doubt of the appropriateness of general jurisdiction there. These two places also have long been recognized in the United States as sufficient bases for general jurisdiction.[52] In contrast, a corporation's statutory seat is a concept from the civil law and is foreign to the United States. Moreover, because of its technicality, there is much controversy over its precise definition.[53] Therefore, including the statutory seat as a jurisdictional basis in a statute for U.S. courts would be inappropriate. The place of central administration, in most situations, would be the same place as the principal place of business activity. In the few situations where they are different, the benefits of allowing the place of central administration as an additional basis for general jurisdiction are outweighed by the costs. An especial difficulty in fixing the place of central administration lies in the modern model of corporation administration. Corporations that do not conduct their central administration at their principal places of business activity often are modern multistate or multinational enterprises with dispersed decisionmaking. Their decisionmaking may take place through video conferences or other remote communication techniques, with each participant located

---

[49] *See Treaty Draft, supra* note 3, art. 18(2)(f) (prohibiting jurisdiction based on "the service of a writ upon the defendant in that State"); *id.* art. 18(2)(i) (prohibiting jurisdiction based on "the temporary residence or presence of the defendant in that State"); Russell J. Weintraub, *How Substantial Is Our Need for a Judgments-Recognition Convention and What Should We Bargain Away to Get It?*, 24 Brook. J. Int'l L. 167, 189–90 (1998) [hereinafter Weintraub I]; Russell J. Weintraub, *Negotiating the Tort Long-Arm Provisions of the Judgments Convention*, 61 Alb. L. Rev. 1269, 1278–79 (1998) [hereinafter Weintraub II].

[50] *E.g.*, Kadic v. Karadzic, 70 F.3d 232, 248 (2d Cir. 1995) (holding that an invitee of the United Nations is not immune from personal serve of process).

[51] *See infra* Proposed Statute § 203(c); *cf. Treaty Draft, supra* note 3, art. 18(3) (similar, but more complicated, provision).

[52] *See, e.g.*, UI&IPA, *supra* note 41, § 1.02.

[53] *See* Rudolf B. Schlesinger et al., *Comparative Law* 384 (5th ed. 1988); *cf. id.* at 418 (6th ed. 1998) (abbreviated discussion).

in a different place.[54] Even if it were possible to determine one place of central administration, it would be questionable to subject the corporation to general jurisdiction there because of the thinness of the contact. Consequently, including central administration as a basis of general jurisdiction would be inappropriate.

As to unincorporated associations and the like, we refine the draft treaty's categorization by treating them separately from corporations. Because by definition they have no place of incorporation, the only appropriate basis for general jurisdiction over unincorporated persons is their one principal place of business activity or administration. This basis of jurisdiction also has long been recognized in the U.S. courts.[55] Here the proposed statute utilizes the vague term "administration" to help handle the variety of legal persons, some of which may not focus on business.

Much more controversial is the proposed statute's elimination of doing business as a basis of general jurisdiction, other than that at an organization's principal place of business activity.[56] Under the doing-business doctrine, which is peculiar to the United States,[57] if at the time of service of process the defendant's business activities in the forum state are extensively continuous and systematic – a level of activity termed "doing business" as opposed to merely "transacting business" – the defendant becomes subject to jurisdiction even on claims that are wholly unrelated to the in-state activities.[58] General jurisdiction based on doing business entails terrible problems of line-drawing and does not conform to the usual rationale of general jurisdiction.[59] Because it requires the defendant to be so active in the forum as to seem a native, it is seldom properly available.[60] This basis of jurisdiction arose to provide appropriate jurisdiction when specific jurisdiction was not yet fully available. Today, courts need resort to it, albeit inappropriately, only when all appropriate

---

54 *See 1997 Synthesis*, *supra* note 40, at 21.

55 *See, e.g.*, UI&IPA, *supra* note 41, § 1.02.

56 *See* ALI International Jurisdiction and Judgments Project, *supra* note 9, at 14–15 (describing this dispute as a possible deal-breaker); Silberman, *supra* note 7, at 175–79 (suggesting a compromise).

57 *See* Reimann, *supra* note 48, at 77, 82–83.

58 *See* Ferens v. John Deere Co., 494 U.S. 516 (1990) (allowing Mississippi to exercise general jurisdiction over a Delaware corporation with its principal place of business in Illinois, for a Pennsylvania accident); Perkins v. Benguet Consol. Mining Co., 342 U.S. 437, 448 (1952) (upholding jurisdiction in an Ohio state-court suit against a Philippine corporation, which was temporarily performing all of its management activities in Ohio while mining was suspended by the effects of war in the Philippines, on a basically unrelated claim); *cf.* Helicopteros Nacionales de Colombia, S.A. v. Hall, 466 U.S. 408, 416–19 (1984) (finding that Texas had no general jurisdiction over a foreign corporation, but not reaching the difficult issue of more specific jurisdiction).

59 *See* Born, *supra* note 48, at 103–16.

60 *See* Helicopteros Nacionales de Colombia, S.A. v. Hall, 466 U.S. 408, 418 (1984) (holding that "mere purchases, even if occurring at regular intervals, are not enough to warrant a State's assertion of *in personam* jurisdiction over a nonresident corporation in a cause of action not related to those purchase transactions"). *But see* Russell J. Weintraub, *International Litigation and Arbitration* 6 (1997) (citing questionable counterexamples).

bases of personal jurisdiction fail to reach the defendant.[61] Given the shortcomings of doing-business jurisdiction, the draft treaty properly abandons this basis of general jurisdiction,[62] and so should the proposed statute. Of course, the more common activity-based jurisdiction that falls more solidly within specific jurisdiction would survive, as provided in the next section.

§ 202. Specific Jurisdiction

(a) Contract

(1) A state has personal jurisdiction over a defendant as to a claim in contract if the claim arose from the defendant's transacting business in that state.

(2) A state has personal jurisdiction over a merchant as to a claim on a consumer contract by a consumer if the consumer habitually resides in that state and the claim arose from or related to the merchant's transacting business in, or purposefully directing other commercial activities to, that state.

(3) A state has personal jurisdiction over an employer as to a claim on an individual employment contract by an employee if the employee was to perform his or her principal obligation in that state.

(b) Tort

A state has personal jurisdiction over a defendant as to a claim in tort if:

(1) the act or omission causing injury occurred in that state; or

(2) the injury occurred in that state and the defendant purposefully directed other activities relating to the tortious injury to that state.

(c) Real Property

A state has personal jurisdiction over a defendant as to a claim arising from the defendant's owning, using, or possessing real property in that state.

(d) Imputed Contacts

In determining jurisdiction under this section:

(1) a state may attribute to the defendant the activities of the defendant's agent if the activities were within the agent's scope of authority;

(2) a state may attribute to the defendant the activities of the defendant's branch if the defendant would be liable for the branch's acts; and

(3) a state may attribute to the defendant the activities of the defendant's co-conspirator if the co-conspirator performed the activities in furtherance of

---

[61] *E.g.*, Frummer v. Hilton Hotels Int'l, 227 N.E.2d 851, 854 (N.Y. 1967); *see* Weintraub I, *supra* note 49, at 187–89 (explaining that elimination of doing-business jurisdiction "will block suit in only a few cases in which the United States has a legitimate interest in providing a forum").

[62] *See Treaty Draft*, *supra* note 3, art. 18(2)(e) (prohibiting general jurisdiction based on "the carrying on of commercial or other activities by the defendant in that State"); Catherine Kessedjian, *Synthesis of the Work of the Special Commission of March 1998 on International Jurisdiction and the Effects of Foreign Judgments in Civil and Commercial Matters*, Hague Conf. Prelim. Doc. No. 9, at 29–30 (July 1998) [hereinafter *1998 Synthesis*]; Weintraub II, *supra* note 49, at 1277–78; Zekoll, *supra* note 48, at 1294–95.

the conspiracy and the defendant was or should have been aware of the activities.

Comment:

a. Contract: This subsection provides for a court's specific jurisdiction for a claim in contract. Subsection (1) establishes the general rule for all kinds of contracts, except for those within exclusive jurisdiction under § 207(d). Subsections (2) and (3) offer economically disadvantaged parties an additional forum to pursue a claim against economically advantaged parties.

In determining which court is the most suitable forum to adjudicate a contract dispute, three different approaches deserve consideration. Under the Brussels Convention, the court with specific jurisdiction is determined by a legal concept: the place of performance.[63] In determining the place of performance, the forum court must first apply its own conflict of law rules to determine the applicable law governing the contract and then apply the governing law to determine whether the contractual obligation in dispute was to be performed in the forum state.[64] This approach is subject to highly technical factors, vulnerable to manipulation, and dependent on which country's law governs.[65] As a result, this approach does not always direct the dispute to an appropriate forum.[66]

The draft treaty uses a different approach. The criterion for contracts relating to the supply of goods is the place where such goods were supplied; for contracts relating to provision of services, the place where such services were provided; and for mixed contracts relating to both the supply of goods and the provision of services, the place where the principal obligation was performed.[67] Although this approach seems preferable to that of the Brussels Convention, it still suffers two major deficiencies. First, given the complexity of modern business transactions, it is difficult to categorize all contracts as involving supply of goods, provision of services, or a mixture.[68] Second, the siting factors established in the draft treaty – for example, the place the goods were supplied – look to only one facet of an often multifaceted business transaction. Such a mechanical approach will sometimes direct a dispute to an inappropriate forum.[69]

---

63 *See* Brussels Convention, *supra* note 4, art. 5(1).

64 *See* Stephen Cromie, *International Commercial Litigation* 8 (1990).

65 *See* Rudolf B. Schlesinger et al., *Comparative Law* 392–93 (5th ed. 1988). For example, under English law the default rule for money obligation on sale of goods is that the payment must be made where the seller is domiciled, while under German law the default rule is that the payment must be made where the debtor is domiciled. *See* Cromie, *supra* note 64, at 8.

66 *See 1997 Synthesis, supra* note 40, at 51 ("The effect of this case law has been a fragmentation of litigation and a proliferation of fora which many people agree should be avoided.").

67 *See Treaty Draft, supra* note 3, art. 6; *cf. id.* art. 9 (activity-based language appearing in brackets as a possible alternative).

68 For example, in a dispute arising from a patent license, it is difficult, if not impossible, to perceive what kind of goods have been supplied or what kind of services have been provided.

69 For example, a buyer in state *A* contracts with a seller in state *B* for sale of goods to be delivered to a third-party beneficiary in state *C*. The contract is negotiated and executed in state *A*. The transaction

The proposed statute therefore takes a third approach. Because a contract, simple or complicated and coming from any of many different contexts, often involves a series of commercial activities, such as negotiation, execution, and performance, and because all of those activities should enter into determining whether a court is appropriate to hear a dispute arising from the contract, it is desirable to use a notion flexible enough to accommodate these varied considerations. But it is necessary to limit the flexible notion in order to ensure that the forum state has a sufficiently close relation with the dispute. Consequently, the proposed statute uses "transacting business" to provide flexibility, but also uses the restrictive phrase "arose from" to ensure a close connection.

This chosen approach follows most states' long-arm statutes, which give their courts specific jurisdiction for claims arising from the defendant's transacting business in the state.[70] One advantage of this wording is that the abundant case law will give useful guidance on its meaning.[71] One disadvantage is that this wording will continue to be unpredictable in application. However, this disadvantage is not as serious as one might first think. Given that specific jurisdiction for a claim in contract between an ordinary party and a big party falls under other provisions[72] and given that an interstate or international contract rarely exists between two ordinary parties, the scope of this provision actually narrows to contracts between two merchants or other big parties. If such contracting parties view predictability as an important value, they are free to insert a choice-of-forum clause in their contract, as is commonly done.[73]

With regard to disputes arising from a consumer contract or an individual employment contract, the draft treaty provides special protection to the economically disadvantaged party.[74] This protection is three-fold: first, the consumer and the

---

between the buyer and the seller has nothing to do with state *C*, except that the goods should be delivered there. In a dispute regarding whether the contract complied sufficiently with the required formalities to be valid, should state *C* be deemed an appropriate forum?

70 Thirty-seven states extend specific jurisdiction over the defendant who transacts business in the forum state. *See* 1 Casad and Richman, *supra* note 42, at 397; *see also* UI&IPA, *supra* note 41, § 1.03(a)(1).

71 *But see* 1 Casad and Richman, *supra* note 42, at 398 ("The sheer number of cases impedes the abstraction of meaningful generalizations about the concept of transacting business under the long-arm statutes.").

72 *See infra* Proposed Statute §§ 202(a)(2)–(3), 207(d).

73 *See id.* § 205.

74 *See Treaty Draft, supra* note 3, arts. 7–8. The draft treaty's special protection covers only consumers and employees. It thus deviates from the Brussels Convention, which also covers insurance policyholders. *See* Brussels Convention, *supra* note 4, arts. 7–12a. But under the draft treaty, consumer contracts include insurance contracts between consumers and insurers. *See 1997 Synthesis, supra* note 40, at 43; *cf. supra* Proposed Statute § 103(c). Therefore, the real difference lies in insurance taken out by non-consumers. Because the rationale for special protection disappears in the non-consumer context, the proposed statute follows the draft treaty's approach. *See* Errol P. Mendes, *The Troublesome Workings of the Judgments Convention of the European Economic Community*, 13 Vand. J. Transnat'l L. 75, 93–95 (1980) (criticizing the inappropriateness of the Brussel Convention's extending special protection to commercial insurance).

employee are given additional forums to sue the merchant and the employer; second, the merchant and the employer have fewer available forums to sue the consumer and the employee than they would otherwise have; and, third, the effectiveness of any forum selection clause is limited. Because these three protections differ in nature, the proposed statute reallocates them to different sections.[75] This section on specific jurisdiction deals only with the additional jurisdiction available to the consumer and the employee.

As to consumers, the draft treaty allows them to sue a merchant in the forum where the consumer habitually resides if "the conclusion of the contract ... is related to trade or professional activities that the defendant has engaged in or directed to that State, in particular in soliciting business through means of publicity, and ... the consumer has taken the steps necessary for the conclusion of the contract in that State."[76] This provision tries to strike a sound balance between protecting the consumer and ensuring the merchant a reasonable forum. The draft treaty thus requires that the merchant have contacts with the consumer's habitual residence to establish jurisdiction there. In essence, it accords with the "purposefully directed" requirement under U.S. jurisdictional law.[77]

The proposed statute therefore follows the draft treaty on this point, while changing the wording to conform to subsection (1). The additional phrases of "related to" and "purposefully directing other commercial activities" are intended to expand jurisdiction over merchants and thus protect consumers.

As to employees, the draft treaty does not treat them as favorably as consumers. The draft treaty allows an employee to bring an action against the employer "in the courts of the State in which the employee habitually carries out his work or in the courts of the last State in which he did so," but if there is no one such state, he is allowed to sue "in the courts of the State in which the business that engaged the employee is or was situated."[78] Unlike a consumer, an employee is not authorized to sue the employer in the court where the employee habitually resides. The reason is that "such jurisdiction would be too favourable to the worker, especially if his or her habitual residence is that where the worker resides after the contract has expired."[79] A reasonable forum to adjudicate a claim by an employee against the employer is the center of the employee's professional activities.[80] This is the forum the draft treaty's wording attempts to specify.

---

75 For the second protection, see *infra* Proposed Statute § 207(d). For the third protection, see *infra id.* § 205(b). For definitions, see *supra id.* § 103.

76 *Treaty Draft, supra* note 3, art. 7(1).

77 *See* Clermont, *supra* note 1, at 124.

78 *Treaty Draft, supra* note 3, art. 8(1)(a).

79 *See 1997 Synthesis, supra* note 40, at 43. *But see* Catherine Kessedjian, *International Jurisdiction and Foreign Judgments in Civil and Commercial Matters*, Hague Conf. Prelim. Doc. No. 7, at 54 (Apr. 1997) ("If the worker does not work in one place only, jurisdiction could be given to the court of his habitual residence at the time the action is brought.").

80 *See 1997 Synthesis, supra* note 40, at 43.

Instead of the phrase "habitually carries out his work," the proposed statute uses the words "the employee was to perform his or her principal obligation" to point more accurately to the center of the employee's professional activities. This wording also avoids the difficult situation where the employee does not habitually carry out the work in one state. Because the state where an employee was to perform his or her principal obligation has a fairly strong connection with the dispute, it is reasonable to subject the employer to jurisdiction there, even if the employee works in several states.

b. Tort: This subsection provides for a court's specific jurisdiction for a claim in tort. In the process of drafting the treaty, some negotiators argued for special rules for different torts.[81] Fearing that such an approach would proliferate threshold litigation, the treaty drafters decided to establish a general rule for all kinds of torts.[82] The proposed statute follows that general approach.

If the tortious act or omission and the resulting injury both occur in the same state, the courts of that state provide an appropriate forum to adjudicate the claim.[83] Controversy arises when the tortious act or omission and the resulting injury occur in different states.[84]

The draft treaty, which on the whole seems a decent compromise in the pursuit of international agreement, takes the position that both of those states have specific jurisdiction.[85] However, it creates various exceptions to the jurisdiction of the injury state. First, the defendant can defeat this jurisdiction by showing that it could not reasonably have foreseen the result.[86] Second, the injury state can remedy only the part of the injury occurring in that state, unless the plaintiff habitually resides there.[87] Third, in cases of antitrust violations and conspiracy to inflict economic loss, the injury state will not have this jurisdiction at all.[88] Even with those exceptions, however, the draft treaty still seems to reach farther than U.S. law currently does.

---

81 *Compare* Kessedjian, *supra* note 79, at 70 (arguing, in light of experience under the Brussels Convention, that a general rule is not workable in complex proceedings and creates too much overlapping jurisdiction), *with 1998 Synthesis, supra* note 62, at 34 (favoring a general rule applicable to all kinds of torts).

82 *See 1998 Synthesis, supra* note 62, at 34 ("It was also noted, however, that there may be danger in such an approach which, by allowing for multiple characterisations from the start, increases the potential for litigation merely for the sake of establishing the jurisdiction of the court.").

83 *See* 1 Casad and Richman, *supra* note 42, at 446–48 (categorizing this situation as an impact tort); *1998 Synthesis, supra* note 62, at 33–34 (stating that all experts agree on this point).

84 *See generally* Ronald A. Brand, *Tort Jurisdiction in a Multilateral Convention: The Lessons of the Due Process Clause and the Brussels Convention*, 24 Brook. J. Int'l L. 125 (1998) (discussing difficulties of tort clause).

85 *See Treaty Draft, supra* note 3, art. 10(1).

86 *See id.* art. 10(1)(b) ("unless the defendant establishes that the person claimed to be responsible could not reasonably have foreseen that the act or omission could result in an injury of the same nature in that State").

87 *See id.* art. 10(4); Ronald A. Brand, *Current Problems, Common Ground, and First Principles: Restructuring the Preliminary Draft Convention Text, supra* p. 75, at 78–9 (criticizing this exception).

88 *See Treaty Draft, supra* note 3, art. 10(2).

The proposed statute likewise treats the state where the tortious act or omission occurs, even if the injury results elsewhere, as an appropriate forum. This jurisdictional basis for specific jurisdiction in tort has long been deemed appropriate in the United States.[89] The proposed statute tightens up the draft treaty's language regarding the injury state, however. It does so to avoid any possible constitutional problems – and doing so has the added benefit of obviating the need for the draft treaty's three exceptions. Under the Due Process Clause's power test,[90] the required minimal contacts must come from the defendant's activities: the defendant must have purposefully availed itself of the privilege of conducting activities in the forum state.[91] In a tort action, the mere fact that the plaintiff suffers injury in the forum is not sufficient to support jurisdiction without minimal contacts on the defendant's part, whether or not the defendant could have foreseen that its out-of-state act or omission would result in injury in that state.[92] Consequently, the proposed statute requires that the defendant direct to that state other activities relating to the tortious injury.

Most states have similar statutes extending jurisdiction over a defendant whose out-of-state act or omission results in an injury in the forum state.[93] The proposed statute differs from those state statutes in two ways. First, rather than enumerate several types of activities,[94] the proposed statute uses the generic term "other activities" to broaden its coverage. Actually, however, those state statutes' enumerated activities do not provide much more certainty than the proposed statute's generic term. Second, the proposed statute counts only activities "relating to" the tortious injury, which is generally not true under those state statutes.[95] Although the leniency

---

89 *See* Restatement (Second) of Conflict of Laws § 36(1) (1971) (amended 1988); UI&IPA, *supra* note 41, § 1.03 cmt. at 363 ("The state where the tortious act or omission occurs will often be the most appropriate location for the trial of the action.").

90 *See* World-Wide Volkswagen Corp. v. Woodson, 444 U.S. 286 (1980); Shaffer v. Heitner, 433 U.S. 186 (1977); Hanson v. Denckla, 357 U.S. 235 (1958).

91 *See* Hanson v. Denckla, 357 U.S. 235, 254 (1958) ("it is essential in each case that there be some act by which the defendant purposefully avails itself of the privilege of conducting activities within the forum State, thus invoking the benefits and protections of its laws"); 1 Casad and Richman, *supra* note 42, at 145.

92 *See* World-Wide Volkswagen Corp. v. Woodson, 444 U.S. 286, 295–97 (1980) (holding that mere foreseeability does not satisfy the power test).

93 *See* 1 Casad and Richman, *supra* note 42, at 462; *see also* UI&IPA, *supra* note 41, § 1.03(4). On the "stream of commerce" problem, see Kevin M. Clermont, *Civil Procedure: Territorial Jurisdiction and Venue* 59–61 (1999).

94 *See, e.g.*, UI&IPA, *supra* note 41, § 1.03(a)(4) ("regularly does or solicits business, or engages in any other persistent course of conduct, or derives substantial revenue from goods used or consumed or services rendered, in this state"); Wis. Stat. § 801.05(4) (1994) ("(a) Solicitation or service activities were carried on within this state by or on behalf of the defendant; or (b) Products, materials or things processed, serviced or manufactured by the defendant were used or consumed within this state in the ordinary course of trade"). Seventeen states have statutes patterned after UI&IPA § 1.03(a)(4), and six states have statutes patterned after Wis. Stat. § 801.05(4). *See* 1 Casad and Richman, *supra* note 42, at 463.

95 *See* 1 Casad and Richman, *supra* note 42, at 464 ("The courts in states whose statutes are based on the Uniform Interstate and International Procedure Act generally have not required such a connection.").

of those state statutes might be appropriate for product liability cases, the proposed statute applies to all kinds of torts. In order to ensure a sufficiently close nexus among the forum, the claim, and the defendant, the statute requires that the defendant's other contacts with the forum relate to the matter in dispute. Furthermore, the restrictive phrase "relating to" somewhat reduces the uncertainty of the generic term "other activities."

c. Real Property: This subsection provides an additional basis of personal jurisdiction for a claim regarding real property. Although the draft treaty does not contain such a provision, this basis is popular in state long-arm statutes.[96] It is useful, for example, in acquiring jurisdiction over out-of-state defendants for disputes arising from the sale of real property.[97]

The fact that the defendant owns, uses, or possesses real property in the state, and the plaintiff's claim arises therefrom, establishes a sufficiently strong nexus among the forum, the claim, and the defendant. Also, the state where the real property is located has a significant interest in exercising jurisdiction in a dispute regarding it. Finally, this provision for nonexclusive personal jurisdiction nicely supplements the later provision for exclusive jurisdiction for nonpersonal remedies regarding the real property:[98] a plaintiff can bring one action where the property lies, without struggling to fit the personal claim into some other provision for personal jurisdiction.

d. Imputed Contacts: This subsection treats specific jurisdiction over the defendant through the imputed contacts of its agent, branch, or co-conspirator. The basic notion is that when the defendant acts through its agent, branch, or co-conspirator, the latter's contacts with the forum may be attributed to the defendant and help subject it to jurisdiction.

An accepted proposition is that to justify personal jurisdiction over a principal, the court may attribute the state-directed activities of the principal's agent.[99] To determine whether an agent-principal relationship exists, the court looks to the ordinary law of agency, asking whether the principal has empowered an agent and whether the agent has acted within the scope of that authority.[100] For jurisdiction, then, the plaintiff must make a prima facie showing of the principal's vicarious liability under the applicable substantive law. The rationale is that if the principal would be substantively liable for the agent's activities, then those activities may contribute to a finding of jurisdiction over the principal.

Indeed, that rationale extends to a variety of contexts where a jurisdictional

96 *See, e.g.*, UI&IPA, *supra* note 41, § 1.03(a)(5).

97 *See* 1 Casad and Richman, *supra* note 42, at 470.

98 *See infra* Proposed Statute § 207(a).

99 *See* UI&IPA, *supra* note 41, § 1.03; 1 Casad and Richman, *supra* note 42, at 476.

100 *See* 1 Casad and Richman, *supra* note 42, at 478 ("Even if the person who acted in the forum state was an agent of the defendant, his actions will not subject the defendant to long-arm jurisdiction unless they were within the scope of the agent's authority.").

argument exists for attributing another's activities to the defendant.[101] Of those contexts, the one giving courts the greatest difficulty is the attribution of state-directed activities by a validly incorporated and formally separate corporation that, along with the defendant, constitutes part of a modern multistate or multinational enterprise. If the affiliate corporation has an agent-principal relationship to the defendant corporation, then the courts will attribute the affiliate's contacts to the defendant.[102] But some courts have gone perceptibly beyond the "agency" standard, coming up with tests that ask, for example, whether the state-directed activities are sufficiently important to the defendant that it would have performed them itself in the affiliate's absence.[103] Such tests, however, seem to be confused stabs at a standard that would conform to the rationale of tying jurisdictional attribution to substantive liability. The proper "alter ego" standard takes the courts into corporate law, asking whether the defendant would be liable for all of the affiliate's acts under the doctrine of piercing the corporate veil, which, in special situations of common control, overcomes the usual limited liability of corporations and merges the corporate entities.[104] If so, then the state-directed activities of the affiliate may contribute to a finding of jurisdiction over the defendant.

The draft treaty has a provision allowing suit where "a branch, agency or any other establishment of the defendant is situated, provided that the dispute relates directly to the activity of that branch, agency or establishment."[105] This is a remarkably unclear provision. First, the drafters are foggy on the meaning of such key terms as "branch," which may or may not include a subsidiary.[106] Second, while the drafters have repeatedly discussed the matter, it is still not clear whether the draft treaty even addresses piercing the corporate veil.[107] Perhaps all this provision does in the draft treaty is to extend specific jurisdiction over legal persons to places where they have a physical presence,[108] a function subsumed in the proposed statute's § 202(a)(1).

To remedy those drafting problems, the proposed statute deviates significantly from the draft treaty. It speaks instead of attributing contacts. The first category is the usual one of the defendant's agent. The second category is the defendant's branch, which here has its natural meaning as any part of the defendant's organization, whether or not a separate legal entity. The third category is the defendant's

---

[101] *See generally* Lea Brilmayer and Kathleen Paisley, *Personal Jurisdiction and Substantive Legal Relations: Corporations, Conspiracies, and Agency*, 74 Cal. L. Rev. 1 (1986).

[102] *See* 1 Casad and Richman, *supra* note 42, at 498–501.

[103] *E.g.*, Gelfand v. Tanner Motor Tours, Ltd., 385 F.2d 116, 121 (2d Cir. 1967).

[104] *See* 1 Casad and Richman, *supra* note 42, at 496–98.

[105] *Treaty Draft, supra* note 3, art. 9. This provision uses essentially the same language as does the Brussels Convention, *supra* note 4, art. 5(5). *See* Nygh and Pocar, *supra* note 3, at 55–57.

[106] *See* Kessedjian, *supra* note 79, at 72 (stressing the need for careful definition).

[107] *See 1998 Synthesis, supra* note 62, at 31–32, 37–38; *1997 Synthesis, supra* note 40, at 33; Kessedjian, *supra* note 79, at 72.

[108] *See* Brand, *supra* note 87, at 100–01.

co-conspirator. The case law under many states' long-arm statutes has recognized this ground for imputing contacts.[109] Because its justification lies in the fact that the defendant and the co-conspirator jointly executed the conspiracy, rather than that the defendant exerted any control over the co-conspirator, additional requirements exist that the co-conspirator's activities were performed in furtherance of the conspiracy and the defendant was or should have been aware of those activities.[110]

§ 203. Permitted Jurisdiction

In accordance with a state's own law, within the limits of the Due Process Clause of the Fourteenth Amendment to the Constitution of the United States, that state may, but need not, exercise specific jurisdiction as to a claim regarding one of the following matters:

(a) domestic relations;

(b) electronic commerce or tort; or

(c) international human rights.

Comment: This section is the graylist of permitted jurisdictional bases.[111] It includes areas where diversity of practice is beneficial at present or where significant changes are foreseeable in the near future.

Jurisdiction in domestic relations is a sprawling and localized field, which includes the oddities of jurisdiction over status, and so is peculiarly resistant to codification.[112] E-claims are, of course, very much in flux.[113] And international human rights has proved a sticking point in the Hague negotiations.[114]

§ 204. Multiple Claims and Parties

(a) A state having jurisdiction as to a claim also has personal jurisdiction over an appearing party as to the claimant's additional claim, the defending party's counterclaim, a cross-claim, or an additional claim interposed by or against an intervening party if the additional claim, counterclaim, or cross-claim arose from the same transaction or occurrence as the primary claim.

(b) A state having personal jurisdiction under § 202 or § 207 over a defending party also has personal jurisdiction over a third-party defendant as to the defending

---

109 *See* 1 Casad and Richman, *supra* note 42, at 481 n. 367.

110 *See id.* at 481 and n. 369 (citing Wahad v. FBI, 132 F.R.D.17 (S.D.N.Y. 1990)).

111 *See supra* text accompanying note 24.

112 *See generally* Carol S. Bruch, *Statutory Reform of Constitutional Doctrine: Fitting* International Shoe *to Family Law*, 28 U.C. Davis L. Rev. 1047 (1995).

113 *See generally Internet: Which Court Decides? Which Law Applies?* (Katharina Boele-Woelki and Catherine Kessedjian eds., 1998); Clermont, *supra* note 93, at 43–47; Joaquim-J. Forner Delaygua, *International Jurisdiction in "Business to Business" On-line Performed Contracts: Lessons from The Hague?, supra* p. 47.

114 *See* Kovar Letter, *supra* note 8, at 9; *supra* text accompanying note 50. *See generally* Kathryn Lee Boyd, *The Inconvenience of Victims: Abolishing Forum Non Conveniens in U.S. Human Rights Litigation*, 39 Va. J. Int'l L. 41 (1998).

party's indemnity, warranty, or contribution claim if it arose from the same transaction or occurrence as the primary claim, unless the primary claimant and the defending party have colluded to infringe the third-party defendant's jurisdictional interests.

(c) *When no court within the United States has jurisdiction over all co-defending parties, a state having personal jurisdiction under § 202 or § 207 over any of them also has personal jurisdiction over the others if the claims against all arose from the same transaction or occurrence and all are persons needed for just adjudication. When no such state exists, a state having personal jurisdiction under § 201 over any of them also has personal jurisdiction over the others if the claims against all arose from the same transaction or occurrence and all are persons needed for just adjudication.*

Comment: This section provides for a court's jurisdiction in multiple-claim and multiple-party litigation. There are two main policies competing in this context. On the one hand, a defendant is entitled to the protection provided by the jurisdiction rules against being haled into an inconvenient forum. On the other hand, public policy dictates that all related disputes should be resolved in a single proceeding to promote judicial economy and avoid inconsistent adjudication. How to adjust jurisdiction in line with a sound balance between the two is the focus of concern.

The draft treaty provides three rules to treat this concern, although they may not all survive the remaining negotiations. First, in the context of multiple defendants, the draft treaty allows a plaintiff to join other defendants in a court of a state where any defendant habitually resides, on two conditions: the plaintiff's claims against the defendants must be "so closely connected that they should be adjudicated together to avoid a serious risk of inconsistent judgments"; and there must be a substantial connection between the forum state and the disputes involving those other defendants.[115] Second, in the context of counterclaims, the court having jurisdiction for the original claim also has jurisdiction for a counterclaim if the counterclaim arises out of the same transaction or occurrence as the original claim.[116] Third, in the context of third-party claims, the court having jurisdiction for the original claim also has jurisdiction for the defendant's claim against a third party for indemnity or contribution if there is a substantial connection between the forum state and the dispute involving the third party.[117] In order to protect a co-defendant's or a third party's interest under an exclusive forum selection agreement, the draft treaty specifically excludes the application of these special jurisdictional rules when the co-defendant or the third party invokes an exclusive forum selection agreement.[118]

In general, then, the draft treaty favors the policy of combining related disputes

[115] *See Treaty Draft, supra* note 3, art. 14(1).

[116] *See id.* art. 15.

[117] *See id.* art. 16(1).

[118] *See id.* arts. 14(2), 16(2); *cf. infra* Proposed Statute § 205(d) (providing a like effect).

in one proceeding,[119] doing so in rules like the Brussels Convention's but with additional protections.[120] The draft treaty's general policy is a desirable one, but its safeguards for the co-defendant and the third-party defendant remain deficient. First, the requirement of "a substantial connection" between the forum state and the dispute involving the out-of-state co-defendant or third-party defendant is unclear and troubling. Second, the draft treaty does not exclude the application of its special multiple-defendant rule if a plaintiff is able to sue the defendants in a court having general or specific jurisdiction over all of them. Third, the draft treaty chooses a less appropriate court, a court with general jurisdiction over any defendant, to adjudicate the plaintiff's claims against all defendants. As a matter of jurisdictional theory, the court's general jurisdiction rests on the connection between the defendant and the forum, while the court's specific jurisdiction also relies on the relationship between the particular dispute and the forum. Because the rationale underlying the multiple-defendant rule is to resolve related disputes in one shot, the court with specific jurisdiction is a more appropriate candidate for handling the lawsuit.

The proposed statute likewise favors the policy of extending the court's jurisdictional reach to combine related disputes in one proceeding. However, the proposed statute tightens the limitations to ensure a close relation among the disputes, to direct the whole lawsuit to an appropriate forum, and to prevent abuse.

On multiple-claim litigation, the proposed statute's extension of jurisdiction covers more kind of claims than does the draft treaty.[121] When a court has territorial jurisdiction, whether personal, in rem, or quasi in rem,[122] the proposed statute authorizes the court to adjudicate any additional claims, on two conditions: the party against whom the claim is interposed must have appeared in the action; and the claim sought to be interposed must have arisen from the same transaction or occurrence as the main claim. Because this kind of additional jurisdiction seeks only to allow related claims among appearing parties, putting no new parties' jurisdictional

---

[119] *See 1998 Synthesis, supra* note 62, at 39 ("Indeed, it was pointed out that this kind of jurisdiction is extremely useful in international litigation, since it avoids multiple proceedings, thereby avoiding irreconcilable judgments."); Kessedjian, *supra* note 79, at 82.

[120] *See* Brussels Convention, *supra* note 4, art. 6. For a detailed introduction to so-called derivative jurisdiction under the Brussels Convention, see Stephen O'Malley and Alexander Layton, *European Civil Practice* 444–55 (1989).

[121] Unlike their attitude toward multiple-party litigation, the Europeans take a narrow view of multiple-claim jurisdiction. *See* Brand, *supra* note 87, at 89–90.

[122] In the situation of jurisdiction in rem or quasi in rem, the effect of this provision is prohibition of the traditional limited appearance. On the one hand, to take an example from true nonpersonal jurisdiction, when a plaintiff seeks to foreclose a mortgage on the defendant's land and the defendant appears to defend the action, the plaintiff should be able to interpose a personal claim to demand the deficiency. On the other hand, given the proposed statute's abolition of much of attachment jurisdiction, *see infra* text accompanying note 174, the old need for limited appearance disappears. Thus, the proposed statute does not permit a limited appearance to defend the action without subjecting to personal jurisdiction on any related personal claim. *See* Clermont, *supra* note 93, at 118–20.

interests at stake, U.S. cases have generally recognized some extent of this jurisdictional basis.[123] Because the proposed statute limits the basis with a transactional test, it should pass constitutional muster – by the conceptualization either that appearance constitutes implied consent to the lawsuit's dimensions permitted under applicable procedural law[124] or, better, that appearance authorizes jurisdiction for additional claims that can reasonably be adjudicated concurrently.[125]

On multiple-party litigation, the general principle under U.S. law, admittedly, is that personal jurisdiction is tested independently for each defendant.[126] If there exists no independent jurisdiction over a co-defendant or third-party defendant, the court normally cannot entertain the dispute involving that new party no matter how compelling the reasons for adjudicating the disputes together. For example, when the court has no independent jurisdiction over a co-defendant who should be joined to accord complete and consistent relief, the court must choose between adjudicating the dispute without joining the co-defendant or dismissing the entire case.[127] Although occasionally U.S. law illogically dispenses with this jurisdictional principle by simply treating special situations as not requiring jurisdiction,[128] the fact remains that current law does not give great consideration to the competing policy of promoting judicial economy and avoiding inconsistent adjudication. Consequently, the proposed statute in parts of this section runs the risk of sometimes going beyond the outer boundary of due process's power test, even though the proposed statute is eminently reasonable. Perhaps the time has come for the Supreme Court to jettison, at least in part, the power test as an unsound scheme for the allocation of territorial

---

123 *See, e.g.*, Adam v. Saenger, 303 U.S. 59 (1938).

124 *See* Restatement (Second) of Conflict of Laws § 34 cmt. c (1971) (amended, with fundamental changes, in 1988).

125 *See* Restatement (Second) of Judgments § 9 (1982) ("when the claim involved arose out of the transaction that is the subject of the pending action or is one that may in fairness be determined concurrently with that action"); Clermont, *supra* note 12, at 460 and n. 236.

126 *See* ALI International Jurisdiction and Judgments Project, *supra* note 9, at 12; Clermont, *supra* note 1, at 96.

127 *See* Fed. R. Civ. P. 19 (compulsory joinder).

128 Examples include the involuntary plaintiff doctrine, *see* Field et al., *supra* note 10, at 1280–81, vouching-in and other extensions of privity, *see id.* at 1179–83, 1205–06, and absent class members, *see id.* at 220 and n. m. The most telling example is vouching-in: if the defendant is entitled to indemnification for liability that might result from the action, the defendant can notify the one liable over to the defendant to appear and defend the action, with the effect of permitting the defendant to assert issue preclusion against the indemnitor in the event that the defendant is found liable to the plaintiff. *See* State Bank v. American Sur. Co., 288 N.W. 7 (Minn. 1939); Restatement (Second) of Judgments §§ 57–58 (1982); Restatement of Judgments § 107(a) cmts. c-i (1942). It is very difficult to explain why the jurisdictional principle should be strictly observed in impleader but totally overlooked in vouching-in, when the functions of the two devices are almost identical. *See* First Nat'l Bank v. City Nat'l Bank, 65 N.E. 24 (Mass. 1902); Ronan E. Degnan and Alan J. Barton, *Vouching to Quality Warranty: Case Law and Commercial Code*, 51 Cal. L. Rev. 471, 477–80 (1963); Paul Stephen Ware, Note, *Vouching: In or Out?*, 42 Wash. and Lee L. Rev. 121 (1985). *But see* Peter A. Gross, Comment, *Constitutional Limits on Vouching*, 118 U. Pa. L. Rev. 237 (1969).

jurisdiction.[129] Or perhaps the Court should simply defer to Congress on this jurisdictional point.[130] Of course, on unusual facts of a particular case, due process's unreasonableness test will apply to prevent a U.S. court from exercising fundamentally unfair jurisdiction.[131]

As to third-party litigation, the proposed statute allows the defending party to implead a third party, but only for an indemnity, warranty, or contribution claim rather than just any kind of secondary liability. Moreover, in order to ensure a sufficient connection between the forum and the third-party defendant, the proposed statute applies only to specific and exclusive jurisdiction and further imposes a transactional test. Lastly, in order to prevent the parties from circumventing the ordinary jurisdictional rules, this special jurisdictional rule is inapplicable when the other parties' purpose is to infringe the third party's jurisdictional interests.[132] Hence, this modest subsection reaches far fewer than all third-party claims and even has a considerably narrower coverage than the Brussels Convention or the draft treaty, which should ensure its constitutionality.

As to multiple-defendant litigation, the proposed statute provides a prioritizing of courts for the claimant to join all co-defendants in one proceeding: first, a court having jurisdiction, either general or specific, over all of the co-defendants the claimant seeks to join; second, a court having specific or exclusive jurisdiction over any co-defendant, but only if the claims against all the co-defendants arose from the same transaction or occurrence and additionally all the co-defendants come within the compulsory joinder notions set out in § 103(e); and finally, a court having general jurisdiction over any co-defendant, subject to the same conditions. The requirement that all claims arise from the same transaction or occurrence functions to ensure not only that the different claims are closely related but also that any basis of specific or exclusive jurisdiction over a co-defendant connects the forum to the other co-defendants. The additional compulsory joinder requirement ensures a compelling need for allowing suit against the out-of-state co-defendants in one co-defendant's home state. Because the claimant has no better forum and cannot receive complete and consistent relief without joining all persons coming in as co-defendants, this jurisdiction is the system's last resort. In essence, this additional requirement turns this jurisdiction into jurisdiction by necessity.[133] Again, then, the proposed statute's limitations should help to uphold its constitutionality.

---

[129] *See* Clermont, *supra* note 1, at 125.

[130] *See id.* at 127; Linda J. Silberman, "*Two Cheers" for* International Shoe *(and None for* Asahi*): An Essay on the Fiftieth Anniversary of* International Shoe, 28 U.C. Davis L. Rev. 755, 766–67 (1995).

[131] *See* Asahi Metal Indus. Co. v. Superior Court, 480 U.S. 102 (1987).

[132] The Brussels Convention contains a similar exception to prevent abuse of its derivative jurisdiction in third-party litigation. *See* Brussels Convention, *supra* note 4, art. 6(2) ("instituted solely with the object of removing him from the jurisdiction of the court which would be competent in his case").

[133] *See* George B. Fraser, Jr., *Jurisdiction by Necessity – An Analysis of the* Mullane *Case*, 100 U. Pa. L. Rev. 305 (1951).

§ 205. Choice of Forum

(a) A state has personal jurisdiction over a defendant as to a claim that the parties have agreed to submit to a court in that state if the agreement is entered or confirmed:

(1) in writing or by any other means of communication that renders information accessible for subsequent reference;

(2) by the course of dealing between the parties; or

(3) by a usage of trade of which the parties were or should have been aware.

(b) Such agreement in a consumer contract or an individual employment contract is effective only if the agreement is entered after the dispute arises or if, but only to the extent, the agreement allows the consumer or the employee to bring the action in a court not otherwise having jurisdiction.

(c) The jurisdiction conferred by such agreement is presumed to be exclusive unless the parties have agreed otherwise.

(d) A state denied jurisdiction under such agreement must decline such jurisdiction or suspend proceedings unless it can exercise jurisdiction pursuant to § 206 or § 207 or unless the states having jurisdiction under the agreement have declined to exercise jurisdiction.

Comment: This provision provides for jurisdiction by forum selection agreement. Four main issues arise under this heading: a forum selection agreement's enforceability, scope, formality, and exclusivity.

With regard to enforceability, the contemporary view is that forum selection agreements are generally enforceable. The draft treaty adheres to this view and prohibits the contracting states' national law from imposing other limitations,[134] even if the forum selection agreement directs the dispute to a state having no connection with any party or the dispute.[135] U.S. law on forum selection has moved from hostility to embrace.[136] Nevertheless, despite the Supreme Court's series of cases upholding forum selection clauses by moving toward a freedom-of-contract paradigm,[137] their enforceability, complicated by the *Erie* problem, still varies significantly across different jurisdictions, ranging from per se unenforceable to per se enforceable.[138] This situation highlights the benefits of the proposed statute. It

---

134 *See* Kessedjian, *supra* note 79, at 62 ("[T]he future Convention forms a single whole, and that States Parties cannot use their national laws, even for [enforceability, which has] been settled by the Convention, and the various national legal systems have nothing further to say on the question.").

135 The thought is that the parties should be able to designate a neutral forum, especially in the context of international trade. *See 1998 Synthesis, supra* note 62, at 35; *1997 Synthesis, supra* note 40, at 27; Kessedjian, *supra* note 79, at 66.

136 *See* Born, *supra* note 48, at 373–77 (tracing the historical development of enforceable forum selection clauses); 1 Casad and Richman, *supra* note 42, at 47–56.

137 *See* Carnival Cruise Lines v. Shute, 499 U.S. 585 (1991); The Bremen v. Zapata Off-Shore Co., 407 U.S. 1 (1972); National Equip. Rental, Ltd. v. Szukhent, 375 U.S. 311 (1964).

138 *See* Born, *supra* note 48, at 378–81 (analyzing different approaches taken by courts to enforceability).

provides an opportunity not only to unify these messy approaches but also to undo some unfortunate decisions.[139] The proposed statute therefore adopts the balanced approach of the draft treaty.

With regard to scope of a forum selection agreement, a well-established rule in the continental countries is that the parties can agree to subject to a court's jurisdiction only their disputes arising "in connection with a particular legal relationship."[140] The draft treaty adopts this limit.[141] U.S. law seems to impose no such limit.[142] Accordingly, the proposed statute departs from the draft treaty, on the view that a limit would produce litigation and that a limit is unnecessary given the section's other protections against overreaching, such as those for consumers and employees.[143]

With regard to formality of a forum selection agreement, the central concern is to ensure that such agreement is genuinely and consciously reached by the parties, on the one hand, and to prevent excessive formality from impeding modern developments of commercial practices, on the other hand.[144] Although the Hague Conference has promulgated a specific convention on choice of forum,[145] the Brussels Convention[146] provides the basic model for the draft treaty.[147] The draft treaty well serves the competing policies on formality. The proposed statute deviates from the draft treaty only to change the wording to the commonly used terms of "course of dealing" and "usage of trade" in U.S. law.[148]

---

139 *See, e.g.*, Carnival Cruise Lines v. Shute, 499 U.S. 585 (1991) (upholding a forum selection clause printed on a passenger ticket). This case has been widely criticized as blind to consumer protection. *See, e.g.*, Patrick J. Borchers, *Forum Selection Agreements in the Federal Courts After* Carnival Cruise: *A Proposal For Congressional Reform*, 67 Wash. L. Rev. 55 (1992) (proposing a statute providing special protections for consumers and employees); *cf.* Rudolf B. Schlesinger, *Jurisdictional Clauses in Consumer Transactions: A Multifaceted Problem of Jurisdiction and Full Faith and Credit*, 29 Hastings L.J. 967, 974 (1978) (arguing that a clause like the one in *Carnival Cruise* would be unenforceable because it violates the notion of fair play and substantial justice). But some would argue that the proposed statute's special protections for consumers and employees go too far by covering sophisticated consumers and senior employees. *E.g.*, Peter D. Trooboff, *Ten (and Probably More) Difficulties in Negotiating a Worldwide Convention on International Jurisdiction and Enforcement of Judgments: Some Initial Lessons*, *infra* p. 263, at 269–70.

140 *See, e.g.*, Brussels Convention, *supra* note 4, art. 17.

141 *See Treaty Draft*, *supra* note 3, art. 4(1).

142 *See* Born, *supra* note 48, at 455 ("Indeed, it is possible, at least as a drafting matter, for parties to agree to settle *all* their future disputes, regardless of connection to a particular agreement, in a designated forum.").

143 *See supra* note 139; text accompanying note 75 (other special treatment of consumers and employees).

144 *See* Kessedjian, *supra* note 79, at 62 ("Developments in domestic law concerning the formal validity of clauses on choice of court indicate that the main emphasis is now on the availability of proof that each party gave free and informed consent to the jurisdictional choice.").

145 *See* Hague Convention on the Choice of Court, Nov. 25, 1965, 4 I.L.M. 348, *available in* <http://www.hcch.net/e/conventions/text15e.html>.

146 *See* Brussels Convention, *supra* note 4, art. 17; O'Malley and Layton, *supra* note 120, at 549 (interpreting Article 17 of the Brussels Convention).

147 *See Treaty Draft*, *supra* note 3, art. 4(2).

148 *See, e.g.*, U.C.C. § 1–205 (1990).

With regard to exclusivity of a forum selection agreement, it is widely recognized that the decision should be left to the parties whether the chosen court has exclusive jurisdiction. Controversies arise when the parties fail to indicate whether the forum selection is exclusive or nonexclusive. The default rule under the draft treaty is that the chosen court's jurisdiction is exclusive "unless the parties have agreed otherwise."[149] Although U.S. courts disfavor exclusive forum selection and tend to take nonexclusive jurisdiction as the default rule,[150] the proposed statute follows the draft treaty, because exclusivity is most often consistent with the contracting parties' intention and is always helpful in preventing parallel proceedings.[151]

§ 206. Appearance by Defendant

(a) A state has personal jurisdiction over a defendant if the defendant appears without objection to jurisdiction asserted in accordance with applicable procedure rules.

(b) A defendant's appearance does not affect any co-defendant's right to object to jurisdiction.

Comment: This section provides for the defendant's submission to a court's jurisdiction by appearance without timely objection. The draft treaty provides that the defendant can raise lack of jurisdiction no later than defense on the merits,[152] so following the law of many countries, although not precisely the U.S. law.[153] The proposed statute deviates somewhat from the draft treaty's standard, using instead the criterion of whether the defendant has raised jurisdiction in accordance with applicable procedure rules. Finally, given that lack of jurisdiction is a personal defense, the proposed statute explicitly provides that a defendant's waiver of jurisdiction will not affect the co-defendant's right to object to jurisdiction.

§ 207. Exclusive Jurisdiction

(a) A state has exclusive nonpersonal jurisdiction in an action for an in rem or quasi in rem remedy on a nonpersonal claim regarding real property, including fixtures, if the real property is located in that state or regarding tangible personal property if the personal property is located in that state with the consent of the defending party. Any judgment rendered in such an action without appearance of the defendant affects only the property.

(b) A state has exclusive jurisdiction in an action with the object of determining the

---

149 *See Treaty Draft, supra* note 3, art. 4(1).

150 *See* Born, *supra* note 48, at 454 ("Courts are usually reluctant to hold that a forum clause is exclusive, and often do so only if a provision includes language specifically excluding litigation in courts other than the chosen forum.").

151 *See* Kessedjian, *supra* note 79, at 66 ("If [there is exclusive jurisdiction], there will be no lis pendens."); *1997 Synthesis, supra* note 40, at 27.

152 *See Treaty Draft, supra* note 3, art. 5.

153 *See* Kessedjian, *supra* note 79, at 64 ("Many national systems have a requirement that any objection of want of jurisdiction must be raised before any defence is argued on the merits.").

validity, nullity, or dissolution of an organization or other legal person if it was organized or formed under the law of that state.

(c) Except for jurisdiction under §§ 205 and 206, a state has exclusive jurisdiction over an action with the object of determining the validity, construction, effects, administration, or variation of a trust created voluntarily and evidenced in writing if the settlor provided in the trust instrument that jurisdiction would lie in that state without indicating it to be nonexclusive and, in the absence of such provision, exclusive jurisdiction over such an action if the trust has its principal place of administration in that state.

(d) Except for jurisdiction under §§ 205 and 206, a state has exclusive personal jurisdiction over a consumer as to a claim on a consumer contract by a merchant if the consumer habitually resides in that state and exclusive personal jurisdiction over an employee as to a claim on an individual employment contract by an employer if the employee habitually resides in that state or performs his or her principal obligation in that state.

(e) A state lacking jurisdiction for an action, or part thereof, under this section must decline such jurisdiction or suspend proceedings unless the states possessing jurisdiction consistent with this section have declined to exercise jurisdiction.

Comment: This section provides for a court's exclusive jurisdiction in certain types of actions, by depriving other courts of general or specific jurisdiction that otherwise would exist. The reason for exclusive jurisdiction is that the designated court has such a close connection with the action that it is able to adjudicate the action most effectively. In addition, protection of certain important public policies in the forum with exclusive jurisdiction is an important justification.[154]

Following the approach of the Brussels Convention,[155] the draft treaty provides exclusive jurisdiction for four types of actions: in rem rights in immovable property; validity of a legal person and its decisions; validity of public register entries; and validity of registered intellectual property rights.[156] Given the nature of this exclusive jurisdiction, it cannot be derogated by a forum selection agreement or waived by the defendant's failure to object to jurisdiction.[157]

The proposed statute provides exclusive jurisdiction for the first two of those types of actions: actions for a nonpersonal remedy, and actions for determining the validity of a legal person. The other two types are omitted, as being too foreign or too federal for inclusion. But the proposed statute collects two more types from elsewhere in the draft treaty: actions concerning a trust,[158] and actions against an economically

---

[154] *See* O'Malley and Layton, *supra* note 120, at 522 (explaining the reasons underlying exclusive jurisdiction in the Brussels Convention); Kessedjian, *supra* note 79, at 48–54 (draft treaty).

[155] *See* Brussels Convention, *supra* note 4, art. 16.

[156] *See Treaty Draft, supra* note 3, art. 12.

[157] *See id.* arts. 4(3), 5(1).

[158] *See id.* art. 11.

disadvantaged party.[159] Because as to these latter two types the justifications for exclusive jurisdiction are lesser, it can be derogated by a forum selection agreement or waived by the defendant's failure to object to jurisdiction.

a. Nonpersonal Remedy: The draft treaty provides that an action targeting "rights in rem in immovable property or tenancies of immovable property" is subject to the exclusive jurisdiction of the state where the property is situated, unless the tenant habitually resides elsewhere.[160] Although the appropriateness of this exclusive jurisdiction is universally recognized,[161] the formulation of the draft treaty does not mesh easily with U.S. law,[162] which deems all rights to be personal and draws only the inherent distinction between nonpersonal remedy and personal remedy. A nonpersonal remedy acts directly on a specific thing. Because in the United States an action on a claim for such a remedy must be based upon the court's jurisdiction over the thing, the jurisdiction is exclusive in the court where the thing is situated.[163]

Accordingly, the proposed statute adopts a different approach by resorting to this notion of in rem or quasi in rem remedy. Nevertheless, as far as real property is concerned, this approach produces essentially the same result as that under the draft treaty.[164] To accommodate U.S. law, however, the proposed statute does not limit exclusive jurisdiction to actions regarding real property, but it does impose two limitations on jurisdiction over personal property. First, in order to avoid the difficulties of categorization and reification, which would allow the states unreasonably to expand jurisdiction, the proposed statute excludes intangible property.[165] Second, in order to prevent abuse of this jurisdiction by the person controlling the property, the proposed statute requires that the personal property be located in the forum state with the consent of the defending party.[166]

By its additional limitation to a "nonpersonal claim," the proposed statute intends to abolish much of attachment jurisdiction, the kind of jurisdiction that comprises

---

159 *See id.* arts. 7–8.

160 *See id.* art. 12(1).

161 *See* O'Malley and Layton, *supra* note 120, at 525; *1997 Synthesis, supra* note 40, at 35.

162 England has a similar problem in the context of the Brussels Convention. *See* O'Malley and Layton, *supra* note 120, at 526 ("What constitutes a right in rem is more readily apparent in civil law than in common law systems .... ").

163 For an explanation of in rem and quasi in rem jurisdiction, see Clermont, *supra* note 93, at 8–9, 63–68.

164 An in rem action to register title to land and a quasi in rem action to partition land, quiet or remove a cloud on title, or foreclose a mortgage or lien fall within the draft treaty. But an in personam action on a land sale contract does not. *See* O'Malley and Layton, *supra* note 120, at 526.

165 For an introduction to categorization and reification problems, see Clermont, *supra* note 93, at 67–69; *see also* Clermont, *supra* note 12, at 425–26.

166 For example, a debtor, who bought a car under lien in New York and then absconded by driving to California, should not be able to sue the lien creditor in California to remove the lien. *See* Shaffer v. Heitner, 433 U.S. 186, 208 n. 25 (1977) (suggesting a constitutional underpinning for this limitation); Clermont, *supra* note 93, at 91. Any immunities, such as the one for loaned artworks, would depend on separate federal statutes. *See* In re Grand Jury Subpoena Duces Tecum Served on the Museum of Modern Art, 719 N.E.2d 897, 906 n. 2 (N.Y. 1999).

actions where the plaintiff has a personal claim against the defendant and seeks to satisfy it by attachment of particular property of the defendant – or by garnishment of an obligation owed the defendant by a third party – without obtaining personal jurisdiction over the defendant. Despite their uniqueness, these actions are traditionally referred to as actions quasi in rem, because they technically concern the interests of particular persons in a designated thing. Their validity in today's world, with the greatly expanded scope of personal jurisdiction, has been seriously questioned.[167] But this distinctive kind of jurisdiction persists in the United States. To satisfy the power test, it must be exercised where the thing is. In the leading case of *Shaffer v. Heitner*,[168] the Supreme Court made clear that all nonpersonal jurisdiction must also pass the unreasonableness test, which means that this jurisdiction is now available only in four, rather special situations: (1) to secure a judgment being sought by the plaintiff elsewhere; (2) to enforce a judgment already rendered for the plaintiff elsewhere; (3) to recover where personal jurisdiction constitutionally exists; or, perhaps, (4) to recover when no other U.S. forum is available. Attachment jurisdiction in the first and second situation is perfectly appropriate, and accordingly the draft treaty would authorize such jurisdiction for security[169] and enforcement,[170] as does the proposed statute.[171] Jurisdiction in the third situation becomes completely unnecessary and inappropriate once the sovereign extends personal jurisdiction to appropriate lengths.[172] Finally, jurisdiction in the fourth situation remains constitutionally shaky. It receives regular criticism, although it actually sees little use.[173] The United States should surrender that use.[174]

b. Legal Person: The draft treaty provides that the state "whose law governs the legal person" has exclusive jurisdiction over an action to determine the validity of the legal person or its decisions.[175] Because that wording differs from the formula for general jurisdiction and raises choice-of-law problems, the proposed statute designates the state of creation for exclusive jurisdiction over an action to determine the validity of the legal person.

Also, because a dispute regarding the validity of the legal person's decisions normally arises between shareholders and managers and because the dispute is often about the organization's mismanagement, exclusive jurisdiction for this kind of

---

167 *See* Paul D. Carrington, *The Modern Utility of Quasi In Rem Jurisdiction*, 76 Harv. L. Rev. 303 (1962).

168 433 U.S. 186 (1977).

169 *See Treaty Draft*, *supra* note 3, art. 13(2).

170 *See 1997 Synthesis*, *supra* note 40, at 41, 61.

171 *See infra* Proposed Statute § 305(c).

172 *See* Michael B. Mushlin, *The New Quasi In Rem Jurisdiction: New York's Revival of a Doctrine Whose Time Has Passed*, 55 Brook. L. Rev. 1059, 1104–27 (1990).

173 *See id.* at 1095–96, 1100.

174 *See Treaty Draft*, *supra* note 3, art. 18(2)(a) (prohibiting jurisdiction based on "the presence or the seizure in that State of property belonging to the defendant, except where the dispute is directly related to that property").

175 *See id.* art. 12(2).

lawsuit seems inappropriate.[176] This subsection of the proposed statute goes far enough already in codifying U.S. law's vague "internal affairs" doctrine.[177] Moreover, given the nature of this kind of action, were it desirable to provide exclusive jurisdiction, the forum where the organization has its principal place of business activity would be a better candidate than the place of creation.[178] Accordingly, the proposed statute leaves actions on the validity of decisions out of the subsection.

c. *Trust*: The draft treaty provides both exclusive and nonexclusive jurisdiction for cases involving trusts. Under the draft treaty, the state designated in the trust agreement has exclusive jurisdiction over an action concerning the validity, construction, effects, administration, or variation of the trust.[179] If there is no such designation, each of three states has jurisdiction: the state where the principal place of administration of the trust is situated; the state whose law is applicable to the trust; and the state with which the trust has the closest connection for the purpose of the proceedings.[180] The scope of all this jurisdiction is subject to two limitations. First, the covered trusts are those created voluntarily and evidenced in writing. This limitation is intended to exclude a trust created by operation of law, such as a constructive trust.[181] Second, these jurisdictional rules apply only to disputes concerning the internal relationships of the trust. This limitation is intended to exclude actions by or against a third party.[182]

The proposed statute generally accepts this approach. However, in the absence of the settlor's choice of forum in the trust instrument, the proposed statute provides only one state with exclusive jurisdiction rather than three states with overlapping jurisdiction. Three reasons support this deviation. First, intricate choice-of-law problems would result from designating the state whose law is applicable to the trust. Designating the state with which the trust has the closest connection would be too open-ended and uncertain. Second, because this jurisdictional rule covers only disputes concerning the internal relationships of the trust, the principal place of administration of the trust is the most appropriate forum. This concept enjoys more certainty

---

176 The same point seems to have been recognized in the process of treaty negotiations. *See 1997 Synthesis, supra* note 40, at 31; Kessedjian, *supra* note 79, at 52.

177 *See* Paul D. Carrington and James A. Martin, *Substantive Interests and the Jurisdiction of State Courts*, 66 Mich. L. Rev. 227, 235 (1967).

178 *See* Kessedjian, *supra* note 79, at 52.

179 *See Treaty Draft, supra* note 3, art. 11(1).

180 *See id.* art. 11(2).

181 *See 1997 Synthesis, supra* note 40, at 45 ("it is preferable for all special rules of the Convention to be limited to trusts created voluntarily in writing as provided by the 1985 Hague Convention"). The draft treaty's treatment of trust jurisdiction is in line with the general principles established in the Hague convention on trusts. Hague Convention on the Law Applicable to Trusts and on Their Recognition, July 1, 1985, 23 I.L.M. 1389, *available in* <http://www.hcch.net/e/conventions/text30e.html>.

182 *See 1997 Synthesis, supra* note 40, at 45.

and captures the idea of the "centre of gravity" of the trust.[183] Third, providing exclusive jurisdiction has the advantage of centralizing the dispute in a single forum. U.S. law recognizes the desirability of joining all dispersed beneficiaries in one proceeding to resolve the trust dispute once and for all.[184]

d. Consumer or Employee: In accordance with the policy of providing special protection to the economically disadvantaged party, the draft treaty restricts the available forums for a merchant or employer to sue the consumer or employee.[185] The proposed statute agrees.[186]

e. Derogation: In order to preserve the appropriate court's jurisdiction, the proposed statute establishes a hierarchy of derogation in §§ 207, 206, and 205.

Title 3 – Ancillary Provisions

§ 301. Limitations Tolling

Any court within the United States dismissing a claim for lack of territorial jurisdiction may, if it be in the interest of justice, provide that the period of limitations be tolled while the claim was pending and for a period of 30 days after it is dismissed, unless applicable law provides for a longer tolling period.

Comment: This section applies when a claim is pursued in one forum, but then dismissed for lack of territorial jurisdiction. Because establishing an interstate transfer system is too big a step to take currently,[187] the proposed statute includes instead this tolling provision, based on the model of 28 U.S.C. § 1367(d).[188] In the context of dismissal for lack of subject-matter jurisdiction, reformers had long advocated a tolling statute.[189] The proposed statute simply provides such a tolling statute in the context of dismissal for lack of territorial jurisdiction. In order to minimize the incentive for parallel proceedings, this section applies in federal as well as state court. In order to curb abuse, the dismissing court has discretion only to toll the limitations period in the interest of justice.

---

183 Kessedjian, *supra* note 79, at 72 ("If no choice is made, jurisdiction should be given to the place of the 'centre of gravity' of the trust.").

184 *See* Mullane v. Central Hanover Bank & Trust Co., 339 U.S. 306 (1950) (upholding the constitutionality of subjecting out-of-state beneficiaries to the jurisdiction of the state where the trustee administers the trust).

185 *See Treaty Draft, supra* note 3, arts. 7(2), 8(1)(b).

186 *See supra* text accompanying note 75 (other special treatment of consumers and employees).

187 *See supra* note 21.

188 *See* Denis F. McLaughlin, *The Federal Supplemental Jurisdiction Statute – A Constitutional and Statutory Analysis*, 24 Ariz. St. L.J. 849, 982–89 (1992) (including discussion in support of the statute's constitutionality).

189 *See* ALI Study of the Division of Jurisdiction Between State and Federal Courts 65–66, 373–74, 453–57 (1969).

The general policy behind this provision is the same as that behind the transfer-of-venue statute in 28 U.S.C. § 1406(a), namely, to allow the dispute to be decided on the merits.[190] An incidental benefit of this provision is that it relieves the pressure on a court to interpret the jurisdictional provisions expansively, allowing the judge to apply the proposed statute with an eye to the long run and dismiss the action without concerns of injustice in the short run.[191]

§ 302. Forum Non Conveniens

A court having jurisdiction under this statute, other than under § 203, may not dismiss or stay the action on the ground of forum non conveniens.

Comment: Once the rest of the proposed statute has narrowed general jurisdiction and refined specific jurisdiction, so that exorbitant jurisdiction is no more, the benefits of forum non conveniens will disappear. But the costs of that doctrine – multiplying expense and delay, increasing uncertainty, unfairly burdening plaintiffs, and facilitating discrimination against foreigners – will remain. Accordingly, the proposed statute abolishes forum non conveniens,[192] except where the old regime persists under the permitted bases of § 203. Of course, the Due Process Clause's unreasonableness test[193] will still apply to prevent a U.S. court from exercising fundamentally unfair jurisdiction.

§ 303. Lis Pendens

(a) Except as provided in subsection (b), a court of a state having jurisdiction in an action must stay the proceedings, or the related part thereof, if when the action commenced a related action was pending in the court of another state within the United States or of the United States and:
  (1) the current proceedings present a claim asserted in that pending action; or
  (2) the current proceedings present a claim that would be a compulsory counterclaim in that pending action.

(b) The second-seised court may refuse to stay, or lift a stay, if in the first-commenced action:
  (1) the plaintiff is seeking only a declaration of nonliability;
  (2) the plaintiff fails to prosecute its case;

190 *See* Goldlawr, Inc. v. Heiman, 369 U.S. 463 (1962) (applying § 1406(a) in the situation of lack of personal jurisdiction and emphasizing that the statute's general purpose is to remove whatever obstacle may impede the adjudication of cases on the merits).

191 *See supra* note 10.

192 At the insistence of the United States, the draft treaty retains a narrow forum non conveniens provision. *See Treaty Draft, supra* note 3, art. 22. But the time has come for the United States to abandon its infatuation with the doctrine. *See* Clermont, *supra* note 1, at 118–21.

193 *See* World-Wide Volkswagen Corp. v. Woodson, 444 U.S. 286 (1980); Shaffer v. Heitner, 433 U.S. 186 (1977); International Shoe Co. v. Washington, 326 U.S. 310 (1945).

(3) a judgment would not be rendered within a reasonable time; or
(4) a judgment would not be recognized in the second-seised state.

(c) Otherwise, a court of a state having jurisdiction in an action may stay the proceedings, or the related part thereof, if a related action is pending in another court and the actions are so closely connected that it is expedient to hear and determine them together.

(d) The court must resume or dismiss the stayed proceedings promptly after the other action terminates.

Comment: In order to avoid parallel proceedings and to foster comity, the draft treaty's "first-seised rule" provides that the court where the action is first initiated should proceed to adjudicate the dispute, while the court where the same action is later brought should stay its proceedings.[194] Because under the rest of the draft treaty the courts' jurisdictional reach is shortened and so the plaintiffs' available forums are restricted, the advantage given to the first-suing plaintiff by the first-seised rule becomes acceptably modest. Consequently, the proposed statute adopts the rule that the second-seised court normally has to stay its proceedings. This subsection (a), then, significantly changes the traditional U.S. doctrine, which either emphasizes the court's obligation to proceed with the case by narrowly limiting the court's power to stay its proceedings or gives the court considerable discretion to decide on an all-things-considered basis whether to stay its proceedings.[195]

Two policies compete regarding the appropriate scope of exceptions. On the one hand, in order to prevent the second court from overly protecting its own citizens,[196] exceptions should be narrowly defined and the court should not be given much discretion to refuse to stay proceedings. On the other hand, it is essential to avoid dictating the inappropriate staying of proceedings. The proposed statute in subsection (b)'s four enumerated exceptions generally follows the draft treaty's approach, which strikes a balance in the middle.

The rest of the section clarifies the obvious. Thus, the court retains most of its inherent discretion to stay its own proceedings.

---

194 *See* Treaty Draft, *supra* note 3, art. 21. For criticism of this rule's inducing a race to the courthouse, see Kessedjian, *supra* note 79, at 86. Of course, in the absence of the rule, there is a similarly undesirable race to judgment. *See* George A. Bermann, *The Use of Anti-Suit Injunctions in International Litigation*, 28 Colum. J. Transnat'l L. 589, 602 n. 58 (1990). On balance, the direction of the draft treaty's rule is desirable. *See* Stephen B. Burbank, *Jurisdictional Equilibration, the Proposed Hague Convention, and Progress in National Law, supra* p. 117, at 132–4.

195 *See* Born, *supra* note 48, at 461–74.

196 For example, the plaintiff sues the defendant in state *A*. The defendant initiates an action against the plaintiff in state *B*, where the defendant lives. To favor the defendant, state *B* refuses to stay its proceedings and renders a judgment before the conclusion of state *A*'s proceedings. For an example of this scenario, see Deutsch v. West Coast Mach. Co., 497 P.2d 1311 (Wash. 1972), the subsequent history of which appears in Andreas F. Lowenfeld, *International Litigation and Arbitration* 186–87 (1993).

In the context of international forum competition, unless the foreign forum is also bound by rules similar to the proposed statute, the justification vanishes for a first-seised rule (or for prohibiting antisuit injunctions). So, in that situation, the ordinary case law remains in force.[197] Parts of this section (and the next) of the proposed statute could, however, be extended geographically if a Hague treaty were adopted.

§ 304. Antisuit Injunctions

A court of a state may not issue an antisuit injunction to forbid a person from pursuing a claim in the court of another state within the United States or of the United States on the ground that the other court is an inappropriate location for suit.

Comment: Antisuit injunctions are undesirable, generally being prohibited or at least discretionarily refused between U.S. courts.[198] Because the proposed statute binds such courts to resolve the problems of parallel proceedings by lis pendens and because the proposed statute otherwise restrains the courts' jurisdictional reach, there is no longer a need for permitting a court to issue an antisuit injunction on the domestic level.[199]

§ 305. Provisional and Final Remedies

(a) A state having jurisdiction under this statute in an action has jurisdiction to order provisional remedies with regard to the action.

(b) A state not otherwise having jurisdiction under this statute nevertheless has jurisdiction to order provisional remedies if:

(1) their enforcement is within that state; and

(2) their purpose is to secure a judgment being sought elsewhere.

(c) A state has jurisdiction to order provisional remedies, or to enforce a judgment or award, with regard to property if the property is located in that state.

---

197 Because there is no statute providing a uniform standard for a court's staying its own proceedings or issuing an antisuit injunction, the courts relying on their inherent powers have developed differing standards. *See* Born, *supra* note 48, at 461–64, 475–77. At the present time, there is no compelling reason for imposing uniform standards in the proposed statute to cover international conflict.

198 *See generally* Larry L. Teply and Ralph U. Whitten, *Civil Procedure* 369–72 (2d ed. 2000) (discussing antisuit injunctions); Edward Dumbauld, *Judicial Interference with Litigation in Other Courts*, 74 Dick. L. Rev. 369 (1970); James P. George, *Parallel Litigation*, 51 Baylor L. Rev. 769 (1999); *cf.* Stone, *supra* note 4, at 145–46 (Brussels Convention).

199 Two reasons for an antisuit injunction are the desire to avoid duplicate proceedings that could result in inconsistent judgments and the need to protect the issuing forum's jurisdiction or public policy. *See* Born, *supra* note 48, at 475–90. The former concern is handled by the proposed statute's general rule requiring the second-seised court to stay its proceedings, and the latter concern is alleviated by the proposed statute's reasonable distribution of territorial jurisdiction among the states. But *see* Burbank, *supra* note 194, at 137–38.

Comment: The proposed statute adopts essentially the same rule as the draft treaty,[200] which follows the general principles established by the Helsinki Resolution of the International Law Association.[201] The kinds of provisional remedies are left to the applicable rules in the various states.[202]

Subsection (b) makes clear that a state having no jurisdiction over the substantive merits of an action nevertheless has jurisdiction to order provisional remedies to maintain the status quo or freeze the defendant's assets. This special jurisdiction can be essential for a plaintiff to secure a judgment.

Although the proposed statute abolishes much of attachment jurisdiction,[203] subsection (c) preserves it for the purposes of security and enforcement. Other bases of jurisdiction under the proposed statute can, of course, be used for security and enforcement as well.

CONCLUSION

The Hague negotiations have handed Congress and the states a great opportunity. They can untangle the mess that is the U.S. law of territorial jurisdiction in civil cases. The basic thrust of reform would be legislation providing that state courts, not only in all international cases but also even in interstate cases, possess jurisdiction if and only if the case's circumstances satisfy the draft treaty's analogous jurisdictional provision.

As a suggestive illustration, this article has forwarded a proposed statute by which Congress would regulate state-court jurisdiction along such lines. We submit that it demonstrates the legal, if not the political, feasibility of jurisdictional reform on the domestic scene.

APPENDIX: PROPOSED STATUTE

Title 1 – General Provisions

§ 101. Scope

This statute applies to all civil actions in the courts of a State, territory, or possession of the United States, the District of Columbia, or the Commonwealth of Puerto Rico, except as otherwise provided in this statute.

---

200 *See Treaty Draft, supra* note 3, art. 13.

201 *See* Kessedjian, *supra* note 79, at 74 and Annex I (reprinting International Law Ass'n, *Provisional and Protective Measures in International Litigation* (1996)).

202 *See generally* George A. Bermann, *Transnational Provisional Relief in the Courts*, in *International Dispute Resolution: The Regulation of Forum Selection* 99 (Jack L. Goldsmith ed., 1997); Catherine Kessedjian, *Note on Provisional and Protective Measures in Private International Law and Comparative Law*, Hague Conf. Prelim. Doc. No. 10, at 14–23 (Oct. 1998). Under the Brussels Convention, the available provisional remedies and their effects are determined by national law. *See* O'Malley and Layton, *supra* note 120, at 649.

203 *See supra* text accompanying note 171.

§ 102. Preemption of State Law

A state may not exercise territorial jurisdiction on bases other than those specified in this statute or in another federal statute of the United States. Except as otherwise provided in this statute, a state must exercise any properly invoked territorial jurisdiction on one of the bases specified in this statute.

§ 103. Definitions

In this statute:

(a) A "state" means a State, territory, or possession of the United States, the District of Columbia, the Commonwealth of Puerto Rico, or a foreign state.

(b) "Habitual residence" means the place where a natural person dwells in the ordinary course of his or her life or a new place to which the person moves with the intention to dwell for an indefinite period.

(c) "Consumer" means a person or an entity that is not a merchant. For a claim on an insurance contract, "consumer" can include the insured, the policyholder, and the beneficiary if not a merchant.

(d) "Merchant" means a person or an entity that engages in the course of its occupation in the particular transaction on which the claim is based, or that otherwise by its occupation holds itself out as having knowledge or skill peculiar to that transaction.

(e) "Person needed for just adjudication" means a person:

 (1) in whose absence complete relief cannot be accorded among those already parties; or

 (2) who claims an interest relating to the subject of the action and is so situated that the disposition of the action in the person's absence may (i) as a practical matter impair or impede the person's ability to protect that interest or (ii) leave any of the persons already parties subject to a substantial risk of incurring double, multiple, or otherwise inconsistent obligations by reason of the claimed interest.

Title 2 – Jurisdictional Bases

§ 201. General Jurisdiction

(a) A state has personal jurisdiction, as to any claim, over a natural person whose habitual residence is in that state.

(b) A state has personal jurisdiction, as to any claim, over an incorporated organization organized under the law of or having its principal place of business activity in that state.

(c) A state has personal jurisdiction, as to any claim, over an unincorporated association or other legal person having its principal place of business activity, or for a non-business entity the principal place of administration, in that state.

§ 202. Specific Jurisdiction

(a) Contract

(1) A state has personal jurisdiction over a defendant as to a claim in contract if the claim arose from the defendant's transacting business in that state.

(2) A state has personal jurisdiction over a merchant as to a claim on a consumer contract by a consumer if the consumer habitually resides in that state and the claim arose from or related to the merchant's transacting business in, or purposefully directing other commercial activities to, that state.

(3) A state has personal jurisdiction over an employer as to a claim on an individual employment contract by an employee if the employee was to perform his or her principal obligation in that state.

(b) Tort

A state has personal jurisdiction over a defendant as to a claim in tort if:

(1) the act or omission causing injury occurred in that state; or

(2) the injury occurred in that state and the defendant purposefully directed other activities relating to the tortious injury to that state.

(c) Real Property

A state has personal jurisdiction over a defendant as to a claim arising from the defendant's owning, using, or possessing real property in that state.

(d) Imputed Contacts

In determining jurisdiction under this section:

(1) a state may attribute to the defendant the activities of the defendant's agent if the activities were within the agent's scope of authority;

(2) a state may attribute to the defendant the activities of the defendant's branch if the defendant would be liable for the branch's acts; and

(3) a state may attribute to the defendant the activities of the defendant's co-conspirator if the co-conspirator performed the activities in furtherance of the conspiracy and the defendant was or should have been aware of the activities.

§ 203. Permitted Jurisdiction

In accordance with a state's own law, within the limits of the Due Process Clause of the Fourteenth Amendment to the Constitution of the United States, that state may, but need not, exercise specific jurisdiction as to a claim regarding one of the following matters:

(a) domestic relations;

(b) electronic commerce or tort; or

(c) international human rights.

§ 204. Multiple Claims and Parties

(a) A state having jurisdiction as to a claim also has personal jurisdiction over an appearing party as to the claimant's additional claim, the defending party's counterclaim, a cross-claim, or an additional claim interposed by or against an intervening party if the additional claim, counterclaim, or cross-claim arose from the same transaction or occurrence as the primary claim.

(b) A state having personal jurisdiction under § 202 or § 207 over a defending party also has personal jurisdiction over a third-party defendant as to the defending party's indemnity, warranty, or contribution claim if it arose from the same transaction or occurrence as the primary claim, unless the primary claimant and the defending party have colluded to infringe the third-party defendant's jurisdictional interests.

(c) When no court within the United States has jurisdiction over all co-defending parties, a state having personal jurisdiction under § 202 or § 207 over any of them also has personal jurisdiction over the others if the claims against all arose from the same transaction or occurrence and all are persons needed for just adjudication. When no such state exists, a state having personal jurisdiction under § 201 over any of them also has personal jurisdiction over the others if the claims against all arose from the same transaction or occurrence and all are persons needed for just adjudication.

§ 205. Choice of Forum

(a) A state has personal jurisdiction over a defendant as to a claim that the parties have agreed to submit to a court in that state if the agreement is entered or confirmed:
  (1) in writing or by any other means of communication that renders information accessible for subsequent reference;
  (2) by the course of dealing between the parties; or
  (3) by a usage of trade of which the parties were or should have been aware.

(b) Such agreement in a consumer contract or an individual employment contract is effective only if the agreement is entered after the dispute arises or if, but only to the extent, the agreement allows the consumer or the employee to bring the action in a court not otherwise having jurisdiction.

(c) The jurisdiction conferred by such agreement is presumed to be exclusive unless the parties have agreed otherwise.

(d) A state denied jurisdiction under such agreement must decline such jurisdiction or suspend proceedings unless it can exercise jurisdiction pursuant to § 206 or § 207 or unless the states having jurisdiction under the agreement have declined to exercise jurisdiction.

§ 206. Appearance by Defendant

(a) A state has personal jurisdiction over a defendant if the defendant appears without objection to jurisdiction asserted in accordance with applicable procedure rules.

(b) A defendant's appearance does not affect any co-defendant's right to object to jurisdiction.

§ 207. Exclusive Jurisdiction

(a) A state has exclusive nonpersonal jurisdiction in an action for an in rem or quasi in rem remedy on a nonpersonal claim regarding real property, including fixtures, if the real property is located in that state or regarding tangible personal property if the personal property is located in that state with the consent of the defending party. Any judgment rendered in such an action without appearance of the defendant affects only the property.

(b) A state has exclusive jurisdiction in an action with the object of determining the validity, nullity, or dissolution of an organization or other legal person if it was organized or formed under the law of that state.

(c) Except for jurisdiction under §§ 205 and 206, a state has exclusive jurisdiction over an action with the object of determining the validity, construction, effects, administration, or variation of a trust created voluntarily and evidenced in writing if the settlor provided in the trust instrument that jurisdiction would lie in that state without indicating it to be nonexclusive and, in the absence of such provision, exclusive jurisdiction over such an action if the trust has its principal place of administration in that state.

(d) Except for jurisdiction under §§ 205 and 206, a state has exclusive personal jurisdiction over a consumer as to a claim on a consumer contract by a merchant if the consumer habitually resides in that state and exclusive personal jurisdiction over an employee as to a claim on an individual employment contract by an employer if the employee habitually resides in that state or performs his or her principal obligation in that state.

(e) A state lacking jurisdiction for an action, or part thereof, under this section must decline such jurisdiction or suspend proceedings unless the states possessing jurisdiction consistent with this section have declined to exercise jurisdiction.

Title 3 – Ancillary Provisions

§ 301. Limitations Tolling

Any court within the United States dismissing a claim for lack of territorial jurisdiction may, if it be in the interest of justice, provide that the period of limitations be tolled while the claim was pending and for a period of 30 days after it is dismissed, unless applicable law provides for a longer tolling period.

§ 302. Forum Non Conveniens

A court having jurisdiction under this statute, other than under § 203, may not dismiss or stay the action on the ground of forum non conveniens.

§ 303. Lis Pendens

(a) Except as provided in subsection (b), a court of a state having jurisdiction in an action must stay the proceedings, or the related part thereof, if when the action commenced a related action was pending in the court of another state within the United States or of the United States and:

(1) the current proceedings present a claim asserted in that pending action; or
(2) the current proceedings present a claim that would be a compulsory counterclaim in that pending action.

(b) The second-seised court may refuse to stay, or lift a stay, if in the first-commenced action:
(1) the plaintiff is seeking only a declaration of nonliability;
(2) the plaintiff fails to prosecute its case;
(3) a judgment would not be rendered within a reasonable time; or
(4) a judgment would not be recognized in the second-seised state.

(c) Otherwise, a court of a state having jurisdiction in an action may stay the proceedings, or the related part thereof, if a related action is pending in another court and the actions are so closely connected that it is expedient to hear and determine them together.

(d) The court must resume or dismiss the stayed proceedings promptly after the other action terminates.

§ 304. Antisuit Injunctions

A court of a state may not issue an antisuit injunction to forbid a person from pursuing a claim in the court of another state within the United States or of the United States on the ground that the other court is an inappropriate location for suit.

§ 305. Provisional and Final Remedies

(a) A state having jurisdiction under this statute in an action has jurisdiction to order provisional remedies with regard to the action.

(b) A state not otherwise having jurisdiction under this statute nevertheless has jurisdiction to order provisional remedies if:
(1) their enforcement is within that state; and
(2) their purpose is to secure a judgment being sought elsewhere.

(c) A state has jurisdiction to order provisional remedies, or to enforce a judgment or award, with regard to property if the property is located in that state.

Part II
Judgments Provisions and the Convention's Future

John J. Barceló III†

The Draft Hague Convention's Judgments Provisions

The judgments provisions of the Draft Convention greatly improve the prospects for recognizing and enforcing judgments across national borders, but only if the judgment is based on one of the Convention's approved grounds for jurisdiction over the defendant. Here is a simplified overview. Parties to the Convention undertake to recognize and enforce final judgments rendered in other contracting states, provided that: (i) the rendering court (F1) based jurisdiction on one of the Convention's whitelist of approved grounds and (ii) none of the Convention's narrow list of grounds for refusing to recognize and enforce a judgment is present. The Convention's grounds for refusing recognition and enforcement primarily concern procedural irregularities (essentially ensuring due process), but they also include incompatibility with "the public policy of the State addressed" (F2).

What follows is a more detailed discussion of the judgments provisions grouped under three headings. The first concerns the documents necessary to make a prima facie showing for recognition or enforcement. The second explains what effect the jurisdictional basis of the foreign judgment has upon the possibilities for recognition or enforcement. The third deals with the limited non-jurisdictional grounds for refusing recognition or enforcement.

Prima Facie Presentation

The Draft Convention instructs a litigant seeking recognition or enforcement to produce certain documents. [Draft Convention Article 29.] The litigant must produce a certified copy of the F1 judgment. If that judgment was taken by default, then the litigant must also produce documents showing that the papers instituting the proceedings (generally a complaint) were notified to the defaulting party. Finally, to ensure finality of the F1 judgment, the litigant must present documents establishing that the judgment is, in F1, either res judicata (in the case of recognition) or enforceable (in the case of enforcement). The burden of proof is expressly on the party seeking to have the F1 judgment recognized or enforced.

---

† William Nelson Cromwell Professor of International and Comparative Law and Elizabeth and Arthur Reich Director of the Leo and Arvilla Berger International Legal Studies Program.

J.J. Barceló and K.M. Clermont (eds.), A Global Law of Jurisdiction and Judgments: Lessons from The Hague, 237–243

JURISDICTIONAL BASIS OF THE FOREIGN JUDGMENT

The papers in the first part of this volume discuss in some depth the different grounds for jurisdiction over the defendant regulated by the Convention. They fall into three categories: (i) grounds of both general and specific jurisdiction approved by the Convention (whitelist); (ii) grounds prohibited by the Convention (blacklist); and (iii) grounds neither approved nor prohibited (gray zone). The fate of a judgment under the Convention is strongly linked to the ground of jurisdiction over the defendant exercised by the F1 court.

The Draft Convention accords almost automatic recognition and enforceability only to those foreign judgments based on one of the whitelist grounds of jurisdiction. Hence the Draft Convention gives considerable incentive to litigants to choose only those courts that satisfy the Draft Convention's jurisdictional rules.

At the same time the Draft Convention permits parties to retain gray-zone grounds of jurisdiction. That is the whole point of a mixed convention: it facilitates final agreement by allowing negotiators to move disputed issues into the gray zone. The Draft Convention is clear that a judgment based on a gray-zone jurisdictional ground falls beyond the regulatory regime of the Convention. [Draft Convention Article 24.] There is no Convention obligation either to enforce or to reject the judgment. Hence the pre-Convention rules in every country presumably would apply. As discussed in the first part of this volume and in the papers in this second part looking to the future, from a U.S. perspective the "doing business" ground of general jurisdiction is a prime candidate for gray-zone treatment. Other countries, however, may disagree because they would prefer "doing business" to be a prohibited ground. It is understandable that not all controversial grounds of jurisdiction can be shifted to the gray zone. One of the benefits that countries adhering to the Convention will hope to receive is protection from exorbitant grounds of jurisdiction. If all controversial grounds of jurisdiction were simply dumped into the gray zone, support for the Convention could be seriously undermined. Although the Draft Convention does not obligate parties to enforce a gray-zone judgment, in practice some countries will to do so, including, at a minimum, F1 itself. Hence, should the gray zone expand past some threshold, the Draft Convention will become less viable.

Concerning blacklist jurisdictional grounds, the Draft Convention is categorical. Parties to the Convention are prohibited from recognizing or enforcing such judgments. [Draft Convention Article 26.] The prohibited grounds are generally those also banned by the Brussels and Lugano conventions-such as nationality of the plaintiff, or the presence in the jurisdiction of any amount of the defendant's property, or being physically served with papers in the jurisdiction.

In view of the importance of the jurisdictional basis of the F1 judgment, it is not surprising that the Draft Convention allows an F2 court to "verify the jurisdiction" of F1. [Draft Convention Article 27(1).] The only constraint is that the F2 court must accept F1's findings of fact on which F1 based its jurisdiction, provided that the judgment was not by default. [Draft Convention Article 27(2).] The Draft

Convention does not expressly regulate which party has the burden of proof on this issue. As a default rule, however, the Draft Convention provides that F2's law governs procedural questions concerning recognition or enforcement. [Draft Convention Article 30.] Hence the Draft Convention is willing to tolerate lack of uniformity on this point, though one would expect that most jurisdictional systems would put the burden of proof on the party attacking the judgment.

Non-Jurisdictional Grounds for Refusing Recognition or Enforcement

One of the Draft Convention's most significant achievements is its restriction of the non-jurisdictional grounds for refusing recognition or enforcement to the six grounds listed in Article 28. The first five of those grounds concern procedural irregularities in F1. The sixth allows F2 to reject the judgment if it is "manifestly incompatible with the public policy of the State addressed" (F2). The efficacy of the Convention could turn heavily on how narrowly or broadly contracting parties interpret this last ground.

Public Policy

It is interesting that these grounds track in a general way the grounds in the New York Convention on the Recognition and Enforcement of Foreign Arbitral Awards. [New York Convention Article V.] The New York Convention similarly restricts the grounds for rejecting a foreign arbitral award to a short list of procedural defects and one catch-all "public policy" ground.[1] The experience under the New York Convention has been largely positive, however, with most contracting parties giving a narrow interpretation to public policy by requiring something akin to a violation of the forum's "most basic notions of morality and justice." [2]

Will that be the experience under the Draft Hague Convention? One is entitled to some skepticism because the New York Convention applies only in a specialized field. Awards typically concern sophisticated business entities engaged in international commercial transactions. Moreover, the parties have voluntarily chosen arbitration as their dispute settlement mechanism. There is not much room here for matters that violate fundamental principles of morality and justice. The Draft Hague Convention sweeps more broadly to include recognition or enforcement of almost any foreign judgment. Since the Draft Convention is not limited to money judgments, one can easily imagine complications surrounding foreign judgments for specific

1 To be more accurate, New York Convention Article V(2) includes as grounds for rejection of a foreign arbitral award both public policy of the enforcing country and the non-arbitrability of the subject matter as determined by F2 law. In reality, however, non-arbitrability can also be seen as a form of public policy violation.

2 Parsons & Whittemore Overseas Co. v. Societe Generale de L'Industrie du Papier (RAKTA), 508 F. 2d 969, 974 (2d Cir. 1974).

performance, injunctions, or other forms of "equitable" relief. And what of a libel judgment in F1 for criticizing the government or a public figure? What about a judgment in F1 for infringing a patent on subject matter not considered patentable in F2? Perhaps such cases will be rare, but the potential range within which value clashes can occur is large.

In sum, one cannot be too confident in predicting easy going for the Draft Convention's public policy concept. But of course no convention would be viable without such a concept.

Damages

In one area that might have been left to public policy the Draft Convention instead provides special rules. Article 33(1) allows F2 to scale back a damage award that is non-compensatory (e.g., punitive damages or an antitrust treble damages award) to a level that could have been awarded in F2. Even as to compensatory damages, Article 33(2) allows F2 to scale them back if F2 finds them "grossly excessive." Damages are not to be scaled back, however, below what could have been awarded in F2 in the same circumstances. Any scaling back is to be done only after F2 takes into account the need to cover "costs and expenses relating to the proceedings" (attorney's fees, court costs, and so on). This last provision attempts to bridge the gap between systems in which attorney's fees and other costs are routinely awarded to the winning party (as in most European systems) and those in which such costs are not generally awarded (as in the United States).

Procedural Grounds

The first five grounds listed in Article 28 for refusing to recognize or enforce a judgment are procedural in nature. *First*, F2 can turn away a judgment if the same parties are litigating the same subject matter in F2, and the F2 action was filed first. *Second*, F2 can privilege one of its own judgments or that of a third state, as long as the third state judgment is capable of being recognized in F2 under the terms of the Draft Convention. *Third*, F2 can reject a judgment resulting from violations of F2's notions of "fundamental principles of procedure". Put more simply, this is a due process requirement, judged by F2's standards. *Fourth*, F2 need not recognize or enforce a judgment if the defendant was not notified of the action in sufficient time to arrange a defense. This is, of course, merely a particularization of the general due process standard. *Fifth*, F2 need not recognize or enforce a judgment obtained by procedural fraud.

Two further comments are in order. First, Article 28 says that "recognition or enforcement of a judgment *may* be refused" (emphasis added) for one of the six listed reasons (five procedural grounds plus public policy). In other words, rejection is a matter of F2's discretion. The Draft Convention does not attempt in any way to guide how that discretion should be exercised. Second, Article 28(2) emphasizes that except for specific provisions in the Draft Convention (e.g., public policy and damages), F2 is not to review the merits of F1's judgment.

The Paris Symposium's Papers on the Draft Convention's Future

The remaining three papers in the volume are devoted to general questions concerning the Draft Convention's future rather than specifically to judgments issues. The latter come into play to some extent, however, because, as we have seen, the Draft Convention links the obligation to recognize or enforce a judgment to that judgment's jurisdictional basis. One of the central issues is the extent to which the negotiating parties will be willing to solve impasses over jurisdictional bases by shifting the impasses into the gray zone, concerning which there is no Convention obligation to recognize or enforce.

Horartia Muir Watt, Professor of Law at the University of Paris I, Panthéon-Sorbonne, in her paper on *New Perspectives for Jurisdiction and Judgments Within Europe: A Critical View*, focuses on changes in European Union law that will change significantly the way the member states of the EU participate in the Hague Conference jurisdiction and judgments project. Because of amendments to the European Community Treaty effected by the Amsterdam Treaty, which came into force in May 1999, the European Union itself now has competence to negotiate treaties on recognition and enforcement of foreign judgments. Professor Muir Watt raises questions about this development under European Union law, including the possibility that aspects of EU institutional law may affect the content of the EU Regulation that will replace the Brussels Convention. (That EU Regulation has now come into force and is included in the Appendix to this volume.) This change in EU law means that in the future EU member states will negotiate as a bloc concerning the Convention.

In the second part of her paper Professor Muir Watt turns to substantive issues arising in cases concerning judgments issues under the Brussels Convention. Although her discussion does not deal directly with the Draft Hague Convention, it is relevant nevertheless because of the many close parallels between the Brussels Convention and the Draft Hague Convention. The former was of course the model for the initial drafts of the latter.

The final two papers in the volume, those by Peter Trooboff and Arthur von Mehren, take a broad view of the Draft Hague Convention project and of the central issues that have arisen and that must be resolved if there is to be a successful treaty. The Trooboff paper views the issues from the perspective of an American international lawyer. The von Mehren paper presents an overview and a perspective on possible approaches for achieving the consensus needed for a successful worldwide treaty.

Peter Trooboff is a senior partner in the Covington & Burling firm in Washington, D.C., former President of the American Society of International Law, and member of the U.S. delegation negotiating the Draft Hague Convention. His paper on *Ten (and Probably More) Difficulties in Negotiating a Worldwide Convention on International Jurisdiction and Enforcement of Judgments: Some Initial Lessons* is written from a U.S. delegate's standpoint. It concentrates on the background factors that shape United States reactions to the project and especially as they contrast with those of its main negotiating counterpart, Europe (or the member states of the European Union).

Several of Trooboff's initial list of difficulties derive from systemic differences in methodology between the American uncodified case-law approach and the rule-oriented, codified European way of doing things. Moreover, the Europeans are already functioning with a successful multilateral jurisdiction and judgments convention, the Brussels (and Lugano) Convention. (The Brussels Convention is of course now converted into an EU Regulation.) The U.S., on the other hand, has never entered such a treaty and has never tried to articulate its standards in workable treaty language. Moreover, Americans view some European practices as inconsistent with American constitutional due process requirements. One example is the Brussels Convention rule allowing a plaintiff to join all unrelated defendants implicated in a single legal or injury-causing event, as long as the plaintiff has good jurisdiction over one defendant in the group. Under the American approach, in general each defendant's links to the forum would have to satisfy constitutional due process requirements.

Perhaps the most contentious cleavage discussed by Trooboff is that between American and European approaches to jurisdiction over business entities. Europeans accept general jurisdiction at the registered office or principal place of business of a corporation. The U.S., on the other hand, treats a corporation as suable on all claims (general jurisdiction) in any jurisdiction in which the corporation does a substantial amount of business–a theory Europeans reject as overreaching. Trooboff also notes that European concerns over exorbitant U.S. grounds for jurisdiction are heightened by a general fear that U.S. judgments are frequently excessive.

On related claims (specific jurisdiction), Europeans look for some form of organizational presence in the jurisdiction–branch, agency, or establishment. The U.S. sees this as inviting formalistic evasion of proper court competence. It would have jurisdiction turn on a business entity's transactional activities connected to the forum state rather than on corporate form. Trooboff notes that there are also differences separating U.S. and European approaches to forum non conveniens and lis pendens.

Beyond the ten numbered difficulties to which Trooboff devotes most of his paper, he closes with several more unnumbered ones. Controversy surrounds various proposals for resolving whether and when the Draft Hague Convention would apply instead of the Brussels regime when a non-EU plaintiff sues an EU defendant in the EU. Others concern e-commerce, human rights claims, and intellectual property issues.

Arthur von Mehren, Harvard's emeritus Joseph Story Professor of Law and like Peter Trooboff a member of the U.S. delegation, authored the final paper in the volume. He believes the current Draft Convention is too ambitious, and so he proposes an approach "more tolerant of differences in practices and values."

Von Mehren notes that the Brussels Convention was the original model for the Hague Conference negotiations. The Brussels Convention fit well in a European context of strong commitment to economic union and shared jurisdictional and choice of law principles. It fits much less well in a global context where the participants' practices and values diverge sharply – as they do in some areas as between the U.S. and Europe – and where strong economic and political bonds are absent. He cites as examples of consensus-breaking divergence the U.S. doing business ground of general jurisdiction – rejected by Europeans – and the European practices for joining defendants or for allowing consumers to sue at their habitual residence. As Trooboff also notes, and as just discussed above, these European practices clash with U.S. constitutional norms. Von Mehren also stresses the absence in a global setting of a judicial institution capable of ensuring uniform interpretation and enforcement of agreed convention norms – the role played in the Brussels context by the Court of Justice of the European Communities.

Professor von Mehren argues that the way forward requires a more wholehearted acceptance of the mixed convention concept. The Brussels Convention was a double convention. It set down required and prohibited grounds of jurisdiction and mandates enforcement of judgments, leaving to F1 responsibility to enforce the agreed-upon jurisdictional grounds under the appellate supervision of the ECJ. A mixed convention would provide for an additional category – the gray zone – for jurisdictional grounds incapable of winning a consensus either in favor of or against acceptance. No convention party would be obligated to recognize or enforce a judgment based on a gray-zone ground of jurisdiction. Thus von Mehren urges a more flexible and open-minded approach, under which – for the sake of substantial progress – nettlesome disagreements could be swept into the gray zone.

The resulting convention would still be valuable. It would make the transnational law of jurisdiction and judgments more transparent. Business planners and litigants would know the approved and enforceable grounds of jurisdiction in major countries world-wide. Moreover, as a practical matter, litigants would have a strong incentive to file claims in approved – as opposed to gray-zone – jurisdictions. Thus, the approved grounds would clearly come to dominate in transnational cases.

Horatia Muir Watt[†]

New Perspectives for Jurisdiction and Judgments Within Europe: A Critical View

This paper does not draw directly on the experience of the Hague Convention. It aims, rather, to highlight important parallel developments within the European Union that affect the position of European member states as far as their relationship to the Hague Conference is concerned. The Commission has, for the past year, been preparing the "communitarization" of rules relating to jurisdiction and recognition of judgments in Europe. One could say that something like a full faith and credit system is being put into place by means of community regulations, which are to replace the present 1968 Brussels Convention and the future (or virtual) "Brussels II" Convention. Various difficulties attend this move, given both the institutional changes brought about by the Amsterdam Treaty and the cultural differences that still divide the various states on jurisdictional and judgment issues.

Background: Pressure to Europeanize Private International Law

Parallel to the Hague negotiations, there has been considerable discussion in Europe as to whether the time is ripe for the Council to develop a body of authentically European private international law. At present, this field is somewhat heterogeneous, comprising international treaties such as the Brussels and Rome Conventions, negotiated by virtue of the mandate conferred on the member states by Article 220 (now Article 293 of the EC Treaty), and isolated provisions of secondary Community law, relating mainly to choice of law, which appear as accessories to substantive legislation in particular areas. Since the European Union is not a federation, individual member states also continue to negotiate and conclude international agreements concerning conflicts of laws and rules of jurisdiction with third states on their own account – for instance within the Hague Conference, of which the Union is not a member as such. The "communitarization" now contemplated would mean the individual states' relinquishing their power to negotiate individually with third states, and the simultaneous transfer to the European Council of exclusive regulatory power in this field. Each of these consequences gives rise to considerable opposition on a national level,

---

† Professor of Law, Université Paris I (Panthéon-Sorbonne).

J.J. Barceló and K.M. Clermont (eds.), A Global Law of Jurisdiction and Judgments: Lessons from The Hague, 245–261

and neither has as yet been enacted;[1] nevertheless, various important developments that have taken place in the field of judicial jurisdiction and recognition of foreign judgments in the past year within the European Union should certainly be considered, within this context, as a first step in that direction on the part of the Community authorities.

Communitarization of the Third Pillar

Such developments are all the direct result of the entry into force of the Amsterdam Treaty, on May 1, 1999, which has brought about what is known in the somewhat mysterious Community jargon as the "Communitarization of the Third Pillar." This enigmatic expression in fact means the incorporation into the EC Treaty a new Title IV (Articles 61 through 70), which gives regulatory power to the Council in fields that previously came within the scope of intergovernmental action (under ex "K3"). Such fields, which include judicial cooperation in civil matters, have thus been transferred from the Third to the First Pillar under the heading of the free movement of persons. Despite various proposals to the contrary, this transfer has not as yet affected the member states' mandate to negotiate international treaties between themselves with a view to fulfilling the aims of the Community, or with third states. Nor does it seem to have entailed the disappearance of the power of the Community Authorities to continue regulating matters of private international law, including jurisdiction and recognition of foreign judgments incidentally, that is, as an accessory to the unification of substantive rules.

From Conventions to Regulations

Soon after the entry into force of the Treaty of Amsterdam, the Commission published two separate proposals purporting to transform the two Brussels Conventions into Regulations. What has been come to be called the "Brussels II Regulation" has now finally been enacted in June 2000. The "Brussels I Regulation" is in the process of being so; to my knowledge, the initial proposal, dated July 14, 1999, has itself been modified on various points to take account of the consultative opinion of the European Parliament and objections brought to bear within the various states, so that the latest version is dated March 2000.[2] These both indicate that their legal foundation is the new Article 61(c) of the EC Treaty. According to this text, the European Council enacts measures relating to judicial cooperation in civil matters under Article 65. The latter provision authorizes the Council (a) to act in order to

[1] Such opposition may indeed explain the delay attending the enactment of the Brussels I Regulation (see below), which is still under discussion to date. The negotiating status of the individual states of the Union with third states within the field covered by the Regulation seems to be particularly problematic.

[2] The Regulation may be enacted by the time this paper is published. Information is available from the European Union website, see <http//:www.europa.eu.int/eur-lex.>.

improve and simplify the recognition of foreign judgments, then (b) to promote the "compatibility" of the rules in force in the various states in the field of conflicts of law and jurisdiction. While the Commission, responsible for preparing the new texts, states that these do no more than "re-format" the content of the existing conventions, thereby suggesting that there are no substantive changes within the text, several significant amendments seem in fact to have found their way into the proposed instruments.

Pros and Cons

Aim of This Paper

Certainly, the Commission's initiative on these points has strong practical arguments to recommend it. In particular, the Brussels II Convention was designed to solve various extremely urgent problems concerning child custody in the aftermath of divorce within the European Union, and although France and Spain had already made moves to ratify the new instrument before the new Regulation was actually enacted,[3] its entry into force could have taken many years, at least if the experience of the Rome Convention (which took eleven years to enter into force) is anything to go by. The efficiency factor is further accentuated by the fact that, with respect to the Regulations, jurisdiction of the European Court is no longer dependant upon the ratification by the individual states of an additional Protocol and extends naturally beyond the mere interpretation of the new instruments to their enforcement – or at least, to the sanction of their violation. Here again, the lesson to be learned from the Rome experience is the need for energetic action, since the Protocol that provides the jurisdiction of the European Court to interpret that Convention is still not in force. More generally, the perspective of the enlargement of the Community obviously makes any move towards simplification of legislative procedures very welcome in principle. However, it is difficult to be entirely satisfied with what has been enacted (Brussels II) and proposed (Brussels I) so far. The aim of this paper is certainly not to put up gratuitous resistance, nor in any way to take part in the "sovereigntist" debate currently waging here, but to look at these developments critically in the hope that certain arguments might be taken seriously before rash action is taken in the haste of putting into place the new post-Amsterdam Europe of "Liberty, Justice and Security."

Layout of This Paper

Before an English-speaking audience, there is clearly no constraint, even if the place of performance is Paris, to follow the French academic tradition of dividing the

3 For France, *see* Acts 2000–209 and 211 of March 8, 2000, JORF of March 9, 2000. For Spain, *see* the information reported by H. Gaudemet-Tallon, "Bruxelles 2: de la convention au règlement communautaire," in *L'actualité du droit international privé de la famille*, Rep. Defrénois, 2000.

presentation of any theme into two parts. It so happens, however, that there are two sorts of considerations that call for attention. The first are institutional and relate to the legal foundation for the new regulation. The second are substantive and relate to problems raised by the Commission's changes to the text of the existing Conventions.

Institutional Issues

Four Issues Debated

The transformation of the two Brussels Conventions into Regulations has given rise to debate on several points, all pertaining to the legal foundation and extent of the Council's regulatory power in the field of civil jurisdiction and judgments. Discussion seems to have been most heated in Germany, where Christian Kohler has for some time, even before the Amsterdam Treaty came into force, been drawing attention to the institutional consequences linked to the inclusion of civil matters within the new First Pillar.[4] In Italy, opposition has also been focused on domestic constitutional issues relating to the fact that in Italy, as opposed to the situation in France, for example, jurisdiction is a matter for parliamentary legislation and not regulation by the executive.[5] In France, the debate was for a long while less articulate; however, recently, Hélène Gaudemet-Tallon has formulated convincing criticism concerning the particular status of the Brussels II Regulation.[6] Four essential issues arise relating to (i) the Council's power of "horizontal" regulation; (ii) the construction of Article 65, which constitutes the legal basis for the proposed regulations; (iii) the question of subsidiarity; and finally (iv) distortions arising from the fact that certain states have a particular status with respect to Title IV.

A Council's Power to Regulate "Horizontally"

The first question concerns the extent to which the Council is really empowered, under the new Title IV of the Treaty, to adopt horizontal regulations concerning civil jurisdiction and recognition of judgments. Briefly, the new First Pillar concerns policies involving the "free movement of persons" within the European Union, which means that the Council's power of regulation seems to be purely functional, or "sectorial," in the sense that such regulation is allowed only insofar as it pursues that particular policy. It is doubtful whether general provisions for jurisdiction and recognition of judgments in civil matters are sufficiently linked to the policy of ensuring the free circulation of persons to justify the exercise of the Council's

4 *See* in particular, Ch. Kohler, "Interrogations sur les sources du droit international privé européen après le traité d'Amsterdam," Rev. crit. DIP 1999.1.

5 L. Mari, Communication before the Academy of Urbino, Paris, 31st March, 2000.

6 *See* Gaudemet-Tallum report, *supra* note 3.

regulatory power to that end. This issue requires some explanation, in light of the recent history of the new Article 65.

Civil Matters as a Foreign Body Within the First Pillar

The new First Pillar, which aims at ensuring the "free movement of persons" within a space of "Liberty, Security and Justice," deals mainly with cooperation in administrative and criminal matters, as part of the "Schengen complex." Judicial cooperation in civil matters was included in the form of an "Addendum" – as what seems much like an afterthought – toward the end of the Amsterdam negotiations. Indeed, in December 1996 ("Dublin II") expressly mentioned that questions of private international law were to be maintained within the sphere of intergovernmental action; it was clearly not intended, initially, that this field participate in the communitarization that affected other fields comprised within the Third Pillar.[7]

The reversal took place in response, it appears, to recent pressure in favor of an authentically European private international law,[8] as opposed to a world-orientated one, developed by means of international treaties within the Hague Conference. This may explain why, at the same time, it was proposed that Article 220(4) be abrogated, signifying that intergovernmental action was no longer appropriate in this field. However, as already indicated, the latter proposal was not followed, and the new Article 293 still clearly allows for negotiation in the future of new international instruments as between member states in the area of private international law. On the other hand, judicial jurisdiction and rules for the recognition of judgments in civil matters were included – alongside measures pertaining above all, to the status of foreign citizens and the prevention of criminality – within the Council's new regulatory jurisdiction pertaining. In such a context, these issues have been described as a "foreign body" within Title IV.[9]

Free Movement of Persons as a Functional Limit to Council's Regulatory Power Under Title IV

This situation, in which the transfer of civil matters to the First Pillar seems to have been somewhat accidental, or at least unforeseen when the design of the Amsterdam Treaty was initially set out, may explain why certain restrictions affecting the Council's regulatory power seem to have been overlooked, and why it now appears that the solutions that have in fact been adopted are less efficient than they were previously, when such matters were still covered by intergovernmental action under ex-K3. Indeed, whereas inside the original Third Pillar, cooperation in civil matters was indicated as a possible object for intergovernmental action, with a view to

---

7 On the history of Title IV, see Ch. Kohler, *op cit*, p. 15.

8 *See* Ch. Kohler, *op cit*, note 22.

9 *See* Ch. Kohler, *op cit*, p. 20.

fulfilling the aims of the Community and *in particular* the free circulation of persons, their transfer to the First Pillar has put such cooperation, as the object of Council's new regulatory power, in the *exclusive* dependency of the free circulation of persons. The communitarization of the Third Pillar has therefore transformed an intergovernmental "horizontal" competence into a purely functional regulatory one entirely linked to the fulfillment of this particular objective. It does seem, therefore, that the scope of the Council's regulatory power is insufficiently extensive to allow it to enact a horizontal regulation on judicial cooperation in civil matters, since such an initiative goes far beyond what is strictly necessary to ensure the free circulation of persons. While this object is, arguably, closely linked to the recognition of foreign judgments concerning the custody of children, for example, it is clearly out of touch with issues such as jurisdiction over contract. This is why it is important that Article 293 should remain a basis for more extensive member state action in pursuit of other community objectives; indeed it may prove equally important that the Council's own regulatory power to adopt rules of private international law as an accessory to unified or harmonized substantive provisions. Of course, the plurality of enactments and instruments adopted on different legal bases, which is clearly the price to pay of avoiding obstruction of future action in the field of private international law, is far from ideal. This is particularly the case when, as we shall see later, various measures that are adopted on different bases, conflict.

The Construction of Article 65

If it is supposed, nevertheless, that the Council is empowered to regulate judicial cooperation horizontally, or that the regulations in question are to be considered a necessary part of the policy promoting the free circulation of persons, a second issue then arises by reason of the wording of Article 65 itself. Does this text provide for anything other than what has been described as mere "softlaw."[10] In other words, does non-binding invitations or measures of encouragement encouragement addressed to the member states, exclusive of any compulsory harmonization on the part of the Council, as in other fields such as mutual recognition of academic programs and diplomas where similar language is used?[11] Although harmonization is not expressly excluded, as it is in the area of education, the language of Article 65 does not make it easy to conclude in favor of the Council's power to adopt a regulation unifying rules of jurisdiction and recognition of judgments. The structure and terms of that text make it necessary to envisage these two issues separately – even though they are undoubtedly part of one functional unit, and any distinction as to the Council's respective power of regulation also appears somewhat arbitrary.

---

[10] *See* Ch. Kohler, *op cit*, p. 15.

[11] *See* for example, Article 149 (ex-Article 126) of the EC Treaty, concerning the action of the Community in the field of education.

Jurisdiction and Choice of Law

Rules of jurisdiction are covered by Article 65(b), which authorizes the Council to promote "compatibility" between national rules of jurisdiction and choice of law. Whether promoting compatibility really includes power to lay down new uniform rules in these two fields may be doubted. Nor indeed is it the same thing to ensure compatibility, on the one hand, and unify existing national rules, on the other. It is thus generally thought that the Council is empowered by Article 65(b) to eliminate the obstacles pertaining to recognition of judgments that get in the way of the proper workings of the interior market. But opinion is divided as to whether this includes measures intended positively to bring state rules together, or whether it merely involves devising means to reduce disharmony. Such means are however easier to imagine in the field of choice of law where they might include techniques such as renvoi, than in the area of jurisdiction. Be that as it may, the unified rules of jurisdiction contained in the new Regulations do indeed seem to overstep what is authorized by the terms of Article 65. Moreover, insofar as the new acts claim merely to reformat the texts of the Conventions, without actually changing their content. It is difficult to see how they can be seen as promoting greater compatibility than that already achieved by means of the Conventions themselves.

Recognition of Judgments

Article 65(a) could, on the other hand, be construed a little more generously. Here, the Council is allowed to improve and simplify procedures for recognition of foreign judgments. Of course, this does not seem to go as far as to imply that it may lay down new recognition procedures in areas where they do not already exist on an intergovernmental basis. In this respect, the enactment of a regulation in a field covered by the Brussels II Convention, which was not – and still is not – in force among the states of the Union, may raise some difficulties. There does not seem to be any doubt, however, that the Council may act with a view to simplify recognition procedures existing under the Brussels I Convention. But it can be argued here that the Council's power is limited to taking certain measure of accessory to improve the working of an existing instrument, which leave that instrument itself untouched.[12] Indeed, doubts have been voiced over the procedures by which an intergovernmental treaty may be modified; should the parallelism of forms not be respected?[13] Such doubts may be eased in the context of the conflict of norms raised by the next issue.

The Derogatory Status of Certain States under Title IV

If the principal advantages of a regulation as compared with an international treaty reside both in the greater efficiency of institutional procedures and the better chances

---

12 *See* Ch. Kohler, *op cit*, p. 19.

13 *See* H. Gaudemet-Tallon, *op cit*; *see* also the text below, concerning doubts as to the primacy of regulations over treaties with conflicting content.

of ensuring uniform application, then the new Regulations again fall short of the mark. Indeed, by means of protocols provided for under Article 69, and annexed to the Amsterdam Treaty, three states (Denmark, Ireland, and the United Kingdom) have opted out of the new Title IV and are therefore not affected with measures relating to cooperation in civil matters enacted on that basis. This is the price to pay of including such matters within the "Schengen complex," that is, among provisions principally dedicated to administrative and criminal law aspects of circulation of persons, provisions that three states are not yet ready to accept. Clearly, however, a specific regime is much less justified in civil matters. Indeed, this explains why Ireland and the United Kingdom have agreed to opt back in as far as civil matters are concerned and to submit voluntarily to the new Regulations.[14] But Denmark, however, has not so agreed; thus the Brussels I Convention will still apply in matters concerning the relationship between that country and the other contracting states. And until the Brussels II Convention (for the adoption of which there is clearly little incentive since the enactment of the regulation) is in force, jurisdiction and recognition of judgments in family matters, between Denmark and the other EU states will be governed by the relevant national rules. Such a situation has been stigmatized as the source of possible discriminations and distortions within the European Union, particularly as the content of the proposed regulations is not identical to that of the conventions. Similar difficulties are, of course, in the relationship between the member states and Switzerland, which will continue to be governed by the Lugano Convention.

Conflicts Between Norms

Such difficulties are made more acute by uncertainty as to the proper solution to apply to conflicts between various supranational norms, involving international conventions between the member states, on the one hand, and secondary community law on the other. The Brussels Conventions themselves contain clauses that provide that each Convention will replace any anterior agreements among the contracting states with the same object (Article 55 for Brussels I; Article 38 for Brussels II). While Brussels I states that it does not affect more specific existing or future agreements relating to jurisdiction and judgments concerning more specialized areas (Article 56) among the contracting states, Brussels II indicates that it prevails over any conflicting agreement, the object of which is different, but which could interfere with the scope of the Convention (Article 39). The solutions thus adopted are certainly in harmony with the generally accepted idea that a more specific treaty must have precedence over a more general one, and a later over a prior one.

But the new Regulations provide for identical solutions, simply replacing the term "Convention" by the term "Regulation." The primacy which the Regulations thus claim for themselves, to varying degrees, over prior agreements – including the

[14] Letters dated August 2, 1999 (United Kingdom) and July 5, 1999 (Ireland).

Brussels Conventions – among the member states – including the Brussels Conventions – calls for discussion. Although it is very often affirmed that the primacy of Community law means that it will override international conventions concluded by the member states,[15] it is debatable whether such a conclusion has any proper legal foundation.[16] Indeed, the Luxembourg Court has ruled that conventions concluded by the Union itself override secondary Community law; it is difficult to see why this solution should not extend to cases where Community regulations conflict with treaties concluded by the member states individually. At least, the contrary cannot simply be deduced from the primacy of community law over conflicting domestic law.[17] In any event, the primacy of Community law is obviously inapplicable to conventions concluded with third states; thus, the new Regulations cannot in any way affect the application of the Lugano Convention as between the member states and Switzerland, nor indeed the existing Brussels I Convention as regards Denmark itself.

Subsidiarity

Article 5 of the EC Treaty (ex-3B) provides that the Community may act only in order to implement a result that the various states are unable to attain otherwise. Although one can hardly disagree with the Commission when it declares that individual state action is insufficient to fulfill the Community's objectives in the field of international judicial cooperation in civil matters,[18] this in no way disqualifies intergovernmental action by way of treaties, which Article 293 (ex-220) still allows, despite the communitarization of the Third Pillar. Therefore, the question clearly arises as to whether the adoption of a regulation is really essential to bring about what has in fact already been very satisfactorily achieved in civil and commercial matters by the Brussels I Convention, and which could equally be well achieved in family matters by the new Brussels II Convention, which currently awaits ratification.[19] As it has also been pointed out, the new Regulations both affect the interests of third states (see Articles 4 and 59 of Brussels I, and Articles 8 and 43 of Brussels II), in respect of which it is hardly clear that the Community has undisputed "external" jurisdiction.[20] Indeed, there is a risk here that the Regulations may conflict with international treaties in force between the various member states and such third states, as within the Hague Conference. Therefore, it is far from certain that the

---

15 *See*, for such an affirmation, E. Jayme and Ch. Kohler, "L'interaction des règles de conflit continues dans le droit derive de la Communauté européenne et des conventions de Bruxelles et de Rome," Rev. crit. DIP 1995.1.

16 H. Gaudemet-Tallon, *op cit*.

17 Primacy affirmed by CJCE March 8, 1978, *Simmenthal*, aff. 106/77.

18 *See* the explanatory comments accompanying the proposed text.

19 *See* above.

20 *See* on this point, H. Gaudemet-Tallon, *op cit*.

Regulations constitute a more satisfactory way of achieving a harmonious result than the international treaties.

These institutional issues may not be invincible; my talents as an institutional lawyer are far too limited to come to any final conclusion here. It does seem to me, however, that such issues are sufficiently serious to merit consideration, an impression that grows even stronger when considering the questions raised by the substantive content of the new Regulations.

Substantive Issues

Important Changes as to Content

Despite the Commission's assurances to the contrary, several of the changes affecting the new texts are more than purely aesthetic. This is not necessarily a bad thing. In the field of jurisdiction, for example, the new text considerably improves the language and structure of the Brussels I Convention Article 5(1), insofar as it now contains special rules applicable to litigation in the field of contracts for the sale of goods and for the provision of services. This enhances certainty in an area where it is sorely needed, and clearly responds to the idea that, in contractual litigation, considerations of convenience and justice point to the jurisdiction of the court at the place of characteristic performance. It is, however, difficult to understand why, as a matter of principle, the analytical framework set out by the well-known *Tessili* and *De Bloos* cases,[21] which clearly goes against such considerations, is nevertheless preserved in the new text, as far as all other contracts are concerned. Be this as it may, the change affecting sale and services is clearly of great practical importance, and could not have been achieved, it appears, by means of interpretation by the European Court of Justice.[22] In the field of foreign judgments, considerable progress has been made in the wording of Article 27(2), which requires non-recognition of judgments entered in default of appearance, when the defendant was not duly served with the document instituting the proceedings in sufficient time to prepare his defense.[23] The text of

21 CJCE October 6, 1976, *Tessili*, aff. 12/76, and October 6, 1976, *De Bloos*, aff. 14/76, which, in order to identify the court with jurisdiction over a contractual dispute under Article 5(1), impose a detour by the law applicable to the contract, which will determine the place of performance of the obligation that gives rise to the claim.

22 At least, the Court has recently maintained its traditional position, as adopted in the *Tessili* case, even though it was suggested by the requesting (French) court that the time had come to prefer a jurisdictional nexus based on characteristic performance (CJCE *Groupe Concorde*, 2000, not yet published, but accessible at <http://www.curia.eu.int>).

23 This cause of refusal has given rise to much opportunistic strategic behavior on the part of certain litigants, since a formal irregularity affecting the service of process under the procedural law of the foreign court suffices to impede the circulation of a judgment, even though the defendant was in fact perfectly well aware of the proceedings brought against him; in many cases, the game consists in allowing foreign proceedings to proceed by default, in order to be able to invoke article 27(2) at the enforcement stage.

Article 41(2) of the proposed Regulation replacing Brussels I (and article 15(c) of the Brussels II Regulation, of which the wording is slightly different) has been changed so as to prevent a defendant from impeding the recognition or enforcement of a foreign judgment by invoking the fact that service was not duly made in accordance with the procedural law of the foreign court, while in fact having had knowledge of the proceedings. Such a modification, which is certainly to be welcomed, seems to be the result of a balancing test, in which the requirements of the fundamental right to defend oneself, are weighed against those of judgment recognition and enforcement.

Recognition and Enforcement Procedures

More important still, however, the new Regulations modify certain rules of procedure, with a view to enhancing the free circulation of judgments within the European Union. Although implemented to a different extent by the proposed texts of the two Regulations, the common idea is to allow recognition and enforcement of foreign judgments on an automatic or quasi-automatic basis. This is clearly a revolution that can hardly pretend to be purely formal, since its effect is to consider the member states as practically one unified territory for enforcement purposes. Two different versions of this innovation, one "soft," one "harder," appear in the texts now under discussion. While the practical difficulties they encounter differ, the most important issue they raise together is whether, at this stage, it is appropriate to eliminate the opportunity of developing a specifically European body of case law concerning the requirements of procedural fairness.

Practical Objections

In the present state of the law, under the Brussels I Convention, judgments given in one member state are not enforceable in another until they have undergone a specific registration or exequatur procedure before a designated court in the state of enforcement. Such a court may not review the foreign judgment on the merits, but is required to investigate whether there are any grounds for refusal of enforcement under Article 27 of the Convention.[24] This provision deals mainly with public policy, lack of proper notice, and conflicting judgments. Only in exceptional cases may enforcing court investigate the jurisdiction of the court rendering judgment or look into the foreign courts' choice of law. At first instance, the court exercises control on these points of it's own motion; the enforcing defendant has no opportunity to challenge the foreign judgment. However, the defendant may lodge an appeal against the enforcement order. While such appeals are in statistically rare, it is important to emphasize that, nevertheless, there has been important recent litigation on questions

[24] Although enforcement is distinct from recognition, which is automatic, the courts of the place where a foreign judgment is being relied on may be called upon, even incidentally, in the course of other proceedings, to check that no grounds for refusal exist.

of procedural fairness, particularly concerning requirements of the right to a fair hearing between persons domiciled in different contracting states. Therefore, although there are many fewer grounds for impeaching foreign judgments than at common law, they nevertheless represent important procedural guarantees, of which the enforcing court is the natural guardian. This is where the new regulations come in.

Proposed Change in Enforcing Court's Role

It is quite true that under the new Regulation that purports to replace the Brussels I Convention, things seem, at first glance, to be very much the same as before in two ways: (a) insofar as the registration or exequatur procedure that conditions enforcement in another member state remains, and (b) as long as the grounds for refusal of recognition, though improved, remain substantially identical.[25] A closer look, however, reveals that the enforcing court, which is required under the Brussels Convention to investigate whether such grounds exist, is now under the new text expressly prevented from so. According to the new Article 37, enforcement is ordered as soon as the court is satisfied that certain formalities have been met. These formalities, indicated in Article 50, are exclusively designed to identify the judgment and ensure that it is accompanied by a translation if the language of the enforcing court differs from that of judgment. Registration has thus become purely mechanical. Under no circumstances may the enforcing court refuse to order enforcement on grounds of public policy.

Procedural Drawback

The modification brought about by the Regulation obviously aims at speedier circulation of European judgments within the Union. Indeed, it is argued that since, statistically, few enforcement orders are actually challenged under Article 27 of the Brussels I Convention, there is little point in obliging the enforcement court to proceed with investigations that prove superfluous in many cases. Such investigations can therefore safely be left to cases at a later stage, that is, to cases where the regularity of the judgment is in fact litigated before the court competent to hear an appeal, which may then impeach the judgment on the ground of the new Article 41. The first objection to such an argument is of a purely practical nature. The efficiency of the new solution is perhaps less certain than it may seem at first sight. Presently, under most national procedural laws, the enforcing court has jurisdiction to order various additional measures that may prove necessary in facilitating the insertion of the foreign judgment in the country of the enforcing court. For instance, a judgment

[25] If not better, since the language of existing Article 27(2) has been improved, as shown above, and the exceptional verification of choice of law (which Article 27(4) allows when a judgment belonging to the scope of the Convention has taken position on a preliminary question of personal status) has disappeared from the new version of the text.

for a sum of money in foreign currency may need converting; a decision on alimony may need updating; interest may need calculating. As long as such questions may, according to the procedural law of the enforcing court allows such questions to be dealt with within the procedural framework imposed by the Brussels Convention, which excludes a full debate between the parties in the first instance, then there is every practical reason to encourage enforcing courts to settle them. From the standpoint of procedural economy, the gain is particularly apreciable when one remembers that even this simplified registration or exequatur procedure requires the services of a local lawyer before the enforcing court. However, with the new system, it seems quite clear that the enforcing court, reduced to a merely administrative authority, can have no jurisdiction to deal with such additional issues. Therefore, a new judicial procedure will therefore be necessary. This is one of the reasons why trans-European consumers, creditors with small value judgments, are felt to be insufficiently considered.[26]

Objection: Suppress Frontiers for Enforcement Purposes

Of course, an objection to this practical argument might be that the Regulation in its present form has not gone far enough. Why not, simply, eliminate frontiers between member states for enforcement purposes and pursue the idea, which has now been under discussion for some time, of a specifically European trans-frontier enforcement order, or, more simply, why not consider that an order made in one state of the Union is directly enforceable in the others? Obviously, such a project is extremely ambitious. Even though language barriers can be overcome by the use of a uniform certificate or model document and translation, there remain very important differences between enforcement procedures in the different states. These differences have until now required necessary the existence of a "filter," in the form of a registration or exequatur procedure, whereby the foreign judgment acquires the same force, and produces the same effects, as a purely domestic judgment. The direct articulation between measures ordered by a foreign judgment and national enforcement procedures may be sticky in many cases. How would a French huissier or bailiff react to an English extraterritorial freezing order, for which French law has no equivalent, without a translating procedure like of exequatur?[27] These practical difficulties may well be overcome, however, as comparative knowledge (if not, as of yet, harmonization of procedure) progresses within Europe. It may also be more realistic to introduce direct enforcement in certain areas where the state of the law, or rather, the types of measures that may require extraterritorial enforcement, are similar in the different states of the Union. Discussion is now under way to amend

26 Filali Osman, "Les actions collectives des consommateurs dans l'Union européenne: Un nouveau défi pour le droit international privé communautaire," in *La circulation des jugements en Europe*, Bruylant, Brussels, 2000.

27 It has recently been submitted that the adaptation required in this example is perfectly conceivable: Gilles Cuniberti, *Les measures conservatoires sur des biens situés à l'étranger*, LGDJ, 2000.

the initial proposal concerning the Brussels II Regulation, so that judgments and measures concerning parental rights of access and custody rendered in one state will be directly enforceable in other Union states.[28]

Further objections arise, however, which call into consideration the role of case law, at the present stage of European integration, in the framing of new requirements relating to the public policy content of procedural fairness.

Public Policy and Procedural Fairness

To deprive the enforcing court any opportunity to investigate the foreign judgments' conformity to these requirements is not only to take the risk, which, as will be seen, has been amply illustrated in recent caselaw, of obliging the enforcing court to recognize a judgment that shocks its sense of procedural fairness, but it is to remove the very possibility of a dialogue, out of which a body of specific European requirements may evolve. *Paradoxically, suppression of national frontiers may, at this stage, impede the development of that very trans-European private international law that the communitarization of the Third Pillar was intended to encourage.* Two points call for particular attention here. First, the Court of Justice has recently construed the recognition requirements laid down by the Brussels I Convention in such a way as to link them unequivocally to those of Article 6(1) of the European Convention of Human Rights. Second, there are cases in which national legislation may still bear the vestige of procedural unfairness, where vigilance and investigation on the part of other member state courts called upon to recognize and enforce foreign judgments can play a fundamental role.

The Fundamental Right to a Fair Trial – Krombach 2000 Case[29]

The defendant, Krombach, is a German doctor who abused and caused the death of a young French girl in Germany. Criminal proceedings in Germany having come to no satisfactory conclusion, and the victim's Father, Bamberski, initiated criminal proceedings before the French courts, in the course of which he also claimed damages for pain and suffering. The French Criminal Court, the Cour d'Assises, decided it had jurisdiction, by reason of the victim's French nationality and ordered Krombach to appear before it. On Krombach's refusal to comply with that order, the French court entered a judgment by default of appearance, pronouncing a criminal sentence and awarding civil damages. Bamberski immediately sought enforcement of the civil award of damages before the German courts. It was then that the *Bundesgerichtshof* put to the European Court of Justice a preliminary question of interpretation to the European Court of Justice, concerning the requirements of procedural fairness under

---

[28] *See* H. Gaudemet-Tallon, *op cit.*

[29] European Court of Justice, May 28, 2000, aff. C-7/98, Krombach v. Bamberski, in Rev. crit. dr. int. privé 2000, 3.

Article 27 of the Brussels I Convention.[30] The difficulty concerned the French default procedure before the Criminal Court (*contumax*). According to French law, once the defendant has refused to comply with the court order to appear, the ensuing default or *contumax* procedure denies the defendant to be represented before the court by a lawyer.[31] It was argued successfully before the European court that such a provision is contrary to the fundamental right to a fair trial.

Architecture of Article 27

Although such a result is hardly surprising, Court of Justice's reasoning is particularly interesting since it involves perhaps for the first time – a construction of the Brussels Convention that is probably contra legem. Indeed, Article 27(1) provides that violation of public policy is a ground for refusal of recognition and enforcement, while Article 27(2) lays down the conditions under which a defendant may oppose recognition and enforcement on procedural grounds. It was long supposed, at least by the national courts, that there were no cases other than the one envisaged by Article 27(2) (under which the defendant had not had sufficient opportunity to organize his defense and a judgment was then entered in default against him), where procedural anomalies would constitute grounds for refusal of recognition and enforcement. According to such an interpretation, the public policy clause of Article 27(1) was reserved for cases involving substantive policies of the forum, that is, reasons for refusal other than procedural unfairness. The reasons that seemed to justify this particular relationship between the two provisions were that (a) the impediments to recognition and enforcement should be allowed only restrictively, in the light of the objective of free circulation of judgments, and (b) the fact that each contracting state had subscribed to the European Convention on Human Rights, thereby considerably reducing the risk of discovering procedural unfairness among the various national laws.

The *Krombach* case not only proved this latter argument to be wrong, but gave the Luxembourg Court the opportunity to state, very clearly, that fundamental procedural rights, those very rights which the European Court of Human Rights at Strasbourg has been progressively reading into Article 6(1) of the European Convention, are now to be read into the public policy clause of Article 27(1). Thus, any violation of the right to a fair trial as understood under the Strasbourg case law must give rise to refusal of recognition and enforcement, even when such violation is not invoked by the defendant before the foreign court. Therefore, it is highly

30 There was also an interesting question here as to the extent to which a judgment given by the courts of the nationality of one of the parties should be refused recognition under the Brussels Convention, insofar as this Convention condemns nationality as a basis for jurisdiction. The European Court rejected such a possibility, as the enforcing court may not investigate the jurisdiction of the court of judgment (except where there has been infringement of one of the grounds of exclusive jurisdiction, notably under Article 16 of the Convention, which was not the case here).

31 Article 630 of the Code of Civil Procedure.

probable that even in such a case, the defendant who actually submitted a defense before the foreign court but is considered himself to be a victim of an unfair trial for reasons other than the circumstances in which he prepared his defense, must also be able to rely on the procedural content of the public policy clause. The sole function of Article 27(2) seems therefore to be to restrict the extent to which a defendant may oppose recognition on the grounds of the absence of proper opportunity to prepare his defense. Be that as it may, it is clear that, in the *Krombach* case, without the opportunity for dialogue provided by the judicial "filter" at the enforcement stage, which made these important developments possible, the fairness of the French *contumax* procedure might never have been called into question.

Public Policy: Question of Perspective

It may seem somewhat strange to hear the notorious public policy clause, usually perceived as both the source and the sign of cultural division, being invoked in favor of positive integration within the European Union, particularly at a time when the trend is clearly towards the abolition of impediments to the free circulation of judgments among member states. *However, the impact of the development of a human rights perspective has very much affected the function of public policy in the private international law of the various European states.* From being an entirely negative or defensive device, it has grown to become instrumental in the development of a new body of common principles, which progressively define the judicial process in terms of fundamental guarantees. These common principles obviously derive from the considerable mass of caselaw from Strasbourg. But their growth also requires a substantial contribution from national courts, both in reviewing domestic cases, and, when the opportunity arises, in their scrutiny of foreign judgments. Indeed, it is here that we have the "outsider's insights,"[32] the eye-opening effect of a foreign view, as in the *Krombach* case.

Further Illustration from Franco-British Litigation

That such a dialogue is still entirely necessary can be illustrated further by a decision given by the French Supreme Court in 1999,[33] while the *Krombach* case was pending in Luxembourg. Here, a French resident, Pordea, brought a defamation claim before the High Court against the *Times* newspaper, but finally abandoned the suit when unable to deposit the 25,000 pounds sterling required by way of caution judicatum solvi. A judgment for costs of 20,078 pounds sterling at a 15 per cent interest rate was then entered against Pordea by default; after various episodes before French courts, the Cour de cassation refused to allow the judgment to cross the Channel.

32 Expression used by B. Markesinis to describe the use of comparative law, in "The Comparatist (or a Plea for a Broader Legal Education)," Yearbook of European Law, 1995, p. 261, Clarendon Press, Oxford, 1996.

33 Cass. Civ. I, 16 March 1999, *Pordea*, Rev. gén. proc. 1999.747, note Muir Watt.

The interesting point here is that the English judgment could not be impeached on grounds of discrimination by reason of nationality, which the European Court had condemned several times in the case of similar national provisions requiring a guarantee from foreign claimants, even when they were citizens of a European country.[34] Here, the English rule expressed no distrust of foreign claimants as such, but required a guarantee designed to cover the risk that a claimant resident abroad might, if unsuccessful before the English courts, disappear home without paying for costs. The very existence of the Brussels Convention, however, makes such a precaution appear excessive where European residents are concerned, since enforcement of any judgment against such claimants may be obtained without difficulty.[35] However, to refuse enforcement, the French Supreme Court referred directly to the fundamental right to a fair hearing under Article 6(1) of the European Convention on Human Rights, considering that the sum required of a foreign-based claimant to gain access to the English courts represented an undue impediment.

It is also remarkable that this decision refers, too, to Article 27(1) of the Brussels Convention, anticipating the European Court's solution offered in the *Krombach* case a year later. While it is certainly regrettable that the European Court was not asked for its own interpretation on the conformity of English rules of procedure with the requirements of procedural fairness, the French court's view of English practice has certainly contributed to the definition of these requirements. It would surely be a great shame to do away with this opportunity for dialogue too soon. And if European legislation in private international matters is to become essentially technocratic, paying attention to judicial wisdom will no doubt prove particularly important.

---

34 CJCE July 1, 1993, *Hubbard*, Rev. crit. DIP 1994.633, note Droz; CJCE Sept. 26, 1996, *Data delecta*, Rev. crit. DIP 1997.33, note Droz; CJCE March 20, 1997, *Hague*, Rev. crit. DIP 1997.283, note Droz.

35 On this point, see G.A.L. Droz, notes quoted above.

Peter D. Trooboff[†]

Ten (and Probably More) Difficulties in Negotiating a Worldwide Convention on International Jurisdiction and Enforcement of Judgments: Some Initial Lessons

There are at least ten underlying reasons why, from the United States' perspective, the Hague Conference project on drafting a global convention on jurisdiction and recognition and enforcement of foreign judgments represents a difficult project. It is useful to identify these factors without trying to predict whether the project is going to succeed or fail. Other presentations in this volume analyze, in greater detail, the issues arising from the current draft of the proposed Hague Convention. This contribution is, therefore, intended as an overview for those who have not lived with this project for the eight plus years in which the United States Delegation has worked on this matter. It is deliberately not a rigorous, technical analysis of specific provisions of the pending draft but rather an effort to explain the background to those issues that are raised by other chapters. Numerous lessons can be drawn from the United States' experience in this negotiation, ranging from general lessons about negotiating treaties in the field of private international law to specific lessons relating to the United States' involvement in the Hague Conference. While I will allude to those lessons, their extraction is an exercise that will await another time and some greater distance.[1]

The first difficulty – the United States has never entered into a convention on the recognition and enforcement of foreign judgments. We tried to work out such an agreement in the 1970s with the British.[2] We failed because, even though we were prepared to accept a provision that would limit damages to some extent, the British

---

† Partner, Covington & Burling, Washington, D.C. The author has served on the United States delegation to the Hague Conference on Private International Law in connection with the proposed convention. These views were not approved by the Department of State and do not necessarily reflect the position of the United States in those negotiations.

1 I am most grateful to John McEvoy of the Faculty of Law at the University of New Brunswick and to the Canadian Council on International Law for inviting me to present an early draft of these thoughts on a panel at the Council's annual meeting in October 1999 in Ottawa and for providing me with a transcript of my informal remarks.

2 *See* P.M. North, *The Draft U.K./U.S. Judgments Convention: A British Viewpoint*, 1 Nw. J. Int'l L. & Bus. 219 (1979).

J.J. Barceló and K.M. Clermont (eds.), A Global Law of Jurisdiction and Judgments: Lessons from The Hague, 263–279

insurance industry was not ready to consider a treaty requiring the enforcement of U.S. judgments in the United Kingdom. A similar effort was undertaken with the French and that, too, did not work.

So in dealing with this effort, we are starting from scratch in the United States. That necessarily means that we face an enormous task in educating the American Bar and our judiciary regarding this subject even if the treaty replicated for the United States the existing common law rulings on recognition and enforcement. As will become evident, the situation is, in fact, far more complicated. The proposed Hague Conference Convention will not necessarily follow existing precedents in every respect; further, the Hague Conference delegations wanted the proposed convention to address when jurisdiction will be asserted over parties from other contracting states and not simply when judgments from such states will be enforced.

A second difficulty is that the United States courts enforce judgments from abroad under a nineteenth century case, *Hilton v. Guyot*,[3] generally without a reciprocity requirement, provided that the originating court has jurisdiction and follows procedures that meet our constitutional due process requirements. In general, American courts have not subjected judgments of the courts of other nations to a separate test to determine whether they are entitled to recognition and enforcement. Rather, the courts of the United States revert to acting as they would if they were confronting a domestic case that raised an issue as to whether the originating court had properly asserted jurisdiction.[4]

At the same time, in Europe and elsewhere in the world, the treatment of foreign judgments varies a great deal – from countries that require treaties to countries that have revision au fond even to this day, from countries that look at least to the choice-of-law to those that look at other procedural or substantive issues, particularly grounds of jurisdiction that do not conform to their practices.[5] So it is a world in which we have, if you will, opened the door to judgments of foreign courts but where many of those same courts have not reciprocated by enforcing our judgments. That difference puts the United States in a weaker bargaining position when we sit at the negotiating table at the Hague Conference. Less than facetiously, several in our delegation have suggested that the bargaining process might be somewhat different if the chair of the judiciary committees in the House or Senate were to introduce in the United States Congress the Reciprocal Enforcement of Judgments Act. I have, in fact, tried drafting such a statute. Such action might well begin to change the dynamics of the negotiating table in The Hague, but there are serious, though not necessarily decisive, policy problems with that approach, notably concerns with

---

3 159 U.S. 113 (1895).

4 Restatement (Third) of the Foreign Relations Law of the United States § 481, Cmts. (c) and (d) and Reporters' n. 1 (1987) (reciprocity holding no longer followed by most courts applying common law).

5 For an excellent recent survey of European practices outside the scope of treaties, see G. Walter and S. Baumgartner (eds.), *General Report in Recognition and Enforcement of Foreign Judgements Outside the Scope of the Brussels and Lugano Conventions* 1 (Kluwer 2000).

denying private rights in the name of forcing greater openness for U.S. judgments in other nations.

A third difficulty within the Hague Conference project is that the Europeans have existing and working conventions that apply to the recognition and enforcement of judgments. When the European Community states sat down and began work on what became the Brussels Convention in the early 1960s,[6] they sought to cover more than just the recognition and enforcement of judgments and bases of jurisdiction solely for that purpose – the so-called "convention simple." Instead, their goal was to write a double convention ("convention double") that establishes jurisdictional rules for the first court that hears the case. That is what the Brussels Convention is, a closed, double-determining convention establishing rules for determining when courts have jurisdiction and ensuring enforcement of the resulting judgments. Further, the European Community, now the European Union, has the European Court of Justice to ensure uniformity in interpretation when cases raise problems under the Brussels Convention.

With the Lugano Convention,[7] essentially the same regime was extended to all of the European Free Trade Association countries as well as the EU states. The non-EU states that are currently parties to the Lugano Convention are Iceland, Norway, Switzerland, and Poland. So a working convention regime exists in Europe among all these countries. As a result, when the United States comes to the bargaining table along with other non-EU states, the starting point of the EU states is, not surprisingly, "Look, we have got something that works. Why don't you just sign it or a substantially similar global convention since the Lugano Convention is for countries in the espace judiciaire européen? Why must we go through this long and difficult exercise delineating how you are different? Our conventions work – go ahead and sign." And there are American academics who say that is what we should do. Not very many, I might add, but there are some. So that is the third problem. There is a reference point for many at the table who are parties to the Brussels and Lugano Conventions, and, as noted below, a certain rigidity that comes from there being such an existing treaty regime.

A fourth reason for the difficulties results from the absence of written rules of jurisdiction in United States law. Our law in this area has developed out of the Supreme Court's litigation interpreting the Due Process Clause of the United States Constitution. The Supreme Court has interpreted the constitutional reach of U.S. jurisdiction in terms that do not lend themselves to statutory drafting, such as "fundamental notions of fair play and substantial justice," "purposeful availment," "reasonableness," and the like. Other states cannot be readily persuaded in a multilateral negotiation to use such terminology in a treaty, especially one that will almost

---

6 Convention on Jurisdiction and the Enforcement of Judgments in Civil and Commercial Matters, Sept. 7, 1968, as amended, 1998 O.J. (C 27) 1 (consolidated text).

7 Convention on Jurisdiction and the Enforcement of Judgments in Civil and Commercial Matters, done at Lugano, 1988 O.J. (L 319).

certainly not be interpreted by a single court. When you start looking for statutes in which United States legislators have written down our notions of jurisdiction, you find some in the long-arm statutes of the states and you find some in the work of the National Conference of Commissioners on Uniform State Laws.[8] None of these efforts focuses on an international treaty under which U.S. courts would agree as to when assertion of jurisdiction would be permitted and which grounds may not be relied upon for suits against persons or entities from other contracting states.

In short, the United States is writing down for the first time notions for which there is not a well-developed language. The challenge is at least as difficult as that which the American Law Institute (ALI) faces in preparing the Restatement on a substantive area of the law, as the ALI is finding its preliminary link to draft a federal statute on this subject. Given the international context, my view is that the challenge presented by the Hague Conference undertaking is considerably greater than that faced in the Restatement context.[9]

A fifth reason for the difficulty is that the Brussels and Lugano Conventions do have rules of jurisdiction in carefully set out, often formalistic, language. These rules have, with only minimal alteration, been carried forward in the European Union regulation that will replace the Brussels Convention on March 1, 2002.[10] In some instances, these rules would result in an unconstitutional assertion of jurisdiction if applied in the United States. Consider, for example, jurisdiction over a defendant, based solely on the place of injury under the interpretation that the European Court of Justice has given to Article 5(3) of the Brussels Convention. Perhaps even more clearly problematic from a U.S. perspective is Article 6 of the Brussels Convention, which subjects a defendant to jurisdiction regardless of contacts with the forum if the defendant is one of several defendants and another of the defendants is domiciled where the court is located. This may be a convenient way to consolidate European litigation, but to Americans, it is an unconstitutional assertion of jurisdiction over a defendant having no contact with a forum. So the Brussels and Lugano Conventions have some rules that are formalistic and also some that present difficult constitutional issues for U.S. negotiators.

Further, the Brussels and Lugano Conventions do not view all grounds of jurisdiction to be on equal footing. Rather, the rule under Article 2 is understood as a

---

8 *See* Uniform Interstate and International Procedure Act § 1.03 (1962) (Personal Jurisdiction Based upon Conduct), 13 Uniform Laws Annotated-Civil Procedure and Remedial Laws 355 (1986) (adopted by 6 states).

9 For elaboration on the role that the American Law Institute may play in relation to the Hague Convention project, either in preparing implementing legislation or in drafting a statute to clarify US recognition and enforcement law if the Hague convention does not succeed, *see* L. Silberman and A. Lowenfeld, *A Different Challenge for the ALI: Herein of Foreign Country Judgments, an International Treaty, and an American Statute*, 75 Ind. L.J. 635 (2000).

10 Council Regulation 44/2001 on Jurisdiction and the Enforcement of Judgments in Civil and Commercial Matters, 2001 O.J. (L 12) 1 (Art. 76 providing for entry into force on March 1, 2002) [hereinafter Council Regulation 44/2001].

"general" rule that permits a suit always at the domicile of the defendant and views the other rules as "special," indeed exceptional.[11] Finally, there sometimes appears to be a bias among the parties to these European conventions in favor of having cases eligible to be heard in a single forum under the jurisdictional rules, possibly because they do not have a doctrine of forum non conveniens under their domestic procedural systems. I will return to this last point in a moment.

The sixth reason why this is a difficult exercise is that, to be frank, United States judgments are feared in the rest of the world. There is genuine concern over the assertion of jurisdiction by United States courts because of the size of the awards that juries in the United States are believed to grant in civil litigation. Empirical evidence to the contrary, newspaper publicity about multimillion dollar judgments for injuries suffered from an overly-hot coffee cup is not readily overcome. Further, there is a perception that United States courts assert jurisdiction in circumstances that courts of other nations would not. As a result, when other countries in the Hague Conference and certainly European countries, came to the table to start this exercise, they had a single, clear objective in mind, which was to limit and restrict to the maximum extent possible, the jurisdiction that the United States courts assert.

Our counterparts at the Hague Conference negotiations characterized the U.S. jurisdiction that they were trying to restrict as "doing business jurisdiction." Now they were not initially using that phrase as a term of art with a precise, generally understood meaning and, as a result, there is a risk of confusion. To sort out the situation, a few words of background are essential. In New York State, doing business jurisdiction is a term of art. In New York courts, doing business jurisdiction is general jurisdiction in which the claim asserted against the defendant is *unrelated* to the activities of the defendant in the jurisdiction. This term is contrasted with "transacting business jurisdiction," which in New York State is a specific jurisdiction, i.e., the cause of action asserted against the defendant is *related* to the activities of the defendant within the jurisdiction.

As is known to anyone who reads American cases, courts almost always begin by determining if they have general jurisdiction. Most often, indeed almost always in international cases, they determine that the defendant has not engaged in the kind of "systematic and continuous" activities that will support general jurisdiction and permit a claim unrelated to the activity in which the defendant is engaged.[12] For that reason, the courts turn to determining if specific jurisdiction exists and, in that connection, weigh not only the extent of the defendant's contacts with the forum but

---

11 *See, e.g.*, H. Gaudemet-Tallon, *Les Conventions de Bruxelles et de Lugano* 55 and 105–06 (Montchrestien 1996) (referring to the "general principle of jurisdiction" under Article 2 of the Brussels Convention under which a defendant domiciled in the territory of a contracting state is "normally" sued before a court of that state and emphasizing the narrow interpretation that the European Court of Justice has repeatedly given to the "exception" to Article 2 embodied in the bases of jurisdiction set forth in Article 5 of the Brussels Convention).

12 Landoil Resources Corp. v. Alexander & Alexander Serus Inc., 918 F.2d 1039, 1043 (2d Cir. 1991) (requiring "continuous, permanent and substantial activity" based on leading treatise and case law).

also the quality of the contacts, i.e., the relationship of those specific contacts to the particular claim against the defendant.

The doing business jurisdiction that our Hague Conference counterparts sought to eliminate was a much less technical or precisely formulated notion. In fact, it was a shorthand reference for the key political objective of many countries to the Hague Conference negotiations. That objective responded to an assertion by industries in other countries that American courts were exercising jurisdiction when they should not have been doing so. In fact, as any student of the cases knows, there are few, if any, cases in which United States courts have asserted jurisdiction against foreign companies based on general jurisdiction, and virtually none in an international setting. Indeed, in the leading recent case, *Helicopteros Nacionales de Columbia, S.A. v. Hall*,[13] the Supreme Court expressly denied jurisdiction over a Peruvian company for purposes of a tort claim arising from a crash in Peru, even though the defendant's activities in the United States were extensive. Those activities included negotiations for virtually all of its helicopter fleet over a seven-year period, purchasing of helicopters and parts, and training of pilots and management personnel. It is also noteworthy that the Supreme Court said the "activities in question were not 'the *kind* of continuous and systematic general business contacts' required by due process to uphold general jurisdiction over a foreign corporation" (emphasis added).[14]

Unfortunately, the other delegates to the Hague Conference were unprepared to furnish examples of U.S. courts asserting general jurisdiction that was unwarranted. This absence of any evidence is notable in light of our repeated offer to receive and review any such cases and attempt to respond, if necessary in the proposed treaty, for any abuses that the cases revealed. Nonetheless, general jurisdiction – when the claim is unrelated to the continuous and systematic activities of the defendant – was clearly a target for those who came to this conference table to try to work out a Hague Conference Convention. At the same time, the American Bar, especially litigators, as they began to see drafts of the proposed convention, have asked why the United States would consider a broad prohibition on general jurisdiction. "To what problem is this an appropriate remedy?" they asked. "What is the quid pro quo that justifies such a major concession, and what is the justification for it?"

In explaining this controversy over general jurisdiction, I make no attempt to place a value judgment about whether seeking its prohibition was a good or bad objective from the perspective of other Hague Conference members. I can say, however, that their objective has influenced the approach that our negotiating

[13] 466 U.S. 408 (1984).

[14] Brilmeyer et al., *A General Look at General Jurisdiction*, 66 Tex. L. Rev. 723, 744 (Mar. 1988) (arguing that the critical distinction should be between the defendant's *intrastate* contacts and its *interstate* activity and that the key point in *Helicopteros* was that the intrastate activity (training of personnel) was limited compared to the extensive interstate activity (negotiating and purchasing of helicopters and parts)). Contrast, as Brilmeyer and her co-authors do, Perkins v. Benguet Consol. Mining Co., 342 U.S. 437 (1952), in which there were extensive *intrastate* activities on which the court relied in finding general jurisdiction over a Philippine corporation.

partners have taken to every aspect of the proposed convention, particularly the definition of the required and prohibited bases of jurisdiction, seeking to narrow the former and broaden the latter. I also express a personal belief that the real objection of industry in other countries to the jurisdiction of U.S. courts has nothing to do with general jurisdiction. Rather, I believe that they have encountered difficulties in cases involving assertions of specific jurisdiction and that those difficulties have much more to do with how the cases are managed (including what motions are filed and whether jurisdictional discovery is avoided) than with how U.S. courts apply the constitutional due-process test. After eight years of negotiations, it is remarkable how much energy certain Hague Conference delegations have devoted to prohibiting, under the proposed convention, a ground of jurisdiction on which virtually no U.S. court has relied in an international case for several decades.

A seventh reason for our difficulties – the rules of the Brussels and Lugano Conventions, by virtue of their quite formalistic approach, exclude many instances in which U.S. courts would assert jurisdiction. For example, Article 5(5) of both conventions permits suit against a legal entity in a state if the claim concerns "a dispute arising out of the operations of a branch, agency or establishment." The implications of this approach cannot be overstated. Absent such a legal presence in another jurisdiction, a non-U.S. company would not be subject to United States jurisdiction, even if it engaged in a broad range of activities within the United States related to the purchase or sale of goods or services to the supply of products that caused tortious injury, violated contract obligations, or infringed on intellectual property rights.

The current Hague Conference negotiation has introduced a new concept to the lexicon of private international law – it is called "activities-based jurisdiction." Time and again United States courts have asserted jurisdiction over defendants that did not have a branch, agency or establishment in the United States but that had engaged in activities in the United States that were found to serve as a constitutional basis for asserting jurisdiction over a claim arising out of those activities. In brief, the U.S. courts base their assertion of personal jurisdiction on the relationship of the defendant to the forum state and not on the particular legal structure of such activity. And the reason for this approach should be clear – absent this assertion of jurisdiction, non-U.S. parties could readily avoid U.S. jurisdiction simply by avoiding particular legal relationships, even though they engaged in extensive marketing or other promotion, negotiation, or performance. The United States could never enter into a convention that does not have some recognition of some kind of activities-based jurisdiction broader than that available when the defendant has followed the formalities of setting up a branch, agency or establishment. As other papers in this volume discuss in greater detail, the October 1999 draft of the proposed Hague Convention brackets in Article 9 language that begins to address, inadequately in my judgment, the need for a clear whitelist provision on activities-based jurisdiction.

The eighth difficulty – though many of the rules in the Brussels and Lugano Conventions were quite appropriate for 1968, when negotiations ended and had relevance for the relatively homogenous social and economic circumstances in the state parties of the European Community at that time, they were designed for a world that, in many ways, no longer exists. Articles 13 and 14 of those conventions protect consumers by allowing them to sue in their domicile, where they bought goods by mail or from the door-to-door salesman who wanted to escape jurisdiction. Article 15 of the Brussels and Lugano Conventions goes further and provides that a consumer is not bound by a choice-of-court provision unless it is entered into after the dispute arises. These same consumer protection concepts appear in Article 7 of the October 1999 draft of the Hague Conference convention.

The Brussels and Lugano Conventions also include certain rules, inserted in 1989, that protect employees working in cross-border situations by permitting them to bring suit where they habitually carried out work or, absent one state of employment, where the employer is or was situated at the time the employee was engaged. In addition, these conventions since 1989 also protect employees by providing that an employer may sue an employee only at the employee's domicile. Finally, like consumers, employees are not bound by a choice-of-court clause until a dispute actually arises. Again, there were certainly good social policy reasons for these provisions in a European context.[15] All of these ideas are embodied in Article 8 of the October 1989 draft of the proposed Hague Conference convention.

These protective provisions for consumers and employees are controversial in two respects. First, they embody social policies not likely to be acceptable worldwide. For example, American, Canadian, Japanese – and, yes, European – multinational corporations regularly assign senior managers, and even middle-management and blue-collar workers, all over the world under contracts that explicitly provide that if an employee wants to file a suit against an employer, the employee must bring it where the employer is domiciled and agrees to adjudicate such disputes.

Assume that a multinational corporation assigns a manager or worker to a three-year assignment in another country, and that the employee has a contract with a choice-of-court provision that refers to the courts of the headquarters of the corporation. Why would such a multinational corporation agree to be subject to suit in the courts where the employee is temporarily assigned, assuming that the state of assignment becomes a party to the Hague Convention? And why should the corporation have its choice-of-court provision rendered ineffective by the new convention? I see little prospect that companies in the United States or companies in many other countries will support their governments' ratification of a convention that does not give effect to the contract provisions employers make with their employees.[16] In my

---

[15] For the background to the 1989 amendments that were the result of jurisprudence of the European Court of Justice and also the provisions of the Lugano Convention, see H. Gaudemet-Tallon, *supra* 11, at 99–100 and 121–24.

[16] For an example of the tenor of likely industry opposition to these employee-protective provisions, see letter of Thomas M.T. Niles, President, U.S. Council for International Business, to Secretary of State Madeleine K. Albright 2 (Oct. 30, 2000) (copy on file with the author) (characterizing the provisions as "extremely controversial" and emphasizing "[b]usinesses and their employees contractual autonomy and certainty with respect to employment contracts").

judgment, it is not likely that the Brussels and Lugano Conventions protective provisions for empolyees will be found as an appropriate basis for consensus in a worldwide agreement.

When we turn to the consumer-protection provisions, the issues become even more complex. These issues are affected by the most important development since the negotiation of the Brussels and Lugano Conventions and the commencement of the Hague Conference negotiations in 1992 – the advent of electronic commerce over the Internet. Providers of goods or services over the Internet say that they do not even know where their consumers are located. Further, and this is their key point, Internet sellers of goods or services argue that, if consumers are willing to "click" agreement to a contract providing that the consumer will not sue the seller where the consumer is located but rather resort to courts of a specified state, that agreement should be binding on consumers. The choice-of-forum clause should be valid, Internet merchants maintain, regardless of where the dispute arises. In short, the e-commerce industry has great difficulties with the kind of consumer-protection notions contained in the 1968 Brussels Convention. Article 8 of the Draft Hague Convention follows the Brussels model and, consequently, has resulted in enormous controversy.

The Hague Conference held one session on e-commerce in Ottawa during 2000 and convened another in Ottowa in February 2001.[17] From that discussion and the subsequent Hague Conference sessions in Basel in December 2000 and Edinburgh in April 2001, a consensus is perhaps beginning to emerge for a Hague Convention rule that would not interfere with the effectiveness of choice-of-court or arbitration clauses in consumer contracts. However, the provision would permit a state party to opt into a regime of greater protection for consumers having their habitual residence in that state. The prospects for such a compromise may, unfortunately, be limited, in view of the Commission of the European Union's rejection of strenuous efforts within the EU to permit the full effect of alternative-dispute provisions in consumer contracts.[18]

A ninth difficulty is that a refusal to assert jurisdiction is a constitutional matter in many countries for reasons arising out of the abuses of World War II. German and other states' constitutions say that if a court has jurisdiction, the judge has an obligation to hear the case. Why? Because, as we all know, there was a period during which judges did not hear cases because of who the defendant was, not having anything to do with neutral principles or juridical philosophy. In these circumstances, it is not easy to find a basis for applying the doctrine of forum non conveniens that

[17] For a summary of the choice-of-forum issue and related points, see Hague Conference on Private International Law (C. Kessedjian), Electronic Commerce and International Jurisdiction (Ottawa Feb. 28–Mar. 1, 2000) 6–8, Enforcement of Judgments, Prel. Doc. No. 12 (Aug. 2000).

[18] Amended Proposed Council Regulation, com (2000) 689 5 (proposing a "stock-taking of alternative dispute-settlement schemes" after the regulation has come into force and calling for a "speeded up" development of such proposals in new Preamble Paragraph 14a of the then proposed regulation).

common law countries such as the United States regard as an important corrective to otherwise applicable jurisdictional rules.

Our colleagues from civil law countries, after some discussion with those of us from common law nations, now have less trouble with our approach of looking at so-called private-interest factors (such as where the evidence, the witnesses and other elements in litigation are located) to determine whether there is a more appropriate forum for a particular case. However, these same colleagues are not persuaded when we ask about public-interest factors, e.g., should our courts spend their time and money and the taxpayers' money on this case? They believe that this is a totally inappropriate consideration and that courts should never question whether hearing a particular case is a wise expenditure of the taxpayers' money, even if there is another forum with a much greater public-policy interest in the controversy.

As things stand now, Article 22 of the Draft Hague Convention includes a forum non conveniens provision, and it is a considerable improvement over the provision in prior drafts. For example, it would permit cases to be referred to non-contracting states, and it would apply even if the forum were not the habitual residence of the defendant. The provision, however, would not apply in the consumer and employment cases and that will be a real problem. Moreover, it imposes a rule that requires the posting of security when the jurisdiction of the more appropriate forum is based on national law rather than the Convention (unless, as seems almost impossible, the defendant shows possession of sufficient assets to satisfy any anticipated judgment in the other state or a state where the resulting judgment could be enforced). An analogous problem appears in the lis pendens provision of Article 21 of the draft convention, assuming, which is hardly self-evident, that it is necessary or desirable to have a race-to-the-courthouse provision of the kind that appears in the Brussels and Lugano Conventions. Again there is an attempt to have the Convention impose rules – in this instance, the race to the courthouse – even when jurisdiction is based on national law rather than on a jurisdictional provision under the Convention. This quasi-regulation of permitted grounds of jurisdiction that, by definition are determined under national law, will likely remain controversial to the end.

The tenth reason for difficulty in negotiating the Convention – even as this project was underway in The Hague, the European Union began a revision of the Brussels Convention. That exercise has moved forward at the same time as the negotiations in the Hague Conference, but on a faster timetable. Under the Treaty of Amsterdam, responsibility for the subject matter of the Brussels Convention became an area of competence for the European Union rather than for member states acting through treaties. It is possible that twelve of the member states will not even sign the Hague Convention if it is successful. Rather, the Convention may be signed on their behalf by the European Union, with only three states, including the United Kingdom and Denmark, signing on their own behalf. The Commission of the European Union is extremely anxious to promulgate in final form its regulation that will accomplish some or all of these results. Thus, the publication of the Council Regulation 44/2001 was a crucial event.[19] This regulation has, if you will, supernationalized this area of activity within the European Union, and that is affecting the substance and the timing of this negotiation at the Hague Conference.

In fact, this list of ten difficulties faced in the present negotiations is too short because there are some larger questions that need to be addressed at this stage in the Hague Conference project and that constitute distinct reasons for our problems. For example, from the very earliest expert group meetings on the proposed convention, we heard complaints about U.S. courts assuming general jurisdiction over cases involving non-U.S. litigants and the problems such assumptions of jurisdiction presented for non-U.S. parties. As is noted, we challenged our colleagues to furnish us with examples of such cases but received not a single report of such a case. Our research shows that the instances in which U.S. courts rely upon general jurisdiction are limited, and that most such cases arise in the U.S. domestic context, e.g., heavy cross-border promotional activity by amusement parks and similar such national market activities. We recognize that many non-U.S. parties object to having to litigate in the United States, but the issue is whether general jurisdiction is the core of the problem. We see little evidence that it is. The incomplete understanding of the interests of those who will be impacted by this convention has seriously affected our capacity to resolve the activities-based jurisdiction issue and has also contributed to the overreaching in Article 18 of the October 1999 draft on prohibited bases of jurisdiction.

Another difficulty results from the willingness of some delegations to press issues without proper preparation in the Special Commission. A good example is the exclusion from Article 10, the whitelist tort provision, of claims based on "injury caused by anti-trust violations, in particular price-fixing or monopolization, or conspiracy to inflict economic loss."[20] There was virtually no discussion of this provision, which the Chair should never have permitted to come to a vote without a more careful study of its terms. The United States strongly objected to the procedure that led to its consideration and approval. When the Antitrust Division of the Department of Justice saw the provision, it nearly recommended that the United States terminate its participation in the Hague Conference negotiations. In the minds of some delegations, so-called "economic" torts should not serve as a sole basis for jurisdiction even when they cause foreseeable injury in another jurisdiction. That is antithetical to nearly 100 years of United States law in the field of competition. At a minimum, the provision deserved much more study than it received.

Perhaps the most difficult "new" issue in the negotiations has been the so-called disconnection clause of the proposed Hague Conference Convention. It could be the subject of another paper. To capture the essence here, the reader should refer to the three proposals that appear in the Annex to the October 1999 draft for Article 37 of the draft Hague Conference Convention and to the attached chart, which attempts

[19] Council Regulation 44/2001, *supra* note 10.

[20] Article 10(2) of the Draft Hague Conference Convention (Oct. 1999).

to summarize two of those provisions (the third simply allowing for reservations to the Convention). It would be difficult to overstate the complexity of these proposals, even as summarized. To make matters easy, simply take two cases on the assumption that the United States, France, and Germany are all parties to the new Hague Conference Convention: (1) a U.S. habitual resident sues a French-incorporated company in a French court; and (2) a U.S. company sues a German-incorporated company in a French court.

As you will quickly see, under the first proposal in Article 37, the issue in each of these cases is that no provision of the Hague Conference Convention has any application in either of them. The Brussels Convention controls in every instance. There are three extremely limited exceptions: when the case happens to involve a contract with a forum-selection clause that designates a non-European Union court; when the case happens to involve an issue that is subject to the exclusive jurisdiction of the courts of a non-EU state; or, when and if the European court would even apply forum non conveniens doctrine and the more appropriate court is a non-EU state, then the Hague Conference Convention would be applicable.

At this point one might reasonably ask, "You mean that you have spent eight years negotiating a convention that does not apply when you bring suit in the courts of another convention state in the European Union?" The answer is, first, that, of course, the United States Delegation thought that it was negotiating a worldwide convention that would take precedence over any regional convention in both of these cases and any other cases involving litigants from parties to the new Hague Convention. This solution would be applicable absent some extremely special circumstances that the U.S. Delegation had yet to identify.

The U.S. Delegation has sought for several years to address this issue, which is known in the European Union as the disconnection clause. Our Hague Conference counterparts from the European Union have responded that the issue is too political to permit resolution at this time. The political issues concern the allocation of authority within the European Union. From the United States' perspective, the issue is much simpler – the Hague Conference Convention should apply in both of the examples unless the case is truly outside the scope of the Convention, e.g., involves parties that are both habitual residents of the same state. To this response, our European Union colleagues explain that the only possible solution would be to work through each of the articles of the Hague Conference Convention and arrive at a disconnection solution in each instance. For the time being, they understand that the United States does not believe that the disconnection issue is all that complex, unless the entire premise of negotiating a global convention is altered to provide multiple exceptions, which would significantly undermine the value of the resulting convention and almost certainly ensure its failure to gain United States ratification.

I have omitted mention of some difficulties that deserve more attention than I can give them in this paper and also some that are common to any multilateral negotiations. As one example of the former, I would refer the reader to the two variants under Article 18(3) that reflect the effort to permit the human rights community to view the Convention as contributing to the important litigation that in recent years they have brought in national courts against individual violators of fundamental international norms. While private international lawyers do not often enter into such issues, there is no choice but to do so in this instance, especially when one considers the strong domestic support that the human rights community has earned in the United States and many other countries that are participants in the Hague Conference negotiation.

Another such example of issues affecting specialists concerns intellectual property rights and, in particular, whether the exclusivity provisions of proposed Article 12(4) are appropriate in a worldwide convention and whether Article 12(6) is a wise exception to any such exclusivity. Under the Brussels Convention, there is controversy about the comparable provision, Article 16(4), which appears to preclude the kind of inter partes infringement action that Article 12(6) would permit. Further, it is unclear whether the solution proposed by Article 12(6) would be suitable for uniform application to all types of intellectual property rights or whether a distinction needs to be drawn between, for example, trademarks, where the rights are established through use, and patents, where the rights are established through registration.[21]

E-commerce, human rights, and intellectual property rights issues illustrate the importance of broad consultation by the U.S. government with sectors of the American Bar, whose interests may be impacted by a treaty having the potential scope of the proposed Hague Conference Convention. To its credit, the Office of the Assistant Legal Adviser for Private International Law has encouraged such a dialogue within the U.S. government and with professional associations, jurists, practitioners including trial lawyers, and industry and consumer advocates throughout the United States. That office has also worked to form a delegation comprising a broad spectrum of representatives of U.S. interests that may be impacted by a Hague Conference Convention. Organizing such consultation and assembling the results into coherent policy choices for the U.S. Delegation require considerable time and resources, probably more than the Legal Adviser anticipated at the outset of the negotiations in 1992. Thus, yet another challenge in the Hague Conference negotiations has been and will be to maintain the necessary infrastructure within the United States to support the delegation to the Conference and, if a convention is successfully worked out at the Conference, the work on drafting implementing legislation.

As to the difficulties in the Hague Conference that are common to all international negotiations, they are well illustrated in an experience of my own. I spent ten hours in a small working group writing the single sentence that is now proposed Article 10(1) simultaneously in French and English. The final product is rather good, given the complexity of the subject matter, but that is a great deal of time for one sentence.

21 *See* Comments of the International Trademark Association in letter from Kimberly L. Muller, President, to Todd Dickinson, Under Secretary of Commerce for Intellectual Property and Director of the U.S. Patent and Trademark Office 5–8 (Dec. 1, 2000) (copy on file with author).

We have only a limited number of members of each delegation and there is only so much that can be accomplished in the available time. Some delegations are accustomed to generating drafts by hand, while others depend on computer so that styles of working differ widely. Finally, even the hardest-working delegation member reaches a point when fatigue overtakes reason and frustration risks undermining prior hard work. These factors are apparent in any multilateral negotiation, but they are real and should not be overlooked. I should add that the skill and expertise of the Hague Conference staff, and their diplomacy from time to time, helps enormously to overcome some of these rather traditional difficulties.

Finally, the U.S. Delegation faced considerable pressure from other Hague Conference members to move to a diplomatic conference on the Convention in October 2000 where the U.S. Delegation was assured that many of our current problems would be solved. In October 1999, the United States refused to join in the consensus in favor of that schedule. As is now well known, the head of the United States Delegation, Jeffrey Kovar, Assistant Legal Adviser for Private International Law, wrote the Secretary General of the Hague Conference in February 2000 to explain why the United States would not agree to holding that diplomatic conference in the fall of that year. To be sure, the Kovar letter caused considerable annoyance and even anger on the part of some of our Hague Conference counterparts.[22] I strongly urge review of the letter itself rather than reliance on third-party summaries, since its tone is far more constructive and substantive than admitted in some unfortunate characterizations. Yes, it was a tough letter, but sometimes such candor and clarity are the only way to inject reality into a negotiation and cause everyone to rethink the premises on which each delegation is operating. In my judgment, the Kovar letter achieved that critical objective.

Since the Kovar letter was sent, there have been, in 2000, two unsponsored exchanges among key participants in the Conference (Geneva and Noordwijk) and two informal negotiating sessions sponsored by the Hague Conference (Washington and Basel). Three more informal sessions occurred in the first months of 2001 (WIPO/Geneva, Ottawa, and Edinburgh). Progress has been slow, but there has been identifiable movement on certain issues, including activities-based jurisdiction. We appear to have regained the collaborative, open spirit that prevailed before the unfortunate votes at the Special Commission sessions in June and October 1999. We also appear to be at least beginning to understand the essential elements of a successful outcome from the diplomatic conference. Can anyone now seriously contend that the delay in the diplomatic conference and its reorganization into a two-stage process, i.e., consensus procedures in June 2000 and voting only at the second stage in 2001, were not essential, or that the considerable time that delegations have devoted in the interim to further negotiation was unnecessary?

---

22 Letter from Jeffrey Kovar, Assistant Legal Adviser for Private International Law, U.S. Dep't. of State, to J.H.A. van Loon, Secretary General, Hague Conference on Private International Law (Feb. 22, 2000) (copy on file with author).

The Hague Conference negotiations may succeed. At this point it is too early to predict the outcome with any certainty. However, one point is clear – the only path to success is through the consensus approach that the delegations have followed at their informal meetings in 2000 and 2001. No participating state or group of states can or should prevail by votes that ignore the legitimate concerns of other delegations. In the end, the issue is not what each delegation has to give up, but rather whether each delegation can take back to its government a balanced and constructive treaty that has a high prospect for acceptance by its bar, its judiciary, and its scholars.

Disconnection Clauses-Article 37 (Annex, October 1999 Draft)[23]

Pending Proposals Analyzed

	Proposal #1	***Proposal #2***
Article 3 (Defendants' Habitual Residence)	Brussels (but Hague applies for non-EU domiciliaries)	**Brussels:** If defendant domiciled in EU State **Hague**: If defendant domiciled in non-EU State[24]
Article 4 (Choice of Court)	Brussels (but Hague applies if non-EU court chosen provided non-EU court accepts jurisdiction)	**Brussels:** Chosen court is EU state (Brussels requires the defendant or plaintiff to be domiciled in EU State) **Hague:** If chosen court is non-EU state (even if defendant is domiciled in the EU)
Article 5 (Defendant Appearance) **Article 6** (Contracts) **Article 7** (Consumer Contracts)	Brussels (but Hague applies if defendant is domiciled in non-EU state; but in consumer contracts, if non-EU defendant has branch in EU State, then Brussels applies; same rule for insurance contracts)	**Brussels:** If defendant is domiciled in EU state **Hague:** If defendant is domiciled in non-EU state Question: What about insurance contracts?

[23] Prepared by Peter D. Trooboff, October 31, 2000, for distribution in Washington, D.C. to an informal meeting of Hague Conference delegations.

[24] The Brussels Convention applies if any of the following Brussels Convention provisions is applicable: exclusive jurisdiction (Br. Art. 16), prorogation (Br. Art. 17), lis pendens/related actions (Br. Arts. 21 and 22), or protective jurisdiction (Br. Arts. 13–15 and 17 (employment)).

Article 8 (Employment Contracts) **Article 9** (Branches/ Activities-Based Jurisdiction) **Article 10**(Torts/Delits) **Article 11** (Trusts)		
Article 12 (Exclusive Jurisdiction)	Brussels (but Hague applies if there is exclusive jurisdiction in a Hague state that is not an EU state)	**Brussels:** If the court with exclusive jurisdiction is an EU state **Hague:** If the court with exclusive jurisdiction is not an EU state and is Hague state (even if the defendant is EU-domiciled)
Article 14 (Multiple Defendants) **Article 15** (Counterclaims) **Article 16** (Third Party Claims)	Brussels (but Hague applies if the defendant is not domiciled in EU State)	**Brussels:** If the defendant is domiciled in an EU state **Hague:** If the defendant is not domiciled in an EU state[25]
Article 18 (Prohibited Grounds)	Hague: if prohibited ground in Hague, Hague prevails (even if Brussels allows); result: Brussels Article 4 excluded (may be the same result as under Proposal #2)	**Brussels:** If the defendant is domiciled in an EU state **Hague:** If the defendant is not domiciled in an EU state (provided that the defendant is habitually resident in a Hague state)

[25] The Brussels Convention applies if any of following Brussels Convention provisions is applicable: exclusive jurisdiction (Br. Art. 16), prorogation (Br. Art. 17), lis pendens/related actions (Br. Arts. 21 and 22), or protective jurisdiction (Br. Arts. 13–15 and 17 (employment)).

Articles 21 and 22 (Lis Pendens/Forum Non Conveniens)	Brussels (but Hague applies if the court favored is a non-EU court and is in a Hague state)	**Brussels:** If the court favored is an EU court **Hague:** If the court favored is a non-EU court and is a Hague state (even if the defendant is EU domiciled)

Arthur T. von Mehren[†]

Drafting a Convention on International Jurisdiction and the Effects of Foreign Judgments Acceptable Worldwide: Can the Hague Conference Project Succeed?

The Background

On October 19, 1996, the states represented at the Eighteenth Session of the Hague Conference on Private International Law voted to include in the agenda of the Nineteenth Session the questions of jurisdiction, and recognition and enforcement of foreign judgments in civil and commercial matters.[1]

In June 1997, a Special Commission on international jurisdiction and the effects of foreign judgments in civil and commercial matters began preparatory work on a convention. In October 1999 after five sessions, during which 86 plenary meetings were held,[2] the Special Commission adopted the Preliminary Draft Convention on Jurisdiction and Foreign Judgments in Civil and Commercial Matters.[3]

In the ordinary course of events, the Hague Conference would convene its nineteenth session in the fall of 2000 to consider the Special Commission's draft. At the session, plenary meetings would be conducted under strict rules of procedure[4] based on the majoritarian principle, which do not encourage reaching consensus through compromise.

In the weeks following the Special Commission's fifth and final session, several delegations questioned the desirability of convening the diplomatic conference in a year's time to consider the Special Commission's draft. The draft does not address definitively certain matters as delicate as they are important, namely, whether, and in what manner, intellectual property rights and electronic commerce should be covered by the Convention.[5] Moreover, for fundamental systemic reasons, some

† Joseph Story Professor of Law, *emeritus*, Harvard University. The author is a member of the U.S. Delegation for the Special Commission. The views expressed are his own and do not necessarily represent U.S. positions.

1 Final Act of the Eighteenth Session, I Proceedings of the Eighteenth Session, Miscellaneous matters 29, at 47 (The Hague, SDU Publishers 1999).

2 Two-week sessions took place in June 1997, June 1998, November 1998, and June 1999; the final session in October 1999 lasted ten days.

3 The text is available on the Internet under <http://www.net/e/conventions/draft36e/html>.

4 *See* Rules of Procedure for Plenary Meetings, Annex to the Minutes of the Opening Session, I Proceedings of the Eighteenth Session, *supra* note 1, at 20–23.

5 A group of experts on electronic commerce convened in Ottawa from February 28 to March 1, 2000 and reconvened in February 2001; an experts meeting was held in collaboration with WIPO in January

J.J. Barceló and K.M. Clermont (eds.), A Global Law of Jurisdiction and Judgments: Lessons from The Hague, 281–291

delegations resisted proceeding on the basis of the October 1999 draft. The United States delegation believed, for example, that the Conference's traditional diplomatic session procedures, with their strong majoritarian bias, were incapable of producing a convention that would be acceptable worldwide; the time for a global convention of the draft's substantive scope, rigor, and complexity had simply not yet come. For a global convention on jurisdiction and recognition to be successful, consensus must be achieved. The scope of such a convention must be more modest and its provisions more tolerant of differences in practices and values than could be any convention largely based on the conceptions, aspirations, and approaches embodied in the Special Commission's preliminary draft.

In a letter dated February 22, 2000, Jeffrey Kovar, Assistant Legal Adviser for Private International Law and head of the U.S. delegation, wrote to J.H.A. van Loon, Secretary General of the Conference, as follows:

> [T]he project as currently embodied in the October 1999 preliminary draft convention stands no chance of being accepted in the United States. Moreover, our assessment is that the negotiating process so far demonstrates no foreseeable possibility for correcting what for us are fatal defects in the approach, structure, and details of the text. In our view there has not been adequate progress toward creation of a draft convention that would represent a worldwide compromise among extremely different legal system.

For these reasons, the United States opposed the scheduling of a diplomatic conference in accordance with the Conference's normal procedures. Kovar proposed instead

> a stocktaking session when delegations can discuss in a frank, informal, and serious way whether there is the desire and political will to depart from the current text and seek new avenues for agreement.

"If there is such a will," the U.S. delegation would propose "a much more open-ended schedule of work ... along with agreement on more consensus-based negotiating methods."

Should it prove impossible to produce a broadly acceptable convention, the United States favored suspension of work on the project.

> [T]his would leave open the possibility that the underlying views and dynamics could mature over time, with the hope that achieving a viable Hague Convention would ultimately be possible.

2001 to address intellectual property issues. See Communication of August 9, 2000 from the Permanent Bureau of the Hague Conference to the National Organs of the Member States, L.C. ON No. 44 (00), 2 (2000); Hague Conference on Private International Law, Conclusions of the Special Commission of May 2000 on General Affairs and Policy of the Conference, Prec. Doc. No. 10 (June 2000), 10.

The Current Situation

As of the summer of 2000, no one can be sure what the ultimate fate of the Special Commission's Preliminary Draft Convention will be. If the European Union states and the United States cannot agree upon a convention sufficiently attractive to make eventual ratification by them a reasonable possibility, the exercise will likely have been of academic interest only.[6]

Can the Special Commission's draft be turned into a convention ratifiable on a worldwide basis? A procedure has been proposed and accepted by the Conference[7] that will test whether the needed consensus can be achieved. The Conference's nineteenth session would be held in two stages. The first stage, a session of not more than two weeks in June 2001, would break new ground procedurally for The Hague's diplomatic conferences; the Conference's Rules of Procedure for Plenary Meetings, which limit debate and apply a strict majority principle, would not apply. The session would instead try to reach consensus on the issues thought to be crucial for a convention acceptable to Europe and to the United States. By the fall of 2000, informal discussions, open to all delegations, would begin to prepare the ground for the June 2001 session. If the results achieved at that session were sufficiently promising – and perhaps even if they were not – a second and final session of two to three weeks would be held in late 2001 or early 2002. The Rules of Procedure for Plenary Meetings would apply to any such session.

Why the Present Impasse?

The issues raised by a convention on jurisdiction and foreign judgments in civil and commercial matters are many, varied, and difficult. Different legal systems have different practices, procedures, and rules. Moreover, in the last decade, the rapid development and spread of commerce and new technologies have raised difficult and still unresolved economic, political, and legal issues in such fields as intellectual property and electronic commerce. But the present impasse has other deep and pervasive causes, as well.

---

6 This is better than nothing; the consultations, as well as their ultimate failure, could serve to further discussion and reform of national laws. See Kevin M. Clermont, Jurisdictional Salvation and the Hague Treaty, 85 Cornell L. Rev. 89 (1999); Linda J. Silberman and Andreas F. Lowenfeld, A Different Challenge for the ALI: Herein of Foreign Country Judgments, an International Treaty, and an American Statute, 75 Ind. L. J. 635 (2000); see also papers by Linda J. Silberman and Kevin M. Clermont and Kuo-Chang Huang in this volume.

7 *See* Communication of August 9, *supra* note 5, announcing that the Nineteenth Session of the Conference would begin in June 2001. The conclusions of the Special Commission of May 2000 on General Affairs and Policy of the Conference (*supra* note 5, at 12) make clear that this session would be "for the purpose of discussing any proposals that have been made, but with out decisions being made at that session, unless consensus or a near consensus is reached on certain proposals. The second, and concluding, part of the Nineteenth Session would be held late in 2001 or early 2002; it would "proceed in the normal way for Diplomatic Conferences" (*ibidem*); *see also id.* at 10–12.

The work of the Special Commission was dominated from the beginning by the model of a regional convention, concluded by legal orders with convergent legal traditions and cultures that reflects a high degree of consensus on basic issues. The economies and legal systems of the original parties to the Brussels Convention – Belgium, France, the Federal Republic of Germany, Italy, Luxembourg, and The Netherlands – had many common elements; furthermore, the Six aspired to economic federation. In addition, they still adhered, at least in principle, to the teachings of Savigny: Each broad category of legal relationships was, ideally, to be regulated by the substantive law of the same legal order regardless of the forum in which the litigation was conducted.[8] This tendency has since been strengthened through unification of choice-of-law rules in the European Union, whether by multilateral conventions (as the Rome Convention on the Law Applicable to Contractual Obligations) or by EU legislation. Where "decisional harmony" – "international uniformity of decisions" – is assured, jurisdictional rules may be seen as essentially outcome-neutral. Accordingly, decisive weight can be given in their design to promote a well-functioning market by ensuring the "free movement of judgments" and providing predictable and easily administered jurisdictional norms. In these circumstances, consensus was both necessary and attainable.

States that later joined the European Community – the United Kingdom, Ireland, and Denmark, in particular – accepted the Brussels Convention as part of a package deal in order to obtain the advantage of membership in an emerging economic and political union. On a worldwide basis, such a union is, at the most, a remote prospect; moreover, fundamentally the negotiating parties at The Hague with respect to certain basic issues hold different views. The Special Commission never fully understood that, to produce a convention acceptable worldwide, compromises would have to be worked out where the concerned legal systems hold significantly different views regarding such fundamental matters as whether, in principle, rules of adjudicatory authority should tend to favor plaintiffs or defendants and whether it is appropriate for judges to exercise considerable or little discretion in invoking adjudicatory authority and recognizing foreign adjudications.

These differences rest in significant measure on a fundamental discordance between the views of the United States and of most, perhaps all, European Union states concerning the role of adjudication in contemporary society. Does adjudication contribute importantly to development of, and adjustments in, civic society? Or are these matters best left in the hands of other non-judicial institutions? Societies that take the former view vest significantly greater creative responsibility and broader, more discretionary adjudicatory authority in their courts than do societies that prefer that development and adjustment to be the responsibility of non-judicial institutions.

To some extent, these differences can be bridged through compromise. Article 33, for example, represents a promising compromise to the vexing problem of the extent to which – if at all – judgments for non-compensatory damages, in particular,

---

8 *See, e.g.*, Jan Kropholler, Internationles Privatrecht 35–41 (3rd ed., Tübingen, Mohr (Siebeck) 1997).

punitive damages, or for compensatory damages that are grossly excessive under the standards of the court addressed, are entitled to recognition and enforcement.[9] Most provisions of paragraph (2) of Article 18 *Prohibited Grounds of Jurisdiction* can be seen as reflecting reciprocal compromises. For example, three exorbitant bases of unlimited general jurisdiction have been foresworn: property, regardless of its value, present in the state (German ZPO, § 23); nationality of the plaintiff (French Code Civil, Article 14); and tag jurisdiction (United States and the United Kingdom).

Compromises have been achieved as well through the various provisions respecting required grounds of jurisdiction. In this area, however, another complication arises. American jurisdictional theory and practice have, for a variety of reasons, developed along lines so different from most European theory and practice that several of the provisions of Chapter II on Jurisdiction – e.g., Article 6 *Contracts* and Article 14 *Multiple Defendants* – are not only theoretically flawed in the American view but also, in various applications, unconstitutional under United States standards.[10] Conversely, many American jurists consider the absence of a general activity-based jurisdiction a serious – even fatal – defect in the Special Commission's draft.[11] Likewise, paragraph (1) of Article 18 *Prohibited Grounds of Jurisdiction* is seen as a potential excessive limitation to the scope of permitted jurisdiction:

> Where the defendant is habitually resident in a Contracting State, the application of a rule of jurisdiction provided for under the national law of a Contracting

---

9 The article provides:

1. In so far as a judgment awards non-compensatory, including exemplary or punitive, damages, it shall be recognized at least to the extent that similar or comparable damages could have been awarded in the State addressed.
2. (a) Where the debtor, after proceedings in which the creditor has the opportunity to be heard, satisfies the court addressed that the circumstances, including those existing in the State of origin, grossly excessive damages have been awarded, recognition may be limited to a lesser amount.
   (b) In no event shall the court addressed recognize the judgment in an amount less than that which could have been awarded in the State addressed in the same circumstances, including those existing in the State of origin.
3. In applying paragraph 1 or 2, the court addressed shall take into account whether and to what extent the damages awarded by the court of origin serve to cover costs and expenses relating to the proceedings.

10 *See* the papers for the Symposium on "Could a Treaty Trump Supreme Court Jurisdiction?", 61 Alb. L. Rev. 1159–1307 (1998); Ronald A. Brand, Due Process, Jurisdiction and a Hague Judgments Convention, 60 U. Pitt. L. Rev. 661 (1999).

11 *See, e.g.*, Andreas F. Lowenfeld, Thoughts About a Multinational Judgments Convention: A Reaction to the von Mehren Report, 57 Law & Contemp. Probs. (No. 3) 289, 296 (1994); Peter D. Trooboff, Proposed Hague Conference General Convention on Jurisdiction and the Recognition and Enforcement of Judgments – Some Thoughts on Finding Solutions to Tough Issues, in Barrás et al. (eds.), E Pluribus Unum – Liber Amircorum Georges A.L. Droz 461, 464–65 (The Hague et al., Nijhoff, 1996). Some authors, however, hope the Hague Convention will lead to the elimination of this basis. See Clermont, *supra* note 6, at 114–15; Stephen B. Burbank, Jurisdiction to Adjudicate: End of the Century or Beginning of the Millennium?, 7 Tul. J. Int'l Comp. L. 111, 119 (1999).

State is prohibited if there is no substantial connection between that state and the dispute.

THE ADVANTAGES OF A MIXED CONVENTION[12]

Clearly, the Brussels Convention was in many respects and at many levels a thoroughly inappropriate model for the work of the Special Commission on international jurisdiction and the effects of foreign judgments in civil and commercial matters. In retrospect, one sees that the Commission should have begun its work not by seeking to adapt Brussels for its purposes, but by exploring what might reasonably be accomplished in a worldwide convention.

From the start of negotiations, the American delegation opposed the use of the Brussels Convention's double-convention format as the basis for of the Special Commission's work.[13] Instead, the Delegation proposed the more flexible and open-ended mixed-convention format.[14] In the delegation's view, the resulting convention would be more widely acceptable than a double convention, which would prescribe the jurisdictional bases that a state must make available and proscribe all other assertions of adjudicatory authority in matters within the Convention's scope.

---

12 The author first discussed the mixed-convention approach in 1993: A. von Mehren, Recognition of United States Judgments Abroad and Foreign Judgments in the United States, 57 RabelsZ 449, 456–459 (1993), and the proposal was further developed in Recognition and Enforcement of Foreign Judgments: A New Approach for the Hague Conference?, 57 Law & Contemp. Probs. (No. 3) 271 (1994); The Case for a Convention-mixte Approach to Jurisdiction to Adjudicate and Recognition and Enforcement of Foreign Judgments, 61 RabelsZ 86 (1997); Remarks by Arthur T. von Mehren upon Receiving the 1997 Leonard J. Theberge Award for Private International Law, 31 Int'l Lawyer 722 (1997); Enforcing Judgments Abroad: Reflections on the Design of Recognition Conventions, 24 Brook. J. Int'l L. 17–29 (1998); Jurisdictional Requirements: To What Extent Should the State of Origin's Interpretation of Convention Rules Control for Recognition and Enforcement Purposes?, in Andreas F. Lowenfeld and Linda J. Silberman (eds.), The Hague Convention on Jurisdiction and Judgments, Records of a Conference Held at New York University School of Law, April 30–May 1, 1999 (Juris Publishing).

13 Brussels provides in Article 3, paragraph (1) that "Persons domiciled in a Contracting State may be sued in the courts of another Contracting State only by virtue of the rules set out in Sections 2 to 6 of this Title [II, Jurisdiction]."

14 Conclusions (drawn up by the Permanent Bureau) of the Special Commission charged with presenting the proposed jurisdiction and recognition project to the Eighteenth Session for inclusion in the Agenda of its Nineteenth Session state that, during the commission's second meeting (June 4–7, 1996),

> several experts reverted to the hypothesis that there might be a series of bases for assuming jurisdiction, described as a 'grey area'. This hypothesis was contested by other delegations, insofar as it called in question the consensus to the effect that the efforts of the Special Commission and of Member States ought primarily to be focused on the establishment of a double convention containing one single list of bases for assuming jurisdiction (called a 'white' or 'green list'), together with competences which were excluded (called 'black' or 'red list').

Conclusions of the Special Commission's second meeting on the recognition and enforcement of foreign judgments in civil and commercial matters, I Proceedings of the Eighteenth Session, *supra* note 1, at 191, col. 2.

The Special Commission's members were thoroughly familiar with single and double conventions. In the absence of strong bonds – in particular, those economic and political in nature – the single convention format is appropriate. Limited to regulating indirect jurisdiction, the single convention reflects the lack of a strong sense of interdependence and the absence of neutral institutions that can control the interpretation and application of each state's international obligations.

Double conventions, on the other hand, regulate both direct and indirect jurisdiction. Jurisdictionally speaking, they divide Gaul into two parts: required and prohibited, those claims of adjudicatory authority that must – and those that must not – be granted. Federal systems, especially the United States, have long provided functional approximations of double conventions;[15] examples of international double conventions were first provided by the Brussels Convention, and later, the Lugano Convention. Double conventions are appropriate and achievable, as well, where the legal orders concerned have relatively common legal traditions and cultures and where economic and political considerations favoring participation count more strongly for the given state than do relevant objections based on its legal tradition and culture. In addition, a neutral institution – in the case of the Brussels Convention, the European Court of Justice – must be available to assure that the member states respect their obligations both in asserting adjudicatory authority and recognizing and enforcing judgments. Where these conditions are not satisfied, however, a more limited approach is necessary and Gaul must ultimately be divided, for purpose of jurisdiction, into three parts:[16] required, prohibited, and permitted.

The single convention and the double convention lie at the two extremes of a spectrum that runs from states essentially without strong political and economic commitments vis-à-vis others to states with such commitments. Mixed conventions come into question as states grow less politically and economically independent, but lack a sufficiently compelling sense of interdependence as well as supervisory supranational institutions. Mixed conventions combine elements from single and double conventions in various ways, depending on the degree of consensus that the participants have reached on the single convention/double convention spectrum.

Under a mixed convention, a contracting state's courts are free to invoke, or not to invoke, any basis of jurisdiction that is neither required nor prohibited. Further,

15 Technically speaking, the American system provides prohibited, but not required, bases; states may, but are not constitutionally required to, invoke jurisdiction unless the claim of adjudicatory authority is constitutionally impermissible. There is, however, a marked tendency for each state to claim adjudicatory authority to the extent constitutionally permitted. Accordingly, in American practice, constitutionally-permitted bases can be seen as equivalent to required bases in the sense that, generally speaking, nearly all states take jurisdiction where the Constitution of the United States permits. States are required to recognize and enforce judgments rendered on such constitutionally-permitted jurisdictional bases under the Full Faith and Credit Clause of the Constitution.

16 Unless one is satisfied with a convention that addresses only recognition and enforcement. For a discussion of why a mixed convention is preferable today to such a convention simple, see A. von Mehren, Enforcing Judgments Abroad, *supra* note 12, at 23–25.

a state is free to recognize and enforce – or deny recognition and enforcement to – judgments resting on permitted bases; the treatment accorded such judgments depends in principle on the general law of the state addressed concerning the recognition and enforcement of foreign judgments.

Had the Special Commission set out from the beginning to draft a mixed convention, when consensus was not reached on whether a given jurisdictional basis should be required or prohibited, the dilemma could have been resolved by treating the ground as a basis that was permitted in the sense that states were not required to provide it. Certain of these bases could still be recognized as grounds entitling a judgment to recognition and enforcement abroad, while others would not.[17] Sharply divergent state practices, which states are unwilling or unable to give up, could thus continue both with respect to the asserting of adjudicatory authority and the recognition and enforcement of judgments without putting into question the Convention as a whole. Acceptance of a subcategory of permitted bases without entitlement to recognition and enforcement allows as well for adaptation and development in jurisdiction and recognition practice in light of technical and economic change. A mixed convention is thus valuable even where it controls neither the use of permitted bases nor the effects abroad of judgments resting on those bases.[18]

Yet the 1996 report, in recommending that a convention on jurisdiction and judgments be placed on the agenda of the Hague Conference,

> favour[ed] the preparation of a double Convention limiting itself, as do the Conventions of Brussels and Lugano, to bases for assuming jurisdiction which are accepted and those which are rejected.[19]

Not until June 14, 1999 – four days before the close of its fourth session – did the Special Commission accept the mixed convention format. At the Sixty-fifth Plenary Meeting of the Special Commission, during the discussion that proceeded the vote on Article 17,[20] which resolved this fundamental issue,

> [s]everal experts noted that the very fact of providing for jurisdictions based on national law indicated that the present negotiations were moving towards the conclusion of a mixed rather than a double convention. Several experts affirmed that they still aspired to a double convention, others noted, however, that it was merely being realistic to recognize that in a global context only a mixed convention could be achieved.[21]

---

[17] I have developed elsewhere in more detail the two possible subcategories of permitted bases of jurisdiction. *See* A. von Mehren, Enforcing Judgments Abroad, *supra* note 12.

[18] *See generally* A. von Mehren, Enforcing Judgments Abroad, *supra* note 12, at 27–28.

[19] I Proceedings of the Eighteenth Session, *supra* note 1, at 63, col. 2.

[20] Article 17 provides:

> Subject to Articles 4, 5, 7, 8, 12, and 13, the Convention does not prevent the application by Contracting States of rules of jurisdiction under national law, provided that it is not prohibited under Article 18.

[21] Report of Meeting No. 65, p. 1.

Although the October 1999 Preliminary Draft is technically a mixed convention, it was essentially drafted as a double convention. The Special Commission clung firmly and long to that model. It is not surprising that the Commission's product remains, in spirit and approach, much more a close-knit double convention than a loose-jointed mixed convention: the draft accepts permitted bases grudgingly; flexibility and room for development are not seen as advantages; most importantly, the draft is largely the result of majoritarian rather than consensus thinking. The Special Commission, in its work, premised a higher degree of consensus among the Hague Conference members than existed, and ignored both the full implication of the fundamental differences in the economic, political, and institutional situation that made the Brussels and Lugano Conventions workable, and the global setting of a Hague convention.

Can the Project Still Succeed?

Drafting an acceptable and workable convention on jurisdiction and recognition and enforcement of foreign judgments has proved a task even more difficult and complex than any Hague delegation had anticipated. A knowledge of law and practice that only specialists possess is required to regulate fairly and effectively the matters to which the Convention would apply today. Drafting provisions that jurists with different legal and cultural backgrounds can be expected to understand and apply correctly is extremely difficult, as well. The unavailability of a court system to interpret and apply a global convention so as to bind the national courts of all contracting states is a serious shortcoming in international convention practice;[22] regrettably, a counterpart to the European Court of Justice – which authoritatively interprets and applies the Brussels Convention – is not available to non-regional international conventions such as emanate from the Hague Conference.[23]

Moreover, the drafting of global conventions is complicated by conceptual and doctrinal differences among national legal systems. Further, it is difficult to persuade

---

22 Consider, for example, the contrasting views of the United States and of European states regarding the meaning of crucial provisions of the Hague Convention of November 15, 1965 on the Service Abroad of Judicial and Extrajudicial Documents in Civil and Commercial Matters, discussed in Schlunk v. Volkswagenwerk A.G., 486 U.S. 694 (1988).

23 The Special Commission considered at some length on several occasions whether institutional arrangements functionally comparable to the European Court of Justice could be worked out for a Hague jurisdiction and recognition convention. *See* Catherine Kessedjian, Synthesis of the Work of the Special Commission of March 1998 on International Jurisdiction and the Effects of Foreign Judgments in Civil and Commercial Matters, Hague Conf. Prelim. Doc. No. 9 (July 1998), p. 45 no. 118. It may be feasible to provide for exchanges of information and occasional meetings to discuss State Parties' decisional law applying to the Convention. Such arrangements can, at best, encourage a greater measure of uniformity interpreted and applied by national courts.

Non-regional international conventions, for example the United Nations Convention on the Recognition and Enforcement of Foreign Arbitral Award of 1958, can, however, be highly successful despite this institutional weakness.

jurists – especially those who actively practice – that change is desirable. Better the devil we know, and have learned to live with, than the devil we know not. Finally, very difficult problems remain to be resolved as to the fit between any future Hague Convention on jurisdiction and enforcement of judgments and other conventions – in particular, Brussels and Lugano – dealing with the same subject matters on a regional basis.[24]

The difficulties noted need not prevent agreement on a convention that could, in time, be widely accepted; they are, however, highly likely to prevent agreement on the desirability vel non of a substantial number of particular jurisdictional bases. The ultimate fate of the Hague project depends on whether a mixed convention can be agreed that leaves control over the assumption of jurisdiction in the state of origin and recognition of the resulting judgments in the state addressed, except where broad consensus is reached respecting, as the case may be, the duty to entertain or, mutatis mutandis, to refuse to entertain, an action and the duty to enforce – or refuse to enforce – the resulting foreign judgment.[25] If international obligations respecting the exercise of direct and indirect jurisdiction are to achieve global acceptability, they must rest on a broad consensus.

Only an instrument drafted in the compromising spirit of a true mixed convention can bridge the gap between the views and practices of the United States and the European Union. Such a convention will be more modest than is a double convention and will not satisfy the jurist's longing for symmetry and completeness. But,

> [b]ecause of its flexible format, a balanced and acceptable mixed convention should be draftable. Such a convention offers reliable, low-cost information to plaintiffs and defendants [respecting where suits can be brought and judgments enforced] and [thus] would improve their lot generally. By designating *required* and *prohibited* jurisdictional bases, it would both encourage the use of higher quality bases and protect defendants against various exorbitant claims of adjudicatory authority. Over time, a well designed mixed-convention should have as well a distinctly beneficial effect on general thinking and practice respecting the exercise of adjudicatory authority and the enforcement of foreign judgments.[26]

The question remains whether the delegations to the Hague Conference have not only the skill and energy, but also the desire, will, and compromising spirit, needed to snatch success from the jaws of failure. During the Special Commission's sessions, the European Union countries displayed an increasing tendency toward block voting.

---

24 *See* Annex to the Special Commission's 1999 Preliminary Draft Convention; Andreas Bucher, Vers une convention mondiale sur la compétence et les jugements étrangers, 122 La Semaine Judicaire II, 77, at 116–18 (2000).

25 This opinion is shared by, e.g., Lowenfeld, *supra* note 11, at 295–96; Harold G. Maier, A Hague Conference Judgments Convention and United States Courts: A Problem and a Possibility, 61 Alb. L. Rev. 1207, 1220–24; Brand, *supra* note 10, at 706.

26 A. von Mehren, Enforcing Judgments Abroad, *supra* note 12, at 28.

This circumstance helps to explain the strong and pervasive effect that the Brussels Convention had on the October 1999 draft. In the long run, block voting is, of course, self-defeating if a convention capable of global acceptance is desired. Whether a sufficiently large and representative group of delegations is prepared to go forward in a spirit of compromise and consensus is, accordingly, a threshold question for the future of a Hague Convention on jurisdiction and recognition.

Assuming that the road to a true mixed convention – and to negotiation in such a spirit – is open, in what measure and what ways could the Special Commission's draft serve as its foundation? Only a few observations on this topic can be ventured here.

The Commission's draft can serve as a convenient and useful structural framework for negotiations. Many of its provisions would require little if any adaptation for use in a more loose-jointed, open-ended mixed convention. On the other hand, certain of the draft's provisions would be highly controversial. Where the controversy respected the propriety of exercising adjudicatory authority, the difficulty might be overcome by treating the claim as permitted rather than required or prohibited. In other cases, the provision could be redrafted in narrower terms, thus allocating a part of the disputed provision to the permitted area, while retaining part as either required or prohibited. Another modification that might make the Convention more broadly acceptable would be to reduce the Convention's range. Limiting the recognition and enforcement provisions' coverage to money judgments would, for example, make the Convention considerably easier to understand and apply.

The October 1999 Hague draft represents a great deal of hard, informed, and intelligent work. Its existence can facilitate and expedite the drafting of a convention appropriate for global use. The Special Commission's labors need not be in vain.

Appendices

Hague Conference on Private International Law
Preliminary Draft Convention on Jurisdiction and Foreign Judgments in Civil and Commercial Matters

Adopted by the Special Commission on October 30, 1999
Amended Version (new numbering of articles)

CHAPTER I

SCOPE OF THE CONVENTION

Article 1

Substantive Scope

1. The Convention applies to civil and commercial matters. It shall not extend in particular to revenue, customs or administrative matters.
2. The Convention does not apply to –
   (a) the status and legal capacity of natural persons;
   (b) maintenance obligations;
   (c) matrimonial property regimes and other rights and obligations arising out of marriage or similar relationships;
   (d) wills and succession;
   (e) insolvency, composition or analogous proceedings;
   (f) social security;
   (g) arbitration and proceedings related thereto;
   (h) admiralty or maritime matters.
3. A dispute is not excluded from the scope of the Convention by the mere fact that a government, a governmental agency or any other person acting for the State is a party thereto.
4. Nothing in this Convention affects the privileges and immunities of sovereign States or of entities of sovereign States, or of international organisations.

Article 2

Territorial Scope

1. The provisions of Chapter II shall apply in the courts of a Contracting State unless all the parties are habitually resident in that State. However, even if all the parties are habitually resident in that State –
   (a) Article 4 shall apply if they have agreed that a court or courts of another Contracting State have jurisdiction to determine the dispute;
   (b) Article 12, regarding exclusive jurisdiction, shall apply;
   (c) Articles 21 and 22 shall apply where the court is required to determine whether

J.J. Barceló and K.M. Clermont (eds.), A Global Law of Jurisdiction and Judgments: Lessons from The Hague, 295–310

to decline jurisdiction or suspend its proceedings on the grounds that the dispute ought to be determined in the courts of another Contracting State.

2. The provisions of Chapter III apply to the recognition and enforcement in a Contracting State of a judgment rendered in another Contracting State.

CHAPTER II

JURISDICTION

Article 3

Defendant's Forum

1. Subject to the provisions of the Convention, a defendant may be sued in the courts of the State where that defendant is habitually resident.
2. For the purposes of the Convention, an entity or person other than a natural person shall be considered to be habitually resident in the State –
   (a) where it has its statutory seat,
   (b) under whose law it was incorporated or formed,
   (c) where it has its central administration, or
   (d) where it has its principal place of business.

Article 4

Choice of Court

1. If the parties have agreed that a court or courts of a Contracting State shall have jurisdiction to settle any dispute which has arisen or may arise in connection with a particular legal relationship, that court or those courts shall have jurisdiction, and that jurisdiction shall be exclusive unless the parties have agreed otherwise. Where an agreement having exclusive effect designates a court or courts of a non-Contracting State, courts in Contracting States shall decline jurisdiction or suspend proceedings unless the court or courts chosen have themselves declined jurisdiction.
2. An agreement within the meaning of paragraph 1 shall be valid as to form, if it was entered into or confirmed –
   (a) in writing;
   (b) by any other means of communication which renders information accessible so as to be usable for subsequent reference;
   (c) in accordance with a usage which is regularly observed by the parties;
   (d) in accordance with a usage of which the parties were or ought to have been aware and which is regularly observed by parties to contracts of the same nature in the particular trade or commerce concerned.
3. Agreements conferring jurisdiction and similar clauses in trust instruments shall be without effect if they conflict with the provisions of Article 7, 8 or 12.

Article 5

Appearance by the Defendant

1. Subject to Article 12, a court has jurisdiction if the defendant proceeds on the merits without contesting jurisdiction.
2. The defendant has the right to contest jurisdiction no later than at the time of the first defence on the merits.

Article 6

Contracts

A plaintiff may bring an action in contract in the courts of a State in which –

(a) in matters relating to the supply of goods, the goods were supplied in whole or in part;
(b) in matters relating to the provision of services, the services were provided in whole or in part;
(c) in matters relating both to the supply of goods and the provision of services, performance of the principal obligation took place in whole or in part.

Article 7

Contracts Concluded by Consumers

1. A plaintiff who concluded a contract for a purpose which is outside its trade or profession, hereafter designated as the consumer, may bring a claim in the courts of the State in which it is habitually resident, if –
   (a) the conclusion of the contract on which the claim is based is related to trade or professional activities that the defendant has engaged in or directed to that State, in particular in soliciting business through means of publicity, and
   (b) the consumer has taken the steps necessary for the conclusion of the contract in that State.
2. A claim against the consumer may only be brought by a person who entered into the contract in the course of its trade or profession before the courts of the State of the habitual residence of the consumer.
3. The parties to a contract within the meaning of paragraph 1 may, by an agreement which conforms with the requirements of Article 4, make a choice of court –
   (a) if such agreement is entered into after the dispute has arisen, or
   (b) to the extent only that it allows the consumer to bring proceedings in another court.

Article 8

Individual Contracts of Employment

1. In matters relating to individual contracts of employment –
   (a) an employee may bring an action against the employer,

(i) in the courts of the State in which the employee habitually carries out his work or in the courts of the last State in which he did so, or
(ii) if the employee does not or did not habitually carry out his work in any one State, in the courts of the State in which the business that engaged the employee is or was situated;

(b) a claim against an employee may be brought by the employer only,
(i) in the courts of the State where the employee is habitually resident, or
(ii) in the courts of the State in which the employee habitually carries out his work.

2. The parties to a contract within the meaning of paragraph 1 may, by an agreement which conforms with the requirements of Article 4, make a choice of court –
(a) if such agreement is entered into after the dispute has arisen, or
(b) to the extent only that it allows the employee to bring proceedings in courts other than those indicated in this Article or in Article 3 of the Convention.

Article 9

Branches [and Regular Commercial Activity]

A plaintiff may bring an action in the courts of a State in which a branch, agency or any other establishment of the defendant is situated, [or where the defendant has carried on regular commercial activity by other means,] provided that the dispute relates directly to the activity of that branch, agency or establishment [or to that regular commercial activity].

Article 10

Torts or Delicts

1. A plaintiff may bring an action in tort or delict in the courts of the State –
(a) in which the act or omission that caused injury occurred, or
(b) in which the injury arose, unless the defendant establishes that the person claimed to be responsible could not reasonably have foreseen that the act or omission could result in an injury of the same nature in that State.
2. Paragraph 1(b) shall not apply to injury caused by anti-trust violations, in particular price-fixing or monopolisation, or conspiracy to inflict economic loss.
3. A plaintiff may also bring an action in accordance with paragraph 1 when the act or omission, or the injury may occur.
4. If an action is brought in the courts of a State only on the basis that the injury arose or may occur there, those courts shall have jurisdiction only in respect of the injury that occurred or may occur in that State, unless the injured person has his or her habitual residence in that State.

Article 11

Trusts

1. In proceedings concerning the validity, construction, effects, administration or variation of a trust created voluntarily and evidenced in writing, the courts of a

Contracting State designated in the trust instrument for this purpose shall have exclusive jurisdiction. Where the trust instrument designates a court or courts of a non-Contracting State, courts in Contracting States shall decline jurisdiction or suspend proceedings unless the court or courts chosen have themselves declined jurisdiction.

2. In the absence of such designation, proceedings may be brought before the courts of a State –
   (a) in which is situated the principal place of administration of the trust;
   (b) whose law is applicable to the trust;
   (c) with which the trust has the closest connection for the purpose of the proceedings.

Article 12

Exclusive Jurisdiction

1. In proceedings which have as their object rights in rem in immovable property or tenancies of immovable property, the courts of the Contracting State in which the property is situated have exclusive jurisdiction, unless in proceedings which have as their object tenancies of immovable property, the tenant is habitually resident in a different State.
2. In proceedings which have as their object the validity, nullity, or dissolution of a legal person, or the validity or nullity of the decisions of its organs, the courts of a Contracting State whose law governs the legal person have exclusive jurisdiction.
3. In proceedings which have as their object the validity or nullity of entries in public registers, the courts of the Contracting State in which the register is kept have exclusive jurisdiction.
4. In proceedings which have as their object the registration, validity, [or] nullity[, or revocation or infringement,] of patents, trade marks, designs or other similar rights required to be deposited or registered, the courts of the Contracting State in which the deposit or registration has been applied for, has taken place or, under the terms of an international convention, is deemed to have taken place, have exclusive jurisdiction. This shall not apply to copyright or any neighbouring rights, even though registration or deposit of such rights is possible.

[5. In relation to proceedings which have as their object the infringement of patents, the preceding paragraph does not exclude the jurisdiction of any other court under the Convention or under the national law of a Contracting State.]

[6. The previous paragraphs shall not apply when the matters referred to therein arise as incidental questions.]

Article 13

Provisional and Protective Measures

1. A court having jurisdiction under Articles 3 to 12 to determine the merits of the case has jurisdiction to order any provisional or protective measures.

2. The courts of a State in which property is located have jurisdiction to order any provisional or protective measures in respect of that property.
3. A court of a Contracting State not having jurisdiction under paragraphs 1 or 2 may order provisional or protective measures, provided that –
   (a) their enforcement is limited to the territory of that State, and
   (b) their purpose is to protect on an interim basis a claim on the merits which is pending or to be brought by the requesting party.

Article 14

Multiple Defendants

1. A plaintiff bringing an action against a defendant in a court of the State in which that defendant is habitually resident may also proceed in that court against other defendants not habitually resident in that State if –
   (a) the claims against the defendant habitually resident in that State and the other defendants are so closely connected that they should be adjudicated together to avoid a serious risk of inconsistent judgments, and
   (b) as to each defendant not habitually resident in that State, there is a substantial connection between that State and the dispute involving that defendant.
2. Paragraph 1 shall not apply to a codefendant invoking an exclusive choice of court clause agreed with the plaintiff and conforming with Article 4.

Article 15

Counter-claims

A court which has jurisdiction to determine a claim under the provisions of the Convention shall also have jurisdiction to determine a counter-claim arising out of the transaction or occurrence on which the original claim is based.

Article 16

Third Party Claims

1. A court which has jurisdiction to determine a claim under the provisions of the Convention shall also have jurisdiction to determine a claim by a defendant against a third party for indemnity or contribution in respect of the claim against that defendant to the extent that such an action is permitted by national law, provided that there is a substantial connection between that State and the dispute involving that third party.
2. Paragraph 1 shall not apply to a third party invoking an exclusive choice of court clause agreed with the defendant and conforming with Article 4.

Article 17

Jurisdiction Based on National Law

Subject to Articles 4, 5, 7, 8, 12 and 13, the Convention does not prevent the application by Contracting States of rules of jurisdiction under national law, provided that this is not prohibited under Article 18.

Article 18

Prohibited Grounds of Jurisdiction

1. Where the defendant is habitually resident in a Contracting State, the application of a rule of jurisdiction provided for under the national law of a Contracting State is prohibited if there is no substantial connection between that State and the dispute.
2. In particular, jurisdiction shall not be exercised by the courts of a Contracting State on the basis solely of one or more of the following –
   (a) the presence or the seizure in that State of property belonging to the defendant, except where the dispute is directly related to that property;
   (b) the nationality of the plaintiff;
   (c) the nationality of the defendant;
   (d) the domicile, habitual or temporary residence, or presence of the plaintiff in that State;
   (e) the carrying on of commercial or other activities by the defendant in that State, except where the dispute is directly related to those activities;
   (f) the service of a writ upon the defendant in that State;
   (g) the unilateral designation of the forum by the plaintiff;
   (h) proceedings in that State for declaration of enforceability or registration or for the enforcement of a judgment, except where the dispute is directly related to such proceedings;
   (i) the temporary residence or presence of the defendant in that State;
   (j) the signing in that State of the contract from which the dispute arises.
3. Nothing in this Article shall prevent a court in a Contracting State from exercising jurisdiction under national law in an action [seeking relief] [claiming damages] in respect of conduct which constitutes –
   [Variant One:
   (a) genocide, a crime against humanity or a war crime[, as defined in the Statute of the International Criminal Court]; or
   (b) a serious crime against a natural person under international law; or
   (c) a grave violation against a natural person of non-derogable fundamental rights established under international law, such as torture, slavery, forced labour and disappeared persons.

   Sub-paragraphs [(b) and] (c) above apply only if the party seeking relief is exposed to a risk of a denial of justice because proceedings in another State are not possible or cannot reasonably be required.]

   [Variant Two:
   a serious crime under international law, provided that this State has established its criminal jurisdiction over that crime in accordance with an international treaty to which it is a party and that the claim is for civil compensatory damages for death or serious bodily injury arising from that crime.]

Article 19

Authority of the Court Seised

Where the defendant does not enter an appearance, the court shall verify whether Article 18 prohibits it from exercising jurisdiction if –

(a) national law so requires; or
(b) the plaintiff so requests; or
[(c) the defendant so requests, even after judgment is entered in accordance with procedures established under national law; or]
[(d) the document which instituted the proceedings or an equivalent document was served on the defendant in another Contracting State.]

or

[(d) it appears from the documents filed by the plaintiff that the defendant's address is in another Contracting State.]

Article 20

1. The court shall stay the proceedings so long as it is not established that the document which instituted the proceedings or an equivalent document, including the essential elements of the claim, was notified to the defendant in sufficient time and in such a way as to enable him to arrange for his defence, or that all necessary steps have been taken to that effect.

[2. Paragraph 1 shall not affect the use of international instruments concerning the service abroad of judicial and extrajudicial documents in civil or commercial matters, in accordance with the law of the forum.]

[3. Paragraph 1 shall not apply, in case of urgency, to any provisional or protective measures.]

Article 21

Lis Pendens

1. When the same parties are engaged in proceedings in courts of different Contracting States and when such proceedings are based on the same causes of action, irrespective of the relief sought, the court second seised shall suspend the proceedings if the court first seised has jurisdiction and is expected to render a judgment capable of being recognised under the Convention in the State of the court second seised, unless the latter has exclusive jurisdiction under Article 4 or 12.
2. The court second seised shall decline jurisdiction as soon as it is presented with a judgment rendered by the court first seised that complies with the requirements for recognition or enforcement under the Convention.
3. Upon application of a party, the court second seised may proceed with the case if the plaintiff in the court first seised has failed to take the necessary steps to

bring the proceedings to a decision on the merits or if that court has not rendered such a decision within a reasonable time.

4. The provisions of the preceding paragraphs apply to the court second seised even in a case where the jurisdiction of that court is based on the national law of that State in accordance with Article 17.
5. For the purpose of this Article, a court shall be deemed to be seised –
   (a) when the document instituting the proceedings or an equivalent document is lodged with the court, or
   (b) if such document has to be served before being lodged with the court, when it is received by the authority responsible for service or served on the defendant.

   [As appropriate, universal time is applicable.]
6. If in the action before the court first seised the plaintiff seeks a determination that it has no obligation to the defendant, and if an action seeking substantive relief is brought in the court second seised –
   (a) the provisions of paragraphs 1 to 5 above shall not apply to the court second seised, and
   (b) the court first seised shall suspend the proceedings at the request of a party if the court second seised is expected to render a decision capable of being recognised under the Convention.
7. This Article shall not apply if the court first seised, on application by a party, determines that the court second seised is clearly more appropriate to resolve the dispute, under the conditions specified in Article 22.

Article 22

Exceptional Circumstances for Declining Jurisdiction

1. In exceptional circumstances, when the jurisdiction of the court seised is not founded on an exclusive choice of court agreement valid under Article 4, or on Article 7, 8 or 12, the court may, on application by a party, suspend its proceedings if in that case it is clearly inappropriate for that court to exercise jurisdiction and if a court of another State has jurisdiction and is clearly more appropriate to resolve the dispute. Such application must be made no later than at the time of the first defence on the merits.
2. The court shall take into account, in particular –
   (a) any inconvenience to the parties in view of their habitual residence;
   (b) the nature and location of the evidence, including documents and witnesses, and the procedures for obtaining such evidence;
   (c) applicable limitation or prescription periods;
   (d) the possibility of obtaining recognition and enforcement of any decision on the merits.
3. In deciding whether to suspend the proceedings, a court shall not discriminate on the basis of the nationality or habitual residence of the parties.

4. If the court decides to suspend its proceedings under paragraph 1, it may order the defendant to provide security sufficient to satisfy any decision of the other court on the merits. However, it shall make such an order if the other court has jurisdiction only under Article 17, unless the defendant establishes that sufficient assets exist in the State of that other court or in another State where the court's decision could be enforced.
5. When the court has suspended its proceedings under paragraph 1,
   (a) it shall decline to exercise jurisdiction if the court of the other State exercises jurisdiction, or if the plaintiff does not bring the proceedings in that State within the time specified by the court, or
   (b) it shall proceed with the case if the court of the other State decides not to exercise jurisdiction.

CHAPTER III

Recognition and Enforcement

Article 23

Definition of "Judgment"

For the purposes of this Chapter, "judgment" means –

(a) any decision given by a court, whatever it may be called, including a decree or order, as well as the determination of costs or expenses by an officer of the court, provided that it relates to a decision which may be recognised or enforced under the Convention;

(b) decisions ordering provisional or protective measures in accordance with Article 13, paragraph 1.

Article 24

Judgments Excluded from Chapter III

This Chapter shall not apply to judgments based on a ground of jurisdiction provided for by national law in accordance with Article 17.

Article 25

Judgments to Be Recognised or Enforced

1. A judgment based on a ground of jurisdiction provided for in Articles 3 to 13, or which is consistent with any such ground, shall be recognised or enforced under this Chapter.
2. In order to be recognised, a judgment referred to in paragraph 1 must have the effect of res judicata in the State of origin.
3. In order to be enforceable, a judgment referred to in paragraph 1 must be enforceable in the State of origin.

4. However, recognition or enforcement may be postponed if the judgment is the subject of review in the State of origin or if the time limit for seeking a review has not expired.

Article 26

Judgments Not to Be Recognised or Enforced

A judgment based on a ground of jurisdiction which conflicts with Articles 4, 5, 7, 8 or 12, or whose application is prohibited by virtue of Article 18, shall not be recognised or enforced.

Article 27

Verification of Jurisdiction

1. The court addressed shall verify the jurisdiction of the court of origin.
2. In verifying the jurisdiction of the court of origin, the court addressed shall be bound by the findings of fact on which the court of origin based its jurisdiction, unless the judgment was given by default.
3. Recognition or enforcement of a judgment may not be refused on the ground that the court addressed considers that the court of origin should have declinedjurisdiction in accordance with Article 22.

Article 28

Grounds for Refusal of Recognition or Enforcement

1. Recognition or enforcement of a judgment may be refused if –
   (a) proceedings between the same parties and having the same subject matter are pending before a court of the State addressed, if first seised in accordance with Article 21;
   (b) the judgment is inconsistent with a judgment rendered, either in the State addressed or in another State, provided that in the latter case the judgment is capable of being recognised or enforced in the State addressed;
   (c) the judgment results from proceedings incompatible with fundamental principles of procedure of the State addressed, including the right of each party to be heard by an impartial and independent court;
   (d) the document which instituted the proceedings or an equivalent document, including the essential elements of the claim, was not notified to the defendant in sufficient time and in such a way as to enable him to arrange for his defence;
   (e) the judgment was obtained by fraud in connection with a matter of procedure;
   (f) recognition or enforcement would be manifestly incompatible with the public policy of the State addressed.
2. Without prejudice to such review as is necessary for the purpose of application

of the provisions of this Chapter, there shall be no review of the merits of the judgment rendered by the court of origin.

Article 29

Documents to Be Produced

1. The party seeking recognition or applying for enforcement shall produce –
   (a) a complete and certified copy of the judgment;
   (b) if the judgment was rendered by default, the original or a certified copy of a document establishing that the document which instituted the proceedings or an equivalent document was notified to the defaulting party;
   (c) all documents required to establish that the judgment is res judicata in the State of origin or, as the case may be, is enforceable in that State;
   (d) if the court addressed so requires, a translation of the documents referred to above, made by a person qualified to do so.
2. No legalisation or similar formality may be required.
3. If the terms of the judgment do not permit the court addressed to verify whether the conditions of this Chapter have been complied with, that court may require the production of any other necessary documents.

Article 30

Procedure

The procedure for recognition, declaration of enforceability or registration for enforcement, and the enforcement of the judgment, are governed by the law of the State addressed so far as the Convention does not provide otherwise. The court addressed shall act expeditiously.

Article 31

Cost of Procedings

No security, bond or deposit, however described, to guarantee the payment of costs or expenses shall be required by reason only that the applicant is a national of, or has its habitual residence in, another Contracting State.

Article 32

Legal Aid

Natural persons habitually resident in a Contracting State shall be entitled, in proceedings for recognition or enforcement, to legal aid under the same conditions as apply to persons habitually resident in the requested State.

Article 33

Damages

1. In so far as a judgment awards non-compensatory, including exemplary or punitive, damages, it shall be recognised at least to the extent that similar or comparable damages could have been awarded in the State addressed.
2. (a) Where the debtor, after proceedings in which the creditor has the opportunity to be heard, satisfies the court addressed that in the circumstances, including those existing in the State of origin, grossly excessive damages have been awarded, recognition may be limited to a lesser amount.
   (b) In no event shall the court addressed recognise the judgment in anamount less than that which could have been awarded in the State addressed in the same circumstances, including those existing in the State of origin.
3. In applying paragraph 1 or 2, the court addressed shall take into account whether and to what extent the damages awarded by the court of origin serve to cover costs and expenses relating to the proceedings.

Article 34

Severability

If the judgment contains elements which are severable, one or more of them may be separately recognised, declared enforceable, registered for enforcement, or enforced.

Article 35

Authentic Instruments

1. Each Contracting State may declare that it will enforce, subject to reciprocity, authentic instruments formally drawn up or registered and enforceable in another Contracting State.
2. The authentic instrument must have been authenticated by a public authority or a delegate of a public authority and the authentication must relate to both the signature and the content of the document.

[3. The provisions concerning recognition and enforcement provided for in this Chapter shall apply as appropriate.]

Article 36

Settlements

Settlements to which a court has given its authority shall be recognised, declared enforceable or registered for enforcement in the State addressed under the same conditions as judgments falling within the Convention, so far as those conditions apply to settlements.

CHAPTER IV

General Provisions

Article 37

Relationship with Other Conventions
[See annex]

Article 38

Uniform Interpretation
1. In the interpretation of the Convention, regard is to be had to its international character and to the need to promote uniformity in its application.
2. The courts of each Contracting State shall, when applying and interpreting the Convention, take due account of the case law of other Contracting States.

[Article 39

1. Each Contracting State shall, at the request of the Secretary General of the Hague Conference on Private International Law, send to the Permanent Bureau at regular intervals copies of any significant decisions taken in applying the Convention and, as appropriate, other relevant information.
2. The Secretary General of the Hague Conference on Private International Law shall at regular intervals convene a Special Commission to review the operation of the Convention.
3. The Commission may make recommendations on the application or interpretation of the Convention and may propose modifications or revisions of the Convention or the addition of protocols.]

[Article 40

1. Upon a joint request of the parties to a dispute in which the interpretation of the Convention is at issue, or of a court of a Contracting State, the Permanent Bureau of the Hague Conference on Private International Law shall assist in the establishment of a committee of experts to make recommendations to such parties or such court.

[2. The Secretary General of the Hague Conference on Private International Law shall, as soon as possible, convene a Special Commission to draw up an optional protocol setting out rules governing the composition and procedures of the committee of experts.]]

Article 41

Federal Clause

ANNEX

Article 37

Relationship with Other Conventions

Proposal 1

1. The Convention does not affect any international instrument to which Contracting States are or become Parties and which contains provisions on matters governed by the Convention, unless a contrary declaration is made by the States Parties to such instrument.
2. However, the Convention prevails over such instruments to the extent that they provide for fora not authorized under the provisions of Article 18 of the Convention.
3. The preceding paragraphs also apply to uniform laws based on special ties of a regional or other nature between the States concerned and to instruments adopted by a community of States.

Proposal 2

1. (a) In this Article, the Brussels Convention [as amended], Regulation [...] of the European Union, and the Lugano Convention [as amended] shall be collectively referred to as "the European instruments".
   (b) A State party to either of the above Conventions or a Member State of the European Union to which the above Regulation applies shall be collectively referred to as "European instrument States".
2. Subject to the following provisions [of this Article], a European instrument State shall apply the European instruments, and not the Convention, whenever the European instruments are applicable according to their terms.
3. Except where the provisions of the European instruments on –
   (a) exclusive jurisdiction;
   (b) prorogation of jurisdiction;
   (c) lis pendens and related actions;
   (d) protective jurisdiction for consumers or employees;
   are applicable, a European instrument State shall apply Articles 3, 5 to 11, 14 to 16 and 18 of the Convention whenever the defendant is not domiciled in a European instrument State.
4. Even if the defendant is domiciled in a European instrument State, a court of such a State shall apply –
   (a) Article 4 of the Convention whenever the court chosen is not in a European instrument State;

(b) Article 12 of the Convention whenever the court with exclusive jurisdiction under that provision is not in a European instrument State; and

(c) Articles 21 and 22 of this Convention whenever the court in whose favour the proceedings are stayed or jurisdiction is declined is not a court of a European instrument State.

Note: Another provision will be needed for other conventions and instruments.

Proposal 3

Judgments of courts of a Contracting State to this Convention based on jurisdiction granted under the terms of a different international convention ("other Convention") shall be recognised and enforced in courts of Contracting States to this Convention which are also Contracting States to the other Convention. This provision shall not apply if, by reservation under Article ..., a Contracting State chooses –

(a) not to be governed by this provision, or

(b) not to be governed by this provision as to certain designated other conventions.

Hague Conference on Private International Law

COMMISSION II

JURISDICTION AND FOREIGN JUDGMENTS IN CIVIL AND COMMERCIAL MATTERS

Nineteenth Session

Summary of the Outcome of the Discussion in Commission II of the First Part of the Diplomatic Conference 6–20 June 2001

Interim Text – Prepared by the Permanent Bureau and the Co-reporters

For the sake of clarity this summary follows the order of the articles as set out in the preliminary draft Convention of October 1999. It is understood that the structure and form of the Convention awaits final discussion.[†]

*Chapter * – Substantive Scope*

Article 1 – Substantive Scope

1. The Convention applies to civil and commercial matters.[1]

It shall not extend in particular to revenue, customs or other[2] administrative matters.[3]

2. The Convention does not apply to –
   (a) the status and legal capacity of natural persons;
   (b) maintenance obligations;
   (c) matrimonial property regimes and other rights and obligations arising out of marriage or similar relationships;
   (d) wills and succession;
   (e) insolvency, composition or analogous proceedings;
   (f) social security;

[†] Note: proposals have only been included if endorsed by Member State delegations.

[1] It has been proposed to add the words 'before courts of Contracting States' at the end of the first sentence. This proposal has not been discussed. Note the statement in Preliminary Document No. 11 (the Nygh/Pocar Report) at p. 31 that there was a consensus in the Special Commission that the application of the Convention should be confined to proceedings before courts. There was no suggestion in the Diplomatic Conference that this consensus should be departed from with the possible exception of authentic instruments (see Art. 35 below). It should be noted, however, that there were proposals to include decisions of certain administrative organs in the scope of Article 12. See footnote 88 below.

[2] It was agreed to add the word 'other' in order to indicate that revenue and customs matters are also of an administrative nature.

[3] A desire was expressed for further clarification of the meaning and scope of 'administrative matters'. An attempt to provide further clarification was made, but this did not achieve consensus. That clarification would also have merged paragraph 3 with paragraph 1.

J.J. Barceló and K.M. Clermont (eds.), A Global Law of Jurisdiction and Judgments: Lessons from The Hague, 311–350

(g)[4] arbitration and proceedings related thereto;[5]
(h) admiralty or maritime matters;
[(i) anti-trust or competition claims;][6]
[(j) nuclear liability;][7]
(k)[8] *Alternative A*
[provisional and protective measures other than interim payment orders;][9]
Alternative B
[provisional or protective measures [other than those mentioned in Articles 13 and 23A];][10]
[(l) rights in rem in immovable property;][11]
[(m) validity, nullity, or dissolution of a legal person and decisions related thereto].[12]

[3. This Convention shall not apply to arbitration and proceedings related thereto, nor shall it require a Contracting State to recognise and enforce a judgment if

---

4 There was general agreement that alternative dispute resolution was also outside the scope of the Convention, except to the extent that it has resulted in a consent judgment or settlement to which the court has given its authority under Article 36, below.

5 If paragraph 3 (see below) was accepted, this sub-paragraph should be deleted.

6 There was general agreement towards the proposal's approach, subject to further study, that certain aspects of what is covered in the United States (including the Sherman Act, the Clayton Act and the antitrust portions of the Federal Trade Commission Act) by the term 'anti-trust claims' such as actions against cartels, monopolisation, abuse of market dominance, horizontal or vertical restraints, mergers and acquisitions, price fixing or price discrimination be excluded from the Convention. On the other hand, it was acknowledged that words such as 'unfair competition' (*concurrence déloyale*) went too far since in certain systems it might include matters such as misleading or deceptive practices, passing off and infringement of marks, copyrights and patents. The problem remains of finding the appropriate terminology to define the area to be excluded and which can be understood at the international level.

7 There is no consensus on this proposed exclusion.

8 This paragraph would be deleted if Article 13 (Alternative A) was adopted.

9 The intention of this Alternative (see the discussion of Article 13 below) is to exclude provisional and protective measures from the scope of the Convention but to ensure that jurisdiction to make interim payment orders remains subject to the list of prohibited jurisdictions. The proponents of this version favour the inclusion of a provision in the chapter on recognition and enforcement to clarify that interim payment orders will not be recognised or enforced under the Convention. No consensus exists on this proposal.

10 This second Alternative is primarily inspired by a wish to exclude provisional and protective measures from the scope of the Convention. It differs from the first Alternative in specifically excluding each of the categories of provisional measures and protective measures by using the word 'or' and by omitting any reference to interim payments. However, the words within the final brackets 'other than those mentioned in Articles 13 and 23A' are put forward as a further option for those who favour a restricted provision for jurisdiction and recognition and enforcement in respect of provisional and protective measures. There is no consensus in respect of any of these options.

11 The exclusion of this matter from the scope of the Convention has been proposed. See Article 12(1) below.

12 The exclusion of this matter from the scope of the Convention has been proposed. See Article 12(2) below.

the exercise of jurisdiction by the court of origin was contrary to an arbitration agreement.][13]

4. A dispute is not excluded from the scope of the Convention by the mere fact that a government, a governmental agency or any person acting for the State is a party thereto.
5. Nothing in this Convention affects the privileges and immunities of sovereign States or of entities of sovereign States, or of international organisations.

Article 2 – Territorial Scope[14]

1. The provisions of Chapter II shall apply in the courts of a Contracting State unless all the parties are habitually resident in that State. However, even if all the parties are habitually resident in that State –
   (a) Article 4 shall apply if they have agreed that a court or courts of another Contracting State have jurisdiction to determine the dispute [provided that dispute is of an international character];[15]
   (b) Article 12, regarding exclusive jurisdiction shall apply;
   (c) Articles 21 and 22 shall apply where the court is required to determine whether to decline jurisdiction or suspend its proceedings on the grounds that the dispute ought to be determined in the courts of another Contracting State.
2. The provisions of Chapter III apply to the recognition and enforcement in a Contracting State of a judgment rendered in another Contracting State.

*Chapter ** – Jurisdiction*

Article 3 – Defendant's Forum[16]

1. Subject to the provisions of the Convention, a defendant may be sued in the courts of [a] [the] State [in which] [where] that defendant is [habitually] resident.

---

[13] This proposal is designed to meet the desire expressed that a judgment given in breach of an arbitration agreement or contrary to an arbitration award not be recognised or enforced. No consensus exists on this proposal.

[14] Another proposal for the amendment of paragraph 1 of this Article has been reproduced as part of Proposal 4 in Annex I.

[15] Concern has been expressed that sub-paragraph a) as it stands, will have the effect of making the Convention applicable to purely domestic situations involving not only parties who were habitually resident within the same State but also involving a legal relationship and a subject matter entirely confined to that State: see the Report of the co-reporters Prel Doc 11 at p. 41, note 40. The words in brackets were proposed to require an international connection. This proposal was opposed, and it was pointed out that it was difficult to define when a dispute was of an international nature and that this might lead to divergent interpretations. The view was also expressed that this issue should be determined only by the selected court. Other suggestions made were: that paragraph a) be deleted with the result that the Convention, including Article 4, would not apply if all the parties to the choice of forum agreement were habitually resident in the same State, or extending Article 22 in order to allow the selected court in such a situation to decline jurisdiction.

[16] There is agreement on the defendant's forum as a forum of general jurisdiction.

[2. For the purposes of the Convention, a natural person shall be considered to be resident –
   (a) if that person is resident in only one State, in that State;
   (b) if that person is resident in more than one State,
      (i) in the State in which that person has his or her principal residence; or
      (ii) if that person does not have a principal residence in any one State, in each State in which that person is resident.][17]

3. For the purposes of the Convention, an entity or person other than a natural person shall be considered to be [habitually] resident in the State –
   (a) where it has its statutory seat;
   (b) under whose law it was incorporated or formed;
   (c) where it has its central administration; or
   (d) where it has its principal place of business.[18]

Article 4 – Choice of Court

1. If the parties have agreed that [a court or] [the][19] courts of a Contracting State shall have jurisdiction to settle any dispute which has arisen or may arise in connection with a particular legal relationship, [that court or those] [the][20] courts [of that Contracting State][21] shall have jurisdiction[, provided the court has subject matter jurisdiction][22] and that jurisdiction shall be exclusive unless the parties have agreed otherwise. Where an agreement having exclusive effect designates [a court or] [the] courts of a non-Contracting State, courts in Contracting States shall decline jurisdiction or suspend proceedings unless the

---

17 The view has been expressed that 'habitual residence' has acquired a too technical meaning in the interpretation of earlier Hague Conventions, particularly the Convention of 1980 on the Civil Aspects of International Child Abduction. Another view favoured continuity of the established concept of 'habitual residence' and feared that 'residence' provided too slight a connection. Reference was made to the appearance of 'the temporary residence [...] of the defendant' in Article 18(2)(i), as it now stands, as one of the prohibited grounds of jurisdiction. If the proposed paragraph 2 were accepted, consequential amendments to other articles would be necessary. It was also suggested that a separate definitions article be drafted. There is no consensus on these points.

18 There appears to be agreement on this paragraph, except for the inclusion of the word 'habitual', see note 17 above. A re-numbering would be required if paragraph 2 were inserted.

19 It has been proposed to delete the reference in paragraph 1 to 'a court' and refer to 'the courts' of the chosen country, to meet the concern that paragraph 1 could allow a court to interpret a choice of forum clause in a contract as conferring jurisdiction on a specific court that it would not otherwise be authorised to exercise under national law. There was a general agreement that a choice of forum clause could only confer jurisdiction over the person of the defendant and not in respect of subject matter outside the competence of the chosen court; see the comments of the Co-reporters in Preliminary Document No 11, at p. 44. However, doubts were expressed whether this proposal was either necessary or appropriate.

20 See note 19, above.

21 See note 19, above.

22 This is an alternative proposal to address the problem referred to in note 19, above.

[court or][23] courts chosen have themselves declined jurisdiction. [Whether such an agreement is invalid for lack of consent (for example, due to fraud or duress) or incapacity shall depend on national law including its rules of private international law.][24]

2. An agreement within the meaning of paragraph 1 shall be valid as to form, if it was entered into –
   (a) in writing or by any other means of communication which renders information accessible so as to be usable for subsequent reference;
   (b) orally and confirmed in writing or by any other means of communication which renders information accessible so as to be usable for subsequent reference;
   (c) in accordance with a usage which is regularly observed by the parties;
   (d) in accordance with a usage of which the parties were or ought to have been aware and which is regularly observed by parties to contracts of the same nature in the particular trade or commerce concerned.[25]
3. Where a defendant expressly accepts jurisdiction before a court of a Contracting State, and that acceptance is [in writing or evidenced in writing], that court shall have jurisdiction.[26]

[4. The substantive validity of an agreement conferring jurisdiction shall be determined in accordance with the applicable law as designated by the choice of law rules of the forum.][27]

5. [The parties cannot be deprived of the right to enter into agreements conferring jurisdiction.][28] [However,] [such agreements and similar clauses in trust instruments shall be without effect, if they conflict with the provisions of Article 7, 8 or 12.][29]

---

23 See note 19, above.

24 This proposal seeks to confirm that the substantive validity of the choice of forum agreement is governed by the national law of the forum seised, including its choice of law rules. It also seeks to confine substantive validity to questions affecting the consent or capacity of the parties as opposed to questions of reasonableness and public policy. Objections were raised, however, that reasonableness could be an element of consent or capacity. It was also pointed out that general rules of contract validity should apply without limitation to consent or capacity. See also paragraphs 4 and 5 and footnotes 27 and 28. There was no consensus in respect of this proposal.

25 This paragraph as redrafted was accepted by agreement. The redraft removes the words 'or confirmed' from the chapeau to sub-paragraph b) where it is more appropriate.

26 This paragraph is intended to deal with the situation where a defendant consents to appear and defend in a jurisdiction other than the chosen one. There was agreement as regards the purpose of this provision, but the view was expressed that the reference to 'writing' should be aligned with paragraph 2.

27 This is an alternative proposal to that discussed in note 24, above. There was no consensus on this proposal.

28 This proposal seeks to make it clear that national law may not prohibit the entry into choice of forum clauses by express prohibition or the use of public policy, except in the cases which may be provided for in the Convention, such as consumer transactions or employment contracts; see the views expressed by the co-reporters in Preliminary Document No 11, at p. 42. This proposal did not receive consensus.

Article 5 – Defendant's Right to Contest Jurisdiction[30]

[The defendant shall have the right to contest jurisdiction under Articles [white list] [at least until] [no later than at][31] the time of the first defence on the merits.][32]

Article 6 – Contracts[33]

[*Alternative A*

1. [Subject to the provisions of Articles 7 and 8,][34] a plaintiff may bring an action in contract in the courts of the State –
   (a) in which the defendant has conducted frequent [and] [or][35] significant activity; [or
   (b) into which the defendant has directed frequent [and] [or] significant activity;][36]

   provided that the claim is based on a contract directly related to that activity [and the overall connection of the defendant to that State makes it reasonable that the defendant be subject to suit in that State].[37]

[*Variant 1*[38]

2. For the purposes of the preceding paragraph, 'activity' means one or more of the following –
   (a) [regular and substantial] promotion of the commercial or professional ventures of the defendant for the conclusion of contracts of this kind;
   (b) the defendant's regular or extended presence for the purpose of negotiating contracts of this kind, provided that the contract in question was performed at least in part in that State. [Performance in this sub-paragraph refers [only]

---

[29] This is the text as it appeared in the preliminary draft Convention of October 1999. The relationship between the choice of forum provisions and consumer transactions and employment contracts still has to be resolved.

[30] See also Article 27A below.

[31] It has been proposed to delete the words 'no later than at' and substitute the words 'at least until' the time of. The purpose of this proposal is to make clear it was a minimum condition. It did not receive consensus.

[32] It has been proposed that this provision be deleted in its entirety as an intrusion into the proper role of national law. No consensus was reached on this issue.

[33] There was no consensus on the basis for jurisdiction in contractual matters. In the material that follows, two basic options are put forward: one alternative refers to activity (with several sub-options) and the other alternative focuses on the place of performance.

[34] This refers to the provisions on consumer transactions and employment contracts on which no decisions have been taken as yet.

[35] This leaves open the question of whether the requirements of frequency and significance should be cumulative or alternative.

[36] This leaves open the question of whether the activity of the defendant should take place within the State of the forum or could be directed from outside that State into the State of the forum.

[37] If the words within brackets are accepted, this would be a condition to be satisfied in addition to that of frequent and/or significant activity.

[38] In this variant the scope of 'activity' would be confined to the activities of promotion, negotiation and performance which are further defined in the following sub-paragraphs.

to non-monetary performance, except in case of loans or of contracts for the purchase and sale of currency];[39]

(c) the performance of a contract by supplying goods or services, as a whole or to a significant part.]

[*Variant 2*[40]

2. For the purpose of the preceding paragraph, 'activity' includes, inter alia, the promotion, negotiation, and performance of a contract.

[3. The preceding paragraphs do not apply to situations where the defendant has taken reasonable steps to avoid entering into or performing an obligation in that State.][41]]]

[*Alternative B*[42]

A plaintiff may bring an action in contract in the courts of a State in which –

(a) in matters relating to the supply of goods, the goods were supplied in whole or in part;

(b) in matters relating to the provision of services, the services were provided in whole or in part;

(c) in matters relating both to the supply of goods and the provision of services, performance of the principal obligation took place in whole or in part.]

[Article 7 – Contracts Concluded by Consumers[43]

1. This Article applies to contracts between a natural person acting primarily for personal, family or household purposes, the consumer, and another party acting for the purposes of its trade or profession, [unless the other party demonstrates that it neither knew nor had reason to know that the consumer was concluding the contract primarily for personal, family or household purposes, and would not have entered into the contract if it had known otherwise].[44]

---

39 The words in brackets, if accepted, would exclude the payment of the purchase price or fee for services rendered from the scope of 'performance'.

40 Under this variant the activities of promotion, negotiation and performance would be within the scope of 'activity' but would not define its parameters.

41 This proposal that would have to be considered whether Variant 1 or 2 was adopted, seeks to protect business parties, including those using electronic commerce, who take measures to avoid entering into obligations in a particular State and thereby avoid becoming subject to the jurisdiction of the courts of that State.

42 This alternative option consists of the text as it appeared in the preliminary draft Convention of October 1999.

43 This Article consists of the first four common paragraphs with three different alternative solutions (including two variants of the second alternative) to meet the desire of some delegations to allow a choice of forum clause in consumer contracts in cases where the relevant law permits this, the agreement complies with the requirements of Article 4, paragraphs (1) and (2), and provided the agreement is valid as to substance under the applicable law. A fourth alternative solution has also been suggested: to exclude business to consumer contracts from the scope of the Convention. For that reason the whole of the Article is placed in square brackets. There is no consensus in respect of any of them either that one or more should be omitted or that any one of them should be preferred.

2. Subject to paragraphs [5–7], a consumer may bring [proceedings] [an action in contract][45] in the courts of the State in which the consumer is habitually resident if the claim relates to a contract which arises out of activities, including promotion or negotiation of contracts, which the other party conducted in that State, or directed to that State, [unless[46] [that party establishes that][47] –
   (a) the consumer took the steps necessary for the conclusion of the contract in another State; [and
   (b) the goods or services were supplied to the consumer while the consumer was present in the other State.][48]]

[3. For the purposes of paragraph 2, activity shall not be regarded as being directed to a State if the other party demonstrates that it took reasonable steps to avoid concluding contracts with consumers habitually resident in the State.][49]

4. Subject to paragraphs [5–7], the other party to the contract may bring proceedings against a consumer under this Convention only in the courts of the State in which the consumer is habitually resident.[50]

[*Alternative A*[51]

5. Article 4 applies to a jurisdiction agreement between a consumer and the other party if the agreement is entered into after the dispute has arisen.[52]

---

44 The purpose of this provision within brackets is to give some protection to the business party, especially in a long distance transaction such as in electronic commerce, where the business party cannot easily ascertain with whom it is dealing or the truthfulness of that person's representations. There was opposition to the insertion of this provision on the ground that it would be very difficult for a consumer to rebut an allegation that the business was unaware that the buyer was a consumer.

45 Not all proceedings brought by consumers are actions in contract. They may be actions for a common law tort or delict, or a civil claim on a ground provided for by a statute enacted for the protection of consumers. Some delegations wanted to confine paragraph 2 to actions in contract. There was no consensus on this point.

46 This is the so-called 'small shop' exception that seeks to protect a business party who has dealt with a foreign consumer, such as a tourist, entirely in its State of habitual residence. The question was raised whether there was a need to make such a provision that could only be of relevance to small transactions that are unlikely to become the subject of proceedings under the Convention.

47 This provision would place the burden of establishing that the two conditions in sub-paragraphs (a) and (b) were fulfilled on the business party. The fear was expressed that the burden would be too high for many small businesses. If this issue was not resolved one way or the other, the question of on whom the burden lies, will remain uncertain and would lead to divergent interpretations. There was no consensus on this point.

48 There was no consensus on whether this condition should be added to that set out in sub-paragraph (a).

49 This proposal seeks to protect business parties, including those using electronic commerce, who take measures to avoid entering into obligations in a particular State and thereby avoid becoming subject to the jurisdiction of the courts of that State. There is no consensus on this provision.

50 This is proposed as the general rule to which Alternatives A to C are exceptions.

51 This Alternative is a revised version of the solution that was presented to the informal discussions held in Edinburgh in April 2001: see Prel Doc 15, Annex III-A. It provides that a choice of forum clause in a consumer contract will be effective if valid under the law of the habitual residence of the consumer and the Contracting State in which recognition and enforcement is sought has made the declaration provided for in the proposed Article 25 bis. For the sake of convenience that proposed Article is reproduced here as part of Alternative A. Several delegations objected to this proposal on

6. Where a consumer and the other party have entered into an agreement which conforms with the requirements of Article 4(1) and (2) before the dispute has arisen, the consumer may bring proceedings against the other party in the courts of the State designated in that agreement.[53]
7. Where a consumer and the other party have entered into an agreement which conforms with the requirements of Article 4(1) and (2) before the dispute has arisen, Article 4 applies to the agreement to the extent that it is binding on both parties under the law of the State in which the consumer is habitually resident at the time the agreement is entered into.[54]

Add at the beginning of Article 25 the words:

'Subject to Article 25 *bis*'

Insert [*Article 25 bis*[55]

1. A Contracting State may make a declaration that it will not recognise or enforce a judgment under this Chapter, or a declaration specifying the conditions under which it will recognise or enforce a judgment under this Chapter, where –
   (a) the judgment was rendered by the court of origin under Article 7(2) [or Article 8(2)];[56] and
   (b) the parties had entered into an agreement which conforms with the requirements of Article 4 designating a court other than the court of origin.[57]

[2. A declaration under this Article may not deny recognition and enforcement of

---

the ground of its complexity, but there was no agreement that it should be omitted from the list of alternatives.

52 This is the provision that appeared as Article 7(3)(a) in the preliminary draft Convention of October 1999. It is not controversial.

53 This repeats the provision that appeared as Article 7(3)(b) in the preliminary draft Convention of October 1999. It is not controversial in so far as it allows the consumer to bring proceedings in the chosen forum in addition to other fora, including the forum under Article 7(2). The controversial issue is whether the proceedings brought by the consumer could be confined to the chosen forum.

54 This provision contains a choice of law provision referring to the law of the consumer's habitual residence the issues of whether the choice of forum clause is lawful as regards each party and whether it is substantially valid (including issues of public policy and reasonableness): see Report of the co-reporters, Prel. Doc. No 11 at p. 42.

55 If accepted, this Article should be placed among the articles dealing with recognition and enforcement.

56 The reference to Article 8(2) will be relevant if this solution is extended to individual contracts of employment.

57 Under this provision a State may declare that it will only recognise or enforce judgments under the Convention that are consistent with a choice of court clause. A State making the declaration would not be bound to recognise or enforce a judgment given in accordance with Article 7(2) if this jurisdiction was incompatible with the choice of court clause. On the other hand, a State not making the declaration would be bound to recognise or enforce a judgment rendered in accordance with Article 7(2) in other Contracting States, including a State that had made the declaration. But a non-declaring State would not be bound to recognise or enforce a judgment rendered by the chosen court, including one of a State that had made the declaration. A concern was expressed at this lack of reciprocity and fear of possible complexities that might be introduced if the declaration also specified conditions.

a judgment given under Article 7(2) [or Article 8(2)] if the Contracting State making the declaration would exercise jurisdiction under the relevant Article in a corresponding case.][58]

3. Recognition or enforcement of a judgment may be refused by a Contracting State that has made a declaration contemplated by paragraph 1 in accordance with the terms of that declaration.]]

[*Alternative B*[59]

[*Variant 1*[60]

5. This provision may be departed from by a jurisdiction agreement provided that it conforms with the requirements of Article 4.
6. A Contracting State may declare that –
   (a) it will only respect a jurisdiction agreement if it is entered into after the dispute has arisen or to the extent that it allows the consumer to bring proceedings in a court other than a court indicated in this Article or in Article 3; and
   (b) it will not recognise and enforce a judgment where jurisdiction has been taken in accordance with a jurisdiction agreement that does not fulfil the requirements in sub-paragraph a).]

[*Variant 2*[61]

5. Article 4 applies to an agreement between a consumer and the other party if the agreement is entered into after the dispute has arisen; or to the extent that the agreement permits the consumer to bring proceedings in a court other than the consumer's habitual residence.
6. A Contracting State may declare that in the circumstances specified in that declaration –

---

58 This provision is intended to prevent States that make a declaration under Article 25 *bis* (1) from denying recognition or enforcement of a judgment when that State does not treat such choice of court provisions as binding on its own consumers.

59 There are two variants in this Alternative. The basic rule is that stated in paragraph 4 above which limits the business party to the forum of the consumer's habitual residence. Both Variants allow a departure from this rule, but differ in whether departure is allowed unless a declaration is made to the contrary (Variant 1) or whether a departure is not allowed unless a State makes a declaration to the opposite effect (Variant 2).

60 Variant 1 allows the parties to depart from the basic rule by an agreement that complies with the requirements of Article 4, but this choice of forum will not be regarded as excluding the forum provided for in paragraph 2 nor will a judgment rendered by the chosen forum (unless the consumer commenced the proceedings there or it coincided with the habitual residence of the consumer) be recognised or enforced in a State that makes a declaration to that effect. That State thereby 'opts-in' into the system of restricted jurisdiction over proceedings brought by the business party against the consumer.

61 Under Variant 2 pre-dispute choice of forum clauses are not binding on consumers except in States that have made a declaration that they will respect such an agreement and that they will recognise and enforce judgments given in pursuance of such agreements. Such States will not recognise and enforce judgments given in breach of choice of forum clauses. Whatever system of declaration is adopted, problems of reciprocity remain.

(a) it will respect a jurisdiction agreement entered into before the dispute has arisen;
(b) it will recognise and enforce a judgment in proceedings brought by the other party given by a court under a jurisdiction agreement entered into before the dispute has arisen;
(c) it will not recognise and enforce a judgment given by a court in which proceedings could not be brought consistently with a jurisdiction agreement entered into before the dispute has arisen.]]

[*Alternative C*[62]
5. Article 4 applies to a jurisdiction agreement between a consumer and the other party if the agreement is entered into after the dispute has arisen.
6. Where a consumer and the other party have entered into an agreement which conforms with the requirements of Article 4(1) and (2) before the dispute has arisen –
   (a) the consumer may bring proceedings against the other party under the Convention in the courts of the State designated in that agreement;
   (b) the consumer may not bring proceedings against the other party under this Convention in any other court, unless the agreement permits the proceedings to be brought in that court;
   (c) the other party may bring proceedings against the consumer under this Convention only if the agreement permits the proceedings to be brought in the courts of the State in which the consumer is habitually resident.]]

Article 8 – Individual Contracts of Employment

This matter was not discussed by Commission II. The Commission agreed that the Working Documents put forward in relation to this subject as well as the draft prepared at the informal discussions in Edinburgh in April 2001 should be reproduced in Annex II to facilitate further discussion. The proposals in Annex II should be viewed in the light of the Alternatives proposed in relation to Article 7 above.

62 This Alternative limits the 'white list' jurisdiction that may be invoked by each of the parties in cases where a choice of forum agreement has been concluded between the parties. In essence there will only be 'white list' jurisdiction if the consumer brings proceedings in the chosen forum. Conversely, there will only be 'white list' jurisdiction in the chosen forum in relation to an action brought by the business party if the chosen forum coincides with the habitual residence of the consumer. If the consumer brings proceedings in the forum provided for under paragraph 2 or in any other 'white list' forum contrary to a choice of forum clause, that forum will be deprived of its 'white list' status. It will then depend on the national law of the forum to determine whether the consumer will be permitted to rely on that jurisdiction and it will also depend on the national law of the State addressed to determine whether a judgment rendered in a State other than that of the chosen forum will be recognised or enforced, even if, in the absence of a choice of forum clause, the court in the State of origin would have exercised a 'white list' jurisdiction, such as a jurisdiction under paragraph 2.

Article 9 – Branches [and Regular Commercial Activity][63]

1. A plaintiff may bring an action in the courts of a State in which a branch, agency or any other establishment of the defendant is situated, [or where the defendant has carried on regular commercial activity by other means,] provided that the dispute relates directly to the activity of that branch, agency or other establishment [or to that regular commercial activity].

[2. For purposes of applying paragraph 1, a legal entity shall not be considered a 'branch, agency or other establishment' by the mere fact that the legal entity is a subsidiary of the defendant.][64]

Article 10 – Torts [or Delicts][65]

1. A plaintiff may bring an action in tort [or delict] in the courts of the State –
   (a) in which the act or omission that caused injury occurred, or
   (b) in which the injury arose, unless the defendant establishes that the person claimed to be responsible could not reasonably foresee that the act or omission could result in an injury of the same nature in that State.[66]

[2. A plaintiff may bring an action in tort in the courts of the State in which the defendant has engaged in frequent or significant activity, or has directed such activity into that State, provided that the claim arises out of that activity and the overall connection of the defendant to that State makes it reasonable that the defendant be subject to suit in that State.][67]

[3. The preceding paragraphs do not apply to situations where the defendant has taken reasonable steps to avoid acting in or directing activity into that State.][68]

---

[63] The matter placed between the brackets has not been discussed pending general discussion of the 'activity jurisdiction' elsewhere. There appears to be general agreement, subject to further clarification (see note 64 below), on the remainder of the paragraph.

[64] It was proposed to delete the term '*nécessairement*' in the French text. It was also proposed to replace the term 'simple' by the term '*seul*' in the French text. There does not appear to be any objection with the interpretation given by the Co-Reporters in Preliminary Document No 11 at p. 56 that a subsidiary, even one that is wholly owned by a parent, will not by that fact alone be regarded as falling within the definition of 'a branch, agency or other establishment'. However, some delegations expressed a fear that the formal incorporation of those comments into the body of the text might be misinterpreted. There is no consensus on this provision.

[65] The deletion of the words 'or delicts' in the title and in the first paragraph has been proposed. The concern was raised that the term includes both civil and criminal offences in some legal systems and may extend the reach of Article 10 or result in other unintended consequences in those systems. There is no consensus on this proposal.

[66] This is the text of the preliminary draft Convention of October 1999. No specific proposals were made to modify this text. However, it was noted that the paragraph would have to remain under consideration in light of e-commerce and intellectual property issues, its relation to activity jurisdiction proposals, and constitutional issues in one State. There was agreement that the material appearing as paragraph 2 in the preliminary draft Convention of October 1999 should be deleted.

[67] This proposal seeks to insert an activity based jurisdiction similar to that proposed in relation to Article 6 Contracts, Alternative A, paragraph 1. There is no consensus on this proposal.

[68] This proposal seeks to protect business parties, including those using electronic commerce, who take measures to avoid entering into obligations in a particular State and thereby avoid becoming subject to the jurisdiction of the courts of that State. There is no consensus on this proposal.

[4. A plaintiff may also bring an action in accordance with paragraph 1 when the act or omission, or the injury may occur.][69]

[5. If an action is brought in the courts of a State only on the basis that the injury arose or may occur there, those courts shall have jurisdiction only in respect of the injury that occurred or may occur in that State, unless the injured person has his or her habitual residence in that State.][70]

Article 11 – Trusts

1. In proceedings concerning the validity, construction, effects, administration or variation of a trust created voluntarily and evidenced in writing, the courts of a Contracting State designated in the trust instrument for this purpose shall have jurisdiction, and that jurisdiction shall be exclusive unless the instrument provides otherwise.[71] Where the trust instrument designates a court or courts of a non-Contracting State, courts in Contracting States shall decline jurisdiction or suspend proceedings unless the court or courts chosen have themselves declined jurisdiction. [The validity of such a designation shall be governed by the law[72] applicable to the validity of the trust.][73]
2. In the absence of such [valid][74] designation, proceedings may be brought before the courts of a State –
   (a) in which is situated the principal place of administration of the trust; or
   (b) whose law is applicable to the trust; or
   (c) with which the trust has the closest connection for the purpose of the proceedings, taking into account in particular the principal place where the trust is administered, the place of residence or business of the trustee, the situation of the assets of the trust, and the objects of the trust and the places where they are to be fulfilled; or
   (d) in which the settlor (if living) and all living beneficiaries are habitually resident, if all such persons are habitually resident in the same State.[75]

---

69 The deletion of this paragraph that appeared as Article 10, paragraph 3 of the preliminary draft Convention of October 1999 has been proposed. There is no consensus on its deletion.

70 The deletion of this paragraph that appeared as Article 10, paragraph 4 of the preliminary draft Convention of October 1999 has been proposed. There is no consensus on its deletion.

71 There was agreement on the insertion of the last sub-sentence in order to bring the provision in conformity with the similar provision found in Article 4, paragraph 1.

72 It was noted that the phrase 'national law' should replace the word 'law' if the Convention consistently uses 'national law' in such cases.

73 The words within brackets were proposed to ensure that the question of the existence and validity of the choice of forum clause would be determined by the law applicable under the choice of law rules of the court seised and not necessarily by any law nominated as the applicable law by the settlor. No consensus was reached on this provision.

74 See note 73 above.

75 Subject to the use of the word 'valid' in the chapeau, this paragraph was approved by consensus.

[3. This Article shall only apply to disputes among the trustee, settlor and beneficiaries of the trust.][76]

Article 12 – Exclusive Jurisdiction

[1. In proceedings which have as their object rights in rem in immovable property or tenancies of immovable property, the courts of the Contracting State in which the property is situated have exclusive jurisdiction, unless in proceedings which have as their object tenancies of immovable property [concluded for a maximum period of six months],[77] the tenant is habitually resident in a different State.][78]

[2. In proceedings which have as their object the validity, nullity, or dissolution of a legal person, or the validity or nullity of the decisions of its organs, the courts of a Contracting State whose law governs the legal person have exclusive jurisdiction.][79]

3. In proceedings concerning the validity of entries in public registers other than those dealing with intellectual property rights, the courts of the Contracting State in which the register is kept shall have exclusive jurisdiction.

Intellectual property[80]

[*Alternative A*[81]

4. In proceedings in which the relief sought is a judgment on the grant, registration, validity, abandonment, revocation or infringement[82] of a patent or a mark, the

---

76 This paragraph did not achieve consensus. It has been proposed that this matter should be left to national law: see the comment of the co-reporters in Preliminary Document No 11, at p. 62 that the disputes covered by this Article are disputes that are internal to the trust.

77 It has been proposed to limit the exclusion of tenancies of immovable property from the exclusive jurisdiction of the State of situation to a lease for a single period not exceeding 6 months. There was no consensus on this proposal.

78 It has been proposed to exclude rights in rem in immovable property and tenancies of movable property from the scope of the Convention. There was no consensus on this proposal.

79 It has been proposed to exclude the validity, nullity, or dissolution of a legal person and decisions related thereto from the scope of the Convention. There was no consensus on this proposal.

80 Three proposals have been made with respect to the treatment of intellectual property in the Convention. The first two appear within general brackets and are each bracketed also (Alternatives A and B). That indicates that there is no consensus on the inclusion of intellectual property within the scope of the Convention or in respect of each of the proposals themselves. For the third proposal, see note 88 below.

81 The main difference between Alternatives A and B is whether proceedings for the infringement of patents and marks and such other rights as may be covered by this provision should fall within the exclusive jurisdiction or not. In addition, for a number of the delegations that favour an exclusive jurisdiction also for infringement under this provision, a satisfactory final or disconnection clause with respect to existing and future instruments regulating jurisdiction, recognition and enforcement for specific areas such as intellectual property is a precondition for including infringement in this Article on exclusive jurisdiction.

82 It was pointed out that, when deciding which proceedings (e.g. infringement proceedings based on provisions of an Unfair Competition Act or of a Patent or Trademark Act, or proceedings concerning certain common law torts such as passing off) were to be covered by 'infringement', the solution should be consistent with the possible exclusion of 'antitrust or competition claims' from the scope of the Convention.

courts of the Contracting State of grant or registration shall have exclusive jurisdiction.[83]

5. In proceedings in which the relief sought is a judgment on the validity, abandonment, or infringement of an unregistered mark [or design], the courts of the Contracting State in which rights in the mark [or design] arose shall have exclusive jurisdiction.]

[*Alternative B*[84]

5A. In relation to proceedings which have as their object the infringement of patents, trademarks, designs or other similar rights, the courts of the Contracting State referred to in the preceding paragraph [or in the provisions of Articles [3 to 16]] have jurisdiction.[85]]

Alternatives A and B

[6. Paragraphs 4 and 5 shall not apply where one of the above matters arises as an incidental question in proceedings before a court not having exclusive jurisdiction under those paragraphs. However, the ruling in that matter shall have no binding effect in subsequent proceedings, even if they are between the same parties. A matter arises as an incidental question if the court is not requested to give a judgment on that matter, even if a ruling on it is necessary in arriving at a decision.][86]

7. [In this Article, other registered industrial property rights [(but not copyright or neighbouring rights, even when registration or deposit is possible)][87] shall be treated in the same way as patents and marks.]

---

83 This paragraph also covers situations where an application for the grant or registration of a patent or mark has been filed.

84 This Alternative does not dispute the proposition in Alternative A that there should be exclusive jurisdiction in respect of proceedings that have as their object the registration, validity, nullity or revocation of patents, trade marks, designs or other similar rights. To that extent paragraphs 4 and 5 would remain if paragraph 5A was accepted. Alternative B refers only to proposed paragraph 5A. Paragraphs 6, 7 and 8 are common to both Alternatives.

85 This provision will have to be excluded from the exceptions stated in Article 17.

86 The purpose of this paragraph is to maintain non-exclusive jurisdiction where a matter otherwise falling within the scope of paragraphs 4 and 5 arises as an incidental question in proceedings which do not have as their object one or more of the matters described in that paragraph. The intention is that any decision made between the parties on such an incidental question will not have a preclusory effect in another State, in other cases when produced by one of the parties. There is no consensus on this paragraph.

87 There is no consensus on the words included within the brackets. Other suggestions are to exclude copyright from the scope of the Convention either in whole or only copyright infringement on-line. Furthermore, the following text was proposed as an alternative: ["In proceedings concerning the infringement of a copyright or any neighbouring right, the courts of the Contracting State under whose laws the copyright or the neighbouring right is claimed to be infringed shall have exclusive jurisdiction"]. This proposal seeks to include copyright within the exclusive jurisdiction of the courts of the Contracting State under whose law a copyright is claimed to have been infringed. This is an alternative to the exclusion of proceedings for the infringement of copyright proposed in paragraph 7 above.

[8. For the purpose of this Article, 'court' shall include a Patent Office or similar agency.][88]

Article 13 – Provisional and Protective Measures[89]

[*Alternative A*[90]

1. A court seised[91] and having jurisdiction under Articles [in the white list] to determine the merits of the case has jurisdiction to order provisional and protective[92] measures.
2. A court of a Contracting State [may] [has jurisdiction to],[93] even where it does not have jurisdiction to determine the merits of a claim, order a provisional and protective measure in respect of property in that State or the enforcement of which is limited to the territory of that State, to protect on an interim basis a claim on the merits which is pending or to be brought by the requesting party in a Contracting State which has jurisdiction to determine that claim under Articles [in the white list].[94]
3. Nothing in this Convention shall prevent a court in a Contracting State from ordering a provisional and protective measure for the purpose of protecting on an interim basis a claim on the merits which is pending or to brought by the requesting party in another State.[95]

---

88 This paragraph might be necessary to ensure that decisions of these organs are covered by the chapter on recognition: see the definition of 'judgment' in Article 23.

89 This Article would be deleted if Alternative A of Article 1(2)(k) was adopted. It would also be deleted if the Alternative B of Article 1(2)(k) was adopted without the reference to Articles 13 and 23A. Some delegations have also suggested that provisional and protective measures should be dealt with in a separate Chapter in the Convention. This would certainly be necessary if no provision were made for the recognition and enforcement of provisional and protective measures.

90 For another proposal in relation to Article 13, see Article 1(2)(k) which proposes that provisional and protective measures be excluded from the scope of the Convention with certain qualifications.

91 It has been suggested that it would be sufficient if a court is seised after a provisional and protective measure is made. This would require the addition of the words 'or about to be seised' or similar.

92 The description 'provisional and protective' is intended to be cumulative, that is to say, the measures must meet with both criteria.

93 A form of words has also been suggested that would make it clear that Contracting States are obliged to provide this jurisdiction, although it was also stressed that this would not interfere with the discretion of the courts of such States either to make or to refuse to make such orders.

94 It was noted that some States, especially those in the Commonwealth other than the United Kingdom, did not provide for jurisdiction to make provisional and protective orders unless the court was seised of jurisdiction to determine the merits of the case. This could operate to the detriment of foreign plaintiffs who sought to 'freeze' assets within the jurisdiction in aid of litigation pending elsewhere. The provision is intended to provide such States with jurisdiction to make such orders based on the existence of property in the forum and limited to the territory of the forum. There was no consensus on this provision.

95 This provision is intended to overcome any restrictions imposed on the exercise of jurisdiction by the courts of Contracting States by the list of prohibited jurisdictions (at present found in Article 18). The provision would also allow the exercise of jurisdiction to make provisional and protective orders under national law without the restrictions imposed by the list of prohibited jurisdictions. It is proposed to remove the reference to Article 13 in Article 17 in order to allow the exercise of such jurisdiction

4. In paragraph 3[96] a reference to a provisional and protective measure means –
   (a) a measure to maintain the status quo pending determination of the issues at trial; or
   (b) a measure providing a preliminary means of securing assets out of which an ultimate judgment may be satisfied; or
   (c) a measure to restrain conduct by a defendant to prevent current or imminent future harm.]

[*Alternative B*[97]
A court which is or is about to be seised of a claim and which has jurisdiction under Articles [3 to 15] to determine the merits thereof may order provisional and protective measures, intended to preserve the subject-matter of the claim.]

Article 14 – Multiple Defendants
It was agreed to delete this Article.

Article 15 – Counter-claims[98]
[Subject to Article 12,][99] a court which has jurisdiction to determine a claim under the provisions of the Convention shall also have jurisdiction to determine a counter-claim arising out of the transaction or occurrence on which the original claim is based [unless the court would be unable to adjudicate such a counter-claim against a local plaintiff under national law].[100]

---

under national law. Some delegations took the view that this paragraph was the only provision on provisional and protective measures that should be included in the Convention.

96 It has been proposed that this definition apply also to paragraphs 1 and 2.

97 This proposal is linked with the second alternative in Article 1(2)(k) which in itself contains the options either to exclude provisional or protective measures entirely from the scope of the Convention or to permit a limited jurisdiction to make such orders. Alternative B provides for such a limited jurisdiction, if so desired.

98 There was agreement that there should be provision for a jurisdiction based on a counter-claim and that this jurisdiction should be one that is entitled to recognition and enforcement under Article 25(1). There was some debate on whether this was already obvious or should be further clarified: see the remarks of the co-reporters in Preliminary Document No 11, at p. 95. The language not within brackets was also approved by consensus.

99 It was agreed that the proposal to add this qualification should remain within brackets pending resolution of the status of Article 12.

100 It was proposed to add the language within brackets to provide for the situation where the counterclaim is outside the subject matter jurisdiction of the court. There was general agreement that a counter-claim could only confer jurisdiction over the person of the defendant and not subject matter jurisdiction (including excess of any monetary limits) which it did not possess under national law. There was some discussion as to whether this was already obvious, or whether the issue which also arises in relation to forum selection clauses, should be dealt with in a general provision, and whether the language proposed within the brackets was adequate for the intended purpose. In relation to the last issue, the following alternative words have been proposed: " [...], unless the court seised does not have subject matter jurisdiction to adjudicate the counter-claim".

Article 16 – Third Party Claims

It was agreed to delete this Article.

Article 17 – Jurisdiction Based on National Law[101]

[Subject to Articles 4, 7, 8, 11(1), 12 and 13,[102]][103] the Convention does not prevent the application by Contracting States of rules of jurisdiction under national law, provided that this is not prohibited under Article 18.

[Article 18 – Prohibited Grounds of Jurisdiction[104]

[1. Where the defendant is habitually resident in a Contracting State, the application of a rule of jurisdiction provided for under the national law of a Contracting State is prohibited if there is no substantial connection between that State and [either] the dispute [or the defendant].[105]][106]

2. [In particular,][107] [Where the defendant is habitually resident in a Contracting State,][108] jurisdiction shall not be exercised by the courts of a Contracting State on the basis [solely of one or more][109] of the following –

[(a) the presence or the seizure in that State of property belonging to the defendant, except where the dispute is directly related to that property;][110]

(b) the nationality of the plaintiff;

(c) the nationality of the defendant;

(d) the domicile, habitual or temporary residence, or presence of the plaintiff in that State;

[(e) the carrying on of commercial or other activities by the defendant in that State, [whether or not through a branch, agency or any other establishment

---

101 Subject to the determination of the material in brackets, this Article was approved by agreement.

102 It has been proposed that the reference to Article 13 be deleted. This will allow the making of provisional and/or protective orders under national law.

103 The question of the existence or exclusivity of Articles 7, 8, 12 and 13 still remain to be resolved.

104 There was no consensus on this provision.

105 It has been proposed to add the words 'either' and 'or the defendant' in order to meet the difficulties in national legal systems where the main emphasis for jurisdictional competence lies on the link between the forum and the defendant, rather than the subject matter of the dispute. There is no consensus on this point.

106 The deletion of the whole of paragraph 1 has been proposed in order to emphasise the basic concept of the Convention that there be a limited number of required bases of jurisdictions that are generally accepted, a limited number of jurisdictional bases so universally disapproved as exorbitant that they should be listed as prohibited jurisdictions, and that any other jurisdiction not listed in either category should remain open for the exercise of jurisdiction under national law (the 'grey zone'). There was no consensus on the deletion of paragraph 1.

107 If paragraph 1 is to be deleted, the words in brackets should also be deleted.

108 If paragraph 1 is to be deleted, the words in brackets should be placed in what is now paragraph 2.

109 It has been proposed to delete the words within the brackets. No consensus exists on this point.

110 It has been proposed to delete sub-paragraph a) entirely. There is no consensus on this issue.

of the defendant,][111] except where the dispute is directly related to those activities;][112]

(f) the service of a writ upon the defendant in that State;

[(g) the unilateral designation of the forum by the plaintiff;][113]

(h) [proceedings in that State for declaration of enforceability or registration or for the enforcement of a judgment, except where the dispute is directly related to such proceedings][114] [initiation of proceedings in that State by the party against whom jurisdiction is claimed, for the purpose of recognising or enforcing a judgment from another State];[115]

[(i) the temporary residence or presence of the defendant in that State;][116]

[(j) the signing in that State of the contract from which the dispute arises;][117]

[(k) the location of a subsidiary or other related entity of the defendant in that State;][118]

[(l) the existence of a related criminal action in that State].[119]

[3. Nothing in this article shall prevent a court in a Contracting State from exercising jurisdiction under national law in an action claiming damages in respect of conduct which constitutes –

[(a) genocide, a crime against humanity or a war crime];[120] [or][121]

(b) a serious crime under international law, provided that this State has exercised its criminal jurisdiction over that crime in accordance with an international treaty to which it is a Party and that claim is for civil compensatory damages for death or serious bodily injuries arising from that crime.[122]

---

111 The addition of the words within the brackets is proposed to make it clear that the presence of a branch, agency or other establishment within the forum should not be a basis for the exercise of general jurisdiction under national law: see the view expressed by the co-reporters in Preliminary Document No 11 at p. 57 that 'such a general jurisdiction is inconsistent with the Convention' (the preliminary draft Convention of October 1999). No consensus was reached on this proposal.

112 It has been proposed to delete sub-paragraph e) entirely. There is no consensus on this issue.

113 It has been proposed to delete sub-paragraph g) entirely. There is no consensus on this point.

114 This was the text as it appeared in the preliminary draft Convention of October 1999.

115 The language within the brackets was proposed as an alternative to the October 1999 text by way of clarification only. However, it was objected that the omission of the words 'except where the dispute is directly limited to such proceedings' had a substantive effect and would deprive the judgment debtor of the opportunity to raise objections directly related to the enforcement, such as part payment of the debt.

116 It has been proposed to delete this sub-paragraph entirely. There is no consensus on this point.

117 It has been proposed to delete this sub-paragraph entirely. There is no consensus on this point.

118 The addition of this item to the list of prohibited jurisdiction has been proposed. There is no consensus on this point.

119 The addition of this item to the list of prohibited jurisdictions has been proposed. There is no consensus on this point: see the comments of the co-reporters in Preliminary Document No 11, at p. 31, footnote 14 and accompanying text.

120 It was proposed to include a reference to the definitions contained in the Statute of the International Criminal Court. However, it was pointed out that this Statute had not as yet entered into force.

121 There was agreement that the material in sub-paragraph a) be placed in separate brackets, because sub-paragraphs a) and b) raised different issues.

Sub-paragraph b) only applies if the party seeking relief is exposed to a risk of a denial of justice[123] because proceedings in another State are not possible or cannot reasonably be required.][124]]

Article 19 – Authority of the Court Seised

1. Where the defendant does not enter an appearance, the court shall verify whether Article 18 prohibits it from exercising jurisdiction if –
   (a) national law so requires; or
   (b) the plaintiff so requests; or
   [(c) the defendant so requests, even after judgment is entered in accordance with procedures established under national law; or]
   (d) [the document which instituted the proceedings or an equivalent document was served on the defendant in another Contracting State]

   or

   [it appears from the documents filed by the plaintiff that the defendant's address is in another Contracting State].[125]

[2. When the jurisdiction of the court seised in a Contracting State is based on or is consistent with a ground of jurisdiction provided for in Articles 3 to 16, a party may request the court to declare so in the judgment.][126]

Article 20[127]

1. The court shall stay the proceedings so long as it is not established that the document which instituted the proceedings or an equivalent document, including the essential elements of the claim, was notified to the defendant in sufficient time and in such a way as to enable him to arrange for his defence, or that all necessary steps have been taken to that effect.

[2. Paragraph 1 shall not affect the use of international instruments concerning the service abroad of judicial and extrajudicial documents in civil or commercial matters, in accordance with the law of the forum.]

[3. Paragraph 1 shall not apply, in case of urgency, to any provisional or protective measures.]

---

122 The original proposal had translated the French '*exercé*' as 'established'. Some favourable comments on the proposal were withdrawn when it was pointed out that the intention was not to say 'established' in English but to restrict the article to situations where criminal jurisdiction is 'exercised'.

123 It was pointed out that the concept of 'denial of justice' was unknown under certain legal systems.

124 There was no consensus on the proposed paragraph 3. It is included in the text within square brackets to facilitate future discussion.

125 It was agreed to place the text of Article 19, paragraph 1, as it appeared in the preliminary draft Convention of October 1999 (including any bracketed material) in the present document.

126 There was no consensus on this proposal.

127 It was agreed to place the text of Article 20, as it appeared in the preliminary draft Convention of October 1999 (including any bracketed material) in the present document.

Article 21 – Lis Pendens

1. When the same parties are engaged in proceedings in courts of different Contracting States and when such proceedings are based on the same causes of action, irrespective of the relief sought, the court second seised shall suspend the proceedings if the court first seised has jurisdiction under Articles [white list][128] [or under a rule of national law which is consistent with these articles][129] and is expected to render a judgment capable of being recognised under the Convention in the State of the court second seised, unless the latter has exclusive jurisdiction under Article 4 [, 11][130] or 12.
2. The court second seised shall decline jurisdiction as soon as it is presented with a judgment rendered by the court first seised that complies with the requirements for recognition or enforcement under the Convention.
3. Upon application of a party, the court second seised may proceed with the case if the plaintiff in the court first seised has failed to take the necessary steps to bring the proceedings to a decision on the merits or if that court has not rendered such a decision within a reasonable time.
4. The provisions of the preceding paragraphs apply to the court second seised even in a case where the jurisdiction of that court is based on the national law of that State in accordance with Article 17.
5. For the purpose of this Article, a court shall be deemed to be seised –
   (a) when the document instituting the proceedings or an equivalent document is lodged with the court; or
   (b) if such document has to be served before being lodged with the court, when it is received by the authority responsible for service or served on the defendant.

   [As appropriate, universal time is applicable.]
6. If in the action before the court first seised the plaintiff seeks a determination that it has no obligation to the defendant, and if an action seeking substantive relief is brought in the court second seised –
   (a) the provisions of paragraphs 1 to 5 above shall not apply to the court second seised; and
   (b) the court first seised shall suspend the proceedings at the request of a party if the court second seised is expected to render a decision capable of being recognised under the Convention.

---

[128] It was agreed to add the words within brackets in order to make it clear that the lis pendens rule only applies when the court first seised exercises jurisdiction under the Convention: see the Report of the co-reporters, Preliminary Document 11, at p. 86.

[129] This proposal sought to make it clear that the lis pendens rule will not only apply where the court first seised is exercising 'white list' jurisdiction as such, but also in the case where that court exercises a jurisdiction under national law in a situation that is consistent with 'white list' jurisdiction, such as proceedings against a defendant who is habitually resident in that State: see Report of co-reporters, Preliminary Document 11, at p. 86. There was no consensus on this point.

[130] There was no consensus on the insertion of a reference to Article 11 (trusts).

7. This Article shall not apply if the court first seised, on application by a party, determines that the court second seised is clearly more appropriate to resolve the dispute, under the conditions specified in Article 22.

Article 22 – Exceptional Circumstances for Declining Jurisdiction

1. In exceptional circumstances, when the jurisdiction of the court seised is not founded on an exclusive choice of court agreement valid under Article 4, or on Article 7, 8 or 12, the court may, on application by a party, suspend its proceedings if in that case it is clearly inappropriate for that court to exercise jurisdiction and if a court of another State has jurisdiction and is clearly more appropriate to resolve the dispute. Such application must be made no later than at the time of the first defence on the merits.
2. The court shall take into account, in particular –
   (a) any inconvenience to the parties in view of their habitual residence;
   (b) the nature and location of the evidence, including documents and witnesses, and the procedures for obtaining such evidence;
   (c) applicable limitation or prescription periods;
   (d) the possibility of obtaining recognition and enforcement of any decision on the merits.
3. In deciding whether to suspend the proceedings, a court shall not discriminate on the basis of the nationality or habitual residence of the parties.
4. If the court decides to suspend its proceedings under paragraph 1, it may order the defendant to provide security sufficient to satisfy any decision of the other court on the merits. However, it shall make such an order if the other court has jurisdiction only under Article 17, or if it is in a non-Contracting State,[131] unless the defendant establishes that [the plaintiff's ability to enforce the judgment will not be materially prejudiced if such an order is not made][132] [sufficient assets exist in the State of that other court or in another State where the court's decision could be enforced].[133]
5. When the court has suspended its proceedings under paragraph 1,
   (a) it shall decline to exercise jurisdiction if the court of the other State exercises jurisdiction, or if the plaintiff does not bring the proceedings in that State within the time specified by the court; or
   (b) it shall proceed with the case if the court of the other State decides not to exercise jurisdiction.
6. This Article shall not apply where the court has jurisdiction only under Article

---

131 It was agreed to insert the words "or if it is in a non-Contracting State" in order to fill a gap in the provision, see the Report of the co-reporters, Preliminary Document 11, at pp. 92–93.

132 The words in the preceding brackets were proposed in substitution of the existing text which were thought to set too high a standard for the defendant to be able to meet on the one hand and still not give the plaintiff the security needed on the other: see the Report of the co-reporters, Preliminary Document 11 at p. 93. There was no consensus on this point.

133 This is the text of the preliminary draft Convention of October 1999.

17 [which is not consistent with Articles [white list]].[134] In such a case, national law shall govern the question of declining jurisdiction.[135]

[7. The court seised and having jurisdiction under Articles 3 to 15 shall not apply the doctrine of forum non conveniens or any similar rule for declining jurisdiction.][136]

*Chapter *** – Recognition and Enforcement*

Article 23 – Definition of "Judgment"

For the purposes of this Chapter, 'judgment' means any decision given by a court, whatever it may be called, including a decree or order, as well as the determination of costs or expenses by an officer of the court, provided that it relates to a decision which may be recognised or enforced under the Convention.[137]

[Article 23A – Recognition and Enforcement of Provisional and Protective Measures[138]

[*Alternative A*

1. A decision ordering a provisional and protective[139] measure, which has been

---

[134] This proposal sought to ensure that the preservation of national rules of *forum non conveniens* will not apply both where the court seised is exercising 'white list' jurisdiction as such, and also in the case where that court exercises a jurisdiction under national law in a situation that is consistent with 'white list' jurisdiction, such as proceedings against a defendant who is habitually resident in that State. There was no consensus on this point.

[135] This paragraph makes it clear that Article 22 does not apply where the court is only exercising jurisdiction under national law. In that case, the court can apply its own rules of *forum non conveniens* or similar (if any). This resolves the question raised by the co-reporters in Preliminary Document 11, at p. 89. It was agreed to insert this paragraph.

[136] This paragraph was proposed to ensure that national rules of forum non conveniens or similar rules would not be used in relation to 'white list' jurisdiction as a means of declining jurisdiction. There was no consensus on this point.

[137] For those delegations that support the complete exclusion of provisional and protective measures from the Convention, no reference to such measures will be necessary in this Article. It has been proposed to include in the Convention provisions both for jurisdiction to take provisional and protective measures and for their recognition and enforcement. As for jurisdiction, it was pointed out that the definition of 'judgment' in Article 23 could be read to include provisional and protective measures. As for recognition and enforcement, proposals are made in Article 23A below.

[138] The two alternatives which do not appear to differ much in substance, provide for the recognition and enforcement of provisional and protective orders made by a court that is seised (or about to be seised) of the substantive dispute. Such a provision is opposed naturally by those delegations that favour exclusion of such measures from the scope of the Convention. But several delegations that favoured the inclusion of a provision relating to such measures in the jurisdictional or procedural part of the Convention, opposed making provision for the recognition and enforcement of provisional and protective orders. Note also that there may be a need to address: the extent to which similar relief is known in the State of the court addressed; and, procedures to safeguard the interests of third parties or of the defendant (e.g. an undertaking to pay damages).

[139] The two descriptions 'provisional' and 'protective' are intended to be cumulative.

taken by a court seised[140] with the claim on the merits, shall be recognised and enforced in Contracting States in accordance with Articles [25, 27–34].

2. In this article a reference to a provisional or protective measure means –
   (a) a measure to maintain the status quo pending determination of the issues at trial; or
   (b) a measure providing a preliminary means of securing assets out of which an ultimate judgment may be satisfied; or
   (c) a measure to restrain conduct by a defendant to prevent current or imminent future harm.]

[*Alternative B*
Orders for provisional and protective measures issued in accordance with Article 13[141] shall be recognised and enforced in the other Contracting States in accordance with Articles [25, 27–34].]]

Article 24 – Judgments Excluded from Chapter III

This Chapter shall not apply to judgments based solely on a ground of jurisdiction provided for by national law in accordance with Article 17, and which is not consistent with any basis of jurisdiction provided for in Articles [white list].[142]

Article 25 – Judgments to Be Recognised or Enforced

1. A judgment based on a ground of jurisdiction provided for in Articles 3 to 13, or which is consistent with any such ground, shall be recognised or enforced under this Chapter.
2. [In order to be recognised, a judgment referred to in paragraph 1 must have the effect of res judicata in the State of origin.][143]
   or
   [A judgment referred to in paragraph 1 shall be recognised from the time, and for as long as, it produces its effects in the State of origin.][144]

---

[140] It was suggested that it would be sufficient if a court is seised after a provisional and protective measure is made as long as it is already seised by the time of recognition and enforcement of the provisional and protective measure is sought abroad.

[141] This refers back to the proposal made as Alternative B in Article 13, above. The order must have been made by a court which is seised or about to be seised of a claim and which has white list jurisdiction to determine the merits thereof.

[142] The addition of the second part of the sentence was accepted by consensus. The additional words make it clear that Chapter III will apply to any judgment based on one or more grounds of jurisdiction, so long as any one of those grounds is consistent with a required basis for jurisdiction under the Convention. For recognition purposes, the application of Article 24 is confined to judgments that can only be based on jurisdiction provided for by national law.

[143] This is the text of paragraph 2 as it appeared in the preliminary draft Convention of October 1999. It was suggested to avoid the use of technical terms such as '*res judicata*' or '*autorité de la chose jugée*' which may not have a uniform meaning in all legal systems.

[144] This text was proposed as an alternative text to paragraph 2 by the Informal Working Group on Article 25. It has been agreed to insert it in the text to facilitate future discussion.

3. [In order to be enforceable, a judgment referred to in paragraph 1 must be enforceable in the State of origin.][145]
   or
   [A judgment referred to in the preceding paragraphs shall be enforceable from the time, and for as long as, it is enforceable in the State of origin.][146]
4. However, recognition or enforcement may be postponed [or refused][147] if the judgment is the subject of review in the State of origin or if the time limit for seeking a review has not expired.

Article 26 – Judgments Not to Be Recognised or Enforced[148]

A judgment based on a ground of jurisdiction which conflicts with Article 4, 5, 7, 8 or 12, or whose application is prohibited by virtue of Article 18, shall not be recognised or enforced.[149]

Article 27 – Verification of Jurisdiction[150]

1. The court addressed shall verify the jurisdiction of the court of origin.
2. In verifying the jurisdiction of the court of origin, the court addressed shall be bound by the findings of fact on which the court of origin based its jurisdiction, unless the judgment was given by default.
3. Recognition or enforcement of a judgment may not be refused on the ground that the court addressed considers that the court of origin should have declined jurisdiction in accordance with Article 22.

Article 27A – Appearance Without Protest

1. If, in the proceedings before the court of origin, –
   (a) the plaintiff claimed that the court had jurisdiction on one of the grounds specified in Articles [white list]; and
   (b) the plaintiff did not claim that the court had jurisdiction on any other ground under national law; and
   (c) the court did not determine that it had jurisdiction under any other ground under national law; and

---

145 This is the text of paragraph 3 as it appeared in the preliminary draft Convention of October 1999.

146 This text was proposed as an alternative text to paragraph 3 by the Informal Working Group on Article 25. It has been agreed to insert it in the text for future discussion.

147 The addition of the words in brackets is proposed in order to ensure that Contracting States are not obliged to recognise or enforce judgments under the circumstances described in this paragraph. The decision whether to postpone or refuse recognition should be left to national law. The proposal has not as yet been discussed.

148 Agreement was reached on this Article subject to further identification of the Articles to which it will apply.

149 Agreement was reached on this paragraph subject to further identification of the Articles to which it will apply.

150 This Article was agreed to.

(d) the defendant proceeded on the merits without contesting jurisdiction,[151]
the defendant shall, in the court addressed, be precluded from contesting the jurisdiction of the court of origin.

2. This Article shall not apply if the courts of a Contracting State other than the State of the court of origin had exclusive jurisdiction under Article 12.[152]

Article 28 – Grounds for Refusal of Recognition or Enforcement

1. Recognition or enforcement of a judgment may be refused [only][153] if –
   (a) proceedings between the same parties and having the same subject matter are pending before a court of the State addressed, if first seised in accordance with Article 21;[154]
   (b) the judgment is inconsistent with a judgment rendered, either in the State addressed or in another State, provided that in the latter case the judgment is capable of being recognised or enforced in the State addressed;[155]
   [(c) the [judgment results from] proceedings [in the State of origin were][156] incompatible with fundamental principles of procedure of the State addressed, [including the right of each party to be heard by an impartial and independent court];][157]
   (d) the document which instituted the proceedings or an equivalent document, including the essential elements of the claim, was not notified to the defendant in sufficient time and in such a way as to enable him to arrange for his

---

[151] The view was expressed that the time limits presently specified in Article 5, above, should be incorporated in sub-paragraph d). There was no consensus on this point.

[152] Apart from the matter noted in note 151, above, there was consensus on this proposed new article. Its purpose is to overcome the difficulty referred to by the co-reporters in relation to the text of Article 5 as it appeared in the preliminary draft Convention of October 1999 (see Preliminary Document No 11, at p. 46) that under the text as it then stood appearance without protest to a jurisdiction exercised pursuant to national law (the 'grey zone') would convert that jurisdiction into required jurisdiction. There was a consensus that this would be an undesirable effect of the previous provision. The effect of the new provision would remove appearance by the defendant from the list of required jurisdictions (the 'white list'), but appearance of the defendant without protest will, if the conditions set out in paragraph 1 are fulfilled, preclude the defendant from contesting the jurisdiction of the court of origin upon the verification of the jurisdiction of that court by the court addressed.

[153] The insertion of the word 'only' has been proposed to make clear that the following list is an exclusive list of grounds for refusal or enforcement, see Preliminary Document No 11, at p. 102. No consensus was reached on the inclusion of this word in the text.

[154] This sub-paragraph was agreed to.

[155] This sub-paragraph was agreed to.

[156] The deletion of the words 'judgment results from' and the insertion of the words 'in the State of origin' has been proposed. This is intended to clarify the provision. Further discussion depends on the decision of the issue raised in footnote 157.

[157] The deletion of this sub-paragraph has been proposed because it would encourage attacks on the impartiality and independence of the court by the losing party in an attempt to delay enforcement. It would also be contrary to the need for mutual trust and confidence among the courts of Contracting States. It may be that, subject to revision, the first part of the sub-paragraph could be acceptable. No consensus was reached on the continued inclusion of the sub-paragraph in its present form.

defence [, or was not notified in accordance with [an applicable international convention] [the domestic rules of law of the State where such notification took place]],[158] unless the defendant entered an appearance and presented his case without contesting the matter of notification in the court of origin, provided that the law of that court permits objection to the matter of notification and the defendant did not object.[159]

(e) the judgment was obtained by fraud in connection with a matter of procedure;[160]

(f) recognition or enforcement would be manifestly incompatible with the public policy of the State addressed.[161]

2. Without prejudice to such review as is necessary for the purpose of application of the provisions of this Chapter, there shall be no review of the merits of the judgment rendered by the court of origin.[162]

Article 29 – Documents to Be Produced[163]

1. The party seeking recognition or applying for enforcement shall produce –
   (a) a complete and certified copy of the judgment;
   (b) if the judgment was rendered by default, the original or a certified copy of a document establishing that the document which instituted the proceedings or an equivalent document was notified to the defaulting party;
   (c) all documents required to establish that the judgment is res judicata in the State of origin or, as the case may be, is enforceable in that State;
   (d) if the court addressed so requires, a translation of the documents referred to above, made by a person [legally][164] qualified to do so.

[2. An application for recognition or enforcement may be accompanied by the form annexed to this Convention[165] and, if the court addressed so requires, a translation of the form made by a person [legally][166] qualified to do so.][167]

---

158 No difficulties were raised about the portion of the sub-paragraph not in brackets. The material within the brackets was put forward as containing two options. The option contained within the first set of brackets would permit the requested court to deny recognition in cases where the applicable international convention was violated, such as the Hague Convention of 1965 on the *Service Abroad of Judicial and Extrajudicial Documents in Civil or Commercial Matters.* The second option would permit the requested court to deny recognition where service was not effected in accordance with the requirements of the law of the State where notification took place. In most cases, but not all, this would coincide with the State addressed. There was no consensus on the acceptance of either option.

159 The addition of the words after the last comma was agreed to, subject to drafting.

160 Agreement was reached on this sub-paragraph.

161 Agreement was reached on this sub-paragraph.

162 Agreement was reached on this paragraph.

163 This Article was approved by consensus as it appeared in the preliminary draft Convention of October 1999. It was noted that drafting changes would have to be made if the proposed amendments to Article 25 were accepted.

164 It was proposed to add the words 'legally'. There was no consensus.

165 A draft of such a form is attached in Annex III as a basis for further discussion.

166 It was proposed to add the words 'legally'. There was no consensus.

3. No legalisation or other formality may be required.
4. If the terms of the judgment do not permit the court addressed to verify whether the conditions of this Chapter have been complied with, that court may require the production of any other necessary documents.

Article 30 – Procedure

The procedure for recognition, declaration of enforceability or registration for enforcement, and the enforcement of the judgment, are governed by the law of the State addressed so far as the Convention does not provide otherwise. [The law of the State addressed must provide for the possibility to appeal against the declaration of enforceability or registration for enforcement.][168] The court addressed shall act [in accordance with the most rapid procedure available under local law][169] [expeditiously].

Article 31 – Costs of Proceedings

1. No security, bond or deposit, however described, to guarantee the payment of costs or expenses [for the procedure of Article 30][170] shall be required by reason only that the applicant is a national of, or has its habitual residence in, another Contracting State.

[2. An order for payment of costs and expenses of proceedings, made in one of the Contracting States against any person exempt from requirements as to security, bond, or deposit by virtue of paragraph 1 shall, on the application of the person

---

167 It was agreed that the nature of the form and whether it should be mandatory, available upon request, or discretionary on the part of the rendering court, required further discussion.

168 This proposal was put forward in order to ensure that there be at least one possibility of an appeal against a decision either to grant or to refuse exequatur or registration. This proposal was opposed on the ground that the provision of a method of challenging or reviewing such a decision should be left to national law. The matter remains unresolved.

169 The language within the brackets was proposed to replace the word 'expeditiously' in the existing text. Its intention was to give expression in the text of the Convention to the comment of the Reporters in Preliminary Document No 11 at p. 110 that Article 30 'obliges Contracting States to use ... the most rapid procedure they possess in their national law'. Concerns were expressed that the proposal would constitute too great an intrusion into national law and that certain rapid procedures that are provided for, for example, in the context of regional arrangements, are not necessarily appropriate in a world wide convention. In a further clarification the Reporters pointed out that such a provision would not oblige a State to use a procedure made available specifically for the purposes of a treaty or arrangement to which that State was a party, but referred to its non-treaty law (droit commun). No consensus was reached on this provision.

170 This addition was proposed with the intention of clarifying the scope of the Article without changing the substance. The necessity for this provision was questioned and fears were expressed about unintended consequences. Reference was also made to Article 16 of the Hague Convention of 1973 on the Recognition and Enforcement of Decisions relating to Maintenance Obligations. Consensus was reached on the substance of this paragraph.

entitled to the benefit of the order, be rendered enforceable without charge in any other Contracting State.][171]

Article 32 – Legal Aid[172]

[Natural persons habitually resident in a Contracting State shall be entitled, in proceedings for recognition and enforcement, to legal aid under the same conditions as apply to persons habitually resident in the requested State.]

Article 33 – Damages

1. A judgment which awards non-compensatory damages, including exemplary or punitive damages, shall be recognised and enforced to the extent that a court in the State addressed could have awarded similar or comparable damages. Nothing in this paragraph shall preclude the court addressed from recognising and enforcing the judgment under its law for an amount up to the full amount of the damages awarded by the court of origin.[173]
2. (a) Where the debtor, after proceedings in which the creditor has the opportunity to be heard, satisfies the court addressed that in the circumstances, including those existing in the State of origin, grossly excessive damages[174] have been awarded, recognition and enforcement may be limited to a lesser amount.
   (b) In no event shall the court addressed recognise or enforce[175] the judgment in an amount less than that which could have been awarded in the State

---

171 The proposal for this paragraph is based on Article 15 of the Hague Convention of 1980 on International Access to Justice and Article 18 of the Hague Convention of 1954 on Civil Procedure. Its purpose is to secure enforcement of an order made by the requested court for the payment of the costs and expenses borne by the judgment debtor in a case where the requested court has rejected enforcement of the judgment on a ground such as the fraud of the judgment creditor upon the court of origin. There was no consensus on this point.

172 It was proposed that this provision be deleted from the Convention because it raised constitutional concerns. Some delegations did not consider the provision essential and it could therefore be deleted. But for yet other delegations it was of great importance. It was suggested that the issue could be resolved through an 'opt-in' provision. There was no consensus on these proposals.

173 The text of paragraph 1 has been approved by consensus and replaces the text of the preliminary draft Convention of October 1999. The working group that produced this text also recommended consideration of reversing the order of paragraphs 1 and 2.

174 The Reporters explained that the statement at p. 114 of Preliminary Document No 11 to the effect that as a general principle 'grossly excessive' was likely to mean 'grossly excessive by the standards of the court of origin', did not mean that the question of whether the damages were grossly excessive should be judged only by the standards of the court of origin. This would depend on the circumstances of each case, especially on whether the judgment creditor was a resident of the State of origin or of the requested State. In the latter case, obviously the standards of the requested State would assume greater importance.

175 The addition of the reference to enforcement here and in other parts of the Article was proposed in order to make clear that the Article applies to both recognition and enforcement, see the comments of the Reporters in Preliminary Document No 11, at p. 113. The proposal was accepted by consensus.

addressed in the same circumstances, including those existing in the State of origin.[176]

3. In applying paragraph 1 or 2, the court addressed shall take into account whether and to what extent the damages awarded by the court of origin serve to cover costs and expenses relating to the proceedings.

Article 34 – Severability

[*Alternative A*

If the judgment contains elements which are severable, one or more of them may be separately recognised, declared enforceable, registered for enforcement, or enforced.][177]

[*Alternative B*

Partial recognition or enforcement

Partial recognition or enforcement of a judgment shall be granted where:

(a) partial recognition or enforcement is applied for; or
(b) only part of the judgment is capable of being recognised or enforced under this Convention; or
(c) the judgment has been satisfied in part.][178]

Article 35 – Authentic Instruments

[*Alternative A*

1. Each Contracting State may declare that it will enforce, subject to reciprocity, authentic instruments formally drawn up or registered and enforceable in another Contracting State.][179]

[*Alternative B*

1. Authentic instruments formally drawn up or registered and enforceable in a

---

[176] It was inquired whether statutory damages (where a statute has determined the amount to be awarded in case of breach), liquidated damages (where a contract has determined the amount to be paid in case of breach) and fixed interest on damages awards would fall within the scope of Article 33 and, if so, whether their character would be compensatory or non-compensatory. The co-reporters indicated that Article 33 would be applicable in such cases and that the classification of such damages as compensatory or punitive would be determined by the requested court. That court would take into account whether the statutory provision in question of the originating forum, or the contractual provision as interpreted according to its governing law, merely sought to estimate what was required to compensate the plaintiff or sought to impose a penalty.

[177] This is the text as it appeared in the preliminary draft Convention of October 1999. It was noted by the co-reporters in Preliminary Document No 11, at p. 115 that this text made no express provision for partial enforcement. Such a provision would allow the court addressed to sever the portion of the judgment which had already been paid or otherwise satisfied.

[178] This is an alternative text which has been included in this document to facilitate future discussion.

[179] This is the text as it appeared in the preliminary draft Convention of October 1999. According to that text States wishing to take advantage of Article 35 should specifically elect to adopt it on the basis of reciprocity with other States making a similar declaration.

Contracting State shall, upon request,[180] be declared enforceable in another Contracting State.][181]

2. The authentic instrument must have been authenticated by a public authority or a delegate of a public authority and the authentication must relate to both the signature and the content of the document.[182]

[3. The provisions concerning recognition and enforcement provided for in this Chapter shall apply as appropriate.][183]

[Article X[184]

Any Contracting State may, at the time of ratification, acceptance, approval of, or accession to, this Convention, or at any time thereafter, make a declaration that it will not apply Article 35, or that it will apply that Article subject to reciprocity.[185]][186]

Article 36 – Settlements[187]

Settlements to which a court has given its authority shall be recognised, declared enforceable, registered for enforcement, or enforced in the State addressed under the same conditions as judgments falling within the Convention, so far as those conditions apply to settlements.

*Chapter **** – General Provisions*

Article 37 – Relationship with Other Conventions

It was agreed that the proposals made in the Annex to the preliminary draft Convention as well as the Working Documents produced for the purposes of the present Session be reproduced in Annex 1 of this Summary.

---

180 Further discussion will be necessary to clarify what is meant by the words 'upon request' or whether the method and form of making the request (in writing, to a court or other instance) should be left to national law.

181 According to this alternative text, Article 35 will apply to all Contracting States in the absence of a declaration as envisaged in the proposed Article X below. No consensus was reached on the version of paragraph 1 to be preferred.

182 This was the text as it appeared in the preliminary draft Convention of October 1999.

183 It was decided that this paragraph should remain within square brackets.

184 This provision is part of Alternative 2 to paragraph 1, above. If accepted, it will probably be placed among the General Provisions of the Convention. If accepted, it will give Contracting States the following options: (1) not to apply Article 35 under any circumstances; (2) to apply Article 35 on condition of reciprocity; or (3) to apply Article 35 without requiring reciprocity, that is, where a Contracting State is prepared to give effect to authentic instruments, although it does not provide for that institution under its domestic law.

185 It remains to be decided whether reciprocity should be required in this proposal.

186 There is no consensus as regards this provision.

187 This Article was approved by consensus.

Articles 38 to 40 – Uniform Interpretation

This matter has not yet been discussed.

Article 41 – Federal Clause

This matter has not yet been discussed.

[Article 42 – Ratification of and Accession to the Convention[188]

[Alternative A

1. This Convention shall become effective between any two Contracting States on the date of entry into force provided that the two States have each deposited a declaration confirming the entry into force between the two States of treaty relations under this Convention.
2. At the time of deposit of its instrument of ratification or accession, or at any time thereafter, each State shall deposit with the depository a copy of its declarations concerning all Contracting States with which the State will enter into treaty relations under the Convention. A Contracting State may withdraw or modify a declaration at any time.
3. The depository shall circulate all declarations received to all Contracting States and to Member States of the Hague Conference.
4. The Hague Conference on Private International Law shall regularly publish information reporting on the declarations that have been deposited pursuant to this Article.]

[Alternative B

1. The Convention shall be open for signature by the States which were Members of the Hague Conference on Private International Law at the time of its Nineteenth Session.[189]
2. It shall be ratified, accepted or approved and the instruments of ratification, acceptance or approval shall be deposited with the Ministry of Foreign Affairs of the Kingdom of the Netherlands.
3. Any other State may accede to the Convention.
4. The instrument of accession shall be deposited with the Ministry of Foreign Affairs of the Kingdom of the Netherlands.
5. The Convention shall enter into force for a State acceding to it on the first day of the third calendar month after the deposit of its instrument of accession.
6. The accession will have effect only as regards the relations between the acceding State and such Contracting States as will have declared their acceptance of the

---

[188] It was agreed that the two following proposals be included in this document in order to facilitate future discussion of this subject. There was no decision on whether there should be a provision dealing with bilateralisation and, if so, what form such a provision should take and how far bilateralisation should extend.

[189] It was requested that consideration be given to a method whereby the European Community could become a party to the Convention.

accession. Such a declaration will also have to be made by any Member State ratifying, accepting or approving the Convention after an accession. Such declaration shall be deposited at the Ministry of Foreign Affairs of the Kingdom of the Netherlands; this Ministry shall forward, through diplomatic channels, a certified copy to each of the Contracting States.

7. The Convention will enter into force as between the acceding State and the State that has declared its acceptance of the accession on the first day of the third calendar month after the deposit of the declaration of acceptance.][190]]

ANNEX I[191]

Article 37 – Relationship with Other Conventions

Proposal 1

1. The Convention does not affect any international instrument to which Contracting States are or become Parties and which contains provisions on matters governed by the Convention, unless a contrary declaration is made by the States Parties to such instrument.
2. However, the Convention prevails over such instruments to the extent that they provide for fora not authorised under the provisions of Article 18 of the Convention.
3. The preceding paragraphs also apply to uniform laws based on special ties of a regional or other nature between the States concerned and to instruments adopted by a community of States.

Proposal 2

1. (a) In this Article, the Brussels Convention [as amended], Regulation [...] of the European Union, and the Lugano Convention [as amended] shall be collectively referred to as "the European instruments".
   (b) A State Party to either of the above Conventions or a Member State of the European Union to which the above Regulation applies shall be collectively referred to as "European instrument States".
2. Subject to the following provisions [of this Article], a European instrument State shall apply the European instruments, and not the Convention, whenever the European instruments are applicable according to their terms.
3. Except where the provisions of the European instruments on –
   (a) exclusive jurisdiction;
   (b) prorogation of jurisdiction;
   (c) *lis pendens* and related actions;
   (d) protective jurisdiction for consumers or employees;

[190] This proposal follows the language of Articles 37 and 38 of the *Hague Convention of 1980 on the Civil Aspects of International Child Abduction.*

[191] Proposals 1–3 were annexed to the preliminary draft Convention of October 1999. Proposal 4 was introduced and discussed at the June 2001 Session.

are applicable, a European instrument State shall apply Articles 3, 5 to 11, 14 to 16 and 18 of the Convention whenever the defendant is not domiciled in a European instrument State.

4. Even if the defendant is domiciled in a European instrument State, a court of such a State shall apply –
   (a) Article 4 of the Convention whenever the court chosen is not in a European instrument State;
   (b) Article 12 of the Convention whenever the court with exclusive jurisdiction under that provision is not in a European instrument State; and
   (c) Articles 21 and 22 of this Convention whenever the court in whose favour the proceedings are stayed or jurisdiction is declined is not a court of a European instrument State.

Note: Another provision will be needed for other conventions and instruments.

Proposal 3

Judgments of courts of a Contracting State to this Convention based on jurisdiction granted under the terms of a different international convention ("other Convention") shall be recognised and enforced in courts of Contracting States to this Convention which are also Contracting States to the other Convention. This provision shall not apply if, by reservation under Article ..., a Contracting State chooses –

(a) not to be governed by this provision, or
(b) not to be governed by this provision as to certain designated other conventions.

Proposal 4[192]

Article 2 – Territorial Scope

Insert the words shown in brackets in the chapeau of paragraph 1, as follows:

1. The provisions of Chapter II shall apply in the courts of a Contracting State unless all the parties are habitually resident in that State [or in the territory of a regional economic integration organisation that is a Contracting Party under Article []]. However, even if all the parties are habitually resident in that [Contracting] State [or Party] –

[...]

Article 37A – Relationship with Conventions in Particular Matters

This Convention shall not affect any conventions to which the Contracting States are or will be parties and which, in relation to particular matters, govern jurisdiction or the recognition or enforcement of judgments.

[192] It was pointed out to facilitate future discussions that Article 37A and Article X could in principle also be extended to cover regional economic integration organisations.

Article 37A – Relationship with Conventions in Particular Matters

This Convention shall not affect the application of any other convention to which the Contracting States are or will be parties and which, in relation to particular matters, governs jurisdiction or the recognition or enforcement of judgments, provided that the application of such other convention shall not affect the rights and obligations under this Convention of any State Party that is not a Party to such other convention.

Article X – Allocation of Jurisdiction Under This Convention

Nothing in this Convention shall affect any rule of a Contracting State regarding the internal allocation of jurisdiction among the courts of that State.

ANNEX II

Proposal 1

Article 8 – Individual Contracts of Employment

1. An employee may bring a claim in matters relating to individual contracts of employment against the employer
   (a) in the courts of the State where the employer has its habitual residence;
   (b) in the courts of the State in which the employee habitually carries out or carried out his work, [unless it was not reasonably foreseeable by the employer that the employee would habitually carry out his work in that State]; or
   (c) if the employee does not or did not habitually carry out his work in any one State, in the courts of the State in which the establishment that engaged the employee is or was situated or in the courts of the State in which the employee carried out the work which has given rise to the dispute.
2. An employer may bring a claim in matters relating to individual contracts of employment against the employee only in the courts of the State in which the employee is habitually resident or in which the employee habitually carries out his work.
3. However, proceedings may be brought before the courts referred to in an agreement which conforms with the requirements of Article 4, paragraphs 1 and 2 –
   (a) if the agreement is entered into after the dispute has arisen;
   (b) to the extent that the agreement allows the employee to choose whether to bring proceedings in the courts referred to in the agreement or in the courts of the State referred to in paragraph 1; or
   (c) to the extent that the agreement is binding on both parties under the law of the State in which the employee carried out the work which has given rise to the dispute and provided that it meets the requirements specified in the declaration made by such State as contemplated in Article X.

Proposal 2

Article 8 – Individual Contracts of Employment

1. In matters relating to individual contracts of employment, an employee may bring a claim against the employer,
   (a) in the courts of the State in which the employee habitually carries out or carried out his work, [unless it was not reasonably foreseeable by the employer that the employee would habitually carry out his work in that State]; or
   (b) if the employee does not or did not habitually carry out his work in any one State, in the courts of the State in which the establishment that engaged the employee is or was situated.
2. An employer may bring a claim against the employee under this Convention only –
   (a) in the courts of the State:
      (i) in which the employee is habitually resident; or
      (ii) in which the employee habitually carries out his work; or
   (b) if the employee and the employer have entered into an agreement to which paragraph 4 b) or c) applies, in the court designated in that agreement.
3. Article 4 applies to an agreement between an employee and an employer only:
   (a) to the extent that it allows the employee to bring proceedings in the courts of a State other than the State referred to in paragraph 2; or
   (b) if the agreement is entered into after the dispute has arisen; or
   (c) to the extent that the agreement is binding on the employee under the law of the State in which the employee is resident at the time the agreement is entered into.

Proposal 3

Article X – Reservation in Respect of Consumer Contracts and Employment Contracts

1. A Contracting State may declare at the time of signature, ratification, acceptance, approval or accession that it will not be bound by Article 7 or 8 of this Convention.
2. A Contracting State which makes a declaration in accordance with the preceding paragraph may also declare that it will not be bound by Chapter III of this Convention in respect of judgments rendered under Article 7 or 8.
3. A Contracting State which makes a declaration in accordance with the preceding paragraphs is not to be considered a Contracting State of this Convention in respect of matters to which the declaration applies.

Note: This proposal is an alternative to Article 25 bis in the Edinburgh Draft Annex III A and Article 8, paragraph 4 c). It could also work well with the present wording of Articles 7 and 8 in the 1999 draft Convention. However, some modifications of the rules of jurisdiction will have to be modified in the Edinburgh Draft.

The purpose of this reservation is to make it possible for States that do not accept special rules about consumers or employees, to opt out from the Convention in this respect.

Under the first paragraph a State can opt out from the jurisdictional rules but not the rules on recognition and enforcement under Chapter III. Consequently, such a State is bound to recognise and enforce judgments rendered under Article 7 or 8. However, the State is not obliged to apply Articles 7 and 8 in relation to jurisdiction.

Under the second paragraph, a Contracting State has the possibility to opt out completely in respect of consumer contracts and/or employment contracts. A State can only make a declaration under this paragraph if it has also made a declaration under paragraph 1. A State that has decided to make declarations under paragraphs 1 and 2 will be regarded as having opted out completely in respect of consumer contracts and employment contracts under the Convention. Therefore such a State cannot apply Articles 7 and 8, and judgments rendered in other Contracting States under Articles 7 and 8 will not be recognised under the Convention in the State that has taken this reservation.

Paragraph 3 makes it clear that a State making reservations under paragraphs 1 and 2 is to be considered a non-Contracting State in respect of matters covered by the reservation.

Proposal 4 "Edinburgh Solution"

Article 8 – Individual Contracts of Employment

1. This Article applies in matters relating to individual contracts of employment.
2. An employee may bring a claim against the employer
   (a) in the courts of the State in which the employee habitually carries out or carried out his work, [unless it was not reasonably foreseeable by the employer that the employee would habitually carry out his work in that State]; or
   (b) if the employee does not or did not habitually carry out his work in any one State, in the courts of the State in which the establishment that engaged the employee is or was situated.
3. An employer may bring a claim against the employee under this Convention only –
   (a) in the courts of the State:
      (i) in which the employee is habitually resident; or
      (ii) in which the employee habitually carries out his work; or
   (b) if the employee and the employer have entered into an agreement to which paragraph 4b) or c) applies, in the court designated in that agreement.
4. Article 4 applies to an agreement between an employee and an employer only:
   (a) to the extent that it allows the employee to bring proceedings in the courts of a State other than the State referred to in paragraph 2; or
   (b) if the agreement is entered into after the dispute has arisen; or
   (c) to the extent that the agreement is binding on the employee under the law of the State in which the employee is resident at the time the agreement is entered into.

Article 25 – Judgments to Be Recognised or Enforced
"Subject to Article 25 *bis* ..."

[Article 25 ***bis***

1. A Contracting State may make a declaration that it will not recognise or enforce a judgment under this Chapter, or a declaration specifying the conditions under which it will recognise or enforce a judgment under this Chapter, where:
   (a) the judgment was rendered by the court of origin under Article 7(2) or Article 8(2); and
   (b) the parties had entered into an agreement which conforms with the requirements of Article 4 designating a court other than the court of origin.
2. [A declaration under this Article may not deny recognition and enforcement of a judgment given under Article 7(2) or Article 8(2) if the Contracting State making the declaration would exercise jurisdiction under the relevant Article in a corresponding case.]
3. Recognition or enforcement of a judgment may be refused by a Contracting State that has made a declaration contemplated by paragraph 1 in accordance with the terms of that declaration.]

ANNEX III

Proposal by the Informal Working Group on Forms

Annex to the Convention

Forms

Form A

Confirmation of Judgment

(Sample form confirming the issuance of a judgment by the Court of Origin for the purposes of recognition and enforcement under the Convention on Jurisdiction and Foreign Judgments in Civil and Commercial Matters (the "Convention"))

(THE COURT OF ORIGIN)

(ADDRESS OF THE COURT OF ORIGIN)

(CONTACT PERSON AT THE COURT OF ORIGIN)

(TEL./FAX/EMAIL OF THE COURT OF ORIGIN)

(PLAINTIFF)

Case / Docket Number:

v.

(DEFENDANT)

(THE COURT OF ORIGIN) hereby confirms that it rendered a judgment in the above captioned matter on (DATE) in (CITY, STATE, COUNTRY), which is a Contracting State to the Convention. Attached to this form is a complete and certified copy of the judgment rendered by (THE COURT OF ORIGIN).[193]

1. Select one or more of the following options:[194]
   A. This Court based its jurisdiction over the defendant(s) on the following article(s) of the Convention, as implemented under the law governing the proceedings of this Court:

      ....

      ....

      ....

   B. This Court based its jurisdiction over the defendant(s) on the following ground of jurisdiction provided for by national law:

      ....

      ....

[193] Article 29(1)(a).

[194] Article 27 (1) – The court addressed shall verify the jurisdiction of the court of origin.

....

....

C. This Court did not identify in the judgment a ground for jurisdiction over the defendant(s):

YES __________ NO __________

2. This Court based its jurisdiction over the defendant(s) on the following findings of fact (*If the findings of fact are stated in the judgment or accompanying decision, indicate the relevant passages of the judgment and the decision*):[195]

....

....

....

....

3. This Court awarded the following payment of money (*Please indicate any relevant categories of damages*):[196]

....

....

....

....

4. This Court awarded interest as follows (*Please specify the rate of interest, the portion(s) of the award to which interest applies, and the date from which interest is computed*):

....

....

....

....

5. This Court included within the judgment the following court costs and expenses (including attorneys fees) related to the proceedings (*Please specify the amounts of any such awards, including where applicable, any amount(s) intended to cover costs and expenses relating to the proceedings within a monetary award*):[197]

....

....

....

....

6. This Court awarded, in whole or in part, the following non-monetary remedy (*Please describe the nature of the remedy*):

....

....

....

[195] Article 27(2) – The court addressed shall be bound by the findings of fact on which the court of origin based its jurisdiction.

[196] Refer to Article 33.

[197] Article 33 (3).

....

7. This judgment was rendered by default:

   YES __________ NO _________

   (*If this judgment was rendered by default, please attach the original or a certified copy of the document verifying notice to the defendant of the proceedings.*)[198,199]

8. This judgment (or some part thereof) is currently the subject of review in (COUNTRY OF THE COURT OF ORIGIN):[200]

   YES __________ NO _________

9. This judgment (or some part thereof) is presently enforceable in (COUNTRY OF THE COURT OF ORIGIN):[201]

   YES __________ NO _________

List of documents:

....

....

....

....

....

....

....

Dated this .... day of .... , 20........

....

Signature and/or stamp by an officer of the Court

---

198 Article 27(2) – If the judgment was by default, then the Court being addressed by this form is not bound by the findings of fact on which the court of origin based its jurisdiction.

199 Article 29(1)(b).

200 Article 25(4).

201 Article 25(3).

EU Regulations

Community legislation in force

Document 301R0044

Council Regulation (EC) No 44/2001 of 22 December 2000 on jurisdiction and the recognition and enforcement of judgments in civil and commercial matters

Official Journal L012, 16/01/2001 P.0001–0023

THE COUNCIL OF THE EUROPEAN UNION,

Having regard to the Treaty establishing the European Community, and in particular Article 61(c) and Article 67(1) thereof,

Having regard to the proposal from the Commission(*1*),

Having regard to the opinion of the European Parliament(*2*),

Having regard to the opinion of the Economic and Social Committee(*3*),

Whereas:

(1) The Community has set itself the objective of maintaining and developing an area of freedom, security and justice, in which the free movement of persons is ensured. In order to establish progressively such an area, the Community should adopt, amongst other things, the measures relating to judicial cooperation in civil matters which are necessary for the sound operation of the internal market.

(2) Certain differences between national rules governing jurisdiction and recognition of judgments hamper the sound operation of the internal market. Provisions to unify the rules of conflict of jurisdiction in civil and commercial matters and to simplify the formalities with a view to rapid and simple recognition and enforcement of judgments from Member States bound by this Regulation are essential.

(3) This area is within the field of judicial cooperation in civil matters within the meaning of Article 65 of the Treaty.

(4) In accordance with the principles of subsidiarity and proportionality as set out in Article 5 of the Treaty, the objectives of this Regulation cannot be sufficiently achieved by the Member States and can therefore be better achieved by the Community. This Regulation confines itself to the minimum required in order to achieve those objectives and does not go beyond what is necessary for that purpose.

(5) On 27 September 1968 the Member States, acting under Article 293, fourth indent, of the Treaty, concluded the Brussels Convention on Jurisdiction and the

J.J. Barceló and K.M. Clermont (eds.), A Global Law of Jurisdiction and Judgments: Lessons from The Hague, 353–382

Enforcement of Judgments in Civil and Commercial Matters, as amended by Conventions on the Accession of the New Member States to that Convention (hereinafter referred to as the "Brussels Convention")(*4*). On 16 September 1988 Member States and EFTA States concluded the Lugano Convention on Jurisdiction and the Enforcement of Judgments in Civil and Commercial Matters, which is a parallel Convention to the 1968 Brussels Convention. Work has been undertaken for the revision of those Conventions, and the Council has approved the content of the revised texts. Continuity in the results achieved in that revision should be ensured.

(6) In order to attain the objective of free movement of judgments in civil and commercial matters, it is necessary and appropriate that the rules governing jurisdiction and the recognition and enforcement of judgments be governed by a Community legal instrument which is binding and directly applicable.

(7) The scope of this Regulation must cover all the main civil and commercial matters apart from certain well-defined matters.

(8) There must be a link between proceedings to which this Regulation applies and the territory of the Member States bound by this Regulation. Accordingly common rules on jurisdiction should, in principle, apply when the defendant is domiciled in one of those Member States.

(9) A defendant not domiciled in a Member State is in general subject to national rules of jurisdiction applicable in the territory of the Member State of the court seised, and a defendant domiciled in a Member State not bound by this Regulation must remain subject to the Brussels Convention.

(10) For the purposes of the free movement of judgments, judgments given in a Member State bound by this Regulation should be recognised and enforced in another Member State bound by this Regulation, even if the judgment debtor is domiciled in a third State.

(11) The rules of jurisdiction must be highly predictable and founded on the principle that jurisdiction is generally based on the defendant's domicile and jurisdiction must always be available on this ground save in a few well-defined situations in which the subject-matter of the litigation or the autonomy of the parties warrants a different linking factor. The domicile of a legal person must be defined autonomously so as to make the common rules more transparent and avoid conflicts of jurisdiction.

(12) In addition to the defendant's domicile, there should be alternative grounds of jurisdiction based on a close link between the court and the action or in order to facilitate the sound administration of justice.

(13) In relation to insurance, consumer contracts and employment, the weaker party should be protected by rules of jurisdiction more favourable to his interests than the general rules provide for.

(14) The autonomy of the parties to a contract, other than an insurance, consumer

or employment contract, where only limited autonomy to determine the courts having jurisdiction is allowed, must be respected subject to the exclusive grounds of jurisdiction laid down in this Regulation.

(15) In the interests of the harmonious administration of justice it is necessary to minimise the possibility of concurrent proceedings and to ensure that irreconcilable judgments will not be given in two Member States. There must be a clear and effective mechanism for resolving cases of lis pendens and related actions and for obviating problems flowing from national differences as to the determination of the time when a case is regarded as pending. For the purposes of this Regulation that time should be defined autonomously.

(16) Mutual trust in the administration of justice in the Community justifies judgments given in a Member State being recognised automatically without the need for any procedure except in cases of dispute.

(17) By virtue of the same principle of mutual trust, the procedure for making enforceable in one Member State a judgment given in another must be efficient and rapid. To that end, the declaration that a judgment is enforceable should be issued virtually automatically after purely formal checks of the documents supplied, without there being any possibility for the court to raise of its own motion any of the grounds for non-enforcement provided for by this Regulation.

(18) However, respect for the rights of the defence means that the defendant should be able to appeal in an adversarial procedure, against the declaration of enforceability, if he considers one of the grounds for non-enforcement to be present. Redress procedures should also be available to the claimant where his application for a declaration of enforceability has been rejected.

(19) Continuity between the Brussels Convention and this Regulation should be ensured, and transitional provisions should be laid down to that end. The same need for continuity applies as regards the interpretation of the Brussels Convention by the Court of Justice of the European Communities and the 1971 Protocol(5) should remain applicable also to cases already pending when this Regulation enters into force.

(20) The United Kingdom and Ireland, in accordance with Article 3 of the Protocol on the position of the United Kingdom and Ireland annexed to the Treaty on European Union and to the Treaty establishing the European Community, have given notice of their wish to take part in the adoption and application of this Regulation.

(21) Denmark, in accordance with Articles 1 and 2 of the Protocol on the position of Denmark annexed to the Treaty on European Union and to the Treaty establishing the European Community, is not participating in the adoption of this Regulation, and is therefore not bound by it nor subject to its application.

(22) Since the Brussels Convention remains in force in relations between Denmark and the Member States that are bound by this Regulation, both the Convention and the 1971 Protocol continue to apply between Denmark and the Member States bound by this Regulation.

(23) The Brussels Convention also continues to apply to the territories of the Member States which fall within the territorial scope of that Convention and which are excluded from this Regulation pursuant to Article 299 of the Treaty.

(24) Likewise for the sake of consistency, this Regulation should not affect rules governing jurisdiction and the recognition of judgments contained in specific Community instruments.

(25) Respect for international commitments entered into by the Member States means that this Regulation should not affect conventions relating to specific matters to which the Member States are parties.

(26) The necessary flexibility should be provided for in the basic rules of this Regulation in order to take account of the specific procedural rules of certain Member States. Certain provisions of the Protocol annexed to the Brussels Convention should accordingly be incorporated in this Regulation.

(27) In order to allow a harmonious transition in certain areas which were the subject of special provisions in the Protocol annexed to the Brussels Convention, this Regulation lays down, for a transitional period, provisions taking into consideration the specific situation in certain Member States.

(28) No later than five years after entry into force of this Regulation the Commission will present a report on its application and, if need be, submit proposals for adaptations.

(29) The Commission will have to adjust Annexes I to IV on the rules of national jurisdiction, the courts or competent authorities and redress procedures available on the basis of the amendments forwarded by the Member State concerned; amendments made to Annexes V and VI should be adopted in accordance with Council Decision 1999/468/EC of 28 June 1999 laying down the procedures for the exercise of implementing powers conferred on the Commission(*6*),

HAS ADOPTED THIS REGULATION:

Chapter I

Scope

Article 1

1. This Regulation shall apply in civil and commercial matters whatever the nature of the court or tribunal. It shall not extend, in particular, to revenue, customs or administrative matters.

2. The Regulation shall not apply to:
   (a) the status or legal capacity of natural persons, rights in property arising out of a matrimonial relationship, wills and succession;
   (b) bankruptcy, proceedings relating to the winding-up of insolvent companies or other legal persons, judicial arrangements, compositions and analogous proceedings;
   (c) social security;
   (d) arbitration.
3. In this Regulation, the term "Member State" shall mean Member States with the exception of Denmark.

Chapter II

Jurisdiction

Section 1

General Provisions

Article 2

1. Subject to this Regulation, persons domiciled in a Member State shall, whatever their nationality, be sued in the courts of that Member State.
2. Persons who are not nationals of the Member State in which they are domiciled shall be governed by the rules of jurisdiction applicable to nationals of that State.

Article 3

1. Persons domiciled in a Member State may be sued in the courts of another Member State only by virtue of the rules set out in Sections 2 to 7 of this Chapter.
2. In particular the rules of national jurisdiction set out in Annex I shall not be applicable as against them.

Article 4

1. If the defendant is not domiciled in a Member State, the jurisdiction of the courts of each Member State shall, subject to Articles 22 and 23, be determined by the law of that Member State.
2. As against such a defendant, any person domiciled in a Member State may, whatever his nationality, avail himself in that State of the rules of jurisdiction there in force, and in particular those specified in Annex I, in the same way as the nationals of that State.

Section 2

Special Jurisdiction

Article 5

A person domiciled in a Member State may, in another Member State, be sued:

1. (a) in matters relating to a contract, in the courts for the place of performance of the obligation in question;
   (b) for the purpose of this provision and unless otherwise agreed, the place of performance of the obligation in question shall be:
   - in the case of the sale of goods, the place in a Member State where, under the contract, the goods were delivered or should have been delivered,
   - in the case of the provision of services, the place in a Member State where, under the contract, the services were provided or should have been provided,

   (c) if subparagraph (b) does not apply then subparagraph (a) applies;
2. in matters relating to maintenance, in the courts for the place where the maintenance creditor is domiciled or habitually resident or, if the matter is ancillary to proceedings concerning the status of a person, in the court which, according to its own law, has jurisdiction to entertain those proceedings, unless that jurisdiction is based solely on the nationality of one of the parties;
3. in matters relating to tort, delict or quasi-delict, in the courts for the place where the harmful event occurred or may occur;
4. as regards a civil claim for damages or restitution which is based on an act giving rise to criminal proceedings, in the court seised of those proceedings, to the extent that that court has jurisdiction under its own law to entertain civil proceedings;
5. as regards a dispute arising out of the operations of a branch, agency or other establishment, in the courts for the place in which the branch, agency or other establishment is situated;
6. as settlor, trustee or beneficiary of a trust created by the operation of a statute, or by a written instrument, or created orally and evidenced in writing, in the courts of the Member State in which the trust is domiciled;
7. as regards a dispute concerning the payment of remuneration claimed in respect of the salvage of a cargo or freight, in the court under the authority of which the cargo or freight in question:
   (a) has been arrested to secure such payment, or
   (b) could have been so arrested, but bail or other security has been given:
   - provided that this provision shall apply only if it is claimed that the defendant has an interest in the cargo or freight or had such an interest at the time of salvage.

Article 6

A person domiciled in a Member State may also be sued:

1. where he is one of a number of defendants, in the courts for the place where any one of them is domiciled, provided the claims are so closely connected that it is expedient to hear and determine them together to avoid the risk of irreconcilable judgments resulting from separate proceedings;
2. as a third party in an action on a warranty or guarantee or in any other third party proceedings, in the court seised of the original proceedings, unless these

were instituted solely with the object of removing him from the jurisdiction of the court which would be competent in his case;

3. on a counter-claim arising from the same contract or facts on which the original claim was basccd, in thc court in which thc original claim is pcnding;
4. in matters relating to a contract, if the action may be combined with an action against the same defendant in matters relating to rights in rem in immovable property, in the court of the Member State in which the property is situated.

Article 7
Where by virtue of this Regulation a court of a Member State has jurisdiction in actions relating to liability from the use or operation of a ship, that court, or any other court substituted for this purpose by the internal law of that Member State, shall also have jurisdiction over claims for limitation of such liability.

Section 3

Jurisdiction in Matters Relating to Insurance

Article 8
In matters relating to insurance, jurisdiction shall be determined by this Section, without prejudice to Article 4 and point 5 of Article 5.

Article 9

1. An insurer domiciled in a Member State may be sued:
   (a) in the courts of the Member State where he is domiciled, or
   (b) in another Member State, in the case of actions brought by the policyholder, the insured or a beneficiary, in the courts for the place where the plaintiff is domiciled,
   (c) if he is a co-insurer, in the courts of a Member State in which proceedings are brought against the leading insurer.
2. An insurer who is not domiciled in a Member State but has a branch, agency or other establishment in one of the Member States shall, in disputes arising out of the operations of the branch, agency or establishment, be deemed to be domiciled in that Member State.

Article 10
In respect of liability insurance or insurance of immovable property, the insurer may in addition be sued in the courts for the place where the harmful event occurred. The same applies if movable and immovable property are covered by the same insurance policy and both are adversely affected by the same contingency.

Article 11

1. In respect of liability insurance, the insurer may also, if the law of the court permits it, be joined in proceedings which the injured party has brought against the insured.

2. Articles 8, 9 and 10 shall apply to actions brought by the injured party directly against the insurer, where such direct actions are permitted.
3. If the law governing such direct actions provides that the policyholder or the insured may be joined as a party to the action, the same court shall have jurisdiction over them.

Article 12

1. Without prejudice to Article 11(3), an insurer may bring proceedings only in the courts of the Member State in which the defendant is domiciled, irrespective of whether he is the policyholder, the insured or a beneficiary.
2. The provisions of this Section shall not affect the right to bring a counter-claim in the court in which, in accordance with this Section, the original claim is pending.

Article 13

The provisions of this Section may be departed from only by an agreement:

1. which is entered into after the dispute has arisen, or
2. which allows the policyholder, the insured or a beneficiary to bring proceedings in courts other than those indicated in this Section, or
3. which is concluded between a policyholder and an insurer, both of whom are at the time of conclusion of the contract domiciled or habitually resident in the same Member State, and which has the effect of conferring jurisdiction on the courts of that State even if the harmful event were to occur abroad, provided that such an agreement is not contrary to the law of that State, or
4. which is concluded with a policyholder who is not domiciled in a Member State, except in so far as the insurance is compulsory or relates to immovable property in a Member State, or
5. which relates to a contract of insurance in so far as it covers one or more of the risks set out in Article 14.

Article 14

The following are the risks referred to in Article 13(5):

1. any loss of or damage to:
   (a) seagoing ships, installations situated offshore or on the high seas, or aircraft, arising from perils which relate to their use for commercial purposes;
   (b) goods in transit other than passengers' baggage where the transit consists of or includes carriage by such ships or aircraft;
2. any liability, other than for bodily injury to passengers or loss of or damage to their baggage:
   (a) arising out of the use or operation of ships, installations or aircraft as referred to in point 1(a) in so far as, in respect of the latter, the law of the Member State in which such aircraft are registered does not prohibit agreements on jurisdiction regarding insurance of such risks;

(b) for loss or damage caused by goods in transit as described in point 1(b);
3. any financial loss connected with the use or operation of ships, installations or aircraft as referred to in point 1(a), in particular loss of freight or charter-hire;
4. any risk or interest connected with any of those referred to in points 1 to 3;
5. notwithstanding points 1 to 4, all "large risks" as defined in Council Directive 73/239/EEC(7), as amended by Council Directives 88/357/EEC(8) and 90/618/EEC(9), as they may be amended.

Section 4

Jurisdiction over Consumer Contracts

Article 15

1. In matters relating to a contract concluded by a person, the consumer, for a purpose which can be regarded as being outside his trade or profession, jurisdiction shall be determined by this Section, without prejudice to Article 4 and point 5 of Article 5, if:
   (a) it is a contract for the sale of goods on installment credit terms; or
   (b) it is a contract for a loan repayable by installments, or for any other form of credit, made to finance the sale of goods; or
   (c) in all other cases, the contract has been concluded with a person who pursues commercial or professional activities in the Member State of the consumer's domicile or, by any means, directs such activities to that Member State or to several States including that Member State, and the contract falls within the scope of such activities.
2. Where a consumer enters into a contract with a party who is not domiciled in the Member State but has a branch, agency or other establishment in one of the Member States, that party shall, in disputes arising out of the operations of the branch, agency or establishment, be deemed to be domiciled in that State.
3. This Section shall not apply to a contract of transport other than a contract which, for an inclusive price, provides for a combination of travel and accommodation.

Article 16

1. A consumer may bring proceedings against the other party to a contract either in the courts of the Member State in which that party is domiciled or in the courts for the place where the consumer is domiciled.
2. Proceedings may be brought against a consumer by the other party to the contract only in the courts of the Member State in which the consumer is domiciled.
3. This Article shall not affect the right to bring a counter-claim in the court in which, in accordance with this Section, the original claim is pending.

Article 17

The provisions of this Section may be departed from only by an agreement:

1. which is entered into after the dispute has arisen; or

2. which allows the consumer to bring proceedings in courts other than those indicated in this Section; or
3. which is entered into by the consumer and the other party to the contract, both of whom are at the time of conclusion of the contract domiciled or habitually resident in the same Member State, and which confers jurisdiction on the courts of that Member State, provided that such an agreement is not contrary to the law of that Member State.

Section 5

Jurisdiction over Individual Contracts of Employment

Article 18

1. In matters relating to individual contracts of employment, jurisdiction shall be determined by this Section, without prejudice to Article 4 and point 5 of Article 5.
2. Where an employee enters into an individual contract of employment with an employer who is not domiciled in a Member State but has a branch, agency or other establishment in one of the Member States, the employer shall, in disputes arising out of the operations of the branch, agency or establishment, be deemed to be domiciled in that Member State.

Article 19

An employer domiciled in a Member State may be sued:

1. in the courts of the Member State where he is domiciled; or
2. in another Member State:
   (a) in the courts for the place where the employee habitually carries out his work or in the courts for the last place where he did so, or
   (b) if the employee does not or did not habitually carry out his work any one country, in the courts for the place where the business which engaged the employee is or was situated.

Article 20

1. An employer may bring proceedings only in the courts of the Member State in which the employee is domiciled.
2. The provisions of this Section shall not affect the right to bring a counter-claim in the court in which, in accordance with this Section, the original claim is pending.

Article 21

The provisions of this Section may be departed from only by an agreement on jurisdiction:

1. which is entered into after the dispute has arisen; or
2. which allows the employee to bring proceedings in courts other than those indicated in this Section.

Section 6

Exclusive Jurisdiction

Article 22

The following courts shall have exclusive jurisdiction, regardless of domicile:

1. in proceedings which have as their object rights in rem in immovable property or tenancies of immovable property, the courts of the Member State in which the property is situated. However, in proceedings which have as their object tenancies of immovable property concluded for temporary private use for a maximum period of six consecutive months, the courts of the Member State in which the defendant is domiciled shall also have jurisdiction, provided that the tenant is a natural person and that the landlord and the tenant are domiciled in the same Member State;
2. in proceedings which have as their object the validity of the constitution, the nullity or the dissolution of companies or other legal persons or associations of natural or legal persons, or of the validity of the decisions of their organs, the courts of the Member State in which the company, legal person or association has its seat. In order to determine that seat, the court shall apply its rules of private international law;
3. in proceedings which have as their object the validity of entries in public registers, the courts of the Member State in which the register is kept;
4. in proceedings concerned with the registration or validity of patents, trade marks, designs, or other similar rights required to be deposited or registered, the courts of the Member State in which the deposit or registration has been applied for, has taken place or is under the terms of a Community instrument or an international convention deemed to have taken place. Without prejudice to the jurisdiction of the European Patent Office under the Convention on the Grant of European Patents, signed at Munich on 5 October 1973, the courts of each Member State shall have exclusive jurisdiction, regardless of domicile, in proceedings concerned with the registration or validity of any European patent granted for that State;
5. in proceedings concerned with the enforcement of judgments, the courts of the Member State in which the judgment has been or is to be enforced.

Section 7

Prorogation of Jurisdiction

Article 23

1. If the parties, one or more of whom is domiciled in a Member State, have agreed that a court or the courts of a Member State are to have jurisdiction to settle any disputes which have arisen or which may arise in connection with a particular legal relationship, that court or those courts shall have jurisdiction. Such jurisdiction shall be exclusive unless the parties have agreed otherwise. Such an agreement conferring jurisdiction shall be either:

(a) in writing or evidenced in writing; or
(b) in a form which accords with practices which the parties have established between themselves; or
(c) in international trade or commerce, in a form which accords with a usage of which the parties are or ought to have been aware and which in such trade or commerce is widely known to, and regularly observed by, parties to contracts of the type involved in the particular trade or commerce concerned.

2. Any communication by electronic means which provides a durable record of the agreement shall be equivalent to "writing".
3. Where such an agreement is concluded by parties, none of whom is domiciled in a Member State, the courts of other Member States shall have no jurisdiction over their disputes unless the court or courts chosen have declined jurisdiction.
4. The court or courts of a Member State on which a trust instrument has conferred jurisdiction shall have exclusive jurisdiction in any proceedings brought against a settlor, trustee or beneficiary, if relations between these persons or their rights or obligations under the rust are involved.
5. Agreements or provisions of a trust instrument conferring jurisdiction shall have no legal force if they are contrary to Articles 13, 17 or 21, or if the courts whose jurisdiction they purport to exclude have exclusive jurisdiction by virtue of Article 22.

Article 24

Apart from jurisdiction derived from other provisions of this Regulation, a court of a Member State before which a defendant enters an appearance shall have jurisdiction. This rule shall not apply where appearance was entered to contest the jurisdiction, or where another court has exclusive jurisdiction by virtue of Article 22.

Section 8

Examination as to Jurisdiction and Admissibility

Article 25

Where a court of a Member State is seised of a claim which is principally concerned with a matter over which the courts of another Member State have exclusive jurisdiction by virtue of Article 22, it shall declare of its own motion that it has no jurisdiction.

Article 26

1. Where a defendant domiciled in one Member State is sued in a court of another Member State and does not enter an appearance, the court shall declare of its own motion that it has no jurisdiction unless its jurisdiction is derived from the provisions of this Regulation.
2. The court shall stay the proceedings so long as it is not shown that the defendant has been able to receive the document instituting the proceedings or an equivalent

document in sufficient time to enable him to arrange for his defence, or that all necessary steps have been taken to this end.

3. Article 19 of Council Regulation (EC) No 1348/2000 of 29 May 2000 on the service in the Member States of judicial and extrajudicial documents in civil or commercial matters(*10*) shall apply instead of the provisions of paragraph 2 if the document instituting the proceedings or an equivalent document had to be transmitted from one Member State to another pursuant to this Regulation.
4. Where the provisions of Regulation (EC) No 1348/2000 are not applicable, Article 15 of the Hague Convention of 15 November 1965 on the Service Abroad of Judicial and Extrajudicial Documents in Civil or Commercial Matters shall apply if the document instituting the proceedings or an equivalent document had to be transmitted pursuant to that Convention.

Section 9

Lis Pendens – Related Actions

Article 27

1. Where proceedings involving the same cause of action and between the same parties are brought in the courts of different Member States, any court other than the court first seised shall of its own motion stay its proceedings until such time as the jurisdiction of the court first seised is established.
2. Where the jurisdiction of the court first seised is established, any court other than the court first seised shall decline jurisdiction in favour of that court.

Article 28

1. Where related actions are pending in the courts of different Member States, any court other than the court first seised may stay its proceedings.
2. Where these actions are pending at first instance, any court other than the court first seised may also, on the application of one of the parties, decline jurisdiction if the court first seised has jurisdiction over the actions in question and its law permits the consolidation thereof.
3. For the purposes of this Article, actions are deemed to be related where they are so closely connected that it is expedient to hear and determine them together to avoid the risk of irreconcilable judgments resulting from separate proceedings.

Article 29

Where actions come within the exclusive jurisdiction of several courts, any court other than the court first seised shall decline jurisdiction in favour of that court.

Article 30

For the purposes of this Section, a court shall be deemed to be seised:

1. at the time when the document instituting the proceedings or an equivalent document is lodged with the court, provided that the plaintiff has not subsequently

failed to take the steps he was required to take to have service effected on the defendant, or
2. if the document has to be served before being lodged with the court, at he time when it is received by the authority responsible for service, provided that the plaintiff has not subsequently failed to take the steps he was required to take to have the document lodged with the court.

Section 10

Provisional, Including Protective, Measures

Article 31
Application may be made to the courts of a Member State for such provisional, including protective, measures as may be available under the law of that State, even if, under this Regulation, the courts of another Member State have jurisdiction as to the substance of the matter.

Chapter III

Recognition and Enforcement

Article 32
For the purposes of this Regulation, "judgment" means any judgment given by a court or tribunal of a Member State, whatever the judgment may be called, including a decree, order, decision or writ of execution, as well as the determination of costs or expenses by an officer of the court.

Section 1

Recognition

Article 33
1. A judgment given in a Member State shall be recognised in the other Member States without any special procedure being required.
2. Any interested party who raises the recognition of a judgment as the principal issue in a dispute may, in accordance with the procedures provided for in Sections 2 and 3 of this Chapter, apply for a decision that the judgment be recognised.
3. If the outcome of proceedings in a court of a Member State depends on the determination of an incidental question of recognition that court shall have jurisdiction over that question.

Article 34
A judgment shall not be recognised:
1. if such recognition is manifestly contrary to public policy in the Member State in which recognition is sought;

2. where it was given in default of appearance, if the defendant was not served with the document which instituted the proceedings or with an equivalent document in sufficient time and in such a way as to enable him to arrange for his defence, unless the defendant failed to commence proceedings to challenge the judgment when it was possible for him to do so;
3. if it is irreconcilable with a judgment given in a dispute between the same parties in the Member State in which recognition is sought;
4. if it is irreconcilable with an earlier judgment given in another Member State or in a third State involving the same cause of action and between the same parties, provided that the earlier judgment fulfils the conditions necessary for its recognition in the Member State addressed.

Article 35

1. Moreover, a judgment shall not be recognised if it conflicts with Sections 3, 4 or 6 of Chapter II, or in a case provided for in Article 72.
2. In its examination of the grounds of jurisdiction referred to in the foregoing paragraph, the court or authority applied to shall be bound by the findings of fact on which the court of the Member State of origin based its jurisdiction.
3. Subject to the paragraph 1, the jurisdiction of the court of the Member State of origin may not be reviewed. The test of public policy referred to in point 1 of Article 34 may not be applied to the rules relating to jurisdiction.

Article 36

Under no circumstances may a foreign judgment be reviewed as to its substance.

Article 37

1. A court of a Member State in which recognition is sought of a judgment given in another Member State may stay the proceedings if an ordinary appeal against the judgment has been lodged.
2. A court of a Member State in which recognition is sought of a judgment given in Ireland or the United Kingdom may stay the proceedings if enforcement is suspended in the State of origin, by reason of an appeal.

Section 2

Enforcement

Article 38

1. A judgment given in a Member State and enforceable in that State shall be enforced in another Member State when, on the application of any interested party, it has been declared enforceable there.
2. However, in the United Kingdom, such a judgment shall be enforced in England and Wales, in Scotland, or in Northern Ireland when, on the application of any

interested party, it has been registered for enforcement in that part of the United Kingdom.

Article 39

1. The application shall be submitted to the court or competent authority indicated in the list in Annex II.
2. The local jurisdiction shall be determined by reference to the place of domicile of the party against whom enforcement is sought, or to the place of enforcement.

Article 40

1. The procedure for making the application shall be governed by the law of the Member State in which enforcement is sought.
2. The applicant must give an address for service of process within the area of jurisdiction of the court applied to. However, if the law of the Member State in which enforcement is sought does not provide for the furnishing of such an address, the applicant shall appoint a representative ad litem.
3. The documents referred to in Article 53 shall be attached to the application.

Article 41

The judgment shall be declared enforceable immediately on completion of the formalities in Article 53 without any review under Articles 34 and 35. The party against whom enforcement is sought shall not at this stage of the proceedings be entitled to make any submissions on the application.

Article 42

1. The decision on the application for a declaration of enforceability shall forthwith be brought to the notice of the applicant in accordance with the procedure laid down by the law of the Member State in which enforcement is sought.
2. The declaration of enforceability shall be served on the party against whom enforcement is sought, accompanied by the judgment, if not already served on that party.

Article 43

1. The decision on the application for a declaration of enforceability may be appealed against by either party.
2. The appeal is to be lodged with the court indicated in the list in Annex III.
3. The appeal shall be dealt with in accordance with the rules governing procedure in contradictory matters.
4. If the party against whom enforcement is sought fails to appear before the appellate court in proceedings concerning an appeal brought by the applicant, Article 26(2) to (4) shall apply even where the party against whom enforcement is sought is not domiciled in any of the Member States.
5. An appeal against the declaration of enforceability is to be lodged within one

month of service thereof. If the party against whom enforcement is sought is domiciled in a Member State other than that in which the declaration of enforceability was given, the time for appealing shall be two months and shall run from the date of service, either on him in person or at his residence. No extension of time may be granted on account of distance.

Article 44

The judgment given on the appeal may be contested only by the appeal referred to in Annex IV.

Article 45

1. The court with which an appeal is lodged under Article 43 or Article 44 shall refuse or revoke a declaration of enforceability only on one of the grounds specified in Articles 34 and 35. It shall give its decision without delay.
2. Under no circumstances may the foreign judgment be reviewed as to its substance.

Article 46

1. The court with which an appeal is lodged under Article 43 or Article 44 may, on the application of the party against whom enforcement is sought, stay the proceedings if an ordinary appeal has been lodged against the judgment in the Member State of origin or if the time for such an appeal has not yet expired; in the latter case, the court may specify the time within which such an appeal is to be lodged.
2. Where the judgment was given in Ireland or the United Kingdom, any form of appeal available in the Member State of origin shall be treated as an ordinary appeal for the purposes of paragraph 1.
3. The court may also make enforcement conditional on the provision of such security as it shall determine.

Article 47

1. When a judgment must be recognised in accordance with this Regulation, nothing shall prevent the applicant from availing himself of provisional, including protective, measures in accordance with the law of the Member State requested without a declaration of enforceability under Article 41 being required.
2. The declaration of enforceability shall carry with it the power to proceed to any protective measures.
3. During the time specified for an appeal pursuant to Article 43(5) against the declaration of enforceability and until any such appeal has been determined, no measures of enforcement may be taken other than protective measures against the property of the party against whom enforcement is sought.

Article 48

1. Where a foreign judgment has been given in respect of several matters and the declaration of enforceability cannot be given for all of them, the court or competent authority shall give it for one or more of them.

2. An applicant may request a declaration of enforceability limited to parts of a judgment.

Article 49

A foreign judgment which orders a periodic payment by way of a penalty shall be enforceable in the Member State in which enforcement is sought only if the amount of the payment has been finally determined by the courts of the Member State of origin.

Article 50

An applicant who, in the Member State of origin has benefited from complete or partial legal aid or exemption from costs or expenses, shall be entitled, in the procedure provided for in this Section, to benefit from the most favourable legal aid or the most extensive exemption from costs or expenses provided for by the law of the Member State addressed.

Article 51

No security, bond or deposit, however described, shall be required of a party who in one Member State applies for enforcement of a judgment given in another Member State on the ground that he is a foreign national or that he is not domiciled or resident in the State in which enforcement is sought.

Article 52

In proceedings for the issue of a declaration of enforceability, no charge, duty or fee calculated by reference to the value of the matter at issue may be levied in the Member State in which enforcement is sought.

Section 3

Common Provisions

Article 53

1. A party seeking recognition or applying for a declaration of enforceability shall produce a copy of the judgment which satisfies the conditions necessary to establish its authenticity.
2. A party applying for a declaration of enforceability shall also produce the certificate referred to in Article 54, without prejudice to Article 55.

Article 54

The court or competent authority of a Member State where a judgment was given shall issue, at the request of any interested party, a certificate using the standard form in Annex V to this Regulation.

Article 55

1. If the certificate referred to in Article 54 is not produced, the court or competent authority may specify a time for its production or accept an equivalent document or, if it considers that it has sufficient information before it, dispense with its production.
2. If the court or competent authority so requires, a translation of the documents shall be produced. The translation shall be certified by a person qualified to do so in one of the Member States.

Article 56

No legalisation or other similar formality shall be required in respect of the documents referred to in Article 53 or Article 55(2), or in respect of a document appointing a representative ad litem.

Chapter IV

Authentic Instruments and Court Settlements

Article 57

1. A document which has been formally drawn up or registered as an authentic instrument and is enforceable in one Member State shall, in another Member State, be declared enforceable there, on application made in accordance with the procedures provided for in Articles 38, et seq. The court with which an appeal is lodged under Article 43 or Article 44 shall refuse or revoke a declaration of enforceability only if enforcement of the instrument is manifestly contrary to public policy in the Member State addressed.
2. Arrangements relating to maintenance obligations concluded with administrative authorities or authenticated by them shall also be regarded as authentic instruments within the meaning of paragraph 1.
3. The instrument produced must satisfy the conditions necessary to establish its authenticity in the Member State of origin.
4. Section 3 of Chapter III shall apply as appropriate. The competent authority of a Member State where an authentic instrument was drawn up or registered shall issue, at the request of any interested party, a certificate using the standard form in Annex VI to this Regulation.

Article 58

A settlement which has been approved by a court in the course of proceedings and is enforceable in the Member State in which it was concluded shall be enforceable in the State addressed under the same conditions as authentic instruments. The court or competent authority of a Member State where a court settlement was approved shall issue, at the request of any interested party, a certificate using the standard form in Annex V to this Regulation.

Chapter V

General Provisions

Article 59

1. In order to determine whether a party is domiciled in the Member State whose courts are seised of a matter, the court shall apply its internal law.
2. If a party is not domiciled in the Member State whose courts are seised of the matter, then, in order to determine whether the party is domiciled in another Member State, the court shall apply the law of that Member State.

Article 60

1. For the purposes of this Regulation, a company or other legal person or association of natural or legal persons is domiciled at the place where it has its:
   (a) statutory seat, or
   (b) central administration, or
   (c) principal place of business.
2. For the purposes of the United Kingdom and Ireland "statutory seat" means the registered office or, where there is no such office anywhere, the place of incorporation or, where there is no such place anywhere, the place under the law of which the formation took place.
3. In order to determine whether a trust is domiciled in the Member State whose courts are seised of the matter, the court shall apply its rules of private international law.

Article 61

Without prejudice to any more favourable provisions of national laws, persons domiciled in a Member State who are being prosecuted in the criminal courts of another Member State of which they are not nationals for an offence which was not intentionally committed may be defended by persons qualified to do so, even if they do not appear in person. However, the court seised of the matter may order appearance in person; in the case of failure to appear, a judgment given in the civil action without the person concerned having had the opportunity to arrange for his defence need not be recognised or enforced in the other Member States.

Article 62

In Sweden, in summary proceedings concerning orders to pay (betalningsföreläggande) and assistance (handräckning), the expression "court" includes the "Swedish enforcement service" (kronofogdemyndighet).

Article 63

1. A person domiciled in the territory of the Grand Duchy of Luxembourg and sued in the court of another Member State pursuant to Article 5(1) may refuse to

submit to the jurisdiction of that court if the final place of delivery of the goods or provision of the services is in Luxembourg.

2. Where, under paragraph 1, the final place of delivery of the goods or provision of the services is in Luxembourg, any agreement conferring jurisdiction must, in order to be valid, be accepted in writing or evidenced in writing within the meaning of Article 23(1)(a).
3. The provisions of this Article shall not apply to contracts for the provision of financial services.
4. The provisions of this Article shall apply for a period of six years from entry into force of this Regulation.

Article 64

1. In proceedings involving a dispute between the master and a member of the crew of a seagoing ship registered in Greece or in Portugal, concerning remuneration or other conditions of service, a court in a Member State shall establish whether the diplomatic or consular officer responsible for the ship has been notified of the dispute. It may act as soon as that officer has been notified.
2. The provisions of this Article shall apply for a period of six years from entry into force of this Regulation.

Article 65

1. The jurisdiction specified in Article 6(2), and Article 11 in actions on a warranty of guarantee or in any other third party proceedings may not be resorted to in Germany and Austria. Any person domiciled in another Member State may be sued in the courts:
   (a) of Germany, pursuant to Articles 68 and 72 to 74 of the Code of Civil Procedure (Zivilprozessordnung) concerning third-party notices,
   (b) of Austria, pursuant to Article 21 of the Code of Civil Procedure (Zivilprozessordnung) concerning third-party notices.
2. Judgments given in other Member States by virtue of Article 6(2), or Article 11 shall be recognised and enforced in Germany and Austria in accordance with Chapter III. Any effects which judgments given in these States may have on third parties by application of the provisions in paragraph 1 shall also be recognised in the other Member States.

Chapter VI

Transitional Provisions

Article 66

1. This Regulation shall apply only to legal proceedings instituted and to documents formally drawn up or registered as authentic instruments after the entry into force thereof.

2. However, if the proceedings in the Member State of origin were instituted before the entry into force of this Regulation, judgments given after that date shall be recognised and enforced in accordance with Chapter III,
   (a) if the proceedings in the Member State of origin were instituted after the entry into force of the Brussels or the Lugano Convention both in the Member State or origin and in the Member State addressed;
   (b) in all other cases, if jurisdiction was founded upon rules which accorded with those provided for either in Chapter II or in a convention concluded between the Member State of origin and the Member State addressed which was in force when the proceedings were instituted.

Chapter VII

Relations with Other Instruments

Article 67

This Regulation shall not prejudice the application of provisions governing jurisdiction and the recognition and enforcement of judgments in specific matters which are contained in Community instruments or in national legislation harmonised pursuant to such instruments.

Article 68

1. This Regulation shall, as between the Member States, supersede the Brussels Convention, except as regards the territories of the Member States which fall within the territorial scope of that Convention and which are excluded from this Regulation pursuant to Article 299 of the Treaty.
2. In so far as this Regulation replaces the provisions of the Brussels Convention between Member States, any reference to the Convention shall be understood as a reference to this Regulation.

Article 69

Subject to Article 66(2) and Article 70, this Regulation shall, as between Member States, supersede the following conventions and treaty concluded between two or more of them:

- the Convention between Belgium and France on Jurisdiction and the Validity and Enforcement of Judgments, Arbitration Awards and Authentic Instruments, signed at Paris on 8 July 1899,
- the Convention between Belgium and the Netherlands on Jurisdiction, Bankruptcy, and the Validity and Enforcement of Judgments, Arbitration Awards and Authentic Instruments, signed at Brussels on 28 March 1925,
- the Convention between France and Italy on the Enforcement of Judgments in Civil and Commercial Matters, signed at Rome on 3 June 1930,
- the Convention between Germany and Italy on the Recognition and Enforcement of Judgments in Civil and Commercial Matters, signed at Rome on 9 March 1936,

- the Convention between Belgium and Austria on the Reciprocal Recognition and Enforcement of Judgments and Authentic Instruments relating to Maintenance Obligations, signed at Vienna on 25 October 1957,
- the Convention between Germany and Belgium on the Mutual Recognition and Enforcement of Judgments, Arbitration Awards and Authentic Instruments in Civil and Commercial Matters, signed at Bonn on 30 June 1958,
- the Convention between the Netherlands and Italy on the Recognition and Enforcement of Judgments in Civil and Commercial Matters, signed at Rome on 17 April 1959,
- the Convention between Germany and Austria on the Reciprocal Recognition and Enforcement of Judgments, Settlements and Authentic Instruments in Civil and Commercial Matters, signed at Vienna on 6 June 1959,
- the Convention between Belgium and Austria on the Reciprocal Recognition and Enforcement of Judgments, Arbitral Awards and Authentic Instruments in Civil and Commercial Matters, signed at Vienna on 16 June 1959,
- the Convention between Greece and Germany for the Reciprocal Recognition and Enforcement of Judgments, Settlements and Authentic Instruments in Civil and Commercial Matters, signed in Athens on 4 November 1961,
- the Convention between Belgium and Italy on the Recognition and Enforcement of Judgments and other Enforceable Instruments in Civil and Commercial Matters, signed at Rome on 6 April 1962,
- the Convention between the Netherlands and Germany on the Mutual Recognition and Enforcement of Judgments and Other Enforceable Instruments in Civil and Commercial Matters, signed at The Hague on 30 August 1962,
- the Convention between the Netherlands and Austria on the Reciprocal Recognition and Enforcement of Judgments and Authentic Instruments in Civil and Commercial Matters, signed at The Hague on 6 February 1963,
- the Convention between France and Austria on the Recognition and Enforcement of Judgments and Authentic Instruments in Civil and Commercial Matters, signed at Vienna on 15 July 1966,
- the Convention between Spain and France on the Recognition and Enforcement of Judgment Arbitration Awards in Civil and Commercial Matters, signed at Paris on 28 May 1969,
- the Convention between Luxembourg and Austria on the Recognition and Enforcement of Judgments and Authentic Instruments in Civil and Commercial Matters, signed at Luxembourg on 29 July 1971,
- the Convention between Italy and Austria on the Recognition and Enforcement of Judgments in Civil and Commercial Matters, of Judicial Settlements and of Authentic Instruments, signed at Rome on 16 November 1971,
- the Convention between Spain and Italy regarding Legal Aid and the Recognition and Enforcement of Judgments in Civil and Commercial Matters, signed at Madrid on 22 May 1973,
- the Convention between Finland, Iceland, Norway, Sweden and Denmark on the

Recognition and Enforcement of Judgments in Civil Matters, signed at Copenhagen on 11 October 1977,
- the Convention between Austria and Sweden on the Recognition and Enforcement of Judgments in Civil Matters, signed at Stockholm on 16 September 1982,
- the Convention between Spain and the Federal Republic of Germany on the Recognition and Enforcement of Judgments, Settlements and Enforceable Authentic Instruments in Civil and Commercial Matters, signed at Bonn on 14 November 1983,
- the Convention between Austria and Spain on the Recognition and Enforcement of Judgments, Settlements and Enforceable Authentic Instruments in Civil and Commercial Matters, signed at Vienna on 17 February 1984,
- the Convention between Finland and Austria on the Recognition and Enforcement of Judgments in Civil Matters, signed at Vienna on 17 November 1986, and
- the Treaty between Belgium, the Netherlands and Luxembourg in Jurisdiction, Bankruptcy, and the Validity and Enforcement of Judgments, Arbitration Awards and Authentic Instruments, signed at Brussels on 24 November 1961, in so far as it is in force.

Article 70

1. The Treaty and the Conventions referred to in Article 69 shall continue to have effect in relation to matters to which this Regulation does not apply.
2. They shall continue to have effect in respect of judgments given and documents formally drawn up or registered as authentic instruments before the entry into force of this Regulation.

Article 71

1. This Regulation shall not affect any conventions to which the Member States are parties and which in relation to particular matters, govern jurisdiction or the recognition or enforcement of judgments.
2. With a view to its uniform interpretation, paragraph 1 shall be applied in the following manner:
   (a) this Regulation shall not prevent a court of a Member State, which is a party to a convention on a particular matter, from assuming jurisdiction in accordance with that convention, even where the defendant is domiciled in another Member State which is not a party to that convention. The court hearing the action shall, in any event, apply Article 26 of this Regulation;
   (b) judgments given in a Member State by a court in the exercise of jurisdiction provided for in a convention on a particular matter shall be recognised and enforced in the other Member States in accordance with this Regulation.

   Where a convention on a particular matter to which both the Member State of origin and the Member State addressed are parties lays down conditions for the recognition or enforcement of judgments, those conditions shall apply. In any event, the provisions of this Regulation which concern the procedure for recognition and enforcement of judgments may be applied.

Article 72

This Regulation shall not affect agreements by which Member States undertook, prior to the entry into force of this Regulation pursuant to Article 59 of the Brussels Convention, not to recognise judgments given, in particular in other Contracting States to that Convention, against defendants domiciled or habitually resident in a third country where, in cases provided for in Article 4 of that Convention, the judgment could only be founded on a ground of jurisdiction specified in the second paragraph of Article 3 of that Convention.

Chapter VIII

Final Provisions

Article 73

No later than five years after the entry into force of this Regulation, the Commission shall present to the European Parliament, the Council and the Economic and Social Committee a report on the application of this Regulation. The report shall be accompanied, if need be, by proposals for adaptations to this Regulation.

Article 74

1. The Member States shall notify the Commission of the texts amending the lists set out in Annexes I to IV. The Commission shall adapt the Annexes concerned accordingly.
2. The updating or technical adjustment of the forms, specimens of which appear in Annexes V and VI, shall be adopted in accordance with the advisory procedure referred to in Article 75(2).

Article 75

1. The Commission shall be assisted by a committee.
2. Where reference is made to this paragraph, Articles 3 and 7 of Decision 1999/468/EC shall apply.
3. The Committee shall adopt its rules of procedure.

Article 76

This Regulation shall enter into force on 1 March 2002.

This Regulation is binding in its entirety and directly applicable in the Member States in accordance with the Treaty establishing the European Community.

Done at Brussels, 22 December 2000.

For the Council
The President
C. Pierret

(*1*) OJ C 376, 28.12.1999, p. 1.
(*2*) Opinion delivered on 21 September 2000 (not yet published in the Official Journal).
(*3*) OJ C 117, 26.4.2000, p. 6.
(*4*) OJ L 299, 31.12.1972, p. 32.
OJ L 304, 30.10.1978, p. 1.
OJ L 388, 31.12.1982, p. 1.
OJ L 285, 3.10.1989, p. 1.
OJ C 15, 15.1.1997, p. 1.
For a consolidated text, see OJ C 27, 26.1.1998, p. 1.
(*5*) OJ L 204, 2.8.1975, p. 28.
OJ L 304, 30.10.1978, p. 1.
OJ L 388, 31.12.1982, p. 1.
OJ L 285, 3.10.1989, p. 1.
OJ C 15, 15.1.1997, p. 1.
For a consolidated text see OJ C 27, 26.1.1998, p. 28.
(*6*) OJ L 184, 17.7.1999, p. 23.
(*7*) OJ L 228, 16.8.1973, p. 3. Directive as last amended by Directive 2000/26/EC of the European Parliament and of the Council (OJ L 181, 20.7.2000, p. 65).
(*8*) OJ L 172, 4.7.1988, p. 1. Directive as last amended by Directive 2000/26/EC.
(*9*) OJ L 330, 29.11.1990, p. 44.
(*10*) OJ L 160, 30.6.2000, p. 37.

Annex I

Rules of jurisdiction referred to in Article 3(2) and Article 4(2) The rules of jurisdiction referred to in Article 3(2) and Article 4(2) are the following:

- in Belgium: Article 15 of the Civil Code (Code civil/Burgerlijk Wetboek) and Article 638 of the Judicial Code (Code judiciaire/Gerechtelijk Wetboek);
- in Germany: Article 23 of the Code of Civil Procedure (Zivilprozessordnung),
- in Greece, Article 40 of the Code of Civil Procedure ...
- in France: Articles 14 and 15 of the Civil Code (Code civil),
- in Ireland: the rules which enable jurisdiction to be founded on the document instituting the proceedings having been served on the defendant during his temporary presence in Ireland,
- in Italy: Articles 3 and 4 of Act 218 of 31 May 1995,
- in Luxembourg: Articles 14 and 15 of the Civil Code (Code civil),
- in the Netherlands: Articles 126(3) and 127 of the Code of Civil Procedure (Wetboek van Burgerlijke Rechtsvordering),
- in Austria: Article 99 of the Court Jurisdiction Act (Jurisdiktionsnorm),
- in Portugal: Articles 65 and 65A of the Code of Civil Procedure (Código de Processo Civil) and Article 11 of the Code of Labour Procedure (Código de Processo de Trabalho),

- in Finland: the second, third and fourth sentences of the first paragraph of Section 1 of Chapter 10 of the Code of Judicial Procedure (oikeudenkäymiskaari/ rättegångsbalken),
- in Sweden: the first sentence of the first paragraph of Section 3 of Chapter 10 of the Code of Judicial Procedure (rättegångsbalken),
- in the United Kingdom: rules which enable jurisdiction to be founded on:
  (a) the document instituting the proceedings having been served on the defendant during his temporary presence in the United Kingdom; or
  (b) the presence within the United Kingdom of property belonging to the defendant; or
  (c) the seizure by the plaintiff of property situated in the United Kingdom.

Annex II

The courts or competent authorities to which the application referred to in Article 39 may be submitted are the following:

- in Belgium, the "tribunal de première instance" or "rechtbank van eerste aanleg" or "erstinstanzliches Gericht",
- in Germany, the presiding judge of a chamber of the "Landgericht",
- in Greece, the "...",
- in Spain, the "Juzgado de Primera Instancia",
- in France, the presiding judge of the "tribunal de grande instance",
- in Ireland, the High Court,
- in Italy, the "Corte d'appello",
- in Luxembourg, the presiding judge of the "tribunal d'arrondissement",
- in the Netherlands, the presiding judge of the "arrondissementsrechtbank";
- in Austria, the "Bezirksgericht",
- in Portugal, the "Tribunal de Comarca",
- in Finland, the "käräjäoikeus/tingsrätt",
- in Sweden, the "Svea hovrätt",
- in the United Kingdom:
  (a) in England and Wales, the High Court of Justice, or in the case of a maintenance judgment, the Magistrate's Court on transmission by the Secretary of State;
  (b) in Scotland, the Court of Session, or in the case of a maintenance judgment, the Sheriff Court on transmission by the Secretary of State;
  (c) in Northern Ireland, the High Court of Justice, or in the case of a maintenance judgment, the Magistrate's Court on transmission by the Secretary of State;
  (d) in Gibraltar, the Supreme Court of Gibraltar, or in the case of a maintenance judgment, the Magistrates' Court on transmission by the Attorney General of Gibraltar.

Annex III

The courts with which appeals referred to in Article 43(2) may be lodged are the following:

- in Belgium,
  (a) as regards appeal by the defendant: the "tribunal de première instance" or "rechtbank van eerste aanleg" or "erstinstanzliches Gericht",
  (b) as regards appeal by the applicant: the "Cour d'appel" or "hof van beroep",
- in the Federal Republic of Germany, the "Oberlandesgericht",
- in Greece, the "...",
- in Spain, the "Audiencia Provincial",
- in France, the "cour d'appel",
- in Ireland, the High Court,
- in Italy, the "corte d'appello",
- in Luxembourg, the "Cour supérieure de Justice" sitting as a court of civil appeal,
- in the Netherlands:
  (a) for the defendant: the "arrondissementsrechtbank",
  (b) for the applicant: the "gerechtshof",
- in Austria, the "Bezirksgericht",
- in Portugal, the "Tribunal de Relação",
- in Finland, the "hovioikeus/hovrätt",
- in Sweden, the "Svea hovrätt",
- in the United Kingdom:
  (a) in England and Wales, the High Court of Justice, or in the case of a maintenance judgment, the Magistrate's Court;
  (b) in Scotland, the Court of Session, or in the case of a maintenance judgment, the Sheriff Court;
  (c) in Northern Ireland, the High Court of Justice, or in the case of a maintenance judgment, the Magistrate's Court;
  (d) in Gibraltar, the Supreme Court of Gibraltar, or in the case of a maintenance judgment, the Magistrates' Court.

Annex IV

The appeals which may be lodged pursuant to Article 44 are the following:
- in Belgium, Greece, Spain, France, Italy, Luxembourg and the Netherlands, an appeal in cassation,
- in Germany, a "Rechtsbeschwerde",
- in Ireland, an appeal on a point of law to the Supreme Court,
- in Austria, a "Revisionsrekurs",
- in Portugal, an appeal on a point of law,
- in Finland, an appeal to the "korkein oikeus/högsta domstolen",
- in Sweden, an appeal to the "Högsta domstolen",
- in the United Kingdom, a single further appeal on a point of law.

Annex V

Certificate referred to in Articles 54 and 58 of the Regulation on judgments and court settlements (English, inglés, anglais, inglese, ...)

1. Member State of origin
2. Court or competent authority issuing the certificate
   2.1. Name
   2.2. Address
   2.3. Tel./fax/e-mail
3. Court which delivered the judgment/approved the court settlement(*1*)
   3.1. Type of court
   3.2. Place of court
4. Judgment/court settlement(*2*)
   4.1. Date
   4.2. Reference number
   4.3. The parties to the judgment/court settlement(*3*)
      4.3.1. Name(s) of plaintiff(s)
      4.3.2. Name(s) of defendant(s)
      4.3.3. Name(s) of other party(ies), if any
   4.4. Date of service of the document instituting the proceedings where judgment was given in default of appearance
   4.5. Text of the judgment/court settlement(*4*) as annexed to this certificate
5. Names of parties to whom legal aid has been granted

The judgment/court settlement(*5*) is enforceable in the Member State of origin (Articles 38 and 58 of the Regulation) against:

Name:

Done at ...., date ......
Signature and/or stamp ......

(*1*) Delete as appropriate.
(*2*) Delete as appropriate.
(*3*) Delete as appropriate.
(*4*) Delete as appropriate.
(*5*) Delete as appropriate.

Annex VI

Certificate referred to in Article 57(4) of the Regulation on authentic instruments (English, inglés, anglais, inglese, ...)

1. Member State of origin
2. Competent authority issuing the certificate
   2.1. Name
   2.2. Address
   2.3. Tel./fax/e-mail
3. Authority which has given authenticity to the instrument

3.1. Authority involved in the drawing up of the authentic instrument (if applicable)
    3.1.1. Name and designation of authority
    3.1.2. Place of authority
3.2. Authority which has registered the authentic instrument (if applicable)
    3.2.1. Type of authority
    3.2.2. Place of authority

4. Authentic instrument
    4.1. Description of the instrument
    4.2. Date
        4.2.1. on which the instrument was drawn up
        4.2.2. if different: on which the instrument was registered
    4.3. Reference number
    4.4. Parties to the instrument
        4.4.1. Name of the creditor
        4.4.2. Name of the debtor
5. Text of the enforceable obligation as annexed to this certificate.

The authentic instrument is enforceable against the debtor in the Member State of origin (Article 57(1) of the Regulation)

Done at ...., date ......
Signature and/or stamp ......

INDEX